On the Edge

THIRD EDITION

On the Edge

THE UNITED STATES IN THE TWENTIETH CENTURY

DAVID A. HOROWITZ
Portland State University

PETER N. CARROLL
Stanford University

WADSWORTH
CENGAGE Learning

Australia • Brazil • Japan • Korea • Mexico • Singapore • Spain • United Kingdom • United States

WADSWORTH
CENGAGE Learning™

On the Edge: The United States in the Twentieth Century, Third Edition
David A Horowitz,
Peter N. Carroll

Publisher: Clark Baxter

Senior Development Editor:
Sue Gleason

Assistant Editor: Paul Massicotte

Editorial Assistant: Richard Yoder

Marketing Manager:
Lori Grebe-Cook

Marketing Assistant: Mary Ho

Advertising Project Manager:
Stacey Purviance

Project Manager, Editorial
Production:Jennifer Klos

Print Buyer: Lisa Claudeanos

Permissions Editor: Bob Kauser

Production Service:
Scratchgravel Publishing Services

Photo Researcher: Laura Molmud

Copy Editor: Chris Thillen

Cover Designer: Qin-Zhong Yu

Cover Image: PhotoDisc/Getty
Images; StockTrek/Getty Images

Compositor:
Scratchgravel Publishing Services

For product information and technology assistance, contact us at **Cengage Learning Customer & Sales Support, 1-800-354-9706**

For permission to use material from this text or product, submit all requests online at **cengage.com/permissions**
Further permissions questions can be emailed to **permissionrequest@cengage.com**

Library of Congress Control Number: 2004102422

ISBN-13: 978-0-534-57186-3

ISBN-10: 0-534-57186-7

Wadsworth
10 Davis Drive
Belmont, CA 94002-3098
USA

Cengage Learning is a leading provider of customized learning solutions with office locations around the globe, including Singapore, the United Kingdom, Australia, Mexico, Brazil, and Japan. Locate your local office at: **international.cengage.com/region**

Cengage Learning products are represented in Canada by Nelson Education, Ltd.

For your course and learning solutions, visit **academic.cengage.com**

Purchase any of our products at your local college store or at our preferred online store **www.ichapters.com**

Printed in Canada
5 6 7 12 11 10 09

CONTENTS

Chapter 5

The Great Depression and New Deal Reform, 1929–1936   *151*

Chapter 6

Democratic Capitalism and the Liberal State, 1937–1941   *181*

Chapter 15

The Turn to Centrism: Bush, Clinton, and Bush, 1988–2003   **507**

PREFACE

On the Edge: The United States in the Twentieth Century is an interpretive history describing the challenges and dilemmas that have confronted the nation during the last century. The book follows two major themes. First, it traces the expansion of national economic and political power at home and abroad. Second, it describes the domestic conflicts and controversies precipitated by such growth.

Seeking a balanced perspective, *On the Edge* provides equitable coverage to elites and out-groups, liberals and conservatives, modernists and traditionalists, and politicians and cultural figures. This history moves beyond the narration of political and institutional leaders to portray the significant historical roles played by nominally powerless people—ranging from the working class and poor to the beleaguered middle class to women and the nation's racial, ethnic, and cultural minorities. It also explores how technology, popular culture, and social innovation have affected mainstream life and institutions.

Our intention is to stimulate the critical perspective of instructors and students by combining narrative and analytic history in jargon-free prose. Although chapters follow a general chronological outline, they are divided into thematic sections to encourage conceptualization and provocative discussion. Each chapter includes several biographical sketches that use the lives of individuals to illuminate important themes of the period.

The third edition of *On the Edge* is presented in a more compact form than earlier versions. The chapters have been reconfigured into chronological units combining political and cultural history. The revision also covers developments to the year 2004. Chapter reading lists in this edition describe recent works of significant interest, followed by an annotated list of additional sources. We have further simplified graphs, charts, and tables for quick reference and easy comprehension. Monetary figures are conveyed in current dollars—the actual value for the period under discussion. A separate volume, *On the Edge: The United States Since 1945*, also is available from this publisher.

David Horowitz wishes to thank Jeff Brown of the Portland State University Department of History for invaluable technical assistance and to express appreciation for the aid, comfort, and sustenance of Gloria Myers Horowitz. Peter Carroll acknowledges the counsel and support of Jeannette Ferrary. The authors offer special thanks to Publisher Clark G. Baxter, Senior Developmental Editor Sue Gleason, and Assistant Editor Paul Massicotte.

Finally, we would like to thank the reviewers of this and previous editions: Clarence Bolt, Camosun College; Robert J. Caputi, Rochester Institute of Technology; Rodney P. Carlisle, Rutgers University; Stacy A. Cordery, Monmouth College; James A. Jolly, Millersville University; Ronald Marcello, University of North Texas; Clay McShane, Northeastern University; Fraser Ottanelli, University of South Florida; Leo P. Ribuffo, George Washington University; and David L. Wilson, Southern Illinois University.

PROLOGUE

The last quarter of the nineteenth century brought an explosion of industrial and financial activity to the U.S. economy that defined new patterns of life. As corporate capitalism took hold, real wages increased and opportunities expanded. Yet market development was uneven and often exacted a horrific price among an increasingly diverse population of workers, farmers, and small property holders. Political leaders either exploited the new conditions or sought genuine responses to them. Most citizens remained both awed and repelled by the dramatic changes introduced by the new world.

CORPORATE REVOLUTION

"An almost total revolution" was taking place "in every relation of the world's industrial and commercial system," observed economist David Wells in 1889. As the gross national product tripled in the last thirty years of the nineteenth century, a corporate restructuring of the U.S. economy emphasized the vitality of big companies. Nationwide business enterprises required enormous amounts of capital and tightly managed organizations. To establish these firms, entrepreneurs raised capital through sales of stock to investors, who then shared in profits generated by professional managers. Under the *Santa Clara* decision of 1886, the Supreme Court provided corporations with the legal status of individuals under the Fifth and Fourteenth amendments to the Constitution, thereby protecting them against government claims on assets or earnings without due process.

New corporations like John D. Rockefeller's Standard Oil Company, which consolidated petroleum refining, increased the scale and efficiency of raw material processing. In the steel industry, Scots immigrant Andrew Carnegie combined innovative methods of ore refining and administration to build the nation's first billion-dollar company. Meanwhile, engineer Frederick

1

Winslow Taylor developed efficient high-speed metal cutters and other tools to achieve industrial "economies of scale" that made the size of a business crucial to its profits. Inventions such as the electric light, telephone, cash register, and elevator further accelerated the market revolution. Raw materials and finished products were distributed by a nationwide system of railroads, whose coordination was facilitated when the railroads agreed to create four standard time zones in 1883.

Although not heavily industrialized, the South played a role in the incorporation of the national economy. Once northern troops withdrew in 1877, southern lawyers, merchants, and business leaders sought to "redeem" the South by opening the region to northern investors and industrialists. The South had "fallen in love with work," *Atlanta Constitution* editor Henry W. Grady exulted in 1886. "Redeemer" regimes in such states as South Carolina, Mississippi, and Georgia lowered taxes, reduced government regulation, cut public services, leased convict labor to mining and railroad interests, and sold or granted millions of acres of land to northern timber and mine operators. Corporate capitalism made its most dramatic gains in the textile mills of the Piedmont hill country in the Carolinas, Georgia, and Alabama, where poor white farmers comprised a captive nonmobile labor force.

The West contributed to the booming economy by providing valuable natural resources in land, minerals, fish, and timber. Six western states from North Dakota to Washington joined the Union between 1889 and 1890. The region had a popular image as a frontier whose proximity to undeveloped nature allowed free play for manly success. Before western riches could be freed for development, however, investors required the federal government to replace the subsistence economy and communal landholding practices of the native inhabitants. Forcing Native Americans to surrender their lands provoked warfare from Northern Plains Sioux, the Apache of the Southwest, and other nations. Yet U.S. military attacks, the slaughter of the bison, western settlement, and railroad expansion ended resistance to white land tenure. The Dawes Act of 1887, which abolished communal ownership of Native American land and divided individual allotments into 160-acre parcels, struck an additional blow to tribal sovereignty.

The western states soon became a magnet for international capital. As mining towns spread across mountain hillsides, the region became one of the most urbanized and ethnically diverse sectors of the nation. Yet economic conditions rarely favored miners in a labor-intensive industry characterized by low wages and the speedup (an accelerated work pace).

The major corporate revolution occurred in the cities, where one-third of the nation's people lived by 1890. In steel-framed skyscrapers, office and administrative functions were consolidated in the downtown core. Electric streetcars or trolleys, which appeared around 1890, increased available labor pools by widening commuter distances. Mass transit also attracted middle-class shoppers to downtown department stores. Cities such as New York, the home of nearly two thousand millionaires by 1892, became showplaces for the new rich. Besides their fabulous mansions, grand hotels, and plush cafes, the great urban centers featured cultural institutions and parks constructed with the help of private benefactors. As a symbol of progress, the future of the metropolis was best expressed in the industrial and technological exhibits of the Chicago World's Fair, the Columbian Exposition of 1893, which conveyed the hope that material progress would produce a harmonious society.

Although corporate capitalism offered lower consumer prices, greater investor flexibility, and more opportunities for white-collar employees, its successes often came at the cost of free business competition. In 1879 Rockefeller's Standard Oil Company organized the nation's first trust, an arrangement by which stockholders from competing companies ceded industry decision-making power to a centralized "trust" in return for increased dividends. By the 1880s, powerful trusts dominated steel, copper, and sugar refining; leather processing; meatpacking; and linseed oil production. Investment banking promoted further consolidation, particularly among rail lines organized by titans like Jay Gould, James Hill, and Cornelius Vanderbilt. Business leaders insisted that natural laws of supply, demand, and competition governed the economy and should not be artificially disrupted by state intervention. Claiming to possess superior energy and initiative, Carnegie and Rockefeller embraced Herbert Spencer's Social Darwinism by portraying the market as a struggle for survival among the most "fit." Capitalists also pursued commercial supremacy through the domination of overseas trade.

The high stakes of corporate competition and the luxurious lifestyles of the social elite prompted Samuel Clemens and Charles Dudley Warner to name their 1873 novel *The Gilded Age.* By the 1880s, 10 percent of the population owned 70 percent of national wealth. Figures for 1890 showed the richest 2 percent earning more than half the nation's aggregate income. Carnegie, who received more than $20 million a year by the end of the century, sought to overcome his reputation as a robber baron by espousing the Gospel of Wealth, a doctrine that portrayed business leaders as trustees of God's abundance, obligated to improve the lives of others. The steel magnate donated nearly 90 percent of his $400 million personal fortune to "self-help" philanthropies such as public libraries; he later created foundations to promote education and world peace.

IMMIGRANTS, WORKERS, AND LABOR PROTEST

A large segment of the nation's industrial and agricultural workforce consisted of migrants from other countries. Between the Civil War and World War I, more than 25 million immigrants from Europe, Asia, and Mexico found their way to the United States. The Irish and the German were the most numerous of these arrivals. Displaced by the enclosure of peasant holdings and widespread potato famine, 5.5 million Irish immigrants arrived on U.S. soil in the century before 1920. Half were women who found jobs in domestic service, factories, and mills. By 1880, one-third of New York City's population was Irish American; Irish children soon outnumbered white Protestants in the Boston public schools. Setting a precedent for subsequent waves of immigrants, the Irish and Germans sought self-protection from nativist hostility through ethnic fraternal and burial societies, community newspapers, parochial schools, neighborhood commercial associations, and political activity.

Irish and German "bosses" used a highly personal style of leadership to win the loyalty of ethnic and working-class voters. Operating on the precinct and ward level, they regularly provided constituents with social services, jobs, and municipal contracts. Machine patrons such as New York's George Washington Plunkitt offered emergency food baskets and aid to victims of fires and other disasters and sponsored recreational activities such as holiday picnics and youth clubs. Leaders like Plunkitt prided themselves on knowing their districts and treating constituents with respect. The ward boss system thrived among Catholic and Jewish immigrants, who came from cultures emphasizing collective charity and group support instead of Protestant individualism.

The highest proportion of foreign-born residents lived in the West. Although the superintendent of the Census did not declare the continental frontier closed until 1890, the Wild West long had been integrated into the urban-industrial frontier. Western agriculture, mining, logging, and processing plants required a huge labor force. German farmers dotted the Plains. Scandinavian loggers worked the fir forests of the northern Midwest and Pacific Northwest. Mountain state mining operations sought Welsh, Polish, German, and Chinese workers. In southern Texas and California, where large-scale agriculture displaced the Mexican population and disrupted landholding patterns, Hispanic men earned subsistence wages in construction while women toiled as poorly paid seasonal field laborers or food processing workers.

Asian immigrants played a major role in the western economy. Between 1868 and 1924, nearly 275,000 Japanese came to Hawaii and California as contract workers, although many eventually succeeded as farmers, orchardists, and gardeners. By 1882, over 100,000 foreign-born Chinese labored as migrant field workers, domestic servants, industrial wage earners, or small business proprietors. Anxieties over Asian labor competition provoked a wave of nativism in the western states. After mobs in Los Angeles lynched eighteen Chinese laborers during the depression of the 1870s, Denis Kearny, the leader of the California Workingmen Party, declared that "the Chinese must go! They are stealing our jobs." In 1885 similar tensions led to the murder of twenty-eight

Chinese in Wyoming. Under the Chinese Exclusion Act of 1882, the first immigration restriction law in U.S. history, the entry of Chinese laborers was prohibited and Chinese Americans were denied naturalization for citizenship.

The industrial revolution's factories, mills, processing plants, mines, construction sites, and railroad yards were extremely dangerous and forced workers to abandon traditional work habits. Factory jobs demanded that repetitious tasks be performed on a strict schedule, a routine that employees found monotonous, impersonal, and demeaning. Many laborers came from rural cultures whose seasonal work rhythms had not prepared them for industrial discipline and efficiency. "The tick of the clock is the boss in his anger," wrote Yiddish poet Morris Rosenfeld. Moreover, society offered workers virtually no protection from the perils of industrial life. Vulnerable to wage cuts and layoffs in an industrial system that killed 100 employees a day, workers received an average $10 in pay for a 59-hour week.

The first successful nationwide labor organization was the Knights of Labor. Formed in the 1860s, the union did not initially support strikes. After local affiliates participated in successful railroad walkouts in the 1870s and 1880s, the Knights attained a membership of 700,000. Yet the union's reputation failed to survive the Haymarket Square riot of 1886, when a dynamite bomb killed eight Chicago policemen at a rally to protest police brutality against striking workers. Following the arrest and conviction of eight anarchist pamphleteers with no connection to the bombing and the execution of four of the defendants, a wave of public hysteria focused on the perceived influx of "European" class struggle. The American Federation of Labor (AFL), an organization of craft unions founded in 1886 by Samuel Gompers, soon replaced the Knights as the dominant force in the labor movement. Espousing a pragmatic philosophy of business unionism, the AFL concentrated on higher wages, job security, and improved working conditions for skilled laborers.

Despite the AFL's acceptance of capitalism, bitter labor disputes disrupted industrial life. After a 20 percent pay cut in 1892, workers at the main Carnegie mill in Homestead, Pennsylvania, affiliated with the AFL and confronted security forces in a shoot-out that resulted in sixteen deaths. When state militia ended the strike, Alexander Berkman, a Russian-born anarchist, wounded Carnegie general manager Henry Clay Frick in an assassination attempt. Meanwhile, the governor of Idaho declared martial law and requested federal troops against striking silver miners. Two years later, consecutive pay cuts at the Illinois plant producing Pullman railroad cars led to a strike by the American Railway Union that spread to the entire midwestern rail system. After dispatching 14,000 troops to maintain order, the federal government issued a court injunction to prevent interference with distribution of the mail by trains. Arrested for contempt as the strike collapsed, union leader Eugene V. Debs spent six months in prison and declared himself a socialist upon his release.

SHARECROPPERS, FARMERS, AND POPULISTS

With the departure of northern troops from the old Confederacy in 1877, southern planters resumed control of the cotton economy. Having lost half their capital in the form of slaves, growers could not absorb the employment costs of field labor, overseers, and drivers. Because recently emancipated slaves often were unwilling to sacrifice autonomy by working for wages, and landlords refused to sell or rent property to them, black families labored for a share of the landlord's crop. In a capital-starved economy in which cotton was the only cash commodity, landlords provided black sharecroppers and tenants with housing, stock, implements, or seed in return for a sizable portion of the proceeds. White-owned country stores intensified African American dependency and debt by extending credit for food, clothing, and supplies in exchange for future crops.

White power over African American sharecroppers and tenants was reinforced by convict labor, 90 percent of whom were black. Trapped in a system from which it was almost impossible to break free, prison laborers built the transportation networks and mined the resources that eased the South into economic modernization and urbanization. Local elites used the pretext of maintaining order in growing commercial centers to tighten racial exclusion codes, particularly in segregating railroad and streetcar transit. Such laws were upheld by Supreme Court rulings that limited civil rights protections guaranteed by the Fourteenth Amendment. Southern politicians prevented any threat to white supremacy by disenfranchising African American voters through a variety of devices including the white primary, the literacy test, the poll tax, and regulations limiting balloting to those whose "grandfathers" had qualified to vote.

As southern governments enforced the economic privileges of wealthy planters, poor white and black farmers turned to populist protest. Vulnerable to the forces of a growing international economy, cotton prices had declined during the 1880s from 30 cents a pound to less than 6 cents. Farmers also objected to paying accelerating debt with the scarce dollars of a contracting currency. The Southern Farmers Alliance, formed in the 1880s by Texan Charles Macune, proposed that small farmers form marketing cooperatives to sell their cotton collectively. Alliance leaders also proposed a subtreasury plan to store crops in government warehouses until market prices improved. With this agenda, the Alliance elected candidates across the South and sent Georgia's Tom Watson to Congress in 1890. Attacking "race antagonism" as a cause of poverty, Watson told biracial audiences that "you are kept apart that you may be separately fleeced of your earnings."

Like southern cotton producers, western wheat growers were tied to prices, interest rates, and monetary policies set outside the region. In response, the National Farmers Alliance of the Northwest, organized in the 1880s, proposed an antimonopoly program of railroad regulation and monetary reform. Such agitation stimulated passage of the Interstate Commerce Act of 1887, which imposed "reasonable" and nondiscriminatory freight rates on the railroads and created the Interstate Commerce Commission (ICC), the first regulatory agency in U.S. history. Agrarian activity also contributed to enactment of the Sherman Antitrust Act of 1890, which prohibited restraint of trade and commerce against the public interest.

Alliance leaders hoped to offset the impact of falling prices on farmers and debtors by expanding the money supply. A coalition of northern and southern activists organized a convention of the People's (or Populist) Party in Omaha, Nebraska, in 1892 and called for the unlimited coinage of silver at one-sixteenth the value of gold. The Populists also advocated government ownership of railroads and utilities, postal savings banks, a federal income tax, and direct election of U.S. senators by voters instead of state legislatures.

The People's Party won five Senate seats in 1892, when Populist presidential nominee General James B. Weaver polled over 1 million (8.5 percent) of the popular vote. Populist appeal intensified when a major economic depression struck in 1893. During the next four years, nearly 500 banks and 15,000 businesses went bankrupt; unemployment leaped to 20 percent. As farm prices sank, profits disappeared, and wages plummeted, thousands of unemployed workers joined Jacob S. Coxey in mounting the first demonstrations in history at the Washington Capitol to demand government creation of public works programs.

THE NEW POLITICS OF THE 1890s

Political activism of the 1890s built upon an extensive body of social and political dissent. In 1879 land reformer Henry George published *Progress and Poverty*, a widely read plea to prevent permanent division of social classes through adoption of a single tax on speculative income. Edward Bellamy's popular *Looking Backward: 2000–1887* (1888) criticized heartless economic competition and envisioned the creation of a cooperative commonwealth. Meanwhile, the Christian perspective of reformer Henry D. Lloyd's *Wealth vs. Commonwealth* (1894) demonstrated how the trusts victimized ordinary people. Populist monetary demands found their way into best-selling books such as William Harvey's Coin's *Financial School* (1894) and *The American People's Money* (1895), by Minnesota activist Ignatius Donnelly.

The depression of the 1890s deepened social divisions and pushed voters into ideological camps. In better times, Republicans and Democrats ran disciplined but nonsubstantive campaigns to mobilize evenly divided supporters

EXHIBIT **P-1   CHRONOLOGY OF MAJOR EVENTS, 1876–1896**

1876	Disputed presidential election between Democrat Samuel J. Tilden and Republican Rutherford B. Hayes
1877	Compromise provides for election of Hayes and withdrawal of federal troops from former Confederacy
1878	Bland-Allison Act requires U.S. Treasury to coin silver currency
1880	Election of Republican President James A. Garfield
1881	Assassination of Garfield; Chester Arthur succeeds
1882	Chinese Exclusion Act
1883	Pendleton Civil Service Act creates Civil Service Commission; Supreme Court invalidates civil rights legislation
1884	Election of Democratic President Grover Cleveland
1886	Haymarket Square Riot, Chicago
1887	Interstate Commerce Act creates Interstate Commerce Commission (ICC); Dawes Act abolishes American Indian tribal sovereignty
1888	Election of Republican President Benjamin Harrison
1890	Sherman Antitrust Act; Sherman Silver Purchase Act; McKinley Tariff
1892	Creation of People's (Populist) Party; Election of Democratic President Grover Cleveland; Homestead Steel Strike
1893	Financial panic and onset of depression of 1893–1897; Repeal of Sherman Silver Purchase Act
1894	Wilson-Gorman Tariff; Pullman Strike
1896	Election of Republican President William McKinley

for patronage and other spoils. In the Midwest, voters tended to split along ethnocultural lines, with evangelical Protestants supporting Republicans and Roman Catholics and German Lutherans backing the Democrats. As southern and western Democrats defected to the Populists or Republicans in the 1894 congressional elections, however, currency reformers organized to take over the Democratic Party. The turning point came in 1896, when thirty-six-year-old William Jennings Bryan of Nebraska galvanized the Democratic National Convention with a passionate plea for free silver. "You shall not press down upon the brow of labor this crown of thorns," cried Bryan, "you shall not crucify mankind upon a cross of gold."

The youngest man in history to be nominated for the presidency by a major party, Bryan embodied the heartland's producer democracy. Such values stressed the government's importance in ensuring autonomy and equality of opportunity in an economy characterized by individual property and freedom of contract. After a long and bitter debate, the People's Party agreed to "fusion" with the Democrats by endorsing Bryan's candidacy; but they selected Georgia's Tom Watson as the vice presidential nominee. This strategy satisfied southern Populists who feared that an independent political party might jeopardize white supremacy. Meanwhile, united Republicans chose veteran Ohio politician William McKinley, a strong advocate of high tariffs and the gold standard, to lead their ticket. As the nineteenth century reached its final years, the nation looked to the future with a mixture of confidence and apprehension.

RECOMMENDED READINGS

Alex Lichtenstein, *Twice the Work of Free Labor: The Political Economy of Convict Labor in the New South* (1996). The author describes how New South modernization depended upon the region's unique peneology-for-profit system.

Gretchen Ritter, *Goldbugs and Greenbacks: The Antimonopoly Tradition and the Politics of Finance in America, 1865–1896* (1997). This book explains why the currency issue was the leading political controversy of the 1890s.

Additional Readings

The rise and consequences of corporate capitalism are described in Olivier Zunz, *Making America Corporate, 1870–1920* (1990), and Alan Trachtenberg, *The Incorporation of America: Culture and Society in the Gilded Age* (1982). For city department stores, see Susan Porter Benson, *Counter Cultures: Saleswomen, Managers, and Customers in American Department Stores, 1890–1940* (1986).

Southern integration with northern capital is described in Edward L. Ayers, *The Promise of the New South: Life After Reconstruction* (1992). See also Harold D. Woodman, *New South, New Law* (1995), and Dwight B. Billings, *Planters and the Making of a "New South"* (1979). For Native American policy in the West, see Robert Wooster, *The Military and United States Indian Policy, 1865–1903* (1988), which can be supplemented by Blue Clark, *Lone Wolf v. Hitchcock: Treaty Rights and Indian Law at the End of the Nineteenth Century* (1995), and Sidney J. Harring, *Crow Dog's Case: American Indian Sovereignty, Tribal Law, and United States Law in the Nineteenth Century* (1994). Western economic development is surveyed in Rodman W. Paul, *The Far West and the Great Plains in Transition, 1859–1900* (1988).

The international dimension to U.S. immigration is addressed in Walter Nugent, *Crossings: The Great Transatlantic Migrations, 1870–1914* (1992). See also Alan M. Kraut, *The Huddled Masses: The Immigrant in American Society, 1880–1921* (1982). For a positive view of urban development, see Stanley K. Schultz, *Constructing Urban Culture: American Cities and City Planning, 1800–1920* (1989). Industrial work culture is described in Bruce Laurie, *Artisans into Workers: Labor in Nineteenth-Century America* (1989), and David Montgomery, *Citizen Worker: The Experience of Workers in the United States with Democracy and the Free Market During the Nineteenth Century* (1993). For labor protest, see Kim Voss, *The Making of Exceptionalism: The Knights of Labor and Class Formation in the Nineteenth Century* (1994); Paul Avrich, *The Haymarket Tragedy* (1984); and Paul Krause, *The Battle for Homestead, 1880–1892: Politics, Culture, and Steel* (1992). See also Carl Smith, *Urban Disorder and the Shape of Belief: The Great Chicago Fire, the Haymarket Bomb, and the Model Town of Pullman* (1994).

Southern agriculture is analyzed in Edward Royce, *The Origins of Southern Sharecropping* (1993), and Gerald David Jaynes, *Branches without Roots: Genesis of the Black Working Class in the American South, 1862–1882* (1986). Sources on convict labor include David M. Oshinsky, *Worse Than Slavery: Parchman Farm and the Ordeal of Jim Crow* (1996); Mary Ellen Curtin, *Black Prisoners and Their World: Alabama, 1865–1900* (2000); and Matthew J. Mancini, *One Dies, Get Another: Convict Leasing in the South, 1866–1928* (1996). For the legal basis of African American disenfranchisement, see the early segments of J. Morgan Kousser, *Colorblind Injustice: Minority Voting Rights and the Undoing of the Second Reconstruction* (1999).

Syntheses of the Populist movement include William A. Peffer, *Populism, Its Rise and Fall* (1992); Robert C. McMath, *American Populism: A Social History, 1877–1898* (1993); and Lawrence F. Goodwyn, *The Populist Moment: A Short History of the Agrarian Revolt in America* (1978). For regional studies, see Steve Hahn, *The Roots of Southern Populism: Yeomen Farmers and the Transformation of the Georgia Upcountry, 1850–1890* (1983), and Jeffrey Ostler, *Prairie Populism: The Fate of Agrarian Radicalism in Kansas, Nebraska, and Iowa, 1880–1992* (1993).

Midwestern antimonopoly sentiment is explored in David Thelen, *Paths of Resistance: Tradition and Democracy in Industrializing Missouri* (1991); Steven L. Piott, *The Anti-Monopoly Persuasion: Popular Resistance to the Rise of Big Business in the Midwest* (1985); and Andrew R. L. Cayton and Peter S. Onuf, *The Midwest and the Nation: Rethinking the History of an American Region* (1990). For ethnocultural politics, see Paul Kleppner, *The Cross of Culture: A Social Analysis* (1978), and *The Third Electoral System, 1853–1892* (1979). A useful analysis of politics appears in Robert Kelley, *The Cultural Pattern in American Politics: The First Century* (1979), which should be supplemented by Michael Lewis Goldberg, *An Army of Women: Gender and Politics in the Gilded Age* (1997). For Bryan, see LeRoy Ashby, *William Jennings Bryan: Champion of Democracy* (1987).

LIFE AT THE START OF THE TWENTIETH CENTURY

As the new century began, the nation had already entered the industrial age. The key economic institution that would dominate the next hundred years was the corporation. This business arrangement, based on immense capital investments, would enable a new managerial class to organize production, distribution, and consumption of goods and services on a vast scale. To harness that capacity, corporate leaders also had to organize large numbers of people to work within that system on all levels. With the need for workers, big cities became the locus of economic power, supplanting the farm and the town in American life. The central values of the older agrarian culture—individualism, free competition, and localism—faced a new context based on technology, bureaucratic consolidation, and national market development. While organizations replaced individuals as the building blocks of modern life, people and institutions adjusted uneasily to a new era. Ethnic, racial, and gender diversity in the expanding labor force upset traditional norms, and new cultural styles emerged.

THE CONSOLIDATION OF CORPORATE CULTURE

Traumatized by the severe depression of 1893–1897, corporate leaders attempted to take control of market forces and reduce competition by consolidating businesses. Between 1897 and 1904, some 3,000 firms merged into 300 giant corporations that controlled 40 percent of national wealth. In 1901 U.S. Steel produced more than 60 percent of the nation's steel, which provided the huge corporation with more income than the federal government. Investment bankers such as J. P. Morgan amassed enormous amounts of money to capitalize corporate mergers. By 1913 the Pujo congressional investigating committee found that a single money trust underwritten by the Morgan and Rockefeller interests held 341 interlocking directorates in 112 separate enterprises. Seventy Americans owned one-sixteenth of the nation's wealth.

Brown Brothers

The assembly line at the Ford Motor Company.

Although some segments of the economy, such as retail trade and food processing, remained more competitive, an important transition from proprietary to corporate capitalism accelerated in railroads, oil, steel, copper, and other industries. By 1917 modern corporations dominated raw materials processing, large-scale manufacturing, distribution, and marketing. Pioneering with new business methods, these integrated enterprises dispersed responsibility under the control of professional managers. These white-collar workers constituted a "new" middle class of non-production personnel that included corporate executives, supervisors, and engineers as well as sales and office employees.

Technological innovation continued to energize economic development. New canning techniques and refrigerated rail cars allowed consumers nationwide to sample a wide variety of meats, fruits, and vegetables from California, Texas, and Florida. Meanwhile, the new century saw the development of electrical appliances such as fans, flatirons, stoves, sewing machines, and clothes washers, as well as the early use of synthetic rayon. In 1901 the eruption of a gusher near Beaumont, Texas, stimulated the modern era of petroleum refining. Two years later Ohio brothers Orville and Wilbur Wright were the first to

EXHIBIT **1-1   AUTOMOBILE REGISTRATION, 1905–1920**
(IN ROUNDED FIGURES)

1905	77,000
1910	458,000
1915	2,332,000
1920	8,132,000

Source: *Historical Statistics of the United States, Colonial Times to 1970* (1975).

successfully fly a power-driven airplane at Kitty Hawk, North Carolina. Such efforts soon were dwarfed by another dramatic development—the automobile.

Although automobiles first appeared as literal "horseless carriages," the replacement of the tiller by the steering wheel and innovations such as the sliding-gear transmission, pneumatic tires, front bumpers, self-starters, headlights, and the four-cylinder engine revolutionized the industry. In 1908 Henry Ford, a Michigan farm boy who had moved to Detroit, unveiled his famous Model T, an inexpensive automobile that the owner could easily drive and repair. Influenced by Frederick Winslow Taylor's principles of scientific management, Ford introduced the moving assembly line in 1914. By cutting the production time for an automobile from 12½ hours to 90 minutes, Ford reduced the average price of a Model T from about $950 to $265. He was soon selling 500,000 cars a year. By 1920, nine million vehicles traveled the nation's highways, whose planning, construction, and maintenance were assigned to the states by the Federal Highway Act of 1916.

By organizing time and motion efficiently, scientific management increased industrial productivity. Nationwide manufacturing output per worker rose 76 percent between 1899 and 1914, although the workforce grew only 36 percent and physical plants only 13 percent. Critics warned that Taylorism dispensed with skilled workers and bypassed craft unions. Yet "efficiency experts" insisted that productivity would increase corporate profits that would benefit workers, too. In Ford's case the mechanized assembly line allowed the automaker to pay selected skilled workers $5 a day, double the prevailing wage in the industry.

Mass management also required efficient administration of the white-collar clerical staff. As the number of office workers doubled between 1900 and 1910 and doubled again by 1920, reaching almost 3 million employees, managers installed time clocks to enforce punctuality. Because women could be paid less than men, employers hired unmarried women stenographers and typists trained in commercial high schools. Unlike male clerks, women office workers did not expect occupational advancement. Their business careers usually ended upon marriage, because many employers, like Ford, refused to keep married women.

Frederick Winslow Taylor (1856–1915)

Folk myth held that Frederick Winslow Taylor, the creator of "scientific management," died with a stopwatch in his hand. Taylor saw himself as a reformer using professional skills to improve the lives of workers and consumers. The son of an established family from Germantown, Penn-

sylvania, Taylor turned to factory work when weak eyesight curbed his formal schooling. By taking night classes, he rose quickly from common laborer to enter the new profession of engineering.

During his career, Taylor received about a hundred patents. His work led to a heat treatment for tools that increased the cutting capacity of steel by 200 to 300 percent. As machines became more efficient, Taylor grew interested in improving the efficiency of workers as well. Armed with a stopwatch, he kept precise records of the time workers needed to accomplish each task and kept track of every motion made during the process. Using such data to identify the elementary operations and to design the most efficient procedures for specific jobs, Taylor sought the "substitution of science for the rule of thumb." In a famous demonstration of his methods, the engineer quadrupled the amount of pig iron a worker could carry in a day.

These "time-and-motion" studies formed the basis of Taylor's theory of scientific management. In the 1890s Taylor started a management

The premium on corporate efficiency extended from production and labor relations to distribution and sale of products. To maximize capital investment and company resources, business required continuous and predictable consumer demand. In 1908, Harvard University founded the first School of Business that offered degrees in business administration (MBAs). "Concentrate," the school's first dean, Edwin Gay, advised students, "not so much on the way production is organized but on the methods of distribution and the widening marketing area." Following such advice, companies like Ford, American Tobacco, and Atlantic and Pacific (A&P) introduced new mar-

consultant business in Philadelphia by distributing a card that read, "Systematizing Shop Management and Manufacturing Costs a Specialty." Bethlehem Steel became his first major client. The first scientific management consultant in the world, Taylor eventually codified his expertise in *Principles of Scientific Management* (1911).

Taylor's ideas were understandably unpopular with workers. Many believed that Taylorism reduced them to the status of machines and made their tasks unbearably monotonous. Others feared that a streamlined manufacturing process would lead to layoffs. Although Taylor advocated strict shop discipline, he insisted that his system would benefit labor. Efficiency meant greater productivity, he argued, leading to shorter hours, higher wages, and lower consumer prices. Smoother procedures also might reduce worker grievances, improving the relationship between labor and management.

Taylor embodied the growing faith among Progressive professionals that scientific rationality could be applied to the solution of social problems. Yet engineers had no control over corporate managers who used Taylor's principles to speed up the workflow and eliminate jobs. Taylor complained in a professional paper in 1909 that the majority of people bitterly opposed improvements in the status quo. The pioneer of scientific management died one year before Henry Ford adopted his principles to the mass production of automobiles and forever changed the American industrial process.

ket research, the integration of manufacturing and wholesaling, and innovative sales programs to achieve great profits.

Advertising emerged as one of the growth industries as expenditures leaped from $542 million in 1900 to nearly $3 billion by 1920. A new breed of professional copywriters and designers boasted, "Advertising is no longer an experiment." Rejecting classical rules that suggested products would sell themselves according to the laws of supply and demand, advertisers deliberately sought to create consumer desires. Benefiting by the growth of mass circulation magazines, such as *Ladies' Home Journal,* ad agencies targeted likely customers—usually women, who bought most of the household items. The agencies cleverly appealed to women's social desires—such as cleanliness, beauty, or sexuality—rather than aspects of the products they sold.

The urban department store became an important aspect of consumer culture. Developed in New York, Philadelphia, and Chicago by nineteenth-century entrepreneurs such as R. H. Macy, John Wanamaker, and Marshall Field, the all-purpose retail outlet adopted corporate methods of administration and management. In a hierarchical environment, male store managers imbued working-class "shopgirls" with sufficient gentility to make them effective sales and clerical workers. Department stores cultivated a loyal following of mainly female customers by educating consumers about innovations in dress styles and cosmetics, home furnishings, and household appliances. To attract poorer city dwellers, department stores also introduced "bargain basements" that relied on rapid turnover of merchandise to make profits at lower prices. By consolidating retail operations, however, big-city emporiums threatened the competitive viability of independent merchants and neighborhood shops.

LIFE IN THE CITY

The industrial economy also stimulated rapid growth of the nation's cities. As industrial jobs attracted workers from the depressed rural economy and immigrants from overseas, the nation's urban population tripled between 1890 and 1920—a growth rate ten times that of the rural population. By 1920, for the first time, more than half the nation's people lived in a town or city, and nearly two-thirds of urban dwellers clustered in the Northeast. New technologies, such as electric trolley lines and underground railways, integrated residential areas and downtown cores, separating neighborhoods along lines of social class.

As cities became more densely populated, sewage problems overwhelmed municipal authorities. In 1916 New York City dumped 500 million gallons of raw sewage into its rivers every day. Barely half the residents of Rochester and Pittsburgh had sewers, and Baltimore and New Orleans had no sewage system at all. Many tenements lacked running water. Meanwhile, poor health practices, malnutrition, and childhood diseases contributed to a U.S. infant mortality rate of 1 in a 100 live births and the lowest public health ranking of any industrialized nation. By replacing horse-drawn vehicles, however, streetcars reduced animal waste (10 pounds a day for each horse) and freed thoroughfares of thousands of animal carcasses each year. Improved sanitation contributed to cures for malaria, yellow fever, typhoid, and diphtheria and to a one-third decline in the national death rate after 1900, although life expectancy for whites was just forty-eight years; for nonwhites, the rate was thirty-three years.

Intense overcrowding and deplorable housing characterized the sprawling slums and ghettos of urban-industrial centers. Five-story tenements, which featured a narrow central staircase surrounded by four apartments on each level, were the customary form of inner-city residential construction in New York City. One section of Manhattan had a population density of 986 persons per acre, a higher figure than contemporary Bombay, India. One observer noted that even the architecture "seemed to sweat humanity at every window and door." Such settings promoted diseases such as tuberculosis and challenged city officials to respond to the dangers of fire, which extensively damaged four major cities and killed as many as seven thousand people annually. Overcrowding and squalor also contributed to soaring crime rates. By 1893 Chicago averaged one arrest per eleven residents and eight times as many murders as Paris.

The urban environment received extensive coverage in "penny press" newspapers. Publishers such as German immigrant Joseph Pulitzer and the patrician William Randolph Hearst—dubbed practitioners of "yellow journalism" due to their use of color comic strips—provided sensational accounts of crime, gossip, scandal, and corruption. Meanwhile, monthly magazines such as *McClure's* and *Cosmopolitan* followed suit. Ida Tarbell's portrait of the Standard Oil monopoly pioneered the genre. Other examples included Thomas W. Lawson's "Frenzied Finance," a description of insurance company fraud, and Jacob Riis's "How the Other Half Lives," a portrait of life in the tenements of the Lower East Side. David Graham Phillips's "The Treason of the Senate" prompted Theodore Roosevelt to deride journalists as "muckrakers," a name that stuck. Lincoln Steffens's *The Shame of the Cities* (1904), which depicted boss rule, and Upton Sinclair's fictional *The Jungle* (1906), which described conditions in Chicago's meat-packing industry, became muckraking classics.

IMMIGRANTS AND NATIVISTS

Nearly 18 million foreign-born people arrived in the United States between 1890 and 1917, all but 3 million during the first fifteen years of the century. Among the newcomers in the West were 130,000 Japanese who arrived between 1900 and 1910 and some 270,000 migrants from Mexico who crossed the border during the century's first two decades. Yet it was the staggering tide of arrivals from Europe that captured national attention and changed the great metropolises of the Northeast and Midwest. By 1910 three-fifths of the residents of the nation's twelve largest cities were "new" immigrants from Europe or their children.

EXHIBIT **1-2**   **U.S. POPULATION, 1880–1920**
(IN ROUNDED MILLIONS, BASED ON DECENNIAL CENSUS)

Year	Population
1880	50.2
1890	62.9
1900	76.0
1910	92.0
1920	105.7

Source: *Historical Statistics of the United States, Colonial Times to 1970* (1975).

The great majority of post–Civil War immigrants originated in northern and western Europe, particularly England, Ireland, Germany, and Scandinavia. During the 1890s, however, more than three-quarters of European arrivals came from eastern, central, and southern Europe. They were mainly peasants and impoverished rural villagers of Roman Catholic, Eastern Orthodox, and Jewish faiths, and few spoke English. Moreover, nearly all the "new" immigrants left societies ruled by repressive and undemocratic governments. They arrived, as social worker Jane Addams put it, "densely ignorant of civic duties."

Native-born residents frequently accused "new" immigrants of migrating for purely material motives and attacked their reluctance to sever links with their native lands. To some extent, demographic statistics supported such charges. Almost half the number of Italians, Greeks, and Slavs who came to the United States between 1890 and 1914 returned home. During the peak immigration years, about one-fourth as many foreigners departed as arrived. Most were male sojourners who planned to earn enough money to return home and buy a small farm or business. Women constituted only one-third of the Catholic entrants from southern and eastern Europe. Immigrants also returned to their native countries in response to unsatisfying prospects or left during years of economic depression, as in 1908. Other newcomers departed because of rampant discrimination or hostility.

This mass immigration provoked a strong nativist reaction among upper-class patricians and a host of pseudoscientific writers who opposed the influx of newcomers. Some racial theorists applied Darwinian metaphors to posit a hierarchy of national and racial groups, suggesting that Europeans could be divided into Teutonic, Alpine, and Mediterranean "races" in descending order. Applying notions common to animal breeding, some warned that hybrid offspring could reassert the latent characteristics of remote ancestors. Nativists such as Francis A. Walker, president of the Massachusetts Institute of Technology, declared that natural selection now worked against the Anglo-Saxon race. "New" immigrants, charged Walker, were "beaten men from beaten races, representing the worst failures in the struggle for existence."

Nativist anxieties included the notion of "race suicide," popularized by political leaders such as Senator Henry Cabot Lodge and Theodore Roosevelt. Warning that the "higher races" would lose the "warfare of the cradle" by having fewer children, Roosevelt lamented that the "greatest problem of civilization is to be found in the fact that well-to-do families tend to die out." Such notions of racial purity received their most coherent expression in Madison Grant's *The Passing of the Great Race* (1916), which celebrated the supremacy of "the white man par excellence" and warned that southern and eastern Europeans threatened the older American stock with "mongrelization."

Immigrants to the Pacific coast from Asian countries faced similar scorn and legal discrimination. The Chinese Exclusion Act of 1882, barring immigration from China, reduced the Chinese American population from 90,000 in 1900 to 60,000 in 1920, of which less than 5 percent were women. Japanese immigrants, who first arrived in Hawaii as contract laborers during the 1890s, were equally unwelcome on the mainland after 1900. West Coast labor unions perceived them as competitors for employment, pushing Japanese immigrants into agricultural work. By 1910, Japanese farmers were growing 70 percent of California's strawberry crop. Local newspapers warned of the "yellow peril." In 1906, San Francisco's school board voted to place Asian children in segregated schools. When this anti-Japanese act became an issue in relations with Tokyo, President Theodore Roosevelt persuaded school authorities to rescind the vote. In exchange, Japan accepted a Gentleman's Agreement of 1907, promising to restrict the immigration of male workers. Even so, in 1913 California passed an alien land law abolishing the right of Japanese-born farmers to own property. The measure undermined Japanese agriculture and remained a sore point for decades.

Ethnic Enclaves

Despite rampant nativism, Irish Americans, the most populous of the "old" immigrants, continued to dominate public life in the cities. By 1900 two-thirds of Irish Americans were citizens, and the group boasted the highest citizenship and voting rates of any immigrant group. Many Irish workers held skilled jobs in the construction and industrial crafts and supported trade unions. Moreover, by 1890, 40 percent of the U.S.-born Irish had white-collar jobs. As the new century began, Irish Americans attended college in greater proportions than their Protestant counterparts.

Politics and public service provided Irish Americans an avenue to middle-class respectability. By 1890 Irish politicians, such as New York's John Kelly, controlled the Democratic Party in the major urban centers of the North— New York, Boston, Chicago, and San Francisco—which contained 30 percent of all the municipal employees in the nation. Such politicians used public payrolls to distribute wealth to communities normally ostracized because of their working-class and Roman Catholic backgrounds. Irish American police, fire-fighters, and civil servants became a mainstay of urban life. By 1910 Irish American women accounted for 20 percent of city public school teachers in the North, whereas many found better-paying white-collar work as secretaries, clerical employees, and nurses.

Irish politicians, civil servants, and trade unionists acted as Americanizing agents and brokers for "new" immigrants who gravitated to the nation's industrial towns and cities. Most newcomers pursued trades they had learned in Europe. For example, Czech immigrants often served as skilled workers and artisans, Portuguese newcomers were traditionally fishermen, and many Greeks and Italians ran fish, vegetable, and fruit markets as well as restaurants and construction companies. In contrast, peasants with Slovakian and Polish backgrounds found jobs in heavy industry.

Members of national groups tended to cluster in ethnic neighborhoods that preserved their native cultures through language, food, music, and religion. Larger ethnic communities developed their own institutions such as stores and banks to provide employment and services for residents. In San Francisco A. P. Gianinni created the Bank of Italy (later, the Bank of America) so that non-English-speaking fish and vegetable peddlers could do business in a congenial facility. Chinese Americans there organized newspapers, local associations, and theaters that made the port city a gateway between China and the United States. Mexican Americans established economic and cultural centers with vigorous newspapers in cities such as San Antonio and Los Angeles. Ethnic groups of all nationalities organized fraternal and benevolent orders, burial societies, mutual-aid groups, and loan and insurance cooperatives.

For Irish, Italian, Polish, Mexican, and some German immigrants, the Roman Catholic Church played a crucial role in maintaining cultural traditions that facilitated adjustment to a new social environment. While diocesan hospitals, cemeteries, and bookstores solidified Catholic identity, the church created an extensive parochial school system to protect children from Protestant influences. By 1900 Catholic institutions provided education from kindergarten to the university level in every major American city. Because parish schools stressed citizenship and English instruction, German, Polish, Italian, and Hispanic Catholics often were denied the use of native languages. Conflicts with the Irish-dominated hierarchy were particularly strong among Italian and Hispanic immigrants, who often felt that the church ignored their festivals and traditional worship habits.

The Jews of the Lower East Side

Like the Irish, whose native land offered only poverty and oppression, Jewish immigrants had little interest in returning to their places of origin in Russia, Poland, and Austria-Hungary. Victimized by violent attacks called pogroms, 2 million Jews fled from eastern Europe to the United States. Unlike other

Hester Street on Manhattan's Lower East Side, the home to a thriving community of Jewish immigrants from eastern Europe.

immigrant groups, the Jews migrated as families (43 percent were women; 25 percent were children under age fourteen). Eastern European custom and law had excluded Jews from owning land and had pushed them into business and artisan trades. Two-thirds of the new Jewish immigrants identified themselves as skilled workers, and more than 70 percent were literate.

Most Jewish immigrants settled in New York City, clustering on Manhattan's Lower East Side. At a time when New York produced 70 percent of the nation's women's clothing and 40 percent of men's clothing, Jews brought their needle skills into the burgeoning garment industry. By 1910 the clothing industry accounted for half of the city's factories and half of its industrial force. Because of the demand for labor, more than 70 percent of New York's Jewish women over age sixteen worked for wages, and these women accounted for one-third of all garment workers. Although the mass production of clothing fostered oppressive labor conditions in unhealthy sweatshops, the system encouraged the democratization of national dress habits, freed many immigrants from destitution, and accustomed many Jewish women to working outside the home.

Jewish culture found unprecedented freedom of expression in the new environment. Yiddish, a German-based dialect spoken in the ghettos of eastern Europe, was the language of poetry, song, drama, and socialist writing that molded secular Jewish culture. Immigration also increased the synagogue's role as a center of Jewish communal life and philanthropy and reinforced Zionism, a religious and political ideology held by Russian and Polish Jews who believed that only a national state in Palestine could offer protection from anti-Semitism.

Despite their exclusion from such prestigious fields as corporate business, banking, and the law, Jewish immigrants experienced more upward mobility than any other immigrant group. Unlike most newcomers, Jews placed more importance on education than on property ownership. By 1910 the Jewish community contained a higher proportion of people over age sixteen who attended school than any other ethnic group. Jews soon ranked first among immigrants in the percentage attending college, which led several Ivy League colleges to impose quotas on Jewish enrollments. Meanwhile, the Anglo-Protestant elite denied Jews entry into exclusive residential neighborhoods, country clubs and resorts, and many private schools.

Nuevos Mexicanos and Native Americans

While U.S.-born educators strove to "Americanize" European immigrants and the children of newcomers adapted to American ways, some native-born groups confronted legal barriers and racial discrimination that blocked their opportunities for assimilation, economic improvement, or political participation. Hispanic residents of the Southwest, for example, whose territory had been invaded by U.S.-owned railroad corporations and ranchers during the late nineteenth century, lost their lands to commercial farms and became day workers in Arizona mines or Texas ranches. Although Hispanics sustained enough strength to win bilingualism in New Mexico's constitution, the dominant Anglos ignored these provisions and taught only English in the public schools after the state entered the Union in 1912.

After 1890, irrigation projects in the Southwest and California stimulated fruit and vegetable production, which in turn created agricultural jobs that attracted immigrants from Mexico. By 1900, some 100,000 Mexicans inhabited the United States, a statistic that doubled in 1910 and doubled again by 1920. Though many Mexicans became permanent residents, many recrossed the border during slack times. Married women also worked in the fields or in domestic service. By 1920, Mexican Americans formed small, struggling communities in cities like Denver and Los Angeles.

Native Americans also faced hard conditions after Congress passed the Dawes Act of 1887, providing for the breakup of tribal landholdings. Poor soil and cheating by white speculators made farming on the 160-acre allotments extremely difficult. The Burke Act of 1906 accelerated land grants to white purchasers by waiving the government's twenty-five-year trusteeship of Native property. By 1917 Native Americans had lost 62 percent of the lands held thirty years earlier.

Believing that Native people were unsuited for civilization, Washington officials reduced federal appropriations for education. When local communities protested the integration of Native children in public schools, the federal government agreed to segregate Native education. The government also changed the curriculum to provide mostly vocational training and encouraged graduates to take jobs as farmworkers (which provided compensation at 89 cents per day). More promising children were sent to private boarding schools that placed great pressure on Native students to abandon their traditional cultures and become Christians. "I have come to the conclusion that this Jesus was an Indian," protested one graduate, the author Charles Eastman, a Santee Sioux. "He was opposed to material acquirement and great possessions. He was inclined to peace. . . . These are not the principles on which the white man has founded his civilization."

MAINTAINING THE RACIAL DIVIDE

"Cannot the nation that has absorbed 10 million foreigners," proposed the preeminent African American scholar W. E. B. Du Bois, "absorb 10 million Negro Americans into that same political life at less cost than their unjust and illegal exclusion will involve?" Political and cultural leaders answered the question in the negative, both in word and deed. Prejudice, discrimination, and violence against blacks dated to slavery days. By 1900, pseudoscientific racist theories added a dimension of respectability to those attitudes. African Americans would confront the most severe antiblack discrimination and violence since the Civil War.

In 1900, 80 percent of the nation's African Americans lived in the South, where three-quarters of the black labor force languished as tenant farmers or sharecroppers in the declining cotton plantation economy. Racial caste restrictions confined the remainder to the lowest-paying jobs as domestic servants, janitors, or day laborers. Such poverty discouraged literacy and encouraged malnutrition. Most whites considered blacks as second-class citizens.

Despite such restrictions, African Americans had managed to create a small middle class of clergy, physicians, educators, funeral directors, barbers, and beauticians, most of whom served their own communities. In 1896, for example, educated middle-class women established the National Association of Colored Women to promote the social and intellectual uplift of their people. In addition, desperate farmworkers were moving in growing numbers into southern towns and cities, where opportunities for economic improvement brought them into greater contact with whites, both as workers and consumers. In 1901, the only African American in Congress—Representative George H. White of North Carolina—described his constituents as "a rising people, full of potential." White leaders in the South took such words as a warning and turned to segregation codes, political disenfranchisement, and terror to protect white supremacy.

Beginning in the 1890s, southern legislatures passed "Jim Crow" laws that imposed racial segregation in transportation, schools, and public places. In the landmark *Plessy* v. *Ferguson* case of 1896, the Supreme Court ruled that such practices were constitutional if facilities were "separate but equal." In this way, the Court reduced the matter of race lines to a simple code of white and black; people of mixed races became legally black. After the ruling, most southern states adopted even stricter codes of segregation that included drinking fountains, toilets, even Bibles used in courts. But in ruling that "separate" must be "equal," the Court left open the possibility of subsequent litigation about the meaning of equality.

The tightening of southern segregation coincided with the introduction of laws designed to eliminate the black vote. The failure of southern Populists to build an interracial coalition against the Democrats during the 1890s revealed the power of white politicians to void black votes through fraud and intimidation. Yet Democrats feared the potential of blacks to tip the balance of power. "When we say the Negro is unfit to rule," explained a North Carolina politician in 1900, "we declare he is unfit to vote." South Carolina's Ben "Pitchfork" Tillman, Mississippi's James "The White Knight" Vardaman, and Georgia's Hoke Smith rose to power in the Democratic Party through demagogic appeals that fused white anxiety over the power of northern corporations to control southern life with blatant race-baiting. Vardaman denounced the black man as "a lazy, lying, lustful animal which no conceivable amount of training can transform into a tolerable citizen." The only effect of education, he said, "is to spoil a good field hand and make an insolent cook."

Such racism inspired fundamental changes in southern state constitutions that effectively denied African Americans the right to vote (not just thwarted their votes by illegal actions). The process began with southern representatives in Congress working to repeal Reconstruction-era statutes that permitted federal oversight of southern elections. (Northern politicians accepted such acts in exchange for southern votes for measures that benefited northern corporations.) Then, in a series of southern state constitutional conventions, Democrats won support of a poll tax, which discouraged political participation by the poor of both races. "Understanding" tests, which demanded an ability to explain portions of the state constitution read aloud by white county clerks, further disenfranchised potential voters. Poor whites could avoid these restrictions through tacit agreements with white officials and "grandfather" clauses that suspended voting requirements for those whose ancestors could vote before 1865. All-white primaries in the one-party South also purged black voters.

Beyond legal restrictions on voting or using public facilities, whites employed sheer violence to keep African Americans in subordinate positions. Between 1884 and 1914, white vigilantes and mobs lynched some 3,600 black men, many in gruesome public rituals purporting to protect the purity of white women from black sexual assault. African American journalist Ida Wells dismissed such allegations and suggested not only that white men sought sexual pleasure from black women but also that white women voluntarily entered sexual relations with black men. For those comments, the Memphis-based Wells had to leave the South forever.

Southern leaders legitimized their racist policies by citing pseudoscientific literature that asserted the biological and cultural inferiority of African peoples. Anthropological works of the period insisted that blacks had "primitive nerve impulses." Such notions led the pioneer psychologist G. Stanley Hall to advise that blacks should be treated by veterinarians instead of physicians. The sociologist Frank Lester Ward speculated that rape involved an unconscious attempt by black men to raise the degraded status of their race.

Notions of Anglo-Saxon supremacy found increasing support in the field of history. Academic scholars such as Woodrow Wilson portrayed Reconstruction as a corrupt attempt by northern "carpetbaggers" to integrate former slaves into social and political life on equal terms. Revisionist sentiments reached popular audiences through novels such as Thomas Dixon's *The Clansman* (1905), which romanticized the creation of the terrorist Ku Klux Klan. Filmmaker D. W. Griffith used the book as the basis for *Birth of a Nation* (1915), one of Hollywood's first full-length motion pictures. Shortly after the movie's White House screening—it was "history written with lightning," said President Wilson—"Colonel" William Joseph Simmons reorganized the Klan as a nostalgic fraternal order.

Although African Americans in the North generally escaped the codified segregation of the southern states, they regularly encountered discrimination in housing, education, and employment. Amid growing racial tensions, African Americans also faced the danger of spontaneous attacks by white mobs. Major race riots shook New York City in 1900 and Springfield, Illinois, the home of Abraham Lincoln, in 1908. When a dozen black soldiers stationed in Brownsville, Texas, reacted violently to racial slurs and harassment in 1906, President Theodore Roosevelt issued blanket dishonorable discharges to three companies of their all-black regiment, including six men who had won the Medal of Honor.

Efforts to control African Americans through segregation, disenfranchisement, and violence reflected white anxieties about the emergence of an autonomous black community. In 1900, Booker T. Washington remained the leader of the nation's African Americans. Born a slave, Washington graduated from a vocational training school for blacks established by northern philanthropists. As head of Alabama's Normal and Industrial Institute at Tuskegee, he instilled the student body with middle-class virtues such as hard work, frugality, cleanliness, and proper manners. Convinced that blacks would fare better as southern artisans or farmers than as northern wage earners, he encouraged

Booker Taliaferro Washington (1856-1915)

Nicknamed "the Wizard" for his mastery of backstage political intrigue, Booker T. Washington was born into slavery, the child of a Virginia plantation cook and their white owner. Washington served as a houseboy until his family moved to West Virginia following emancipation. After

Brown Brothers

working briefly in salt furnaces and coal mines, the former slave found a position as a house servant for a wealthy general and was taught to read by the officer's wife, a former New England schoolteacher. Attending the Hampton Institute in Virginia, a teacher training school for "colored" students, he internalized the work ethic that would direct his life efforts.

Washington combined a small grant from the state of Alabama with donations from northern philanthropists to found a "normal" school for African Americans at Tuskegee in 1881. Convinced that slavery had left blacks dependent on whites, he instilled strict discipline and training in skills and crafts to prepare pupils for economic self-sufficiency in the rural South. As Tuskegee's student body grew to 1,500, industrialists like Andrew Carnegie and John D. Rockefeller consulted the school director on donations to other African American vocational institutions. In 1895, Washington's reputation for reliability brought him an invitation to address Atlanta's Cotton States and International Exposition.

students to accept a separate social status from whites. As Washington became the conduit for northern contributions to African American schools and the distributor of meager black political patronage, he appeared before the Atlanta Cotton Exposition of 1895 to assure the leaders of the New South that "in all things purely social" the races could "be separate as the fingers, yet one as the hand in all things essential to mutual progress."

As the southern plantation cotton economy stagnated and white racial hysteria escalated, blacks began migrating to the North. Railroad promotions and exhortations by African American newspapers such as the *Chicago Defender* alerted black migrants to new opportunities in auto plants, steel mills,

The Atlanta speech cemented Washington's position as the nation's foremost African American leader. Reiterating calls for hard work, economic improvement, and self-help, the Tuskegee educator told blacks to "cast down your bucket where you are." By temporarily accepting a separate social status for African Americans and minimizing political demands, Washington offered an accommodationist strategy for southern race relations. Yet his emphasis on black education contradicted racial demagogues who believed that schooling was wasted on people of color. Convinced that political rights would follow economic success, Washington formed the National Negro Business League in 1900. He summarized the self-help strategy in the widely acclaimed autobiography, *Up from Slavery* (1901), and won an invitation to dine with President Theodore Roosevelt at the White House. Quietly, Washington bought stock in black newspapers and financed court challenges to racial segregation.

As segregation laws, voter disenfranchisement, and lynching spread across the South, Washington's supporters claimed that the Tuskegee director had gained essential assistance from whites in a period of dangerous racial tension. Yet northern African American critics feared that vocational training would permanently relegate black workers to marginal status, that accommodation sacrificed racial pride, and that Washington used his extensive patronage powers to ostracize opponents. Despite such controversies, the distinguished principal of Tuskegee remained a symbol of African American aspiration, dignity, and self-mastery long after his death in 1915.

and packing houses, even though most of the openings turned out to be in menial service jobs. Changing economic circumstances produced new concerns over civil rights. In 1905 W. E. B. Du Bois, a history and sociology professor at all-black Atlanta University, organized a conference of community leaders dedicated to "Negro freedom and growth." Meeting on the Canadian side of Niagara Falls, thirty-one conferees endorsed a declaration by Du Bois and Boston activist William Monroe Trotter that Booker T. Washington's style of racial accommodation had to be replaced by protest.

The first African American to earn a Ph.D. from Harvard, Du Bois accused the powerful Washington of failing to adjust to the urban-industrial age,

William Edward Burghardt Du Bois
(1868–1963)

"The problem of the twentieth century," the eminent black scholar W. E. B. Du Bois declared in 1900, "is the problem of the color line." Born in Massachusetts, Du Bois earned undergraduate degrees from Fisk University and Harvard before receiving a Harvard Ph.D. in history

after writing a dissertation on the slave trade. He began his academic career in 1894 teaching classical languages at Ohio's all-black Wilberforce University. He then became an assistant instructor of sociology at the University of Pennsylvania, where he completed a pioneering study of Philadelphia's African American community. Between 1897 and 1910, Du Bois served as professor of economics and history at Atlanta University, another African American institution.

As a young instructor, Du Bois had complimented Booker T. Washington's Atlanta Exposition address as "a word fitly spoken." However, traumatized by a well-publicized Georgia lynching in 1899 and moved by participation in the first Pan African Conference in London in 1900, Du Bois rejected Washington's accommodationist strategies. In *The Souls of Black Folk* (1903), the scholar melded academic and partisan prose in a penetrating view of U.S. race relations. "The Negro is a sort of seventh son," he wrote, "born with a veil, and gifted with second sight in

insisting that blacks could never achieve economic success without political power. He proposed to challenge racial discrimination under the leadership of a college-educated elite of African Americans he called "the Talented Tenth." This approach won support from a group of white reformers who shared a commitment to equal rights for blacks. In 1909 Du Bois joined social worker Lillian Wald, activist Mary White Ovington, socialist William English Walling, Rabbi Stephen Wise, and several reform-minded journalists in organizing the National Association for the Advancement of Colored People (NAACP), the nation's first civil rights organization. As editor of its magazine, *The Crisis*, Du Bois became the nation's leading voice of African American rights.

this American world." Every African American was "an American, a Negro; two souls, two thoughts." Du Bois criticized Washington's toleration of disenfranchisement and racial segregation and called for a "talented tenth" to lead African Americans to social inclusion.

Seeking to focus political protest, Du Bois convened a 1905 conference dedicated to "Negro freedom and growth." Despite Booker T. Washington's opposition, delegates issued Du Bois's Declaration of Principles, co-written with Monroe Trotter, which was a clear and forthright demand for full citizenship rights for African Americans. After several yearly "Niagara movement" meetings, Du Bois joined a group of white reformers and Progressives in 1909 to form the National Association for the Advancement of Colored People.

Designed as an interracial movement to gain civil and social rights for African Americans, the NAACP chose Du Bois as its director of publicity and research and as the editor of its monthly magazine, *The Crisis*. He used this position to spread ideas on political empowerment and race pride among African Americans participating in the Great Migration from the South. A sign of Du Bois's influence came in 1917 when the brilliant editor organized New York City's silent march against lynching. By then, his editorials and articles had helped to spread the NAACP across both North and South, making it the most important African American institution in the nation and Du Bois its leading proponent.

THE PLIGHT OF WORKING PEOPLE

African Americans, Nuevos Mexicanos, and European immigrants shared one common denominator: the prosperity of early twentieth-century capitalism rested on the labor of ordinary men, women, and children. Although the incorporation of new technologies created opportunities for engineers, production supervisors, and white-collar managers, corporate mergers and mechanization replaced many skilled jobs. Most workers continued to earn paltry wages for long hours under hard working conditions. At the turn of the century, one economist estimated that 60 percent of all men did not earn enough to maintain a family. By 1916 almost two-thirds of the nation's people owned only 5 percent of national wealth.

No event publicized the horrors of industrial work more vividly than the 1911 fire at the Triangle Shirtwaist Company in New York City. The blaze began on the top floor of a ten-story building one Saturday afternoon as the workers—several hundred Italian and Jewish immigrant women—prepared to leave. The women jammed against the exits, but management had locked the doors to keep employees from stealing fabric and consorting with union organizers. When the elevators filled, some women leaped into the shafts, where their bodies jammed the machinery. Dozens more climbed to the roof and, holding hands, jumped to their death. The tragedy claimed the lives of nearly 150 young women. A few days later, 80,000 people marched in a somber funeral procession. A subsequent investigation blamed company man- agement as well as the building and fire departments and resulted in passage of some fifty laws designed to improve factory safety.

As the Triangle fire demonstrated, women workers were an essential part of industrial labor. The number of women who worked outside the home grew from 5 million in 1900 to 7 million ten years later, making women one-fifth of the nation's workforce. Yet social restraints prohibited married women, espe- cially of the middle and upper classes, from obtaining paying jobs. As a result, most women who worked outside the home were either single or lacked any other support. Female workers had a hierarchy of preferred employment. The best educated became teachers or nurses (with a small number of doctors and lawyers). Graduates of high school entered the clerical field or, in descending order, chose retail sales, factory work, or domestic service; the latter occupa- tion claimed 40 percent of the female labor force in 1900. Racial segregation limited these choices further. In department stores, for instance, white women sold goods by day; by night, black women washed the floors.

Child labor proliferated. In 1900, 10 percent of all girls between the ages of ten and fifteen and 20 percent of boys of the same age held jobs. "The most beautiful sight we see is the child at labor," declared Coca-Cola founder Asa Candler. By 1913 roughly one-fifth of the nation's children earned their own livings. Even when states adopted laws regulating child labor, they typically permitted twelve-year-old children to work ten hours a day (see Chapter 3 for federal child labor legislation).

Labor abuses also increased in southern manufacturing, where 62 per- cent of the labor force worked in low-wage extractive industries. As consumer demand for ready-made cigarettes spread, producers such as the American Tobacco Company rationalized tobacco processing in the Carolinas and Vir- ginia and employed marginalized farmers in company plants at subsistence wages. With investment in cotton manufacturing increasing sevenfold be- tween 1880 and 1900, southern mills surpassed New England's as the largest

EXHIBIT **1-3   CHILDREN AGED 10–15 IN THE U.S. WORKFORCE, 1890–1910**
(IN ROUNDED MILLIONS)

1890	1.5
1900	1.8
1910	1.6

Source: *Historical Statistics of the United States, Colonial Times to 1970* (1975).

processors of raw cotton spun into fiber and woven fabric. The ranks of southern textile workers grew from 17,000 to 100,000. During the 1890s child labor increased 130 percent in southern mills.

Because families survived by acting as working units in an economy with few skilled positions, mill employees resented efforts to regulate their children's labor or the enforcement of school attendance laws. Adult women also remained an important part of the mill economy. However, southern mill wages were among the lowest in the nation, and male family members were compelled to join the workforce so that earnings could be pooled and company housing shared. Living in primitive and racially segregated mill villages that maintained a rural flavor, most southern mill hands worked sixty-hour weeks. Black employees toiled under similar conditions but were assigned the most menial tasks.

Mexican American workers in Texas and the Southwest also faced exploitative conditions. The replacement of the old ranch economy by large-scale commercial operations forced many Mexicans into agricultural wage labor, tenant farming, railroad construction, or mining. Meanwhile, the federal government initiated a series of dam-building projects to irrigate more than a million acres of southwestern agricultural land. During the first years of the century, commercial interests began to use holdings in Texas, Arizona, and southern California for large-scale cultivation of cotton and vegetables.

As outside investment promoted mechanized agriculture and forced Mexican peasants off the land, and as Mexico's refugees fled the revolutionary turmoil of the 1910s, agribusiness employers tapped an additional labor supply. The new Mexican Americans, or Chicanos, joined displaced producers above the Rio Grande to become a permanent migrant workforce that traveled across the country cultivating and picking crops as they ripened. Landowners paid the lowest possible wages and housed temporary adult and child field workers in shacks with primitive facilities. To keep wages low and discourage strikes, corporate growers persuaded Congress to waive immigration restrictions on farmworkers in 1917.

EXHIBIT **1-4**   **U.S. PER CAPITA INCOME, 1895–1915**
(IN ROUNDED DOLLARS)

1895	200
1900	246
1905	299
1910	383
1915	398

Source: *Historical Statistics of the United States, Colonial Times to 1970* (1975).

A RISING LABOR MOVEMENT

Coinciding with the era of corporate prosperity and a rising cost of food, labor problems stimulated a surge in union membership from 800,000 in 1900 to 2 million in 1917. During this period, John Mitchell's United Mine Workers (UMW) gained recruits with a series of well-publicized walkouts in the Pennsylvania and West Virginia coal mines (see Chapter 2). However, American Federation of Labor (AFL) craft unions thrived even more by organizing skilled workers who faced the speedups that accompanied mechanization and scientific management strategies.

Some of the most protracted union struggles involved the garment industry. In 1900 Jewish labor activists organized the International Ladies Garment Workers Union (ILGWU), which mobilized mainly female apparel employees. The union lost a bitter struggle against the Triangle Shirtwaist Company in 1910, when company guards beat women strikers. After Chicago police killed ten women demonstrators in a citywide walkout later in the year, the ILGWU lost a second strike. Yet a successful organizing drive in 1911 brought stability to the industry by pioneering the use of arbitration procedures to settle disputes. Meanwhile, socialist Sidney Hillman's Amalgamated Clothing Workers combined a conciliatory approach to management with innovative union practices such as cooperative housing and banking.

Common laborers in the South faced greater challenges. In Atlanta, where one-fifth of the labor force was organized, cotton mill workers joined a strike led by the United Textile Workers of America and the AFL in 1914–1915. Subjected to piecework, long hours, low wages, and competition from child labor, Atlanta mill workers were unified by kinship ties and republican values. After a walkout precipitated by the discharge of fellow unionists, strikers managed to arrange visits by representatives of the Department of Labor and the U.S. Commission on Industrial Relations. Still, the workers lost the bitter strike when management used blacks to evict them from company-rented housing.

More violent conflicts erupted in the West, where the Western Federation of Miners (WFM) became a major force in the 1890s. When the union struck the Colorado coal fields in 1903, the Mine Owners Association launched a campaign of terror, forced the governor to declare martial law, and precipitated a bloody civil war. The WFM benefited by forming alliances with Mexican American miners, whose *mutualista* benevolent associations promoted ethnic solidarity. In 1913, the union organized a fifteen-month strike of Greek, Italian, Slavic, and Mexican miners at Ludlow, Colorado. The bitter struggle reached a climax in April 1914 when the Colorado Fuel and Iron Company evicted strikers from company housing and the governor summoned the National Guard. After shootouts between workers and company police, Guardsmen exploded bombs above a miners' tent colony and attacked mine families with machine-gun fire, killing thirteen adults and five children. The Commission on Industrial Relations subsequently blamed mine owners for "ruthless suppression of unionism." A shaken John D. Rockefeller Jr., whose family had a 40 percent interest in the company, adopted public relations tactics and initiated a program of employee representation, union recognition, and higher wages.

The most controversial labor organization of the era was the Industrial Workers of the World (IWW) or Wobblies, organized in 1903 by WFM leader "Big Bill" Haywood and other socialists. Bluntly declaring that "the working class and the employing class have nothing in common," the IWW rejected the use of labor contracts as well as political action. Instead, charismatic organizers like Haywood and Joe Hill sought to create an all-embracing union of workers that would employ "direct action" to achieve a classless society. Under Haywood's leadership, the Wobblies mobilized miners, loggers, and migrant workers in the West and used songbooks, hymns, and "free speech" crusades to create worker solidarity. The IWW also organized sit-down strikes against General Electric, staged a walkout of silk workers in Paterson, New Jersey, and unionized the textile mills of Lawrence, Massachusetts.

Business leaders saw union demands as illegal restraints of worker contracts and used federal courts to uphold antilabor injunctions under the Sherman Antitrust Act. The labor movement also suffered from the reluctance of U.S. workers to develop class loyalty. At a time when consumer values held the promise of upward social mobility, labor collectivism implied the permanence of a worker's status. As access to the pleasures of popular culture came within reach of millions of working people, efforts to link the labor movement with republican, producer, or socialist values were not always successful.

The ethnic and cultural diversity of the working class made it even more difficult to forge labor unity. Besides a number of mutually antagonistic nationalities and social groups, racial tensions limited the movement. When Japanese and Mexican farmworkers struck in California in 1903, for example, the participation of Asian workers prompted the race-conscious AFL to refuse to charter the union. Most AFL groups were racially exclusive and rejected women, ethnic minorities, and unskilled labor. Such policies limited union growth and encouraged excluded groups such as African Americans to act as strikebreakers. Gender also affected the struggle because the task orientation and personal nature of female jobs in retail sales, clerical service, and domestic work discouraged collective bargaining.

SOCIALISTS, ANARCHISTS, AND CULTURAL RADICALS

The militancy of organized labor sparked greater support for a vibrant socialist movement. Organizing the Socialist Party of America in 1900, union activist Eugene Debs brought together industrial workers, urban ethnic minorities, agrarian monetarists, radical intellectuals, and middle-class reformists. "While there is a lower class," declared Debs, "I'm in it. While there is a criminal class, I'm of it. While there's a soul in prison, I am not free." To confront corporate power, the Socialist leader espoused a pragmatic agenda of workplace democracy and participation in elections. Theoreticians like Daniel De Leon argued that revolutionary industrial unions could develop sufficient class consciousness to elect political leaders and eventually turn government over to working-class syndicates. Meanwhile, the skillful Marxist oratory of New York's Morris Hillquit appealed to the Socialist Party's autonomous immigrant branches and readers of its foreign-language press.

Socialists won control of the International Association of Machinists in 1907. Yet Samuel Gompers and building trade unions prevented a similar takeover of the AFL. Following Debs's desire to build a mass movement that crossed class lines, the party abandoned the call to nationalize private land in 1910 and expelled the syndicalist followers of De Leon two years later. With a membership of nearly 120,000 in 1912, the party sought legitimacy by running a nationwide slate of candidates. By endorsing municipal ownership of public utilities such as gas, water, and sewer systems, Socialists elected over 300 municipal officers. The party also placed 33 members in state legislatures and sent Victor Berger, a German American from Milwaukee, to Congress. Running as a fourth-party candidate, Debs received almost a million votes for president (6 percent of the total) in 1912 (see Chapter 2).

Some radicals were attracted to anarchism, a philosophy that saw the state as an oppressive instrument serving the propertied classes. Utopian collectivists such as Emma Goldman, Alexander Berkman, and Johann Most disparaged property ownership and sought to dismantle all power structures. Adhering to the "propaganda of the deed," a few anarchists like Berkman advocated the use of violence or armed rebellion to appropriate property for collective use to create a cooperative society.

A feminist, "free-love" opponent of wedlock, and a pacifist, Goldman carried the spirit of anarchism into the cultural realm. "If I can't dance," she once told a gathering of radicals, "I don't want to be part of your revolution." Goldman filled her *Mother Earth* magazine with denunciations of marriage, organized religion, and bourgeois politics as extensions of male power. Women "must no longer keep their mouths shut and their wombs open," she declared. Goldman's pamphlet, "Why the Poor Should Not Have Children," resulted in her arrest in 1915 after a birth-control lecture in Portland, Oregon. Meanwhile, Charlotte Perkins Gilman emerged as the new century's leading critic of gender roles. In *Women and Economics* (1898) and *The Man-Made World* (1911), Gilman dismissed housekeeping as the "smallest, lowest, oldest" task in the world and argued that women should be free to join the paid workplace.

The 1910s produced an outpouring of political dissent and free-spirited bohemianism that marked the rebellion of a generation rejecting Victorian hierarchy and genteel propriety. Seeking refuge in artistic havens such as New York's Greenwich Village and Taos, New Mexico, middle-class rebels such as Floyd Dell and Waldo Frank deployed Marxist criticism to attack capitalism and adopted Sigmund Freud's notions about sexual repression to discredit "puritanism." "We feel social injustice as our fathers felt personal sin," exclaimed Randolph Bourne, a dissenting essayist who celebrated the potential flowering of youthful idealism. Radical poets, novelists, artists, intellectuals, journalists, and cartoonists found a welcome outlet in Max Eastman's magazine, *The Masses*, published between 1911 and 1917.

NEW FAMILIES AND POPULAR CULTURE

The nature of work in industrial society and the shift to city living transformed family patterns, altered gender roles, and created a new class of consumers. The trend away from rural farms and small businesses meant that middle-class urbanites relied less on the family as an economic unit of survival. Family size continued to drop as the national birthrate declined from 44.3 per thousand to 27.7 per thousand between 1860 and 1920. The reduction in pregnancies coincided with increased use of contraceptives by middle-class women, a practice advanced by birth control advocate Margaret Sanger.

Wider economic opportunities for middle-class women coincided with a gradual increase in the divorce rate from 5 percent in 1880 to 10 percent nearly four decades later. Enhanced personal freedom for women translated into a greater educational opportunity; by 1920, 47.3 percent of all college students were women. The importance of education in the white-collar workplace lengthened the period between physical maturity and economic independence. Elementary school attendance grew steadily between 1898 and 1914, and high school and college enrollment doubled. By 1917, thirty-eight states had enacted laws requiring young people to remain in school until age sixteen.

The extended period of schooling encouraged the emergence of a distinct peer culture. Psychologist G. Stanley Hall labeled this stage of life "adolescence," asserting that modern industrial society required an intermediate period of disciplined physical development and postponed sexuality. For working-class families, the increase of single women in the workforce brought concerns about the loss of traditional patriarchal control of their daughters. After the passage of laws raising the legal age of sexual consent, working-class parents accounted for half the cases brought to court to contest voluntary sexual relations of their children. The courts usually favored the parents' claims, though many unmarried women left home because of abusive environments.

As the average work week for middle-class employees decreased from fifty-six to forty-one hours between 1900 and 1920, a growing number of urban consumers became increasingly attracted to youthful imagery and pursuits. Display advertising emphasized women with vigor and hourglass dimensions popularized by Charles Dana Gibson's smart-looking "girls." Portrayals of healthy male bodies, which in the nineteenth century had viewed fat as a sign of success, now stressed muscularity and strength. College football became a middle-class fad, and professional baseball found its way to the major industrial cities. Meanwhile, amusement parks appeared on city outskirts. The new centers featured arcades, carousels, roller coasters, food concessions, live orchestras, and dance pavilions. New York's Coney Island, which attracted more than a million people on hot summer days, provided a holiday spirit for working-class families seeking Sunday release from jobs.

Middle-class consumers sought more respectable entertainment through the purchase of sheet music to play on parlor pianos. Beginning in the 1890s, publishers in New York's "Tin Pan Alley" district used mass-production techniques to market popular songs. By 1915 the industry was selling 200 million music sheets a year. After 1900 a new form of music called "rag" or "ragtime" crossed racial, ethnic, and class lines. First played by a German musician in Missouri, ragtime was popularized by the African American composer and pianist Scott Joplin. Fusing syncopated African-derived rhythm with European melody, the new music spread from clubs and brothels to amusement parks and dance halls, where it blended with blues and jazz forms emanating from the black South. As urban men and women mixed together in the informal atmosphere of the dance palace, others sought entertainment in the ethnic humor and benign sexuality of the vaudeville stage.

The new century's most revolutionary form of entertainment was the motion picture. After George Eastman pioneered the photographic process in the 1880s, Thomas Edison developed a movie camera and kinetoscope. Silent pictures like the sixty-second production *The Kiss* (1896) appeared in the penny arcades of urban vice districts. Once films could be projected on walls or screens, director Edwin W. Porter made *The Great Train Robbery* (1903), the first film with a consistent plot line. A group of immigrant Jewish entrepreneurs, including Samuel Goldwyn and Adolph Zukor, then moved exhibitions to "nickelodeon" (5 cents a ticket) storefronts in tenement neighborhoods. By 1908 the nation contained nearly 10,000 movie establishments. Seeking to expand their audience, exhibitors took over vaudeville stages and built their own theaters.

Leaving the East Coast for Hollywood to escape harsh weather, high costs, production restrictions, and troublesome labor unions, movie entrepreneurs consolidated casting, production, distribution, and exhibition. By 1913, serials such as *The Perils of Pauline* and *Ruth of the Rockies* were smash hits. Director Mack Sennett featured the "Keystone Kops" in a series of "slapstick" comedies that parodied police and social authorities. Filmmakers showcased selected "stars" such as Lillian Gish, Mary Pickford, and Charlie Chaplin. As movie attendance reached 10 million people a year by the mid-1910s, Chaplin and Pickford negotiated million-dollar contracts.

Chaplin's brilliant portrait of the "little tramp," an underdog in baggy pants, resonated with millions of immigrants and rural migrants who faced snobbery and middle-class hostility in strange environments. Yet Hollywood also learned to engage middle-class audiences. Director Cecil de Mille brought a touch of class to films like *The Cheat* (1915), the same year that D. W. Griffith's controversial *Birth of a Nation* riveted audiences with a three-hour history lecture. Actors like Mary Pickford and her frequent co-star Douglas Fairbanks flaunted new styles of material consumption in lavish romance stories. By 1920 the motion picture industry had become a major influence on popular consumer tastes and values.

PRAGMATIST PHILOSOPHERS AND REALIST ARTISTS

As the middle class faced the tensions and dislocations of the urban-industrial life, the literary and artistic conventions of the Victorian era began to fade. Although sentimental, romantic, and moralistic art remained popular, young writers and artists increasingly found such optimism out of place. In literature, a "Little Renaissance" emerged around a cluster of younger writers known as realists and naturalists. Theodore Dreiser, the son of a German immigrant, exploded the confines of the Victorian novel in *Sister Carrie* (1900) by realistically depicting a young woman's corruption by city life. Dreiser sustained the book's pessimistic tone and frank sexual themes in *The Financier* (1912) and *The Titan* (1914). Other naturalists included Stephen Crane, Frank Norris, Willa Cather, and Ellen Glasgow.

Similar shifts took place in American poetry. In the 1910s a new generation of young poets rebelled against the Victorian genteel tradition by experimenting with new methods and more contemporary themes. In 1912 Harriet Monroe founded the influential journal *Poetry,* which published works by Robert Frost, Edgar Lee Masters, e. e. cummings, Carl Sandburg, Amy Lowell, and Edna St. Vincent Millay. Although the perspectives of the new poets differed, they drew their material and use of language from the experiences of common people.

Modern art also shattered Victorian sensibilities. Painters like John Sloan and George Bellows depicted the harshness of the contemporary world so forcefully that critics named their style the Ashcan school. "Forget about art," realist Robert Henri told his students, "and paint pictures of what interests you." In 1913 the exhibitor (and photographer) Alfred Stieglitz helped to organize the Armory Show, an exhibition that included abstract paintings by Marcel Duchamp, Henri Matisse, and Pablo Picasso. Introducing cubism and expressionism, the show dramatized the break with nineteenth-century formalism and heralded the artist's new demand for freedom to explore the internal dimensions of modern life.

A similar rejection of nineteenth-century certainties contributed to the development of a distinctively national philosophy: pragmatism. As expressed by Harvard psychologist and philosopher William James, pragmatism rejected the validity of absolutes and fixed principles, suggesting an open-ended universe. James argued that ideas should be tested by their workability and that an idea contained meaning only in relation to the consequences precipitated by believing the proposition. "What in short," James asked, "is the truth's cash value in experiential terms?"

Pragmatism found an effective advocate in Columbia University educator John Dewey, who applied its tenets to group activity and social action. Calling himself an "instrumentalist," Dewey considered authoritarian teaching methods such as rote memorization, strict routine, and the mastery of a sharply defined body of knowledge inappropriate to the learning experience. He denounced beliefs in absolute truth as "the ultimate refuge of the stand patter." Instead, Dewey suggested that schools be democratically organized and rooted in direct experience and that they serve as agents of social reform as well as vehicles for transmitting culture. Such ideas reflected a growing faith among urban professionals that public education could stabilize the social order. Works by historian Charles Beard and economist Thorstein Veblen also illustrated the faith that "progressive" technicians and reformers could apply rational planning to offset vested interests and mere precedent.

SOCIAL JUSTICE

"Jesus Christ knew a great deal . . . about organizing society," reform-minded minister Washington Gladden observed in the 1890s, "and the application of his law to industrial society will be found to work surprisingly well." Gladden's

Social Gospel inspired many "progressive" Christians to embark on projects of social reform. Preaching that spiritual regeneration led to social justice, Gladden believed that government promotion of communal property ownership could reduce class conflict. Protestant theologian Walter Rauschenbusch expanded on Gladden's notions in the influential *Christianity and the Social Crisis* (1907). Arguing that social environment shaped personal character, Rauschenbusch called for an activist ministry among the urban poor. Similar views were embraced by Roman Catholics who adhered to Pope Leo XIII's 1893 encyclical on economic and social justice.

Middle-class women in the cities played the dominant role in the era's social crusades. Liberated by smaller families and increased leisure time, many joined organizations seeking to restore morality to public life. The General Federation of Women's Clubs, which focused on improving working conditions for women and children, grew from a membership of 50,000 in 1898 to more than a million by 1914. At a time when half of women college graduates did not marry, dedicated single women like Jane Addams made careers in the newly developed field of social work. In 1889 Jane Addams helped start Hull House, a pioneer settlement house. The project aimed to provide working-class residents of a Chicago neighborhood with diverse services including child care, a library, meeting rooms, and classes in housekeeping, cooking, music, and art. Attracting women professionals to serve and live with the urban poor, Addams made the settlement house an advocate of positive social change. By 1910, four hundred such agencies existed in the United States.

Settlement leaders helped energize a community of social feminists. Working with the National Child Labor Committee, they lobbied thirty-one state legislatures to prohibit children younger than fourteen from working in factories, and those less than sixteen from working in mines. Social feminists also managed to eliminate night work and shifts of more than eight hours a day for some young workers. Reformers broke new ground when twenty-two state legislatures established programs that paid child support to widows or abandoned wives. In addition, women professionals secured the inclusion of the Children's Bureau in the Department of Commerce and Labor in 1912. Meanwhile, Florence Kelley's National Consumers' League and the National Woman's Trade Union League won passage of women's minimum wage bills in fifteen states and maximum hour laws in thirty-nine states. In *Muller* v. *Oregon* (1908), Louis D. Brandeis cited expert testimony on the effect of extended labor on women's health to convince the Supreme Court to uphold a ten-hour daily work limit for female workers. Viewed as a "progressive" decision, the ruling provided a constitutional basis to limit women's equality in the workplace until the 1960s.

Purity and Social Feminism

Social reform often overlapped the purity crusade. The movement for moral purification had roots in pre–Civil War evangelical temperance campaigns

Margaret Higgins Sanger (1883-1966)

Feminist and birth control advocate Margaret Higgins was the sixth of eleven children born to an Irish Catholic family in the factory town of Corning, New York. Precluded by financial and social pressures from attending medical school, she became a nurse and then married shortly

Culver Pictures

after graduation, despite her assertion that "marriage was akin to suicide."

As an obstetric nurse, Sanger saw numerous cases of self-inflicted abortion among patients on the poverty-stricken Lower East Side of Manhattan. One woman she nursed to recovery begged her doctor for contraceptive information only to be told, "Tell Jake to sleep on the roof." Sanger subsequently recalled that when the patient died six months later during a second abortion attempt, she "came

to a sudden realization that my work as a nurse and my activities in social science were entirely palliative and consequently futile and useless to relieve the misery I saw all about me."

"No woman can call herself free who does not own or control her body," wrote Sanger. Convinced that women could take control of their lives only by first achieving reproductive freedom, she dedicated herself to the cause of "birth control," a term she herself coined. Sanger spent a year studying contraception, and then in 1914 began publication of *Woman Rebel,* a journal whose masthead read, "No Gods; No Masters." Identifying with Greenwich Village socialists and anarchists like Emma Goldman and the followers of the Industrial Workers of the World

that sought to uplift the individual. Believing that personal character and disciplined families depended on a wholesome social environment, moral reformers targeted the liquor trade as a threat to stable family life. The Women's Christian Temperance Union (WCTU), founded by Frances Willard in 1874, had enrolled 2 million members by 1900. Meanwhile, activists at Ohio's Oberlin College formed the Anti-Saloon League in 1893. Its goal was to win passage of an amendment to the U.S. Constitution that would prohibit the sale and distribution of alcoholic beverages.

(IWW), Sanger asserted that the "new woman" would gain "the highest possible fulfillment of her desires on the highest possible plane" when she became "absolute mistress of her own body."

Sanger advocated the diaphragm because it gave women control over reproduction. Her efforts attracted the attention of Anglo-Protestant women eager to limit the size of their families and anxious to control the growing immigrant population in the cities. Indeed, despite her early radicalism, Sanger consistently received a more sympathetic hearing from the middle class than from the working class. Yet birth control provoked intense opposition from purity moralists, the Roman Catholic Church, and male leaders like Theodore Roosevelt. Sanger's use of specific terms such as *gonorrhea* and *syphilis* made her early publications even more controversial.

After Sanger was indicted in 1914 on nine counts of sending birth control information through the mail, she fled to Europe. There she met English psychologist Havelock Ellis and inspected birth control clinics in Holland. When she returned home two years later, the federal government dropped the charges against her. Nevertheless, Sanger soon provoked authorities by opening the first U.S. birth control clinic in Brooklyn, New York. Although Sanger went to jail for thirty days, the case helped to lay the groundwork for future court rulings permitting physicians to dispense contraceptive advice "for the prevention and cure of disease." Abandoning her radical ties after World War I, Sanger increasingly relied on support for the birth control crusade from social elites seeking to reduce the ranks of the "unfit" among the immigrant working class.

The purity crusade also targeted prostitution. Red-light districts existed openly in post–Civil War cities. Many young female newcomers found themselves either coerced or enticed into prostitution, which could bring six times the earnings of wage labor. Reformers such as Elizabeth Blackwell and Caroline Wilson, two of the first women physicians, and Antoinette Blackwell, the first woman ordained as a Protestant minister, campaigned against the "double standard" that allowed white men to have promiscuous relations but insisted that their wives avoid extramarital liaisons. By abolishing "white slavery," reformers hoped to destroy the sexual marketplace. To aid urban newcomers, activists also supported organizations such as the Young Men's Christian Association (YMCA), the Young Women's Christian Association (YWCA), and the Traveler's Aid Society.

Reformers' concern for the morality of young women prompted new laws to oversee the private lives of teenagers and working adolescents. Although most states raised the age of legal consent for sexual activity and imposed penalties for statutory rape, reformers also advocated juvenile courts and reformatories to prevent sexuality before marriage. Hoping to guide young women toward "correct" behavior, such measures also provided jobs for women social workers, police, and prison staff. In 1908 Portland, Oregon, hired Lola G. Baldwin as the nation's first municipally paid policewoman to prevent sex crimes.

Purity crusaders treated prostitution as a public health issue. As pathologists isolated the organisms that caused syphilis and gonorrhea, blood tests revealed that diseased persons could pass "silent infections" to unsuspecting partners. Responding to pressure from social hygienists, many cities established vice commissions to investigate sex crimes and banned commercial prostitution. In 1910 Congress passed the Mann Act, making transportation of a woman to another state for immoral purposes a federal crime.

Purity crusaders failed to achieve a consensus about contraception. Public health workers such as Margaret Sanger saw "birth control" as a means of preventing the ill effects of excessive pregnancies. Radical feminists such as Emma Goldman hoped that contraception would give women greater control over their lives. Other advocates sought to reduce high birthrates among immigrants and the poor. Yet many purity reformers saw birth control as an affront to women's role as nurturer and feared that carefree sexuality would lead to promiscuity. Conservative reform groups, such as the New York Society for the Prevention of Vice, campaigned against sending contraceptive or abortion medications through the mail. Sanger was forced to close her first birth-control clinic in 1916 when she faced indictment on obscenity charges. Two years later a Supreme Court ruling permitted doctors to distribute birth-control information, although state laws still prohibited the sale of contraceptives.

Concerned that new forms of entertainment popularized sexual promiscuity, purity crusaders and social workers cooperated in promoting wholesome recreation. Their efforts resulted in stricter licensing of cabarets, curbs of liquor sales on dance floors, and the stationing of policewomen at amusement parks. Reformers also worried that motion pictures, by glamorizing crime and sexuality, might lower moral standards among immigrants and working-class youth. Social workers John Collier and Jane Addams supported the National Board of Review in 1908 to preview films and eliminate objectionable material. In 1910 San Francisco censors rejected thirty-two films—including *Saved by a Sailor, In Hot Pursuit,* and *The Black Viper*—as "unfit for public exhibition." By the early 1920s, dozens of cities and eight states had created similar commissions to monitor the fantasies presented on the screen.

Prohibition and Woman's Suffrage

Purity reformers also crusaded against the dangers of substance abuse. The use of narcotics such as opium, morphine, and cocaine had grown steadily during the nineteenth century. Physicians often prescribed diluted opium, a substance readily available in patent medicine. The soft drink Coca-Cola contained small amounts of cocaine until 1903. By the turn of the century, the United States had about 250,000 narcotics addicts.

The rapidly developing health-care professions supported efforts to regulate narcotics. Eager to establish professional standards of practice, doctors and pharmacists embraced the idea that widespread drug use was socially harmful. The American Medical Association and the American Pharmaceutical Association insisted that only professionals with appropriate credentials should dispense drugs. Responding to this pressure, Congress passed the Pure Food and Drug Act in 1906 and initiated federal regulation of the pharmaceutical industry. Three years later, the United States prohibited the importation of opium. In 1914 the Harrison Narcotics Act stipulated that narcotics could be used only for medical purposes and required federal registration of all drug producers as well as a doctor's prescription for all drugs.

Despite the broad scope of the social justice and purity crusades, alcohol remained the main focus of social reformers. In the South, evangelical Protestants denounced the use of liquor as a sin. Social service and health-care professionals joined the campaign. Industrialists such as Henry Ford portrayed drinking as an obstacle to efficient production. The National Safety Council, founded by corporate interests in 1912, dramatized this point by noting the connection between alcohol use and industrial accidents.

Prohibition had distinct social implications for crusaders eager to universalize Anglo-Protestant notions of rationality, efficiency, and discipline. In northern cities, where reformers tied the liquor trade to ethnic political machines and working-class saloons, the crusade against alcohol targeted immigrants accustomed to moderate drinking during holidays and family celebrations. In the South the drinking controversy intersected with racial politics when white supremacists asserted that abstinence would prevent African American men from raping white women. Meanwhile, social feminists in all regions used the alcohol issue to initiate discussion of spousal abuse and neglect by drunken husbands.

With evangelical churches as a base, prohibitionists had persuaded two-thirds of the counties in the South to "vote dry" by 1907. Supporters like William Jennings Bryan praised antiliquor laws as a triumph of the democratic majority over the corrupt and exploitative liquor interests. The movement's power reflected the effectiveness of the Anti-Saloon League, which organized itself as a nationwide lobby and dispersed professional agents to influence public officials. By 1909 six states had passed prohibition laws. Four years later the Webb-Kenyon Act permitted dry states to stop the transportation of liquor across their boundaries. By 1917, when supporters sought congressional approval for an amendment to the Constitution, nineteen states already had enacted alcohol prohibition legislation.

By pitting the organized power of women's civic groups and purity organizations against liquor interests and urban electoral machines, prohibition brought middle-class women into the political arena and dramatized the potential power of the women's vote. Within six years of its founding in 1890, the National American Woman Suffrage Association (NAWSA) had seen four western states grant women the vote. The three Pacific Coast states joined them between 1910 and 1912, although national support for women's suffrage grew slowly. As NAWSA's membership surpassed 75,000 in the early 1910s, professional women and female college students began to link the vote to economic independence and sexual freedom. Yet when social worker Alice Paul led a noisy suffrage protest in Washington in 1913, political leaders like the newly elected President Woodrow Wilson refused to encourage the movement.

NAWSA sought to reassert leadership over the suffrage crusade in 1915 by electing Carrie Chapman Catt as its president. A veteran campaigner, Catt retreated from the radicals' attempts to challenge conventional gender roles and social inequality. Instead, suffragists joined with purity crusaders, arguing that they would be better able to exert a "womanly influence" for reform if women possessed the franchise. Catt had once implored Anglo-Protestants to "cut off the vote of the slums and give it to women." She now expanded this strategy to appeal to nativist and racial sentiments of the white middle class. Hostile to ethnic voters of the industrial cities, NAWSA also rejected requests by black women's groups in the South for inclusion in the suffrage crusade. Although Catt's "insider strategy" caused ethnic, racial, and class rifts in the movement, NAWSA's membership leaped to 2 million by 1917.

These protest campaigns reflected a broader desire among diverse groups to improve and uplift industrial society. Most reformers considered themselves "progressive," though the label disguised positions, such as immigration restriction or racial segregation, that looked backward to the nineteenth century. But as social issues associated with industrial expansion and urban growth demanded attention, conservatives and liberals alike looked to the political arena for a resolution of social problems. Some issues, such as sanitation and health reform, could be handled on the local level; broader issues, such as suffrage or prohibition, became part of state legislative politics. And some issues, such as economic regulation, proved to be national in scale, demanding the involvement of Congress, the White House, and the Supreme Court.

AMERICAN HISTORY RESOURCE CENTER

To explore documents, images, audio and video clips, articles, and commentary related to the material in this chapter, visit the source collections at ushistory.wadsworth.com and and use the Search function with the following key terms:

W. E. B. Du Bois   Eugene Debs
Theodore Roosevelt   Women's Suffrage
Booker T. Washington

RECOMMENDED READINGS

William Leach, *Land of Desire: Merchants, Power and the Rise of a New American Culture* (1993). Focusing on mass marketing in the urban age, the book explores innovations in advertising, sales, and popular culture.

Grace Elizabeth Hale, *Making Whiteness: The Culture of Segregation in the South, 1890–1940* (1998). The author places racial segregation at the turn of the century in the context of social and economic development, resulting in white/black separation.

Gail Bederman, *Manliness and Civilization: A Cultural History of Gender and Race in the United States, 1880–1917* (1995). This analysis of male/female images treats gender relations within the framework of racial ideology.

Christine Stansell, *American Moderns: Bohemian New York and the Creation of a New Century* (2000). This study of cultural radicalism looks at the intellectual avant-garde and its response to the new industrial society.

Additional Readings

The life of J. P. Morgan provides a fine introduction to corporate finance in an age of unregulated banking: see Jean Strouse, *Morgan: American Financier* (1999). Corporate consolidation is explored in Alfred D. Chandler Jr., *Scale and Scope: The Dynamics of Industrial Capitalism* (1990). For technological developments, see James R. Beninger, *The Control Revolution: Technological-ization and the Economic Origins of the Information Society* (1986). Industrial management is the subject of Daniel Nelson, *Frederick W. Taylor and the Rise of Scientific Management* (1980), and Olivier Zunz, *Making America Corporate, 1870–1920* (1990). For changes in mass marketing, see Jackson Lears, *Fables of Abundance: A Cultural History of Advertising in America*

(1994), and Pamela Walker Laird, *Advertising Progress: American Business and the Rise of Consumer Marketing* (1998). See also the pioneering Robert Wiebe, *The Search for Order, 1877–1920* (1968).

Immigration is described in Alan M. Kraut, *The Huddled Masses: The Immigrant in American Society, 1880–1921* (1982). John Higham, *Strangers in the Land: Patterns of American Nativism, 1860–1925* (1955), is the standard work on anti-immigrant thought but should be supplemented by Ronald Takaki, *A Different Mirror: A History of Multicultural America* (1993). For the experience of Asian settlers, see Sucheng Chan, *This Bittersweet Soil: The Chinese in California Agriculture, 1869–1910* (1987), and Robert A. Wilson and Bill Hosokawa, *East to America: A History of the Japanese in the United States* (1980). Government policy toward Native Americans is described in Frederick Hoxie, *A Final Promise: The Campaign to Assimilate the Indians, 1880–1920* (1984). For Mexican Americans, see George J. Sanchez, *Becoming Mexican American: Ethnicity, Culture and Identity in Chicano Los Angeles, 1900–1945* (1993). The Irish American experience is explored in Paul Messbarger, *Fiction with a Parochial Purpose: Social Use of American Catholic Literature, 1884–1900* (1970). Among works on immigrant Jews are Gerald Sorin, *A Time for Building: The Third Migration, 1880–1920* (1992), and Susan A. Glenn, *Daughters of the Shtetl: Life and Labor in the Immigrant Generation* (1990).

Racial segregation is described in Leon F. Litwack, *Trouble in Mind: Black Southerners in the Age of Jim Crow* (1998); Glenda Elizabeth Gilmore, *Gender and Jim Crow: Women and the Politics of White Supremacy in North Carolina, 1896–1920* (1996); and Stephen Kantrowitz, *Ben Tillman and the Reconstruction of White Supremacy* (2000). For the attack on black voting, see Michael Perman, *Struggle for Mastery: Disfranchisement in the South, 1888–1908* (2001). Violent enforcement of white supremacy is the subject of Philip Dray, *At the Hands of Persons Unknown: The Lynching of Black America* (2002). For the antilynching position, see Patricia A. Schechter, *Ida B. Wells-Barnett and American Reform, 1880–1930* (2001).

Northern migration by African Americans is portrayed in Nicholas Lemann, *The Promised Land: The Great Black Migration and How It Changed America* (1991), and James R. Grossman, *Land of Hope: Chicago, Black Southerners, and the Great Migration* (1989). For contrasting approaches to African American politics, see Louis Harlan, *Booker T. Washington: The Wizard of Tuskegee* (1983), and David Levering Lewis, *W. E. B. Du Bois: Biography of a Race, 1868–1919* (1993). See also Carolyn Wedin, *Inheritors of the Spirit: Mary White Ovington and the Founding of the NAACP* (1998).

Descriptions of industrial work can be found in William Lazonick, *Competitive Advantage on the Shop Floor* (1990). For specific studies, see David Von Drehle, *Triangle: The Fire That Changed America* (2003), and Patricia A. Cooper, *Once a Cigar Maker: Men, Women, and Work Culture in American*

Cigar Factories, 1900–1919 (1987). Southern labor conditions are addressed in David L. Carlton, *Mill and Town in South Carolina, 1880–1920* (1982). See also Jacqueline Jones, *Labor of Love, Labor of Sorrow: Black Women, Work, and the Family from Slavery to the Present* (1985). For women's new occupational roles, see Lisa M. Fine, *The Souls of the Skyscraper: Female Clerical Workers in Chicago, 1870–1930* (1990), and Susan Porter Benson, *Counter Cultures: Saleswomen, Managers, and Customers in American Department Stores, 1890–1940* (1986).

A shop-floor perspective on working-class politics can be found in David Montgomery, *The Fall of the House of Labor* (1987). For the labor movement, see Michael Kazin, *Barons of Labor: The San Francisco Building Trades and Union Power in the Progressive Era* (1987). The AFL is covered in Julia Greene, *Pure and Simple Politics: The American Federation of Labor and Political Activism, 1881–1917* (1998). Regional labor protest can be found in Gary M. Fink, *The Fulton Bag and Cotton Mills Strike of 1914–1915* (1993), and Alan Derickson, *Workers' Health, Workers' Democracy: The Western Miners' Struggle, 1891–1925* (1988). An attempt to "uplift" workers is described in Thomas Winter, *Making Men, Making Class: The YMCA and Workingmen, 1877–1920* (2002).

For the cultural ramifications of labor protest, see John Clendenin Townsend, *Running the Gauntlet: Cultural Sources of Violence against the IWW* (1986). See also David Roediger, *The Wages of Whiteness: Race and the Making of the American Working Class* (1991). For the influence of unions on government policy, see the relevant segments of Melvyn Dubofsky, *The State and Labor in Modern America* (1994).

The Socialist movement is the subject of Nick Salvatore, *Eugene Debs, Citizen and Socialist* (1990); Mary Jo Buhle, *Women and American Socialism, 1870–1920* (1983); and L. Glen Sevetan, *Daniel De Leon: The Odyssey of an American Marxist* (1979). For anarchism, see Candace Serena Falk (ed.), *Emma Goldman: A Documentary History of the American Years* (2003), and Marian J. Morton, *Emma Goldman and the American Left* (1992). For the bohemians, see Douglas Clayton, *Floyd Dell: The Life and Times of an American Rebel* (1994), and Mary V. Dearborn, *Queen of Bohemia: The Life of Louise Bryant* (1996). See also Robert A. Rosenstone, *A Romantic Revolutionary: A Biography of John Reed* (1990).

Innovations in family structure are summarized in the relevant segments of John D'Emilio and Estelle B. Freedman, *Intimate Matters: A History of Sexuality in America* (1988). See also Elaine Tyler May, *Great Expectations: Marriage and Divorce in Post-Victorian America* (1980).

For urban culture, see Stephen J. Ross, *Working-Class Hollywood: Silent Film and the Shaping of Class in America* (1998); Kathy Peiss, *Cheap Amusements: Working Women and Leisure in Turn-of-the-Century New York* (1986); and Robert W. Snyder, *The Voice of the City: Vaudeville and Popular Culture in New York* (1989). For amusement parks, see John F. Kasson, *Amusing the Million: Coney Island at the Turn of the Century* (1978). Popular songs are explored in sections of Ian Whitcomb, *After the Ball: Popular Music from Rag to Rock* (1982). For ragtime, see Peter Gammond, *Scott Joplin and the Ragtime Era* (1976). See also Ronald L. Morris, *Wait Until Dark: Jazz and the Underworld, 1890–1940* (1988). Introductions to motion pictures include Charles J. Maland, *Chaplin and American Culture: The Evolution of a Star Image* (1989), and Richard Schikel, *D. W. Griffith: An American Life* (1984).

Ferment in the visual arts is addressed in Martin Green, *New York 1913: The Armory Show and the Paterson Strike Pageant* (1988). The literary rebellion is treated in Jay Martin, *Harvests of Change: American Literature, 1865–1914* (1967). For intellectual change, see David W. Noble, *The Progressive Mind, 1890–1917* (1981). Dewey's ideas are explained in Alan Ryan, *John Dewey and the High Tide of American Liberalism* (1995). The Anglo-American context of Progressive thought is explored in James Kloppenberg, *Uncertain Victory: Social Democracy and Progressivism in European and American Thought, 1870–1920* (1986). For the plight of reformers and experts, see Leon Fink, *Progressive Intellectuals and the Dilemmas of Democratic Commitment* (1997).

An account of the social gospel movement can be found in Paul T. Phillips, *A Kingdom on Earth: Anglo-American Social Christianity, 1880–1940* (1996), and George Marsden, *Fundamentalism and American Culture: The Shaping of Twentieth-Century Evangelicalism, 1870–1925* (1980). For social justice activism, see David B. Danbom, *"The World of Hope": Progressives and the Struggle for an Ethical Life* (1987). Labor reform is outlined in Elizabeth Anne Payne, *Reform, Labor, and Feminism: Margaret Dreier Robins and the Women's Trade Union League* (1988).

For social service professionals, see Kathryn Kish Sklar, *Florence Kelley and the Nation's Work: The Rise of Women's Political Culture, 1830–1900* (1995), and Robyn Muncy, *Creating a Female Dominion in American Reform, 1890–1935* (1991). Social settlement centers are the subject of Doris Groshen Daniels, *Always a Sister: The Feminism of Lillian D. Wald* (1989); Mina Carson, *Settlement Folk: Social Thought and the American Settlement Movement, 1885–1930* (1990); and Rirka Shpak Lissak, *Pluralism and Progressives: Hull House and the New Immigrants, 1890–1919* (1989). See also Elisabeth Israels Perry, *Belle Moskowitz: Feminine Politics and the Exercise of Power in the Age of Alfred E. Smith* (1987), and Gloria E. Myers, *Municipal Mother: Portland's Lola Greene Baldwin, America's First Policewoman* (1995).

The movement to regulate adolescent sexuality is treated in Mary E. Odum, *Delinquent Daughters: Protecting and Policing Adolescent Female Sexuality in the United States, 1885–1920* (1995). For antiprostitution campaigns, see David J. Langum, *Crossing over the Line: Legislating Morality and the Mann Act* (1994), and Barbara Meil Hobson, *Uneasy Virtue: The Politics of*

Prostitution and the American Reform Tradition (1987). The birth-control controversy is addressed in the relevant segments of Linda Gordon, *Women's Body, Women's Right: A Social History of Birth Control in America* (1976). For the antiliquor crusade, see Richard F. Hamm, *Shaping the Eighteenth Amendment: Temperance Reform, Legal Culture, and the Polity, 1880–1920* (1995); K. Austin Kerr, *Organized for Prohibition: A New History of the Anti-Saloon League* (1985); and Joseph Gusfield, *Symbolic Crusade: Status Politics and the American Temperance Movement* (rev. ed., 1986).

Ties between purity activism and women's suffrage are explored in Janet Zollinger Giele, *The Paths to Women's Equality: Temperance, Suffrage, and the Origins of Modern Feminism* (1995). See also Rosalind Rosenberg, *Beyond Separate Spheres: The Intellectual Roots of Modern Feminism* (1982). The suffrage campaign is examined from different perspectives in Ellen Carol DuBois, *Harriot Stanton Blatch and the Winning of Woman Suffrage* (1997); Christine A. Lunardini, *From Equal Suffrage to Equal Rights: Alice Paul and the National Woman's Party, 1910–1928* (1986); and Linda G. Ford, *Iron-Jawed Angels: The Suffrage Militancy of the National Woman's Party, 1912–1920* (1991). See also Aileen Kraditor, *The Ideas of the Woman Suffrage Movement, 1890–1920* (1965), and Sara Hunter Graham, *Woman Suffrage and the New Democracy* (1996).

THE POLITICS OF PROGRESSIVE REFORM, 1896–1912

The emergence of an industrial society had profound consequences for local, state, and national politics. Successful corporate modernizers and middle-class professionals believed that government administration and policies would benefit by embracing business values of efficiency, expert leadership, and social stability. By contrast, small farmers and independent business interests felt threatened by big corporations and saw politics as a means to regulate corporate power and enhance a competitive economy. Meanwhile, urban social reformers and ethnic politicians acted to protect working people and expand social welfare programs. Finally, a sizable group of political idealists, including Wisconsin's Robert F. La Follette, educator John Dewey, social worker Jane Addams, and journalist Herbert Croly, advocated political reforms to strengthen the nation's democratic traditions.

These complex and often competing motivations produced what contemporaries called "progressivism," a political movement of energy and intensity but with a variety of objectives, some of them controversial and contradictory. In harnessing political power to bring change, progressives believed they would improve the public good and enhance community interests, though their outlook sometimes ignored important class and cultural differences. Yet progressivism expressed an inspiring optimism about democracy that set the tone of political action at the turn of the century.

THE ELECTION OF 1896

The conflict between rural, small-town America and industrial society dominated the election of 1896, pitting Nebraska's Populist-Democrat William Jennings Bryan against big business Republican candidate William McKinley of Ohio. Bryan's campaign had about $300,000 to spend; McKinley's campaign manager Mark Hanna raised $3.5 million, mostly from big business

EXHIBIT **2-1**   **ELECTION OF 1896**

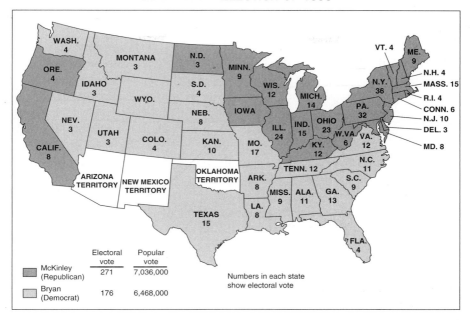

	Electoral vote	Popular vote
McKinley (Republican)	271	7,036,000
Bryan (Democrat)	176	6,468,000

Numbers in each state show electoral vote

groups. The silver-tongued Bryan barnstormed the country, traveling 18,000 miles by train to address 3 million people in a sustained plea for tariff and currency reform. Portraying industrial wage earners as independent producers who sold their labor to employers, Bryan used revivalist rhetoric to persuade voters to join an evangelical crusade for populist and rural values. By contrast, Hanna distributed millions of political pamphlets attacking Bryan as a radical. Instead of campaigning, McKinley stayed at home in Canton, Ohio, and delivered bland front-porch speeches to 750,000 visitors who traveled, often at the expense of big companies, to meet the politician. Hanna introduced corporate merchandising techniques to erode traditional party loyalty and appeal to voters as independent consumers. Afterward, Theodore Roosevelt remarked that Hanna had sold McKinley "as if he were a patent medicine."

Packaged as the candidate of prosperity and inclusion, McKinley insisted that high tariffs would ensure "a full dinner pail" by protecting industrial workers from underpaid foreign competition. By addressing anxiety about depression, unemployment, and wage cuts, McKinley sought the support of ethnic and urban voters formerly repelled by Republican temperance crusades and anti-Catholicism. The Republicans also courted midwestern farmers, who viewed the tariff as protection against foreign agricultural imports. By targeting economic growth, the McKinley campaign demonstrated that Bryan's pleas for free silver and the restoration of traditional social values were not central issues for most of the nation's electorate. Although Bryan carried twenty-four states and nearly 48 percent of the popular vote, working-class and big-city voters gave McKinley a 51 percent majority.

McKinley fulfilled the promise to protect domestic industry and agriculture by signing the Dingley Tariff of 1897. Republicans also maintained the gold standard, enacting the Currency Act of 1900. Simultaneously, the failure of European wheat crops and the discovery of gold in Alaska restored prosperity by increasing farm exports, expanding the money supply, and spurring industrial output. Business leaders also drew important lessons from the economic crisis of the 1890s. Although the Sherman Anti-Trust Act of 1890 had limited monopolistic corporate cooperation "in restraint of trade," a Supreme Court ruling in the *Knight* case of 1895 held that single businesses were safe from antitrust suits. Instead of making deals with their rivals to control the marketplace, companies began merging to form giant corporations. Big business could now seek larger markets both at home (where the new advertising industry flourished) and overseas where potential customers could be found.

COMMERCIAL EXPANSION AND THE ROAD TO EMPIRE

Hoping to sustain economic recovery, Republicans embraced an expansionist foreign policy. As business and farm groups sought new outlets for the nation's surplus, corporate leaders brought the domestic economy into a global marketplace by seeking foreign markets, raw materials, and investment opportunities. Pressure for a more assertive foreign policy also came from a group of upper-class patricians that included Captain Alfred Thayer Mahan, Theodore Roosevelt, Henry Cabot Lodge, and John Hay. This elite viewed expansion as a stimulus to national vitality. "Americans must now begin to look outward," wrote Mahan, a naval officer and author of *The Influence of Sea Power upon History* (1890). Emphasizing U.S. needs for defense against rival powers, Mahan called for a large navy to secure strategic sea-lanes, overseas markets, and unity at home. Because of Mahan's influence, Washington developed a modern navy by 1898.

The patrician leadership also worried about losing its own vitality. As immigrants poured into the country, many feared that the nation's Anglo-Saxon heritage would be diluted and their patriarchal manhood weakened. "I should welcome almost any war," declared Theodore Roosevelt, "for I think this country needs one." Roosevelt and his colleagues focused increasingly on the faltering Spanish Empire in the Caribbean and the Pacific as an opportunity for U.S. expansion. Between the 1860s and the 1890s the public repeatedly expressed support for Cuba's rebellion against Spanish colonialism. When fighting resumed in 1895 and Spain responded with harsh military repression, the yellow journalism of William Randolph Hearst and Joseph Pulitzer inflamed national opinion by providing sensationalist coverage of Spanish concentration camps, brutality, and rape. When artist Frederic Remington cabled Hearst from Havana that hostilities were not imminent, the publisher responded, "You furnish the pictures and I'll furnish the war."

Just beginning to recover from the depression in 1898, corporate leaders feared that a Caribbean war might again upset the economy. Yet they also worried about the uncertainty generated by Cuba's independence movement and Spain's inability to end the uprising. Long interested in constructing a commercial waterway across the isthmus of Central America to tie Atlantic seaports to the markets of the Pacific and Asia, U.S. officials had important strategic interests in the region. Moreover, the State Department and the military warned that expansion-minded Germany might fill the vacuum caused by Spain's retreat from Cuba. Meanwhile, as civil war wracked Cuba in 1897, McKinley signed an annexation treaty with a revolutionary regime that had been created by U.S. interests in Hawaii, although a bloc of "anti-imperialists" prevented immediate ratification in the Senate.

THE SPANISH-AMERICAN WAR AND THE OPEN DOOR POLICY

McKinley was the last Civil War veteran to reside in the White House; he was not anxious to go to war. But as Spain's repression of Cuban rebels threatened U.S. citizens and property, he sent the battleship *Maine* to Havana. Two weeks later the ship exploded and sank, killing 260 U.S. sailors. A naval court attributed the explosion to an external mine, but could not fix responsibility; studies made in the 1970s suggest that the cause of the explosion was inside the ship, perhaps the result of spontaneous combustion. But despite the mystery, U.S. newspapers screamed, "Remember the *Maine*," and the yellow press depicted the blast as the work of Spanish agents. War hawks, or "jingoists," in Congress demanded that the president rescue "national honor." Forced to defend his "backbone" and his "manhood," McKinley finally requested a declaration of war in April 1898, even though Spain was meeting U.S. demands for an armistice and an end to concentration camps. In its war resolution, Congress recognized Cuban independence and demanded Spain's withdrawal. To demonstrate its honorable motives, Congress also adopted the Teller Amendment, rejecting any interest in annexation and asserting that the island would be left to its people. For the first time in U.S. history, Washington justified foreign intervention to save people from the abuses of their leaders, although the Cuban rebels were on the verge of success without outside assistance.

© Bettmann/CORBIS

A sensational contemporary lithograph graphically depicts the sinking of the U.S. battleship *Maine* in Havana harbor, an event that helped to initiate the Spanish-American War.

The war was extremely popular at home. Secretary of State John Hay characterized the conflict as a "splendid little war." The Navy took the strategic initiative when Commodore George Dewey defeated the Spanish fleet in the Philippines in one day. In Cuba an army of 17,000 soldiers included the "Rough Riders," a cavalry unit under the command of Colonel Leonard Wood and Lieutenant Colonel Theodore Roosevelt. By the time U.S. troops landed in Cuba, local guerrillas already held large parts of the island. Yet the celebrated Rough Riders took heavy casualties while storming Santiago's strategic San Juan Hill. Before a climactic battle at Santiago, however, the Navy defeated the Spanish fleet, and Spain soon surrendered, ending the 4-month war.

Although benefiting from Cuban soldiers who fought courageously against Spanish troops, U.S. General William Shafter refused to allow the Cubans to participate in the truce ceremonies. Instead of obtaining independence, Cuba remained under U.S. military occupation. In addition, U.S. forces proceeded to take the island of Puerto Rico with minimal fighting. Although U.S. war fatalities amounted to a mere 379, more than five thousand soldiers died from tropical diseases, inadequate sanitation, and rotten meat. Purity crusaders also condemned the incidence of prostitution, race mixing, and venereal disease. Yet the popular crusade united the country, stimulated U.S. nationalism, and invigorated the desire for overseas empire.

EXHIBIT **2-2** **THE U.S. PACIFIC EMPIRE, 1899**

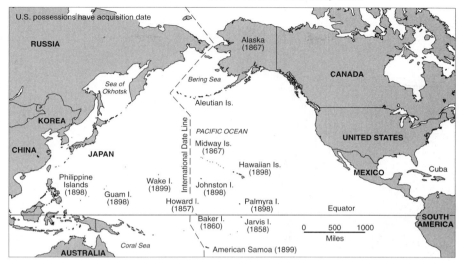

Once the Spanish-American War began, McKinley convinced Congress to pass a joint resolution authorizing the annexation of Hawaii. Under the Paris Peace Treaty of 1898, Spain not only relinquished control of Cuba but also ceded the Philippines, Guam, and Puerto Rico to the United States. The nation now stood on the brink of a territorial empire. Yet nineteenth-century traditions of nonintervention and self-determination clashed with the expansionist aspirations of the McKinley administration. The Anti-Imperialist League, formed in 1898, opposed Senate ratification of the Paris Peace Treaty and attempted to build a coalition opposed to the annexation of overseas territory. Led by William Jennings Bryan, former presidents Benjamin Harrison and Grover Cleveland, industrialist Andrew Carnegie, labor leader Samuel Gompers, and intellectuals such as William James, William Graham Sumner, and Mark Twain, the league denounced the building of an empire as a violation of the nation's most fundamental values.

Anti-imperialists feared that a nation with colonial commitments could not preserve liberty at home. Many southern Democrats also objected to the annexation of colonies whose "colored" population might corrupt the purity of the white race. Opponents of territorial expansion argued that U.S. trade could be extended without the acquisition of colonies or the use of military force. However, imperialists insisted that only annexation could provide the military security necessary to pursue trade opportunities against competing nations in the Caribbean, Pacific, and East Asia. The resulting 57–27 vote in favor of the Paris treaty barely met the two-thirds requirement for Senate ratification, but steered the nation toward a new emphasis on foreign expansion.

Library of Congress

Four thousand U.S. soldiers died in the four-year struggle to "pacify" the Philippines.

The peace treaty gave Cuba only nominal independence. Three years later, the United States forced Cubans to accept the Platt Amendment to the Cuban constitution. This proviso gave Washington broad authority over Cuban domestic affairs, allowed the United States to establish a permanent naval base at Guantanamo Bay, and permitted U.S. military intervention at will. These conditions reversed the terms of Congress's original war resolution: the creation of an independent Cuba. By then, U.S. leaders believed an independent Cuba would threaten the nation's strategic position in the Caribbean.

In the Philippine Islands, insurgents led by Emilio Aguinaldo—who was half Filipino, half Chinese—turned their struggle against Spain into a war for independence against the United States. Facing sustained guerrilla opposition, U.S. troops responded with extensive military operations throughout the Philippine archipelago. Although fighting was often sporadic, the Army frequently used harsh measures against the civilians believed to be supporting the guerrillas, placing many in concentration camps, destroying villages and crops, and adopting torture tactics that the United States had condemned in Spanish-occupied Cuba. Aguinaldo's narrow political base and strategic mistakes limited Filipino resistance. As in Cuba, the Army also attempted to improve conditions on the islands by building roads, schools, and sewers. By 1902, when Washington announced the end of the insurrection, the war had claimed more than 200,000 Filipino and over 4,000 U.S. lives. Fighting continued for another decade against the Moros, or Muslims, on the southern Philippine Islands.

Although the United States had pacified the Caribbean and had established military outposts in Hawaii, Guam, and the Philippines, its position in East Asia remained weak. In 1899 Secretary of State John Hay issued the first in a series of Open Door Notes. Seeking to protect U.S. business in Asia, Hay requested Japanese and European governments to refrain from discriminatory trade practices in their spheres of influence in China. When nationalist Chinese students attacked foreign embassies and massacred western missionaries during the "Boxer Rebellion" of 1900, the United States sent 2,500 troops to join the major powers in restoring order. Fearing that the crisis might lead to abandonment of the Open Door policy, Hay issued a second note supporting China as a "territorial and administrative entity" and endorsing "equal and impartial trade." By ruling out U.S. colonial ambitions and an extended presence in China, the secretary sought to assure domestic critics that the Philippine mistake would not be repeated. Although the United States lacked the naval power to enforce the Open Door policy, Europe and Japan acquiesced because they hoped to avoid war over the division of China.

URBAN PROGRESSIVES AND REFORMERS

While Washington politicians looked overseas to strengthen the economy and reinvigorate the national identity, many reformers hoped to revitalize democratic politics by eliminating corruption and inefficiency in local governments. Led by established middle- and upper-class Anglo-Protestant Republicans, including many women involved in the social purity and suffrage campaigns, progressive reformers challenged powerful patronage machines such as New York's Tammany Hall, which by the 1890s controlled a payroll of $12 million and more jobs than Carnegie Steel. By fixing police appointments, machine bosses received bribes from liquor, prostitution, gambling, and other vice operations. City officials also sold municipal contracts for public transit lines, road construction, and public utilities. In 1903 corporate bribes for New York City franchises surpassed $470 million.

Although Tammany politician George Washington Plunkitt defended such activity as "honest graft," critics charged that corruption placed intolerable burdens on municipal treasuries and taxpayers. Beginning in the 1870s, urban reformers such as E. L. Godkin, editor of *The Nation*, proposed to attack patronage by using merit examinations for public employees. The Civil Service Act of 1883 established such tests for a small percentage of federal job seekers. When Republicans declined to support expansion of civil service reform in the 1884 presidential election, several so-called mugwumps deserted the party. One Republican patrician, Theodore Roosevelt, remained loyal to the national ticket but embraced the crusade against municipal corruption. As head of the New York Board of Police Commissioners, Roosevelt personally toured police beats to curtail graft and vice on the city's Lower East Side.

Such progressive activists believed that municipal government should serve the "public interest." Rejecting nineteenth-century notions of a self-regulating and apolitical marketplace, the reformers sought to modernize and rationalize city government by using trained professionals. Advocates of urban revitalization celebrated middle-class ideals of civic virtue, social responsibility, and citizenship, which they hoped to substitute for the ethnic and class loyalties that buttressed the boss system. They believed an educated, informed public would make good political decisions.

Urban reform received a boost when machine politicians in Galveston, Texas, could not respond effectively to the devastating effects of a tidal wave in 1900. The disaster led to the restructuring of the city government. Under the Galveston Plan, voters selected at-large city commissioners, each of whom administered a different part of the municipal bureaucracy. Instead of relying on patronage to fill positions, the city instituted civil service examinations to place hiring power in government agencies instead of ward syndicates. Emphasizing efficiency, planning, and expert rule, the Galveston Plan professionalized the urban administration and encouraged a citywide perspective among officials.

As the newly organized National Municipal League popularized the commission system and called for the replacement of elected mayors by appointed city managers, muckraking exposés of urban political corruption reinforced the drive for reform. "The misgovernment of the American people is misgovernment *by* the American people," proclaimed Lincoln Steffens in *The Shame of the Cities* (1904). "The spirit of graft and lawlessness is the American spirit." Publicity about nationwide corruption reinforced activist reform mayors like Seth Low of New York City, Joseph Folk of St. Louis, James D. Phelan of San Francisco, and Mark Fagan of Jersey City. By 1909, one hundred U.S. municipalities had adopted the commissioner or manager form of government. Following the lead of reformers such as Detroit's Hazen S. Pingree, Toledo's Samuel M. Jones, and Cleveland's Thomas L. Johnson, many cities lowered public utility and transit rates. Seeking to minimize costs and reduce graft, two-thirds of the nation's cities owned and operated municipal waterworks by 1915.

To run local governments effectively, urban reformers introduced city planners, public health officials, sanitary engineers, housing officers, community development advisers, and corporate experts. They also initiated the use of the secret ballot, moved voting from saloons to public schools and libraries (a move strongly supported by women reformers and suffragists), created non-partisan contests, and established residency requirements for voter registration. Yet progressive electoral reform diluted the voting impact of immigrant and working-class districts and depersonalized urban politics, which helped to produce a 20 percent decline in voter participation in municipal elections between 1890 and 1920.

When problems exceeded the scope of local government, progressives sought solutions in state capitals. In the South, Democrats supported the direct primary, alcohol prohibition, workers' compensation, and regulation of railroads and other utilities. Yet the most dramatic advances came in the North. Between 1898 and 1910 Republican reform governors in Oregon, South Dakota, Wisconsin, Iowa, and Missouri challenged boss control of legislatures and party conventions by approving such procedural reforms as the direct primary (to nominate candidates by popular votes), the referendum (which permitted voters to approve legislation), and the voters' initiative (which allowed voters to propose legislation). The embodiment of state progressive reform was Wisconsin, where insurgent governor Robert M. La Follette demanded a "new citizenship" to place "public interest" above corrupt influences. Using university-trained experts to staff regulatory agencies, La Follette laid the groundwork for the "Wisconsin Idea" and the state's reputation as "the laboratory of democracy."

Progressive reform also produced Governor Joseph Folk's "Missouri Idea," a program that used the power of the law to restrain bribery, bossism, and excessive corporate power. Folk's administration passed legislation to regulate lobbyists, railroads, and insurance companies and pressed trusts such as Standard Oil to refrain from monopoly practices or price gouging. Seeking to compel corporations to submit to regulation in the public interest, Republican insurgents such as Albert B. Cummins, Albert J. Beveridge, Charles Evans Hughes, and Hiram W. Johnson rode reform waves to the governorships of Iowa, Indiana, New York, and California, respectively. As the arena of progressive reform shifted to national politics, all but Hughes would eventually join La Follette on the floor of the U.S. Senate.

Northern progressives also sponsored legislation to ameliorate social problems, such as regulating the labor of women and children. Such ideas conflicted with the laissez-faire principle that workers and employers should be free to enter working agreements without government constraints. But many progressives believed that a woman's work should not interfere with her primary maternal responsibilities or imperil her health. In 1908, the issue reached the U.S. Supreme Court in *Muller v. Oregon.* Using sociological evidence rather than legal precedents, progressive lawyer Louis Brandeis persuaded the Court to allow special protections for women, such as shorter hours. Praised as a "progressive" decision, the ruling became a legal justification for limiting women's equality in the workforce until the 1960s.

Brandeis's legal strategy reflected an experimental outlook among progressives in politics. Unlike Socialists, who called for government ownership of railroads, or Republican conservatives, who demanded a completely free marketplace, progressives opted for public regulation of corporations, hoping that laws could be adjusted over time to remedy deficiencies. This view hinged not on the strength of political interest groups and lobbies, but on the power of public opinion to seek a common civic good that might change over time.

ROOSEVELT AND CORPORATE PROGRESSIVISM

Renominated as the Democratic presidential candidate in 1900, William Jennings Bryan challenged the Republican Party's support of imperial expansion. A self-governing republic "can have no subjects," proclaimed Bryan. "Every citizen is a sovereign, but . . . no one cares to wear a crown." But despite considerable dissent against the continuing war in the Philippines, most voters believed the Senate had settled the issue when it approved annexation of the islands. Meanwhile, Republicans accepted Theodore Roosevelt as President McKinley's running mate. Returning prosperity and the successful war against Spain brought the incumbents 52 percent of the vote versus the Democrats' 45 percent. Six months after McKinley's inauguration, however, anarchist Leon Czolgosz shot the president at point-blank range at the Pan-American Exposition in Buffalo. McKinley died a few days later. "Now look," exclaimed grief-stricken Mark Hanna as Theodore Roosevelt assumed the nation's highest office, "that damned cowboy is president of the United States!"

Roosevelt brought new vigor and imagination to the White House. The son of a wealthy, established New York family, he was born to comfort and poor health. He shook off the sickliness of his youth with a commitment to the strenuous life and grew to adulthood with a conviction that violence and struggle remained basic ingredients of the human condition. The purpose of a man, Roosevelt said, was to "work, fight, and breed." Suspicious of industrial wealth, he welcomed war as "something to think about which isn't material gain." Yet although he was known as a soldier, cowboy, and big-game hunter, Roosevelt also had earned distinction as an author of historical works on westward expansion and naval history.

The new president brought the same emphasis on manly action to political affairs. "Roosevelt, more than any other man living . . . was pure act," exclaimed his contemporary, historian Henry Adams. At a time when most patricians of the upper class shunned politics, the energetic New Yorker saw the pursuit of public office as a social responsibility and zestfully embraced his task. He served a term in the New York State assembly and sat on the United States Civil Service Commission. After returning from the Spanish-American War, the popular Roosevelt won election as governor of New York. Republican Party bosses, fearful of the governor's progressive leanings, persuaded McKinley to remove Roosevelt from the state by placing him on the 1900 ticket. McKinley's assassination made the forty-two-year-old Roosevelt the youngest president in U.S. history.

The dynamic Theodore Roosevelt addresses a crowd in Vermont in 1903.

The new incumbent viewed the presidency as the powerful focal point of the political process and as a national symbol. Roosevelt used the office as a "bully pulpit" from which he could set the national agenda, define the public interest, and mold public opinion. The president realized that a popular and public-relations-minded chief executive could skillfully use the press to build new kinds of political support not available to predecessors. Deliberately personalizing the office, he presented himself as a tribune of the people who was ready to act decisively on their behalf. For example, the White House took the initiative in dealing with Congress by sending drafts of proposed bills to Capitol Hill and then lobbying vigorously for the legislation's passage.

Roosevelt used the presidency to advance a "corporate progressivism" that accepted the existence of big business but used the state to regulate it in the public interest. "Our aim is not to do away with corporations," he told Congress. "On the contrary, these big aggregations are the inevitable development of modern industrialism, and the effort to destroy them would be futile." Yet Roosevelt feared that irresponsible and greedy management would encourage social unrest and radical politics. Accordingly, the president decided to revitalize the Sherman Anti-Trust Act. In particular, he targeted the Northern Securities Company, a huge holding company that resulted from a bitter stock fight among the Rockefeller interests, J. P. Morgan, and railroad barons James J. Hill and E. H. Harriman. Roosevelt denounced the resulting

Ida Minerva Tarbell (1857-1944)

At a time when social conventions usually bound women to traditional roles, Ida Tarbell rejected domestic life to become a journalist. Fascinated by science from girlhood, she entered Pennsylvania's Allegheny College as a biology student in 1876 and was determined to pursue a career, but

Brown Brothers

she soon discovered that in science there was "almost nothing" open to women. Upon graduation, Tarbell became a teacher, entering a profession more accessible to women, but she fled the classroom and its "killing schedule" after two years. She then took a job in a magazine office and began to write.

Tarbell's combination of patient study, objective observation, and fair-minded ethics made her a leading muckraker of the early twentieth century. Prodded by the publisher of *McClure's Magazine*, she spent five years doing research and interviews for a story about Standard Oil, the "mother" of trusts. The resulting nineteen articles for *McClure's* and the two-volume *History of the Standard Oil Company* (1904) portrayed a pattern of corporate bribery, fraud, coercion, double-dealing, and outright violence that added up to a searing indictment of the morality of the big corporations.

Tarbell saw herself as a reporter who gathered facts that spoke for themselves. Uncomfortable with characterizations as the "Joan of Arc of

monopoly of western rail lines as precisely the sort of behavior that big business should avoid. In response, he ordered government attorneys to use the Sherman Act to file suit against Northern Securities for restraint of trade.

Despite protests by Morgan, the administration pursued the antitrust action and won its case before the Supreme Court in 1904. Although the two syndicates ultimately shared control of nearly all western rail lines, the Northern Securities decision modified the *Knight* case and gave new vitality to the Sherman Act. Roosevelt subsequently initiated forty other antitrust actions, thereby earning a reputation as a "trust buster." Nevertheless, he preferred to deal with the trusts through negotiation rather than legal action. In 1903 the president secured legislation that established the Department of Commerce and Labor, including a Bureau of Corporations. Roosevelt directed the agency to regulate large corporations instead of breaking them up through antitrust

the oil industry," she took little interest when the federal government began an antitrust suit against Standard Oil in 1907. Although the *McClure's* series brought discussion of trust regulation into the homes of the middle class, Tarbell remained a conservative in many areas. Despite her own experience with gender discrimination, she gave only tepid support to women's issues and criticized assertive feminist leaders for their alleged insensitivity to the importance of home and family. Warning young women of "the essential barrenness of the achieving woman's triumph," she sparked angry outcries from activists like writer Helen Keller.

During the 1910s Tarbell turned to writing sympathetic portraits of industrial leaders like Henry Ford and Frederick W. Taylor. Scientific management and mass production, she insisted, set the foundation for a viable welfare capitalism and industrial peace, a theme she would expand upon during the New Era of the 1920s. Committed to nineteenth-century ideals of individualism and personal morality, Tarbell remained suspicious of what she called "the most dangerous fallacy of our times," the belief that "we can be saved . . . by laws and systems." A classic progressive, Ida Tarbell never abandoned her skepticism toward interest group politics and collective militancy. Believing in personal accountability, she preferred to trust the "fair play" of the great men she described in her biographies.

litigation and personally asked the chief executives of U.S. Steel and the International Harvester Company to cooperate with the new bureau.

Through "gentlemen's agreements," firms allowed the Bureau of Corporations to investigate their procedures and recommend more responsible business practices. Those who refused to comply faced the threat of antitrust action. When attorneys for Standard Oil and the American Tobacco Company declined to cooperate with the bureau, Roosevelt turned to the Sherman Act. In 1911 the Supreme Court upheld the dissolution of both companies. Yet under the "rule of reason," the Court found that restricted competition did not constitute an illegal restraint of trade unless a company used unfair methods to eliminate competitors or dictated prices that violated the public interest.

Roosevelt hoped to preserve corporate stability and discourage a strong socialist movement by urging business leaders to accept labor unions that

Marcus Alonzo Hanna *(1837–1904)*

Ohio industrialist, corporate progressive, and Republican Party stalwart, the gregarious Marcus Hanna belonged to the party of Lincoln almost from its founding. His mildly reformist Quaker family opposed slavery and supported Republican policies favorable to business. Recognizing the value of close links between industry and public policy, Hanna considered personal and community profits to be indistinguishable and used government power to advance his financial interests. Accordingly, he campaigned against political bosses in Cleveland to protect his holdings in the city's street railway system. A born politician, Hanna later accepted the bosses as allies to ensure their support in future battles.

Eager for greater influence, Hanna actively sought the role of president maker. He chose Ohio Republican Representative William McKinley as his protégé in the 1880s. McKinley's scruples and faintly idealistic political style fascinated Hanna. The congressman's support for high tariffs and flexible views on the currency question added to his appeal. Always the loyal subordinate, Hanna helped McKinley win the Ohio governorship in 1891. He then managed McKinley's successful drive to the White House in 1896 by contributing vast sums of his own money and raising millions more from corporate leaders.

worked within the capitalist system. His approach paralleled that of the influential National Civic Federation (NCF). Founded by Mark Hanna in 1900, the NCF sought harmony between labor and management and urged corporations to recognize social responsibilities by promoting trust regulations, workers' compensation, and company welfare programs. To win the support of organized labor, Hanna invited Samuel Gompers of the American Federation of Labor (AFL) to serve as vice president of the NCF.

These developments shaped Roosevelt's reaction to the anthracite coal strike of 1902. Under the leadership of John Mitchell and the United Mine Workers (UMW), miners walked off the job and demanded a 10 to 20 percent wage increase, an 8-hour day, and management's recognition of the union. Mine owners refused to bargain and tried to end the walkout by using strikebreakers and private security forces. Public opinion tilted toward the workers, especially

Hanna pursued his own ambitions when he entered the U.S. Senate in 1897. Yet he exerted more influence on national affairs when he took an active role in 1901 in founding the National Civic Federation (NCF) as a forum for corporate progressivism. Eager to avoid price competition and to contain the boom-and-bust cycle, the NCF pledged to reduce the conflict between capital and labor and to seek the social solidarity required by a democracy. The organization pursued its agenda by endorsing such reforms as trust regulation and workers' compensation.

After McKinley's death, business interests touted Hanna as the next logical choice for the Republican presidential nomination, but the ambitious Theodore Roosevelt blocked his path. During the anthracite coal strike of 1902 Hanna asked financier J. P. Morgan to pressure the mine owners to settle with the union, a gesture consistent with Hanna's acceptance of labor organizations as partners in industrial harmony. Nevertheless, when Roosevelt stepped forward and succeeded in taking credit for resolving the coal dispute, the new president solidified his primacy in the Republican Party.

Hanna died in Washington in 1904. His greatest legacy was not his fortune or the ill-fated McKinley presidency but the progressive agenda of the National Civic Federation. In the name of corporate self-interest, Mark Hanna played a central role in moving America's business community toward stability and essential reform.

after owner George Baer proclaimed publicly that "God in His Infinite Wisdom has given control of the property interests" to the mine owners. When the dispute threatened coal supplies for the coming winter, Roosevelt summoned both sides to a conference at the White House to settle their differences. The mine owners' refusal to accept mediation outraged the president, who threatened to seize the mines and use the army to mine coal. That warning prompted conservatives such as banker J. P. Morgan to pressure the owners to compromise. Ultimately, the miners received a 10 percent raise and a 9-hour day, but the owners raised prices by 10 percent and refused to recognize the union.

Roosevelt insisted that he had given both labor and management a "square deal" while protecting the public interest. In a marked departure from government policy in previous industrial disputes, the president had accepted the legitimacy of labor demands and forced the leaders of a major industry to

EXHIBIT 2-3   THE SQUARE DEAL

1902	Newlands Reclamation Act
1903	Department of Commerce and Labor created
	Bureau of Corporations created
	Elkins Act (regulates railroad rates)
1906	Hepburn Act (regulates railroad rates)
	Pure Food and Drug Act
	Meat Inspection Act

recognize those claims. Nevertheless, Roosevelt did not champion unions. Exasperated by the shortsightedness of the mine owners, the president asked if they "realize they are putting a very heavy burden on us who stand against socialists; against anarchic disorder?"

Roosevelt's most consistent use of executive power came in the area of natural resources. Emphasizing the efficient use of resources rather than the preservation of virgin wilderness, the president sought to withdraw most federally owned forests from unplanned economic exploitation by private interests. Western congressional representatives opposed this scheme because it threatened economic growth. To reconcile these politicians to his policy, Roosevelt promised that the government would build dams and irrigation systems throughout the West. Accordingly, the Newlands Reclamation Act of 1902 opened millions of acres of desert land to production by using the proceeds from western public land sales to finance construction and maintenance of irrigation projects. Ranchers and growers also accessed cheap water through dams constructed by the Bureau of Reclamation.

Roosevelt's passion for conservation and pride in the nation's heritage led him to dedicate sixteen national monuments, five national parks, and fifty-one wildlife refuges as areas off-limits to economic development. Seeking comprehensive use of natural resources, the president transferred public lands from the Department of the Interior to the Department of Agriculture, where his friend Gifford Pinchot headed the Bureau of Forestry. Like Roosevelt, Pinchot believed that timber resources were essential to the nation's economic development but required planned use under the supervision of government professionals. Both leaders insisted that scientific management of forests could maximize their use by loggers, ranchers, and vacationers and avoid wasteful exploitation of resources.

THE SQUARE DEAL

Roosevelt faced the electorate in 1904 as a president willing to use the federal government to eliminate inequities in national life. Voters responded to the "Square Deal" by giving him 57 percent of the vote and a victory over Democratic candidate Alton B. Parker, a New York state judge. As someone who saw the government as "the most effective instrument in advancing the interests of the people as a whole," Roosevelt moved to expand the federal bureaucracy and the power of the presidency. A prime achievement came in the complex area of railroad regulation, where both agrarian radicals and middle-class reformers had long sought effective control of rates.

Even in his more cautious first term, Roosevelt had supported the Elkins Act of 1903, which outlawed rebates from railroads to large shippers. However, the president preferred to base industry regulation on bureaucratic review rather than on specific legislation. Consequently, he secured passage of the Hepburn Act in 1906, which increased the jurisdiction of the Interstate Commerce Commission (ICC) and provided the commission with greater authority to set transportation rates. Many railroad executives supported regulation as a step toward greater economic stability. Rates administered by the federal government limited price competition among lines and freed a national industry from inconsistent regulation by the states. Reforms such as the Hepburn Act typified the pursuit of an ordered economy by corporate progressives and their allies.

The Roosevelt administration also backed consumer protection legislation. Responding to the efforts of the government's chief chemist, Harvey Wiley of the Department of Agriculture, Congress passed the Pure Food and Drug Act of 1906. The law prohibited the production and sale of adulterated goods and banned false labeling of food and drug items. Business interests accepted the measure because they hoped to reduce competition from specious patent medicine companies and improve consumer confidence in their own products. Roosevelt also signed the Meat Inspection Act of 1906, which established federal supervision to ensure that packers met sanitation standards set by the government. Consumers had been alerted to industry abuses by the writings of muckraker Upton Sinclair. Large meatpackers accepted the new law because it imposed standards of production that they could meet more easily than smaller competitors could, and because better products would improve sales in European markets.

Despite such achievements, the Roosevelt presidency faced a crisis when a stock market crash in 1907 brought a rash of business failures and the collapse of major New York banks. When J. P. Morgan organized the financial community to stop the run, the administration allowed Morgan's U.S. Steel Company to violate antitrust laws by absorbing a Tennessee mining subsidiary. Roosevelt signed the Aldrich-Vreeland Act of 1908, which gave national banks additional flexibility in backing their notes and established a National Monetary Commission to study the banking system. By his final year in office, however, the president faced a Congress that had rejected his bills to supervise corporate competition, to regulate railroad securities, to establish income and inheritance taxes, to limit court injunctions against labor unions, and to establish the 8-hour day for federal employees.

Increasingly hostile to the "stalwart" or conservative wing of the Republican Party, Roosevelt attacked conservative judges for blocking unions, state workers' compensation laws, and the regulation of women's working conditions by the states. The president saw himself as the opponent of both the "fool radicalism" of socialists and the selfishness of "malefactors of great wealth." Pressing the nation's people to give up the idealized nineteenth-century marketplace of small farms and independent businesses, Roosevelt urged the acceptance of large corporations and labor unions and the creation of a national bureaucracy to regulate the activities of both. Only energized government, he believed, could fulfill the nation's destiny for greatness.

ROOSEVELT AND WORLD POWER

Roosevelt came to the White House hoping to consolidate the strategic and commercial gains of the Spanish-American War. One goal was building a canal through Central America. The president believed that U.S. and Caribbean peoples shared an interest in peace, democracy, economic development, and security against the incursions of European powers. Roosevelt insisted that a U.S.-controlled canal would permit Latin America to develop as a prosperous region independent of outside forces and capable of upholding "civilized values." In a period of transition spanning the geographic isolation of the nineteenth century and the total warfare of World War I, the president sought to steer U.S. foreign policy toward global modernization.

Working outside formal channels through personal diplomacy, Roosevelt first invited British cooperation in the construction of the Central American canal. Just two months into his presidency in 1901, the United States and Britain signed the Hay-Pauncefote Treaty, in which Britain renounced interest in the isthmus project and sanctioned construction and fortification of a canal by the United States. Roosevelt then signed the Hay-Herran Treaty with Colombia in 1903, thereby securing permanent rights to a canal zone through the middle of the Colombian province of Panama. When proponents of a canal route across Nicaragua joined with those seeking more compensation from Washington, however, the Colombian Senate unanimously rejected the agreement. Furious, Roosevelt complained, "you could no more make an agreement with the Colombia rulers than you could nail currant jelly to the wall."

After meeting with Roosevelt, Philippe Bunau-Varilla, the chief engineer of an earlier French canal venture, convinced Panamanian leaders that the United States would support a move for independence in the long-restless province. Deployment of U.S. warships to the region contributed to the success of the Panamanian rebellion. Washington quickly signed the Hay-Bunau-Varilla Treaty of 1903, which provided the new republic of Panama with the same $10 million and supplemental fee schedule that had been offered to Colombia. Congress ratified the agreement the following year. "I took the Canal Zone and let Congress debate," Roosevelt later boasted. After military physicians learned to reduce the incidence of malaria and yellow fever among isthmus construction teams, the U.S. Army Corps of Engineers completed the 40-mile-long lock canal, which opened in 1914.

The president nourished U.S. assertiveness in the Western Hemisphere with his 1904 announcement of the Roosevelt Corollary to the Monroe Doctrine. Alarmed by the intervention of European nations in Latin America to collect debts and advance competing business interests, Roosevelt broadened the Monroe Doctrine from a statement opposing further European colonization to a sweeping assertion of the U.S. right to intervene in the internal affairs of hemispheric neighbors. "If we intend to say 'Hands off' to the powers of Europe," the president asserted, "then sooner or later we must keep order ourselves." The Roosevelt Corollary declared that the United States would exercise "an international police power" when "chronic wrongdoing" or "impotence" resulted "in a general loosening of the ties of civilized society." Roosevelt applied the corollary for the first time in 1905, when he sent troops to Santo Domingo to forestall a revolution that would benefit German shipping interests.

Concerned with guaranteeing the Open Door policy, the Roosevelt administration sought to contain the spread of Japanese power in Asia. In 1905 the president grasped an opportunity to mediate the Russo-Japanese War of 1905 by negotiating the Treaty of Portsmouth. Roosevelt's efforts won him the Nobel Peace Prize the following year. Yet his work proved futile when the collapse of the Chinese Empire and the swift emergence of Japan subsequently altered the balance of power in the region. To demonstrate U.S. naval power, Roosevelt sent sixteen battleships on a 45,000-mile voyage that included a stop in Yokohama, Japan. Although the Root-Takahira Treaty of 1908 compelled Washington to accept Japanese restrictions on the Open Door policy in Manchuria, Japan agreed to respect the policy in the rest of China.

Roosevelt also supported the balance of power in Europe by restraining the expansion of German influence. At the Algeciras Conference of 1906, the president mediated a European imperial conflict by supporting British and French interests in North Africa. The resulting agreement not only strengthened the informal alliance among the United States, Britain, and France but guaranteed access to the potentially rich region for U.S. business interests. Secretary of State Elihu Root used the conference to remind developing nations of their obligations to ensure life, property, public order, and equal trade opportunities. By combining diplomacy and his self-described "big stick," Roosevelt framed a foreign policy directed toward a stable world order and an open door for U.S. corporations.

TAFT AND THE PROGRESSIVES

When Roosevelt left the White House in 1909, he handed control of the Republican Party and the progressive movement to William Howard Taft, a talented administrator and lawyer. Taft had served as governor-general of the Philippines, secretary of war, and presidential confidant under Roosevelt. With the president's enthusiastic support, Taft easily won the Republican nomination as the candidate best suited to consolidate the reforms of his predecessor. Meanwhile, the Democrats nominated William Jennings Bryan, who ran a third campaign under the populist slogan "Shall the people rule?" Speaking for the "producing classes," Bryan embraced the direct primary, popular election of U.S. senators, the graduated income tax, federal licensing of corporations, federal guarantees of bank deposits, campaign finance reform, and woman's suffrage. Nevertheless, Taft rode Roosevelt's popularity to an easy victory of 52 percent to 43 percent.

After the election, Roosevelt promptly vanished on a lengthy African safari, where the famous conservationist took dozens of trophies. Unlike the physically fit Roosevelt, Taft weighed more than 300 pounds and was given to nothing more strenuous than golf, a sport not yet popular with the general public. Taft also lacked Roosevelt's gift for public relations and self-promotion. Nor could he stir a crowd or charm the press. Having campaigned on a promise to administer Roosevelt's reform with efficiency, the new president preferred to consolidate existing gains rather than to offer new initiatives. "The lesson must be learned," he declared, "that there is only a limited zone within which legislation and governments can accomplish good."

Despite Taft's reluctance to exert government power for reform, the Department of Justice continued antitrust activity, filing ninety suits and forty indictments against large companies. The president even proposed that corporations be held to federal licensing standards and that a new agency be created to regulate corporate behavior. Taft further responded to the reform agenda by signing legislation to establish postal savings banks, originally demanded by the Populists. The president also approved the establishment of the Children's Bureau in the Department of Commerce and Labor. Despite such achievements, tensions between old-guard and progressive Republicans tested Taft's limited political skills. At a time when progressive sentiment surged nationally, the chief executive offered the country confused and unproductive leadership that finally destroyed his presidency.

The issue of tariff reform illustrated the growing split within the party. Calling Congress into special session in 1909, Taft requested a moderate reduction of the high Dingley Tariff of 1897. However, the president outraged Republican progressives from the Great Plains states when he accepted the Payne-Aldrich Tariff, which actually raised the rates on manufactured goods, thereby threatening crop exports. Taft further offended progressives by replacing James R. Garfield, Roosevelt's conservation-minded secretary of the interior, with western corporate attorney Richard Ballinger. Believing that public lands should either be protected or returned to developers, Ballinger released millions of acres to private ownership or reservoir use against the wishes of Gifford Pinchot, Roosevelt's director of national forests. When Pinchot organized the National Conservation Association to protest such policies, Taft fired him in 1910. Investigated by a Congress that was increasingly hostile to the administration, Ballinger resigned the following year.

The split between the president and congressional progressives deepened because of the controversy regarding House Speaker Joe Cannon, a staunch conservative. Under the leadership of Nebraska's George W. Norris, Republican insurgents sought to weaken Cannon's dictatorial powers. Taft initially supported the revolt and called Cannon "dirty and vulgar." Because he needed the speaker's cooperation for tariff reform, however, the president broke with the insurgents in 1910 and dismissed them as "yelping and snarling." When the rebels stripped Cannon of his power to make committee assignments, the president's political image suffered.

Taft's foreign policy also generated conflict with the progressives. Although Roosevelt had not hesitated to assert U.S. military power in Panama and Santo Domingo, he had always insisted that moral issues were involved in U.S. interventions. However, Taft and Secretary of State Philander C. Knox hoped to minimize European influence in Latin America by encouraging U.S. investment in the region. Consequently, the Taft administration advocated "dollar diplomacy," a foreign policy that unashamedly placed the resources of the Departments of State, War, and the Navy at the disposal of the nation's financial interests. Taft assured the business community that the government would engage in "active intervention to secure for our merchandise and our capitalists opportunity for profitable investment." Acting on such promises, the president sent troops to deal with perceived threats in Nicaragua, Guatemala, Honduras, and Haiti.

By the middle of his term, Taft faced a growing progressive insurgency. One of the most pressing reform demands was the federal income tax. After repeal of Civil War income taxes in the early 1870s, congressional Democrats and Populists reinstated the provision in 1894, only to have the Supreme Court overturn it the next year. When Democrats and insurgent Republicans managed to add the tax to the 1909 tariff, Republican regulars tried to stall the proposal by turning it into a constitutional amendment that would need approval by the states. Yet the strategy failed when the Democrats captured several key state legislatures in 1910. As a result, enough states ratified the income tax provision to enable it to become the Sixteenth Amendment in 1913.

Congressional interest in reform skyrocketed in 1910 when Democrats gained ten Senate seats and took control of the House for the first time in eighteen years. Working with Republican insurgents like Minnesota's Charles A. Lindbergh, House reformers authorized an investigation of the nation's financial and banking resources in 1912. The sensational Pujo Committee inquiry exposed the interlocking directorates of the Morgan and Rockefeller interests and revealed that control of credit had been consolidated in a "money trust." Insurgents also played a major role in passing the Seventeenth Amendment. Ratified by the states in 1913, the measure finally implemented the Populist proposal that U.S. senators be selected by popular vote rather than by the state legislatures.

Taft's political problems deepened as Roosevelt reentered public life in 1910. The ex-president now embraced the ideas outlined in Herbert Croly's *The Promise of American Life* (1909). Advocating a "new nationalism," Croly accepted large corporations and overseas markets as the key to national prosperity. Nevertheless, he sought a safety net for working people through a federal social welfare state administered by trained professionals. Government business regulation and collective bargaining by trade unions would also offset corporate power. Roosevelt had expressed these notions in a 1910 speech, "The New Nationalism," in which he described the executive branch of government as the steward of public welfare and proposed to regulate corporations in the national interest. "Our country means nothing unless it means the triumph of a real democracy," he declared.

THE ELECTION OF 1912

Learning that his successor had betrayed the progressive cause, Roosevelt began to distance himself from the Taft regime. The former president finally broke with Taft in 1911 when the White House initiated antitrust proceedings against U.S. Steel, whose merger with a subsidiary had been approved by Roosevelt four years earlier. The president's action not only reversed the promise made to his predecessor, but made Roosevelt appear to be a tool of Wall Street instead of a progressive. Enraged by the perceived treachery of his protégé, Roosevelt decided to seek the Republican nomination for the presidency. On Lincoln's Birthday in 1912 the former president added a new phrase to the national political lexicon when he announced, "My hat is in the ring."

Roosevelt faced two competitors for the Republican nomination. President Taft represented industrialists, bankers, and stalwart party loyalists who favored high tariffs and a minimum of government interference in the economy. Robert La Follette, the founder of the National Progressive League, was an anti–corporate progressive who appealed to small businesspeople and independent farmers. La Follette advocated corrupt-practices legislation to curb the trusts and democratic reforms such as the initiative, referendum,

EXHIBIT **2-4**   **ELECTION OF 1912**

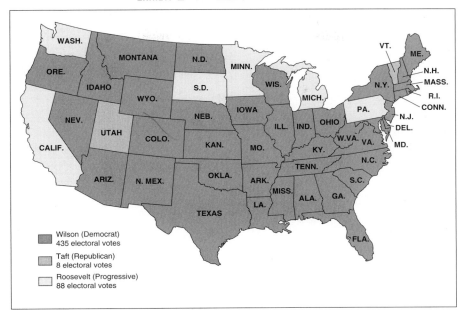

Wilson (Democrat)
435 electoral votes

Taft (Republican)
8 electoral votes

Roosevelt (Progressive)
88 electoral votes

and direct primary. In contrast to his two rivals, Roosevelt embraced corporate progressivism, an approach that accepted large corporations if they were offset by government agencies working to ensure social justice.

As personal problems contributed to the fading of La Follette's campaign, Taft and Roosevelt found themselves in a bitter battle that would leave the Republican Party in shambles. Enormously popular with the rank and file, the former president easily defeated his successor in the thirteen states that conducted presidential primaries, including Taft's native Ohio. At the Chicago convention, however, control rested with the party leadership, most of whom supported the incumbent Taft. When La Follette delegates sought to undercut Roosevelt by siding with Republican stalwarts in a credentials fight, Roosevelt and his backers marched defiantly from the hall, and Taft won the nomination on the first ballot. Roosevelt refused to accept defeat. Arranging for financial backing from newspaper publisher Frank A. Munsey and former Morgan partner George W. Perkins, the former president summoned party dissidents and business and professional reformers to launch a new party, the Progressives.

Insisting that he was eager for the contest, Roosevelt gave the fledgling movement a permanent nickname when he declared himself to be "as strong as a bull moose." With near religious fervor, delegates roared their unanimous approval of his nomination. "We stand at Armageddon," thundered Roosevelt,

EXHIBIT **2-5   VOTER PARTICIPATION IN PRESIDENTIAL ELECTIONS, 1896–1912 (PERCENTAGE OF ELIGIBLE VOTERS)**

1896	79.3
1900	73.2
1904	65.2
1908	65.4
1912	58.8

Source: *Historical Statistics of the United States, Colonial Times to 1970* (1975).

"and we battle for the Lord." Progressives chose popular California governor Hiram W. Johnson as the vice presidential candidate. The party platform called for federal regulatory agencies, prohibition of child labor, the 8-hour day, and democratic reforms, including woman's suffrage and the popular election of senators. Winning support from luminaries such as social worker Jane Addams and journalists Walter Lippmann and Herbert Croly, Roosevelt dismissed those "who had taken on the impossible task of returning to the economic conditions that obtained nearly sixty years ago."

As the party that stood to gain from the Republican split, the Democrats united behind New Jersey reform governor Woodrow Wilson after forty-five ballots. The southern-born son of a Presbyterian minister, Wilson had made his career in the North. Earning a Ph.D. in government at Johns Hopkins University, he began an academic career that led him to the presidency of Princeton University in 1902. Eight years later, embittered by a long struggle over the future of the graduate school, Wilson resigned and ran for the governorship of New Jersey. In a state already notorious for its corrupt politics, Wilson built a strong record of progressive reform.

The Democratic nominee drew political support from two contradictory sources. First, he was the candidate of agrarian and small business reformers, often from the South and West, who hoped to restrain the growth of large corporations. Wilson promised to restore competition through a "New Freedom" of lower tariffs, banking reform, and government dismantling of unfair and inefficient trusts. "What this country needs above everything else," he declared, "is a body of laws which will look after the men who are on the make rather than the men who are already made." Defending an economy of small business competition, the candidate insisted, "If America is not to have free enterprise, then she can have freedom of no sort whatever."

The second source of Wilson's support came from urban progressives and labor activists, who hoped to use government experts to impose efficiency, rationality, and responsibility on large corporations instead of dissolving them. These constituents believed that Wilson's pledge to preserve "free enterprise" was consistent with the candidate's promise to tolerate "reasonable" business combinations. "Nobody can fail to see," he had proclaimed in 1911, "that modern business is going to be done by corporations—the old-time individual competition is gone by." Supporters from both wings of the party nevertheless accepted Wilson's commitment to stop the use of antilabor injunctions by federal courts.

The Socialist Party also competed for the loyalty of reformers. Meeting in Indianapolis, the Socialists nominated Eugene Debs for the presidency and endorsed unemployment insurance and old-age pensions as well as government ownership of railroads, grain elevators, mines, and banks. As a party demanding democratization of the political order, the Socialists advocated a single-term presidency, elimination of the Senate, and removal of the Supreme Court's power of judicial review. With virtually no campaign organization, Debs received more than 900,000 votes, or 6 percent of the popular tally.

Despite Socialist inroads among working-class voters in the industrial cities, the election of 1912 revolved around the two major parties and the Progressives. Taft, who hardly campaigned, only managed to place third with a mere 23 percent of the vote. Roosevelt finished second by winning 27 percent of the popular ballot. Wilson received less than 42 percent of the total vote but benefited from strength in the South and growing popularity in the cities to carry the Electoral College by a resounding 435–88.

Through the Republican split, Woodrow Wilson became only the second Democrat to win the White House since the 1850s. Combined with Roosevelt's popularity, the victory demonstrated the strength of progressive sentiment among the general electorate. A large majority of voters agreed that concentration of wealth threatened personal autonomy and needed to be monitored by an activist government. The new president now faced the challenge of translating that impulse into a coherent program of legislation and policy.

AMERICAN HISTORY RESOURCE CENTER

To explore documents, images, audio and video clips, articles, and commentary related to the material in this chapter, visit the source collections at ushistory.wadsworth.com and and use the Search function with the following key terms:

Theodore Roosevelt	USS *Maine*
Taft	Ida Tarbell
Woodrow Wilson	Rough Riders

RECOMMENDED READINGS

Steven J. Diner, *A Very Different Age: Americans of the Progressive Era* (1998). This overview of the period places politics in the context of economic and social change.

Kristin L. Hoganson, *Fighting for American Manhood: How Gender Politics Provoked the Spanish-American and Philippine-American Wars* (1998). Focusing on the public debate about foreign policy at the turn of the century, this book explores the relationship between war and the ideology of manhood.

Kathleen Dalton, *Theodore Roosevelt: A Strenuous Life* (2002). Examining the private and public lives of the progressive president, this biography stresses Roosevelt's commitment to an invigorated citizenry.

Jonathan M. Hansen, *The Lost Promise of Patriotism: Debating American Identity, 1890–1920* (2003). This study of progressive ideas—focusing on Eugene V. Debs, Jane Addams, and W. E. B. Du Bois, among others—explores differing views of society, government, foreign affairs, and war.

Additional Readings

For a survey of politics in the 1890s, see H. W. Brands, *The Reckless Decade: America in the 1890s* (1995). Bryan's role in the election of 1896 is described in LeRoy Ashby, *William Jennings Bryan: Champion of Democracy* (1987); the McKinley campaign is covered in Lewis L. Gould, *The Presidency of William McKinley* (1980).

The ideology of foreign policy leaders emerges in Warren Zimmermann, *First Great Triumph: How Five Americans Made Their Country a World Power* (2002). See also Michael H. Hunt, *Ideology and U.S. Foreign Policy* (1987), and Kenneth J. Hagan, *The People's Navy: The Making of American Sea Power* (1991). For U.S. expansionism, see Thomas D. Schoonover, *The United States in Central America, 1860–1911: Episodes of Social Imperialism and Imperial Rivalry in the World System* (1991); Ivan Musicant, *The Banana Wars: A History of United States Military Intervention in Latin America from the Spanish-American War to the Invasion of Panama* (1990); and David Healy, *Drive to Hegemony: The United States in the Caribbean, 1898–1917* (1988).

For the conflict with Spain, see Joseph Smith, *The Spanish-American War: Conflict in the Caribbean and the Pacific, 1895–1902* (1994). Two books that place the war in the context of the Cuban revolution are Louis A. Perez, *Cuba Between Empires, 1878–1902* (1983), and *The War of 1898: The United States in History and Historiography* (1998). A military history of the Pacific conflict is Brian McAllister Linn, *The Philippine War: 1898–1902* (2000). The controversy over annexation is the subject of Robert Beisner, *The Anti-Imperialists, 1898–1900* (1968). See Stuart Creighton Miller, *"Benevolent As-*

similation": The American Conquest of the Philippines, 1899–1903 (1982); Glenn May, *Social Engineering in the Philippines: The Aims, Execution, and Impact of American Colonial Policy, 1900–1913* (1980); and Peter W. Stanley and John Curtis Perry, *Sentimental Imperialists: The American Experience in East Asia* (1981).

The optimism of progressive reform in the cities (and its continuing relevance today) is the theme of Kevin Mattson, *Creating a Democratic Public: The Struggle for Urban Participatory Democracy During the Progressive Era* (1998), and Peter Levine, *The New Progressive Era: Toward a Fair and Deliberative Democracy* (2000). See also Michael McGerr, *The Decline of Popular Politics: The American North, 1865–1928* (1986). For the conflict between city bosses and reformers, see John Allswang, *Bosses, Machines, and Urban Voters: An American Symbiosis* (1977). Portraits of reform journalists can be found in Louis Filler, *Muckraking and Progressivism in the American Tradition* (rev. ed., 1995). For general accounts of progressive reform, see Robert Wiebe, *The Search for Order, 1877–1920* (1968); Samuel P. Hays, *The Response to Industrialism, 1885–1914* (1957); and Arthur Link and Richard L. McCormick, *Progressivism* (1983). City reform in the South is explored in Lawrence H. Larsen, *The Rise of the Urban South* (1985).

For progressive reform in the states, see Steven L. Piott, *The Anti-Monopoly Persuasion: Popular Resistance to the Rise of Big Business in the Midwest* (1985), and David Thelen, *Paths of Resistance: Tradition and Democracy in Industrializing Missouri* (1991). The La Follette reform movement is the subject of Thelen's *The New Citizenship: Origins of Progressivism in Wisconsin, 1885–1900* (1972), and *Robert La Follette and the Insurgent Spirit* (1976). See also Bernard A. Weisberger, *The La Follettes of Wisconsin: Love and Politics in Progressive America* (1994). For the South, see Dewey Grantham, *Southern Progressivism: The Reconciliation of Progress and Tradition* (1983), and William A. Link, *The Paradox of Southern Progressivism, 1880–1930* (1992).

Corporate progressivism is explored in several studies, including Jeffrey Lustig, *Corporate Liberalism: The Origins of Modern Political Theory, 1890–1920* (1982); Morton Keller, *Regulating a New Economy: Public Policy and Economic Change in America, 1900–1933* (1990); and Charles Forcey, *Crossroads of Liberalism: Croly, Weyl, Lippmann, and the Progressive Era, 1900–1925* (1961). For the integration of business priorities and reform politics, see Gabriel Kolko, *The Triumph of Conservatism: A Reinterpretation of American History, 1900–1916* (1963), and James Weinstein, *The Corporate Ideal in the Liberal State, 1900–1918* (1969). A more comprehensive application of this thesis can be found in Martin J. Sklar, *The Corporate Reconstruction of American Capitalism, 1890–1916: The Market, the Law, and Politics* (1988), and in *The United States as a Developing Country: Studies in U.S. History in the Progressive Era and the 1920s* (1992). For the impact of radical farmers on federal legislation, see Elizabeth Sanders, *Roots of Reform: Farmers, Workers, and the American State, 1877–1917* (1999).

A good starting point for Roosevelt scholarship is Lewis L. Gould, *The Presidency of Theodore Roosevelt* (1991), and *Reform and Regulation: American Politics from Roosevelt to Wilson* (1986). Biographical treatments include Edmund Morris, *Theodore Rex* (2002); David McCullough, *Mornings on Horseback* (1981); John Milton Cooper Jr., *The Warrior and the Priest: Woodrow Wilson and Theodore Roosevelt* (1983); and John Morton Blum, *The Republican Roosevelt* (1954). For a study of Roosevelt as the embodiment of a white male identity crisis, see Sarah Watts, *Rough Rider in the White House: Theodore Roosevelt and the Politics of Desire* (2003).

For Roosevelt's foreign policy, see Richard H. Collin, *Theodore Roosevelt, Culture, Diplomacy, and Expansionism* (1985), and *Theodore Roosevelt's Caribbean: The Panama Canal, the Monroe Doctrine, and the Latin American Context* (1990). See also Frederick W. Marks, *Velvet on Iron: The Diplomacy of Theodore Roosevelt* (1982), and Akira Iriye, *Pacific Estrangement: Japanese and American Expansion, 1897–1911* (1972). The building of the Panama Canal is described in David McCullough, *The Path Between the Seas* (1977).

For Taft, see Paolo Colletta, *The Presidency of William Howard Taft* (1973), and the relevant sections of Gould, *Reform and Regulation,* which also summarizes the election of 1912. Wilson's successful presidential campaign is captured in Arthur Link, *Woodrow Wilson and the Progressive Era, 1910–1917* (1954). See also Cooper, *The Warrior and the Priest,* and Sklar, *Corporate Reconstruction of American Politics.*

The Roosevelt and La Follette campaigns are described in the previously listed studies of the two leaders. For the Debs candidacy, see Nick Salvatore, *Eugene Debs: Citizen and Socialist* (1990).

WILSONIAN REFORM AND GLOBAL ORDER, 1912–1920

Progressive reform culminated in the presidency of Woodrow Wilson. Building on precedents set by Theodore Roosevelt, the Democratic President Wilson emerged as a legislative activist, developing detailed programs and providing executive leadership in Congress. Despite earlier campaign oratory, Wilson accepted the importance of big corporations and sought primarily to regulate them. His domestic program fulfilled many progressive promises.

Federal power also expanded in the realm of global affairs. Continuing the Open Door policy of the late 1890s, Wilson blended reformist political ideology and economic expansion into a quest for international order. "We created this nation," said President Wilson, "not to serve ourselves, but to serve mankind." Although the dream of collective security remained unfulfilled in his lifetime, this visionary president established the major patterns of twentieth-century foreign policy in an emerging global economy.

WILSON AS CORPORATE PROGRESSIVE

Having prevailed in 1912 under the reformist slogan, "New Freedom," Wilson sought to unify the country behind the progressive notion of the "public interest." A strong admirer of the British parliamentary system, he believed that the president, like the prime minister, should take a vigorous role in leading his party and securing legislation. "The nation as a whole has chosen him," he said of the president, "and is conscious that it has no other political spokesman. His is the only voice in national affairs." The first White House occupant since John Adams to address Congress in person, Wilson devised a legislative program and pushed aggressively for its passage. He installed a private telephone line linking the White House with the Capitol and dispatched lobbyists to gain support for administration initiatives. Wilson also used patronage to reward backers and punish opponents. He recognized the press as

EXHIBIT **3-1**   **WILSONIAN DOMESTIC REFORM, 1913-1916**

1913	Underwood Tariff Act
	Federal Income Tax Act
	Federal Reserve Act (created FRB—Federal Reserve Board)
1914	Clayton Antitrust Act
	Federal Trade Commission Act (created FTC)
1916	Adamson Act (8-hour day for railroad workers)
	Workers' Compensation for Federal Employees
	Rural Credits Act
	La Follette Seamen's Act
	Child Labor Act

a crucial link to the people and became the first president to hold news conferences.

On his first day in office Wilson boldly summoned Congress into special session and called for downward revision of the tariff. The controversial proposal attracted immediate support from farmers and consumers who had failed to gain tariff reform during the Taft years and from industrialists who wanted lower rates for imported raw materials. Exporters and shippers hoped that rate reductions would encourage reciprocity abroad, thereby stimulating foreign trade. After Wilson's forceful leadership built a solid majority, the Underwood-Simmons Act of 1913 incorporated the first significant tariff reform since before the Civil War.

The new tariff played a key role in changing the national revenue base. Because the Sixteenth Amendment now permitted federal income taxes, Democrats proposed a tax on personal earnings to replace funds lost through tariff reductions. The income tax also obliged the wealthy to pay a larger share of government expenses and thereby reduce class tensions. Imposing a 1 percent personal and corporate tax with a rate of up to 7 percent for earnings greater than $500,000, the measure exempted the first $4,000 in family income from taxation. The graduated income tax gave the federal government unprecedented sources of revenue and prepared the way for an expanded social and military role in the years ahead. Yet only 0.5 percent of the population was obliged to file returns (2 percent of the workforce), and by 1916 only 9 percent of the government budget came from income levies.

Declaring that "the great monopoly in our country is the money monopoly," Wilson kept Congress in session to consider banking reform. After the revelations of the congressional Pujo Committee (see Chapter 2), labor attorney Louis Brandeis had written a series of articles titled *Other People's Money and How the Bankers Use It*, which criticized the concentration of financial resources. Anti–corporate progressives such as Robert La Follette demanded

The only Ph.D. ever to reach the White House, Woodrow Wilson became the most eloquent political leader of his time.

government control of a new banking system. Meanwhile, corporate progressives such as Virginia Senator Carter Glass hoped to decentralize and rationalize the financial apparatus and leave authority with private lenders. Acknowledging that most local banks lacked the resources to provide adequate credit to farmers, Brandeis worked with Wilson to devise a regulatory structure that blended federal supervision with banker control at the regional level.

Congress proceeded to pass the Federal Reserve Act of 1913, the most important domestic legislation of the Wilson presidency. The new system created twelve Federal Reserve banks, which represented the nation's geographic regions. All banks that operated nationally were required to invest part of their capital in the Federal Reserve bank in their district, and state banks could do the same. A Federal Reserve Board, appointed by the president, decided on the rate of interest to be paid to the regional Federal Reserve by investor banks. If the board wanted to encourage expansion, it lowered the interest rate, which made it easier to borrow money; if it wanted to curb inflation, it raised interest rates. The Federal Reserve System also provided reserves to cover local financial crises and established the nation's first coordinated check clearance procedures.

Wilson turned to the explosive issue of the trusts in 1914. By then he had begun to shift his view of corporations by replacing the small business ethic of the New Freedom with the corporate progressivism of Theodore Roosevelt's New Nationalism. Again influenced by Brandeis, Wilson pushed for passage of the Clayton Antitrust Act. The bill closed loopholes in existing legislation by barring interlocking directorates, price discrimination, and holding companies among competing firms. The Clayton Act fulfilled the New Freedom promise to discipline monopolistic corporations, but it also demonstrated Wilson's commitment to corporate progressivism. Supported by the National Civic Federation and the Chamber of Commerce, the law targeted the "destructive competition" that prevented corporate planning. To the relief of corporations operating under various state and judicial guidelines, the Clayton Act clarified the limits of business competition by specifying what constituted "unfair practices."

The president drew a sharp distinction between big business and monopoly. "A trust is an arrangement to get rid of competition," he explained, "and a big business is a business that has survived competition by conquering in the field of intelligence and economy." To regulate those differences, in 1914 Congress passed the Federal Trade Commission (FTC) Act, which empowered a new regulatory agency to conduct investigations and issue restraining orders to prevent "unfair trade practices." By stressing administrative regulation instead of antitrust prosecution, the president rejected his earlier commitment to restoring competition. Wilson now embraced the progressive concept of regulation in the public interest through scientific review of data by business experts.

Through the Clayton Act and the FTC, the administration fostered the stability sought by corporations but policed the market to prevent flagrant collusion or fraud. By sustaining the distinction between "reasonable" and "unreasonable" restraint of competition, Wilsonian reform institutionalized the Supreme Court's 1911 "rule of reason" (see Chapter 2). Antitrust legislation now required prosecutors to prove that corporate offenders were attempting to establish monopolies. Because most of Wilson's FTC appointments were corporate attorneys, the administration initiated few antimonopoly suits and encouraged negotiated settlements with private firms. By using government bureaus to set predictable ground rules for corporate competition, the administration effectively ended the debate over the legitimacy of big business. Advocates of government regulation would continue to base their proposals on the Wilsonian model of reform.

WILSON AND THE LIBERAL STATE

With the creation of the Federal Trade Commission (FTC), Wilson considered his legislative tasks complete; but political pressures forced him to take further reform initiatives. At first the president backed away from proposals

EXHIBIT **3-2**   ELECTION OF **1916**

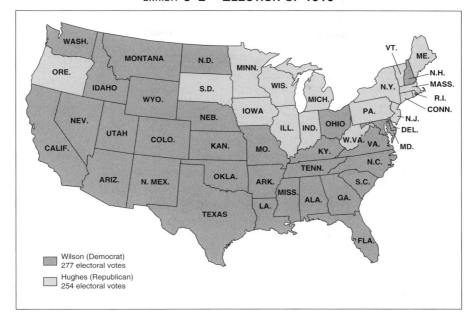

Wilson (Democrat)
277 electoral votes

Hughes (Republican)
254 electoral votes

that appeared to benefit only special interests as opposed to broader, national concerns. After the opposition Republicans gained in the 1914 congressional elections, Wilson began to change his position as the 1916 presidential contest approached. As the leader of a minority party, he recognized the importance of building a coalition and threw the power of the presidency into that effort. Wilson saw the White House as a neutral broker among the economy's organized interests. Accordingly, the Clayton Act specifically exempted labor unions and agricultural organizations from antitrust prosecution and restricted the use of court injunctions against union activities.

Wilson built upon this legacy in 1916 by signing laws to improve the conditions of merchant seamen, to regulate child labor, and to provide workers' compensation for federal employees. He also approved the Adamson Act, which reduced the workday to 8 hours for railroad employees. Passage of a federal highway bill added to his legislative record. The president set further precedent by establishing the federal government as the source of credit for needy farmers. Responding to pressure from southern representatives and agrarian reformers, Wilson signed the Rural Credits Act of 1916, creating a Federal Farm Loan Board to subsidize credit banks. Congress also authorized creation of the nation's first agricultural extension service.

As Wilson sought reelection in 1916, he positioned himself as a progressive who involved professional experts in government. His nomination of Louis Brandeis to the Supreme Court bolstered this image. By placing the first Jew

Louis Dembitz Brandeis (1856–1941)

"A lawyer who has not studied economics and sociology is very apt to become a public enemy," declared Louis Brandeis. Born in Louisville, Kentucky, and the son of German-Jewish immigrants, Brandeis reshaped twentieth-century jurisprudence by defending the interests of working

Brown Brothers

people against corporate power. A successful private law practice made him a millionaire by the age of fifty and freed him to devote time to public issues. The bloody Homestead steel strike of 1892 marked a turning point in his career. Concluding that "organized capital hired a private army to shoot at organized labor for resisting an arbitrary cut in wages," Brandeis committed himself to assisting the working class.

His most important contribution came in the U.S. Supreme Court decision, *Muller* v. *Oregon* (1908). Representing the state of Oregon in a suit challenging the constitutionality of a law setting a maximum workday of 10 hours for women, Brandeis brushed aside legal principles with a cursory three-page summary. "There is no logic that is properly applicable to these laws except the logic of facts," he argued. He used over 100 pages to document expert opinion concerning the adverse impact of excessive working hours on the health of women. The Brandeis Brief marked the first use of sociological data in a Supreme Court case and revolutionized legal argument. "My, how I detest that man's ideas," wrote conservative Justice George

on the Court, the president gained support from working-class and ethnic voters in the big cities. Yet Wilson's progressivism had clear limits. Southern born and bred, the Democratic president exhibited little sympathy for African Americans. One month after taking office, Wilson's postmaster general ordered the segregation of postal employees, a practice that spread through the federal bureaucracy. In federal buildings blacks and whites now had to use segregated facilities, and federal officials dismissed African Americans from public jobs simply on grounds of race. When a delegation of black leaders pleaded with Wilson to reverse such policies, the irate president ended the "insulting" conversation. Indeed, Wilson praised D. W. Griffith's racist film,

Sutherland. "But he is one of the greatest technical lawyers I have ever known."

Politically independent, the progressive Brandeis supported both Republicans and Democrats for national office. In 1912 he initially endorsed Robert La Follette for the Republican presidential nomination, but later supported Woodrow Wilson when the Republicans divided. He subsequently became a close adviser to Wilson. Brandeis played a major role in shaping the Federal Reserve Act of 1913 by insisting that the banking system must ultimately be placed under the control of the federal government instead of the financial community. He also figured strongly in the development of the administration's antitrust policy by drafting the Federal Trade Commission Act of 1914.

Wilson risked controversy by nominating Brandeis to a seat on the Supreme Court in 1916. Unlike most justices, Brandeis had held no previous public office, and his legal work on behalf of social causes had given him a reputation as a radical. As the Senate Judiciary Committee spent four months reviewing the nomination, conservative business and political interests strongly opposed confirmation. Seven past presidents of the American Bar Association, including former secretary of state Elihu Root and former president William Howard Taft, argued that Brandeis's career as an advocate proved his lack of judicial temperament. Ultimately, Brandeis served on the bench for twenty-three years. His richly detailed opinions continued to express the Progressive faith that government regulations and social justice legislation were required to address national problems.

Birth of a Nation, which was partly based on his own history of the American people. Nor did the White House sympathize with the suffragist movement. Wilson insisted that the woman's vote required state legislation, not federal action. Electoral pressure in 1916 forced him to endorse women's suffrage, but feminists satirized the president's slogan, "He Kept Us Out of War" with their own: "He Kept Us Out of Suffrage."

To challenge Wilson, Republicans nominated Charles Evans Hughes, a progressive who had resigned his Supreme Court seat to run for the presidency. Wilson adopted the slogan "peace, prosperity, and progressivism." Yet his campaign may have fallen short if Hughes had not inadvertently snubbed

California Republican and former Progressive vice presidential candidate Hiram Johnson. The election produced a narrow 277–254 Democratic majority in the Electoral College. In the closest contest since 1876, Wilson won only 49.4 percent of the popular vote.

INTERVENTION IN LATIN AMERICA

Aware of the importance of foreign markets for domestic prosperity, Wilson saw Latin America as a region for economic expansion. The enactment of a low-tariff policy increased the nation's foreign trade, and amendments to the Federal Reserve Act stimulated investment overseas. Between 1900 and 1915, U.S. exports doubled to $3 million and foreign investment tripled to $3 billion. Much of this expansion occurred south of the border. What Wilson called the "righteous conquest of foreign markets" justified the use of political and military power to assure stability for capital investment and social progress.

"There are times in the history of nations," explained the president, "when they must take up the crude instruments of bloodshed in order to vindicate spiritual conceptions." Like Theodore Roosevelt, Wilson saw Latin America as the arena where military force might be used to sustain moral values. U.S. influence, he believed, would not only raise the economic standard of living but also "uplift" the "lower" people. In this way, he viewed intervention in the nation's historic sphere of influence as a step toward democracy, stability, order, and constitutional government.

Although Wilson and Secretary of State William Jennings Bryan repudiated dollar diplomacy, Washington escalated military intervention in the Caribbean and Central America by sending troops to occupy Cuba, Santo Domingo, and Nicaragua. Wilson dispatched the marines to Haiti to pressure the government to sign a treaty that ensured U.S. control of the country's finances, public works, army, and foreign relations. Concerned with the security of the Caribbean as war inundated Europe, the president instructed Denmark to sell the Virgin Islands to the United States in 1916 or to face their forcible seizure by U.S. forces.

Wilson's grandest scheme for forcing progress on Latin America involved Mexico, where democratic forces had begun a revolution in 1911. When General Victoriano Huerta led a successful counterrevolution two years later, Wilson refused to recognize the dictatorship—he called it "a government of butchers"—on the grounds that it lacked popular support. Never before had the United States refused to recognize an existing government. "I am going to teach the South American governments to elect good men," Wilson declared. He then threw U.S. support behind General Venustiano Carranza and ordered the navy to seize the Mexican port of Vera Cruz to prevent Huerta from receiving arms. But when Carranza's army failed to control the chaotic fight-

EXHIBIT **3-3**   **EXPORTS OF GOODS AND SERVICES, 1912–1916**
(IN ROUNDED BILLIONS OF DOLLARS)

1912	2.7
1916	6.0

Source: *Historical Statistics of the United States, Colonial Times to 1970* (1975).

ing that raged throughout the country, Wilson turned to General Francisco (Pancho) Villa, a charismatic bandit and revolutionary reformer.

Magazine readers in the United States had received firsthand accounts of Villa's exploits, but when Carranza regrouped and pushed Villa into the mountains of northern Mexico in 1915, Wilson switched sides and recognized the Carranza government. Villa then complicated the situation by shrewdly playing on Mexican resentment of U.S. meddling. In a deliberate act of provocation, Villa crossed the border in 1916 and burned the town of Columbus, New Mexico, killing nineteen people. Outraged, Wilson placed General John J. Pershing in command of a punitive expedition and ordered the army to pursue Villa. Pershing led 7,000 U.S. soldiers 300 miles into Mexico, but President Carranza demanded that Washington respect Mexican sovereignty. A humiliated Wilson finally called off the futile mission in 1917 as the United States became increasingly concerned with Europe.

NEUTRALITY AND THE EUROPEAN CRISIS

Conflicts in the Western Hemisphere could not match the violence across the Atlantic. Three years earlier, in 1914, the assassination of the Hapsburg prince Franz Ferdinand by Slavic nationalists had plunged Europe into the first continental war in a century. The conflict arrayed the Allies (Britain, France, and Russia) against the Central Powers (Germany and the Austro-Hungarian Empire). Wilson promptly proclaimed a policy of neutrality and called the clash "a war with which we have nothing to do, whose causes cannot touch us." He asked the public to be "neutral in fact as well as in name" and "impartial in thought as well as action."

The president's plea failed to acknowledge important U.S. interests in the war. Since the 1890s, U.S. foreign policy leaders had seen Germany rather than Britain as the greatest potential threat to national security because of commercial competition in Latin America and Asia. Strong cultural ties linked the United States and Britain, particularly among the Anglo-Protestant officials of the State Department. Wilson himself greatly admired the British people and their institutions. Predictably, within months of the outbreak of hostilities, the president privately admitted that the United States might have to take an active part in the fighting if Germany appeared likely to win.

EXHIBIT **3-4**   TOTAL U.S. INTERNATIONAL INVESTMENT, 1908–1919
(IN ROUNDED BILLIONS OF DOLLARS)

1908	2.5
1914	5.0
1919	9.7

Source: *Historical Statistics of the United States, Colonial Times to 1970* (1975).

Wilson also believed that the preservation of democracy and prosperity at home depended upon maintaining an open door to the markets, raw materials, and investments of world commerce. In Asia the Japanese already had thwarted U.S. efforts to invest private capital in major railroad projects in China and Manchuria. As an economic recession deepened in 1914, marketplace issues tended to draw the United States into the Allied camp. Because the war disrupted the productive capacity of Europe, the demand for U.S. industrial and agricultural products increased enormously and boosted trade with the Allies from $825 million in 1914 to $3.2 billion in 1916.

U.S. financiers invested in the war by offering huge loans to Britain and France. Proclaiming that money was "the worst of contrabands," Secretary of State Bryan had instituted a ban against loans to the belligerents in 1914, but Wilson modified the order by permitting banks to offer short-term credit to the Allies. In 1915 the president allowed lenders to extend loans to European governments in a controversial decision that he never put in writing. Despite his desire to maintain neutrality, Wilson's convictions concerning the importance of foreign trade led him to permit the Federal Reserve to guarantee these obligations. By 1917, bankers had loaned $2.5 billion to Britain and France. "Our firm had never for one minute been neutral," a Morgan banker later explained. "From the start we did everything we could to contribute to the cause of the Allies." In contrast, U.S. trade with the Central Powers dwindled, and loans to Germany totaled only $300 million.

While these economic patterns developed, Republican leaders pressed Wilson to initiate a program of military preparedness. But the president hoped that a neutral United States might be in a position to shape the peace. Blending idealism with his desire for economic expansion, Wilson believed that the terrible costs of the war would teach the European powers the necessity of ending imperial competition and allow the United States to provide leadership in forging a peace settlement based on international cooperation and free trade. "We are the mediating nation of the world," Wilson declared. "We are compounded of all the nations of the world. We are, therefore, able to understand all nations."

While Wilson awaited the opportunity to initiate a better world, the actions of the warring countries challenged U.S. neutrality. Once hostilities broke out, Britain and Germany each tried to impose blockades on the other's ports. As Britain became an important market for U.S. goods and capital, the Royal Navy mined the entrance to the North Sea and curbed neutral trade with Germany. Washington did not challenge the British blockade.

German efforts to retaliate brought a different response, drawing severe U.S. complaints. The British blockade relied on conventional naval warfare and seldom claimed civilian casualties. But since Germany could not challenge the British navy on the open sea, the Germans adopted a new type of warfare that employed the U-boat, or submarine, to destroy Allied shipping. As deadly as it could be to surface vessels, the submarine was extremely vulnerable to attack, especially when it surfaced. The U-boat therefore became a weapon of stealth and surprise that could not easily avoid threatening the rights of neutral shippers. German submarine warfare soon resulted in great loss of U.S. property and claimed numerous civilian casualties, including U.S. citizens.

Germany's effort to cut British supply lines played into the hands of Allied propaganda. Because Britain controlled the only transatlantic cable, the Allies determined the flow of war news to the United States. U.S. newspapers readily accepted the British interpretation of events, including numerous stories of German atrocities, all of which confirmed the image of Germany as an outlaw nation. British propaganda portrayed the Germans as "Huns," a savage people who severed the hands of Belgian babies and raped women. Other stories that related the loss of innocent lives in the attacks of German submarines further outraged the public.

Wilson's neutrality policy rested on ambiguous and unrealistic assumptions. The president viewed British and German offenses differently. Moreover, he demanded that merchants have the unimpeded right to turn a profit in a war zone while assuming no risks for their actions. The fate of the *Lusitania* illustrated the problems of such a policy. In May 1915 a German submarine sank the British passenger liner within sight of the Irish coast and caused the deaths of 1,198 passengers, including 128 Americans. Theodore Roosevelt denounced the sinking as an "act of piracy," although the *Lusitania* almost certainly used its passengers as a shield for the munitions it carried for the British war effort.

Wilson responded to the sinking by sending a strongly worded protest to the German government. Secretary of State Bryan, angered by the president's unwillingness to criticize similar British violations of neutrality, resigned from office, denouncing the idea that "ammunition intended for one of the belligerents should be safeguarded in transit by the lives of American citizens." Many congressional representatives supported the McLemore Resolution, which warned citizens not to travel to Europe. But Wilson refused to accept any limitations on the rights of neutral nations. By rejecting such restrictions, the president placed himself in a position that required defense of those rights.

In 1915 the Germans acceded to Wilson's demands and promised not to attack passenger ships, but they increased strikes on armed British merchant vessels, which had been ordered to attack submarines on sight. In 1916 Germany announced it would fire on Allied shipping without warning. A few weeks later a submarine torpedoed the *Sussex,* an unarmed French passenger ship, injuring several U.S. citizens. When Wilson delivered an ultimatum that called for Germany to stop sinking merchant and passenger ships unless it wished to risk U.S. intervention, Berlin responded affirmatively with the Sussex Pledge. Yet the president realized how precarious the balance between peace and war had become. "Any little German lieutenant can put us into war at any time by some calculated outrage," he admitted.

THE COMING OF WAR

In seeking to protect neutral rights on the seas, Wilson embraced the idea of mobilizing the armed forces. In the years after 1900, the army and navy had developed centralized staff systems. The Dick Act of 1903 furthered military consolidation by placing state militias, renamed the National Guard, under federal control. In 1916, the president toured the country to win support for a $500-million preparedness program that included creation of the Reserve Officers' Training Corps (ROTC) on the nation's college campuses. Congress responded by passing the National Defense Act of 1916 and a naval appropriations measure. Rejecting the use of bonds as too burdensome on ordinary taxpayers, Congress financed the package through the Revenue Act of 1916, the first major income and inheritance tax in U.S. history.

By 1916, a coalition of British sympathizers, beneficiaries of wartime prosperity, and belligerent nationalists pressed Wilson to intervene in World War I. Yet many citizens wanted the nation to remain at peace. German Americans with cultural ties to their homeland and Irish Americans who despised British colonialism spoke loudly against U.S. involvement. Social justice progressives like Jane Addams also opposed intervention because they feared the war's effects on domestic reform and preferred peaceful resolution of international disputes. Organizations such as the Carnegie Endowment for International Peace had successfully urged presidents Roosevelt, Taft, and Wilson to sign arbitration treaties with the major powers, which resulted in agreements with all except Germany.

The largest group of noninterventionists consisted of midwestern and western farmers and business interests. Removed from European financial and trade ties, they saw the overseas conflict as an imperial struggle that had no bearing on small producers and distributors in the domestic economy. Such agrarian and nationalist views found expression in the Nonpartisan League, a political lobby group that emerged in the north-central and mountain states and boasted a membership of 220,000. Its influence contributed to a powerful noninterventionist bloc in Congress. Wilson actively appealed to these voters in 1916.

As his second term began, the president decided to make another effort to mediate the European conflict. Earlier in the war, he twice had sent his personal representative Colonel Edward House to negotiate between the two sides, but to no avail. The Germans resented the pro-Allied bias of the U.S. position, and the British and French believed they would win the war. By 1915, the cost of the conflict had risen so high that neither side would consider a negotiated peace. In late 1916 Wilson tried again by inviting the belligerents to state their terms for peace. Germany made no public response, although it wanted Lithuania, Poland, Belgium, and the Belgian Congo. The Allies insisted on German withdrawal from Belgium, the return of Alsace-Lorraine to France, substantial monetary compensation, Germany's overseas colonies, and division of the Hapsburg Empire into national groups.

Frustrated and impatient, Wilson seized the moment to make a dramatic appeal for the warring countries to end the war. In an address to Congress in January 1917, the president called for a "peace without victory." Expressing ideals of self-determination and free international trade, he urged world leaders to embrace a global marketplace guaranteed by freedom of the seas, military disarmament, and international cooperation to preserve world order. The proposal demonstrated Wilson's visionary eloquence, but failed to break the European stalemate. Peace prospects rapidly deteriorated. With the war deadlocked on the western front and the British blockade creating severe shortages, German leaders met with Kaiser Wilhelm and voted to revoke the Sussex Pledge and resume unrestricted submarine warfare. The ships of neutral nations would be as vulnerable as those of the adversaries. Germany recognized that this escalation would jeopardize relations with Washington, but hoped to win the war before the United States could establish a military presence in Europe.

Wilson promptly severed diplomatic relations with Germany. The president then asked Congress to pass the Armed Ship bill, authorizing the arming of merchant ships. Seeking to build public support, he released the Zimmerman note, a secret German dispatch recently intercepted by the British. Sent from the foreign secretary of Germany to its Mexican embassy, the Zimmerman note directed Berlin's ambassador to encourage Mexico to attack north of the border if the United States entered the European war. Germany offered to help Mexico recover Texas, New Mexico, and Arizona. One day after publication of the Zimmerman note, the House overwhelmingly approved the Armed Ship bill. Yet in the Senate, a bipartisan coalition of noninterventionists led by Wisconsin's Robert M. La Follette and Nebraska's George W. Norris organized a session-ending filibuster that prevented a vote on the measure. Infuriated at this obstacle to military preparedness and executive prerogative, Wilson denounced the "little group of willful men" who had blocked his proposal and proceeded to arm the merchant vessels by executive order.

The world crisis intensified. In Russia, the overthrow of czarist government in March 1917 introduced a constitutional government. With this republic, the

Allied coalition was no longer tainted by partnership with a despotic ally. That month, German submarines sank three U.S. merchant ships in a single day. Meanwhile, Wilson received a telegram from the U.S. ambassador to Britain warning that French and British solvency had to be protected to "prevent the collapse of world trade." In April the president rode down Pennsylvania Avenue with a cavalry escort to ask Congress for a declaration of war. In a powerful address, Wilson told the country that "the right is more precious than the peace." The world, he said, "must be made safe for democracy."

Wilson left the chamber during a roaring ovation. Yet the anguish of the moment surfaced when the president asked an aide why anyone would cheer a message that would bring so much death. In Congress antimilitarists in the South joined midwestern and western noninterventionists to oppose the war. Denouncing the conflict as an effort to secure the interests of bankers and arms makers, La Follette scoffed at "patriots" who were "back of the thirty-eight corporations most benefited by the war effort." After four days of angry debate, six senators and fifty representatives voted against the declaration of war.

THE DOUGHBOYS AND MILITARY VICTORY

U.S. intervention in 1917 came at a crucial time in the Great War. Two and a half years of fighting on the western front had produced a frustrating stalemate and enormous casualties. The first Russian revolution of March 1917 had diminished Russia's ability to sustain the eastern front, which would free the Central Powers to divert more forces against the depleted British and French troops. Unrestricted submarine warfare compounded Allied problems. In April 1917 Britain had only a six-week supply of food, and the U-boats were sinking 900,000 tons of shipping each month.

But despite Wilson's enthusiasm to play a significant role, Washington faced numerous administrative problems, not least being the recruitment of an army. Reflecting a progressive outlook, Wilson rejected a volunteer army (favored by ex–Rough Rider Theodore Roosevelt) and insisted on a selective service system that would permit the government to organize and deploy a military force. The president wanted this army to represent the larger society, not simply the less privileged classes. Backed by patriotic parades, bands, and political speeches—backed, in short, by community pressure—the Selective Service Act of 1917 enabled the army to draft 3 million soldiers from all walks of life. Although some 300,000 men evaded the draft and 23,000 sought conscientious objector status, another 2 million enlisted voluntarily. Tens of thousands of women also served in the Army Nursing Corps, as navy clerks, and as civilian employees (clerks, telephone operators, canteen workers) for the army. Sixty percent of the soldiers would be noncombatants, serving as laborers and clerks. The military used intelligence tests to assess the capability of

EXHIBIT **3-5**   **U.S. TROOPS ON THE WESTERN FRONT, 1918**

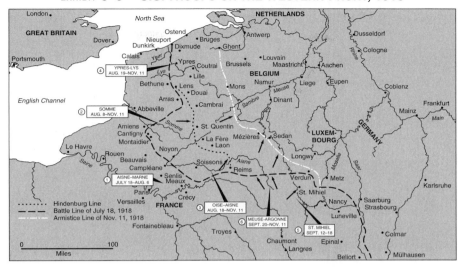

recruits (and discovered that one-third were illiterate). Thus the "doughboys" would be shaped to government specifications.

To command the American Expeditionary Force (AEF), Wilson appointed General John J. Pershing, who had led U.S. troops in Mexico. A career professional, Pershing refused to commit troops to combat until they had completed their training. He also was under strict orders from the president to keep the AEF independent of British and French command to preserve U.S. bargaining power in postwar negotiations. On July 4, 1917, a token force of AEF troops landed in France, as one officer proclaimed, "Lafayette, we are here!" These men were untrained for trench combat and mechanized tank warfare. Even one year later, with only 350,000 troops in place, the AEF was hardly prepared to mount independent operations. The Allies provided nearly all the AEF's artillery and much of its ammunition. Only 40 percent of its supplies came from the United States.

Anticipating that U.S. troops would not be fully mobilized until the following year, Germany mounted a spring offensive in 1918. Wilson and Pershing agreed to the appointment of French General Ferdinand Foch as supreme commander and allowed the AEF to be deployed in Lorraine, where the possibility of a German breakthrough appeared minimal. But U.S. troops arrived at Chateau-Thierry and Belleau Wood in time to engage in trench warfare and contribute to the Allied defense that stalled the German advance. In July 1918 the Allies mounted a counteroffensive, and by September the U.S. First Army pushed the Germans out of the St. Mihiel salient. However, although the AEF held a 9–1 manpower advantage in the southern sector to which it was assigned, Pershing's failure to support infantry attacks with artillery

George Creel (1876-1953)

As the United States entered World War I, Woodrow Wilson asked George Creel to chair the Committee on Public Information (CPI). Uncertain of initial support for the overseas conflict, Wilson hoped that the agency could use new public relations and advertising techniques to

Brown Brothers

build a consensus of support. By establishing the committee under Creel's leadership, the president authorized the first government propaganda agency in U.S. history.

The son of a former Confederate army officer, George Creel struggled through an early career as a journalist until he founded a Kansas City newspaper early in the century. A staunch Progressive, he threw himself into muckraking by denouncing the city's political machine and demanding a variety of reforms to improve public services, to protect workers, and to make the political process more responsive to middle-class interests. Creel was an admirer of Woodrow Wilson, and he supported the president's reelection bid in 1916 by writing some effective political tracts. Impressed by Creel's Progressive credentials and powers of persuasion, Wilson assigned him the task of interpreting U.S. war aims for audiences at home and abroad.

Creel immediately recruited a core of public relations practitioners, journalists, professional historians, and entertainment figures to set in motion a campaign of "moral publicity." Organizing public rallies and parades to support the military effort and encourage the sale of govern-

resulted in heavy casualties. In the fall of 1918, one million doughboys participated in the Allied drive along a 200-mile front through the Argonne Forest. After forty-seven days, the Germans were forced to seek a cease-fire when the imperial government dissolved.

By the time World War I ended at 11:00 AM on November 11, 1918, Germany had lost 1.8 million people and the Hapsburg Empire, 1.2 million. Among the Allies, the Russians suffered 1.7 million deaths, the French nearly 1.4 million, and the British Empire, 947,000. Another 20 million Europeans

ment war bonds, the CPI mobilized 75,000 public speakers and distributed millions of pamphlets, press releases, and drawings.

The CPI chair also exercised authority over the export of films and publications, manipulating these cultural products to ensure that the "wholesome life of America" received exposure throughout the world. Creel and his associates painted Americans as virtuous and Germans as villains in films like *The Prussian Cur* and *The Kaiser: The Beast of Berlin*. Through advertisements in popular magazines, the CPI encouraged citizens to report anyone who "spreads pessimistic stories, cries for peace, or belittles our efforts to win this war." Creel also persuaded the press to engage in voluntary censorship. Meanwhile, the foreign section of the CPI worked to influence European public opinion by portraying Wilson as a hero who would bring political redemption to the world. As part of this effort, the agency bribed European newspaper editors, subsidized European publishers, and provided free copies of American propaganda.

Creel turned the CPI into a vehicle for imposing cultural conformity as well as political unity. Like many Anglo-Protestants, he feared the cultural pluralism practiced by many European immigrants. The CPI clearly insinuated that the use of languages other than English was unpatriotic. Indeed, Creel's memoir, *How We Advertised America* (1920), celebrated the new professions of advertising and public relations and their ability to create a mass society in which all individuals shared a uniform set of values. Given the dominance of class, sectional, and selfish interests before 1917, observed Creel, the war had "come at the right time for the preservation and interpretation of American Ideals."

were wounded. U.S. fatalities totaled 112,432—half from disease, especially from a global flu epidemic. Untold thousands bore the consequences of poison gas, tuberculosis, and shell shock. Although the Allies bore the brunt of the fighting, the United States helped to defeat Germany by securing the North Atlantic sea-lanes against the submarine, permitting the shipment of men and supplies to the front. The timely arrival of AEF soldiers sustained Allied morale and tipped the balance of power. Most important, President Wilson was positioned to influence a lasting European settlement.

ORGANIZING FOR VICTORY

The U.S. military contribution required an immense mobilization of economic and human resources. The first task was financing a war that would ultimately cost $32 billion. With great fanfare that blended modern public relations techniques and political pressure, the government launched a series of Liberty Bond drives that netted $23 billion in loans from individual subscribers. This reliance on bonds, by taking money out of circulation, had secondary advantages of limiting consumer demand for war commodities as well as cooling inflation. Under pressure from La Follette and other insurgents, Congress raised billions in additional revenue with new taxes on "excess profits," high incomes, and luxuries.

Mobilization gave corporate progressives the opportunity to create a working partnership between government and private business. Under the War Finance Corporation, headed by treasury secretary and presidential son-in-law William Gibbs McAdoo, government became the ultimate source of private investment capital. In turn, the War Industries Board (WIB) set production goals for corporations in war industries and controlled the flow of raw materials so war output would have top priority. Led by financier Bernard Baruch, the WIB promoted a "new competition" among large firms by allowing price-fixing, collusive bidding, and guaranteed profits. In blurring the line between government and industry, Baruch introduced a form of national economic planning in which the state served as the partner and facilitator of business rather than its regulator. Among the benefits given to business was a 1917 tax law that treated corporate advertising as a tax-deductible expense, a public subsidy that endures.

Under Herbert Hoover, a mining engineer turned public servant, the Food Administration oversaw agricultural production and distribution. The agency set high prices for commodities to encourage production and then purchased the entire crop. As large harvests of midwestern wheat and southern cotton went to feed and clothe U.S. and Allied troops, agricultural income jumped 30 percent. Anxious to avoid excessive bureaucratic regulation, Hoover encouraged the voluntary cooperation of private citizens with a federal agency. Through an elaborate public relations effort, the Food Administration persuaded millions to solve problems of agricultural distribution by avoiding meat or wheat consumption for several days each week. The successful campaign enabled the agency to supply domestic, military, and foreign consumers without resorting to compulsory rationing.

Similar forms of centralized planning were applied by the Fuel Administration, which distributed coal to both citizens and defense plants, and by the Railroad Administration, which provided central management of a private system owned by several companies. Meanwhile, the Webb-Pomerene Act of

EXHIBIT **3-6**   PUBLIC DEBT OF THE U.S. FEDERAL GOVERNMENT, 1916–1919 (IN ROUNDED BILLIONS OF DOLLARS)

1916	1.2
1917	3.0
1918	12.5
1919	25.5

Source: *Historical Statistics of the United States, Colonial Times to 1970* (1975).

1918 authorized corporations to coordinate price and marketing policies in overseas trade. The Edge Act of 1919 allowed bankers to cooperate to control investments abroad. Such measures seemed to confirm the progressive faith in government planning based on expert leadership.

Progressives also used the war emergency to integrate organized labor into the corporate economy. When war first began in 1914, the reduction of immigration from Europe had created a labor shortage, enabling U.S. workers to press for better wages and rights of collective bargaining. Because government contracts guaranteed business profits, companies passed the rising cost of labor to taxpayers and consumers. But rising prices and business reluctance to recognize unions provoked the largest number of strikes in U.S. history. During the war years, over three thousand strikes occurred annually and involved millions of workers. In the western states, the militant Industrial Workers of the World (IWW) organized workers in mining, logging, even agriculture.

With the nation at war, American Federation of Labor (AFL) leader Samuel Gompers saw an opportunity to calm the labor wars and gain respectability. Gompers had supported Wilson's preparedness program. Once Congress declared war, the federation worked with the government War Labor Board (WLB) to obtain labor's goals of better wages, shorter hours, increased union membership, and a voice in shaping government policy. Influenced by Gompers, the WLB encouraged the formation of unions and collective bargaining in return for labor's cooperation in the war effort. Wilson also created the U.S. Employment Service, which placed nearly 4 million workers in war-related jobs. Government intervention prevented discrimination against union employees and preserved wage standards throughout the war.

Cooperation with the administration helped to double union membership to 5 million. As the annual gross national product grew from $48 billion to $91 billion between 1916 and 1920, the average annual wage of workers rose from $600 to $1,400, although the doubling of the cost-of-living index largely absorbed the increases. Nevertheless, unions worked with the WLB to prod corporations to institute the 8-hour day and comparable pay for women. Proposals for federal pensions for the elderly and unemployment insurance died, however, because opponents linked them with German welfare policies or with socialism.

As the AFL became a respectable "business" union, Gompers ignored political attacks on the more militant Socialists and IWW "Wobblies," whose members faced prison for opposing the war. The AFL also neglected new members of the workforce. When large agricultural growers persuaded Congress to end immigration restrictions for Mexican field workers in 1917, leaders of the IWW's Agricultural Workers Order were in jail, and no union offered to protect the "temporary" Mexican workers' rights. Similarly, when unprecedented numbers of African American workers migrated from the South into industrial cities, the AFL made no effort to recruit black labor.

Nor did unions welcome women workers. Although the war did not attract many new women workers, working women took the opportunity to shift from unskilled, low-paid jobs in domestic services and found better work as clerks, drivers, and factory workers. Entering previously male-only occupations, women often faced sex discrimination and harassment in the workplace. Most innovations ended with the war. "The same patriotism which induced women to enter industry," one union leader advised, "should induce them to vacate their positions after the war."

GENDER AND RACE IN WARTIME

The changes of wartime society, new labor demands, and the persistence of progressive ideals broadened opportunities for both women and racial minorities. Besides finding better jobs in the civilian workforce, about 16,500 experienced women (mostly single whites at an average age around 30) enlisted in the Army Nurses Corps, the Red Cross, or as civilian employees overseas. Some middle-class women served on the home front with government agencies, such as the Food Administration. Suffragist leaders Carrie Chapman Catt and Anna Howard Shaw demonstrated their patriotism by joining the Women's Committee of the Council of National Defense. Other feminists, like anarchist Emma Goldman and socialists Kate Richards O'Hare and Rose Pastor Stokes, went to jail for their political dissent. Pacifists like Jane Addams, who had helped found the Woman's Peace party in 1915, were effectively silenced after Congress voted for war.

For women social purity reformers, World War I facilitated fulfillment of the crusade against liquor. Wartime shortages justified reduced consumption of grains used for beer and whiskey, and economic mobilization underscored the need for a sober workforce. The war also intensified the desire to "Americanize" new immigrants by imposing Anglo-Protestant values of sobriety, particularly because German Americans ran most of the large breweries and distilleries. In 1917 Congress approved the Eighteenth Amendment, which ended the sale of alcoholic beverages; the states completed its ratification two years later. Purity crusaders also focused on preventing sexual promiscuity between

African American infantrymen test their gas masks shortly after arriving in France.

soldiers and single women, and the American Social Hygiene Association helped to create the Commission on Training Camp Activities. The government agency not only provided troops with regular medical examinations and vene-real disease information but also employed federal agents to place 35,000 women in detention centers for the war's duration on prostitution charges.

The importance of women to the war effort led the administration to en-dorse woman's suffrage. Wilson previously had ordered the arrest of White House picketers, including Alice Paul of the Congressional Union, who protested that no war could be a struggle for democracy as long as women lacked the vote. Officials treated Paul and her supporters roughly and force-fed them in jail when they went on hunger strikes. Although confrontational tac-tics did not mobilize masses of women, they enabled suffrage leaders such as Carrie Chapman Catt to portray the mainstream movement as more cautious and reasonable. With Wilson's support, Congress approved the Nineteenth Amendment in 1919, which gave women the vote. Within a year, the provision was ratified and nearly doubled the number of citizens eligible to vote.

World War I also brought opportunities for racial minorities. Some 400,000 African Americans joined the army, forming 13 percent of that service; the navy accepted 5,000; the marines none. Forced to serve in segregated units on seg-regated bases, most black soldiers received noncombat assignments that de-manded strenuous manual labor, such as stevedores and road builders. Their of-ficers were almost entirely white. The army originally intended to use blacks only as laborers, but the NAACP successfully pressured the service into organizing black combat units and establishing a black officers' training camp. Ironically, the first black regiments sent to Europe fought as part of the French army. By contrast, Native Americans were integrated into the services and took especially dangerous assignments as scouts, snipers, and messengers. Native language speakers used telephones to thwart German spies. In 1919 Congress made honorably discharged Native veterans full citizens, a precedent for the granting of universal citizenship to Native Americans in 1924.

On the home front, the war created job opportunities in northern centers of steel production, meatpacking, and other industries. These labor demands accelerated the Great Migration of African Americans, a massive population shift that ultimately relocated nearly half the nation's black population from southern farms to northern and western cities in the next half-century. Despite blacks' involvement in the war effort, Wilson refused to reconsider the segregation of the federal civil service. Nor did the president speak publicly against lynching. Nevertheless, African American leaders like W. E. B. Du Bois hoped to improve the position of blacks by supporting the war. He urged African Americans to "close our ranks shoulder to shoulder with our own white fellow citizens . . . fighting for democracy." Meanwhile, the NAACP tested discrimination cases in the courts. In 1915 the Supreme Court agreed to overturn the grandfather clause in southern voting laws. Two years later the Court outlawed residential segregation ordinances (though many localities ignored the ruling).

The wartime experience encouraged a new assertiveness among African Americans. Blacks in northern cities were free of the more stifling aspects of southern legal segregation and used the franchise to elect local politicians. More dramatically, the war offered liberation from domestic segregation for black soldiers, some of whom were accepted as social and sexual equals in France. When race riots erupted in twenty-five cities during the bloody summer of 1919, blacks fought back against white aggression. In the South, whites reacted violently to the sense of pride among returning black soldiers, some of whom were lynched in uniform. In the North, the riots stemmed from whites' fear that blacks were taking scarce jobs and that black residents would disrupt white neighborhoods. Such tensions would inspire mass movements of African American racial pride and separatism in northern black communities during the 1920s.

THE WAR AGAINST DISSENT

Demanding full public support for the war, the Wilson administration devoted unprecedented resources to shape mass opinion. Wilson appointed journalist George Creel to organize the Committee on Public Information (CPI), the first government propaganda agency. Employing 150,000 people, the CPI distributed 75 million pieces of print literature and appointed 75,000 "Four-Minute Men" to give brief patriotic speeches at public gatherings. The agency persuaded popular entertainers such as Charles Chaplin, Douglas Fairbanks, and Mary Pickford to sell war bonds at public rallies. Private groups such as the National Security League, which drew its members from the academic community, supplemented the government's efforts by solidifying support for the European crusade on college campuses. Such pressure led marginal social groups, such as members of Oklahoma's so-called Five Civilized Tribes and New York's nonsocialist Jewish labor unions, to buy bonds to demonstrate their loyalty.

Despite such efforts, many citizens criticized U.S. participation in the war. "War is the health of the state," warned radical essayist Randolph Bourne in 1918. Socialist Party leader Eugene Debs portrayed the war as a defense of transatlantic capitalism and condemned Wilson's attack on civil liberties. After the Socialists labeled the war a "crime against humanity," they took 30 percent or more of the vote in the 1917 municipal elections in industrial cities such as Chicago, Dayton, Toledo, and Buffalo. In Oklahoma, where struggling tenant farmers and sharecroppers accounted for the nation's highest proportion of Socialist Party members, more than 400 rioting protestors refused to be drafted. Debs's antiwar speech at the Socialist Party convention of 1918 would bring the presidential candidate a ten-year prison sentence.

Opposition to the war was particularly strong in the Midwest, where large numbers of residents quietly resisted bond drives, ignored food pledge campaigns, and sought to evade conscription. Robert La Follette, Idaho senator William E. Borah, and a group of southern representatives bitterly opposed compulsory military service. Joining with William Jennings Bryan, La Follette demanded heavy taxation of war profits to conscript capital instead of labor. Both men called for future referenda of the electorate before Congress declared war. Accused of giving aid and comfort to the enemy, La Follette received the condemnation of the faculty of the University of Wisconsin in his home state. He also faced charges that would remove him from the Senate, which were dismissed only after a 51–21 vote of the full body.

Pressure for conformity heightened concerns about the nation's cultural heterogeneity. By 1917, foreign-born residents or the children of immigrants accounted for one-third of the population, and many were recent arrivals from the countries that formed the Central Powers. Nativist anxieties surfaced in 1917 when Congress added a literacy test for new immigrants, overriding a presidential veto. Yet Wilson signed immigration laws that permitted authorities to deport aliens who belonged to revolutionary organizations.

The administration also responded to dissent by supporting repressive legislation. The Espionage Act of 1917 prohibited any action that might be construed as aiding the enemy or discouraging military service. The law authorized the postmaster general to exclude "treasonable" publications from the mail. Under these provisions, the government imprisoned Debs and banned the mailing of Socialist periodicals. Movie producer Robert Goldstein received a ten-year prison sentence because his film *The Spirit of '76* showed British soldiers attacking U.S. civilians during the Revolutionary War. In 1918 Congress passed the Sedition Act, which made it a crime to "utter, print, write, or publish any disloyal, profane, scurrilous, or abusive language" about the armed forces. The Socialist Party faced indictments and the arrest of more than 1,500 members for criticizing the government.

Radicals and pacifists became targets of government persecution. Under the leadership of "Big Bill" Haywood, the Industrial Workers of the World (IWW) rejected both the American Federation of Labor's craft unionism and the Socialist Party's commitment to gradual political reform. The government used troops to break IWW strikes in Washington and Montana and arrested 165 IWW leaders for organizing workers in the lumber, mining, and farm industries. Haywood avoided imprisonment only by fleeing to Russia. Government repression also led to prison terms for 400 conscientious objectors to military service; the administration recognized only members of pacifist churches such as the Quakers and Mennonites for conscientious objector status.

After the war, the Supreme Court upheld the constitutionality of such repressive measures. In the *Schenck* case (1919), the Court ruled that protection of free speech did not apply during wartime. This decision sustained the conviction of a Socialist Party official who had mailed circulars that questioned the constitutionality of conscription. As Justice Oliver Wendell Holmes argued in a unanimous opinion, "The most stringent protection of free speech would not protect a man falsely shouting fire in a crowded theater and causing a panic." Holmes stated that the Court could deny free speech when a "clear and present danger" existed to public safety and national security. The high Court also upheld the Espionage Act conviction of Eugene Debs for telling an audience that the "master" class made wars while the "subject" class fought them. In *Abrams* v. *the United States* (1919), a split Court upheld the Sedition Act as a legitimate attempt to prevent disaffection during wartime.

Government efforts to suppress dissent encouraged private citizens to attack antiwar critics. In Indiana a jury dismissed charges against a man who had shot someone for yelling, "To hell with the United States." Occasionally, such vigilantism received semiofficial sanction. When IWW copper miners went on strike in Bisbee, Arizona, in 1917, a local sheriff treated the 1,200 Mexican Americans as subversives and used vigilantes to deport them to the desert south of the border. Meanwhile, the Justice Department issued cards to the 250,000 members of the American Protective League (APL) that identified the holders as federal agents and permitted them to spy on neighbors and monitor nonconformists.

German Americans faced special harassment. War hysteria translated German measles into liberty measles, dachshunds into liberty pups, and sauerkraut into liberty cabbage. More ominous forms of repression included the suspension of German-language publications, prohibition of the teaching of German, and physical attacks on German speakers. Some employers dismissed German Americans from their jobs, while mobs beat suspected "Huns" and intimidated them into purchasing war bonds.

THE LEAGUE OF NATIONS AND A NEW WORLD ORDER

President Wilson saw U.S. involvement in World War I as a step toward creating a stable international order. Yet his vision of postwar peace and prosperity collided with the emergence of a new Soviet Union following a second Russian revolution in 1917 that brought the Bolshevik or Communist Party to power. Withdrawing from the coalition against the Central Powers, the new Russian leaders repudiated secret Allied treaties to divide the territorial gains of the war. Instead, the Bolsheviks called for peace through international socialist revolution.

Wilson responded to these revolutionary ideas in January 1918, in a speech to Congress outlining Fourteen Points for a prospective settlement. The president's plan called for disarmament, freedom of the seas, open diplomacy, and self-determination for colonized nations and the people of Europe. Most important, Wilson proposed a new international organization, a League of Nations, to enforce the new world order.

Convinced that his Fourteen Points could bring lasting peace, the president led the U.S. delegation to the Versailles Peace Conference that convened in 1919. Bolstered by the academic experts of the American Peace Commission, Wilson arrived in Europe amid enormous popular acclaim. Yet British Prime Minister David Lloyd George and French Premier Georges Clemenceau were reluctant to abandon their demands for national security and economic compensation. "How can I talk to a fellow who thinks himself the first man in 2,000 years to know anything about peace on earth?" asked the skeptical French leader. Given the enormous financial and human costs absorbed by the Allies, Wilson's only bargaining chip at Versailles remained his personal appeal to the war-weary people of Europe.

Despite the president's insistence on "peace without victory," Wilson shared Allied fears of communism. Bolshevik leader V. I. Lenin had declared that the future of the industrial world belonged to socialism. According to this analysis, capitalist nations would continue to fight wars among themselves as they competed for overseas markets and raw materials until the working class took control and instituted a cooperative global system. This vision of a communist world order defied Wilson's hopes for an international market economy built on democratic freedoms. As communist uprisings threatened to spread throughout Europe, the president sought to contain revolution within

EXHIBIT **3-7**   **U.S. INTERVENTION IN RUSSIA**

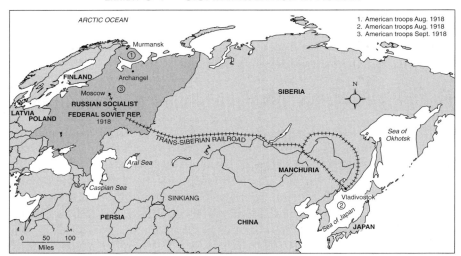

Russia. Without consulting Congress or the public, Wilson had authorized secret expenditures to finance the anti-Bolshevik "White" armies while embargoing trade with Soviet Russia. In the summer of 1918 the president ordered
U.S. troops to Russia to join military attachments from France, Britain, and
Japan. Supposedly sent to keep supplies from falling into German hands, foreign forces occupied northern Russia and Siberia until June 1919 and occupied Manchuria until April 1920.

Some 4,500 U.S. soldiers participated in fighting around Archangel and
suffered about 500 casualties, but the president claimed "we are not at war
with Russia." Wilson hoped that their presence would "liberate" the Russian
people. The military venture revealed the president's vision of international
cooperation, a precursor of the collective security he saw as the heart of a future global order. Yet his concern about communism forced him to compromise with the Allies on his peace plan. The result was the Treaty of Versailles,
a document that violated much of the spirit and substance of the Fourteen
Points. A peace negotiated in secret by the victors, the settlement ignored
freedom of the seas and violated the principle of self-determination. Under its
provisions, Britain, France, and Japan divided Germany's colonies among
themselves and refused to consider dissolving their own empires. Whereas
Germany and Austria lost sovereignty over non-German peoples of Europe,
the treaty's new national boundaries placed many German-speaking people in
the newly formed nations of Central Europe and in Italy.

Far from supporting a peace without victors, Versailles imposed harsh
penalties on the defeated Germans, who had to accept guilt for the war, pay

$35 billion in reparations, and limit the size of their armed forces. Yet Wilson accepted the treaty because it included his cherished proposal for a League of Nations. Defining U.S. freedom and welfare in global terms, the president had used military power to ensure the adoption of essential principles of international law and commerce. He now hoped to use the league to create a stable world order in which disputes between nations might be resolved without violence. In a dangerous and revolutionary political environment, Wilson insisted that no international peace mechanism could work without a system of collective security. Accordingly, Article X of the League Covenant required member nations to defend the territorial integrity and political independence of all participants against external aggression.

Wilson returned to the United States facing a difficult struggle to gain Senate ratification of the treaty. Having chosen to lead his country's delegation to France, the president had left no political buffer between himself and the final treaty; he had to accept responsibility for its limitations. Moreover, because Wilson had omitted Republicans from the delegation, the treaty lacked bipartisan support, and hostile Republicans controlled both houses of Congress.

Three groups of senators objected to U.S. participation in the League of Nations. First, eastern Republicans, led by Henry Cabot Lodge, a personal adversary of Wilson, opposed ratification for political and ideological reasons, believing that the League would threaten the nation's independence. Second, a coalition of sixteen "irreconcilable" eastern Republicans and western progressives refused to endorse the league under any circumstances. Led by La Follette, Borah, and California's Hiram Johnson, these senators feared that U.S. troops would be used to bolster the "tottering" governments of imperial Europe. Third, thirty-five Republican "reservationists" approved membership in the league only without the controversial Article X that provided for collective security. This group maintained that obligations to the Allies threatened national sovereignty and tied the nation to the European status quo.

Because public opinion appeared to support Wilson, Lodge offered to recommend league membership with reservations affirming U.S. autonomy. But instead of negotiating with his critics, Wilson mounted a strenuous speaking tour in September 1919 to build public enthusiasm for an unamended treaty. Midway through his trip, the president collapsed. Rushed back to Washington, he suffered a paralyzing stroke. With the president unable to assume his responsibilities for two months, First Lady Edith Galt Wilson and White House physician Cary Grayson became the only links between the president and the outside world. Wilson's physical collapse destroyed the slim chance of compromise with the reservationists.

When the Senate considered a resolution to pass the treaty with the Lodge reservations in November 1919, Wilson ordered Democrats to invoke

John ("Jack") Reed (1887-1920)

The offspring of a wealthy family from Portland, Oregon, John Reed was one of two U.S. citizens to be buried inside Soviet Russia's Kremlin Wall. "This proletarian revolution will last . . . in history," he proclaimed of the 1917 upheaval that brought the Communists to power in Moscow, "a pillar of fire for mankind forever."

John Reed's odyssey began at Harvard, where the ambitious but physically fragile westerner donned a cheerleader's uniform and published short stories in the college literary magazine. Settling after graduation in New York City, he embraced the bohemian lifestyle of Greenwich Village. Yet a friendship with muckraking journalist Lincoln Steffens pushed him toward a commitment to political activism and social causes. He joined the staff of Max Eastman's radical journal, *The Masses*. In 1913 he was jailed while covering a strike in Paterson, New Jersey, by the Industrial Workers of the World (IWW). The experience led him to organize artists and writers to stage a giant Madison Square Garden Pageant for the union's benefit.

Reed attracted national attention as a writer when he went to Mexico to report on the major social revolution of the era. He spent four months in the desert with Pancho Villa and became known for his ability to match the general's drinking exploits. Reed sent back a series of brilliant dispatches that captured the tedium and the horror of combat. His book *Insurgent Mexico* (1914) established him as the foremost war cor-

customary party loyalty and defeat the measure. Although the Senate adopted the treaty with the Lodge reservations in 1920, a bipartisan coalition of Wilson loyalists and irreconcilables prevented ratification by the necessary two-thirds majority. The United States signed a separate peace treaty with Germany two years later. As the nation retreated from internationalism and high-minded idealism, the president's party lay in tatters.

respondent of his time. When World War I erupted, Reed immediately left for Europe to report on the western front and returned a second time to visit the eastern war zone. His writing portrayed the bloody conflict as a capitalist civil war.

Returning to the United States, Reed further identified with the revolutionary struggle. Soon after marrying, Reed and his new wife, writer Louise Bryant, sailed for Russia and arrived in Petrograd on the eve of the Bolshevik Revolution of 1917. Reed cultivated a close friendship with Soviet leader Lenin and threw himself into the revolutionary process. His classic *Ten Days That Shook the World* (1919), a journalistic diary of the tumultuous events of the November revolution, provided a stirring and optimistic account of the communist takeover as a triumph of the working class.

Reed's antiwar articles and speeches soon precipitated persecution by the U.S. government. Unintimidated, he and Bryant testified before a Senate committee on behalf of U.S. support for the new Soviet state. After an American Communist Party was organized in 1919, Reed formed his own Communist Labor Party, seeking to build a revolutionary workers' movement outside the mainstream labor organizations favored by the Soviets. Nevertheless, he was forced to flee the United States when the government levied sedition charges against him. After being jailed for three months in Finland for traveling with a forged passport, Reed finally reached Moscow. Demoralized by the Communist state's rigid bureaucracy and exhausted from his travels and activities, Reed contacted typhus and died in 1920. He was buried in the Kremlin as a hero of the revolution.

RED SCARE

Social tensions generated by the war escalated in the first years of peace. Concerned that inflation outstripped wage increases, more than 4 million workers took part in 3,600 strikes in 1919 alone. That year the most ambitious general strike in U.S. history gripped Seattle and aroused fears that European class conflict had returned with the doughboys. That fall, coal miners defied the leadership of the United Mine Workers and successfully struck for better wages. Meanwhile, the AFL organized all aspects of steel production and led 375,000 workers in the industry's first strike since 1892. Union organizers focused on better wages, 8-hour workdays, and improved working conditions; companies portrayed the conflict as inspired by radicals and used black and Mexican strikebreakers to end the protest. In Boston, police responded to the firing of AFL unionists in their ranks by walking out, prompting Massachusetts Governor Calvin Coolidge to declare, "There is no right to strike against the public safety by anybody, anywhere, anytime."

A series of terrorist threats coincided with the labor unrest of 1919. In the spring, postal officials discovered mail bombs addressed to John D. Rockefeller, Supreme Court Justice Holmes, and other powerful political and corporate leaders; the bombs were intended for delivery on May Day. The following month, bombs exploded within minutes of each other in eight cities. One of those explosions shook the home of Attorney General A. Mitchell Palmer and startled his neighbor, Assistant Secretary of the Navy Franklin D. Roosevelt. Despite a lack of evidence, the public associated such anarchy with the union movement.

Labor unrest, threats of terrorism, and fears about the Bolshevik Revolution provoked a postwar Red Scare. In 1918 two small communist parties emerged in the United States. Suspecting that Soviet doctrines might find fertile ground among working-class immigrants, the Wilson administration organized to fight the "red" threat. Attorney General Palmer named J. Edgar Hoover, a Justice Department attorney, to head an antiradical division. Meanwhile, Palmer ordered the arrest of labor leaders, peace activists, socialists, communists, and alien dissenters. On a single evening in January 1920 federal agents detained six thousand people, held many without charges, and subjected scores to police brutality. Although the government released most of the arrested activists, it deported more than 500 aliens. As thousands of New Yorkers cheered from the docks, the USS *Buford*—the so-called Soviet Ark— sailed for Finland with 249 aliens, among them anarchists Emma Goldman and Alexander Berkman.

Palmer's actions were part of a nationwide persecution of radicals to eliminate "alien" influences and ideologies. The New York state legislature expelled five Socialists. Milwaukee Socialist Victor Berger, who once joked that the only results of the war were the influenza epidemic and inflation, was denied his seat in the U.S. House of Representatives despite winning two consecutive elections. Twenty-eight states enacted sedition laws, which resulted in the arrest of 1,400 people and the conviction of 300. Some states required public schoolteachers to sign loyalty oaths, and local communities banned politically controversial books from their libraries. Radicals became targets of vigilante violence. After a shoot-out between IWW activists and American Le-

EXHIBIT **3-8**   **U.S. PER CAPITA INCOME IN DOLLARS, 1914–1920**

1914	389
1916	473
1918	740
1920	860

Source: *Historical Statistics of the United States, Colonial Times to 1970* (1975).

gionnaires in Centralia, Washington, in 1919, a mob of veterans castrated IWW organizer Wesley Everest and lynched him from a railroad bridge.

Perceiving a link between foreigners and radicalism, many conservatives endorsed immigration restrictions. The Immigration Act of 1920 punished aliens for possessing subversive literature or contributing to seditious groups. By 1920, thirty-five states had outlawed organizations that supported antistate activities. The American Legion, founded as a service club of veterans, launched a campaign against communist and radical influence. Anti-immigrant sentiments also surfaced in the arrest in 1920 of Nicola Sacco and Bartolomeo Vanzetti, two Italian Americans with ties to the violent anarchist community, for armed robbery outside Boston. Although civil libertarians protested that the defendants' political views led to their prosecution, both were found guilty and executed for their crimes.

Despite such fervor, the Red Scare had run its course by mid-1920. Palmer appeared ridiculous after his warnings of a May 1 uprising of revolutionaries proved unfounded. As labor unrest quieted, as the radical movement splintered, and as the Soviet threat appeared more remote, public interest in subversives dissipated. Yet as the era of Wilsonian liberalism ended, many citizens appeared tired of the burdens of internationalism and reform at home. In choosing political leaders, voters in the coming decade would shy away from assertive executives, from reformist rhetoric, and from global commitments.

AMERICAN HISTORY RESOURCE CENTER

To explore documents, images, audio and video clips, articles, and commentary related to the material in this chapter, visit the source collections at ushistory.wadsworth.com and and use the Search function with the following key terms:

Louis Dembitz Brandeis   World War I
George Creel   Versailles Treaty
Woodrow Wilson   John J. Pershing

RECOMMENDED READINGS

Robert H. Zieger, *America's Great War: World War I and the American Experience* (2000). A concise synthesis of political, social, and military issues, this book grounds the war in the progressive experience.

Jennifer D. Keene, *Doughboys, the Great War, and the Remaking of America* (2001). A study of civilian soldiers and military bureaucracy, the book also explores the subsequent impact of World War I veterans.

Susan Zeiger, *In Uncle Sam's Service: Women Workers with the American Expeditionary Force, 1917–1919* (1999). With a fresh look at a neglected subject, the author explores women's involvement in the war effort.

John Milton Cooper Jr., *Breaking the Heart of the World: Woodrow Wilson and the Fight for the League of Nations* (2001). This study examines Wilson's last crusade, carefully balancing personal factors, political issues, and historical context.

Additional Readings

Wilson's contribution to domestic reform is favorably evaluated in Kendrick A. Clements, *The Presidency of Woodrow Wilson* (1992). Arthur Link, editor of the Wilson papers, has written a multivolume biography titled *Woodrow Wilson* (1947–1965). See also the works listed in Chapter 2 dealing with corporate progressivism. For income tax reform, see John F. Witte, *The Politics and Development of the Federal Income Tax* (1985), and Robert Stanley, *Dimensions of Law in the Service of Order: Origins of the Federal Income Tax, 1861–1913* (1993).

For Wilson's Latin American policy, see Frederick S. Calhoun, *Power and Principle: Armed Intervention in Wilsonian Foreign Policy* (1986), and David Healy, *Drive to Hegemony: The United States in the Caribbean, 1898–1917* (1988). U.S. involvement in Mexico is the focus of John S. D. Eisenhower, *Intervention: The United States and the Mexican Revolution, 1913–1917* (1993), and P. Edward Haley, *Revolution and Interventionism: The Diplomacy of Taft and Wilson with Mexico, 1910–1917* (1970). A thorough examination of Wilson's policy toward Asia is Roy W. Curry, *Woodrow Wilson and Far Eastern Policy, 1913–1921* (1968).

U.S. involvement in World War I has provoked a tremendous outpouring of historical literature. See Jan Willem Schulte Nordholt, *Woodrow Wilson: A Life for World Peace* (1991); Paul Fussell, *Woodrow Wilson and World War I, 1917–1921* (1985); and Thomas J. Knock, *To End All Wars: Woodrow Wilson and the Quest for a New World Order* (1992). Neutrality and preparedness are discussed in Manfred Jonas, *The United States and Germany* (1984); Patrick Devlin, *Too Proud to Fight: Woodrow Wilson's Neutrality* (1975); and

Michael Pearlman, *To Make Democracy for America: Patricians and Preparedness in the Progressive Era* (1984). Wilson's covert warfare on the Russian front is described in David S. Foglesong, *America's Secret War Against Bolshevism: U.S. Intervention in the Russian Civil War, 1917–1920* (1995). For antiwar sentiment, see Kendrick A. Clements, *William Jennings Bryan: Missionary Isolationist* (1982), and John M. Cooper Jr., *The Vanity of Power: American Isolationism and the First World War, 1914–1917* (1969).

Military affairs are discussed in David Trask, *The AEF and Coalition Warmaking, 1917–1918* (1993), and Eric J. Leed, *No Man's Land: Combat and Identity in World War I* (1979). Other descriptions of the fighting include Edward M. Coffman, *The War to End All Wars* (1969); Russell Weigley, *The American Way of War* (1973); and Henry De Weerd, *President Wilson Fights His War* (1968). For army life, see Laurence Stallings, *The Doughboys* (1973); A. E. Barbeau and Florette Henri, *The Unknown Soldiers: Black American Troops in World War I* (1974); and Thomas Britten, *American Indians in World War I* (1997). For wartime dissent, see Christopher C. Gibbs, *The Great Silent Majority: Missouri's Resistance to World War I* (1988). For the plight of German Americans, see Frederick Luebke, *Bonds of Loyalty* (1974).

For home front issues, see David P. Kennedy, *Over Here: The First World War and American Society* (1980), and Ronald Schaffer, *America in the Great War: The Rise of the War Welfare State* (1991). Industrial mobilization is surveyed in Robert D. Cuff, *The War Industries Board: Business-Government Relations during World War I* (1973). For domestic propaganda, see Stephen Vaughn, *Holding Fast the Inner Lines: Democracy, Nationalism, and the Committee on Public Information* (1980), and Leslie Midkiff DeBauche, *Reel Patriotism: The Movies and World War I* (1997). The life of women in wartime is assessed in Maurine W. Greenwald, *Women, War, and Work: The Impact of World War I on Women Workers in the United States* (1980); Barbara Steinson, *American Women's Activism in World War I* (1982); and Kathleen Kennedy, *Disloyal Mothers and Scurrilous Citizens: Women and Subversion during World War I* (1999). For the war's impact on African Americans, see James R. Grossman, *Land of Hope: Chicago, Black Southerners and the Great Migration* (1989), and William Tuttle, *Race Riot: Chicago in the Red Summer of 1919* (1970).

On the peace process, see Arthur Walworth, *Wilson and His Peacemakers: American Diplomacy at the Paris Peace Conference* (1986). A critical perspective can be found in Lloyd C. Gardner, *Safe for Democracy: The Anglo-American Response to Revolution, 1913–1923* (1984). See also William Widenor, *Henry Cabot Lodge and the Search for an American Foreign Policy* (1980).

Postwar political repression receives treatment in Robert Murray, *The Red Scare* (1955). See also Richard Polenberg, *Fighting Faiths: The Abrams Case, the Supreme Court, and Free Speech* (1987); Paul L. Murphy, *The*

Meaning of Free Speech: First Amendment Freedoms from Wilson to FDR (1972); and William Preston, *Aliens and Dissenters: Federal Suppression of Radicals, 1903–1933* (1963). For communism, see Robert A. Rosenstone, *A Romantic Revolutionary: A Biography of John Reed* (1990). Other immigrant radicals are treated in Paul Avrich, *Sacco and Vanzetti: The Anarchist Background* (1991).

THE POLITICS AND CULTURE OF THE JAZZ AGE, 1920–1928

"America's present need is not heroics but healing, not nostrums but normalcy," declared Republican presidential candidate Warren G. Harding in 1920. Yet the following decade was characterized by intensive economic change and social controversy. As business experienced a spectacular boom between 1922 and 1929, confident corporate leaders proclaimed a New Era in human affairs. Nevertheless, technological change, cultural diversity, and new behaviors prompted many Americans to reassert traditional social values and ethnic identities. Although two popular Republican presidents achieved a degree of political harmony, the 1920s initiated the first culture war of the twentieth century.

THE NEW ERA AND THE CORPORATE ECONOMY

At the height of post–World War I prosperity, the U.S. Chamber of Commerce exulted that ordinary citizens had been "transported to a new world." Innovative technologies, rising wages, merchandising and distribution advances, and professional management pointed toward permanent affluence and stability. The secret to the decade's 40 percent growth in gross national product (GNP) lay in consumer spending. Adapting wartime methods to domestic needs, corporate laboratories used innovative technologies to produce new corporate goods including plastics, cosmetics, and automobile tires. DuPont, a major war contractor and the world's largest industrial company, developed artificial fibers like rayon. As synthetic compounds became widespread components of clothing, carpets, and upholstery, researchers developed cellophane to package other mass-produced goods.

"His god was Modern Appliances," Sinclair Lewis wrote of the leading character in *Babbitt* (1922), a satirical novel of small-town life in the consumer era. After World War I, electrical manufacturers shifted emphasis from

EXHIBIT **4-1**   **U.S. PASSENGER CAR REGISTRATION, 1920–1928**
(IN ROUNDED MILLIONS)

1920	8.2
1924	15.5
1928	21.6

Source: *Recent Economic Changes* (1929).

large-scale industrial equipment to household items. General Electric and other companies generated mass-produced appliances such as washing machines, refrigerators, electric irons, toasters, and vacuum cleaners. GE also played a key role in using vacuum tube technology to develop the radio, which won recognition in 1920 when a station in Pittsburgh was the first to broadcast the results of a presidential election. As business journalists predicted that "the magic genii of electricity" would relieve human drudgery and democratize leisure, electric consumption nearly tripled.

The most revolutionary development of the New Era economy was the automobile; its initial proponent, Henry Ford, was the leading folk idol of the age. Ford's Model T, which sold for below $300 by decade's end, offered instant mobility and status for millions of consumers of modest means. "I'll go without food before I'll see us give up the car," a working-class wife in Indiana told researchers. Yet it was General Motors executive Alfred P. Sloan Jr. who revolutionized the industry by decentralizing management, changing models every year, and offering consumers a chance to forge personal identities by choosing among variably priced and sized cars. Auto producers nearly doubled their annual sales during the postwar decade. When the boom ended, two of every three American households owned a motor vehicle.

The boom in consumer spending reflected new marketing appeals, such as advertising and installment purchases. Eighty percent of all personal credit was extended to women homemakers. Spending on household goods, which tripled between 1909 and 1929, was encouraged by the billion-dollar-a-year advertising industry. "The American conception of advertising," explained Madison Avenue's Bruce Barton, "is to arouse desires and stimulate wants, to make people dissatisfied with the old and out-of-date." Heralding a "democracy of goods," merchandisers invoked notions of psychological growth to offer the promise of youth and magical self-transformation through their products. Advertisers also sought to address the anxieties accompanying urban life by marketing therapeutic solutions for intestinal disorders, skin irregularities, body odors, and other personal problems.

Chain stores were a key component of New Era marketing. Emphasizing nationally advertised brand-name products, chains charged cheaper prices because they made bulk purchases and provided no credit or delivery services. The Great Atlantic and Pacific Tea Company (A&P) had first used the concept to revolutionize the nineteenth century grocery trade. Postwar retailers such as Boston department store and "bargain basement" innovator Edward A. Filene promoted the new form of retailing as an example of consumer democracy. Between 1918 and 1929, firms such as J. C. Penney and Woolworth moved into the variety field and the number of chain outlets increased more than fivefold.

Harvard economist Thomas Nixon Carver proclaimed that the freedom to choose among technology's varied and affordable products gave consumers a new economic democracy. The *Magazine of Business* even boasted that the "average woman" prized the vacuum cleaner and electric iron more than the vote or the promises of political reformers. Indeed, former muckrakers Lincoln Steffens and Ida Tarbell agreed that scientific management and mass distribution had revitalized society. Business optimism remained so high that General Motors vice president John J. Raskob proposed to democratize investment by selling stock market certificates on the installment plan. "Nobody can become rich by saving," exclaimed Raskob.

Some corporate leaders sought a stable workforce by applying a "human approach to industry" through "welfare capitalism." As overall wage rates advanced modestly in the New Era, larger companies improved working conditions, provided fringe benefits like profit sharing or pension plans, and hired industrial relations psychologists. Welfare capitalism helped to halve employee turnover in the postwar decade. As a new generation of managers portrayed themselves as trustees for the public and their employees, business schools sought to professionalize corporate administration. Pursuing the advantages of cooperative research, industrial efficiency programs, and coordinated public relations, American companies formed more than four thousand trade associations in the postwar decade.

AUTOMOBILES, CITIES, AND SUBURBS

Optimism about big business could be seen in the world's tallest structure, the Empire State Building. This skyscraper, completed in 1930, was a powerful symbol of technology and the urban age. The 1920 census reported for the first time that more than half the nation's people lived in communities of at least 2,500 people. In the following decade, over 70 percent of population growth took place in metropolitan areas, where land values more than doubled. The most extensive activity occurred in widely dispersed "automobile" cities like Los Angeles, Dallas, and Kansas City. Hard-surfaced roads, lower taxes, and cheap property also attracted businesses to the suburbs, where population doubled during the decade. Developers accommodated the middle-class flight from urban congestion and crime by building bungalows and small homes equipped with garages for commuters. Spacious shopping centers with free parking soon followed.

Automobile culture exerted a costly influence on older cities. A coalition of auto industry groups, road builders, and land developers convinced municipal authorities that motor vehicles would create new channels of commerce, open surrounding areas to development, and reduce congestion in central cities. Urban governments responded by underwriting the cost of city street paving and building highways to the suburbs. Automobile mania contributed to the decimation of electric streetcar transit, whose national ridership peaked in 1923. Trolleys and interurban electric rail lines could not maneuver in traffic, required taxpayer subsidies, charged high fares, and had a reputation for poor service. As commuters supported the building of public highways, gasoline-powered buses with rubber tires began to replace the old trolley system.

Car ownership gave ordinary people a sense of identity; it was as much a symbol of success and status as home ownership. Driving also increased options for personal choice, a matter of concern to moral critics. Although auto advertisements promised to "bring the family together," the recreational aspects of automobility stressed pleasure and individual whim, not family or communal solidarity. Traditional authorities complained that mobile families deserted small towns to take vacation trips. By providing young people unchaperoned intimacy, moreover, cars afforded enough autonomy and privacy to raise additional controversy. The once sacred family, noted one expert, had degenerated into a "physical service station." Ministers linked the automobile to rising crime rates and excesses such as joyriding on the Sabbath. Nashville's Salvation Army even claimed that the misfortunes of unwed mothers in its maternity homes could be traced to "predatory drivers."

HARDING, HOOVER, AND HUGHES

When Republican presidential candidate Warren Harding called for a period of restoration and adjustment in 1920, he was addressing a citizenry exhausted from the burdens of World War I, industrial strife, and the Red Scare. Harding was an undistinguished senator from Marion, Ohio, where he owned a small printing establishment. When he won the Republican presidential nomination as a compromise candidate, he pictured himself as a "white-haired progressive" who had adopted scientific management in his own firm. Rank-and-file delegates pushed Harding into awarding the vice presidential slot to Massachusetts governor Calvin Coolidge, who had won national acclaim by breaking the Boston police strike of 1919.

Harding's campaign emphasized nostalgia for prewar stability and hometown virtue. "Too much has been said of bolshevism in America," he proclaimed. The candidate suggested that international peace and corporate pros-

EXHIBIT **4-2**   **U.S. URBAN AND RURAL POPULATION, 1920–1930**
(IN ROUNDED MILLIONS)

	Urban	Rural
1920	54.2	51.8
1930	68.9	53.8

Source: *Historical Statistics of the United States, Colonial Times to 1970* (1975).

perity would reduce domestic strife and build a national consensus. Although Harding spoke only fleetingly of issues such as lower taxes and a high tariff, his relaxed confidence and sense of goodwill prevailed at the polls. The Republican ticket took over 60 percent of the popular vote in defeating Ohio Governor James M. Cox and his running mate, assistant Navy secretary Franklin D. Roosevelt, Theodore's cousin. Cox's popular tally surpassed Woodrow Wilson's victorious total of 1916, but the Republicans nearly doubled their previous vote. Carrying every state outside the South as well as Tennessee, Harding and Coolidge swept to a 404–127 margin in the Electoral College.

Increased balloting in the 1920 election resulted from the enactment of woman's suffrage. Yet voter participation never surpassed 57 percent in the decade's presidential contests, a continuation of low turnout dating back to the first years of the century. Participation rates were lowest in large industrial cities, where working-class ethnics were concentrated. Poor turnout suggested pervasive apathy to national political issues and the reluctance of eligible women from immigrant families to defy cultural prohibitions against political engagement. As a result, Republicans won a plurality of 1.6 million votes in the nation's twelve largest cities and added to their majorities in both houses of Congress. Clearly, Woodrow Wilson's success in unifying the South, West, and East behind the Democratic Party had not survived World War I.

Harding sought to reduce political discord by pardoning Socialist Party leader Eugene Debs, who had been imprisoned under wartime sedition laws. Despite his incarceration, Debs ran for president in 1920 and matched the 900,000 votes he had received in 1912 with 3.4 percent of the tally. Harding invited Debs to the White House, where the two chatted and smoked cigars. Yet the new administration was most clearly known for its commitment to the conservative fiscal policies of Secretary of the Treasury Andrew Mellon, a multimillionaire Pittsburgh industrialist and financier. "I have never viewed taxation as a means of rewarding one class of taxpayers or punishing another," declared Mellon. To the contrary, the treasury secretary joined Budget Director Charles G. Dawes, a Chicago banker, in pursuing policies that would lower taxes in order to free investors to use their capital to create jobs and prosperity. Mellon persuaded Congress to repeal the wartime excess-profits tax on

EXHIBIT **4-3**   **ELECTION OF 1920**

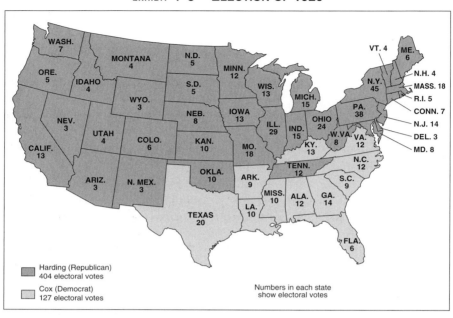

WASH. 7
MONTANA 4
N.D. 5
VT. 4
ME. 6
ORE. 5
IDAHO 4
MINN. 12
N.H. 4
NEV. 3
WYO. 3
S.D. 5
WIS. 13
MICH. 15
N.Y. 45
MASS. 18
R.I. 5
UTAH 4
NEB. 8
IOWA 13
OHIO 24
PA. 38
CONN. 7
CALIF. 13
COLO. 6
KAN. 10
ILL. 29
IND. 15
W.VA. 8
VA. 12
N.J. 14
DEL. 3
MD. 8
ARIZ. 3
N. MEX. 3
OKLA. 10
MO. 18
KY. 13
N.C. 12
TENN. 12
ARK. 9
S.C. 9
TEXAS 20
LA. 10
MISS. 10
ALA. 12
GA. 14
FLA. 6

Harding (Republican)
404 electoral votes

Cox (Democrat)
127 electoral votes

Numbers in each state
show electoral votes

corporations and to cut maximum income surtaxes to 50 percent, although it also raised postage rates, excise taxes, and licensing fees.

The conservative tone of the Harding presidency was exhibited by the choice of former president William Howard Taft to be chief justice of the Supreme Court. Yet the administration's most popular figure was Secretary of Commerce Herbert Hoover, the World War I food administrator and European relief coordinator. The commerce secretary believed that America's corporate structure and democratic heritage could be reconciled through the promotion of voluntary organizations such as trade associations, professional societies, farm marketing groups, and labor unions. "We are passing from a period of extremely individualistic action into a period of associational activities," he declared in *American Individualism* (1922), his plan to combine personal initiative and social efficiency. Hoover sought to preserve the "American System" by using the federal government to coordinate and support cooperative self-help groups.

At Hoover's suggestion, Harding convened a Washington conference on unemployment in 1921 when a postwar recession halved industrial output and unemployment soared to 12 percent. The meeting marked the first time a president had called attention to joblessness. As more than 200 cities created emergency relief groups, Congress allotted funds for public works and passed a Federal Highway Act to provide the first matching grants for state road construction. The conference also commissioned an analysis of business cycles by the independent National Bureau of Economics Research. Hoover subsequently endorsed the Capper-Volstead Act of 1922, which exempted agricultural marketing associations from antitrust legislation and qualified them for government loans.

Under Hoover's leadership, the Department of Commerce assumed the regulation of radio and aviation. The bureau also pursued Hoover's interest in industrial standardization and the compilation of commercial statistics, policies facilitated by *Maple Flooring Association* v. *U.S.* (1925), a case in which the Supreme Court upheld the exchange of information within trade associations. Looking to promote prosperity through an "open door" for global markets, the commerce secretary reorganized the department to focus on the commodities most often sold overseas. To support these efforts, he used commercial attachés to help U.S. manufacturers gain access to raw materials and worked with U.S. oil corporations in gaining lucrative overseas refining concessions. Secretary of State Charles Evans Hughes played an even larger role in coordinating diplomacy with domestic business interests. To encourage overseas investment, Hughes sent private bankers on credit missions and directed the State Department to approve international loans before they were submitted to public subscription.

Emphasizing financial engagement instead of military commitments, the State Department also sponsored disarmament talks among the major powers. The Washington Armaments Conference of 1921–1922 fixed the number of U.S., British, and Japanese battleships and cruisers at a ratio of 5:5:3. The three nations also agreed to respect each other's Pacific island possessions, to honor the Open Door in China, and to recognize existing boundaries in East Asia. Although the United States was militarily weak in the Pacific, it anticipated that its economic power would be sufficient to contain Japan's regional ambitions (see Chapters 6 and 7).

TROUBLED LABOR AND SOCIAL REFORMERS

By 1929, occupations in communications, retail sales, and similar fields accounted for nearly one-fourth of the nation's employment. A substantial proportion of these service workers were women, many recent entries into the job market. White-collar employees tended to see themselves as members of the middle class and often associated labor unions with manual workers, with whom they felt few ties. The labor movement also suffered from the decline of blue-collar employment in older industries such as coal mining and the garment trades. In contrast, mass-production fields such as automobile manufacturing drew heavily upon semiskilled immigrants and rural migrants, whom union activists ignored until the 1930s. Labor's difficulties were compounded by a reluctance to recruit women, African Americans, and Mexican Americans.

The labor movement also had to contend with rising antiunion sentiment among national elites. Once the War Labor Board disbanded in 1919, the

National Association of Manufacturers (NAM) organized an "open shop" campaign to eradicate the "closed shop," a practice that required workers to hold union cards before getting a job. The plan devastated labor solidarity, particularly in the Midwest and South. In 1921, the Supreme Court upheld the use of injunctions against steel unions and harshly limited picketing rights. That same year, federal troops crushed a United Mine Workers (UMW) strike against "yellow dog" contracts prohibiting union membership among new workers, and the Supreme Court held the union liable for damages. Labor faced another defeat in the decade's largest strike in 1922, when 400,000 members of the AFL's railroad shopcraft unions brought transportation to a halt—only to lose the conflict when a federal court issued an injunction against union picketing.

As union membership declined in the 1920s, structural problems in industry threatened worker morale. In new mass-production factories such as automaking and electrical parts, priorities on productivity, efficiency, and speed often resulted in the replacement of older and experienced personnel with unskilled laborers. Despite the enlightened approach of some managers, critics suggested that industrial workers were becoming dehumanized automatons, endlessly repeating specific tasks and losing all control over work routines. Meanwhile, management used progressive rhetoric about social efficiency and cooperation to promote company unions and to maintain control on the shop floor. "I will not permit myself to be in a position of having labor dictate to management," declared Bethlehem Steel's Charles Schwab. Predictably, corporate officials delegated little responsibility to company unions and prevented them from addressing wage and hour issues.

Social feminists and women's reform groups fared little better in contesting business supremacy. Between 1912 and 1923, activists won passage of fifty state minimum wage laws for female workers. Yet in *Adkins* v. *Children's Hospital* (1923), the Supreme Court ruled that such legislation violated the contractual rights of laborers. Reformers faced additional frustration over the crusade to ban child labor. One year after the Court rejected a federal child labor law in 1918, Congress placed prohibitive taxes on products manufactured by underage workers. The Court, however, cited the Constitution's interstate commerce clause to declare the statute an unwarranted regulation of labor. Stunned into action, social welfare activist Florence Kelley mobilized the National Child Labor Committee and won congressional approval of a suitable constitutional amendment in 1924. Yet when the Roman Catholic Church warned of the dangers of government interference with parental discretion, ratification in key industrial states failed overwhelmingly.

Despite such setbacks, the Cable Act of 1922 guaranteed citizenship for native-born women who married immigrants eligible for naturalization. Expanding upon the power of the vote, reformers sought state regulation of consumer and family issues. After activists organized the nonpartisan League of

Women Voters in 1920, the group worked with the Women's Joint Congressional Committee, a coalition embracing nearly every important women's organization in the country, to serve as a legislative clearinghouse. In the traditional South, social feminists helped to institute state budget reforms, created commissions to protect children, and agitated for improved working conditions for women in textile mills. In 1921 Congress passed the Sheppard-Towner Maternity and Infancy Protection Act. Although the bill covered only medical education and did not extend to actual services, it created the twentieth century's first federal welfare program. During the program's 8-year tenure, modest support of state health training clinics helped to bring about a decline in national infant and maternity mortality rates.

INSURGENT FARMERS, SMALL BUSINESS, AND TEAPOT DOME

Women reformers scored another victory in 1921 by working with family farm and small business interests to win approval for the Packers and Stockyards Act and the Grain Futures Act, two laws that regulated monopoly practices keeping meat and bread prices high. Yet independent agriculture fared poorly in the 1920s. As the federal government quit buying farm products after World War I, growers found themselves burdened by excessive acreage, expensive machinery, and sinking commodity prices. The Federal Reserve Board's decision to raise the discount (interest) rate in 1920 intensified small agriculture's plight by forcing local bankers to call in farm loans. When the Esch-Cummins Transportation Act of 1920 returned the railroads to private control and permitted higher shipping rates, the farm economy suffered further. Natural disasters, such as the infestation of Georgia cotton by the boll weevil (beetle) and drought on the Northern Plains, added to agriculture's poor state.

The resulting farm depression resulted in southern cotton farmers experiencing their worst decade since the 1860s. As producers in both North and South found it impossible to market growing surpluses at a profitable rate, the combined value of agricultural acreage plummeted by nearly half in the 1920s, while farm mortgage debt rose and bankruptcies multiplied. By 1930, 42 percent of the agrarian labor force leased its property as tenants or sharecroppers, and 1 million families had left the land. In response to the disaster, rural members of Congress organized a farm bloc. The group was unable to prevent passage of the Fordney-McCumber Tariff of 1922, which restored protective rates on industrial goods to prewar levels. Yet farm politicians loudly demanded protection for commodity prices through creation of a government agency to sell agricultural surplus overseas.

EXHIBIT **4-4**   **U.S. PER CAPITA INCOME IN DOLLARS, 1920–1929**

1920	860
1923	760
1926	826
1929	847

Source: *Historical Statistics of the United States, Colonial Times to 1970* (1975).

Like independent farmers, small business interests objected to the Harding administration's coziness with powerful corporations. Alerted by independent oil refiners regarding a case of potential collusion in 1923, Republican Robert La Follette pressed the Senate to create a special committee to hold hearings on the government's relationship with major domestic oil producers. Testimony revealed that Secretary of the Interior Albert B. Fall secretly had leased valuable government petroleum reserves, including the Teapot Dome area of Wyoming, to favored interests. In return, Fall had received more than $300,000 in bribes. A special government prosecution team also discovered multimillion-dollar graft in the newly created Veterans Bureau and kickbacks to Attorney General Harry Daugherty. The "Teapot Dome" scandal ultimately sent Fall and other officials to prison, forced Daugherty's resignation, and led to the suicide of two presidential appointees.

THE ELECTION OF 1924

"I cannot hope to be one of the great presidents," Warren Harding once confided, "but perhaps I may be remembered as one of the best loved." Demoralized by early evidence of the betrayal of friends in his "Ohio Gang," the popular president suffered a stroke while on a West Coast tour in 1923 and died a few days later. Responsibility for restoring the government's integrity fell to Vice President Calvin Coolidge. A dour and canny politician, Coolidge kept silent about Teapot Dome until 1924, when he replaced Attorney General Daugherty with Harlan Fiske Stone, a highly esteemed former dean of Columbia Law School. Stone sought to professionalize government service by appointing J. Edgar Hoover to the directorship of the Bureau of Investigation with a mandate to adopt new procedures like fingerprinting. Responding to the relaxation of political tensions in the mid-1920s, Stone instructed Hoover to discontinue antiradical surveillance.

As Coolidge prepared for the 1924 election, he consolidated his position within the Republican Party and among the nation's voters. Pressed by northeastern members of Congress to end an anthracite coal strike that threatened winter fuel supplies, the president permitted the governor of Pennsylvania to

EXHIBIT **4-5**   ELECTION OF **1924**

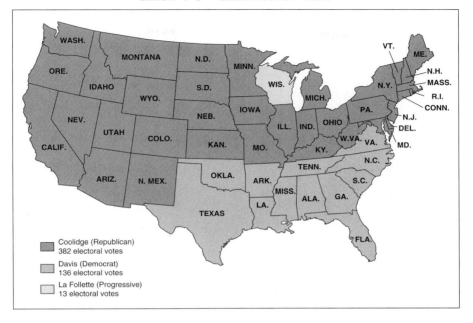

- Coolidge (Republican)
  382 electoral votes
- Davis (Democrat)
  136 electoral votes
- La Follette (Progressive)
  13 electoral votes

arrange a labor settlement favorable to the miners. As a result, Coolidge was not held responsible for the price increases passed on to consumers. He also appealed for the support of Republican progressives by publicly embarrassing U.S. Steel into abandoning the 12-hour work day. Coolidge further signaled independence from corporate interests by signing the Oil Pollution Act of 1924, which provided modest fines for polluting coastal waters. He made another gesture to reformers by offering the vice presidential nomination to progressive Idaho senator William Borah. When Borah declined, the president chose Budget Director Charles Dawes.

Acknowledging that "the chief business of the American people is business," the Republican nominee rode New Era prosperity with the slogan "Keep Cool with Coolidge." In an era of easy money and frenzied speculation, Coolidge embodied virtues of Yankee austerity and respectability. The president's clear and distinct speaking voice, broadcast during the election year on monthly radio addresses, earned him a rating as one of the nation's most popular radio personalities. Coolidge faced little competition from the Democratic Party. Stymied by deep ideological and cultural divisions, the Democrats nominated Wall Street attorney John W. Davis, a political unknown, as their presidential candidate and Charles Bryan, the brother of William Jennings Bryan, as his running mate.

Coolidge's most spirited opposition came from Robert La Follette's Progressives. Rejecting Farmer-Labor or socialist alternatives, La Follette

Robert M. ("Fighting Bob") La Follette
(1855–1925)

There were no silk hats at the funeral of Robert La Follette, a Senate ally noted in 1925. At the age of seventy, the nation's leading political crusader and progressive had died only months after capturing one-sixth of the popular vote in the 1924 presidential election. La Follette's creed,

another colleague told the Senate, was his faith "in the average common sense of the masses." Burton K. Wheeler, the late senator's Progressive Party running mate, later claimed that La Follette ranked with Jefferson and Lincoln as the three greatest characters produced in U.S. history.

Born in a log cabin, La Follette graduated from Wisconsin's new state university and went on to defy the Republican machine by winning three congressional elections in the 1880s. The short, stocky, and square-jawed firebrand managed to build his own political organization by using university graduates and student volunteers to offset the power of the railroad corporations and timber interests. By 1900 La Follette had won the Wisconsin governorship. He proceeded to institute the direct primary, civil service reform, increased corporate taxes, and new state regulatory commissions.

La Follette was sent to the U.S. Senate in 1905; there, he continually emphasized the chasm between the "people" and the "interests." By 1917 he was convinced that New York monied interests had taken over transportation, banking, industry, and commerce and that the nation's growing involvement in Europe was a product of "financial imperialism." La Follette bitterly resisted the nation's drift into World War I,

accepted the new party's presidential nomination and named Senator Burton K. Wheeler, a progressive Montana Democrat, as his vice presidential choice. Unlike Theodore Roosevelt's Progressives of 1912, La Follette's movement attacked large corporations. "The great issue before the American people today," declared La Follette's platform, "is control of government and industry by private monopoly." The Progressives condemned Republican tax and tariff policies, criticized "mercenary" foreign policy, and called for stricter regulation of business. Appealing to independent farmers by supporting federal aid

then opposed conscription and wartime repression and crusaded for war profits taxes and future war referenda. He also helped to defeat U.S. membership in President Wilson's League of Nations.

In the early 1920s La Follette warned that membership in the World Court would cement the alliance between international bankers and the tottering empires of Europe. He organized "people's" lobbies to demand that Washington retract the rate increases and tax breaks granted to his old adversary, the railroads. Retaining his Senate seat by an unprecedented three-to-one margin in 1922, he helped to organize a new Progressive Party and became its presidential standard-bearer two years later.

Tired, aging, without a party apparatus, and outspent twenty to one by Coolidge Republicans, La Follette nevertheless mounted a monumental campaign against corporate capitalism. His Progressive coalition embraced Republican agrarian insurgents, old Populists, urban liberals, and independent socialists, as well as labor leaders from the railroad brotherhoods and trade unions. La Follette and Wheeler focused on the producer values of traditional entrepreneurs and farmers by relentlessly attacking monopoly. In an explicit rejection of the dominance of the two major parties by big-money interests, the candidate promised "to restore government to the people."

The Progressive ticket took second place in ten states and sixty-seven industrial counties. "Fighting Bob" was succeeded in the Senate by his son, Robert M. La Follette Jr., and the family legacy persisted through protests against the ties between corporate capital at home and pressures for increased militarism overseas.

to agriculture, the Progressives also proposed government ownership of railroads and hydroelectric dams as well the abolition of labor injunctions.

Demonstrating a strong showing for a poorly funded third party, La Follette and Wheeler won one-sixth of the popular vote. Yet Republican pronouncements of "Coolidge or Chaos" resulted in continued domination of the urban vote and an easy victory for the president. Outpolling his Democrat opponent by 54 percent to 29 percent, Coolidge took the Electoral College by a one-sided 382–136–13.

COOLIDGE ECONOMICS AND BANKER DIPLOMACY

Buoyed by the electoral mandate for conservative economic policies, treasury secretary Mellon proceeded with tax relief for the affluent. The Revenue Act of 1926 wiped out the gift tax, cut estate taxes by half, and trimmed the surtax on incomes. Two years later, reduced corporate tax rates enabled the Treasury to award refunds to large firms. Mellon's program halved government spending and reduced the national debt by one-third. The Federal Trade Commission (FTC) also reflected the administration's friendliness toward corporate interests. In 1920 the Supreme Court had ruled that U.S. Steel's large size and monopoly status did not violate the "rule of reason," because prosecutors had not proven that the corporation engaged in overt coercion or predatory practices. Once Coolidge appointed corporate attorney and lumber lobbyist William E. Humphrey as FTC chair in 1925, the regulatory agency investigated only cases in which unfair practices were explicitly detrimental to the public interest, held private hearings, and routinely referred informal "stipulations" to trade practice conferences.

Coolidge attempted to balance the administration's pro-business approach by signing the Watson-Parker Act of 1926, a precedent-setting measure that recognized collective bargaining for railroad workers but prohibited strikes during a 60-day mediation period. The administration also responded to public needs when commerce secretary Hoover organized emergency aid to the victims of a catastrophic Mississippi River flood in 1927. Coolidge also signed the Jones-Reid Act of 1928, which appropriated federal funds for levees, drainage basins, and spillways in one of the first steps toward government management of river ecology.

Like its predecessor, the Coolidge administration saw international diplomacy as an extension of domestic financial policy. Seeking a stable and peaceful Europe, the State Department focused on close relations with Britain and France and the reintegration of postwar Germany into the western market. Under the Dawes Plan of 1924, the former Allies reduced German war reparations, while Washington cut Allied debt to the United States government by 40 percent. The deal was facilitated by the willingness of J. P. Morgan and other private bankers to offer over a billion dollars in economic reconstruction loans to Germany.

The State Department also promoted overseas trade. By 1929, the U.S. economy accounted for nearly 16 percent of all global exports, with particularly strong activity in car parts, oil products, and machinery. Latin America emerged as a major U.S. outlet in the postwar era. Loans to the region, often tied to the purchase of U.S. goods or services, exceeded those extended to Germany after 1924. By the close of the decade, Latin Americans bought nearly half their imports from their northern neighbor. Multinational U.S.

mining concerns like the Guggenheim syndicate and agribusinesses like United Fruit invested heavily, exerting economic and political influence in this underdeveloped part of the world.

To support its economic dominance, the United States continued to intervene militarily. At the Pan American Conference of 1923, Washington invoked the Monroe Doctrine to defeat an attempt to outlaw unilateral intervention in the region. Although Coolidge withdrew troops from the Dominican Republic the next year, he dispatched the Marines to Honduras to overcome "anarchy" and sent them into Nicaragua in 1926 when civil war erupted among the nation's political factions. Yet once Coolidge sent former secretary of war Henry L. Stimson to negotiate a settlement for peaceful elections the following year, the Nicaraguan rebels agreed to disarm while the Marines trained a nonpolitical national guard.

Coolidge scored another success in Mexico, whose government was preparing to nationalize oil fields and mines. Although independent oil developers talked of a Bolshevik threat, Standard Oil and major banks warned that provocative action could injure long-range economic interests in Mexico. When Senate noninterventionists won a unanimous vote recommending arbitration of the controversy, Coolidge appointed a representative of J. P. Morgan as ambassador with instructions to bring about a peaceful settlement. Conciliatory efforts resulted in Mexican recognition of mining and petroleum rights granted to foreign companies before 1917. Banker diplomacy had resolved a dangerous dispute without military intervention.

Open to nonmilitary approaches to achieving political stability, the State Department worked with peace activists such as Jane Addams, attorney Salmon O. Levinson, and Congregational minister Frederick J. Libby for an international treaty to denounce the use of war as an instrument of national policy. Believing that such an agreement could strengthen the "machinery" for resolving disputes among nations and set an important precedent, the peace lobby convinced Secretary of State Frank B. Kellogg to transform proposals for a U.S.-French nonaggression pact into a multinational accord. Sixty-two nations signed the Kellogg-Briand Pact of 1928, which won an 85–1 vote of approval in the U.S. Senate after intense lobbying by women's peace groups and ultimately resulted in Nobel Peace Prizes for both Kellogg and Addams.

ETHNIC DIVERSITY

Although New Era administrations sought to unify the nation through economic growth, the diverse U.S. population remained divided by long-standing ethnic rivalries. By 1930, 30 percent of Americans were foreign-born residents or their children. Most ethnic groups preferred to live in urban enclaves that offered community assistance and self-help programs. Roman Catholics, who numbered 36 percent of the nation's people by decade's end, maintained religious and communal traditions through a variety of church institutions. Pressured by the presence of large numbers of southern and eastern Europeans, the Catholic hierarchy acceded to the creation of "nationality" parishes. Euro-Americans sustained ethnic ties through local movie houses, theaters, record shops, and retail stores that offered familiar goods and easy credit. Only the cohesiveness of Jewish ghettos began to decline as socially mobile Jews moved to newer residential areas beyond the reach of traditional religious and Yiddish organizations.

Ever since the 1880s, immigrants had constituted the semiskilled employment pool for industrial expansion. The vast majority of working-class ethnics remained factory laborers or menial service and clerical operators. By the 1920s, however, many of America's second-generation ethnics had moved up to skilled or supervisory industrial work or become educated professionals. Others overcame discrimination in mainstream financial institutions by using kinship networks and ethnic credit unions to raise enough capital to start small businesses. Street paving and construction were two ethnic enterprises that often received contracts granted by urban political bosses.

Although World War I disrupted the flow of immigration from Europe, the migration of workers from south of the U.S. border was encouraged by southwestern agriculture, railroad, and mining concerns. About 10 percent of the population of Mexico, more than 1 million people, moved north in the first three decades of the twentieth century. Ninety percent of Mexican Americans lived in the Southwest, where many worked as low-wage seasonal workers harvesting cotton, vegetables, and fruits. Exploited by cost-conscious commercial farmers, migrant families seldom benefited from government regulation, social agencies, and public schooling.

By 1930, more than half of Mexican immigrants spoke no English and less than 6 percent of adults had achieved U.S. citizenship. Yet major centers of Chicano culture emerged in southwestern cities such as San Antonio and Los Angeles. The Mexican American community also extended to Chicago and the Midwest, where laborers were recruited for jobs in packing houses and rail yards. With the gradual emergence of an urban Mexican American middle class, civic leaders began to transform traditional "mutualista" societies into civil rights lobbies. In Texas, for example, the League of United Latin American Citizens (LULAC) mobilized against public school segregation.

Asian Americans also faced severe discrimination. From the first exclusion laws of the 1880s until 1943, the Chinese population declined from over 300,000 to 80,000. In contrast, the number of Japanese Americans grew to over 275,000, a result of the influx of "picture brides" (Japanese women who came to the United States to marry husbands to whom they had sent photographs). Even after Tokyo stopped granting visas to prospective brides in

1919, fourteen states passed alien land laws, preventing Asians from owning landed property. Upholding the constitutionality of such legislation in the *Ozawa* (1922) and *Thind* (1923) cases, the Supreme Court declared that Asian American immigrants were ineligible for citizenship. The Cable Act of 1922 even stipulated that native-born women of any race who married Asian men would lose their own citizenship. Under the Immigration Quota Act of 1924, aliens ineligible for naturalization were prohibited from entering the United States. Affronted by anti-Asian racism, the Japanese government staged massive "Humiliation Day" and "Hate American" rallies.

Native Americans who served in World War I earned the right of citizenship, setting a precedent for the passage of the Snyder Act of 1924, which gave full citizenship to all native people. Yet the Bureau of Indian Affairs (BIA) and other federal agencies continued to cooperate with developers seeking to exploit reservation lands and resources. Even after Congress created the Pueblo Lands Board to compensate Nuevos Mexicanos for lands illegally given to whites, the panel colluded with speculators, railroad interests, and cattle companies to assess tribal properties below fair market value. Federal policy also proved hostile to American Indian cultural traditions. Seeking to "Americanize" reservation tribal life, the commissioner of Indian affairs ordered the prohibition of religious dancing, specifically targeting the Hopi Snake Dance and the Plains Indians Sun Dance.

BLACK METROPOLIS AND THE HARLEM RENAISSANCE

When black nationalist Marcus Garvey proclaimed, "Up you mighty Race! You can accomplish what you will!" he reflected both the promise and the adversity of African American life in the 1920s. Encouraged by the job opportunities of wartime mobilization, the New Era boom, and advancement of the idea of a "black metropolis" by community leaders and newspaper editors, African Americans left the rural South in unprecedented numbers between 1915 and 1928. Altogether, the Great Migration brought 1.2 million southern blacks to northern and western cities. By 1930, New York and Chicago contained African American communities of more than 225,000 each. Although hampered by a lack of working capital, black businesses, newspapers, and storefront churches thrived in the new environment. Yet the black metropolis presented mixed prospects.

Because African Americans were among the last migrants to the industrial cities, many of the available jobs involved menial tasks at low pay. Black workers served as sweepers and firemen in midwestern steel plants. In Detroit, where the African American population increased sixfold in the 1920s, Henry Ford pioneered the hiring of blacks on the assembly line, but mostly in unskilled positions. Although urbanization produced a black working class adapted to modern industry, African Americans held only 2 percent of the white-collar and skilled jobs in the country by 1930. Racial discrimination also forced black migrants to live in racially defined neighborhoods. Despite the Supreme Court's prohibition of residential segregation ordinances in 1917, white neighborhood associations resorted to restrictive covenants that barred property holders from selling to blacks.

Northern landlords contributed to the growth of urban ghettos by squeezing profits from declining neighborhoods without improving properties. Rents in New York's Harlem, for example, doubled between 1919 and 1927. Yet population density and death rates far exceeded that of the rest of the city. Migration and the struggle for economic survival also disrupted the stability of families; although African American women could find jobs as domestics, black men faced hiring discrimination. Consequently, African Americans in migrant neighborhoods experienced higher rates of desertion, divorce, and illegitimacy than did whites. Prostitution, gambling, bootlegging, the numbers racket, and narcotics addiction all became part of the impoverished inner-city environment in the 1920s.

Despite these difficulties, black pride, habit, and the need for mutual protection led to efforts to "advance the race" by promoting economic self-sufficiency through racial clubs, fraternal orders, and mutual aid societies. The most significant organization for black working people in northern ghettos was the Universal Negro Improvement Association (UNIA). Founded in 1914 by Marcus Garvey, a Jamaican, the UNIA enrolled about 100,000 members at its peak, although Garvey claimed as many as 2 million. Heralding an "Africa for the Africans," Garvey proclaimed that an elite number of African Americans might go to Liberia to teach the necessary skills to redeem the continent from European colonialism. To accomplish this, he organized a Black Star Steamship Line to establish commercial links between the United States, the West Indies, and Africa. Garvey also called for support of African American businesses in a "buy black" campaign and established grocery chains, restaurants, laundries, a hotel, a black doll factory, a printing plant, and a newspaper.

Condemned by established African American leaders such as W. E. B. Du Bois for its reliance on flamboyant parades and decorated uniforms, Garvey's black nationalism nevertheless brought hope to a generation embittered by the harsh realities of the urban promised land. After several UNIA businesses failed through mismanagement, federal prosecutors indicted Garvey for selling fraudulent stock. Although he protested that white business associates had betrayed him, Garvey alone was convicted. After two years in federal prison, the charismatic leader was deported in 1927—at the insistence of Federal Bureau of Investigation Director J. Edgar Hoover—as an alien who had committed a felony.

In contrast to Garvey's black nationalism, civil rights groups such as the National Association for the Advancement of Colored People (NAACP) and the Urban League struggled for equal treatment under the law. Lobbyists succeeded in winning passage of the Dyer Anti-Lynching Bill in the House of Representatives in 1921, only to see southern Democrats kill the measure in the Senate. In Ohio and Indiana, activists mobilized against segregation in the public schools. In contrast, enfranchised African Americans in northern cities resorted to politics to win jobs and protect community interests. By supporting Republican Mayor Bill Thompson, blacks obtained one-fourth of Chicago's postal service jobs and elected Oscar DePriest as the North's first African American member of Congress.

"I am a Negro—and beautiful," exclaimed Harlem poet Langston Hughes at mid-decade. Inspired by the potential of the black metropolis, African American writers, intellectuals, and artists expressed a new racial pride and militancy. Their movement celebrated the advent of the "New Negro" and a "Harlem Renaissance." The stark verses of poets such as Hughes, Sterling Brown, and James Weldon Johnson borrowed from the oral traditions of African American spirituals, blues, and speech. Claude McKay brought these techniques to fiction in *Home to Harlem* (1928), an odyssey of the black working class. Jean Toomer's *Cane* (1923) vividly captured the life of poor southern blacks. As coeditor with Zora Neale Hurston and Wallace Thurman of the literary magazine *Fire!* Hughes announced that "we younger Negro artists intend to express our dark-skinned selves without fear or shame." Traditional African forms also entered the work of young black painters and sculptors.

Renewed race pride also found expression in popular culture. Although radio provided few outlets for African Americans in the 1920s, commercial recording companies tapped a huge market by releasing "race records" by blues artists such as Ethel Waters and Bessie Smith. Similarly, black and white film companies produced "race movies" distributed exclusively to African American audiences. Yet jazz provided the central expression of postwar black culture. In Chicago, where public sentiment resisted Prohibition enforcement, nightclubs featured innovative musicians such as King Oliver, Louis Armstrong, and Thomas ("Fats") Waller. Harlem's rent parties, clubs, and dance halls also attracted a variety of performers, including pioneer swing orchestra leaders such as Fletcher Henderson, Chick Webb, and Duke Ellington.

THE JAZZ AGE, HOLLYWOOD FLAPPERS, AND SPORTS HEROES

As a symbol of the Jazz Age, Harlem became a favorite spot for "slumming parties" by New York's white social elite and adventurous college students. Hot spots like the Cotton Club, which featured exotic musical floor shows with light-skinned female dancers, served exclusively white audiences seeking

James Weldon Johnson (1871–1938)

A central figure in the Harlem Renaissance of the 1920s, James Weldon Johnson devoted his life to the celebration of African American culture. Born in Jacksonville, Florida, he attended preparatory school and college at all-black Atlanta University. Returning home in 1894, he became

principal of an African American grade school, founded a black city newspaper, and proceeded to study law with a white attorney. He became the first African American admitted to the Florida bar by court examination.

Johnson and his brother Rosamond also began an illustrious musical career. After collaborating on a series of black dialect songs and comic operas, the duo penned "Lift Every Voice and Sing" for a school assembly dedicated to Abraham Lincoln; the piece later won acclaim as the unofficial Negro national anthem. Shortly after 1900, the Johnsons left for New York City, where they entered the black vaudeville stage, composed over 200 ragtime ditties, and wrote a major musical. Wary of the era's popular but demeaning "coon" songs and minstrel shows, lyricist Johnson aspired to bring "a higher degree of artistry" to pieces like "Under the Bamboo Tree" (1902), which sold nearly a half-million sheet music copies.

Between 1906 and 1913 Johnson forged ties with the Republican Party to win appointments as U.S. consul to multiracial Venezuela and

the "primitive spontaneity" of black entertainers. Carl Van Vechten's *Nigger Heaven* (1925), a white bohemian view of Harlem orgies and seduction, quickly sold 100,000 copies. The Jazz Age, remarked Langston Hughes, embodied "a vogue in things Negro."

Popular music conveyed the enormous influence of African American jazz. White radio listeners learned about the new musical genre through Paul Whiteman, the self-styled "King of Jazz," whose orchestra broadcasts featured Iowa cornetist Bix Beiderbecke and the relaxed styles of vocalist Bing Crosby. Dance bands favored lighthearted novelty tunes such as "Yes, We Have No Bananas" (1923) and "Yes, Sir, That's My Baby" (1924). Yet songwriters like Ira and George Gershwin artfully fused spiritual and sexual love themes by

Nicaragua. In his free time, he worked on *The Autobiography of an Ex-Colored Man* (1912), an anonymously published story of a light-skinned black who passed for white and observed the nation's racial foibles. Returning to the United States, Johnson joined the *New York Age*, the city's oldest African American newspaper, as a leading editorial writer. Moved by W. E. B. Du Bois's call for social activism, he became field secretary for the NAACP in 1916 and expanded the organization's chapters five-fold within three years. When war tensions led to a massacre of blacks in East St. Louis, Illinois, in 1917, he helped to organize the silent parade of nearly 30,000 protesters down New York's Fifth Avenue. As the NAACP's first African American executive secretary, Johnson lobbied for U.S. military withdrawal from predominantly black Haiti and led the campaign to win House passage of the Dyer Anti-Lynching Bill of 1921.

Johnson believed that the blending of the races would be more palatable if society acknowledged the cultural contributions of African Americans. After editing several anthologies of black poetry and hymns, he published his own work of verse in 1927. *God's Trombones—Seven Negro Folk Sermons* used the free cadence of an old black preacher to capture the rhythm and texture of black speech. To further his work as a cultural architect, Johnson completed *Black Manhattan* (1930), an informal history focusing on African American contributions to the arts. He then took up a career as professor of literature at Fisk University. When Johnson issued his autobiography, *Along This Way*, in 1933, he ranked as the spiritual father of the Harlem Renaissance.

combining blues influences with introspective lyrics. Renditions of "torch" songs like "Someone to Watch Over Me" (1926) often appealed to single women entering the romantic marketplace. Popular music won particular support among middle-class collegiates, whose peer culture sought independence from family influence and traditional mores.

At a time when more Americans attended movies on Sunday than church, Hollywood films reinforced Jazz Age themes. By the end of the decade, the productions of the eight major studios were garnering over 70 million weekly admissions: young women went to the movies an average forty-six times a year. Enhanced by a glamorous star system, alluring theater palaces, and deeply affecting imagery, motion pictures assumed the status of a secular religion.

Jazz Age "flappers" posing with a "flivver," the ubiquitous automobile.

Comic film artists such as Charlie Chaplin, Harold Lloyd, and Buster Keaton delighted audiences by satirizing pretentious authority and moral hypocrisy. Yet motion picture producers sought a middle-class audience by emphasizing sexual and romantic themes in films featuring European stars such as Rudolph Valentino (*The Sheik*, 1920) and Greta Garbo (*The Temptress*, 1926). At the same time, Cecil B. DeMille and other producers worked with homegrown female performers such as Clara Bow, Joan Crawford, and Gloria Swanson to convey the breezy sexuality of the "flapper," the embodiment of the modern American woman.

As early as 1915, journalist H. L. Mencken had used the term *flapper* to describe brazen and volatile young women who sought sexual satisfaction, social equality, and personal freedom. Flappers "bobbed" their hair short and exposed their legs with short dresses that also flattened their chests, hid their waists, and narrowed their hips. Conveying the impression of boyish women in energetic motion, they insisted on the right to drive cars, to wear exaggerated makeup, to use slang, to smoke cigarettes in public, to drink in the company of men, and to frequent illegal speakeasies. On the screen, the "moderns" were best represented by Joan Crawford's frantic version of the Charleston in *Our Dancing Daughters* (1928). Emphasizing the importance of a romantic "personality," Hollywood films taught that successful marriages depended upon mutual recognition of sexual and emotional needs: if men would overcome their obsession with work, women would abandon their preoccupation with purity.

As the corporate workplace offered an avenue to the luxuries of consumerism, popular culture sought to provide middle-class men with vicarious excitement through spectator sports. The romanticization of 1920s athletic heroes was facilitated by the development of a national sports media in newspapers, magazines, and radio. College football with its tribal ritualism dominated campus life and provided fans with mythic heroes such as University of Illinois halfback Harold ("Red") Grange. Yet the greatest sports figures came from the ethnics and poor whites, who gravitated to professional prize fighting and baseball. Irish American heavyweight Jack Dempsey thrilled boxing fans with a ferocious style of combat reminiscent of street brawls. And Babe Ruth, raised in a Catholic boys' home in Baltimore, made baseball the national pastime as the New York Yankees' home-run slugger.

Nostalgia for traditional male roles and media publicity both figured in the most celebrated event of the Jazz Age: Charles A. Lindbergh's solo flight across the Atlantic Ocean in 1927. Taking off from Long Island, New York, Lindbergh piloted his single-engine *Spirit of St. Louis* nonstop for 33.5 hours without instruments. As two continents awaited word of the tiny plane's landing at an airfield near Paris, the White House ordered a battleship to return the aviator and his craft to the United States. Once newspapers celebrated the daunting courage of the Lone Eagle, 4 million people turned out to see the youthful Minnesotan parade down New York City's Broadway and be showered with reams of stock exchange ticker tape. By combining personal ingenuity with sophisticated machine technology, the shy adventurer stirred the public imagination by suggesting that individuals could still play a dynamic role in society.

YOUTH CULTURE AND THE LOST GENERATION

"None of the Victorian mothers," wrote the novelist F. Scott Fitzgerald of campus culture in *This Side of Paradise* (1920), "had any idea how casually their daughters were accustomed to be kissed." Although only 12 percent of college-age youth attended institutions of higher learning by the end of the 1920s, enrollment had tripled since the start of the century. Fitzgerald enthralled readers with a description of an affluent collegiate peer culture that accepted the consumption of liquor and cigarettes as marks of adulthood. Freed from the constraints of family and community, unchaperoned couples explored the new freedoms of dating and "petting." Fitzgerald's fiction romanticized speakeasies, where a diverse clientele consumed illegal liquor, rubbed elbows with gangsters, danced to "hot" orchestrations, and sought

Francis Scott Key Fitzgerald *(1896–1940)*
Zelda Sayre Fitzgerald *(1900–1948)*

The fiction of F. Scott Fitzgerald, as well as the writer's entire career and marriage to Zelda Sayre, epitomized the cultural turbulence that shook traditional values during the "Jazz Age," a term Fitzgerald invented. Catapulted to fame by the publication of his first novel, *This*

Side of Paradise (1920), Fitzgerald depicted "a new generation grown up to find all Gods dead, all wars fought, all faiths in man shaken."

Fitzgerald, who was born in St. Paul, Minnesota, left the wholesome but bland Midwest for the sophistication of the East. First he lived as an undergraduate at Princeton (he quit without graduating in 1917), then as an army officer, and later as an advertising writer in New York. Captivated by wealth, extravagance, and the wholesale rejection of Victorian morality, the novelist and storyteller dispassionately depicted a younger generation preoccupied with booze, sex, jazz, and easy money. For a time, the author's overnight literary success enabled him to fulfill his version of the American Dream.

Fitzgerald met Zelda Sayre while stationed in her home town of Montgomery, Alabama. Zelda symbolized the rich, beautiful, outrageous flapper type that attracted the young military officer. Wild and zany, she held ambitions of escape as a ballet dancer. Together they set off for

sexual adventure. The unofficial anthem of this underground culture was "Making Whoopee" (1928), an irreverent reflection upon marriage and divorce whose title became a common phrase for sex.

As the movies, radio, popular music, and national magazines popularized the consumer ethic, questions of sexual propriety pervaded postwar society. Sexual activity among the young prompted open discussion in *The Revolt of Modern Youth* (1925), a controversial work by Judge Ben Lindsey, the founder of Denver's juvenile court system. A second book, *The Companionate Marriage* (1927), called for the use of contraception and divorce by mutual consent for childless couples. Although Lindsey believed that psychological counseling and sex education would prevent broken homes and reduce youth

Paris, where they lived at the core of the expatriate literary community and joined in repudiating the provincial values of small-town America. Yet the extravagant lifestyle of Paris and New York haunted Fitzgerald and compromised his work, compelling him to write popular short stories for money while publishing the novels *The Beautiful and the Damned* (1922) and *The Great Gatsby* (1925).

Scott and Zelda's marriage also faced difficulties, precipitated in part by Fitzgerald's view of flappers as "brave, shallow, cynical, impatient, turbulent, and empty." Confronting her husband's dominating success, Zelda lost herself in alcohol and suffered a series of emotional breakdowns requiring hospitalization. While confined, Zelda completed the novel *Save Me the Waltz* (1932), the Gatsby story told from a woman's perspective, but she remained institutionalized for the rest of her life. Fitzgerald moved to Hollywood in the late 1930s to write movie scripts, but continued to drink and never recaptured the popularity he had earlier attained.

Through their work and lifestyles, the Fitzgeralds represented the modern revolt against traditional values while paradoxically lamenting the loss of old certitudes. To the aphorism "You can't repeat the past," Fitzgerald's Gatsby exclaims, "Why of course you can! . . . I'm going to fix everything just the way it was before." Yet for all their bravado, F. Scott and Zelda knew otherwise and suffered a relentless sense of failure.

crime, critics associated his proposals with the antics of a generation gone wild and a civilization without ethical bearings. Moralists noted that divorce had doubled between 1914 and 1929 and become one-sixth as frequent as marriage. Equally disturbing were studies suggesting that women born after 1900 were twice as likely to engage in premarital sex as were those born earlier.

The relative sexual freedom of the 1920s reflected the increased availability of condoms, jellies, and the diaphragm. These devices were promoted by the American Birth Control League as a means of containing family size, alleviating sexual guilt, and freeing married women for life outside the home. Despite the huge interest in birth control techniques expressed by college students, married couples became the leading beneficiaries of the revolution in sexual practice. In 1929 one survey reported that three-fourths of married women in their early thirties used contraceptives. Nevertheless, twenty-two states still restricted or forbade the dissemination of birth control devices.

The most important symbol of postwar youth was the lost generation, a name that expatriate Gertrude Stein gave to the exile artists, writers, and intellectuals who flocked to Paris in the 1920s. Writers such as Stein, Ernest Hemingway, F. Scott and Zelda Fitzgerald, John Dos Passos, and Malcolm Cowley drifted to postwar Europe to find artistic inspiration. They also sought escape from the materialism and puritanism they despised in America. As children of the middle class, they were, in Cowley's words, "strangers in their own land." The rebels castigated conventional culture as hopelessly stupid and materialistic. Yet they reserved their most intense wrath for the moral guardians of society, whom they condemned as "philistines" for failing to separate art from morality. *American Mercury* editor H. L. Mencken memorably savaged such targets as the "booboisie."

The meaningless brutality of World War I presented the intelligentsia with a powerful metaphor of disillusionment. Hemingway's bitter novels, *The Sun Also Rises* (1926) and *A Farewell to Arms* (1929), described the lost generation's reaction to the ideological sham and cant of its elders. War "kills the very good and the very gentle and the very brave impartially," he wrote. One of the author's protagonists confessed to being "always embarrassed by the words 'sacred,' 'glorious,' and 'sacrifice.'" Only death was an absolute in a world devoid of believable political ideology. Such cynicism carried over into views of postwar technology and economic progress. Social critics such as Edmund Wilson, Harold Stearns, Van Wyck Brooks, and Lewis Mumford attacked the monotony of the skyscraper and the assembly line. Meanwhile, imagist poets such as Ezra Pound, T. S. Eliot, Hart Crane, and Amy Lowell portrayed modern existence as an absurd wasteland.

"I love my country, but I don't like it," novelist Sinclair Lewis once explained. The first U.S. author to receive the Nobel Prize for Literature, Lewis published *Main Street* in 1920. "It is dullness made God," the midwesterner wrote of life on the Great Northern Plains. His portrait of a married woman's attempt to overcome the conventions of small-town tribalism sold 400,000 copies within weeks. When Lewis's *Babbitt* (1922) drew a biting portrait of a complacent midwestern booster, the title introduced a new term of derision into the language. In *The Great Gatsby* (1925), F. Scott Fitzgerald dissected the superficial materialism and spiritual poverty of the Jazz Age social elite. Adhering to the teachings of Viennese psychoanalyst Sigmund Freud, the lost generation sought liberation from emotional repression and conformity, embracing a bohemian code that welcomed the violation of social and artistic convention.

SOCIAL FEMINISM AND THE PURITY CRUSADE

Influenced by popular ethics of consumerism, young middle-class women of the 1920s often rejected the demands for sacrifice, social commitment, and sisterhood advanced by earlier Progressive Era reformers. Striving for personal satisfaction, many hoped to pursue careers while maintaining life-defining attachments to their families. Advertisers reinforced these expectations by picturing middle-class homemakers as "model consumers" and household business managers. Although merchandisers touted home appliances such as vacuum cleaners and electric irons as liberating women from domestic chores, labor-saving devices simply raised the standards of cleanliness for the tedious and unpaid tasks of housework.

Despite the feminist agenda, middle-class women entered the job market at a slow pace. Although the number of female college graduates tripled in the 1920s, women constituted only 21 percent of the nation's workers at decade's end: the proportion who worked outside the home remained one in four, a ratio that barely wavered between 1910 and 1940. Women in all occupations averaged less than 60 percent of the earnings of male counterparts. Moreover, they comprised no more than one-seventh of the nation's professionals and normally worked in "female" fields as nurses, teachers, librarians, or social workers. Most professions and many civil service exams excluded women outright. As medical schools limited female admissions, the proportion of women training to be physicians declined. By the end of the decade, one-third of all women workers continued to labor as domestic servants.

The political views of women activists divided between social feminists who sought to aid women as a class and those who hoped to advance their sisters as individuals. Such dichotomies explain why social reformers opposed the efforts of Alice Paul's National Woman's Party to pass a constitutional equal rights amendment. Brought before Congress in 1923 and annually throughout the postwar decade, the proposal sought to extend sexual equality to all areas of law, public policy, and employment. Yet some feminists denounced the measure because it would eradicate remaining protections for female workers. Reformers also confronted a conservative reaction against government social welfare. When officials in the Children's Bureau came under fire for allegedly desiring to collectivize national family life, Congress acceded to demands by the American Medical Association (AMA) and other critics by repealing the Sheppard-Towner Act in 1929.

Reacting to popular culture trends, purity reformers exerted a greater impact on public policy than social feminists did. In Utah, lawmakers introduced a proposal to fix women's skirts three inches above the ankle. Several midwestern legislatures considered bans on Sunday baseball games, boxing matches, and public dances. In Boston, the Roman Catholic Church cooperated with the Protestant social elite to ban sexual realism in novels such as Theodore Dreiser's *An American Tragedy* (1925). Popular music was another target. "Does Jazz Put the Sin in Syncopation?" asked Mrs. Marx Obendorfer, national chair of the General Federation of Women's Clubs. The *Ladies Home Journal* complained of "cheap, common tawdry music" that brought moral ruin. Racial anxieties over African rhythms and the sensuality of "vulgar" instruments led New York State to enact the Cotillo Act of 1922, which established municipal regulation of jazz music and dancing. Sixty cities soon banned jazz from dance halls.

Purity reformers were particularly concerned about the movies. Reacting to the perception that motion pictures taught techniques of flirtation and kissing, the sociologist Edward A. Ross contended that the silver screen made young people "sex-wise, sex-excited, and sex-absorbed." In the aftermath of a series of sex and drug scandals in Hollywood involving stars such as Fatty Arbuckle, industry leaders recruited Republican Postmaster General Will H. Hays in 1922 to head the Motion Picture Producers and Distributors Association. Hays reviewed films and scripts and scrutinized the moral background of performers. While public relations efforts slowed down the threat of government censorship, women's clubs and social workers stepped up their campaign for a federal motion picture commission to protect youthful audiences from harmful pictures.

PROHIBITION AND THE FUNDAMENTALISTS

Prohibition was the most controversial feature of the postwar purity crusade. The Eighteenth Amendment, which took effect in 1920, outlawed the manufacture, sale, importing, or transportation of intoxicating liquors, defined as any beverage containing .5 percent alcohol. As a "noble experiment," Prohibition sought to unify the nation around Anglo-Protestant values of sobriety, social efficiency, and civic virtue. Yet the results were mixed. After per capita consumption of alcohol dropped in the early 1920s, it returned to two-thirds its original level by the end of the decade. By then, bootleggers were providing consumers with an annual $500 million in illicit intoxicants by tapping industrial alcohol supplies. Urban officials often declined to challenge the casual use of beer and wine. Critics soon charged that Prohibition constituted class legislation, promoting more crime and corruption than it deterred.

"The only subjects that are getting any attention from the 'political minded,'" observed a Los Angeles college newspaper editor in 1926, "are Prohibition, Birth Control, and the Bible Issue." By the early 1920s, a massive revival of traditional faith had come to play a major role in the nation's Protestant denominations. Represented by the World's Christian Fundamental Association (WCFA), which claimed 6 million members by 1927, evangelicals challenged the spread of "modernist" church teachings that accepted rationalist philosophy and Darwinian evolutionary thought. When 155 Baptist ministers agreed to a conference on basic theology in 1920, Curtis Lee Laws, a religious newspaper editor, coined a new term by urging participants "to do royal battle for the Fundamentals."

Insisting that the Bible was "inerrant" in its original form, fundamentalists sought to save civilization from wrenching cultural change. One preacher, Presbyterian William ("Billy") Sunday, a former professional baseball player, mixed denunciation of sinners and intellectuals with acrobatics to convert an estimated 300,000 people in twenty years. Fundamentalist critics complained that postwar biology texts presented Darwinian theory as scientific fact and offended those who accepted the story of Genesis as the cornerstone of Christian faith. Between 1921 and 1929, organizers introduced 41 antievolution bills before 21 statehouses. When one bill passed in Tennessee as a symbolic gesture, the American Civil Liberties Union (ACLU) challenged the law as a free speech infringement. The ensuing trial of high school biology teacher John Scopes pitted Clarence Darrow, the nation's leading defense attorney, against the famed William Jennings Bryan, retained by the WCFA as a prosecutor.

"It is better to trust the Rock of Ages," proclaimed Bryan, "than to know the age of rocks." As a committed populist and peace activist, the Great Commoner hoped to show that the doctrine of evolution paralyzed social reform because it emphasized struggle and conflict instead of Christian love. But when Bryan testified for the prosecution, he violated his own rule about interpreting scripture when he acknowledged that God may have created the Earth in six time periods rather than days. The logical inconsistency had no impact on the Scopes conviction. Yet when Bryan died in his sleep five days later, the national press portrayed the heavily publicized "monkey trial" as a triumph of the scientific rationalism of the "experts" over "old-time religion." Once the verdict was reversed on a technicality, the Tennessee law remained in effect until 1966.

NATIVISTS AND THE KU KLUX KLAN

Like Darwinists, immigrants were frequently portrayed as a threat to democracy and social order. "Most of the bootleggers . . . appear to be foreigners," announced sociologist Harry Pratt Fairchild in *The Melting Pot Mistake* (1926), a polemic that linked Catholic and Jewish ethnics to radicalism, crime, prostitution, machine politics, labor unions, and unseemly tenement life. Henry Ford promoted these ideas in *The International Jew,* a four-volume tract that sold 500,000 copies in the early 1920s. Based on forged documenta-

Aimee Semple McPherson (1890–1944)

When Aimee Semple McPherson opened a Pentecostal temple in Los Angeles on New Year's Day, 1923, she demonstrated that Protestant fundamentalism did not confine itself to the remote corners of the Appalachian Mountains. McPherson's church embodied the compassionate

side of a creed that attacked evolutionary theory for promoting a materialistic world ruled by force instead of love.

McPherson had fashioned herself into an evangelical faith healer. She had been converted at the age of seventeen by Robert Semple, an itinerant preacher. The two married and left to pursue missionary work in China; but Semple died, and the young widow returned home. After an unhappy marriage to a grocery salesman, Aimee decorated her "gospel automobile" with religious slogans and set out for California.

The "foursquare gospel" of Aimee Semple was an outgrowth of the Protestant pietistic tradition. It appealed to people of little education and small means, to worshippers brought up in the revivalist spirit of the evangelical churches. Most of McPherson's followers were retirees, transplanted from the Midwest and elsewhere, who responded enthusiastically to simple sermons of love and faith healing.

McPherson made Los Angeles the headquarters for countless cross-country revival tours. In tents, churches, and public auditoriums nationwide, she spread the word that the Jazz Age was speeding to hell. Endorsed in 1921 by the mayor of Denver, she filled that city's coliseum

tion once prepared for the czar of Russia, Ford outlined a global Jewish conspiracy whose activities ranged from high finance to production of decadent flapper skirts and "skunk cabbage" jazz. As a mechanized economy reduced labor needs, industrialists formerly opposed to immigration restriction now joined trade unions and groups like the American Legion and Ku Klux Klan in arguing that the influx of foreigners should be regulated.

Such a consensus emerged with the passage of an emergency immigration measure in 1921. Three years later, Congress voted for the Immigration Quota Act, creating a gradual timetable to limit migration from outside the

with 12,000 people nightly for a month. The following year McPherson addressed a secret klavern of the Oakland Ku Klux Klan. Once her Pentecostal temple opened in Los Angeles, her religious enterprises expanded to include a Bible college, a publishing house, branch churches, and overseas missions. In 1924 she purchased Los Angeles's third radio station.

The distinguishing feature of McPherson's gospel remained her belief that a Jazz Age preacher must "fight fire with fire." She became the first woman to deliver a sermon over the radio. In San Diego she scattered religious tracts and handbills from an open biplane. The Los Angeles temple provided telephone callers with the time of day as a free service.

McPherson merged the magic of Hollywood spectacle with religious ecstasy. She dressed in long white gowns that dramatically offset her cascading blond hair. Temple services used full orchestras, choirs, elaborate costumes, and colorful pageantry to portray biblical stories in theatrical fashion. Preacher McPherson once illustrated a sermon entitled "The Green Light Is On" by riding a motorcycle down the temple's center aisle.

The evangelist's fusion of traditionalism and modernism brought press outrage when she disappeared in 1926, only to be linked to a Mexican abortion and an affair with the temple radio operator. Despite her involvements in lawsuits and succeeding scandals, McPherson's followers continued to pay homage to "Everybody's Sister." She remained a symbol of Anglo-Protestant nostalgia for a purer and simpler age, free of overintellectualized theology and relativistic moral values.

Western Hemisphere to 150,000 people a year. Using a sliding quota based on the number of each nation's inhabitants living in the United States between 1890 and 1920, the law drastically reduced immigration from eastern and southern Europe and formalized the ban on the influx of the Japanese. In contrast, the statute's failure to regulate migration from the Western Hemisphere meant that Mexican and Canadian labor could flow unimpeded. Canadians soon comprised 35 percent of immigrants to the United States.

The Ku Klux Klan was the prime advocate of immigration restriction. Organized in Atlanta in 1915, the second Klan admitted "native born, white,

EXHIBIT **4-6   CHANGING PATTERNS OF IMMIGRATION TO THE UNITED STATES, 1921–1929 (IN ROUNDED FIGURES)**

	1921	1925	1929
Northwestern Europe and Canada	204,000	182,000	134,000
Central, eastern, and southern Europe	521,000	69,000	90,000

Source: *Historical Statistics of the United States, Colonial Times to 1970* (1975).

gentile Americans" who embraced racial supremacy and patriotic loyalty. Members took secret oaths of allegiance and wore white robes and hoods to fulfill prescribed ritual and maintain anonymity. The Klan initially spread across the Deep South in a response to the influx of black migrants to the region's cities and to the new pride among returning African American war veterans. Local lodges organized masked parades to discourage black voting and occasionally directed vigilante actions against African Americans considered overly assertive. A series of newspaper exposés and congressional hearings brought the Klan a broader following after 1921. When Texan Hiram Wesley Evans took over as imperial wizard, the organization evolved from a confederation of local vigilantes into a disciplined national movement that attracted 2–6 million followers.

Heralding the flag, the Constitution, and the Bible as its central symbols, the Klan invoked "100 percent Americanism" and "traditional values." KKK rallies, marches, and picnics built a cohesive brotherhood of white Protestants in favor of Prohibition, the public schools, and immigration restriction. Knights saw themselves as guardians of public virtue in a period in which urban commercial and political elites often colluded with vice and criminal syndicates. In cities such as Buffalo, Youngstown, Indianapolis, Dallas, Denver, and Anaheim, the Klan ignored ethnic targets to focus on Anglo-Protestant business and political leaders who impeded its efforts to place purity crusaders in control of local government, police, and public schools. Klanswomen formed their own statewide organizations to engage in charity drives and monitor troubled families and public dance halls.

Insisting that the Klan opposed mob terrorism, Evans credited the secret order for the precipitous decline of southern lynchings in the 1920s. To gain public legitimacy, the imperial wizard organized mass rallies such as the 1925 parade of 80,000 uniformed followers in Washington, D.C. As a bipartisan group, the Klan helped to elect seven governors and three U.S. Senators and took over nearly every key office in Indiana. By a single vote out of 1,038 cast, Klan political clout prevented the 1924 Democratic National Convention from denouncing the secret order by name. Yet KKK secrecy, lingering vigilantism, scandals in Indiana, and the organization's divisive effect on communities re-

The Ku Klux Klan marches through the streets of Washington, D.C., in 1925.

vitalized doubts about its commitment to law and order. Once the Immigration Quota Act removed the urgency from the anti-immigrant crusade, Klan membership quickly dissipated.

THE ELECTION OF 1928

The ethnocultural tensions of the Jazz Age found their way into politics in 1924 when Governor Al Smith of New York, a Roman Catholic and "wet" opponent of Prohibition, lost the Democratic presidential nomination after 102 ballots. Smith represented business interests in the Democratic Party whose opposition to the liquor laws stemmed from hostility to federal regulatory power. In contrast, southern and western Democrats embraced Prohibition as a proper example of government's social welfare role. Four years later, Democrat treasurer and corporate leader John J. Raskob assured Smith's nomination by merging the party's two wings around a states' rights position. By proposing nonenforcement of the Fifteenth Amendment, which extended equal voting rights to African Americans, Raskob won southern support and toleration of the candidate's anti-Prohibition views. Significantly, black delegates at the 1928 convention in Houston were segregated behind a chicken-wire fence.

EXHIBIT **4-7**   ELECTION OF 1928

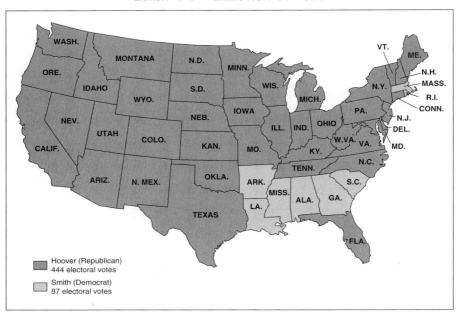

Hoover (Republican)
444 electoral votes

Smith (Democrat)
87 electoral votes

Secretary of Commerce Herbert Hoover emerged as the Republican nominee. Like Henry Ford, Hoover bridged the gap between big business and traditional values. As wartime food and relief coordinator, Hoover had combined the humanitarian zeal of a Quaker background with the administrative skills of a venture capitalist. Once he overcame the opposition of farm-bloc Republicans, Hoover campaigned with the slogan of the New Day. "We in America are nearer to the final triumph over poverty than ever before in the history of any land," he proclaimed. In contrast, the Democrats failed to generate enthusiasm among struggling farmers and manual workers.

Smith's prospects also were hurt by his Prohibition views, which prompted some voters to connect him to corrupt political machines, suspect Catholicism, and working-class crudeness. As Kansas newspaper editor William Allen White observed, critics viewed the Democratic candidate as threatening the "whole Puritan civilization which has built a sturdy, orderly nation," Such sentiment played a role in delivering several states in the once solidly Democratic South to the Republican Party. On Election Day, Smith succeeded in carrying only six states in the Deep South and the heavily Catholic states of Massachusetts and Rhode Island. Taking more than 58 percent of the popular vote, Hoover dominated the Electoral College, 444–87.

Protestant traditionalists rejoiced that voters had rejected the influence of urban politics. The country was "not yet dominated by its great cities," noted the *St. Paul Pioneer Press,* "Main Street is still the principal thoroughfare of the nation." Yet the Smith candidacy was a turning point in U.S. political history. In generating participation by nearly 57 percent of eligible voters, the highest rate since 1916, the Democrats doubled their 1924 vote and embraced the ethnic electorate. For the first time since 1892, the party won more ballots in the nation's twelve largest cities than the Republicans did. By initiating this electoral revolution, Smith and Raskob moved the Democratic Party toward the politics of urban constituencies. Ironically, two Catholic conservatives had facilitated the conversion to political liberalism that would dominate the following decade and put an end to the culture wars of the Jazz Age.

American History Resource Center

To explore documents, images, audio and video clips, articles, and commentary related to the material in this chapter, visit the source collections at ushistory.wadsworth.com and and use the Search function with the following key terms:

James Weldon Johnson	Gertrude Stein
Prohibition	F. Scott Fitzgerald
Ku Klux Klan	Aimee McPherson

Recommended Readings

Roland Marchand, *Creating the Corporate Soul: The Rise of Public Relations and Corporate Imagery in American Big Business* (1998). This book emphasizes how New Era corporations used traditional imagery in advertising and public relations to sustain consumer trust and goodwill.

Ann Douglas, *Terrible Honesty: Mongrel Manhattan in the 1920s* (1995). The author offers an exploration of the full range of Jazz Age cultural modernism with special focus on the relationship between black and white artists and writers.

Edward J. Larson, *Trial and Error: The American Controversy Over Creation and Evolution,* 3rd ed. (2003). The debate over Darwinism in the 1920s is a central topic of this balanced description of the strains between science and popular sentiment.

Charles W. Eagles, *Democracy Delayed: Congressional Reapportionment and Urban-Rural Conflict in the 1920s* (1990). This revisionist account ties the ethnocultural divisions of the postwar Democratic Party to disputes over government power.

Additional Readings

The most useful syntheses of the New Era and postwar political culture are Ellis W. Hawley, *The Great War and the Search for a Modern Order: A History of the American People and Their Institutions*, 2nd ed. (1997), and Lynn Dumenil, *The Modern Temper: American Culture and Society in the 1920s* (1995). Jazz Age consumerism is described in the relevant sections of Jackson Lears, *Fables of Abundance: A Cultural History of Advertising in America* (1994); Susan Strasser, *Satisfaction Guaranteed: The Making of the American Mass Market* (1989); and Roland Marchand, *Advertising the American Dream: Making Way for Modernity, 1920–1940* (1985). For automobile culture and the suburbs, see Kenneth T. Jackson, *The Crabgrass Frontier: The Suburbanization of the United States* (1985), and Scott Bottles, *Los Angeles and the Automobile: The Making of the Modern City* (1987).

The Republican presidencies of the 1920s are best approached through the revisionist scholarship on Herbert Hoover, particularly Joan Hoff Wilson, *Herbert Hoover: The Forgotten Progressive* (1975), and David Burner, *Herbert Hoover: The Public Life* (1978). For Republican leaders as reformers, see the appropriate chapters of Martin J. Sklar, *The United States as a Developing Country: Studies in U.S. History in the Progressive Era and the 1920s* (1992). Small business and rural agitators are described in the relevant segments of David A. Horowitz, *Beyond Left and Right: Insurgency and the Establishment* (1997). See also Eugene M. Tobin, *Organize or Perish: America's Independent Progressives, 1913–1933* (1986), and David B. Danbom, *"The World of Hope": Progressives and the Struggle for an Ethical Public Life* (1987).

A summary of postwar labor appears in the appropriate segments of Robert H. Zeiger, *American Workers, American Unions, 1920–1985* (1986). For southern industrialism, see the relevant sections of Jacquelyn Dowd Hall et al., *Like a Family: The Making of a Southern Cotton Mill World* (1987), and Jack Temple Kirby, *Rural Worlds Lost: The American South, 1920–1960* (1987). The role of postwar women workers is portrayed in segments of Alice Kessler-Harris, *Out to Work: A History of Wage-earning Women in the United States* (1982); Margery Davies, *Women's Place Is at the Typewriter: Office Work and Office Workers, 1870–1930* (1982); and Lisa M. Fine, *The Souls of the Skyscraper: Female Clerical Workers in Chicago, 1870–1930* (1990). See also the relevant chapters of Susan Porter Benson, *Counter Cultures: Saleswomen, Managers, and Customers in American Department Stores, 1890–1940* (1986).

For the Coolidge presidency, see Robert K. Murray, *The Politics of Normalcy: Government Theory and Practice in the Harding-Coolidge Era* (1973). Postwar foreign policy is the subject of Warren I. Cohen, *Empire Without Tears: America's Foreign Relations, 1921–1933* (1987), and Frank Costigliola, *Awkward Dominion: American Political, Economic, and Cultural Relations with Europe, 1919–1933* (1985). For corporate internationalism, see Joan Hoff Wilson, *American Business and Foreign Policy, 1920–1933* (1985), and segments of Akira Iriye, *The Globalizing of America, 1913–1945* (1993). Noninterventionist sentiment is surveyed in Robert David Johnson, *The Peace Progressives and American Foreign Relations* (1995).

The response of European ethnics to New Era consumerism and popular culture is explored in Lizabeth Cohen, *Making a New Deal: Industrial Workers in Chicago, 1919–1939* (1990). For the Jewish experience, see the early chapters of Henry L. Feingold, *A Time for Searching: Entering the Mainstream, 1920–1945* (1992), and the later segments of Elizabeth Ewen, *Immigrant Women in the Land of Dollars: Life and Culture on the Lower East Side, 1890–1925* (1985). Mexican American culture is described in the relevant segments of Sarah Deutsch, *No Separate Refuge: Culture, Class, and Gender on an Anglo-Hispanic Frontier in the American Southwest, 1880–1940* (1987), and David Montejano, *Anglos and Mexicans in the Making of Texas, 1836–1986* (1987). Hispanics, Asians, and Native Americans are portrayed in the relevant chapters of Ronald Takaki, *A Different Mirror: A History of Multicultural America* (1993).

The urbanization of African Americans is explored in the relevant segments of August Meier and Elliot Rudwick, *From Plantation to Ghetto* (1976). For the era's most influential African American, see Judith Stein, *The World of Marcus Garvey: Race and Class in Modern Society* (1986), but also consult the early chapters of David Levering Lewis, *W. E. B. Du Bois: The Fight for Equality and the American Century, 1919–1963* (2000). Accounts of the Harlem Renaissance include Lewis, *When Harlem Was in Vogue* (1988); Cary D. Wintz, *Black Culture and the Harlem Renaissance* (1988); and Houston Baker, *Modernism and the Harlem Renaissance* (1987).

For Hollywood's impact on popular attitudes, see the relevant sections of Lary May, *Screening Out the Past: The Birth of Mass Culture and the Motion Picture Industry* (1980), and Robert Sklar, *Movie-Made America: A Cultural History of American Movies* (1975). These works can be supplemented by Sumiko Higashi, *Cecil B. De Mille and American Culture: The Silent Era* (1994); Richard Koszanski, *An Evening's Entertainment: The Age of the Silent Picture, 1917–1928* (1992); and Billie Melman, *Women and the Popular Imagination in the Twenties: Flappers and Nymphs* (1988). For Jazz Age fashions, see segments of Claudia Kidwell and Margaret C. Christman, *Suiting Everyone: The Democratization of Clothing in America* (1986), and Valerie Steele, *Fashion and Eroticism: Ideals of Feminine Beauty from the Victorian Era to the Jazz Age* (1985). A cultural history of popular music can be found in Kathy J. Ogren, *The Jazz Revolution: Twenties America and the Meaning of Jazz* (1989).

The ties between modern art, jazz, abstract music, science, fiction, and poetry are explored in Robert McCrunden, *Body and Soul: The Making of American Modernism* (2000). Postwar cultural and literary ferment is the topic of Stanley Coben, *Rebellion Against Victorianism: The Impetus for Cultural Change in 1920s America* (1991). For the era's alienated artists and writers, see Marc Dolan, *Modern Lives: A Cultural Re-reading of the "Lost Generation"* (1996).

A useful overview of postwar women's history can be found in Dorothy M. Brown, *Setting a Course: American Women in the 1920s* (1987). See also Nancy F. Cott, *The Grounding of Modern Feminism* (1987). The influence of social work is depicted in the relevant chapters of Don Kirschner, *The Paradox of Professionalism: Reform and Public Service in Urban America, 1900–1940* (1986). Evolving male roles are addressed in sections of Peter G. Filene, *Him/Her Self: Sex Roles in Modern America* (1986).

A pioneer study of postwar cultural conflict can be found in Don S. Kirschner, *City and Country: Rural Responses to Urbanization in the 1920s* (1970). The liquor controversy is discussed in Norman H. Clark, *Deliver Us from Evil: An Interpretation of American Prohibition* (1976). For the impact of religion, see the relevant sections of George M. Marsden, *Fundamentalism and American Culture: The Shaping of Twentieth Century Evangelicalism, 1870–1925* (1980). Three excellent case studies of the 1920s Klan are Leonard J. Moore, *Citizen Klansmen: The Ku Klux Klan in Indiana, 1921–1928* (1991); Nancy MacLean, *Behind the Mask of Chivalry: The Making of the Second Ku Klux Klan* (1994); and Shawn Lay, *Hooded Nights on the Niagara: The Ku Klux Klan in Buffalo, New York* (1995).

The ethnocentric fervor of the postwar era is treated in William G. Ross, *Forging New Freedoms: Nativism, Education, and the Constitution, 1917–1927* (1994). Anti-Jewish sentiment is discussed in segments of Frederic Cople Jaher, *A Scapegoat in the Wilderness: The Origins and Rise of Anti-Semitism in America* (1994), and Leonard Dinnerstein, *Antisemitism in America* (1994). For descriptions of the Democratic Party's battles over urbanism and Prohibition, see Paula Eldot, *Governor Alfred E. Smith: The Politician as Reformer* (1981), and Douglas B. Craig, *After Wilson: The Struggle for the Democratic Party, 1920–1934* (1992).

THE GREAT DEPRESSION AND NEW DEAL REFORM, 1929–1936

Seldom has a leader assumed the reins of power with as great a reputation for administrative experience and humanitarian accomplishment as Herbert Hoover. Riding the crest of New Era prosperity, Hoover marveled that the presidency was "the inspiring symbol of all that is highest in America's purpose and ideals." Yet the lofty aspirations of this Republican administration would be torn apart by the most severe economic downtown in U.S. history. After traditional remedies failed to bring economic recovery, the public endorsed a liberal political philosophy that sanctioned an unprecedented federal government role in business affairs and the lives of ordinary people. Despite controversies over welfare spending and bureaucratic regulation, Franklin D. Roosevelt's New Deal would create the conditions for economic recovery and leave a lasting legacy on U.S. politics and society.

HOOVER'S NEW DAY

Seeking to balance the interests of producers, trade groups, and consumers, Herbert Hoover began his presidency by convening a special session of Congress to address the continuing agricultural depression. As an alternative to subsidies demanded by farm groups, Hoover agreed to the Agricultural Marketing Act of 1929, a measure that promoted the sale of crops through marketing cooperatives eligible for government loans. Under the jurisdiction of the Federal Farm Board, the administration created government stabilization agencies to buy surplus crops. Ironically, by influencing the distribution and price of farm goods, the most ambitious federal program in peacetime violated Republican creeds of limited government.

Having addressed the contentious farm problem, Hoover sought to heal the nation's divisions over Prohibition. By 1929, the wealthy DuPont family had injected financial aid and new leadership into the Association Against the

Prohibition Amendment, the leading advocate of repeal. Conservative Democrats like the DuPonts and John Raskob hoped that eradication of the Eighteenth Amendment would reduce federal regulatory power and allow tax receipts from the sale of legalized alcohol to shrink income and inheritance taxes. A report released in 1931 by former attorney general George W. Wickersham acknowledged that Prohibition had been hindered by illegal syndicates and public apathy or hostility. Yet the president avoided a confrontation with Republican purity crusaders by opposing any move to rescind the "noble experiment."

Continuing the direction of foreign policy under Harding and Coolidge, the Hoover administration sought to expand opportunities for global markets and investments. Concerned about European financial stability, the president sent General Electric chair Owen D. Young and financier J. P. Morgan to renegotiate the payment of World War I reparations and loans. Under the Young Plan of 1929, Germany received credits from private bankers in the United States and an extended period of time to pay a reduced amount of compensation to its wartime enemies. In turn, Washington's European allies were granted the chance to renegotiate their debts to the U.S. government.

The Young Plan signaled that New York City had replaced London as the center of world banking. To enhance this advantage, the administration promoted economic and technical cooperation with its "good neighbors" in Latin America, where the president had led a goodwill tour shortly before taking office. Forging a new approach to the region, the United States recognized all existing governments south of the border and refused to intervene when a revolution broke out in Cuba. "We cannot slay an idea or an ideology with machine guns," declared Hoover. Under the leadership of Secretary of State Henry Stimson, developing nations would be left alone if they honored the "sanctity of contracts" and fulfilled "international obligations." The president ordered a gradual military withdrawal from Haiti. In Nicaragua, where the Marines faced harassment by nationalist guerrillas aligned with General Cesar August Sandino, Hoover called the troops home in 1933.

THE CRASH OF '29

Despite warnings from farm belt politicians and small business interests of excessive Wall Street speculation, Hoover believed that White House leadership could help to balance the economy's diverse interests. Nevertheless, events moved beyond the president's control and severely tested his faith in national institutions and the principle of limited government. On Black Tuesday—October 29, 1929—securities on the New York Stock Exchange, the leading indicator of investor confidence, dropped $14 billion in value, a loss equivalent to $120 billion in today's money. Within two weeks, losses had nearly doubled,

wiping away two-fifths of the value of all equities. "I sat in my back office, trying to figure out what to do," a newspaper publisher remembered of the crash.
"To be explicit, I sat in my private bathroom. My bowels were loose from fear."

The Wall Street collapse stemmed from the same financial practices that
had contributed to the boom. Through unregulated business arrangements,
small investors had generated paper profits by buying stocks for as little as 10
percent of face value. Many then borrowed additional funds by using stock as
collateral, inviting disaster should the value of securities fall. Structural weaknesses also played a role in the crash. New England and rural sections of the
South, Midwest, and Mountain West experienced sinking demand for such
products as coal, timber, cotton textiles, and shoes. These losses were aggravated by poor revenues from shipping and railroads, an indirect result of high
tariffs and reduced foreign trade. A wave of mergers worsened conditions by
forcing thousands of companies out of business. By 1929, half of all nonbank-
ing corporate wealth rested in the hands of 200 conglomerates. Finally, poor
distribution of purchasing power devastated key industries such as residential
construction and auto manufacturing.

THE GREAT DEPRESSION

"We now know they are not magicians," popular writer Gerald Johnson observed of the New Era business elite as unemployment and business bankruptcies escalated. The same could have been said of the nation's political
leaders. Hoover first described the economic disaster as a temporary "depression" instead of a "panic" or "crisis" because he hoped to ease public fears.
"There is more to fear from frozen minds than frozen assets," lectured Secretary of the Treasury Ogden L. Mills. Focusing on the importance of morale,
the White House insisted that corporate maintenance of production, employment, and high wages would sustain the conditions for prosperity. Within
weeks of the crash, Hoover called leading corporate officials to Washington to
win voluntary cooperation. The president also created a host of emergency
agencies and bureaus to address rising unemployment and the need for relief.
Declaring in 1930 that "we have passed the worst," the White House nevertheless expanded outlays for municipal and state public works and requested
funds for the construction of federal buildings.

Despite the administration's efforts, tariff and monetary policies sabo-
taged recovery. Pressed by the farm bloc for protection from foreign competition, Hoover signed the Smoot-Hawley Tariff of 1930, raising the duties on
agricultural products by 70 percent and increasing rates for industrial goods.
More than a thousand professional economists urged the president to veto the
bill as a detriment to foreign trade. Yet Republican partisan interests and nationalist impulses prompted Hoover to approve the measure. The Federal

EXHIBIT **5-1**   **GROSS NATIONAL PRODUCT, 1929–1933**
(IN ROUNDED BILLIONS OF DOLLARS)

1929	103
1933	56

Source: *Historical Statistics of the United States, Colonial Times to 1970* (1975).

Reserve Board also discouraged economic growth when in 1931 it belatedly reacted to excessive stock market speculation and corporate debt by raising interest rates. As consumer demand continued to slacken, industrialists had no alternative but to disregard promises to sustain output; instead, they cut production and laid off workers.

"We are going through a period when character and courage are on trial," declared Hoover, "where the very faith that is within us is under test." Yet investors continued to lose confidence in the nation's financial institutions, a circumstance aggravated by the collapse of the European credit system. When Hoover declared a one-year moratorium on the collection of German and Austrian war debts in 1931, several European nations sought to rescue their weakening currencies by taking them off the gold standard. This development led foreign investors to sell off U.S. equities for more valuable gold. In turn, the withdrawal of funds from New York money markets hurt the U.S. financial system. By 1932, nearly six thousand banks with assets of $4 billion were insolvent.

Ironically, large manufacturers and retailers of household consumer items and foodstuffs avoided financial disaster after 1929. Yet these businesses were unable to compensate for the slide of heavy-industry and agricultural components. By 1932 the market downturn had become known as the Great Depression, and the nation's banking and industrial sectors lay in ruins. Statistics told the grim story: overall investment plummeted by almost 90 percent, exports dropped to a third of their former level, farm receipts sank by nearly 60 percent, and the gross national product fell by nearly half. As more than 100,000 companies went into bankruptcy, industries like auto manufacturing and construction functioned at below one-fourth their former capacities. Meanwhile, the Federal Farm Board had been unable to stop the slide in agricultural prices and had lost $500 million.

The human effects of the Depression were devastating. By the end of 1932, average wages had declined by over 40 percent and the unemployment rate was surging toward 25 percent: joblessness in single-industry cities such as Akron and Toledo reached a paralyzing 60 to 80 percent. As one-third of the nation sank into poverty, a Chicago journalist described "a crowd of some fifty men fighting over a barrel of garbage." During one year alone, New York City apartment landlords evicted 200,000 families. At least 1 million transients, one-fifth of them children, were roaming the nation's highways, railroad yards, and migrant camps. Residents of big-city shantytowns sarcastically

EXHIBIT **5-2 U.S. UNEMPLOYMENT, 1929–1932**
(PERCENTAGE OF CIVILIAN LABOR FORCE)

1929	3.2
1930	8.7
1931	15.9
1932	23.6

Source: *Historical Statistics of the United States, Colonial Times to 1970* (1975).

referred to their settlements as "Hoovervilles"; newspapers used to cover sleeping vagrants were known as "Hoover blankets."

As breadlines and soup kitchens became a mainstay of urban life, the Great Depression left lasting scars. Fear, noted one magazine writer, had become "the dominant emotion of contemporary America—fear of losing one's job, fear of reduced salary or wages, fear of eventual destitution and want." Although employment no longer was part of the natural order of life, jobless workers often saw their plight as a sign of individual failure. Economic dependence forced young couples to postpone weddings and led to a dramatic drop in marriage rates. As children became an added burden, contraceptive sales boomed and birth rates sank to the lowest point in the nation's history. Meanwhile, the International Apple Shippers' Association supplied produce on credit to veterans to sell on street corners for five cents apiece; such salespeople were not classified as unemployed.

THE BURDENS OF ECONOMIC HARDSHIP

The financial catastrophe was particularly harsh for people who already led a marginal existence. In urban immigrant enclaves, the crisis exhausted the informal ethnic welfare and religious networks built up during prosperity. Depression conditions pushed more than half the Mexican American population of the Southwest to the cities. Fearing increased job competition, the Department of Labor endorsed the deportation of illegal immigrants. In Texas, authorities extended the sweep to all Mexican laborers while Colorado declared martial law and turned away Mexican job seekers at state borders. Police roundups in Los Angeles forced members of the nation's largest Chicano community, including U.S. citizens, to flee the country. With support from the American Federation of Labor (AFL) and the American Legion, moreover, midwestern state officials "repatriated" 600,000 people—half the area's Mexican community—by providing mandatory train tickets to the southern border.

Economic pressures further compromised the welfare of American Indians. According to a 1928 federal report, 37 percent of Native American children normally died before the age of three. Among American Indians,

84 percent earned less than $200 a year before the Depression, which cut income by another 25 percent. Such poverty and a 36 percent illiteracy rate encouraged exploitation by the Bureau of Indian Affairs (BIA) and other federal officials. In 1930, for example, the Federal Power Commission permitted Montana utility interests to develop a hydroelectric site on the Flathead Indian Reservation without just compensation to Native residents. Two years later, Senate investigators reported that the Pueblo Lands Board had colluded with speculators, railroad interests, and cattle companies to under-assess New Mexico tribal lands.

By 1934, Native American landholdings had dwindled to barely one-third of their size at the time of the Dawes Act in the 1880s. Government agencies also assaulted tribal cultures by abolishing "pagan" rituals and transporting male students to distant boarding schools for "Americanization." Only at the insistence of reformer John Collier were young men permitted to leave the academies to participate in traditional religious rites.

The Great Depression played havoc with the lives of African Americans, whose unemployment rate was triple that of whites. Blacks fared most poorly in the rural South, where nearly half lived. As cotton prices sank to the lowest levels in forty years, banks and insurance companies foreclosed one-third of the region's cotton farms. A government report described the standard of living among southern sharecroppers and tenants as "below any level of decency." As part of the southern racial caste system, state laws excluded blacks from jury service, while poll taxes, literacy tests, and white primaries kept African Americans from voting. Outside the legal system, strict rules of conduct prevented race mixing. Southern whites addressed blacks by first names, insisted that African American servants or messengers use the rear door, and strictly prohibited physical contact between black men and white women.

Southern communities enforced racial segregation through intimidation, violence, and lynching. National attention focused on Scottsboro, Alabama, in 1931 when local authorities convicted nine African American teenagers on scant evidence of raping two white female prostitutes on a freight train. As eight of the defendants faced death penalties, the Communist Party took up the case—leading to a reversal by the U.S. Supreme Court, which ruled that the defendants had been denied a fair trial because African Americans were excluded from Alabama juries. In another victory, civil rights activists joined the AFL in blocking the Supreme Court nomination of white supremacist and antilabor judge John J. Parker.

DEPRESSION PROTEST

The collapse of the economy compelled artists, writers, and intellectuals to address the suffering of ordinary people. *Tobacco Road* (1932), Erskine Caldwell's best-selling novel and a Broadway play, universalized the plight of Georgia sharecroppers. Political dramas such as Clifford Odets's *Waiting for Lefty* (1935) captured audience sympathies for the labor movement. Meanwhile, authors like Sidney Hook, George Soule, and Stuart Chase produced widely read books that dissected the weaknesses of the capitalist economy. The Communist Party attracted a large number of intellectuals by advocating the use of collective discipline in overcoming "class privilege." Marxist literary critics such as Edmund Wilson, Granville Hicks, and Michael Gold argued that writers could participate in the struggle to create a workers' state if they abandoned "bourgeois" individualism and adapted their work to the class conflict.

Through "proletarian" novels such as Jack Conroy's *The Disinherited* (1933) and Robert Cantwell's *Land of Plenty* (1934), politically committed writers tied accounts of unemployed drifters, ethnic slum-dwellers, and striking workers to "class conscious" political action. In one variant of the genre, socialist James T. Farrell portrayed the epic hopes and struggles of a single family of poor Irish Catholics in the *Studs Lonigan* trilogy (1936). Another massive work, John Dos Passos's *U.S.A.* (1930–1936), incorporated social realism and radical consciousness into a modernist collage of historical and fictional events. Feminist authors such as Tillie Olsen and Meridel Le Sueur discarded sentimental gender conventions to recount the particular burdens that the Depression placed on working-class women.

Such sentiments influenced the content of Hollywood motion pictures in the early years of sound. *King Kong* (1933), which opened with a woman standing on a breadline, drew huge audiences with its depiction of the destruction of the Empire State Building, a symbol of New Era prosperity. Gangster films such as *Public Enemy* (1931) and *Little Caesar* (1930) featured working-class actors like James Cagney and Edward G. Robinson, who induced viewers' sympathy for characters who struggled to overcome adversity. In *I Am a Fugitive from a Chain Gang* (1932), Paul Muni portrayed an innocent man victimized by a corrupt court system. Films with hardened actresses like Marlene Dietrich and Jean Harlow questioned sexual propriety and moral hypocrisy. Meanwhile, comic performers like W. C. Fields, Mae West, and the Marx Brothers starred in hilarious parodies of middle-class pretensions.

To convey the struggles of working-class life, radical writers adopted a documentary style of journalism. When the Communist Party led a strike of nearly 300,000 textile workers in the North Carolina and Tennessee hill country, prominent literary figures such as Edmund Wilson, Theodore Dreiser, and John Dos Passos reported on the bleak working conditions, squalid housing, and antilabor violence of the company mill towns. Similar dispatches detailed the repressive campaign against protesting miners in the Kentucky coal fields as well as Henry Ford's use of extralegal violence against union activists in the automobile industry.

In large cities like New York and Chicago, the Communist Party mounted neighborhood rent strikes, staged massive hunger marches, and formed unemployed councils to gain benefits for destitute families. In the rural South and

West, the party focused on marginalized racial and ethnic minorities. Operating in a white supremacy state with a violent Ku Klux Klan, Communists organized the biracial Alabama Sharecroppers Union (ASU), only to face repeated attacks by local deputies. In Arkansas, the Socialist Party recruited 25,000 members into the racially integrated Southern Tenant Farmers Union (STFU). Radicals in California supported Mexican American and Filipino farmworkers and won sporadic union victories through the use of roving pickets.

Hard times also propelled small producers and retailers to political activism. Hurt by the fall of commodity prices, midwestern growers formed the militant Farmers Holiday Association in 1932. The movement's first protest came in Iowa, where angry dairy farmers barricaded highways to stop underpriced milk from getting to market. Meanwhile, the National Farmers Union vainly pressed Congress for cost-of-production guarantees. Independent merchants turned to politics by organizing against the chain stores, which they condemned as a product of Wall Street speculation and the cause of the Depression. In 1930, local retailers mounted 400 "trade-at-home" campaigns. By 1931, ten states had taxed chain outlets and Congress was saturated with proposals to outlaw chain price-cutting.

The Depression dramatically increased populist suspicion of political and financial elites. In 1932 Texas Democrat Wright Patman demanded that Congress consider the impeachment of Treasury Secretary Andrew Mellon, accused of advancing favors to a petroleum conglomerate. The controversy ended only when President Hoover appointed Mellon as ambassador to Great Britain. Meanwhile, auditors revealed that Swedish entrepreneur Ivar Krueger, who had shot himself in Paris, had forged $100 million in bonds sold to investment houses in the United States. The Senate soon opened an inquiry into foreign bond and security transactions. As popular radio commentator Charles E. Coughlin, a Michigan Roman Catholic priest, attacked "banksters," Hoover demanded an investigation of the stock exchange. A resulting Senate inquiry exposed insider trading and fraud as well as shady business practices in the faltering public utility field.

HOOVER'S SEARCH FOR RECOVERY

As unemployment, homelessness, and hunger overwhelmed the capacities of private charities and public agencies, Hoover became the first president in U.S. history to respond to an economic emergency with federal assistance. He began in 1931 by asking the newly elected Democratic Congress for $2.25 billion for public works, the most costly domestic program to that time. Contractors started work on a massive dam on the Colorado River—a project soon named for the president. Desperate to revive the economy before the next election, Hoover increased the credit supply by permitting the government to use com-

EXHIBIT **5-3 HOOVER'S RECOVERY PROGRAM**

1930	Agricultural commodity stabilization corporations created by Federal Farm Board
1931	$2.25 billion public works program
1932	Federal Home Loan Bank Act (created Federal Home Mortgage Board)
	Emergency and Relief Construction Act ($2.3 billion in public works and relief loans to states)
	Reconstruction Finance Corporation (RFC), $2 billion capitalization
	Norris–La Guardia Anti-Injunction Act

mercial paper instead of gold to back Treasury certificates. He signed the Federal Home Loan Bank Act, which created a central board in Washington to fund twelve regional banks offering loans to distressed mortgage lenders. To please industrial workers, Hoover agreed to the Norris–La Guardia Act of 1932, thereby fulfilling organized labor's historic desire to outlaw court injunctions against strikes, boycotts, and union picketing.

The president's recovery plan centered on the Reconstruction Finance Corporation (RFC), the first federal agency to fight an economic depression. Initially funded in 1932 at $500 million, the RFC was authorized to borrow $2 billion in federal money to provide emergency loans to financial institutions, railroads, and farm mortgage associations. At the insistence of congressional Democrats, the corporation received permission to loan nearly another $2 billion to local and state governments for public works and relief.

The RFC demonstrated that the White House had abandoned the laissez-faire or noninterventionist approach to government activism. Yet the administration's policies failed to stimulate economic recovery. Insisting that investor morale depended upon balanced budgets and government fiscal integrity, Hoover retreated into isolation. "No president must ever admit he has been wrong," he confided. Ruling out further spending, Hoover vetoed Senator George W. Norris's popular bill to build government power facilities on the Tennessee River. He also rejected a program of industrial stabilization and economic coordination proposed by General Electric president Gerard Swope. The Swope Plan sought to give federally supervised trade associations the power to fix prices, control production, and regulate business practices. It also included a provision for federal old-age, life, and unemployment insurance. Yet Hoover objected that excessive government power would lead to a permanent socialist bureaucracy.

The president's limited government philosophy led him to oppose all schemes for direct federal relief. Indeed, the RFC spent only 10 percent of the funding earmarked for state aid to the needy. Clinging to traditional notions of Anglo-Protestant personal accountability, the White House warned that direct help to the jobless would invite bureaucratic control and assure

Fiorello H. La Guardia (1882–1947)

Fiorello La Guardia was a short and stocky man with a loud voice. His mother was Jewish, and his father was an Italian American Protestant. La Guardia spoke six foreign languages. He broke into politics as a Theodore Roosevelt Progressive. To win support for a campaign to enter

Congress, the new politician offered free legal services to immigrant pushcart peddlers, delivery men, and shopkeepers. La Guardia mobilized letter carriers and garment workers and pulled flophouse voters out of bed before Tammany Hall Democrats were awake on Election Day. He won the Italian-Jewish district of East Harlem by 247 votes and went to Washington in 1916 as a Republican.

La Guardia's constituents hailed from southern and eastern European villages with few individualistic traditions. Victimized by a dehumanizing industrial system in America, they sought government assistance. As an urban evangelist of the 1920s, La Guardia agitated for old-age pensions, unemployment insurance, shorter workdays, workers' compensation, and laws against child labor. He also campaigned against high prices levied by corporate middlemen. Rising to speak during a House debate about rising profits in the meat industry, La Guardia pulled from his pocket a lamb chop, then a steak, then a tiny roast. "What workman's family can afford to pay three dollars for a roast of this size?" he screamed.

The fiery Republican was not a disciplined party member or a cheerleader for the celebrated New Era. Instead, he displayed a streetwise in-

bankruptcy of the Treasury. Hoover's experiences as European relief administrator and coordinator for the Mississippi Flood emergency had strengthened a sincere belief in voluntarism and local control. Yet the president appeared to be oblivious to the suffering caused by the Depression. The administration encountered additional criticism when it insisted on raising taxes to offset government spending, a strategy that depleted potential investment capital and purchasing power.

stinct for detecting unwarranted privilege. By 1923 La Guardia had joined rural progressives in denouncing government friendliness toward corporate monopoly and in opposing high tariffs, antilabor injunctions, and tax benefits for the wealthy. La Guardia led the House attack on President Coolidge's plan to sell the Muscle Shoals Dam to Henry Ford and joined with Senator Norris to campaign for public power. He supported Senator Borah's opposition to military occupation of Nicaragua, and demanded the impeachment of treasury secretary Andrew Mellon. "I would rather be right than regular," he once explained.

Republican House leaders stripped La Guardia of all committee assignments in 1924. He attended the Progressive Party convention that year and rose to tell La Follette's followers that "I speak for Avenue A and 116th Street, instead of Broad and Wall." Denied the Republican renomination for his House seat, he was returned to Congress by Progressive and Socialist party ballots. Yet La Guardia broke with the purity concerns of many progressive reformers when he ridiculed federal censorship of the movies and bitterly attacked immigration restriction legislation. He also demonstrated ethnic resentment toward Prohibition by manufacturing beer in his capitol office and defying police to arrest him.

La Guardia's unique contribution was his understanding that the immigrant working class of the large cities constituted a vital component of a new coalition for reform. The crowning achievement of his congressional career was coauthorship of the Norris–La Guardia Act of 1932, which banned the use of injunctions to prevent strikes and abolished "yellow dog" contracts that obligated workers to shun unions.

As Hoover prepared for reelection during the summer of 1932, over 15,000 unemployed World War I veterans marched on Washington, D.C., as part of the Bonus Expeditionary Force (BEF). The protesters hoped to convince the Senate to approve a bill authorizing immediate payment of a veterans' bonus scheduled for 1945. When the proposal was rejected, two thousand marchers remained at their shantytown on government property at Anacostia Flats. After clashes killed two veterans and two police officers,

The Bonus Expeditionary Force, dispersed by federal troops in Washington, D.C., in the summer of 1932.

Hoover directed the Army to use restrained methods to disassemble the encampment. Chief of Staff Douglas MacArthur ignored presidential orders and deployed tanks, tear gas, infantry, cavalry, and machine guns to forcibly eject the veterans and burn the settlement. The routing of the Bonus Army and the placement of locks on White House gates gave the impression that the embattled Hoover had become a prisoner of the presidency.

THE ELECTION OF 1932

Sensing victory at the polls, the Democratic Party turned to New York's Franklin Delano Roosevelt for the presidential nomination. A distant cousin of Theodore, the candidate had graduated from exclusive Groton and Harvard, studied law at Columbia, served as assistant secretary of the Navy in Woodrow Wilson's administration, and was the unsuccessful Democratic candidate for vice president in 1920. The following year, Franklin Roosevelt suffered an attack of poliomyelitis; he remained unable to walk without assis-

EXHIBIT **5-4**   **ELECTION OF 1932**

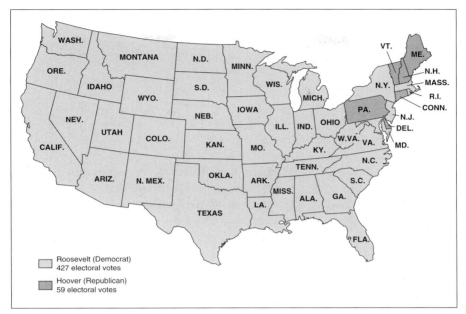

Roosevelt (Democrat)
427 electoral votes

Hoover (Republican)
59 electoral votes

tance for the rest of his life, although he disguised this condition in public. After returning to political life, Roosevelt twice won election as governor of New York. As a progressive, Roosevelt sponsored unemployment relief, labor and banking reform, state hydroelectric power, and conservation measures. He won the 1932 presidential nomination on the third ballot.

The Democratic platform called for direct federal relief for the unemployed, but demanded a 25 percent cut in federal spending. To satisfy fiscal conservatives, the party proposed to repeal Prohibition and balance the federal budget with revenue from the sale of liquor. Yet Roosevelt pinned his quest for the presidency on the need for "bold persistent experimentation" in behalf of the "forgotten man at the bottom of the economic pyramid." Breaking precedent, he flew to the Chicago party convention to accept the nomination personally. "I pledge you," he told the delegates, "I pledge myself, to a new deal for the American people." Assuring the business community that he would restore market vitality, Roosevelt promised that the New Deal would embrace a "changed concept of the duty and responsibility of government toward economic life." To demonstrate his belief in planning by professionals, the candidate announced that he would use a "brains trust" of university experts for advice on public policy.

Hoover responded to the Democratic campaign by warning that his opponent's low-tariff policies would guarantee that "the grass will grow in the streets of a hundred cities" and "weeds will overrun the fields of a million

Owen D. Young *(1874–1962)*

As the Democratic Party searched for a candidate to contest Herbert Hoover for the presidency in 1932, considerable support emerged for Owen Young, one of the country's top industrial and financial figures. Born on a farm in upstate New York, Young attended a one-room school-

house before graduating from St. Lawrence University in 1894. He hoped to enter Harvard Law School but settled on attending Boston University when school officials in Cambridge discouraged his plans to attend classes while working part-time. After graduation Young joined a Boston law firm and cultivated clients in the burgeoning electric industry. These contacts led to an offer to join General Electric as general counsel and vice president in 1913.

As a corporate attorney, Young assumed responsibility for negotiating patent disputes and labor conflicts. The young vice president maintained that worker unrest extended beyond wage and hour issues to intangible psychological concerns such as employee powerlessness. An influential figure in the emerging fields of industrial and public relations, he was named chair of General Electric's board of directors in 1922.

By the mid-decade, Young not only presided over the largest electric products corporation in the world but also sat on the board of powerful General Motors. He also served as executive committee chair for the Radio Corporation of America (RCA), which he had organized in

farms." Although Roosevelt never presented a clear program to end the Depression and even criticized his rival's public spending, voters responded to the New Yorker's warmth, assertiveness, and sense of experiment. Described by contemporary reports as less rebellious than drifting, the electorate rejected the apparent impotence of Republican leadership and gave Roosevelt 57 percent of the popular tally. Hoover carried only six states. Socialist Norman Thomas, a Presbyterian minister, received nearly 900,000 votes.

1919 by pooling radio technologies developed by several companies. With the progressive Gerard Swope as its president and with Young as its chair, General Electric increased its emphasis on consumer sales of large appliances instead of on capital goods for industry. Young stressed a "new capitalism" that fostered cooperation with both government and labor and that reflected private industry's need to cultivate long-range goodwill. He expanded employee profit sharing, pensions, and life and unemployment insurance. Corporate managers, he insisted, had become trustees for workers, consumers, and the general public.

Young's great moment came in 1927 when he delivered the dedication address for Harvard University's expanded Graduate School of Business. In a widely quoted speech, the industrial titan declared that management finally had taken its place as a profession. Business schools would provide the data for enlightened decision making and rational policy, he proclaimed, while trade associations would shape corporate morality by enabling administrators to honor ideals of service and social responsibility. The next year Young told college students that the New Era would usher in "a world of new experiment" that would ensure comfort and economic advancement for consumers as well as a "cultural wage" to permit intellectual self-development among workers.

The author of the Young Plan for European financial recovery and an advocate of efforts to enhance Depression purchasing power at home, Owen Young personified the consistency between progressive ideals and a consumer-oriented management class.

THE NEW DEAL

As Franklin Roosevelt prepared to assume the presidency, thousands of financial institutions verged upon bankruptcy; depositors engaged in bank "runs" to withdraw savings before they were lost. The disaster prompted twenty-nine states to legislate banking moratoriums that restricted the removal of assets. Three midwestern states also suspended farm mortgage foreclosures. "It is

EXHIBIT **5-5   FIRST ONE HUNDRED DAYS OF THE NEW DEAL (MARCH–JUNE 1933)**

- Abandonment of Gold Standard by Executive Action
- Civil Conservation Corps Reforestation Relief Act (created CCC—Civilian Conservation Corps)
- Federal Emergency Relief Act (created FERA—Federal Employment Relief Administration)
- Agricultural Adjustment Act (created AAA—Agricultural Adjustment Administration)
- Tennessee Valley Authority Act (created TVA—Tennessee Valley Authority)
- Federal Securities Act
- Home Owners Refinancing Act (created HOLC—Home Owners Loan Corporation)
- Glass-Steagall Banking Act
- Farm Credit Act (created FCA—Farm Credit Administration)
- National Industrial Recovery Act (created NRA—National Recovery Administration—and PWA—Public Works Administration)

impossible to contemplate the extent of the human suffering and the social consequences of a denial of currency and credit," a New York financier privately warned the president-elect. Roosevelt directly responded to the crisis in his inaugural address. "The only thing we have to fear is fear itself—nameless, unreasoning, unjustified terror," he declared. He promised to ask for "broad executive power to urge war against the emergency, as great as the power that would be given to me if we were in fact invaded by a foreign foe."

Stabilizing the nation's banks, Roosevelt declared a four-day national bank "holiday" that prohibited all financial transactions and exports of gold and silver. He then convened a special session of Congress, which responded immediately with the Emergency Banking Act of 1933. This law gave the White House extraordinary powers to regulate currency and authorized the Treasury to inspect banks and issue licenses and federal loans to sound institutions. Eight days after the inauguration, the president went on radio to deliver his first "fireside chat." Roosevelt assured 60 million listeners that it was safe to return savings to the reorganized banks, and deposits rapidly exceeded withdrawals. "Capitalism was saved in eight days," presidential adviser Raymond Moley subsequently observed. The Glass-Steagall Act of 1933 subsequently separated commercial from investment banking, expanded Federal Reserve regulations on financial speculation, and created the Federal Deposit Insurance Corporation (FDIC) to insure bank deposits of $5,000 or less.

By using government power to remedy defects in the private market, Roosevelt hoped to restore deflated prices, stimulate production, and speed recovery. Weeks after taking office, the president announced that he had taken the country off the gold standard by prohibiting gold exports. A year later, he received the authority to set the price of gold and devalue the dollar through

EXHIBIT **5-6   THE NEW DEAL, 1934**

- Gold Reserve Act
- Farm Mortgage Refinancing Act (created FFMC—Federal Farm Mortgage Corporation)
- Securities Exchange Act (created SEC—Securities and Exchange Commission)
- Communications Act (created FCC—Federal Communications Commission)
- Frazier-Lemke Farm Bankruptcy Act
- National Housing Act (created FHA—Federal Housing Authority)

---

the Gold Reserve Act. The Silver Purchase Act allowed the Treasury to establish a bimetal basis for the currency, a long-standing demand of monetary radicals. The New Deal also initiated stock market reform through the Securities Act of 1933, which required brokers to file investment information with the Federal Trade Commission (FTC) and held company directors liable for improper practices. The next year Congress created the Securities and Exchange Commission (SEC) to regulate and license stock exchanges.

Like Hoover, Roosevelt faced a crisis in agriculture stemming from declining commodity prices. Fears of inflation had prompted the House of Representatives to reject a bill to set crop prices above the "cost of production." One day before a scheduled strike by the Farmers Holiday Association, Congress enacted the Agricultural Adjustment Act of 1933. The law established government price supports to ensure prices for basic commodities, a guarantee that farm prices would maintain the same ratio to nonfarm prices as they had in the boom years of 1909 to 1914. To deal with overproduction, the bill created the Agricultural Adjustment Administration (AAA), which awarded subsidies to farmers in return for agreements to limit cultivated acreage, an arrangement financed by a processing tax on each producer's surplus.

"Kill every third pig or plow every third row under," proclaimed the AAA. The agency oversaw the slaughter of 6 million pigs and destruction of one-fourth of the nation's cotton crop in its first year of existence. Nevertheless, farmers remained adamant about the need for low-interest capital. Seeking to placate this important constituency, the administration created the Commodity Credit Corporation to loan money to growers against the value of crops taken out of production. Another bureau, the Farm Credit Administration (FCA), consolidated all federal agencies dealing with agricultural loans and refinanced one-fifth of all farm mortgages. By 1935, basic crop prices and aggregate farm income had doubled, while agricultural debt dropped by $2 billion.

Responding to the crisis induced by one thousand residential mortgage bankruptcies a day, Congress created the Home Owners Loan Corporation (HOLC) in 1933. The agency issued government bonds to refinance over 1 million mortgages, rescuing 10 percent of the nation's owner-occupied houses from default or foreclosure. To aid the faltering home construction industry,

Congress established federal programs to insure long-term mortgages, lower down-payment requirements, and regulate home loan interest rates. Government activism in the housing field encouraged the spread of single-family residences in suburban communities, where federal underwriters believed financial risk was minimal.

RELIEF, RECOVERY, AND REGULATION

In contrast to his predecessor, Roosevelt had promised direct federal relief to the unemployed. One of the administration's first accomplishments was to get Congress to create the Federal Employment Relief Administration (FERA). Under director Harry L. Hopkins, the agency quickly spent $4 billion on cash stipends and work programs to assist more than 20 million people and dispatched another $500 million for state and local relief. Not satisfied, Roosevelt placed Hopkins in charge of a second agency, the Civil Works Administration (CWA), which spent another billion dollars to hire millions of workers. Still another program, the Civilian Conservation Corps (CCC), combined employment relief and conservation principles by putting 2.5 million young men to work in tasks ranging from reforestation and flood control to range improvement and soil erosion prevention. Structured along military lines, the popular corps stressed discipline, outdoor experience, and national service.

A second conservation agency, the Tennessee Valley Authority (TVA), organized a public power project embracing a seven-state river basin. First promoted by Nebraska senator George W. Norris and opposed by Hoover, the massive undertaking coordinated the construction of nine government dams for flood control and the provision of cheap hydroelectric power for fertilizer and explosives factories. An independent public corporation, the TVA used resource experts to promote soil conservation and reforestation. Although private utilities opposed the project, the experiment showed that government-generated electric power could stimulate private investment, agricultural development, and consumption. Under its auspices, thousands of rural homesteads became electric appliance customers. The TVA also provided a yardstick for setting reasonable and fair utility rates.

Roosevelt's most difficult task centered on restoration of industrial prosperity. When the business community opposed a Senate bill to reduce unemployment by legislating a 30-hour week, the White House urged Congress to pass a substitute measure that would raise prices, end destructive competition, and introduce industry-wide planning. The heart of the law freed corporations from antitrust provisions and created the National Recovery Administration (NRA) to supervise the enforcement of self-regulating industrial codes. These agreements allowed competing companies to set common marketing and labor policies. Section 7(a) of the legislation extended collective bargaining rights and the 40-hour week to approximately half the nation's workforce. Assigning blue eagle placards to participating businesses, the recovery program won massive publicity through huge parades and media extravaganzas.

THE LABOR QUESTION

Despite the extensive scope of the New Deal, Roosevelt's impatience with the slow pace of recovery prompted him to turn in 1935 to a "second New Deal" of massive public works and employment programs. The Works Progress Administration (WPA) was designed to stimulate purchasing power through the creation of jobs. Under its terms, state and local governments were required to use strict means and eligibility tests, including a 16 percent ceiling on positions for women, to provide public sector employment at wages purposely set below prevailing rates. Careful not to compete with the private market, the WPA rebuilt a decaying national infrastructure of highways, bridges, sewers, airports, and post offices. It also provided the first public sponsorship of the arts by hiring dramatists, writers, musicians, and artists. Under its wing, the National Youth Administration (NYA) offered jobs, training, citizenship classes, and educational stipends to unemployed youth. By 1942, the largest and most expensive jobs program in history had put 7 million people to work.

Shortly after enactment of the WPA, the NRA collapsed—a victim of competing interest groups. As consumers objected to high prices set in NRA codes, union leaders contended that employers were evading required labor guarantees. Meanwhile, corporate officials complained of excessive regulation of wages and prices, and small businesses charged that powerful firms dominated the code authorities. Such contention became moot when the Supreme Court ruled in the *Schecter* case (1935) that the NRA involved an improper transfer of legislative power from Congress to the president and an unconstitutional attempt to regulate industry within individual states. Infuriated, Roosevelt snapped that "we have been relegated to a horse and buggy definition of interstate commerce." Six months later, the Court invalidated the AAA when it concluded that the processing tax on farmers involved an improper extension of government authority.

The eradication of the NRA left labor unions with no collective bargaining rights in a period of increased worker discontent. Low wages, layoffs, and speedups had led to another walkout of mill employees in the southern textile industry. On the West Coast, militant maritime workers had struck the docks and mounted a general strike in San Francisco. In southern California, Communist organizers had organized a protest of Mexican American field workers, only to be defeated when growers formed the Associated Farmers and resorted to vigilante violence and police repression. Employees in the mass-production industries had benefited from 1920s welfare capitalism; but as

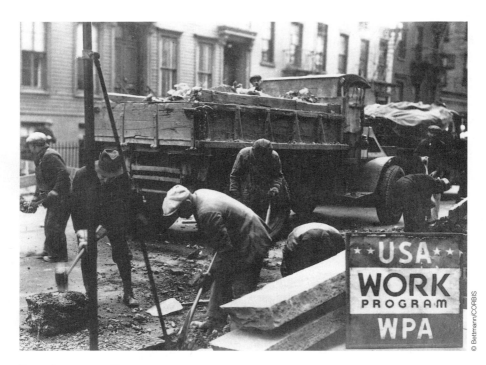

The WPA in action. The Works Progress Administration employed more than 7 million Americans between 1935 and 1942.

management cut back on benefits, workers looked to the labor movement for help. Accustomed to working with a diversity of ethnic and racial groups, the rank and file responded positively when labor activists said that Roosevelt wanted them to join unions to assist recovery. By 1935, more than 1,700 labor organizations were actively recruiting at processing plants, mills, and mass-production factories.

Seeking industrial harmony and enhanced purchasing power of the work-force through collective bargaining, Roosevelt supported New York Senator Robert Wagner's bill to outlaw "unfair labor practices" as "must legislation." Considered the Magna Carta of the union movement, the National Labor Relations Act of 1935 upheld the right of workers to join labor organizations and to bargain collectively through representatives of their own choosing. The law bound employers to recognize duly elected union agents and forbade them from firing workers for union organizing. It also prohibited company unions, employer blacklists, the use of labor spies, and other union-busting practices. A National Labor Relations Board (NLRB) was empowered to supervise bar-gaining elections, investigate unfair employer practices, issue cease and desist orders, and review arbitrary firings. Although the statute did not initially apply

EXHIBIT **5-7** **THE NEW DEAL, 1935**

- Emergency Relief Appropriation Act (created WPA—Works Progress Administration)
- Soil Conservation Act (created Soil Conservation Service)
- Resettlement Administration (RA), created by executive order
- Rural Electrification Administration (REA), created by executive order
- National Youth Administration (NYA), created by executive order
- National Labor Relations Act (created NLRB—National Labor Relations Board)
- Social Security Act
- Banking Act of 1935 (created Open Market Committee of Federal Reserve System)
- Public Utility Holding Company Act
- Frazier-Lemke Mortgage Moratorium Act
- Wealth Tax Act

to employees in agriculture, domestic service, public employment, or intrastate commerce, it initiated a historic shift in favor of workers' rights.

Empowered by passage of the Wagner Act, the AFL sanctioned United Mine Workers President John L. Lewis to form a Committee for Industrial Organizations (CIO), later known as the Congress of Industrial Organizations, to recruit mass-production employees. Instead of enrolling members along craft lines, the CIO organized all the workers in each industry. The new unions found an enthusiastic reception among a broad following of European ethnics, southern whites, African Americans, Hispanics, and women. Responding directly to shop-floor grievances and insisting on workplace rights, industrial unions provided workers with a vital ally against the arbitrary policies of corporate management.

GRASSROOTS RADICALS

Despite strides toward recovery, Roosevelt's New Deal faced a variety of critics. In Minnesota, Governor Floyd Olson, a self-described radical who headed the Farmer-Labor Party, fashioned a militant image by threatening state legislators with martial law if they failed to pass a farm mortgage relief bill. Governor Philip La Follette, who organized Wisconsin's Progressive Party, attracted widespread publicity by enacting the nation's first unemployment insurance. In California, socialist Upton Sinclair ran for governor as a Democrat in 1934, although state business leaders defeated the candidate's attempt to win the election on an "end poverty" platform.

One of the most extreme attacks on the New Deal came from monetary radical Father Charles E. Coughlin, whose weekly radio sermons reached a

Huey ("The Kingfish") Long (1893–1935)

Louisiana's Huey Long was the revered leader of the most popular rural insurgency since the Populist crusades of the 1890s. As a folk hero to poor southern farmers and villagers, Long focused on Depression issues to broaden his appeal until he appeared to threaten Franklin Roosevelt's

reelection to the White House in 1936. His earthy sarcasm and impatience with privilege created nightmares for vested interests from Baton Rouge to Washington.

Long came out of the pine-studded uplands of northern Louisiana, the home of pious Baptists with a long tradition of populism. At the age of twenty-five, he won election as state public service commissioner. Long used his power to decrease streetcar and telephone rates and to penalize Standard Oil.

He attacked the oil colossus in an effective campaign for governor in 1924, but the Ku Klux Klan's opposition denied him victory. Four years later, the brash upstart captured the populist vote with the campaign slogan, "Every Man a King," and won the governorship.

As governor, Long initiated massive highway and hospital construction, distributed free textbooks to the public schools, and set up night classes for poor whites and blacks. To finance these reforms, he resorted to deficit spending and levied heavy taxes on oil refineries. He also established an awesome patronage machine, leading the state house of

national audience of nearly 40 million listeners. An early Roosevelt supporter, Coughlin attracted a large following of lower-middle-class Catholics in northeastern and midwestern cities. Accusing the White House of ties to finance capital as well as communism, the radio priest contrasted the alleged betrayal of international bankers and industrial union leaders with the dignity of working people and independent entrepreneurs. Forming the National Union for Social Justice in 1934, Coughlin demanded that Congress replace the Federal Reserve with a publicly owned national bank.

Louisiana's Huey Long, nicknamed "The Kingfish," was the most colorful and effective New Deal opponent. Upon assuming his Senate seat in 1932, Long launched an ambitious "Share Our Wealth" scheme. Focusing on mal-

representatives to charge him with unauthorized use of state funds and to impeach him in 1929. Although the senate failed to convict Long, the populist firebrand claimed that Standard Oil had persecuted him, and he tightened control of the state. He subsequently prevailed upon the legislature to surpass local authorities by awarding the governor personal control of police and teaching appointments, the militia, the courts, election agencies, and tax-assessing bodies. Critics accused him of running a dictatorial police state that terrorized political enemies.

When Long went to Washington as a senator in 1932, he said he intended to cut the great American fortunes down to "frying size." An early supporter of Franklin Roosevelt, he turned against the National Recovery Administration's alleged threats to small business and called the president "a liar and a faker." Long argued that New Deal agricultural policies compelled rich landlords to force black tenants off the land. He also complained that congressional efforts to control public utilities were as effective as trying "to regulate a rattlesnake." Nevertheless, it was Long's "Share Our Wealth" program that received national attention. Comparing the rich to cannibals, the Louisiana populist advocated tax reform and a guaranteed income to alleviate the Depression's poor distribution of purchasing power.

By 1935 a secret poll by the Democratic Party indicated that Long might take 4 million votes as a third-party candidate in the coming presidential race. Just a month after he announced his candidacy, however, the Kingfish was assassinated as a result of a personal dispute.

distribution of wealth as the main issue before the nation, he promised to tax away all personal fortunes greater than $5 million and all yearly earnings over $1 million. Long insisted that every family should have a guaranteed income— enough to buy a $5,000 homestead, a car, and a radio. He called for pensions for the elderly and free college tuition for "worthy" youth. To bolster purchasing power, Long proposed a massive public works program, a federal minimum wage, and a 30-hour work week.

By 1935, Share Our Wealth clubs had spread across the country; there were 27,000 clubs, with a combined membership reaching into the millions. Long popularized his ideas with folksy ridicule of the rich and comical parodies of urbane New Dealers. Fashioning the slogan, "Every Man a King," he planned to run for president in 1936. Indeed, Democratic tacticians feared that Long might capture 3 or 4 million votes on a third-party ticket and throw the election into the House of Representatives. In September 1935, however, the popular senator was assassinated by the enraged relative of a Louisiana political adversary.

Populist criticism of Roosevelt centered on demands for an old-age pension system. By 1935, twenty-nine states were providing monthly payments to the elderly. Nevertheless, social security advocates such as California physician Dr. Francis E. Townsend pushed for a comprehensive federal program. Townsend argued for creation of an old-age revolving pension fund that would grant $200 a month to every retired person over the age of sixty who spent the entire sum. The Townsend Plan was to be financed by a 2 percent tax on business transactions. Townsendites insisted that their program would stimulate spending and lower unemployment by reducing the size of the labor force. Organizing along evangelical and patriotic lines, supporters gathered millions of signatures to press the White House into action.

THE WELFARE STATE

Roosevelt responded to the groundswell for old-age pensions by appointing a Committee on Economic Security, headed by Secretary of Labor Frances Perkins, the first woman to hold a cabinet office. The panel confirmed that declining death rates, a contracting economy, and smaller families had increased the dependency of the elderly. With White House backing, Congress enacted the landmark Social Security Act of 1935, providing those over the age of sixty-five with monthly federal pensions from a self-supporting federal fund. Unlike social welfare plans in other industrial nations, Roosevelt's old-age insurance depended upon a contributory system of payroll taxes on both employers and workers. The law also established the first federal unemployment insurance. Funded by a payroll levy on employers and administered by the states, the program excluded agricultural and domestic laborers.

Because old-age and unemployment insurance were modeled on contributory plans in the private sector, their accompanying benefits were viewed as legitimate entitlements for workers. In contrast, Aid to Dependent Children (ADC), another social security plan, treated poor women and mothers as social dependents rather than deserving recipients. Designed by social work professionals in the Children's Bureau, ADC provided federal matching funds to states to continue "mother's pension" payments to single women who maintained "suitable homes." Because planners underestimated the number of households headed by poor women, inadequate appropriations led to severe means and morals screening, and medical benefits were excluded from coverage. Nevertheless, Social Security provided public health services and med-

EXHIBIT **5-8**   **GROSS NATIONAL PRODUCT, 1933–1936**
(IN ROUNDED BILLIONS OF DOLLARS)

1933	55.6
1936	82.5

Source: *Historical Statistics of the United States, Colonial Times to 1970* (1975).

EXHIBIT **5-9**   **U.S. UNEMPLOYMENT, 1933–1936**
(PERCENTAGE OF CIVILIAN LABOR FORCE)

1933	24.9
1934	21.7
1935	20.1
1936	16.9

ical assistance to mothers and children in economically distressed areas as well as aid to physically disabled children.

The White House reacted to another populist demand—the redistribution of income—by calling for enactment of a wealth tax, although the president quietly concurred when Congress settled on a minor revenue measure. Emulating Father Coughlin, Roosevelt also addressed banking reform yet agreed to a bill that simply allowed the Federal Reserve Board to set reserve requirements and oversee interest rates. The administration took a stronger stand when it backed Senator Burton K. Wheeler's legislation to regulate the electric power and natural gas industry, in which twelve companies controlled almost half the nation's energy. The Public Utility Holding Company Act of 1935 created the Federal Power Commission (FPC) to monitor interstate electric power transmissions and authorized the Federal Trade Commission to supervise natural gas rates. As its most radical feature, the act required the Securities and Exchange Commission to prohibit holding companies from controlling local energy providers through financial "pyramids" and set a five-year "death sentence" for the dissolution of firms failing to end such practices.

As the 1936 election approached, Roosevelt reached out to nonurban voters. An executive order established the Rural Electrification Administration (REA) to supply isolated communities with public power. The White House also agreed to North Dakota Representative William Lemke's controversial bill to refinance bankrupt farm mortgages. Stung by charges that agricultural production quotas had led to the eviction of 300,000 southern sharecroppers, the president set up the Resettlement Administration (RA) to relocate a small number of tenants and poor farmers in experimental homestead communities. In response to Great Plains drought and dust storms, moreover, Roosevelt lobbied for creation of the Soil Conservation Service, which dispatched agents to promote practices such as contour plowing, rotation of crops, and gully planting. Once the Supreme Court invalidated the AAA, the president approved the Soil Conservation and Domestic Allotment Act of 1936, which distributed benefit payments to growers who participated in government programs to prevent farmland erosion.

THE ELECTION OF 1936

Roosevelt's most formidable political challenge came from conservatives. After the Twenty-First Amendment repealed Prohibition in 1933, Democratic opponents of federal regulation like the DuPont family and John Raskob organized the American Liberty League. Under the leadership of Al Smith, the group solicited business support by denouncing New Deal welfare programs, high taxes, and government controls. Conservatives charged that the Roosevelt administration's minority-bloc politics were ruining the country. "The trouble with this recognition of class war," complained former Woodrow Wilson official Newton Baker, "is that it spread like a grease stain and every group . . . demands the same sort of recognition." Anti-Roosevelt sentiment among the social elite was so intense that some critics refused to utter the president's name, simply referring to him as "that man in the White House."

Although some corporate leaders cooperated with Roosevelt and participated in White House business councils, the Republican Party took up the anti-big-government cry in 1936 when it nominated Governor Alfred Landon of Kansas for the presidency. Claiming that regulated monopoly had replaced free enterprise and that the New Deal was unconstitutional, Republicans called for a balanced federal budget and transfer of relief programs to "nonpolitical" local agencies. Roosevelt adamantly rejected such criticism. Professing faith in "the capitalist system," he claimed that "the true conservative seeks to protect the system of private property and free enterprise by correcting such injustices and inequities as arise from it." Business had to be saved "from the selfish forces which ruined it," he insisted.

Incensed that two-thirds of major newspapers had endorsed Landon, Roosevelt denounced "economic royalists" who hid behind a professed defense of national interest to protect their own power. In a final campaign speech in New York, the president declared that the legions of "organized money are unanimous in their hate for me—and I welcome their hatred." If "the forces of selfishness and lust for power" had met their match in his first term, he shouted, the second term would certainly confront them with "their master." Yet the main Democratic message was that a competent and caring administration had set recovery in motion. By defining liberalism as the philosophy of government generosity, the president looked for broad support among voters, particularly in poor regions like the South, where the Depression emphasized the need for federal assistance. Roosevelt also gained vital financial and organizational support from the powerful CIO campaign lobby, Labor's Non-Partisan League.

Although the conservative *Literary Digest* predicted a Republican victory, Election Day brought a spectacular triumph for the Democrats. Registering the greatest presidential electoral majority since 1820, Roosevelt won 61 percent of the popular vote and swept every state except Maine and Vermont. William Lemke, the Union Party candidate representing supporters of Huey Long, Father Coughlin, and Dr. Townsend, received a mere 2 percent of votes cast. In Congress, the Democrats captured nearly 80 percent of the House and an even larger margin of the Senate. The White House now stood triumphant over its political adversaries. Having forged a broad electoral coalition, including southern and western farmers, urban union workers, European ethnics, middle-class liberals, the poor—and for the first time, a majority of black voters—Roosevelt Democrats hoped to extend the reform mandate to a widening circle of the nation's people.

AMERICAN HISTORY RESOURCE CENTER

To explore documents, images, audio and video clips, articles, and commentary related to the material in this chapter, visit the source collections at ushistory.wadsworth.com and and use the Search function with the following key terms:

Great Depression	Wagner Act
New Deal	Fiorello La Guardia
Social Security Act	Huey Long

RECOMMENDED READINGS

David Kennedy, *Freedom from Fear: The American People in Depression and War, 1929–1945* (1999). A broad narrative covering the social impact and political consequences of two of the twentieth century's most defining periods.

Lizabeth Cohen, *Making a New Deal: Industrial Workers in Chicago, 1919–1939* (1990). Key sections of this pioneering work explain how European ethnics and African Americans adapted to waning social resources in the early Depression.

Thomas Doherty, *Pre-Code Hollywood: Sex, Immorality, and Insurrection in American Cinema, 1930–1934* (1999). This study explores the profusion of sex, crime, scandal, and irreverent comedy in the relatively unregulated motion pictures of the early 1930s.

David Plotke, *Building a Democratic Order: Reshaping American Liberalism in the 1930s and 1940s* (1996). The author concludes that New Deal success stemmed from a mix of state regulation, political party activism, and grassroots social movements.

Additional Readings

The foundations of Herbert Hoover's presidency are outlined in Ellis W. Hawley, *The Great War and the Search for a Modern Order: A History of the American People and Their Institutions, 1917–1933* (rev. ed., 1992). Accounts placing the Republican president in the New Deal tradition include William J. Barber, *From New Era to the New Deal: Herbert Hoover, the Economists, and American Economic Policy, 1921–1933* (1985), and Alan Dawley, *Struggles for Justice: Social Responsibility and the Liberal State* (1991). Hoover's business policies are treated in Robert F. Himmelberg, *The Origins of the National Recovery Administration: Business, Government, and the Trade Association Issue, 1921–1933* (1975).

General studies of the stock market crash include Robert S. McElvaine, *The Great Depression, 1919–1941* (1984), and John A. Garraty, *The Great Depression* (1986). The appropriate sections of Peter Fearon, *War, Prosperity, and Depression: The U.S. Economy, 1917–1945* (1987), demonstrate longer economic trends that led to the collapse of the economy. See also Michael Bernstein, *The Great Depression: Delayed Recovery and Economic Change in America, 1929–1939* (1987).

Depression influence on African Americans can be found in John B. Kirby, *Black Americans in the Roosevelt Era: Liberalism and Race* (1980), and Harvard Sitkoff, *A New Deal for Blacks: The Emergence of Civil Rights as a National Issue* (1978). For southern blacks and the Communist Party, see James M. Goodman, *Stories of Scottsboro* (1994), and Robin D. G. Kelley, *Hammer and Hoe: Alabama Communists during the Great Depression* (1990). Communist involvement among farmworkers is described in Lowell K. Dyson, *Red Harvest: The Communist Party and American Farmers* (1982).

The repression of Hispanics is the subject of Abraham Hoffman, *Unwanted Mexican Americans in the Great Depression: Repatriation Pressures, 1929–1939* (1974), which can be supplemented with segments of Rodolfo Acuña, *Occupied America: A History of Chicanos* (5th ed., 2004). Excellent case studies include Sarah Deutsch, *No Separate Refuge: Culture, Class, and Gender on an Anglo-Hispanic Frontier in the American Southwest, 1880–1940* (1987), and Vicki L. Ruiz, *Cannery Women, Cannery Lives: Mexican Women, Unionization, and the California Food Processing Industry, 1930–1950* (1987).

See also portions of David Montejano, *Anglos and Mexicans in the Making of Texas, 1836–1986* (1987).

Government policy toward Native Americans is treated in Lawrence C. Kelly, *The Assault on Assimilation: John Collier and the Origins of Indian Policy Reform* (1983), and Graham D. Taylor, *The New Deal and American Indian Tribalism: The Administration of the Indian Reorganization Act, 1934–1945* (1980). For the experiences of immigrants and ethnic minorities, see the relevant segments of Ronald Takaki, *A Different Mirror: A History of Multicultural America* (1993). Descriptions of the plight of women can be found in Blanche Wiesen Cook, *Eleanor Roosevelt, Volume 1: 1884–1932* (1992), and the general works of women's history listed at the end of Chapter 6.

Socially conscious Depression art and journalism are described by William Stott, *Documentary Expression and Thirties America* (1973), while the dilemmas of intellectuals are surveyed in Richard Pells, *Radical Visions and American Dreams: Culture and Social Thought in the Depression Years* (1973). See also Terry A. Cooney, *The Rise of the New York Intellectuals: Partisan Review and Its Circle* (1986); Alexander Bloom, *Prodigal Sons: The New York Intellectuals and Their New World* (1987); and Alan Wald, *The New York Intellectuals: The Rise and Decline of the Anti-Stalinist Left from the 1930s to the 1980s* (1987). Accounts of early 1930s radicalism can be found in the relevant segments of Fraser Ottanelli, *The Communist Party of the United States: From the Depression to World War II* (1991), and Robbie Lieberman, *"My Song is My Weapon": People's Songs, American Communism, and the Politics of Culture, 1930–50* (1989). A more critical assessment appears in Harvey Klehr, *The Heyday of American Communism: The Depression Decade* (1984).

Useful overviews of the Roosevelt era include Anthony Badger, *The New Deal: The Depression Years, 1933–1940* (1989), and Wilbur J. Cohen, *The Roosevelt New Deal* (1986). Case studies of federal activism include Donald R. Brand, *Corporatism and the Rule of Law: A Study of the National Recovery Administration* (1988); Walter L. Creese, *TVA's Public Planning: The Vision, the Reality* (1990); and Richard A. Reiman, *The New Deal and American Youth: Ideas and Ideals in a Depression Decade* (1992). Government environmental activity is treated in A. L. Owen, *Conservation under FDR* (1983), while the welfare state is the focus of William R. Brock, *Welfare, Democracy, and the New Deal* (1988). See also Linda Gordon, *Pitied but not Entitled: Single Mothers and the History of Welfare, 1890–1935* (1994). Theodore Rosenof, *Patterns of Political Economy in America: The Failure to Develop a Democratic Left Synthesis, 1933–1950* (1983), explores the limits of New Deal reform.

The labor movement is the subject of Stanley Vittoz, *New Deal Labor Policy and the American Industrial Economy* (1987), and James A. Hodges, *New Deal Labor Policy and the Southern Cotton Textile Industry, 1933–1941* (1986). Labor activism is described in Robert H. Zeiger, *American Workers,*

American Unions, 1920–1985 (1986). For dockworkers, see Bruce Nelson, *Workers on the Waterfront: Seamen, Longshoremen, and Unionism in the 1930s* (1988), and Howard Kimeldorf, *Reds or Rackets? The Making of Radical and Conservative Unions on the Waterfront* (1988). The Depression's impact on the South is explored in Jack Temple Kirby, *Rural Worlds Lost: The American South, 1920–1960* (1987), and Pete Daniel, *Breaking the Land: Transformation of Cotton, Tobacco, and Rice Cultures Since 1880* (1985). For westward migration, see James N. Gregory, *American Exodus: Dust Bowl Migration and Okie Culture in California* (1989).

Theodore Saloutos, *The American Farmer and the New Deal* (1982), explores agrarian unrest. The social perspectives of independent producers are examined by Catherine McNicol Stock, *Main Street in Crisis: The Great Depression and the Old Middle Class on the Northern Plains* (1992), and David A. Horowitz, *Beyond Left and Right: Insurgency and the Establishment* (1997). Useful biographical accounts include Alan Brinkley, *Voices of Protest: Huey Long, Father Coughlin, and the Great Depression* (1982); Glen Jeansonne, *Messiah of the Masses: Huey P. Long and the Great Depression* (1992); and John E. Miller, *Governor Philip F. La Follette, the Wisconsin Progressives, and the New Deal, 1930–1939* (1982). Clyde P. Weed, *The Nemesis of Reform: The Republican Party During the New Deal* (1994), provides a detailed account of anti–New Deal politics.

DEMOCRATIC CAPITALISM AND THE LIBERAL STATE, 1937–1941

"I see one-third of a nation ill-housed, ill-clad, ill-nourished," Franklin Roosevelt declared in his second-term inaugural address. Promising to eliminate poverty and make every person the subject of government concern, the president declared that his generation had a "rendezvous with destiny." New Deal officials believed that the 1936 election landslide had given them a mandate to engage in social and economic planning to benefit needy groups and restore consumer spending. Yet Roosevelt's second term was marked by divisive controversy over the direction and extent of liberal policy. By the time the president completed his first eight years in office, attention had shifted to disturbing developments overseas.

THE SECOND TERM

Optimistic about the prospects of reform, Roosevelt proceeded to satisfy diverse constituencies. To rescue the ailing soft coal industry, the president signed the Guffey-Vinson Act of 1937, which restored the NRA's competitive codes. Responding to the steady decline of farm ownership, the White House convinced Congress to create the Farm Security Administration (FSA). The agency provided $500 million in long-term, low-interest loans to tenants, sharecroppers, and agricultural laborers. It also built health-care facilities and sanitary camps for migrant workers and regulated their wages and work hours. To address the urban housing crisis, Congress established the U.S. Housing Authority, which it authorized to extend loans to public agencies for slum clearance and the construction of low-rent housing projects.

Roosevelt's highest priority targeted structural reforms in the federal government. The president began by requesting enactment of an executive reorganization bill recommended by a special White House committee on administrative management. The proposal called for the appointment of additional

Oval Office assistants and assertion of increased presidential control over the federal agencies and civil service. Its most controversial feature required a two-thirds majority of Congress to override future executive reorganization plans. Denouncing "sycophants" and "professorial nincom-poops" who advised Roosevelt without input from others, congressional skeptics questioned the president's "dictatorial ambitions." When a diluted version of the bill finally won approval in 1939, the new Executive Office of the President did little more than dislodge control of the budget bureau from the Treasury Department.

The belated victory of White House reorganization could not disguise the fact that the administration suffered a devastating defeat over efforts to restructure the federal courts. Angered that the Supreme Court had declared the NRA and AAA unconstitutional and fearing that the Wagner Act and social security might be next, Roosevelt introduced legislation in 1937 to allow the president to appoint an additional Supreme Court justice for each judge who did not retire at age seventy. Because six Court members already had reached that age, the plan could have increased the panel's membership from nine to fifteen. Many Democrats and progressive Republicans joined conservative groups like the Committee to Uphold Constitutional Government in opposing the measure as a presidential attempt to "pack" the Court and destroy the balance of power among the branches of government. After Democrat Burton Wheeler produced a statement from Chief Justice Charles Evans Hughes that the Court had sufficient numbers to manage its caseload, a bipartisan Senate majority easily squashed the reorganization plan.

Political controversies over executive and judicial reform were intensified by increasing strife between labor and management. As industrial corporations defied the terms of the constitutionally untested Wagner Act, 500,000 workers affiliated with CIO organizing committees occupied plants and factories between 1936 and 1937 in a paralyzing series of "sit-down" strikes. Instead of mounting picket lines outside factories, workers simply stopped working inside the plants. The struggle climaxed at the General Motors plant in Flint, Michigan, when police opened fire on workers who threatened to blow up the facility. When the Democratic governor refused to execute a court injunction against the takeover, Roosevelt pressured General Motors to negotiate with the CIO's United Auto Workers. Shortly thereafter, U.S. Steel, a bitter opponent of industrial unionism, settled with the steel workers union.

Although conglomerates like General Motors and U.S. Steel reluctantly accepted collective bargaining, smaller industrialists felt threatened by union wage demands and labor's participation in hirings and promotions. When the Steel Workers Organizing Committee broadened its campaign in the Little Steel Strike of 1937, the union met fierce resistance. In a 1937 demonstration at Republic Steel in Chicago, police fired on workers and their families, killing ten. Following several other defeats in the industry, the mass-production

Strikers riot at Fisher Body plant sit-down protest, Cleveland, 1937.

unions abandoned sit-downs, which the Supreme Court ruled illegal in 1939. Nevertheless, labor's cause was vindicated by a Senate subcommittee— headed by Robert M. La Follette Jr.—which found that Republic Steel and other firms had resorted to extralegal violence to squash strike activity. By the end of the decade, CIO strength reached 2.8 million members and nearly one-fourth the nonfarm workforce belonged to labor unions.

Workplace tensions complicated administration efforts to replace the defunct National Recovery Administration (NRA) labor codes with federal wages and hours legislation. Alarmed at union organizing in the textile industry, southern Democrats insisted that higher pay scales would erase the competitive advantage afforded employers by the region's relatively modest living costs. When CIO leader Sidney Hillman joined Roosevelt aides in drafting the Fair Labor Standards Bill, rural interests delayed passage of the measure until 1938. Nevertheless, the last significant New Deal reform gradually placed industrial workers under the nation's first minimum wage (forty cents an hour) and permanent 40-hour week requirements. Banning employees between the ages of sixteen and eighteen from "hazardous" occupations, the statute fulfilled a long-standing Progressive Era goal by prohibiting goods produced by those under sixteen from interstate commerce. Another provision, affecting mainly female workers, banned home labor in the garment trades.

EXHIBIT **6-1   THE NEW DEAL, 1936–1938**

1936	Soil Conservation and Domestic Allotment Act
	Robinson-Patman Anti-Price Discrimination Act
1937	Bankhead-Jones Farm Tenant Act (created FSA—Farm Security Administration)
	Miller-Tydings Enabling Act
	Wagner-Steagall National Housing Act (created USHA—United States Housing Authority)
1938	Agricultural Adjustment Act (created FCIC—Federal Crop Insurance Corporation)
	Fair Labor Standards Act

MANAGING THE LIBERAL STATE

Pioneering government management of the peacetime economy, New Deal reform centralized federal power. Creation of the Federal Deposit Insurance Corporation, for example, inadvertently made most bank theft a federal crime under the jurisdiction of the Federal Bureau of Investigation (FBI). Highly publicized arrests of bank robbers such as John Dillinger accustomed citizens to the idea of a national police force. After the son of Charles and Anne Lindbergh was abducted and murdered in 1932, Congress gave the FBI jurisdiction over kidnapping. Roosevelt furthered government police powers when he requested secret investigations of domestic Nazis and Communists for "subversive activities." Although the Federal Communications Act of 1934 made telephone wiretapping illegal, the White House insisted that the FBI have authority to conduct electronic eavesdropping in security investigations.

The administration's most extensive use of government power centered on management of the economy. Concerned at the start of the second term that federal spending might induce inflation and inflame political opponents, the president abruptly cut public works. To White House dismay, the decision caused the most precipitous economic decline in U.S. history. As unemployment soared from 7 to 11 million in the six months after August 1937, jobless rates surpassed 50 percent for youth between the ages of sixteen and twenty. Equally demoralizing, the stock market lost two-thirds of the ground gained since the bleak days of 1933. The dismal economic climate compelled the popular Home Owners Loan Corporation to foreclose 100,000 mortgages—10 percent of those it had refinanced.

Roosevelt initially blamed the recession on the persistence of monopoly. Private enterprise was "ceasing to be free enterprise," and was "becoming a cluster of private collectivisms," he declared. Presidential rhetoric was rein-

EXHIBIT **6-2   U.S. FEDERAL BUDGET DEFICITS, 1933–1939**
(IN ROUNDED BILLIONS OF DOLLARS)

1933	2.6
1936	3.4
1939	2.8

forced by Assistant Attorney General Thurman Arnold's antitrust suits against corporate price collusion. Noting that six industrial firms accounted for almost one-fourth the profits of the nation's one thousand largest corporations, small business leaders and western Republican progressives pressed for further action. The White House responded by appointing a Temporary National Economic Committee (TNEC), although the highly touted panel failed to agree on a definition of *monopoly* and ultimately confined its recommendations to technical changes. Desperate to win the confidence of the business community, Roosevelt turned to a more conciliatory approach to restoring prosperity.

Beginning in 1938, administration leaders followed the advice of Utah banker and Federal Reserve Governor Marriner Eccles, who opposed antitrust regulation or reliance on heavy taxation to redistribute wealth. Instead, Eccles advocated fiscal management and public spending as tools encouraging full employment and sustained purchasing power. Intent on assisting potential consumers without raising taxes, New Dealers turned to deficit spending theories popularized by British economist John Maynard Keynes, who held that public expenditures could serve as a substitute for private investment during recessions. Once massive relief programs, social welfare subsidies, government credits, and increased public works had restored economic growth, enhanced tax revenues would erase remaining budget deficits.

Although New Deal fiscal policy did not extend to the states, where regressive sales and gasoline taxes cut into mass purchasing power, Roosevelt adopted the Keynesian model in 1938 by reducing corporate taxes and retreating from antitrust activity. To bolster consumer spending, Congress appropriated an extra $3 billion for the Works Progress Administration (WPA) and relief. Another project, organized through the Federal Surplus Relief Corporation and state welfare agencies, simultaneously subsidized agriculture and the poor by distributing unsold produce in the nation's first food stamp program. Furthering the administration's desire to treat producers as potential consumers, Roosevelt signed a second Agricultural Adjustment Act in 1938, guaranteeing federal price supports with Treasury funds instead of the processing tax. Through the Commodity Credit Corporation, growers received government loans if they took surplus crops off the market. The Federal Crop Insurance Corporation (FCIC) allowed farmers to use cotton or wheat to pay for insurance against natural disasters.

EXHIBIT **6-3**   **U.S. GOVERNMENT SOCIAL WELFARE SPENDING, 1933–1939**
(IN ROUNDED BILLIONS OF DOLLARS)

Year	Welfare Spending	Percentage of Gross National Product
1933	4.5	7.9
1939	9.2	10.5

Source: *Historical Statistics of the United States, Colonial Times to 1970* (1975).

EXHIBIT **6-4**   **U.S. GROSS NATIONAL PRODUCT, 1936–1939**
(IN ROUNDED BILLIONS OF DOLLARS)

1936	82.5
1939	90.5

Source: *Historical Statistics of the United States, Colonial Times to 1970* (1975).

Expanded government authority increased the federal budget from $2 billion in 1933 to $5.2 billion six years later. Ironically, the consolidation of political power was facilitated by the Supreme Court. Despite striking down the NRA and AAA, the Court had gradually been moving toward limiting liberty of contract in favor of regulatory law. Two months after Roosevelt introduced the judicial reorganization bill, justices upheld a Washington state minimum wage law by a single vote. Endorsement of the Wagner Act and the Social Security Act soon followed. As deaths and retirements allowed the president to seat liberals such as Hugo Black, Felix Frankfurter, and William O. Douglas, the Court continued to broaden its definition of the "stream of commerce" within congressional jurisdiction. Federal management of the economy in the public interest had become a matter of political choice instead of legal controversy.

DEMOCRATIC PLURALISM

Roosevelt defended public investment as an ingredient of political liberalism, a philosophy of generous welfare for the many, in contrast to conservatism, which he defined as limited government for the selfish few. Rather than painting the New Deal in radical terms, White House planners portrayed federal activity as essential to the health of the capitalist economy and a stable middle class. In the South and West, government dams, hydroelectric plants, harbor improvements, and land reclamation projects contributed to prosperity by freeing entrepreneurs from dependence on outside investors. In turn, federal mortgage financing benefited the construction trade, which experienced a tripling of annual housing starts during the Roosevelt years. White House in-

EXHIBIT **6-5**   **U.S. UNEMPLOYMENT, 1937–1941**
(AS A PERCENTAGE OF THE CIVILIAN LABOR FORCE)

1937	14.3
1938	19.0
1939	17.2
1940	14.6
1941	9.9

Source: *Historical Statistics of the United States, Colonial Times to 1970* (1975).

EXHIBIT **6-6**   **U.S. ANNUAL PER CAPITA INCOME IN DOLLARS, 1929–1941**

1929	847
1932	465
1935	567
1938	651
1941	934

Source: *Historical Statistics of the United States, Colonial Times to 1970* (1975).

terest in encouraging middle-class home ownership was demonstrated by the Resettlement Administration's erection of model "greenbelt towns" in suburban communities.

The New Deal's modest steps toward inclusion were mirrored in the moderate nature of working-class demands. Although rank-and-file members of the industrial unions were willing to follow militant leaders in confronting management at the point of production, they often agreed to contracts that stabilized relations with employers. Ultimately, seniority rights, grievance mechanisms, freedom from arbitrary firings, and improved wages and fringe benefits were more important to workers than reduction of the work week or control of production planning. Viewing union dues payments as a guarantor of fair labor practices, most employees accepted practical definitions of "business unionism." Because union officials were contractually responsible for shop discipline and the prevention of spontaneous walkouts, they insulated workers from decision making, a practice that depoliticized rank-and-file union members without weakening support for collective bargaining.

Women workers were an integral part of the industrial labor movement, both as union members and as spouses involved in movement activities. Nevertheless, as the Depression economy pushed women into the labor force, conservative social values encouraged married women to stay at home. Secretary of Labor Frances Perkins characterized women who worked "without need" as a menace to society. As 82 percent of a national poll opposed women taking jobs if their husbands worked, twenty-six state legislatures considered

Frances Perkins (1880–1965)

An interviewer frustrated by Frances Perkins's caution once described Roosevelt's labor secretary as a "colorless woman who talked as if she had swallowed a press release." Yet the first female cabinet member in U.S. history was a passionate reformer who exemplified the integration of the social service professions in government.

As a young Mount Holyoke College student at the turn of the century, Perkins was electrified by a speech made by Progressive Era social activist Florence Kelley. The experience inspired her to join the National Consumers' League and the crusade against child labor. A professional social worker who worked with Jane Addams at Hull House, Perkins lobbied for child labor laws in the New York legislature, where she met future patrons of her career such as Alfred E. Smith and Franklin D. Roosevelt.

Expanding her efforts for safer working conditions, Perkins won appointment to New York's State Industrial Commission after Smith became governor in 1918. When Roosevelt became the next state executive, he made Perkins his chief advisor on labor matters, a position that she used to urge him to enact unemployment relief following the crash of 1929. Once elected president, Roosevelt named Perkins to his cabinet.

Aware of her pioneering role, Perkins intended to be taken seriously. "Many good and intelligent women . . . dress in ways that are very at-

bills prohibiting the employment of married women. In addition to WPA quotas for women, federal law stipulated that only one family member could be hired for a civil service job.

Social attitudes assured that women workers remained in the job force in about the same proportions as in the 1920s. At the same time, women's share of professional positions dropped, and three-quarters of women professionals remained teachers and nurses. In industry, women workers earned from one-half to two-thirds the male wage scale and were concentrated in low-paying textile mills and clothing factories. Yet the willingness of women to perform menial tasks lowered their unemployment rates in comparison to men. White women also benefited when corporations replaced old machinery and con-

tractive and pretty," she once commented, "but don't invite confidence in their common sense, integrity, or sense of justice." Regularly outfitted in a plain black dress, a white bow, and trim hat, Perkins took pride in a colleague's remark that she was "the best man in the cabinet." Despite her own career, the secretary of labor denounced affluent women who sought outside employment during the Depression. "Any woman capable of supporting herself without a job," she declared in 1930, "should devote herself to motherhood and the home."

A strong advocate of unemployment relief through public works, Perkins headed Roosevelt's Committee on Economic Security in 1934. Convinced that social insurance was a "great forward step" in the "liberation of humanity," the labor secretary pushed the panel toward endorsement of a national old-age and survivor's insurance plan, a prototype of the Social Security Act. She also drew upon female colleagues from the Progressive Era children's welfare movement to write the child employment provisions of the Fair Labor Standards Act of 1938.

Perkins reacted coolly to the Wagner Act's endorsement of unionization and collective bargaining. In her own words, she "never lifted a finger" for the measure because she had "very little sympathy" for organized labor. Despite aloofness from union activists and feminists, however, Perkins helped to transform liberalism into a creed serving working people and demonstrated that women had a key role to play in public affairs.

verted skilled "male" tasks to routine "female" labor. Enhanced rates of recovery in light industry, the service sector, and clerical work further broadened opportunities for female employees.

By joining unions, voting as Democrats, and sustaining prosperity as consumers, most industrial workers felt that they were entitled to jobs and government programs regulating capitalism in the name of fairness. New Deal rhetoric buttressed this inclusiveness by welcoming southern and eastern Europeans into the national mainstream. As 1920s restriction laws reduced anxieties over the influx of "new immigrants," Democratic Party officials rewarded the electoral support of Catholic and Jewish voters with political patronage. Under Roosevelt, one of every nine government jobs went to a

EXHIBIT **6-7**   **U.S. LABOR UNION MEMBERSHIP, 1936–1940**
(IN ROUNDED MILLIONS)

1936	4.1
1938	6.1
1940	7.3

Source: *Historical Statistics of the United States, Colonial Times to 1970* (1975).

Catholic or Jew, as opposed to one of every twenty-five under Hoover. Non-Protestants also received 30 percent of the president's federal judgeships, including the Supreme Court appointment of Felix Frankfurter, a Jew.

Discrimination against Catholics and Jews persisted in elite professions, social clubs, and residential neighborhoods, but could surface anywhere: the U.S. Olympic team benched two Jewish runners in deference to Nazi Germany's hosting of the 1936 games. Nevertheless, the White House made a point of celebrating unity and ethnic diversity at home. Mastering the press conference and broadcasting sixteen "fireside chats" in eight years, President Roosevelt became the first national leader to convey the concept of multiple American faiths and a Judeo-Christian heritage. Although inclusion rarely embraced African Americans, Hispanics, or Asians by name, ethnic and cultural unity became a predominant feature of New Deal rhetoric and attracted censure by social conservatives fearing the erosion of Anglo-Protestant supremacy.

A CULTURE OF ADVERSITY AND HOPE

The Great Depression simultaneously promoted austere values and aspirations toward a better life. Following the repeal of Prohibition, eight states chose to remain dry and others adopted local option. As hard times increased anxieties over social behavior, the Narcotics Bureau initiated a highly publicized campaign against marijuana use, which tied it to crime, vice, and degeneracy. In New York City, police stepped up harassment of homosexual "deviants" in gay bars. Meanwhile, psychologists reported alarming rates of sexual impotence among unemployed men no longer serving as family breadwinners. As financial difficulties discouraged large families and contraceptive usage spread, 1930s marriage and birth rates declined—with divorce occurring twice as often as matrimony.

Despite Depression adversity, popular media continued to romanticize motherhood and home. One survey suggested that three-fifths of women college students hoped to marry within two years of graduation. Although organizations such as the League of Women Voters encouraged political involvement, little support emerged for a separate women's agenda. Instead, social feminists like Frances Perkins and Democratic Party activist Molly Dewson focused on gender-neutral issues such as public housing, abolition of child labor, federal regulation of working conditions, and Social Security entitlements for male breadwinners. Veteran activist Eleanor Roosevelt emerged as the nation's most important social justice advocate. Refashioning the ceremonial role of "first lady," the president's wife lobbied the White House to appoint more women to diplomatic posts, to promote civil rights protections, and to provide government assistance for needy African Americans, the poor, women, and children.

Struggling business enterprises also reflected hard times. Forced to compete for a shrinking consumer dollar, radio and magazine advertising highlighted insecurities over health or personal attractiveness. In the grocery trade, independent merchants competed with chain stores by offering discount prices, converting to self-service, and encouraging bulk purchases that could be stored in home refrigerators. Automobile giant General Motors sought to reinvigorate sales by announcing annual model changes. Surprisingly, Depression personal debt declined as both lenders and borrowers became extremely cautious.

The economic catastrophe encouraged popular culture entertainments that distracted Americans from mundane realities. Major radio networks broadcast a mixture of news commentaries, religion and nationality shows, "soap opera" dramas, mysteries, westerns, ethnic comedies, and variety hours to hundreds of nationwide affiliates. Swing dance bands led by personalities like Count Basie and Bennie Goodman riveted millions with live "remotes" from big-city ballrooms and night spots. To cut production costs, local radio stations hired "disc jockeys" to play recorded versions of Tin Pan Alley and Broadway favorites between advertising pitches. Popular fare ranged from upbeat morale boosters such as "On the Sunny Side of the Street" (1930) and "Pennies from Heaven" (1936) to plaintive expressions of affirmation such as "Try a Little Tenderness" (1932) and "Over the Rainbow" (1939). Sustaining hope amid adversity, broadcasting unified national speech and taste.

The motion picture industry remained the nation's primary creator of unifying myths and dreams. By 1939, nearly two-thirds of the population attended at least one movie a week. For a five- or ten-cent ticket, audiences could experience Walt Disney cartoons, Shirley Temple comedies, or children's adventures like *The Wizard of Oz* (1939). Others preferred extravagant musicals by directors like Busby Berkeley, who brought the techniques of the Broadway revue to the screen by combining intricate choreography with arresting visuals. Movie vocalists such as Bing Crosby and Alice Faye immortalized the songs of Tin Pan Alley's top composers, while dancing teams like Fred Astaire and Ginger Rogers displayed their exhilarating grace in many popular movies.

Although the major studios occasionally tackled social issues, as in *Grapes of Wrath* (1940), Depression-era motion pictures more often stressed

Walt Disney *(1901–1966)*

Two months after President Roosevelt told the nation that "the only thing we have to fear is fear itself," Americans started humming, whistling, and singing a hit tune entitled "Who's Afraid of the Big Bad Wolf." The song came from the sound track of Walt Disney's animated

cartoon, *The Three Little Pigs* (1933), and served as a metaphor for the national resolve to overcome the Depression. Disney's extraordinary success during this period of crisis reflected his skill in defining popular anxieties and in resolving them with Hollywood-style happy endings.

Disney was born in Chicago but spent several impressionable years on a farm in Missouri. Lonely as a boy, he befriended the barnyard animals and later relied on those childhood friendships as the inspiration for his cartoon animation. In the 1920s Disney produced crude animated films in Kansas City, mostly for commercial advertisers, but could not succeed financially. He moved to Hollywood in 1923 and established an independent production company to make a variety of animated features, including *Plane Crazy* (1928), the first Mickey Mouse cartoon.

Disney's films embraced the tension between modern values and rural nostalgia. While his domesticated and human-appearing animals

optimistic themes with populist overtones. The predominance of sex and crime in early 1930s movies had come under attack by the Legion of Decency, a petition campaign in which 11 million Roman Catholics pledged to boycott "indecent" movies. Concerned in 1934 with falling box office receipts, film industry heads responded to the protest by organizing the Production Code Administration under NRA auspices. Under the so-called Hays Code, named for movie czar Will H. Hays, elements of "good" in films were to balance "evil," while "bad" acts were to be followed by punishment or reform. The code also prohibited portraits of homosexuality, interracial sex, abortion, incest, or drug use, and eliminated profanity, including the word *sex,* from screen language.

evoked a lost age of farming communities, the cartoons themselves depended on new, sophisticated technologies, including synchronized sound and color. The popularity of Disney features in the 1930s illuminated the subliminal anxieties produced by the economic crisis. In a typical cartoon plot, rooms fell apart, houses exploded, or, as in *The Sorcerer's Apprentice,* inanimate objects developed a mind of their own and created utter chaos. Yet the familiar order usually was restored. Disney fantasies also provided psychological escape. In such popular movies as *Snow White and the Seven Dwarfs* (1937) or *Fantasia* (1940), viewers found refuge from the sobering world outside the theater. Yet even films like *Bambi* (1942) hinged on an underlying anxiety about the precariousness of life in the modern world.

A product of the white, Anglo-Protestant Midwest, Disney remained committed to traditional values. His creative work depended on his characters' ability to establish control over chaos; however irrational their means, reason always prevailed in the end. The producer's sentimental vision appealed to a people uncertain of the country's values and worried about its economic future. Like many of the nation's cultural pioneers, Disney expressed his genius through an uncanny synthesis of modernism and tradition, a fusion that anticipated the phenomenal success of his entertainment enterprises in the years following World War II.

Hollywood's conformity to Hays Code restrictions resulted in the "golden age" of American cinema. "Screwball comedies" such as *It Happened One Night* (1934), *Bringing up Baby* (1938), and *The Philadelphia Story* (1940) made fun of the elite but suggested that social class was defined by morally accountable character, not wealth. Historical and political dramas like *Gone With the Wind* (1939) and Frank Capra's *Mr. Smith Goes to Washington* (1939) stressed the importance of humility, common sense, decency, and toughness of spirit. "A free people can beat the world at anything," declared one of Capra's films. Bonding with on-screen characters who conveyed this spirit, Depression audiences made performers such as Jimmy Stewart, Henry Fonda, Cary Grant, and Katharine Hepburn true superstars.

EMBATTLED MINORITIES

As non-European peoples sought to benefit from New Deal pluralism, African American athletes and entertainers gained a foothold in popular culture. Public acceptance of blacks broadened when track star Jessie Owens defied Adolf Hitler's racial theories by winning four gold medals at the 1936 Olympics in Berlin—and when African American heavyweight boxing champ Joe Louis scored a first-round knockout of Germany's Max Schmeling two years later. Jazz artists such as Louis Armstrong, "Fats" Waller, and Billie Holiday received widening acclaim; and Hollywood productions such as *Imitation of Life* (1934) and *Green Pastures* (1936) overcame racial stereotypes with serious treatments of black characters.

Such cultural advances were slow to translate into substantive gains. Yet northern African Americans benefited from the spread of chain stores, whose hiring of black clerks and use of standardized goods and prices minimized exploitive practices. As a result of prodding by civil rights groups such as the NAACP and the Urban League, African Americans shared in the distribution of New Deal work relief: northern blacks received relief at three times the rate of whites. African American participation in the Social Security pension program also signaled a step toward full citizenship. Yet even in the North, the Depression economy underscored racial prejudice and excluded blacks from many jobs. When federal officials redlined or undervalued older and racially mixed neighborhoods, inner-city homeowners could not refinance mortgages or improve properties. Police abuse aggravated tensions, leading to major race riots in Harlem and Detroit. The bitterness and violence of ghetto life were portrayed in black novelist Richard Wright's *Native Son* (1940).

Conditions in the race-conscious South were far more oppressive than in the North. By promoting mechanized operations and mandating reductions of cultivated acreage, New Deal agricultural policy encouraged white landlords to evict tenants. As rural blacks sought jobs or relief in surrounding towns and cities, southern Democrats used their power in Congress to maximize control over the regional labor force. Social Security initially excluded farmworkers and domestic servants and conferred on local authorities the eligibility decisions for unemployment insurance and aid to dependent families. As a concession to white supremacy, housing and public facilities in Tennessee Valley Authority (TVA) model towns and southern Civilian Conservation Corps (CCC) camps remained racially segregated.

Antiblack violence constituted the most persistent feature of southern racism. When a series of vigilante murders aroused the NAACP and the biracial Association of Southern Women for the Prevention of Lynching, northern liberals reintroduced federal antilynching legislation. Politically beholden to the southern wing of the Democratic Party, Roosevelt remained silent when a states'-rights filibuster in the Senate defeated the measure. Nevertheless, New Deal reformers and industrial union leaders often cooperated with African American activists, as in the National Negro Congress, created in 1936 by black labor organizer A. Philip Randolph. Eleanor Roosevelt also supported efforts to involve the federal government in the protection of civil rights. When the Daughters of the American Revolution refused to rent Washington, D.C.'s only concert stage to black opera singer Marian Anderson in 1939, Roosevelt resigned from the group and organized an Easter Sunday recital on the steps of the Lincoln Memorial. The crowd of 75,000 marked the first mass civil rights protest in the nation's history.

Depression conditions proved equally challenging for Mexican Americans. In the southwestern food processing industry, where three-quarters of the workforce was comprised of women, organizers built a powerful CIO affiliate that negotiated benefits such as maternity leave, company-provided day care, and paid vacations. Community activists in Texas and California focused on long-range issues such as public education, voter registration, civil rights, and entrance into the professions. The broader agenda reflected the fact that most of the nation's Mexican Americans had been born in the United States. Seeking to develop middle-class leaders who could align the Mexican labor movement with New Deal reform, CIO organizer Luisa Moreno founded the Spanish-Speaking Congress in 1938.

American Indians may have faced the most difficult obstacles to social inclusion. Once reformer John Collier became Commissioner of Indian Affairs in 1933, the federal government undertook an "Indian New Deal" to reverse detribalization and preserve Native American culture and resources. Collier established the Emergency Conservation Work Program, known as the "all-Indian CCC." He then persuaded Congress to pass the Indian Reorganization Act of 1934, which guaranteed principles of reservation home rule by requiring tribal governments to draft and ratify new constitutions. The law sought economic self-sufficiency for Native peoples by reversing the Dawes Act and returning Indian land tenure to tribal title. Under the terms of this act, the federal government provided financial aid to support Indian college education and promote the study of Native American culture.

Despite Collier's insistence that tribal cooperation and communal experience provided an alternative to the alienation of industrialized society, conservative critics condemned the Indian New Deal as a "sovietization" of reservation existence. Many Native Americans distrusted the commissioner's plan as well, but more than two-thirds of the tribes voted to participate. Having won freedom of contract for tribal agreements, reservation leaders set up self-governing corporations and worked with the Bureau of Indian Affairs (BIA) in establishing cooperative businesses and adopting conservation measures. Nevertheless, federal land policies frequently clashed with tribal traditions, BIA funding dwindled, and some government officials continued to deny legal rights to tribal authorities. Dismayed at the slow pace of progress, activists like author D'Arcy McNickle agitated for the creation of a national Indian political lobby.

THE RADICAL CULTURAL FRONT

"There is no longer I, there is WE," essayist Dorothy Parker remarked of the conversion of Depression artists and writers to social causes. Focusing upon the masses, the nation's leading painters turned to documenting ordinary life. Edward Hopper portrayed the solitude and alienation of urban dwellers in scenes of late-night restaurants and theater lobbies. Reginald Marsh depicted seedy venues like dance halls, honky-tonks, and downtown movie houses. Alice Neel's bleak portraits of New York's Spanish Harlem captured the despair of Depression families. Drawn to political activism, Ben Shahn produced paintings, posters, and murals that satirized the social elite and celebrated working-class radicals like Sacco and Vanzetti. Regionalists like Iowa's Grant Wood and Missouri's Thomas Hart Benton, in turn, applied realist perspectives to the natural landscape, while New Mexico's Georgia O'Keeffe used desert landscapes to accent colorful surrealistic canvases.

Documentary realism found its way into the most memorable fiction of the later 1930s. Margaret Mitchell's *Gone with the Wind* (1936), reproduced as a landmark motion picture, mixed conventional racial stereotyping with the saga of a white southern woman's struggle for survival during the Civil War. John Steinbeck's *Grapes of Wrath* (1939), made into a popular film the following year, sympathetically portrayed the exodus of impoverished Dust Bowl migrants to the California orchards. No radical, Steinbeck nevertheless implied that life lost meaning for ordinary people when capitalism severed traditional ties to the soil and community.

The documentation of American life found a ready outlet in New Deal agencies seeking to create an uplifting public culture. To democratize the arts and place them on a self-supporting basis, the WPA established community arts centers, mounted traveling gallery exhibits, provided free concerts, and offered classes in regional folklore and handicrafts. Under the Federal Arts Project, the government hired unemployed painters to create murals for post offices, schools, and other public buildings. WPA grants underwrote the work of composers such as Aaron Copland, who incorporated traditional folk melodies into suites, ballets, and symphonies for public performance.

Unemployed authors were retained by the WPA's Federal Writers Project to produce oral narratives, state guidebooks, and community histories. Through the Federal Theater Project, drama groups staged moderately priced plays that included "living newspapers," improvised productions incorporating contemporary political events and audience participation. The Farm

Dorothea Lange's photograph of California refugees from the Dust Bowl drought of the mid-1930s, taken for the Farm Security Administration.

Security Administration (FSA) funded conservation-minded film documentaries like Pare Lorentz's *The River* (1937) and *The Land* (1941), artfully combining the New Deal planning ethic with realistic descriptions. The FSA also published James Agee's and Walker Evans's *Let Us Now Praise Famous Men* (1941), a stark photo-essay about Alabama sharecroppers, as well as the work of photographer Dorothea Lange, who produced intimate portraits of ordinary people bravely coping with the Depression.

In large cities like New York, a radical political culture emerged around the Communist Party. By organizing youth clubs, schools, and summer camps, the party educated young people with ideals of socialism, labor solidarity, racial tolerance, and international brotherhood. Through Communist organizations like the "John Reed Clubs," aspiring African American and white ethnic writers prepared for literary careers. Radical workers' theaters, proletarian literary magazines, and craft cooperatives provided alternatives to commercialized entertainment while building support for progressive political and labor causes. The radical cultural front helped to acculturate members of immigrant and minority groups to the broader concerns and standards of American society.

When fascism threatened to spread across Europe at mid-decade, the political left reached out to broaden its base by building coalitions with liberals in a "popular front." In 1935, literary critic Kenneth Burke told the American Writers' Congress that progressives needed to shift their focus from "the worker" to "the people." Emphasizing democratic humanism and inclusion instead of proletarian revolution, party members positioned themselves as the leading opponents of fascist dictatorship, a policy that appealed to Jewish liberals and other European refugees from Nazi persecution. The Popular Front cultivated allies by respecting ethnic diversity, campaigning against racism and lynching, and supporting the industrial union movement. As Communists and "fellow travelers" rallied to New Deal reform, the CIO, and Democratic candidates, party leader Earl Browder explained that communism was "twentieth century Americanism." By 1940, Communist activists comprised 10 percent of the CIO union leadership.

Although Communist Party membership never surpassed 55,000 in the 1930s, the movement had an enormous impact on popular culture. Like their New Deal allies, radical activists used the media to democratize the arts. Seeking to illustrate the dangers of fascist manipulation of the masses, producers like Orson Welles adopted modernist techniques of collage and excerpting to live theater, radio, and the movies. Others, like black novelist Richard Wright and mystery writer Dashiell Hammett, inserted everyday language and experience into their stories. Less heralded authors and dramatists depicted the human costs of capitalism through profiles of marathon dancers, prostitutes, migrant laborers, or unemployed workers. Creating a distinctive brand of class consciousness, the radical cultural front left a legacy of sympathy for urban ethnics and the plight of working-class underdogs.

THE ANTI–NEW DEAL COALITION

The relative success of Roosevelt reforms and the growing threat of overseas fascism led intellectuals like literary critic Alfred Kazin and poet Archibald MacLeish to conclude that democracy and individual rights were best preserved in America. Yet New Deal ties to radical culture ferment, ethnic diversity, and centralized government sparked political controversies and social divisions. Distrustful of federal fiscal management, small business advocates blamed deficit spending for inflation and high interest rates and condemned low consumer prices. Such concerns led Congress to pass the Robinson-Patman Act of 1936, which outlawed manufacturers' discounts to large distributors and chain stores. In 1937, the Miller-Tydings Act permitted states to pass fair-trade laws to control chain price-cutting. By 1939, twenty-seven legislatures had enacted regulations or taxes to contain the retail giants.

In contrast to small business defenders, Roosevelt believed that recovery depended on spreading consumer purchasing power and labor union strength across the nation. Consequently, the president campaigned for several reform Democrats in the southern congressional primaries of 1938. When opponents accused him of attempting to "purge" his own party, however, the strategy backfired and conservative Senate incumbents like Georgia's Walter F. George, South Carolina's "Cotton Ed" Smith, and Maryland's Millard Tydings won easy victories. Roosevelt's political woes deepened in the congressional elections when Republicans scored substantial gains.

After 1938 the White House faced a bipartisan majority in Congress— committed to budget retrenchment, private enterprise, and states' rights. This powerful anti–New Deal bloc spoke for nonurban and small business interests that saw labor and welfare programs primarily benefiting the ethnically and racially diverse cities. These politicians were convinced, as Texas House Democrat Martin Dies Jr. stated, that the period of emergency was "at an end." Republican Senator Robert A. Taft of Ohio spoke for many of his colleagues when he complained that Roosevelt's executive agencies had monopolized legislative and judicial powers and were issuing regulations without accountability. Indeed, House Republicans charged that "swivel chair" experts and planners in the Washington bureaucracy had fostered a permanent dependence on high taxes, wasteful spending, and government collectivism.

Congressional conservatives attacked the New Deal by slashing WPA appropriations and passing the Hatch Act of 1939, which outlawed election activity by federal employees and prohibited them from soliciting campaign contributions from welfare recipients. The anti-Roosevelt coalition also targeted White House ties to the Communist Party. In 1934 the House of Representatives had organized a committee on subversive activities to probe the German-American Bund, a Nazi group espousing an anti-Semitic and fascist agenda. Four years later, Martin Dies convinced Congress to reconstitute the panel. Under Dies's leadership, the House Committee on Un-American Activities (HUAC) investigated Communists, "fellow travelers," and "radicals and crackpots" who allegedly had infiltrated New Deal agencies. Finding evidence of communist involvement in the Federal Theater Project, the committee prevailed upon the House to terminate the experiment.

New Deal opponents adamantly objected to the Roosevelt administration's sponsorship of industrial unionism. Hostility to the labor movement was particularly strong in the South, where the CIO was organizing previously nonunion textile mills and supporting civil rights reform. Conservatives singled out the National Labor Relations Board (NLRB) for cooperating with industrial democracy. After an extensive inquiry, a special House committee concluded that the labor board was staffed with Communists whose administrative decisions supported the CIO at the expense of employers and AFL craft unions.

Conservatives were not alone in disparaging the Communists. The party attracted widespread criticism from liberals for ties to the Soviet Union and for manipulative and deceptive tactics. AFL officials complained that Communist loyalists practiced "dual unionism" by forming secret caucuses in labor groups. National Negro Congress leader A. Philip Randolph walked out of his own civil rights organization when white Communists assumed control. As international tensions and fears of subversion accelerated in 1940, conservatives won passage of the Smith Act, which prohibited advocacy of the forceful overthrow of the government or membership in any group that advanced such teachings.

THE PERILS OF THE OPEN DOOR

By the time New Deal opponents began to set the congressional agenda, troubling events in Europe and Asia overshadowed domestic concerns. Convinced that the restoration of prosperity depended on expanding overseas markets and investments, Roosevelt endorsed the principles of the Open Door policy in international relations. This strategy sought free trade for all nations, with equal access to raw materials and financial partnerships. Latin America provided the prime opportunity for such an approach. Framing the conditions for regional prosperity, the White House announced a Good Neighbor Policy in 1933 based on mutual respect and the shared economic interests of hemispheric partners. Although Washington maintained friendly ties with corrupt dictators in Nicaragua and Cuba, marine contingents left Haiti and Nicaragua, and the United States abandoned the interventionist Platt amendment in Cuba.

The administration pursued a cooperative image in Latin America by ratifying the Buenos Aires Convention of 1936, which obliged all signers to submit regional conflicts to arbitration. Two years later, Washington declined to intervene in a dispute between U.S. oil companies and the government of Mexico. Yet the most important facet of the Good Neighbor Policy came in trade. Beginning in 1934, Congress enacted a series of reciprocal trade acts that empowered the president to halve tariffs on Latin American imports in return for rate reductions on U.S. exports. To provide southern partners with funds to purchase U.S. products, Roosevelt established the Export-Import Bank. By strengthening North America's dominance over the hemisphere's weaker economies, however, reciprocal trade encouraged Latin American business interests to look to Europe for more lucrative opportunities.

New Deal officials believed that a peaceful and prosperous Europe held the key to economic recovery. The administration had hoped to arrange bilateral trade reductions with European allies at the London Economic Conference of 1933, but ran into resistance when the gold-standard nations insisted on first enacting currency stabilization. Roosevelt sought larger export markets for the United States by recognizing the Communist Soviet Union. Yet conditions on the Continent continued to deteriorate. Under the leadership of Adolf Hitler, who assumed absolute power in 1933, German National Socialists (Nazis) demanded a revision of the Versailles Treaty to reestablish their nation as a great power. When the French refused, Hitler withdrew from the League of Nations and announced a rearmament program.

By subsidizing German corporations and winning bilateral agreements from trading partners, the National Socialists intensified competition for U.S. markets in Latin America and cut into U.S. exports to Germany. The Nazis directly threatened Roosevelt's notion of a world community of consumer democracies dedicated to human rights and economic growth. Defying the international community, Hitler established a one-party dictatorship that proclaimed the supremacy of the Aryan "master race," called for the creation of a pan-Germanic "Third Reich," and predicted the ultimate annihilation of national enemies like Jews and Communists. In 1936 Berlin defied Versailles Treaty provisions for German disarmament by reoccupying the Rhineland and entering a military alliance with the fascist government of Italian dictator Benito Mussolini.

Italian forces had invaded the east African nation of Ethiopia in 1935. Although Britain and France declined to intervene in the conflict, the League of Nations condemned Mussolini's aggression, prompting Rome to withdraw from the organization. European tensions were compounded by the situation in East Asia, where Japan easily had defeated Chinese armies in Manchuria in 1931 and converted the province into a protectorate. Refusing to recognize the puppet regime, the United States invoked the Open Door policy in the Stimson Doctrine. Japan ignored such protests. Instead, Tokyo responded to the escalating arms race in Europe by proposing a revision of the Washington Naval Conference of 1921–1922. Nursing nationalist resentments toward U.S. immigration policy, Japan decided to unilaterally expand its fleet when Washington and London declined its overtures.

THE SEARCH FOR NEUTRALITY

Roosevelt's response to the European and Asian crises were severely limited by the persistence of noninterventionist sentiment at home. Most Americans believed that the United States had been tricked into participation in World War I. During the mid-1930s, Senate investigations headed by North Dakota's Republican Gerald P. Nye revealed extensive wartime profiteering by munitions manufacturers and bankers, implying close connections between the arms industry, international finance, and presidential foreign policy. Walter

Millis's best-seller, *Road to War* (1935), popularized the idea that the nation had been lured into the military conflict by a combination of business profiteering, debt entanglement, and Allied propaganda.

Public distrust of bankers and arms interests directly affected U.S. foreign policy. When Roosevelt responded to the conquest of Ethiopia by requesting power to stop arms sales to aggressor nations, Congress blocked any increase in executive power. Instead, noninterventionists passed the Neutrality Act of 1935, which required the president to impose an arms embargo on all warring countries and to notify U.S. citizens that passage on ships owned by belligerent nations would be at their own risk. These provisions attempted to prevent even accidental involvement in foreign conflicts by eliminating the factors that supposedly had drawn the United States into World War I. Reluctantly signing a measure that deliberately narrowed presidential options, Roosevelt warned that the law's "inflexible provisions might drag us into war instead of keeping us out."

Following formalization of the German-Italian alliance in 1936, the White House asked Congress for greater discretion in applying the Neutrality Act. Instead, the ghosts of World War I resurfaced with a new ban on loans to warring countries. When the Spanish Civil War erupted later in the year, foreign policy issues threatened to tear apart the New Deal political coalition. Although Hitler and Mussolini provided crucial military support to the right-wing rebels led by General Francisco Franco, and the Soviet Union and Mexico aided the Spanish republic, Britain, France, and the United States adopted a noninterventionist stance. The effect was to deny supplies to Spain's elected government. Such a policy infuriated liberals and leftists, who viewed the conflict as a moral battleground between the forces of democracy and the legions of fascism. In contrast, many working-class Catholics saw Franco as a defender of the traditional social order against a government associated with land reform, anticlericalism, and cooperation with communists.

Although Gallup polls found more sympathy in the United States for the Spanish loyalists than the fascists, Roosevelt hesitated to offend Catholic constituencies in the Democratic Party. State Department officials perceived the socialist republic as a potential threat to U.S. investors. Consequently, when Congress passed a joint resolution in 1937 prohibiting the export of munitions to either side, the president imposed an arms embargo and forbade civilians from traveling to Spain. Violating the law, 2,800 young U.S. men and women volunteered to join the Abraham Lincoln Brigade to defend the Spanish republic. The crusade won wide support from intellectuals like poet Langston Hughes, dramatist Lillian Hellman, and novelist Ernest Hemingway, whose highly acclaimed *For Whom the Bell Tolls* (1940) captured the idealistic spirit of a struggle in which one-third of the Brigade volunteers died. Meanwhile, American businesses broke the neutrality laws by selling war materiel to

Franco. With superior arms and no U.S. opposition, the fascist allies triumphed in Spain in 1939.

Caught between developing aggression abroad and public desire to keep the nation out of foreign conflicts, Roosevelt assured voters that "we are not isolationists except insofar as we seek to isolate ourselves completely from war." Nevertheless, business interests tied to international trade feared that neutrality would interfere with the development of new markets. Seeking to balance these counterpressures, presidential adviser Bernard M. Baruch suggested a revision of the Neutrality Act that incorporated the chain-store practice of cash-and-carry. As enacted by Congress in 1937, the new law permitted the sale of nonmilitary products to nations at war, but required belligerents to pay cash and to transport their goods in their own ships. Because cash-and-carry favored nations with strong navies and large cash reserves, Britain and France, not Germany, were the potential beneficiaries. The law also required a mandatory embargo on arms sales to all warring countries.

While Congress tried to perfect neutrality laws, Japan attacked the northern provinces of China in 1937. Appealing to Asian nationalism, the Japanese promised to create an East Asia Co-Prosperity Sphere that would exclude the European colonial powers from Chinese markets and resources. Such a sphere of influence paralleled Nazi expansion in central Europe, British control of the Commonwealth nations, and U.S. dominance of Latin America. Yet Roosevelt remained committed to the Open Door policy in Asia and supported an independent China. Backed by strong anti-Japanese public opinion, the president bypassed the neutrality law by refusing to acknowledge that a state of war existed between Japan and China. This decision enabled the administration to extend trade credits to China to finance anti-Japanese resistance. Yet such assistance remained limited because the president wished to avoid an open break with Tokyo.

The White House worried nonetheless about the strength of noninterventionist sentiment. To counteract what he called "isolationism," the president spoke out in 1937 against the "epidemic of world lawlessness" and called for a "quarantine" of aggressor nations. Although he offered no specific plan, Roosevelt publicly admitted for the first time that war might become necessary. Interventionist newspapers praised the president, but public opinion prevented any change of policy. "It's a terrible thing," he later said, "to look over your shoulder when you are trying to lead—and to find no one there." When Japanese planes attacked a U.S. gunboat in China, the White House accepted Tokyo's apology and cash compensation. Meanwhile, Democratic Representative Louis Ludlow of Indiana sponsored a constitutional amendment in 1938 to require a public referendum before Congress could declare war. Under extreme pressure from the administration, House leaders barely managed to return the measure to committee in an extremely close vote.

THE DEBATE OVER INTERVENTION

The United States watched nervously as conservative leaders in Britain and France accepted Germany's takeover of Austria in 1938. Six months later, Hitler demanded the western portion of Czechoslovakia. Fearing another European war, the British and French governments clung to the hope that Nazi Germany could serve as a barrier against Soviet communism. In what became known as the diplomacy of "appeasement," Britain's Prime Minister Neville Chamberlain took the initiative in drafting the Munich Pact of 1938. Under its terms, the German-speaking sector of Czechoslovakia was ceded to Berlin in exchange for Hitler's promise to expand no further. Demoralizing antifascists worldwide, the agreement persuaded the Soviet Union that the Western Allies wanted Germany to expand eastward. When Nazi troops occupied the rest of Czechoslovakia early in 1939, Britain and France issued no protest, although they promised to protect Poland from aggression and began to rearm.

As German expansion threatened world order, Roosevelt increased the U.S. military arsenal with particular attention to the air force. The White House hoped that air power could deter Nazi aggression without requiring a large and unpopular army. Realizing that the United States might become a supplier of military equipment to its European allies, the president secretly approved a plan to manufacture French warplanes. Yet Roosevelt's rearmament designs remained ambiguous and modest, partly because he feared that public disclosure could arouse congressional opposition. In turn, insufficient military preparedness made the White House wary of involvement in European controversies. As Germany began to threaten Poland in 1939, the Western Allies abandoned appeasement. To eliminate the danger of a two-front conflict, Hitler signed a nonaggression pact with Soviet leader Josef Stalin in August 1939. Five days later, on the first of September, Germany invaded Poland. Within two days, Britain and France declared war on the Nazi state.

The outbreak of World War II intensified Roosevelt's belief that France and Britain must defeat Germany to preserve European stability while confirming his commitment to stay out of the conflict. To reconcile the contradiction, the president emphasized that support of Great Britain would protect U.S. interests without embroiling the nation in hostilities. Roosevelt promptly called Congress into special session in September 1939 to repeal the arms embargo. As the nation engaged in a dramatic debate about U.S. interests, Senate defenders of neutrality such as Gerald Nye and Robert M. La Follette Jr. warned that any revision of the law would bring the United States into war. Yet interventionists in both political parties organized well-funded lobbying groups, and Congress repealed the arms embargo. The new Neutrality Act still prohibited U.S. vessels from entering war zones, but permitted belliger-

EXHIBIT **6-8**   **THE ROAD TO WAR, 1931–1939**

1931	Japan occupies Manchuria
1933	Japan withdraws from League of Nations
	Adolf Hitler's National Socialists assume power in Germany
1934	German rearmament
1935	Italy invades Ethiopia
	U.S. Neutrality Act invokes arms embargo
	Nye Munitions Investigation convenes
1936	Italy withdraws from League of Nations and enters alliance with Germany
	Germany reoccupies the Rhineland
	Spanish Civil War begins
1937	Japan attacks northern China
	U.S. Neutrality Act invokes "cash-and-carry" for nonmilitary aid
	Roosevelt "quarantine" speech
1938	Munich Conference accepts German annexation of Austria and parts of Czechoslovakia
	Germany annexes all of Czechoslovakia
1939	Russo-German Nonaggression Pact
	Germany invades Poland
	Great Britain and France declare war on Germany
	U.S. Neutrality Act invokes cash-and-carry for military aid

ents to purchase military supplies on a cash-and-carry basis, effectively placing the United States in the Allied camp.

When German armies invaded Norway, Denmark, the Low Countries, and France in the spring of 1940, the battle between interventionists and neutralists intensified. As Nazi troops blitzed toward Paris, Roosevelt warned against "the illusion that we are remote and isolated." Noninterventionists such as Democratic Senator Burton K. Wheeler of Montana derided the notion that Germany could ever mount an invasion of the Western Hemisphere. Yet while Wheeler and noninterventionists in both parties called for a negotiated peace, Congress approved increased defense appropriations to prepare for war. The president sought bipartisan support by appointing two Republican internationalists to the cabinet: Henry Stimson as secretary of war, and Frank Knox, the Republican vice presidential candidate in 1936, as secretary of the navy. The fall of France in June 1940 brought a dramatic rise in pro-British sentiment, but opinion polls showed that 82 percent of the public still opposed direct intervention.

Charles A. Lindbergh *(1902–1974)*

The most prominent opponent of U.S. intervention in World War II was aviation pioneer Charles Lindbergh. Since winning international acclaim for his solo flight from New York to Paris in 1927, the flier had been the object of almost unceasing public scrutiny. Lindbergh's suspicions of both

the public and the press were confirmed by the spectacle surrounding the kidnap-murder of his son in 1931. Four years later he and his wife, writer Anne Morrow Lindbergh, fled to Europe, where they lived for eight years.

During the 1930s Lindbergh made four trips to Nazi Germany to inspect the nation's air industry. "The German aviation development is without parallel," he wrote. By 1938, he considered Germany "probably the strongest air power in Europe." With war im-

minent the next year, the family returned to the United States, where Lindbergh entered the public debate over U.S. involvement in the European conflict. Lindbergh's father, a member of the House of Representatives, had strongly opposed U.S. intervention in World War I, and the younger Lindbergh maintained a profound skepticism about European entanglements. The aviator's conservative leanings and Republican connections also led him to suspect that Franklin Roosevelt was a devious and deceitful man who was exploiting the world crisis to expand his own power.

More troubling was Lindbergh's thinking about the comparative merits of the United States and Nazi Germany. "We Americans are a primitive people," he told *Life* magazine. "We do not have discipline.

As German planes bombed British cities and German submarines sank vessels in the Atlantic during the summer of 1940, Prime Minister Winston Churchill pleaded for U.S. naval assistance. Roosevelt responded with an executive agreement granting Britain fifty overage navy destroyers in return for British bases in the Western Hemisphere and London's promise never to surrender the fleet. The "destroyers for bases" deal symbolized U.S. commitment to the British cause. Yet noninterventionists such as the popular aviator

Our moral standards are low." In contrast, Lindbergh viewed Germany as marked by "a strength and vigor which it is impossible to overlook." Compounding these views was the aviator's rabid anticommunism. "An alliance between the United States and Russia should be opposed by every American, every Christian, and by every humanitarian in this country," he declared shortly after Hitler invaded the Soviet Union.

Convinced that the democracies were deteriorating morally and that German airpower would dominate the war, Lindbergh advocated a negotiated peace between Berlin and Great Britain. Yet critics detected a tinge of anti-Semitism in the aviator's assertion that Jewish groups were working with the British and the Roosevelt administration to push the United States into war through their "large ownership and influence in our motion pictures, our press, our radio, and our government." Such statements undercut Lindbergh's claims that Roosevelt's undeclared naval war in the North Atlantic was tipping the balance of power between the executive and legislative branches and subverting American democracy.

Noting the president's use of subterfuge to advance policies far ahead of public opinion, Lindbergh predicted that participation in the war would radically change America. He warned that to defeat Germany the United States would have to become a "uniformed and regimented nation," possibly for generations. Indeed, questions about the legitimate scope of U.S. involvement in conflicts abroad, the formulation of foreign policy under cover of secrecy, and the growing militarization of public life would remain permanent fixtures of American society in the decades after World War II.

Charles Lindbergh argued that the arrangement weakened national defense and would lead to U.S. involvement in the European conflict. In September 1940, war opponents organized the America First Committee. With financial backing from business interests serving the domestic market, the organization enrolled more than 800,000 Americans, mostly midwesterners. Public speakers like Lindbergh and Nye spread the message through mass rallies and radio broadcasts that war would bring only dictatorship, militarism, and collectivism.

Despite the popularity of the noninterventionist position, the brutality of German militarism, the Nazi violence against civilians, and the persecution of the Jews strengthened the interventionist cause. Twelve days after the creation of America First, Congress approved the first peacetime draft in U.S. history. The profound sense of national crisis permitted the president to seek an unprecedented third term in 1940. Within the Republican Party, interventionists prevailed in a bitter fight and nominated Wendell Willkie, a Wall Street lawyer who supported aid to Britain and the draft. Roosevelt's campaign denounced noninterventionists as "appeasers" and pictured the struggle against Nazi aggression as one of "people versus dictatorship." Edward R. Murrow's live radio broadcasts from London focused sympathy on civilian victims of the German air assault. Yet the president promised to stay out of Europe. "Your boys," he reaffirmed on the eve of the election, "are not going to be sent into any foreign wars."

On Election Day, Roosevelt took nearly 55 percent of the popular vote and became the first president to serve more than two terms. The White House then announced that a British victory was essential to "national security" and that the United States must become "the great arsenal of democracy." In his State of the Union address of January 1941, Roosevelt appealed for defense of "Four Freedoms—freedom of speech and expression, freedom of religion, freedom from want, and freedom from fear." For most citizens this rhetoric defined World War II as a conflict between freedom and tyranny rather than a defense of national interest.

To the Brink of War

With Britain running out of capital and the United States forbidden by neutrality law from extending credit, the White House faced the problem of moving supplies across the Atlantic. Roosevelt responded with the "Lend-Lease" proposal. Introduced early in 1941, Lend-Lease gave the president unprecedented power to sell, transfer, or lease military equipment and other goods to any nation whose defense he deemed essential to U.S. security. Roosevelt compared the program to lending a neighbor a garden hose to put out a fire before it spread to one's own house. Nevertheless, in one of the most intense debates in the history of Congress, noninterventionists insisted that the White House was asking for dictatorial power that would bring the nation into war. In a bitter reference to New Deal farm policy, Senator Wheeler warned that Lend-Lease would plough under every fourth American boy. Despite these warnings, Congress approved the measure, authorizing $7 billion to send supplies to Britain and its allies.

As critics predicted, Lend-Lease destroyed the fiction of U.S. neutrality. German success in sinking Allied vessels placed increasing pressure on the

EXHIBIT **6-9**   **THE ROAD TO WAR, 1940–1941**

1940	Germany occupies Denmark, Norway, Low Countries, and France
	Japan occupies French Indochina (Vietnam)
	U.S. establishes economic sanctions against Japan
	Germany, Italy, and Japan sign Axis military pact
	U.S. builds two-ocean navy and enacts first peacetime draft
	Roosevelt wins third presidential term
	Battle of Britain
1941	Lend-Lease provides U.S. aid to Britain
	Germany invades Soviet Union
	United States and Britain sign Atlantic Charter
	Undeclared war in the Atlantic
	Repeal of U.S. neutrality law permits arming of merchant ships

United States to assure the delivery of goods to Britain. Roosevelt then assumed unprecedented presidential powers. Invoking the notion of "hemispheric defense," he extended the American neutral zone halfway across the Atlantic and ordered the navy to inform the British of the presence of German ships and planes. The president also signed an executive agreement with the Danish government in exile that provided for U.S. bases in Greenland. When Hitler astounded the world by invading the Soviet Union in June 1941, Roosevelt immediately extended Lend-Lease to the new ally.

Soviet dictator Josef Stalin's reputation for repression and duplicity made him a controversial recipient of U.S. assistance, prompting noninterventionist leader Charles Lindbergh to admit that "with all her faults," he preferred an alliance with the Germans rather than one "with the cruelty, Godlessness, and the barbarism that exist in the Soviet Union." Yet Roosevelt believed that only a total defeat of Germany could prevent Hitler's Third Reich from conquering the world and that nothing should stand in the way of eliminating the Nazi threat. Such thinking mirrored the position of intellectuals like theologian Rheinhold Niebuhr, who argued that social democrats must overcome peace-loving sentiments and employ coercive power to defeat totalitarian foes.

Meeting on a battleship off Canada's Newfoundland coast in August 1941, Roosevelt and Churchill signed the Atlantic Charter. Because Hitler's armies had recently invaded the Soviet Union, Roosevelt hoped to forestall any agreement under which Churchill and Stalin might divide Europe into spheres of influence at the expense of the United States. According to the charter's provisions, the British and the Americans denied any desire for territorial gain and invoked the "four freedoms" to express universal principles of self-determination. The agreement also asserted the right of all nations to "equal terms to the trade and to the raw materials of the world." Roosevelt and

Churchill dramatized this commitment to the Open Door policy by pledging to create a postwar system of collective security to enforce it.

As German submarines attacked Atlantic shipping, including U.S. vessels, Roosevelt worried that Britain might lose the war. Resolved to move ahead of public opinion, he extended the range of convoys to Iceland, a policy that brought the merchant marine directly into conflict with Hitler's warships. After the destroyer *Greer* exchanged fire with a German submarine in September 1941, the president announced that U.S. ships would "shoot on sight" German vessels in the so-called neutral zone. Americans could not "go on living happily and peacefully in a Nazi-dominated world," he warned. Carefully hiding the fact that the *Greer* had tried to sink the submarine, Roosevelt won wide support for the undeclared war in the Atlantic. In November Congress revised the Neutrality Act to allow armed merchant ships to enter the war zone.

Hitler was too involved in the European war to directly confront the military power of the United States. Yet the German invasion of the Soviet Union and attacks against the British, French, and Dutch had strengthened Japan's position in Asia by distracting its most important rivals and weakening European control of the region's resource-rich colonies. Roosevelt had demonstrated official disapproval of Tokyo's occupation of northern China by terminating the U.S.-Japanese trade agreement in 1939. As Japan prepared to invade northern Indochina the next year, the president embargoed the sale of aviation gasoline and scrap iron. Yet Japanese leaders believed that economic self-sufficiency was essential to Japan's political and cultural survival and chose to defy the United States by moving troops into Indochina. In response, Roosevelt tightened the economic screws by embargoing all iron and steel. Japan then signed a tripartite military assistance pact with Italy and Germany.

Not ready for an open break with the United States, Japan opened diplomatic negotiations in the spring of 1941. Yet neither nation was prepared to accept the other's terms. Adhering to the Open Door policy and long concerned about the Japanese "peril," Roosevelt insisted on Tokyo's departure from the Asian mainland before full trade relations could be restored. In contrast, Japan's commitment to the East Asia Co-Prosperity Sphere prevented acceptance of a policy that compromised access to regional oil, rubber, and tin supplies. When the Japanese invaded southern Indochina in July 1941, Roosevelt promptly embargoed oil shipments and froze Japanese assets. Left with limited ability to fuel its industrial system and empire, Tokyo faced a crucial choice. It could either abandon plans for Asian expansion or attempt to seize oil from the Dutch East Indies and Britain's Malay Peninsula. Yet Roosevelt had already assured Churchill that the United States would not tolerate an attack on British possessions in Asia. The stage was set for a historic confrontation in the Pacific.

AMERICAN HISTORY
RESOURCE CENTER

To explore documents, images, audio and video clips, articles, and commentary related to the material in this chapter, visit the source collections at ushistory.wadsworth.com and and use the Search function with the following key terms:

Frances Perkins	Charles Lindbergh
FDR	Dust Bowl
Hitler	

RECOMMENDED READINGS

G. Edward White, *The Constitution and the New Deal* (2000). This important work places the "constitutional revolution" of the late 1930s into historical context by describing how the Supreme Court gradually expanded federal regulatory power.

Robert C. Lieberman, *Shifting the Color Line: Race and the American Welfare State* (1998). The author outlines the political and social context of the two-tiered New Deal welfare state with emphasis on the treatment of African American clients.

Michael Deming, *The Cultural Front: The Laboring of American Culture in the Twentieth Century* (1997). Focusing on the centrality of labor in Popular Front rhetoric, this book shows how the left steered popular culture toward the concerns of ordinary people.

Walter LaFeber, *The Clash: A History of U.S.-Japan Relations* (1997). This superbly crafted analysis explores the context of U.S. involvement in World War II in relation to economic competition and strategic conflict in East Asia.

Additional Readings

Many of the listings for the Depression and the Roosevelt era in the previous chapter carry over to Chapter 6. Segments of Robert H. Zieger, *John L. Lewis: Labor Leader* (1988), and *The CIO, 1935–1955* (1995), explain the industrial union's transition from militancy to accommodation. Daniel Nelson, *American Rubber Workers and Organized Labor, 1900–1941* (1988), offers further insight into the CIO. Communist influence in the labor movement is described by Roger Keeran, *The Communist Party and the Auto Workers Union* (1980). For working-class culture in the late 1930s, see the relevant segments of John Bodnar, *Workers' World: Kinship, Community, and Protest in an Industrial Society, 1900–1940* (1982).

Roosevelt's legacy of deficit spending is the subject of Mark Hugh Leff, *The Limits of Symbolic Reform: The New Deal and Taxation, 1933–1939* (1984), and Alan Brinkley, *The End of Reform: New Deal Liberalism in Recession and War* (1995). For the consequences of fiscal policy for development in the South and West, see Jordan A. Schwarz, *The New Dealers: Power Politics in the Age of Roosevelt* (1993). The Supreme Court's role in validating New Deal legislation is described in Jeffrey D. Hockett, *New Deal Justice: The Constitutional Jurisprudence of Hugo L. Black, Felix Frankfurter, and Robert H. Jackson* (1996).

Works on government sponsorship of the arts after 1935 include Marlene Park and Gerald E. Markowitz, *Democratic Vistas: Post Offices and Public Art in the New Deal* (1984); James Curtis, *Mind's Eye, Mind's Truth: FSA Photography Reconsidered* (1989); and Barbara Melosh, *Engendering Culture: Manhood and Womanhood in New Deal Public Art and Theater* (1991). For art history, see the relevant segments of Donald Goddard, *American Painting* (1990), and the provocative Frances K. Pohl, *Framing America: A Social History of American Art* (2002). A cross-disciplinary approach to Depression culture appears in Alice G. Marquis, *Hopes and Ashes: The Birth of Modern Times, 1929–1939* (1986).

Hollywood's response to the Hays Code is described in Leonard J. Leff and Jerold L. Simmons, *The Dame in the Kimono: Hollywood, Censorship, and the Production Code from the 1920s to the 1960s* (1990). For the industry's relationship to audiences, see the relevant portions of John Izod, *Hollywood and the Box Office, 1895–1986* (1988). The social function of 1930s film is the subject of Richard Maltby, *Harmless Entertainment: Hollywood and the Ideology of Consensus* (1983). See also Joseph McBride, *Frank Capra: The Catastrophe of Success* (1992). Depression-era radio is treated in Fred J. MacDonald, *Don't Touch That Dial! Radio Programming in American Life from 1920 to 1960* (1979). Popular musical tastes are outlined in portions of Ian Whitcomb, *After the Ball: Popular Music from Rag to Rock* (1982). For jazz, see John Edward Hasse, *Beyond Category: The Life and Genius of Duke Ellington* (1993).

The participation of African American leaders in the New Deal political coalition and labor movement is described by Nancy J. Weiss, *Farewell to the Party of Lincoln: Black Politics in the Age of Franklin D. Roosevelt* (1983); Sarah E. Wright, *A. Philip Randolph: Integration in the Workplace* (1990); and Paula F. Pfeffer, *A. Philip Randolph: Pioneer of the Civil Rights Movement* (1990). For the growth of the civil rights movement among Mexican

Americans, see Mario T. Garcia, *Mexican-Americans: Leadership, Ideology, and Identity, 1930–1960* (1989).

An extensive literature on 1930s women's history includes Susan Ware, *Beyond Suffrage: Women in the New Deal* (1981), and *Holding Their Own: American Women in the 1930s* (1982). See also Winifred D. Wandersee, *Women's Work and Family Values, 1920–1940* (1981). For women and social welfare, see Linda Gordon, *Pitied but not Entitled: Single Mothers and the History of Welfare, 1890–1935* (1994). Blanche Wiesen Cook, *Eleanor Roosevelt, Volume 2: 1932–1939* (1999), offers a useful portrait of the First Lady's social activism.

The Popular Front's antifascist crusade is portrayed by Peter N. Carroll, *The Odyssey of the Abraham Lincoln Brigade: Americans in the Spanish Civil War* (1994). For the international context, see Douglas Little, *Malevolent Neutrality: The United States, Great Britain, and the Origins of the Spanish Civil War* (1985). The rise of populist conservatism is treated in Leo P. Ribuffo, *The Old Christian Right: The Protestant Far Right from the Great Depression to the Cold War* (1983), and Michael Kazin, *The Populist Persuasion, an American History* (1995). For the anti–New Deal coalition, see Ronald L. Feinman, *Twilight of Progressivism: The Western Republican Senators and the New Deal* (1981), and Ronald A. Mulder, *The Insurgent Progressives in the United States Senate and the New Deal, 1933–1939* (1979). Opposition to New Deal planning is discussed in David A. Horowitz, *America's Political Class Under Fire: The Twentieth Century's Great Culture War* (2003).

An overview of Roosevelt's international relations can be found in Robert Dallek, *Franklin D. Roosevelt and American Foreign Policy, 1932–1945* (1979), which can be supplemented by Waldo Heinrichs, *Threshold of War: Franklin D. Roosevelt and American Entry into World War II* (1988). The economic assumptions of U.S. foreign policy are surveyed in Patrick J. Hearden, *Roosevelt Confronts Hitler: America's Entry into World War II* (1987). Roosevelt's China policy is the subject of Michael Schaller, *The U.S. Crusade in China, 1938–1945* (1979). For hemispheric relations, see Irwin F. Gellman, *Good Neighbor Diplomacy: United States Policies in Latin America, 1933–1945* (1979).

The most comprehensive treatments of the noninterventionist movement are Justus Doenecke, *Storm on the Horizon: The Challenge to American Intervention, 1939–1941* (2000), and *The Battle Against Intervention, 1939–1941* (1997).

WORLD WAR II: WAR AGAINST FACISM AND THE SEARCH FOR GLOBAL ORDER

Early Sunday morning on December 7, 1941—"a date," said President Franklin D. Roosevelt, "that will live in infamy"—Japanese airplanes flew above the U.S. naval base at Pearl Harbor in Hawaii and began to attack the Pacific fleet, military airfields, and army barracks. Catching the base by surprise, the planes destroyed or damaged eight battleships, three cruisers, and 347 aircraft and caused nearly 3,500 U.S. casualties while sustaining minimal losses. The next day, President Roosevelt announced that a state of war existed, and he vowed to lead the country to "absolute victory." Enraged by the "sneak attack," Congress promptly voted a formal declaration of war (the only dissenter was pacifist Republican Jeannette Rankin). Three days later, Germany and Italy joined Japan and declared war on the United States, and the same day, December 11, Congress responded in kind.

U.S. participation in the war against fascism—which began with the German invasion of Poland on September 1, 1939, and ended with the Japanese surrender on September 2, 1945—emerged as a watershed in the nation's history, separating the prewar economic crisis from postwar affluence and dividing prewar neutrality from postwar interventionism. The war involved more private citizens—soldiers, civilian employees, workers, and consumers—in government activities than ever before. Total warfare saw industrial production double, increasing from $91 billion to $166 billion, and created 15 million new jobs. The war also expanded the federal government's powers. These changes laid the foundation for the postwar national security state, which demanded large military budgets and political consensus on the home front. The war had immense costs in terms of dollars, casualties, and disruption of ordinary lives. Yet ultimate victory not only served to justify the losses but also resulted in growing U.S. responsibility for global stability. For the next generation, World War II stood both as a warning against military weakness and as a reminder of U.S. industrial power.

THE PACIFIC STRATEGY

The conflict between Japan and the United States reflected decades of political and economic competition in the Pacific as well as deep racial antagonism. Pearl Harbor accentuated those feelings. Public opinion polls showed that large majorities wanted prompt vengeance against Japan. But Roosevelt took a global view of the war and insisted that Germany represented a greater threat to U.S. interests. "Defeat of Japan does not defeat Germany," he said, but "defeat of Germany means the defeat of Japan, probably without firing a shot or losing a life." Indeed, Japan's limited resources—its inability to sustain war without imported oil, rubber, or steel—assured its ultimate defeat, as some Japanese militarists acknowledged. But if Germany won in Europe, then Japan might hope for outside assistance.

Roosevelt never wavered from a Europe-first military strategy. Yet Japanese advances in the Pacific during 1942, to the dismay of public opinion, seemed to put the nation in a precarious position. One week after Pearl Harbor, U.S. forces surrendered Guam and, a week after that, capitulated at Wake Island. The Japanese then moved quickly into the Dutch East Indies, conquered the British naval base at Singapore, and advanced into the Gilbert and Solomon Islands. These setbacks climaxed in the capture of U.S. troops at Corregidor and Bataan in the Philippines—a strategic and psychological blow. The Japanese compelled U.S. prisoners of war to march fifty-five miles to prison camps, which resulted in thousands of deaths. When confirmed publicly in 1944, such atrocities intensified anger against Japan and justified total warfare against the Japanese people.

Despite the disaster at Pearl Harbor, however, the Japanese failed to destroy aircraft carriers and vital shore installations. Moreover, U.S. intelligence had broken Japanese naval codes, enabling the Navy to anticipate enemy operations. Within months, a restored naval fleet successfully engaged the Japanese in the Battle of the Coral Sea (May 1942) and at Midway (July 1942), using air power to destroy Japanese aircraft carriers, cruisers, and destroyers. These naval victories effectively ended Japanese expansion in the Pacific. By 1943 U.S. forces, backed by Australians and New Zealanders, began to reverse Japanese conquests. In a series of bloody island encounters, U.S. troops drove the Japanese from Guadalcanal in the Solomon Islands (January–February 1943), from Tarawa in the Gilbert Islands (November 1943), and from the Marianas (summer 1944). By February 1945, forces under the command of General Douglas MacArthur fulfilled his 1942 promise, "I shall return," and recaptured the Philippines, though with heavy casualties. In 1945, fierce Japanese resistance on the islands of Iwo Jima (where nearly 5,000 Americans and 21,000 Japanese were killed) and Okinawa (where more than 11,000

EXHIBIT **7-1**   **THE WAR AGAINST JAPAN, FINAL PHASE, 1944–1945**

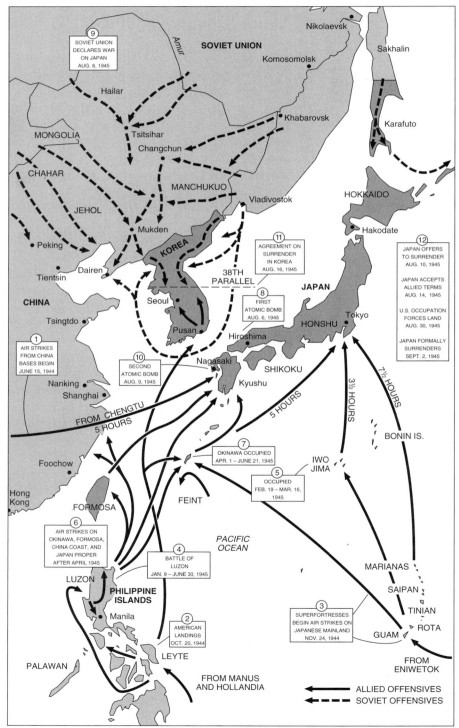

ALLIED OFFENSIVES
SOVIET OFFENSIVES

Americans and more than 110,000 Japanese were killed) alarmed military leaders and the public. The use of suicide *kamikaze* pilots suggested that fanatic Japanese would fight to the death to save Japan's home islands.

Each advance brought U.S. aircraft closer to Japanese cities, which became easy targets for mass bombardments. As early as 1942, General James Doolittle led an air raid on Tokyo, boosting U.S. morale. By mid-1944, U.S. bombers began attacking dispersed strategic targets in the cities. Weather conditions often prevented accuracy, and the incendiary bombs created dreadful firestorms that killed thousands of civilians. Such tactics served both to punish what was perceived as a fanatical enemy and to soften Japan for an amphibious landing after the defeat of Germany.

THE WAR IN EUROPE

In the European theater of operations political considerations played a greater role in shaping military strategy. Each of the Allied nations—the Soviet Union, Britain, and the United States—saw its own national interest as paramount. Reeling under the German advance, the Soviet Union needed military assistance and pleaded for a second front in western Europe to deflect German forces. Soviet leader Josef Stalin also wanted a postwar settlement that would protect his country from future invasions from central Europe. Besides defeating Germany, British Prime Minister Winston Churchill wanted to preserve the British colonial empire, including trade advantages with Commonwealth nations and the Middle East. For his part, Roosevelt wanted above all a quick defeat of Germany and Japan with minimal U.S. casualties; politically, he hoped to replace European spheres of influence—whether British or Soviet—with equal access to international trade for all nations.

These differences had important effects on military strategy. While Stalin pressed for a second front, U.S. generals advised a concentrated buildup of forces in Europe until an invasion of the continent could be mounted. However, Churchill, anxious for any victory and desiring to protect the Mediterranean, persuaded Roosevelt to support an invasion of North Africa, even though it would mean delay of a second front. The operation enabled the White House to deflect public demands to fight Japan first. Moreover, such action would show Stalin the Anglo-American commitment to defeat Germany, forestalling a separate Soviet truce.

In November 1942, the first U.S. troops landed in North Africa. After gaining early victories, U.S. military leaders opted to keep casualties low by accepting a negotiated settlement. General Dwight Eisenhower proceeded to reach an armistice with French Admiral Jean Darlan that permitted the pro-Nazi French to remain in power. By allowing Nazi collaborators to go unpunished, the deal outraged the U.S. public, although French patriots soon assassinated Darlan.

Beachhead assaults accounted for most U.S. battle casualties in the Pacific theater. These marines discard their life jackets as they charge from a landing craft to form a secure line.

The successful North African campaign eliminated German threats to Middle Eastern oil, protected shipping in the Mediterranean, and provided a base for the invasion of Italy. Soon afterward, Roosevelt and Churchill met at Casablanca, Morocco, in January 1943 and announced a policy of "unconditional surrender"—partly to divert criticism of the Darlan deal and partly to thwart any secret negotiations between Stalin and Hitler. Military advisers criticized the term *unconditional surrender* because they feared it would harden enemy resistance. However, Roosevelt wanted to demonstrate his sincerity to Stalin despite the delay in implementing the second front. While U.S. and British troops suffered light casualties in North Africa, Soviet armies engaged in savage warfare on the eastern front. Long before the Western Allies met large German forces, the Soviet army had devastated the German military, and the Soviet Union lost more than 25 million people. Still, the United States hoped for Soviet aid in the war against Japan after the defeat of Germany.

U.S. and British forces finally invaded Europe in the summer of 1943. Landing in Sicily and mainland Italy, Allied troops encountered hard fighting along the Italian coast. Mussolini soon fell from power and was replaced by Marshal Pietro Badoglio, who conditionally surrendered in September 1943. In agreeing to negotiate with Badoglio, U.S. and British leaders recognized his potential as an anticommunist force in postwar Italy. The Western Allies excluded the Soviet Union from the Allied Control Commission in Italy and answered Stalin's protests by arguing that the Soviet army had not participated in the Italian campaign. This decision set an important precedent for Soviet policy in

EXHIBIT **7-2   WESTERN EUROPEAN THEATER, 1942–1945**

1. Allied landings, North Africa, Nov. 8, 1942
2. Surrender Tunisia, May 13, 1943
3. Allied landings Sicily, July 10, 1943
4. Allied landings Italy, Sept. 9, 1943
5. Italian surrender, Malta, Sept. 29, 1943
6. Allied landings Normandy, June 6, 1944
7. Allied landings southern France, Aug. 15, 1944
8. Paris liberated, Aug. 25, 1944
9. German surrender, Reims, May 7, 1945

eastern Europe. Meanwhile, after the surrender of Italian forces, German units entered Italy, where they fought against Allied troops until 1945.

Buoyed by success in Italy, the Big Three—Roosevelt, Churchill, and Stalin—met at Teheran in November 1943 and agreed to open a second front in France the next spring. They also agreed to a temporary division of postwar Germany into zones and prepared to claim reparations for the cost of the war. In addition, Stalin promised to declare war on Japan soon after the German defeat.

As the Allies prepared to invade France in the spring of 1944, U.S. and British aircraft began bombing factories and transportation routes on the European continent, a policy that caused thousands of civilian deaths. Although postwar studies found that the raids barely disrupted German industry, bombing proved more successful in destroying crucial oil resources and rail transportation. The destruction of German air forces also facilitated Allied landings

Audie Murphy *(1924–1971)*

For Audie Murphy, as for thousands of other young people his age, the formative experiences of his life were the Great Depression of the 1930s and the Great War of the 1940s. One of eleven children born to a family of Texas sharecroppers, Murphy grew up amid tragedy and poverty. As

the Dust Bowl destroyed his land, Murphy's father abandoned the family; Murphy's mother, a woman he described as "a sad-eyed, silent woman" who "toiled eternally," died soon after. The younger children went to an orphanage, and sixteen-year-old Murphy drifted through a series of dead-end jobs.

A kid with nothing to lose, Murphy saw World War II as his chance to make something of his life, and he tried to enlist on his eighteenth birthday. The Marine Corps and the Army Air Corps rejected him because he was too small, but he finally got a place in the infantry. The new private assured himself that his assignment was only temporary until he could find a more suitable and more daring role as a glider pilot.

Instead, Murphy spent a harrowing two and a half years as a combat infantryman in North Africa, Italy, and France. His most celebrated moment came in February 1945, when he climbed atop a burning tank and turned its machine guns on an advancing wave of German attackers and blunted the assault. His heroics earned him the Medal of Honor and a host of other decorations as well. By the end of the war Murphy had achieved the rank of second lieutenant and become the most decorated

on the beaches of Normandy on D-Day—June 6, 1944—the largest amphibious military operation in history. After tough fighting in northern France, the Allies moved eastward, racing to destroy German armies. Meanwhile, Soviet armies pressed into Germany from the east, killing or capturing more Germans in the two months after D-Day than were stationed in all of western Europe.

As the Allies approached victory in Europe, the Big Three met at Yalta in February 1945 to plan a postwar political settlement. At a time when the defeat of Japan seemed both difficult and remote, Stalin repeated his promise to

U.S. combat veteran. His brief, sparely written memoir, *To Hell and Back*, attracted attention in Hollywood and became a movie of the same title. Murphy portrayed himself in the film and launched a career in Grade B films in which he usually played a cowboy or soldier.

The young man who had gone to war seeking glory, however, was acutely aware that he had found very little of it. For him, military conflict was brutal and inescapable. "I see war as it is," he later wrote, "an endless series of problems involving blood and guts." Of his original company of 235 men, only Murphy and one other man escaped the conflict without injury. As he later affirmed in his GI catechism, "I believe in the force of a hand grenade, the power of artillery, the accuracy of a Garand. I believe in hitting before you get hit, and that dead men do not look noble." His return to civilian life was marked by stress and disillusionment. The war had "branded" him, Murphy recalled, and for years afterward he was unable to sleep at night without a pistol under his pillow. The medals he had won were meaningless to him, and he gave most of them away to children.

Searing as it was, Murphy's experience was atypical for most U.S. soldiers of his era. Although 16 million men and women served in the armed forces, only one in eight saw combat duty; and U.S. fatalities, while surpassing 400,000, remained a fraction of those suffered by other belligerents. Nevertheless, the psychological effects of unconditional warfare against ruthless dictators left a lasting impression on the nation's life and simultaneously affected and compromised the postwar search for "normalcy" and security.

enter the Pacific war. This move lessened the importance of China in ending the war. No longer worried about Chinese support, Roosevelt and Churchill agreed to compensate the Soviets with the Kuril Islands north of Japan as well as economic rights in Manchuria. The Allies also reaffirmed the temporary partition of Germany, including the division of Berlin into occupied zones. They could not agree about the amount or the nature of German war reparations.

The main problem at Yalta involved Poland—the country whose defense had triggered World War II in 1939. To protect the Soviet Union's western boundary, Stalin demanded recognition of territory taken from Poland during

At Yalta, the "Big Three" (left to right): Prime Minister Winston Churchill, President Franklin Roosevelt, and Soviet Premier Josef Stalin.

his alliance with Hitler (1939–1941). To compensate Poland, Germany would surrender areas of eastern Prussia. Stalin also demanded a friendly Polish government on his vulnerable border, an idea Roosevelt and Churchill reluctantly accepted. The Western Allies did convince Stalin to broaden the Polish government to include some Poles who had established a noncommunist government in exile in London and to permit "free and unfettered elections" as soon as possible. Yet in Poland as in Italy, the Allies did not have an equal stake. Roosevelt understood that the Soviet Union would dominate eastern Europe, particularly because the delayed opening of the second front gave the Soviet army control of the territory east of Germany.

Although the Big Three made major decisions without consulting all the affected nations, Roosevelt believed that an international organization, the United Nations, was essential to keep the peace. A disciple of former president Woodrow Wilson, Roosevelt believed that collective security would be meaningless without the participation of the great powers. Whereas Wilson had envisioned a league of all nations, Roosevelt suggested that "Four Policemen"—the United States, the Soviet Union, Great Britain, and China—would provide greater stability and called for their permanent seating in what would become the United Nations Security Council. Unlike Wilson, Roosevelt worked to gain bipartisan support for the United Nations in Congress. Indeed, Roosevelt's hope of winning congressional approval of the United Nations led him to conceal the pro-Soviet Polish settlement, which he knew would be unpopular.

By 1945, public opinion strongly supported U.S. leadership in the United Nations. Plans for the international organization were first drafted at the Dumbarton Oaks Conference in Washington in 1944. The new international league included a Security Council in which each of the Big Four held veto power. By assuring no infringement of U.S. sovereignty, this power helped win congressional support of the United Nations. Congress also ratified U.S. participation in the Bretton Woods (New Hampshire) Agreement of 1944, by which the United States sought to ensure postwar economic stability and free trade through the creation of the World Bank and the International Monetary Fund.

Roosevelt's vision of the postwar world reflected the realities of military power and his view of U.S. self-interest. As a proponent of free international trade, he opposed returning Indochina to France and expected Britain to move toward decolonization. Yet the defeat of Japan would create a power vacuum in Asia. Roosevelt envisioned the rise of an independent China free from European imperialism and strong enough to provide a buffer against the Soviet Union. In elevating China, Roosevelt exaggerated the role of Chiang Kai-shek as a force for national unity. Numerous U.S. diplomats in China had condemned the ineptitude of Chiang's regime and had stressed the importance of a coalition government with Chinese communists. Roosevelt rejected this advice. His decision assured the continuation of the civil war that had raged in China since the 1920s. Roosevelt's dislike of diplomatic formalities also undermined his hopes for decolonization. His unwillingness to issue clear directives about Indochina, for example, gave his subordinates no guidelines for future policy. These omissions assumed critical importance when Roosevelt died suddenly in April 1945.

WARTIME MOBILIZATION

"If you . . . go to war . . . in a capitalist country," said Secretary of War Henry Stimson, "you have to let business make money out of the process or business won't work." During the 1930s, the economy had lagged in Depression conditions, but the nation possessed a mighty industrial potential that soon exceeded all expectations. Once war began, a marriage between government and business brought astounding results. One year after Pearl Harbor, the United States was producing more war materiel than were all its enemies combined. With 1943 levels of production, replacing all the aircraft lost at Pearl Harbor would take only two days. U.S. shipyards built 5,800 vessels, mostly cargo ships and tankers, reducing the building time of a Liberty ship to 56 days. Such achievements restored public confidence in business and undermined Depression-era critics who doubted that capitalism could survive without major changes. In turn, corporate leaders learned the advantages of cooperation with the federal government. Indeed, Washington provided two-thirds of the $26 billion spent on wartime plants and equipment.

Roosevelt had recognized the importance of preparing industry for war as early as 1938, but had not adopted a specific plan. In 1939 the president appointed a War Resources Board, but noninterventionist opinion prompted him to ignore its report. Other bureaucracies followed: an Advisory Commission for National Defense, which was later replaced by the Office of Production Management; the Office of Price Administration, which supervised price controls; and the Supply Priorities and Allocations Board, which dealt with problems of industrial conversion. These agencies started moving the economy toward wartime production. During 1941 arms manufacturing increased 225 percent.

Roosevelt's efforts to administer the wartime economy mirrored the improvisational strategy of the New Deal. After Pearl Harbor, the president created the War Production Board (WPB), which set production goals and priorities for the allocation of resources and raw materials. Other decisions involved coordinating supplies for the civilian economy, the military, and Lend-Lease. Amid much bureaucratic struggle, the military managed to bypass civilian oversight of procurement and obtained control of supply purchases, which created relationships between the Pentagon and private business that lasted into the postwar era. Meanwhile, Lend-Lease accounted for nearly $50 billion in materiel shipped overseas (60 percent to Britain; 20 percent to the Soviet Union; the rest to other countries).

In developing the war economy, the government had to convince private business to set aside peacetime production. Many industrialists feared that conversion to war-related manufacturing would cause overproduction, leading to a postwar depression. Others were reluctant to abandon civilian-oriented production that was stimulated by wartime jobs and consumer spending. To win business confidence, the White House appointed corporate leaders to "dollar-a-year" positions on the War Production Board and other agencies and encouraged administrators to adopt policies that would reduce the risks associated with conversion to a wartime economy.

Headed by Donald M. Nelson of Sears, Roebuck, the War Production Board awarded $175 billion in "cost-plus" contracts that guaranteed fixed profits. The federal government also financed some $800 million a year in private research and development programs at businesses and universities. More

EXHIBIT **7-3   NATIONAL DEFENSE SPENDING, 1941–1945**
(IN ROUNDED BILLIONS OF DOLLARS)

1941	14.0
1943	78.9
1945	95.2

Source: *Historical Statistics of the United States, Colonial Times to 1970* (1975).

than fifty firms and schools received contracts worth $1 million or more. Government funds supported expensive technological projects at Cal Tech's Jet Propulsion Laboratory as well as the top-secret atomic energy programs at Los Alamos, New Mexico; Hanford, Washington; and Oak Ridge, Tennessee. Wartime scientists and engineers in government-funded university laboratories achieved breakthroughs in electronic digital computing that would lay the foundation for an enormous postwar industry.

Government policy encouraged industrial mobilization by abandoning antitrust actions against war-related businesses and offering contractors generous tax deductions. For example, defense contractors were allowed to take possession of commercial assets leased from the government after five years and were awarded tax write-offs for expenses incurred in reconverting the property to civilian production. Wartime excess profits taxes collected by the Internal Revenue Service were returned to companies to defray reconversion costs. Such subsidies amounted to the greatest capital expansion in U.S. history and provided the foundation for economic growth in the postwar era.

Wartime production and investment policies generally favored big businesses over small firms. Two-thirds of military contracts went to just 100 companies. Large corporations had greater access to government agencies and more experience with extensive procurement contracts. Although the administration responded to complaints by creating the Smaller War Plants Corporation, the government's primary objective remained maximum industrial efficiency. During World War II, industrial production increased 96 percent, while net corporate profits doubled. Equally important, half a million small businesses disappeared, some of them absorbed by 1,600 corporate mergers.

The war demanded tremendous quantities of natural resources such as petroleum. One armored battalion, for example, used 17,000 gallons of gasoline to move 100 miles; the Fifth Fleet consumed 630 million gallons of oil in less than two months. U.S. oil companies met these huge demands in return for protection from government interference, including immunity from antitrust suits, and a dominant voice in making national oil policy. Petroleum corporations also expanded production in the Middle East to lessen the drain on domestic oil reserves. This decision required direct government support

EXHIBIT 7-4   GROSS NATIONAL PRODUCT, 1941–1945
(IN ROUNDED BILLIONS OF DOLLARS)

1941	124.5
1943	191.6
1945	211.9

Source: *Historical Statistics of the United States, Colonial Times to 1970* (1975).

such as Lend-Lease aid to Saudi Arabia. Such government assistance enabled the industry to produce 6 billion barrels of oil during the war. However, postwar petroleum policy, including increasing dependence on foreign oil, remained in private hands.

MOBILIZING PEOPLE

"Every single man, woman, and child," said Roosevelt as he led the nation into war, "is a partner in the most tremendous undertaking of our American history." Congress had limited the peacetime army to 375,000 men, but the first draft law of 1940 added another 800,000. After Pearl Harbor, volunteers rushed to enlist in all services; but the draft provided the bulk of U.S. soldiers. By war's end 16 million people had served in the armed forces. Of these, 12 percent participated in combat; 25 percent never left the country. The new army included 700,000 African Americans, who served in segregated units, and 25,000 Native Americans—including Navajo codetalkers—who were fully integrated. Nearly 300,000 women volunteered for the Women's Army Auxiliary Corps (later renamed Women's Army Corps—WAC) and the Navy's WAVES (Women Accepted for Volunteer Emergency Service). As noncombatants, the WACs did traditional women's work as clerks, cooks, operators, and servants. To avoid upsetting public opinion, WAC Director Oveta Culp Hobby enforced policies that presented women soldiers as feminine and chaste; black WACs remained segregated.

On the home front, the mobilization of the workforce demanded even larger numbers. Between 1940 and 1947, 25 million people (21 percent of the population) left home for another county or state. The nation's rural population dropped by 6 million, falling from 24 to 18 percent of the total population. As the federal government invested $70 billion in wartime industries in the West, 7 million Americans moved across the Mississippi, half of them going to the Pacific Coast. California gained 3.5 million residents during the 1940s. The search for wartime jobs drew 750,000 African Americans from the South, reducing the region's share of the black population from 77 percent to

EXHIBIT **7-5**   **CIVILIAN UNEMPLOYMENT RATES, 1939–1945**

1939	17.2%
1941	9.9%
1943	1.9%
1945	1.9%

Source: *Historical Statistics of the United States, Colonial Times to 1970* (1975).

68 percent. Meanwhile, 40,000 Native Americans left their reservations for war work. This migration permanently changed the character of all regions.

Wartime jobs effectively ended the Great Depression. Although 8 million workers (17 percent of the labor force) remained unemployed in 1939, most soon found jobs. By 1942, other previously unemployable workers—teenagers, the elderly, minorities, and women—also began to find work. The number of government civilian employees jumped from 950,000 in 1939 to 3.8 million in 1945. By then, 7 million new workers had jobs on the home front.

Opportunities for better jobs ironically encouraged frequent worker turnover, causing shortages in crucial industries. To oversee such problems, Roosevelt created a War Manpower Commission, but the agency lacked enforcement powers, and absenteeism and job mobility remained common. In 1944 the turnover rate in manufacturing industries was 82 percent. As in the Depression, however, labor disruptions were more than offset by time-saving machinery that increased individual productivity. The Department of Agriculture estimated that farm productivity increased 25 percent per work hour between 1939 and 1945 because of mechanization, land consolidation, and use of chemical fertilizers. In the Southwest the need for farm and railroad workers led the government to negotiate with Mexico to recruit contract laborers. This "bracero" (manual labor) program brought the United States more than 200,000 Mexicans, who accepted low wages for temporary work.

The shortage of labor provided opportunities for rural African Americans. Displaced by farm machines or seeking better jobs, large numbers of southern blacks moved to urban centers. Yet as the war began, many still confronted racial discrimination in employment, even in government programs and within the armed services. "It is against company policy to employ them as aircraft workers or mechanics . . . regardless of their training," declared the president of North American Aviation in a typical statement. "There will be some jobs as janitors for Negroes."

Challenging such discrimination, A. Philip Randolph, president of the Brotherhood of Sleeping Car Porters, called for a protest march on Washington in 1941. The proposal embarrassed the president and in June 1941 forced Roosevelt to issue Executive Order 8802 prohibiting job discrimination in war

Asa Philip Randolph *(1889–1979)*

A. Philip Randolph, a dignified and soft-spoken man who served as president of a small union of railroad sleeping car attendants, ranked as the nation's single most important African American leader of the 1930s and '40s. By 1941 Randolph's efforts to build a mass movement of black

working people elicited the first federal proclamation concerning people of color since the Civil War.

Born in Jacksonville, Florida, Randolph departed on a steamboat for New York City in 1911. A devout follower of civil rights advocate W. E. B. Du Bois, he believed himself to be among the "talented tenth" of African Americans that Du Bois had described. Randolph took night classes at City College and gravitated toward socialism. In 1915 he

helped to launch the *Messenger,* a radical black magazine that opposed participation in World War I until African Americans achieved equality at home. These efforts resulted in his being questioned by the Justice Department for potential violations of the Espionage Act.

Randolph's career took a new direction when black railroad porters asked him to organize a union in 1925. Ever since emancipation, the Pullman Company had hired black men only as porters, believing that subservient and congenial former slaves would accept insults and demands from white passengers. Pullman was the largest private employer of blacks in the nation, and Randolph hoped to show that his people could build and sustain an organization to pursue their own economic

industries and creating a Fair Employment Practices Committee to investigate complaints. During the war years, the FEPC successfully challenged numerous cases of racial discrimination. Yet Roosevelt worried about antagonizing southern Democrats in Congress and the military and therefore declined to order the desegregation of the armed services, government departments, or labor unions. The California Supreme Court finally outlawed segregated unions in 1945, but West Coast African Americans continued to encounter racial restrictions in housing and public accommodations. Despite these disadvantages, some 2 million blacks eventually found work in war industries.

survival without permitting whites to choose their leaders. The Brotherhood of Sleeping Car Porters organized half the Pullman porters and maids within three years and won higher monthly salaries, respectful treatment, and an end to demeaning tipping.

Randolph's success catapulted him into national black leadership in the 1930s. As president of the National Negro Congress, he called for a new deal for the nation's "submerged tenth" and urged African Americans to join the growing industrial union movement. Randolph reasoned that black struggles for social justice paralleled the efforts of white workers and liberal allies. Yet he also pointed out that "the salvation of the Negro . . . must come from within." Accordingly, when the Roosevelt administration failed to heed protests against racial discrimination in defense work, Randolph threatened to lead a march of 100,000 black working people to the capital in 1941.

Despite pleas for restraint from white liberals, Randolph insisted that "there are some things Negroes must do alone." His strategy rested on the understanding that Washington would be compelled to contrast pluralist democracy with Nazi creeds of Aryan supremacy. When President Roosevelt summoned the black leader to ask whether he could deliver the promised protesters, Randolph never hesitated. One week before the scheduled march, Roosevelt issued Executive Order 8802, which forbade job discrimination by government contractors and created a Fair Employment Practices Committee. Although wartime enforcement proved to be inconsistent, Randolph helped to lay the foundations of the postwar civil rights revolution by popularizing the concept of mass demonstrations led and organized by African Americans.

The labor crisis also catapulted women into new jobs. Although women constituted 25 percent of the prewar workforce, middle-class opinion disapproved of working women. Even as the nation prepared for war, private contractors often refused to hire women. To encourage women's employment, the Office of War Information supported a domestic propaganda campaign to make women's work appear patriotic. Most women worked because they needed the wages and appreciated the opportunity to take better-paying jobs normally reserved for men. A considerable proportion of black women also moved from domestic to industrial occupations, although they remained in the lowest wage brackets. Between 1941 and 1945, 6.5 million women entered the labor force—a 57 percent increase. By the war's end 36 percent of all civilian workers were women.

Women were entitled to the same pay as men for the same work, but most earned the minimum wage and were usually excluded from management positions. Businesses often segregated women into "female" jobs, which paid less than "male" jobs. These practices reflected the prevailing belief that war work was temporary, intended not to encourage women's independence or accelerate their working careers but simply to support the men at war. Although a government survey showed that 75 percent of women wished to retain their jobs, business and union leaders agreed that women should give up their jobs to returning veterans. "Americans may no longer believe that a woman's place is in the home," sociologist Jerome Bruner observed, "but more important, we believe even less that a man's place is on the street without a job."

Taking advantage of worker shortages, organized labor aggressively enrolled new union members. Between 1939 and 1945 union membership nearly doubled, and unions claimed 15 million organized workers. The number of women union workers quadrupled to 3 million by 1944. After Pearl Harbor, unions adopted a no-strike policy but continued to press for higher wages. To deal with disputes, Roosevelt created new government agencies that regulated wages, hours, and working conditions. The National War Labor Board attempted to control wage inflation by establishing a cost-of-living standard, but wage limits did not apply to overtime work. Although hourly wages increased 24 percent during the war, weekly earnings rose 70 percent. In exchange for no-strike agreements and wage limits, organized labor accepted policies that encouraged workers to join unions.

Despite these gains, numerous unauthorized wildcat strikes occurred, even in war industries, and affected 3 million workers in 1943. A national coal miners' strike that year threatened the entire economy. Such walkouts intensified antilabor sentiment. In 1943 Congress responded by passing, over Roosevelt's veto, the Smith-Connally Labor Act, which imposed a thirty-day cooling off period before workers could go on strike, prohibited strikes in war industries, and banned union contributions to political parties. Despite such rules, U.S. workers participated in nearly 10,000 spontaneous walkouts between 1944 and 1945.

THE HOME FRONT

With business booming and workers earning large paychecks, the economy faced runaway inflation. In 1942 the Office of Price Administration froze most consumer prices. Yet food prices continued to climb. Congress then passed the Anti-Inflation Act of 1942, which regulated farm prices and wages and

EXHIBIT **7-6**   **CONSUMER PRICE INDEX, 1941–1945**
(1967 = 100)

1941	44.1
1943	51.8
1945	53.9

Source: *Historical Statistics of the United States, Colonial Times to 1970* (1975).

stabilized the economy. During the last two years of the war, consumer prices increased by less than 2 percent.

To conserve scarce materials, the government instituted a rationing program for canned goods (because of tin shortages), rubber, gasoline, coffee, shoes, sugar, meat, butter, and fuel oil. Most civilians saw personal sacrifices as part of the patriotic effort, although people with cash could violate the rules in an illegal black market. The government also organized scrap campaigns to collect used goods such as tires and cans. More effective were mass campaigns by Hollywood celebrities to encourage the purchase of war bonds. Through payroll deduction plans and bond drives, sales reached $135 billion, $40 billion of which was purchased by small investors. Bond sales discouraged inflation by absorbing consumer dollars.

During four years of war, the federal government spent $321 billion, ten times as much as World War I cost. Taxation financed more than 40 percent of the total bill (further reducing consumer purchasing power). The Revenue Act of 1942 increased tax rates and broadened the tax base to include lower-income workers for the first time. The measure increased corporate taxes to 40 percent and raised excess profits taxes to 90 percent, although loopholes and generous interpretations frequently lowered these rates in practice. The law also instituted the payroll withholding tax, keeping dollars out of consumers' hands. Taxes on high personal income and excess profits produced a substantial temporary redistribution of personal income. The top 5 percent income bracket declined in relative economic worth as its control of disposable income diminished. At the same time, full employment and the increase in two-income families brought greater purchasing power to poorer people. The number of families earning less than $2,000 a year was halved, whereas the number of those making more than $5,000 a year increased fourfold.

Commodity shortages and rationing cut across class lines: People with money could not always find what they wanted to buy. In 1942, for example, the government ordered the automobile industry to stop making cars and light trucks and switch to making tanks and airplanes. Unable to purchase consumer goods, workers put their wartime earnings into personal savings accounts, which would later provide the capital for heavy postwar consumer spending. Wartime advertising also directed attention from shortages to postwar opportunities. "Ordnance Today, Washers Tomorrow," boasted the Easy

EXHIBIT 7-7   FEDERAL BUDGET DEFICITS, 1940–1945
(IN ROUNDED BILLIONS OF DOLLARS)

1940	2.9
1945	47.6

Source: *Historical Statistics of the United States, Colonial Times to 1970* (1975).

Washing Machine Company. The Cessna Aircraft Company predicted that the "Family Car of the Air" would enable weekend golfers to tee off 500 miles from home "after the war."

Without available consumer goods, people with money purchased entertainment. By 1945, Hollywood movie attendance reached 80 million customers a week. The government's Office of War Information, using the power to censor overseas screenings, supported pro-war movies while eliminating unfavorable portrayals of the nation. One government-backed documentary series—Frank Capra's *Why We Fight* films—described the war as "a common man's life and death struggle against those who would put him back in slavery. We lose it, and we lose everything." Hollywood movies were equally patriotic—celebrating U.S. allies, deprecating the enemy, and inspiring sacrifices on the home front. War films—*Sahara* (1942) and *Pride of the Marines* (1945), for example—depicted U.S. soldiers as a melting pot of nationalities, stressing the combat role of white ethnics and nonwhite minorities.

Popular images of U.S. enemies paralleled the course of the war. In 1942, 600,000 Italian Americans had not become naturalized citizens and legally were "enemy aliens," but only a few suspected fascists were arrested for the duration of the war. Roosevelt, aware of the ethnic antagonism of World War I, hoped to limit attacks against white ethnics. He also appreciated the power of the Italian vote in the 1942 congressional elections. On Columbus Day, the president revoked the enemy alien status of most Italian Americans and eased procedures for naturalization. In a similar election situation in 1944, Roosevelt announced both a loan and relief supplies for the defeated Italian enemy, then viewed as an ally against the German occupiers. Films, such as *Sahara,* differentiated between the Italian people and Italy's fascist government and helped prepare the public for the lenient treatment of Italy in 1943.

In contrast, mass media portrayed Nazis and Japanese as ruthless savages. Because the administration played down anti-German feeling, the media distinguished between Nazis and other Germans. "They despise the world of civilians," said *Life* magazine of the German military. "They wear monocles to train themselves to control their face muscles." Hollywood used such stereotypes to scoff at Nazi stupidity, encouraging audiences to laugh at the world conquerors. Depictions of the Japanese were humorless. Partly because of anger at Japanese atrocities and partly because of anti-Asian racism, movies and advertisements portrayed this enemy as subhuman. In dehumanizing the Japanese, however, the media recognized friendly Asian people, especially Chinese and Filipinos. No longer would all Asians be lumped together as "Orientals."

POLITICS IN WARTIME

Despite media pleas for national unity and ethnic cooperation, political disagreements undermined Roosevelt's search for consensus, especially after the 1942 elections increased conservative strength in Congress. The new majority proceeded to dismantle such New Deal agencies as the Civilian Conservation Corps, the National Youth Administration, and the Works Progress Administration. In 1943, Roosevelt announced what he could not prevent: "Dr. New Deal" had been replaced by "Dr. Win the War." By 1945, federal spending had leaped nearly ten times above prewar levels to $95 billion, and the number of civilian employees in the federal government had tripled to nearly 4 million. After numerous investigations, Congress attempted to reverse government growth by limiting Office of Price Administration spending and by abolishing the National Resources Planning Board, an executive bureau that supported deficit spending to fund a postwar social welfare state.

Despite his difficulties with Congress, the president continued to hope for postwar reform. In 1944 Roosevelt proposed an economic "bill of rights," arguing that the nation could not "be content if some fraction of our people . . . is ill-fed, ill-clothed, ill-housed and insecure." The president also demanded legislation for liberal veterans' benefits. By 1944, about 1 million veterans had returned from the armed services, many of them injured or unable to adjust to civilian life. Congress responded by enacting the Servicemen's Readjustment Act, known as the "GI Bill of Rights," a landmark measure that provided unemployment, Social Security, and educational benefits to veterans. By providing college scholarships, home loans, and life insurance, the GI Bill reintegrated veterans into civilian society and helped stimulate postwar prosperity by increasing their purchasing power.

Roosevelt's problems with conservatives dominated the 1944 presidential election. Vice President Henry A. Wallace, an outspoken liberal, had offended regular party bosses as well as southern Democrats. Roosevelt prudently dropped Wallace and chose Senator Harry S Truman of Missouri as his running mate. Truman had gained popularity as chairman of the Senate War Investigating Committee, which had exposed government waste and war profiteering. Republicans nominated Governor Thomas E. Dewey of New York, often identified with the party's Wall Street wing, to challenge Roosevelt's bid for a fourth term. Dewey endorsed a bipartisan foreign policy, including a postwar United Nations, and accepted such New Deal programs as Social Security, unemployment benefits, and collective bargaining. In the election the Democrats benefited from the campaign support of the Congress of Industrial Organizations' Political Action Committee, which brought out the labor vote. This urban electorate provided Roosevelt's margin of victory. Although the president's popular vote slipped below 54 percent of the total, Roosevelt took advantage of the wartime mood of crisis to win an unprecedented fourth term.

BATTLES ON THE HOME FRONT

Roosevelt's efforts to minimize political disturbances nevertheless accentuated important divisions in U.S. political and cultural life. Concerned about threats to national security from pro-Nazi, pro-fascist, and pro-communist groups, the White House approved an FBI domestic intelligence program that violated traditional civil liberties, arranged for the possible arrest of so-called subversives, and permitted the military to discriminate against political radicals. The administration also engineered a "Brown Scare" to preserve the "free world" from Nazi subversion. Roosevelt pressed Catholic leaders to silence the acerbic anti-Semitic broadcasts of radio priest Father Charles Coughlin. The Department of Justice mounted a mass sedition trial, accusing thirty defendants of conspiring with Nazi Germany to undermine the loyalty of the armed forces. Yet the proceedings were marred by insufficient evidence and ended in an embarrassing mistrial in 1944. Although the Soviet Union fought as an ally, the government suspected—correctly in some cases—that communist sympathizers were working with spies to acquire military and diplomatic secrets. Making no distinctions between criminal activities and political dissidence, the FBI and the military treated all communists as dangerous, which laid the foundation for the postwar "Red Scare."

Government indifference to civil rights in wartime appeared most blatantly in the arrest of more than 110,000 West Coast Japanese Americans. Alarmed by Pearl Harbor and Japanese victories in the Pacific, journalists and political leaders falsely reported that California Japanese had conspired with the Japanese enemy and planned further subversion at home. When none occurred, California Attorney General Earl Warren used this demonstrable loyalty as counterproof: "We are just being lulled into a false sense of security," he told Congress, "and the only reason we haven't had disaster in California is because it has been timed for a different date." Racism played a large role in this disregard for Japanese American civil rights. "It's a question of whether the white man lives on the Pacific or a brown man," admitted one farmer anxious to get rid of Japanese American competition. The commanding general of the West Coast area, John DeWitt, simply stated, "A Jap's a Jap. . . . It makes no difference if he is an American citizen." However, the army assumed that 150,000 Japanese Americans in Hawaii, necessary to the islands' wartime economy, were loyal and need not be detained or removed.

Roosevelt shared this distrust of Japanese Americans. Disregarding counter advice from military and civilian leaders, in 1942 the president issued Executive Order 9066, which required the internment and relocation of all Japanese on the West Coast. Two-thirds of the affected people were U.S. citizens by birth (under the Naturalization Act of 1924, Japanese immigrants could not become citizens). Many second-generation Japanese Americans, or Nisei, wished to prove their loyalty by complying with the order. Others protested vigorously: "Has the Gestapo come to America? Have we not risen in righteous anger at Hitler's mistreatment of the Jews? Then, is it not incongruous that citizen Americans of Japanese descent should be similarly mistreated and persecuted?"

Forced to sell their property at short notice—usually to unscrupulous buyers—the Japanese were herded into detention centers and then relocated into ten concentration camps in remote, often bleak parts of the country. Despite serious constitutional questions concerning the rights of citizens, the American Civil Liberties Union hesitated to defend the Japanese. Moreover, government officials conspired to present tainted evidence to the Supreme Court, which in the *Korematsu* case of 1944 upheld the relocation on grounds of military necessity. In the *Endo* decision, however, the Court ruled that citizens could not be detained once their loyalty had been established. By then the administration understood that internment was no longer necessary. Yet the president delayed closing the concentration camps for five months because he feared that release of Japanese American prisoners might hurt his reelection bid in 1944. Litigation would continue into the 1980s, when surviving Japanese American prisoners received economic compensation from the federal government for a wartime loss of $400 million in property. Despite these abuses of government power, 18,000 Nisei volunteered for military service and fought heroically in a segregated unit in the European theater of war. However, several thousand Japanese Americans, angered by their treatment, disavowed U.S. citizenship and returned to Japan after the war.

In contrast to internment, pleas for national unity enabled Native Americans to obtain equal treatment with whites and provided African Americans with reasons to challenge racial prejudice. Whereas the theme for blacks in World War I had been W. E. B. Du Bois's summons to "close ranks," African American leaders in World War II launched a "Double V" campaign: "Declarations of war do not lessen the obligation to preserve and extend civil liberties" at home. Randolph's March on Washington movement did not disband but persisted as an all-black pressure group. Meanwhile, the NAACP increased its membership ninefold to 450,000 during the war. In 1942 nonviolence advocate James Farmer founded the Congress of Racial Equality (CORE), which used sit-ins to desegregate public facilities in Chicago and Washington, D.C. "Not since Reconstruction," concluded Gunnar Myrdal's massive study of racism, *An American Dilemma* (1944), "has there been more reason to anticipate fundamental changes in American race relations."

Changes came slower than Myrdal predicted. In the military, African Americans, like Japanese Americans, served in segregated units; and the Red Cross separated "colored" blood from "white." (Ironically, a black physician, Charles Drew, had originally developed blood transfusion techniques.) Military policy, explained one general, "is simply transferring discrimination from everyday life into the Army." Believing that African Americans could not make good soldiers, the army assigned blacks to labor units and denied them opportunities for promotion and prestigious duties such as flying. Despite proven battlefield valor, no African Americans received Medals of Honor during World War II (although in 1997 President Bill Clinton belatedly awarded the nation's highest military honor to seven African American heroes of that war). To their humiliation, black soldiers discovered that Nazi prisoners of war could use public eating facilities in places where African American soldiers in uniform were denied service. Such treatment provoked numerous race riots on and off military bases (two-thirds of blacks were stationed in the South). In one notorious case, black athlete Jackie Robinson was court-martialed—and acquitted—for refusing to sit in the back of a bus.

African Americans also faced racial problems at home. A public opinion poll taken at the beginning of the war found that 18 percent of blacks admitted pro-Japanese feelings; in a similar poll, when asked to choose between complete racial equality or a German victory, the vast majority of southern white industrialists preferred a Nazi victory. In northern Detroit, whites rioted in 1942 to prevent blacks from living in a federally funded housing project. Whites also initiated "hate" strikes to protest the entry of blacks into factories and shipyards. In 1943 Detroit exploded in a two-day riot that left 35 dead and more than 700 injured. In Philadelphia, trolley car workers went on strike to protest integration, leading the federal government to send armed troops to break the strike. Major race riots also occurred in New York's Harlem, Texas, Ohio, and Massachusetts.

Despite these conflicts, World War II represented an ideological turning point in U.S. race relations. The repudiation of Nazi racism, reinforced at the war's end by the discovery of the infamous death camps, challenged all racist assumptions. In 1943 the American Bar Association admitted its first black member. That year Congress passed legislation accepting Chinese immigration and naturalization, a reversal of racial exclusion policies established in 1882. In 1944 the Supreme Court overturned the white primary, which had served to disenfranchise black voters in most southern states. In Hollywood movies, the "Sambo" stereotypes of the 1930s were replaced by serious depictions of African Americans, and Chinese were shown as responsible allies. Within the military, moreover, religious chaplains of diverse faiths cooperated in providing spiritual care for soldiers, stressing interfaith toleration. These precedents provided the bedrock for civil rights movements of the postwar era.

Just ten years before Pearl Harbor, the Supreme Court referred to the country as a "Christian nation." Although Roosevelt had appointed many Jews to important positions in government before the war, Jewish Americans faced open prejudice in business, social life, and education. Immigration laws established quotas that discriminated against Jews even when Jewish refugees from Nazi persecution faced death as the only alternative. Despite growing evidence that Germans were systematically destroying European Jews as well as other "undesirables" such as Gypsies and homosexuals, Roosevelt did not move to facilitate the admission of Jewish refugees from Europe until 1944.

Complacency about Nazi treatment of Jews ended abruptly with revelations of the European Holocaust in 1945. Images of Nazi concentration camps—emaciated survivors, piles of dead and naked victims, mountains of human hair, eyeglasses, shoes—demonstrated the full horror of racism and modern war. This massive evil defied easy explanation. In 1945 most citizens recognized that the nation had reached a watershed in racial attitudes. Nazi anti-Semitism undermined U.S. anti-Semitism and discredited public assertions of racial "inferiority." To be sure, race prejudice did not disappear from the land, but no longer did public racist assertions seem acceptable, at least against whites.

Other forms of ethnic antagonism endured. Spanish-speaking, brown-skinned Mexican Americans of the Southwest and southern California continued to face segregated housing, higher unemployment, and lower wages. "Why teach them to read and write and spell?" a Los Angeles elementary school principal remarked in a typical dismissal; "they'll only pick beets anyway." Although most Mexican Americans lacked familiarity with such government agencies as the Fair Employment Practices Committee, middle-class activists in the League of United Latin American Citizens saw the war as an opportunity to advance civil rights for their constituents. Adopting the slogan "Americans All," a new generation of Mexican American leaders identified with the democratic aspirations of their adopted country. Similarly, thirty Native American tribes organized into the National Congress of American Indians in 1944.

During the war, teenage Mexican Americans formed "pachuco" gangs and dressed in lavish outfits known as zoot suits. Such clothing, like teenage slang and music, offered a visible protest against conformity to white standards. "The zoot suit was not a costume or uniform from the world of entertainment," explained Harold Fox, the Chicago retailer who introduced the fashion. "It came right off the street and out of the ghetto." Yet in July 1943 rumors that pachucos had beaten a sailor prompted a four-day race riot in Los Angeles as white servicemen attacked zoot-suiters. The fiasco showed that Mexican Americans, like Japanese Americans, lacked the power to defend their communities. Yet Mexican American and African American youth—

including the young Malcolm X—continued to wear zoot suits to assert their cultural independence.

Hostility toward zoot-suiters revealed not only ethnic antagonism but also a general anxiety about the nation's youth. As opportunities in the workforce improved, educators noted a simultaneous increase in teenage runaways, truancy, and high school dropouts. Police reported a dramatic rise in teenage sexual crimes. Such trends paralleled an increase in teenage marriages, the tendency for adolescents to "go steady" at a younger age, and the finding that more younger women were sexually active. Indeed, sex researcher Alfred Kinsey found that infidelity increased in only one social group: very young married women. These changes reflected the pressures of wartime—the shortage of young men, opportunities for independence, and fears associated with military service.

The liberalization of sexual behavior reinforced a conservative countertrend—the celebration of the traditional family. After the Depression decade, wartime prosperity encouraged an increase in marriage and birth rates. Although war mobilization brought more married women into the workforce, women of childbearing age tended to remain at home. Moreover, the appeal for women workers emphasized the temporary nature of wartime employment. "Mother, when will you stay home again?" asked a daughter in one industrial ad campaign; "some jubilant day mother will stay home again, doing the job she likes best—making a home for you and daddy, when he gets back." Even when war undermined traditional expectations about women and the family, ideal sexual roles remained unchanged.

"Home," wrote the front-line journalist Ernie Pyle, "the one really profound goal that obsesses every one of the Americans marching on foreign shores." Whereas the doughboys of World War I were seen as heroic adventurers, the soldiers of World War II appeared as civilians in uniform who were eager to resume prewar activities. Yet the war profoundly disrupted traditional family life. With 16 million men and women in the military, more than 18 percent of U.S. families had at least one relative in the armed forces, and the 400,000 U.S. war dead meant that more than 180,000 children lost their fathers. Child-care centers remained inadequate, and conservatives criticized working mothers for threatening the stability of the home. Popular songs, such as "Don't Sit Under the Apple Tree (with Anyone Else but Me)," expressed sexual anxieties about disrupted relationships and encouraged the hope that life would revert to prewar conditions after the war.

World War II nevertheless altered the relationship between government and the ordinary citizen. Bureaucratic control of the economy, the broadening of the tax base, government-funded advertising campaigns, federal support of technological research and development, the vast expansion of the armed services—these developments did not disappear at the war's end. Equally important, the conflict inspired a new definition of national security. The defeat of noninterventionism between 1939 and 1941 produced a new consensus that the national interest had a global dimension. To most citizens, the two oceans no longer protected the republic from its enemies; an adverse event anywhere in the world could be a threat to national security. This redefinition in turn demanded a strong and vigilant government dominated by an alert executive branch.

TRUMAN AND TRUCE

One month before World War II ended in Europe, the sudden death of Franklin D. Roosevelt thrust Harry Truman into the White House. Although he lacked Roosevelt's experience and skill, Truman inherited the delicate diplomatic responsibility for settling the peace. Unlike Roosevelt, Truman hoped to obtain postwar concessions from the Soviet Union. Roosevelt had pragmatically accepted the vague language of Yalta, but the new president insisted that the Soviet Union adopt the U.S. interpretation of wartime agreements. Truman offended the Allies further when, after the formal German surrender on May 8, 1945 (VE Day), the president abruptly halted Lend-Lease, although British and Soviet protests persuaded Truman to reverse the order.

Worried about the deterioration of U.S.-Soviet relations, the new president eagerly anticipated a summit conference with Allied leaders. Expecting fresh information about the top-secret military project to build an atomic bomb, Truman speculated that the weapon might give the United States greater leverage in winning concessions from the Soviets. Truman arranged to meet at Potsdam in mid-July 1945, the same week the first atomic bomb would be tested in New Mexico. As scientists developed the atomic bomb, Roosevelt had shared the secret with the British, who made important scientific contributions; but he refused to divulge the secret project to Stalin, even though he knew that spies already had passed information to the Russians. Roosevelt's decision indicated his belief that Britain would be a postwar ally, but the Soviet Union might not. Truman shared that assumption. The new president never seriously questioned the use of the atomic bomb against Japan. Military and political leaders predicted that the weapon would forestall an invasion of Japan and save many lives. Despite public concern about the term *unconditional surrender,* Washington ignored moral issues; bombings of Dresden and Tokyo already had claimed more victims than would die in atomic blasts.

The Potsdam meeting failed to resolve U.S.-Soviet disagreements. With news of the successful atomic bomb test, Truman tried to persuade Stalin to alter the political arrangement in eastern Europe, where procommunist parties prevailed in areas occupied by the Soviet Army. Stalin refused to change these governments and viewed Truman's request as a betrayal of the earlier agreements. At Potsdam the Big Three did agree to partition Germany, but again failed to resolve the question of German reparations for war damages. Final treaties were delayed until a later meeting of foreign ministers.

By the Potsdam conference, Japan faced imminent defeat. In July 1945 the Japanese made overtures through the Soviet Union, indicating a willingness to sue for peace. Truman feared that altering demands for "unconditional surrender" would cause political firestorms at home, and he issued a warning that Japan faced destruction. When the Japanese did not respond, the president allowed military decisions to proceed. On August 6, 1945, a single atomic bomb incinerated the Japanese city of Hiroshima, killing about 100,000 civilians. On August 9 the Soviet Union declared war on Japan. The same day, the United States dropped another atomic bomb on Nagasaki. The Japanese then sought immediate peace and agreed to surrender on August 14, provided only that the Japanese emperor be retained. When Truman accepted that condition, World War II was over. In a ceremony held aboard the U.S. battleship *Missouri* on September 2, 1945, Japan signed a formal treaty of surrender.

"Ours is the supreme position," exulted the *New York Herald Tribune*. "The Great Republic has come into its own; it stands first among the peoples of the earth." Such confidence belied a certain dread of what World War II had wrought. The tremendous slaughter of human beings, the destruction of cities, the ravishing of the earth—all stood as solemn warnings about human survival. World War II proved the genuine possibility of annihilation—not just of national enemies but of all humanity. "Never again" became the nation's watchword, a worldview that would shape U.S. policy for the next half-century.

The difficulty in reaching international agreements at Yalta and Potsdam contrasted with Allied unanimity in punishing German war criminals. During World War II, Nazi Germany had violated accepted rules of warfare by indiscriminately killing civilians, by instituting reigns of terror in occupied countries, and by implementing horrible genocidal policies, including the murder of 6 million European Jews. The Allies convened an International Military Tribunal at Nuremberg, Germany, in August 1945 to bring Nazi war criminals to trial. The national interests of the judges—U.S., Soviet, British, and French—precluded a completely fair accounting. Yet in judging twenty-two Nazi defendants, the Nuremberg tribunal established the principles of modern warfare: Wars of aggression, violations of traditional warfare, and inhuman acts constituted war crimes; individuals accused of crimes were entitled to judicial trials; and individuals remained accountable for their criminal actions even though they only followed the orders of superiors. These precedents promised to protect civilian populations from military terror. Since then, history has shown the limitations of the Nuremberg precedent. The Grand Alliance of World War II did not long outlive the circumstances that had created it.

American History Resource Center

To explore documents, images, audio and video clips, articles, and commentary related to the material in this chapter, visit the source collections at ushistory.wadsworth.com and and use the Search function with the following key terms:

Harry Truman	United Nations
Hiroshima	Asa Philip Randolph
Pearl Harbor	WWII

Recommended Readings

Williamson Murray and Allan R. Millett, *A War to Be Won: Fighting the Second World War* (2000). A thorough study of military history, this volume describes the relationships between economic mobilization and wartime strategy and operations.

Warren F. Kimball, *Forged in War: Roosevelt, Churchill, and the Second World War* (1997). A study of wartime diplomacy, this book offers a balanced assessment of Allied decisions.

Greg Robinson, *By Order of the President: FDR and the Internment of Japanese Americans* (2001). The author places the internment program in the context of race conflict and examines Roosevelt's complicity in the outcome.

Library of America, *Reporting World War II: American Journalism, 1938–1946* (1995). This two-volume anthology of wartime reportage offers a vivid depiction of wartime attitudes, fears, and expectations.

Additional Readings

The most complete treatment of Roosevelt's foreign policy is Robert Dallek, *Franklin D. Roosevelt and American Foreign Policy, 1932–1945* (1979). More critical is Frederick W. Marks III, *Wind Over Sand: The Diplomacy of Franklin Roosevelt* (1988). See also Walter LaFeber, *The Clash: A History of U.S.-Japan Relations* (1997). Ideological differences are emphasized in John W. Dower, *War Without Mercy: Race and Power in the Pacific War* (1986), and Akira Iriye, *Power and Culture: The Japanese-American War, 1941–1945* (1981). Roosevelt's China policy is treated in Michael Schaller, *The U.S.*

Crusade in China, 1938–1945 (1979). The attack on Pearl Harbor is examined thoroughly in Gordon W. Prange, *At Dawn We Slept* (1981).

The issues of wartime diplomacy are described in Gaddis Smith, *American Diplomacy During the Second World War, 1941–1945* (1965), and Warren F. Kimball, *The Juggler: Franklin Roosevelt as Wartime Statesman* (1994). More specific is Raymond G. O'Connor, *Diplomacy for Victory: FDR and Unconditional Surrender* (1971). An outstanding study of international relations pertaining to Asia is Christopher Thorne, *Allies of a Kind: The United States, Britain and the War Against Japan, 1941–1945* (1978). The origins of the United Nations are covered well in Robert A. Divine, *Second Chance: The Triumph of Internationalism in America During World War II* (1967). Roosevelt's limited interest in Nazi genocide is documented in David S. Wyman, *The Abandonment of the Jews: America and the Holocaust, 1941–1945* (1984). Wartime diplomacy involving the atomic bomb is described in Gar Alperovitz, *The Decision to Use the Atomic Bomb and the Architecture of an American Myth* (1995), and Martin J. Sherwin, *A World Destroyed: The Atomic Bomb and the Grand Alliance* (1975). For studies of the last phase of the war, see John D. Chappell, *Before the Bomb: How America Approached the End of the Pacific War* (1997), and Leon V. Sigal, *Fighting to a Finish: The Politics of War Termination in the United States and Japan, 1945* (1988).

For U.S. military leadership, see two fine biographies: Stephen E. Ambrose, *Eisenhower*, volume 1 (1983), and Forrest C. Pogue, *George C. Marshall*, volumes 4–5 (1968, 1973). A good analysis of U.S. air strategy is Michael S. Sherry, *The Rise of American Air Power* (1987). For the U.S. combat role in Europe, see Stephen E. Ambrose, *D-Day, June 6, 1944: The Climactic Battle of World War II* (1994). The perspective of the average soldier is presented in Lee Kennett, *G.I.: The American Soldier in World War II* (1987). For women's experiences in the military, see Leisa D. Meyer, *Creating GI Jane: Sexuality and Power in the Women's Army Corps During World War II* (1996).

Good introductions to home-front issues include John W. Jeffries, *Wartime America: The World War II Home Front* (1996); Doris Kearns Goodwin, *No Ordinary Time: Franklin and Eleanor Roosevelt: The Home Front in World War II* (1994); and Richard Polenberg, *War and Society: The United States, 1941–1945* (1972). For workers' experience, see George Lipsitz, *Rainbow at Midnight: Labor and Culture in the 1940s* (1994). The war's impact on the New Deal is the subject of Alan Brinkley, *The End of Reform: New Deal Liberalism in Recession and War* (1995). Wartime oil policy is studied in Michael B. Stoff, *Oil, War, and American Security: The Search for a National Policy on Foreign Oil, 1941–1947* (1980). Business values are treated in Howell John Harris, *The Right to Manage: Industrial Relations Policies of American Business in the 1940s* (1982). A study of the Office of War Information is Allan M. Winkler, *The Politics of Propaganda* (1978).

Fresh approaches to domestic issues appear in Lewis A. Erenberg and Susan E. Hirsch, editors, *The War in American Culture: Society and Consciousness During World War II* (1996). See also the oral histories in Studs Terkel, *The Good War* (1984). Military censorship is described in George H. Roeder Jr., *The Censored War: American Visual Experience During World War II* (1993). For efforts to ease racial tension, see Barbara Dianne Savage, *Broadcasting Freedom: Radio, War, and the Politics of Race, 1938–1948* (1999). Wartime advertising is the subject of Frank Fox, *Madison Avenue Goes to War: The Strange Military Career of American Advertising, 1941–1945* (1975). For the movie industry, see Clayton R. Koppes and Gregory D. Black, *Hollywood Goes to War: How Politics, Profits, and Propaganda Shaped World War II Movies* (1987); Allen L. Woll, *The Hollywood Musical Goes to War* (1983); and Thomas Doherty, *Projections of War: Hollywood, American Culture, and World War II* (1993). Wartime musical tastes are discussed in Lewis Erenberg, *Swinging the Dream: Big Band Jazz and the Rebirth of American Culture* (1998). For poetic commentary, see Harvey Shapiro, editor, *Poets of World War II* (2003).

The impact of war on society is examined in the relevant chapters of Richard Polenberg, *One Nation Divisible: Class, Race, and Ethnicity in the United States* (1980). For organized labor, see Nelson Lichtenstein, *Labor's War at Home: The CIO in World War II* (1983). Studies of the war's regional impact include Alan Clive, *State of War: Michigan in World War II* (1979); Marc Scott Miller, *The Irony of Victory: World War II and Lowell, Massachusetts* (1988); and Marilynn S. Johnson, *The Second Gold Rush: Oakland and the East Bay in World War II* (1993). Broader in scope is Gerald D. Nash, *The American West Transformed: The Impact of the Second World War* (1985).

The ordeal of Japanese Americans is examined by Roger Daniels, *Concentration Camps USA: Japanese-Americans and World War II* (1971), as well as by Edward Spicer et al., *Impounded People: Japanese-Americans in the Relocation Centers* (1969), a report originally written in 1946 for the War Relocation Authority. For critical appraisals of the internment program, see Eric L. Muller, *Free to Die for Their Country: The Story of Japanese American Draft Resisters in World War II* (2001), and Richard Drinnon, *Keeper of Concentration Camps: Dillon S. Myer and American Racism* (1987). Books that study other alien groups are John Christgau, *"Enemies": World War II Alien Internment* (1985), and Stephen Fox, *The Unknown Internment: An Oral History of the Relocation of Italian Americans During World War II* (1990).

Maurice Isserman, *Which Side Were You On: The American Communist Party During the Second World War* (1982), examines the radical left. For analysis of the radical right, see Leo P. Ribuffo, *The Old Christian Right: The Protestant Far Right from the Great Depression to the Cold War* (1983). For the government surveillance programs, see Richard Gid Powers, *Secrecy and*

Power: The Life of J. Edgar Hoover (1987), and Athan G. Theoharis and John Stuart Cox, *The Boss: J. Edgar Hoover and the Great American Inquisition* (1988).

Government efforts to manage race conflict are the subject of Daniel Kryder, *Divided Arsenal: Race and the American State During World War II* (2000). See also Richard Dalfiume, *Desegregation of the Armed Forces, 1939–1953* (1969). Harvard Sitkoff, *A New Deal for Blacks* (1978), describes the March on Washington Movement. Also helpful are African American oral histories edited by Mary Penick Motley in *The Invisible Soldier* (1975). For Native Americans, see Kenneth William Townsend, *World War II and the American Indian* (2000), and Alison R. Bernstein, *American Indians and World War II: Toward a New Era in Indian Affairs* (1991).

The implications of women's wartime experiences are explored in Ruth Milkman, *Gender at Work: The Dynamics of Job Segregation by Sex during World War II* (1987); Maureen Honey, *Creating Rosie the Riveter: Class, Gender, and Propaganda during World War II* (1984); and Karen Anderson, *Wartime Women: Sex Roles, Family Relations, and the Status of Women During World War II* (1981). A good comparative study is Leila Rupp, *Mobilizing Women for War: German and American Propaganda, 1939–1945* (1978). The war's impact on children is the subject of William M. Tuttle, Jr., *"Daddy's Gone to War": The Second World War in the Lives of America's Children* (1993). For the pacifist movement, see Lawrence S. Wittner, *Rebels Against War: The American Peace Movement, 1941–1960* (1969). For religious thought, see the relevant chapters of Martin E. Marty, *Modern American Religion*, volume 3, *Under God, Indivisible, 1941–1960* (1996).

For the Nuremberg trials, see Bradley F. Smith, *Reaching Judgment at Nuremberg* (1977), and Telford Taylor, *Nuremberg and Vietnam: An American Tragedy* (1970).

THE SEARCH FOR SECURITY, 1945–1949

On August 6, 1945, President Harry S Truman, successor to the late Franklin D. Roosevelt, announced that the United States had just exploded a new weapon—an atomic bomb—over the Japanese city of Hiroshima. After another atomic weapon incinerated the city of Nagasaki, Japan agreed to surrender, ending World War II, the most devastating war in human history, on August 14 (VJ Day). The defeated Axis countries—Germany and Japan—lay in ruins. The victorious Allies had also suffered huge casualties, including 25 million Russians who perished. Nazi concentration camps had killed about 10 million people, including 6 million Jews, in an unprecedented human holocaust. American casualties were relatively low: 405,000 U.S. soldiers had died; 800,000 more were wounded. The war had barely even touched North America.

"Ours is the supreme position," exulted a New York newspaper as the war came to an end. "The Great Republic has come into its own; it stands first among the peoples of the earth." The nation's massive wartime production had provided the materials for victory and proven the immense power of its economic system. The formation of the World Bank and the International Monetary Fund in 1944 promised to bring stability to overseas economic relations and reduce the national rivalries that had led to military aggression. Political leaders looked to an interrelated international marketplace to prevent the conditions that had caused the Great Depression of the 1930s. The United States also tried to implement democratic principles of self-government in other countries, although international agreements and global power relations would limit success. Nevertheless, the founding of the United Nations in 1945 suggested that international cooperation would protect the national interests of member nations and prevent another world war.

The Allies also determined to establish international rules of justice that would discourage, or at least punish, the crimes committed by German militarists. In 1945 the Allies convened the International Military Tribunal at Nuremberg, Germany, to bring Nazi war criminals to trial. In convicting twenty-two Germans of war crimes, the tribunal upheld basic principles of warfare: Wars of aggression and inhuman acts constituted war crimes; individuals accused of crimes were entitled to judicial trials; and individuals remained accountable for their actions even though they were following orders of superiors. These legal principles endeavored to create a postwar world of peace and justice.

American optimism was tempered, however, by new realities of global power. Six days after the atomic bombing of Hiroshima, radio commentator Edward R. Murrow observed, "Seldom, if ever, has a war ended leaving the victors with such a sense of uncertainty and fear, with such a realization that the future is obscure and that survival is not assured." Just as the war against fascism had obliged the United States to develop awesome military and industrial power, the crisis had taught American leaders that they could never again retreat into the shell of isolationism that had limited U.S. involvement in world affairs during the 1930s. Recognizing that the nation's security depended on worldwide military, economic, and political interests, Presidents Roosevelt and Truman—and most of the public—expected the United States to become a major factor in postwar international relations. Yet despite such expectations, serious disagreements among the Allies, especially with the Soviet Union, left many unsolved problems to threaten the peace. Within two years of victory, the nation faced another global war—the "Cold War"—that altered the scope of government activity and changed political life on the home front.

Harry Truman stood at the center of the postwar puzzle. The Missouri-born politician had served two full terms as senator but just five weeks as vice president before becoming president when Franklin Roosevelt died suddenly. Anyone who succeeded the charismatic Roosevelt would have suffered by comparison, but Truman's blunt style and the unusual crises he faced created the appearance of presidential ineptness. His popularity ratings, which began at 87 percent when he took office in April 1945, dropped to 50 percent a year later and slid to 32 percent by the November 1946 congressional elections. Yet as the Cold War intensified in 1947, his bold—some would say acerbic—leadership restored his image and reputation. In 1948 his presidential campaign defied the public opinion odds, and his election surprised almost everyone but Truman himself. As president, he realized that the decisions he made often had grave and dangerous consequences—as a sign in his White House office said, "The Buck Stops Here." His sheer determination set the tone of the postwar presidency.

REBUILDING CIVILIAN SOCIETY

The sudden end of World War II accentuated the difficulties of restoring civilian society. Although Roosevelt's New Deal programs of the 1930s had enlarged government responsibility for economic policy and social welfare,

Washington had failed to resolve the problems of massive unemployment until the nation began to mobilize for war. The abrupt termination of wartime contracts in August 1945, together with the demobilization of 12 million soldiers, raised fears of another economic depression.

Anticipating such problems, Congress had passed the Servicemen's Readjustment Act of 1944 (known as the GI Bill of Rights), which allowed veterans a year's unemployment benefits, education scholarships, insurance, and home loans. Such assistance, limited to military veterans, was as far as Congress was willing to go toward guaranteeing social welfare benefits for postwar society. The measure served to reintegrate veterans into civilian life and increased their purchasing power to support the economy. To provide work for returning veterans, moreover, the government joined business leaders and labor unions in forcing women to surrender their wartime jobs for domestic roles. "Nobody's job is safe," a woman salesclerk learned in Hollywood's classic 1946 film, *The Best Years of Our Lives.*

Truman addressed the public's fears of depression in a twenty-one point program presented to Congress in September 1945. "The ultimate duty of government," he said, "is to prevent prolonged unemployment." The president proceeded to ask Congress to enact full-employment legislation, which would guarantee jobs in times of unemployment as well as a package of liberal measures, such as a permanent Fair Employment Practices Commission (FEPC), public housing, higher minimum wages, and urban redevelopment. This ambitious program soon collided with a conservative Congress led by southern Democrats and northern Republicans opposed to government intervention in the economy. "It is just a case of out–New Dealing the New Deal," complained one Republican leader of Truman's agenda. Fearing "creeping socialism," Congress instead passed the Employment Act of 1946 that promised "maximum" rather than "full" employment. Yet even that measure offered few benefits. Although the law committed the federal government to maximize employment—and created the Council of Economic Advisors—neither Truman nor his successors supported the creation of government jobs to ease unemployment. The abrupt layoff of women workers brought no government response.

Truman's economic choices were also limited by earlier decisions. Wartime government had relied on the expertise of corporate leaders—"dollar-a-year" men—who remained on the payrolls of their private corporations while making economic policy for the nation. Their primary commitment to big business triggered a bitter debate about the reconversion to a civilian economy. As the need for war materials declined in 1944, the War Production Board recommended that small businesses that were losing war contracts reconvert to peacetime production while larger corporations would continue to meet military needs. Corporate leaders vigorously resisted this proposal because they did not want small firms to gain advantages in the transition to civilian production. Unwilling to slacken war manufacturing, military leaders backed the major war contractors. This alliance delayed economic reconversion until 1945, thereby protecting the wartime expansion of big business but also extending shortages of civilian goods when the war ended.

Slighting the problems of small business, the War Production Board lifted wartime regulations as soon as hostilities ended. The abrupt termination of government control over scarce resources benefited larger corporations that had stockpiled such materials. Because they were unable to obtain basic manufacturing resources, many small producers folded or sold out to bigger firms. Large corporations took advantage of Washington's generous reconversion sales and bought government-built plants and resources at a fraction of their cost. Such subsidies ensured that the biggest companies would continue to dominate the economy. The Federal Trade Commission (FTC) reported in 1947 that 2,450 independent mining and manufacturing firms had disappeared since 1940 because of mergers and acquisitions. Congress eventually responded to small business pressure by creating the Small Business Administration in 1953, but most government contracts still went to the largest corporations.

Truman's efforts to maintain wartime price controls to prevent runaway inflation also provoked wide opposition. After four years of government regulation, consumers resented continued shortages. But the lifting of some price controls in 1945 prompted huge jumps in prices, which offended consumers even more. In addition, price controls contained substantial loopholes that aggravated shortages. Because companies made greater profits from expensive goods than from cheaper ones (for example, gowns rather than housedresses), manufacturers preferred to produce high-priced goods.

The resulting shortage of necessities led to skyrocketing prices and an illegal black market. Nearly half the nation's lumber sales in 1946 occurred illegally. Yet lifting controls on building materials stimulated construction of profitable industrial plants without alleviating residential housing shortages. Builders and real estate brokers made enormous profits as house prices soared overnight. Shortages and inflation emerged as the major political issues during the 1946 elections as congressional conservatives opposed extension of wartime regulations and Truman demanded consumer protection. Yet despite soaring prices, voters that year rejected government controls. As a result, most price controls ended by 1947, and the consumer price index increased 30 percent between mid-1946 and 1948.

LABOR UNIONS AND ECONOMIC STABILITY

Rising prices stimulated worker unrest. During the war, labor unions had adopted a no-strike pledge and members benefited by improved wages and overtime pay. But the war's end reduced weekly take-home pay at the same time that price inflation undermined purchasing power. By the fall of 1946,

EXHIBIT **8-1   GROSS NATIONAL PRODUCT, 1946–1950**
(IN ROUNDED BILLIONS OF DOLLARS)

1946	212
1950	288

Source: *Economic Report of the President* (1988).

average weekly wages in real dollars had dropped to Depression levels. Such sacrifices contrasted with the immense profits made by businesses during the war. In 1945, Philip Murray, head of the steelworkers' union, pointed out that steel company stockholders had received more than $700 million in dividends during the war. "Contrast this," he said, "with the financial position of America's 475,000 steelworkers."

Labor tensions exploded with a wave of strikes even before the Japanese surrender. During the summer of 1945, 5 million workers called some 4,600 stoppages that amounted to nearly 120 million days of lost labor. Labor strikes quickly spread to the nation's basic industries, such as oil, automobiles, steel, and coal. Some labor protests became "general strikes," involving communities that sympathized with the unions. The strikes brought workers substantial increases, including the new cost-of-living adjustments (COLA) that keyed wages to inflation. But the result contributed to inflationary trends. A 15 percent wage increase for steelworkers led to a $45-per-ton hike in steel prices. Meanwhile, consumers expressed outrage at the inconveniences caused by the strikes.

Truman decided to draw the line. When railroad workers voted to strike in May 1946, effectively paralyzing the nation's transportation, the president seized the railroads. Then he asked Congress for legislation to authorize court injunctions to keep workers on the job, to allow the army to operate the trains, and to permit the drafting of strikers into the military to force them to work. Although the walkout ended before Congress could act, the proposal brought wide criticism. "In his angry determination to get the trains running on time again," protested the liberal *Nation*, "Truman took . . . a leaf from the book of another man who made railroad history, Benito Mussolini." Nonetheless, Congress approved the use of court injunctions to stop certain strikes.

Truman soon used government power to end a coal strike by John L. Lewis's United Mine Workers (UMW). Several times during the war, this union had broken labor's no-strike pledge. When Lewis called another strike in 1946, Truman seized the mines and ended the walkout by accepting an inflationary settlement. Six months later, the UMW defied the government again by calling a strike. Unlike Roosevelt, who in wartime had met Lewis's demands, Truman obtained an injunction and a $3.5 million judgment against the union (and another $10,000 judgment against Lewis), which forced the UMW to surrender. According to a Gallup poll, the president's antiunion stand increased his popularity.

Economic quarrels continued to undermine Truman's position as the 1946 elections approached. Liberals scorned the failure to maintain price controls and his hostility to unions; Republicans criticized him for promoting big government, for administrative ineptness, and for laxity in protecting federal agencies from communist influence. "The choice which confronts Americans," advised the Republican national chairman, "is between Communism and Republicanism." New Republican candidates, such as Joseph R. McCarthy of Wisconsin and Richard M. Nixon of California, appealed to popular fears of communist subversion.

Widespread disapproval of strikes, inflation, and bureaucracy fueled mounting criticism of Democratic leadership. Organized labor, the backbone of the New Deal, resented Truman's lack of support; African Americans, who had recently aligned with Democrats, saw little to praise when the president failed to address a wave of violence against black veterans in the South. Both groups avoided the polls in 1946. And with the simple campaign slogan "Had Enough?" Republicans won in a landslide, gaining a congressional majority in both houses for the first time since 1928. McCarthy and Nixon stood among the victors.

Once in control of the Eightieth Congress, Republicans established a working alliance with southern Democrats to thwart civil rights legislation and to block Truman's other liberal measures, such as public housing, federal aid to education, higher Social Security payments, and certain farm benefits. Ohio Senator Robert Taft, a leader of the conservative Old Guard, told Republicans "to cast out a great many chapters of the New Deal, if not the whole book." But divisions between Republican moderates and conservatives undermined the party's strength. Truman vetoed seventy-five bills, and Congress managed to override only five.

One of those exceptions was the controversial Taft-Hartley Act of 1947, which limited labor union activities. To reduce the number of strikes, the law allowed government to seek injunctions against strike action and provided for a sixty-day "cooling-off" period during which federal mediators would try to settle disputes. To weaken the unions, Taft-Hartley also prohibited "closed" shops (which forced employers to hire only union members) but permitted "union" shops (in which all employees had to join a union after being hired). Taft-Hartley responded to community-wide general strikes by prohibiting secondary boycotts, jurisdictional strikes, and certain "unfair labor practices." The law also required union leaders to certify that they were not members of the Communist Party or other "subversive" groups. Truman, seeking to restore his support among labor unions, criticized the law as "vindictive" and vetoed the bill; but in a show of conservative muscle, Congress easily overrode the veto. Truman's opposition, however, helped him regain the support of organized labor.

Taft-Hartley established the legal framework of labor-management relations for the remainder of the century. On the state level, federal legislation encouraged passage of "right-to-work" laws, which permitted "open" shops, in which workers did not have to join a union. The enforced cooling-off period and the threat of government injunctions (used seventeen times by President Truman and his successor, President Dwight Eisenhower) forced unions and businesses to seek negotiated settlements that would ensure economic stability. Thus union and business leaders increasingly negotiated long-term, industry-wide contracts that included cost-of-living increases and other welfare benefits. "We need the union to ensure enforcement of the contract we have signed," explained one business executive, "to settle grievances, to counsel employees in giving a fair day's work, . . . to help increase productivity." By the early 1950s, union membership reached the highest level in U.S. history. At the same time, 80 percent of Americans described themselves as middle class. Indeed, economists attributed the rapid increase in manufacturing productivity to peaceful labor-management relations and the decline of class conflict.

The emphasis on industry-wide stability sometimes led union leaders to ignore the local problems of rank-and-file workers, and unauthorized ("wild-cat") strikes targeted both employers and unresponsive union leaders. Worker participation in union elections declined from 82 percent before World War II to 58 percent in 1958, a trend that continued in the next decades. While critics complained about labor leaders' "passion for respectability," congressional investigation unearthed widespread corruption in managing union funds. The Landrum-Griffin Act of 1959 required unions to file economic statements with the Department of Labor.

Union leaders often neglected the problems of unorganized workers, especially in the new white-collar jobs. Many unions ignored women workers, who were seen as competition for male jobs, and all-white local unions opposed opening membership to racial minorities. Instead, the rival American Federation of Labor (AFL) and Congress of Industrial Organizations (CIO) unions debated jurisdictional issues and raided each other's membership. Although union membership increased from nearly 15 million in 1945 to 18 million a decade later, the proportion of unionized workers declined 14 percent by 1960. The desire for worker stability began to minimize the differences between the AFL and the CIO. In 1955 the two unions merged into the AFL-CIO. Yet five years later organized labor accounted for less than one-third of all nonfarm workers; by 2000, the ratio had fallen to one-sixth.

FARMS AND FOOD

Although political leaders agreed to restrain the independence of labor unions, divisions between liberal Democrats and conservatives of both parties limited government programs for other constituencies. Southern and western farmers, who were among the poorest Americans during the 1930s, had benefited from federal assistance under the New Deal but generally held conservative views about social policy. As a former farm boy, Truman well understood the problems of small farmers. His liberal agenda proposed a soil conservation program, subsidies for school lunches, farm tenant loans, and crop insurance. But congressional conservatives attacked this extension of government services and reduced or cut the administration's program. Later, Truman would tell North Carolina farmers, "You stand for the Democratic farm program or you stand for the Republican wrecking crew." However, federal agricultural programs generally benefited large corporate agribusinesses more than family farmers.

Such results reflected basic changes in postwar farming. During the war, food producers recognized the profitability of mechanization and land consolidation. By investing in farm machinery and hybrid crops that could be handled by machines, farmers needed fewer workers. Farmers also increased their use of chemical fertilizers, pesticides, additives, and antibiotics. This type of farming was expensive; poorer farmers could not compete, and wealthier farmers acquired ever-larger holdings. Between 1949 and 1959, farm production increased 6 percent per year as the farm population declined and the number of farms dwindled.

Government assistance to corporate farming encouraged these patterns. In the early postwar years, federal loans to war-torn Europe subsidized the export of farm surpluses. After European farming recovered, the Agricultural Acts of 1948 and 1949 established government price supports for sales of basic crops. In 1956 Congress authorized payment for not planting certain crops, and the Soil Bank Act of 1956 provided reimbursements for converting crop land into noncommercial conservation acreage. Larger farms gained most. "The majority of farm people derive little or no benefit from our agricultural price support legislation," stated a presidential economic report; "those with the higher incomes are the main beneficiaries." Meanwhile, the reduction in government rice allotments and the replacement of sharecroppers with hired labor and tractors stimulated an exodus of millions of poor whites and blacks from the rural South.

Technological agriculture encouraged consumption of mass-produced food. As consumers bought more processed and frozen foods, food processors such as Birdseye dictated which crop strains would be planted, leading to a decline in the number of available seed and food varieties. Franchise restaurant chains, which also proliferated in this period, preferred standardized menus, which created another vast market for single strains of produce. Meanwhile, average per capita consumption of dairy products, fresh fruits, and fresh vegetables declined. Since processed food needed nutritional additives and preservatives to maintain the food's value, each edible pound cost as much as 30 percent more than naturally grown food. Corporate consolidation similarly affected beverage consumption. In the beer industry the number of breweries steadily declined. Such changes encouraged the homogenization of eating and drinking habits in all regions.

THE TECHNOLOGICAL FRONTIER

Wartime engineering and scientific research provided the model for postwar technological development. The introduction of radar and jet propulsion, the use of pesticides such as DDT, the effectiveness of "miracle drugs" such as penicillin, and the emergence of synthetic compounds as substitutes for scarce resources such as rubber all testified to the importance of research for social progress. In popular wartime imagery the scientist and the engineer appeared as heroic figures.

The atomic bomb dwarfed these technological accomplishments. Although the bomb appeared to prove U.S. invincibility in war, the use of nuclear weapons raised profound questions about uncontrolled scientific investigation. During the war the government had classified atomic energy research (the "Manhattan Project") as top secret, although physicists around the world understood the theoretical basis of the bomb. In 1945 U.S. scientists predicted that other countries could develop similar weapons in three to five years. However, President Truman preferred to believe the opinion of military leaders who claimed that the United States could monopolize atomic bombs for at least twenty years. The president therefore rejected recommendations to share atomic research with the Soviet Union. Both Congress and public opinion supported this position. The Atomic Energy Act of 1946 established the Atomic Energy Commission (AEC) and placed control of nuclear research and development in civilian hands.

J. Robert Oppenheimer, the head of the Los Alamos research team that developed the atomic bomb, expressed widely held anxieties about the future of scientific research: "In some sense, which no vulgarity, no humor, no overstatement can quite extinguish," he said, "the physicists have known sin; and this is a knowledge which they cannot lose." The realization that atomic science could bring human annihilation spread through the popular culture. Hardly a Hollywood movie of the postwar era lacked some reference to the bomb and its potential destructiveness. Indeed, a new film genre—later named *film noir* (dark film)—now celebrated a different type of hero who inhabited a world of moral ambiguity, uncertainty, and fear. Movies such as *Force of Evil* (1948), *They Live By Night* (1949), and *D.O.A.* (1950) depicted characters trapped by pressures they scarcely understood. Such themes also appeared in postwar science fiction, which enjoyed a remarkable revival. Authors such as Isaac Asimov and Ray Bradbury wrote futuristic stories involving human beings seeking to avert ultimate catastrophe.

The serious scientist now appeared as an ambivalent character, simultaneously capable of bringing salvation or annihilation. "To the average civilized man of 1950," wrote the editor of *Scientific American,* "science no longer means primarily the promise of a more abundant life; it means the atomic bomb." Although nearly all nuclear research involved military work, the AEC launched a public relations division in 1947 to counter public fears. With private contractors such as General Electric and Westinghouse, the agency sponsored public programs suggesting that atomic energy would be used for social betterment and minimized the harmful effects of testing and radiation.

Despite pervasive anxieties about atomic research, the public generally welcomed technological innovations for domestic consumption. Rayon, nylon, and Dacron increasingly replaced cotton and wool. In home furnishings, plastics supplanted wood and leather. Artificial flavors, colors, and preservatives became staples of the U.S. diet. (Most synthetics, however, were derivatives of petroleum products and depleted nonrenewable resources and left nonbiodegradable waste.) Another innovation was the fluoridation of water, which reduced tooth decay. When given the choice of voting for fluoridation, nearly all local communities initially rejected the proposals; but by 1963, 50 million people—25 percent of the population—were drinking fluoridated water. During the postwar decade, the United States replaced Europe as the prime manufacturer of precision scientific instruments. New medical technologies included kidney dialysis machines (1945), artificial heart valves (1953), and electronic heart pacemakers (1957). Meanwhile, new antibiotics such as streptomycin and aureomycin helped to control infectious diseases. Most dramatically, the introduction of Dr. Jonas Salk's poliomyelitis vaccine in 1955 effectively eliminated a dreaded disease that had claimed 55,000 victims each year.

Advances in technology reinforced public optimism about unlimited progress. A few ecologists, such as William Vogt and Fairfield Osborn, warned about the limits of available resources; but the public accepted corporate assurances that applied science would solve such technological problems. Consumers supported both the automobile industry's high-horsepower engines and the petroleum industry's high-octane gasoline, although with added auto body weight, automobile fuel efficiency fell as low as 10 miles per gallon.

Jet aircraft and missiles, electronic transistors, and computers testified to the expanding technological frontiers of the postwar era. Committed to national security and military preparedness, the federal government spent billions of dollars in research and development (R&D), some of it financing university research. Aircraft manufacturing, one of the leading growth industries, drew 80 percent of its business from military contracts. The government also backed electronics, which grew 15 percent per year, making it the fifth largest industry by 1960. Secret military programs for nuclear weapons, missiles, and cryptography demanded complicated mathematical calculations that sparked the computer industry. The first World War II–era computers occupied 15,000 square feet and used 18,000 radio tubes. The introduction of the transistor by Bell Laboratories in 1947 paved the way for miniaturization. Although the federal government purchased most electronics for military programs, computers entered the industrial marketplace in 1951.

Military needs also justified generous government help for the petroleum industry. Accepting the industry's argument that security depended on preserving domestic reserves while exploiting foreign oil, the government waived antitrust regulations to permit development of Middle Eastern oil and devised generous tax credits to subsidize private contracts with Saudi Arabia. Under the Truman administration's Marshall Plan of 1947 (see The Truman Doctrine on page 269), the United States refinanced a major shift in western European energy consumption from coal to petroleum. This step provided a $384 million subsidy to U.S. oil companies and made the Western Allies dependent on imports. In addition, Congress enacted mandatory petroleum import quotas in 1950, which kept cheap foreign oil from lowering domestic prices. In supporting the oil industry, government agencies continued the World War II practice of awarding contracts to the largest corporations. Only 4 percent of R&D funds reached small businesses. Although convenient for government administrators, dealing with big business did not reduce costs. Without competitive bidding, federal budgets routinely had to absorb business cost overruns.

PEACE AND PLENTY

While government leaders struggled to rebuild the postwar economy, most citizens focused on personal concerns of security and prosperity. For the generation that came of age during the Depression and World War II, however, government assistance provided considerable support. Most important was the GI Bill of Rights, which allowed veterans to obtain private homes through government-insured mortgages that required small down payments and allowed extended periods for repayment. In addition, government-funded scholarships gave veterans unprecedented opportunities for educational advancement. Between 1945 and 1950, 6 million veterans (half the nation's total) used nearly $13 billion of government money to enroll in colleges, universities, and vocational training programs. Postwar surveys found that about 20 percent of college-bound veterans would not have returned to school without federal aid.

Women also entered colleges in high numbers, but without veterans' benefits they formed a smaller percentage of college students than they did before the war. Still, the influx of students encouraged colleges to expand facilities, open branch campuses, offer evening instruction, and adjust their curricula to accommodate older students, many of whom held jobs and supported families. By underwriting tuition bills, federal funds boosted the

King Hiram ("Hank") Williams (1923–1953)

"Don't worry," country singer Hank Williams once confided to a concert crowd, "nothing's gonna turn out right no how." Williams grew up in small Alabama towns during the Depression. He was raised by a strong-willed mother who introduced him to the hymns and gospel tunes of the fundamentalist Baptist Church. As a boy,

APWide World Photos

Williams sold peanuts and newspapers and shined shoes. He formed his own "hillbilly" band when he was fourteen years old, combining the influence of black street musicians and the commercial sound of prominent country stars. After Williams won an amateur-night contest in Montgomery in 1937, he formed the Drifting Cowboys band and played the "blood buckets"—the rough southern Alabama honky-tonk clubs.

After working in the shipyards during World War II, Williams traveled to Nashville to become a songwriter. As the war relocated southern blacks and whites to defense plants and military bases, and as jukeboxes spread across the country, rhythm and blues and country music became national phenomena. Fusing gospel, blues, and honky-tonk, Williams won a recording contract in 1947 and produced his first hit, "Move It On Over," an up-tempo tune that influenced the structure of early rock and roll. The next year he joined the *Louisiana Hayride*, a country music radio show from Shreveport, Louisiana, that appealed to workers in the booming regional oil and gas industry.

expansion of academia and established a precedent for later support of education. In addition, the appearance of more ethnically diverse students eroded the homogeneity that had dominated elite campuses.

THE BIRTH OF THE SUBURBAN BOOM

Ex-servicemen and their wives produced the most remarkable population explosion in U.S. history. Taking their cue from a popular 1945 song "Gotta Make Up for Lost Time," veterans rushed to get married and settle down with

Following his smash hit, "Lovesick Blues," Williams reached the top of his profession in 1949 and made regular guest appearances on Nashville's *Grand Ole Opry*. He sold 11 million records between 1949 and 1953, using his unpolished, light voice to master blues techniques such as falsetto singing and call-and-response. He won the devotion of working-class fans because he appeared to "live" his music. "When a hillbilly sings a crazy song," he once explained, "he feels crazy. . . . He sings more sincere than most entertainers because the hillbilly was raised rougher. . . . You got to have smelt a lot of manure before you can sing like a hillbilly."

Williams bonded with audiences by sharing the sense of betrayal and abandonment often inflicted by romance. By conveying emotions of loneliness and despair, love songs such as "Your Cheating Heart" and "Cold Cold Heart" relieved listeners of postwar insistence on domestic bliss. Williams expressed another form of release through drinking songs such as "Jambalaya," which celebrated immediate pleasure over the rigors of delayed gratification and middle-class propriety.

Although the singer poured out his personal problems in music, he was unable to stop a descent into alcoholism. On New Year's Day 1953, eight months before his thirtieth birthday, Hank Williams suffered a fatal heart attack. A biracial crowd of more than 20,000 gathered in Montgomery as leading country music stars conducted a gospel tribute to the fallen performer. By portraying pain and joy as the common denominators of life, Williams became a legendary figure in working-class culture and had an enormous impact on all forms of popular music.

their families. The national birthrate had begun to rise as prosperity returned in 1940, but in May 1946, nine months after the war ended, the number of births soared and remained high until 1957. Demographers found that the "baby boom" resulted from couples marrying younger, thereby increasing the years of marital fertility and producing more third and fourth babies. Yet the number of families with five or more children declined, which suggested a greater willingness to use birth control. Pushed by the baby boom, the nation's population grew from 140 million in 1945 to 152 million in 1950. Such growth also reflected the slightly declining death rate, which resulted from medical advances that extended longevity.

EXHIBIT **8-2**   **BIRTHRATES, 1940–1950**

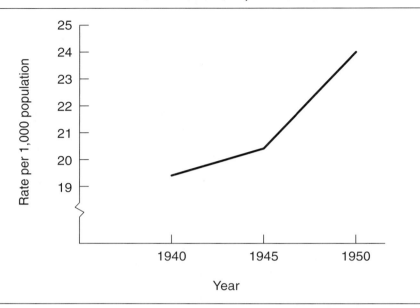

The burst of population accelerated long-term patterns of geographic mobility. Attracted by industrial expansion during World War II, workers and their families had flocked to the southwestern and western states. In Texas the growth of the petrochemical industry, stimulated by the increased use of oil and natural gas, encouraged a 30 percent population growth. In Arizona, Tucson and Phoenix mushroomed into sizable cities, selling the advantages of a warm, sunny climate. Yet when asked in 1956, "Which city would you most like to live in?" more Americans responded: "Los Angeles." California, home of the prospering aircraft and electronics industries, attracted more than 5 million people between 1940 and 1960, doubled in size, and surpassed New York as the most populous state in 1963.

The baby boom soon underscored what many considered the nation's most serious domestic problem: a shortage of housing. Since the Depression, residential construction had virtually ended, and by 1945 the nation's housing was worth 7 percent less than in 1929. Returning veterans often had to share dwellings with other families, camp out in public facilities, or accept substandard rooms in converted chicken coops or Quonset huts. Postwar shortages of building materials and the inflation of real estate prices accentuated the shortage. Responding to the crisis, congressional liberals joined Republican Robert Taft in proposing federal support of public housing. But a coalition of antigovernment conservatives, including Senator Joseph McCarthy, and private builders, such as William Levitt, challenged public housing as a socialist or communist scheme. Instead, these conservatives argued that private enterprise could solve the housing shortage, with federal assistance under the Federal Housing Authority (FHA) or Veterans Administration.

Private builders like Levitt stepped into the breach. Levitt purchased large tracts of land in the suburban fringes of big cities, such as New York's Long Island, and drew on his experience as a war contractor to develop a system of mass-producing standardized housing at affordable prices. He used specialized work crews, interchangeable designs, prefabricated materials, and package deals that included interior appliances, landscaping, and legal fees to produce four-and-a-half room, Cape Cod–style houses for $8,000 in 1949. Many were financed by veterans' loans, which required minimal down payments and offered government-protected finance charges. To keep prices low, the designs eliminated dining rooms, basements, and attics as well as unnecessary trim. Efficient production methods enabled the builder to erect one four-room house every sixteen minutes!

Between 1947 and 1951 Levitt built more than 17,000 dwellings in Levittown, Long Island, and converted a potato field into a community of 75,000 residents. When critics complained that the structures were monotonously repetitive, the developer offered different exterior paint, curved streets, and homes placed at slightly different angles. Such housing, imitated by builders around the nation, benefited from new standardization within the appliance and home-furnishing industries.

This postwar suburban boom rested on government financing of housing loans, highways, and sewer systems. Federal tax deductions for mortgage interest—what was, in effect, a tax break for middle-class housing—annually exceeded $1 billion. The mixture of private enterprise and government policy enabled most of the nation's families to own their residences for the first time in U.S. history. Although some social critics lamented the bland uniformity of suburban lifestyles, promoters stressed the value of individual home ownership. "No man who owns his own house and lot can be a Communist," Levitt declared.

The distance from downtown areas made the use of automobiles a suburban necessity. Auto registration jumped from 26 million in 1945 to 40 million in 1950, a trend that continued for decades. The increase in driving encouraged the spread of fast-food restaurants, drive-in theaters, shopping centers, motels, mobile home parks, and gasoline service stations. Although fuel prices remained low (about 25 cents per gallon), automobiles brought other costs such as increased national dependence on foreign oil and worsening air pollution. In 1947 journalist John Gunther boasted that Los Angeles used electricity to produce "clean industry" and uncontaminated air. Yet within one decade the city's auto exhaust had added a new and permanent aspect to the local environment—smog that was deemed a hazard to public health.

In suburbia, mobility became more valued than community attachments. As families grew, suburbanites readily moved to larger homes. Residential change often mirrored the interchangeability of jobs in an increasingly white-collar service economy. The proliferation of chain stores reflected this trend. As chains increased their share of total food sales from 29 percent to 44 percent in the ten years after 1948, nearly 100,000 independent groceries disappeared. Corporate managers, Gunther noted, never become "a real ingredient in the life of a community."

NEW ISSUES OF GENDER AND SEXUALITY

The baby boom and the rise of suburban living reflected a renewed emphasis on the role of women as wives, mothers, and homemakers. Although women had readily accepted paid labor during the war, most surrendered their jobs, willingly or not, to returning veterans in 1945–1946. Popular magazines and movies insisted that a woman's proper place was in the home. In the film *Mildred Pierce* (1945), for example, the ambitious, self-employed working mother proves to be a failure as a parent; in the supposedly sensitive picture *The Snake Pit* (1949), rebellion against domesticity appears as a form of mental illness. A popular psychology book of 1947, *Modern Woman: The Lost Sex*, explained that "a mature woman without children is the psychological equivalent of a man without the male organ." Such statements had a practical effect. Surveys of women college students found that most enrolled not for careers but to find husbands. Two-thirds of postwar college women quit school before obtaining their BA's.

Despite such pressure, however, female employment began to rise sharply in 1947 and returned to World War II levels by 1950, establishing a trend that would continue through the century. The increasing proportion of working women reflected new social patterns. Although women traditionally had worked until marriage and then left the workforce, the new female workers were married and had children who were attending school (and so needed less supervision). Increasingly, households included two working parents. Before World War II, working wives and mothers usually came from the poorest classes of society; but in the postwar period, an increasing number of middle-class women found jobs even when their husbands earned substantial incomes.

Working women emphasized financial necessity as a motive for their employment. Despite the emphasis on women's domesticity, the national divorce rate had spiked in 1946, as hasty wartime marriages collapsed, and remained substantially higher than prewar divorce rates. Widows, unmarried mothers, and women who were divorced, separated, or deserted headed about 7 percent of U.S. households in 1950. Most worked as secretaries, salesclerks, or semiskilled workers—occupations that labor unions usually ignored—and earned lower salaries than men did for similar tasks. Women-headed households were among the poorest in the nation. Moreover, because postwar real wages remained lower than wartime earnings until 1955, families needed additional incomes to acquire goods and services. In middle-class households the demand for luxury items or a private home encouraged two-income families.

Dissatisfaction with traditional marriage also reflected a conflict between sexual values and sexual behavior. In 1948 Alfred Kinsey of Indiana University published a major research study, *Sexual Behavior in the Human Male,* followed five years later by a similar study of women. Both became best-sellers. Kinsey tilted his research sample to support the unconventional conclusions he wished to dramatize. Yet at a time when traditional morality advocated premarital virginity, Kinsey's statistical data showed that most men and nearly 50 percent of the women interviewed had experienced premarital intercourse. Fully 95 percent of the study's adult white males claimed to have committed at least one "illegal" sexual activity. Half the men and 26 percent of the women reported that they had experienced extramarital sexual relations. Kinsey concluded that two-thirds of the marriages studied had serious sexual problems, and he speculated that sexual incompatibility caused 75 percent of divorces.

The Kinsey report also pointed to surprising patterns of homosexual behavior: 37 percent of the men and 13 percent of the women interviewed said they had participated in at least one postadolescent homosexual encounter. Such figures reflected the growth of homosexual communities in most major cities after World War II. Yet the proliferation of gay lifestyles did not produce greater tolerance of homosexuals. Police raids and blackmail plagued the gay population, and the federal government viewed homosexuals in the military and government as susceptible to compromise by foreign agents. Thousands of homosexuals lost government jobs during the 1940s and 1950s. Although homosexuals would form self-protective groups, such as the Mattachine Society (1951) and the Daughters of Bilitis (1955), fear of exposure prevented them from effectively defending their rights.

Free expression of sexuality among youth prompted social conservatives to warn about the collapse of traditional morality and a new national malaise—juvenile delinquency. Newspapers luridly described teenage crimes, most of which involved underage drinking, premarital sex, and driving without a license. Critics such as FBI Director J. Edgar Hoover blamed juvenile delinquency on working mothers and warned that youth crime would increase unless society strengthened the family, home, church, and local community. President Truman joined a chorus of politicians who urged working mothers to end the crime wave by returning to the home. In fact, however, New York City arrest rates for children under the age of sixteen lagged far behind those reported in the first two decades of the century. Sociologists insisted that poverty caused juvenile crime and advocated slum clearance and social welfare programs as solutions. In addition, Dr. Kinsey said that teenage sexuality appeared normal and healthy and called for greater tolerance from parents and law enforcement authorities.

Kinsey's advice reinforced the message adults received from the most popular pediatrician of the postwar era—Dr. Benjamin Spock, whose book, *Baby and Child Care,* first published in 1946, has sold more than 22 million copies. "Trust yourself," Spock told anxious parents. "Don't be overawed by what the experts say. Don't be afraid to trust your common sense." Although earlier government child-rearing pamphlets had recommended strict regimens, Spock called for flexibility. His respect for children led critics to denounce his "permissiveness" although Spock advocated firm parental control based on love and understanding.

POSTWAR GLOBALISM

Although the postwar years saw more Americans entering the middle class and focusing on personal problems of family life, the country's political leaders increasingly worried about the difficulty of stabilizing global affairs and assuring national security. Indeed, some scholars have speculated that the emphasis on domesticity on the home front reflected the extreme uncertainty of the global arena. For politicians and private citizens alike, the new world of atomic bombs introduced fearful prospects of mass death. And the promise of a lasting peace gradually and frustratingly gave way to endless conflicts with the nation's former wartime ally, the Soviet Union. By the end of the decade, the American people found themselves waging a "cold war" to preserve their way of life.

Despite widespread approval of participation in the United Nations, public demands for rapid demobilization and military budget cuts in 1946 showed a limited commitment to global involvement. Such pressure forced Truman to reduce the size of the armed forces from 12 million to 3 million within a few months. The president's failure to reach postwar agreements with the Soviet Union contributed to his loss of popularity, but public suspicion of world communism enabled him to develop an increasingly militant and internationalist position. His primary postwar goal was to secure the nation from foreign threat—militarily or economically. "We must face the fact that peace must be built on power," Truman said in 1945, "as well as upon good will and good deeds." Such power depended on military strength as well as on a stable economic environment. The huge expenditure of natural resources during the war underscored the importance of protecting the nation's access to raw materials.

"Our foreign relations inevitably affect employment in the United States," explained Secretary of State James F. Byrnes in 1945. "Prosperity and depres-

sion in the United States just as inevitably affect our relations with other nations of the world." To ensure access to markets and resources and to prevent
economic stagnation at home, postwar leaders advocated a worldwide system
of free trade that would include the Soviet Union. "Peace, freedom, and world
trade are indivisible," Truman remarked. "We must not go through the thirties again."

This economic approach to foreign affairs partially reflected the social
background of many of the nation's policymakers in the postwar period. Leading State Department officials such as Dean Acheson and John Foster Dulles
often had personal ties to the nation's largest corporations and held powerful
positions as corporate lawyers, financiers, or big-business executives. For example, the names of five of the six secretaries of state between 1945 and 1960
and of five of the six secretaries of defense between 1947 and 1960 appear in
the *Social Register* of the nation's richest families. Such men, appointed by
both Democratic and Republican presidents, formulated a foreign policy that
expressed and protected the values of the corporate elite. "I am an advocate
of business," conceded Secretary of Defense James Forrestal in 1947. "Calvin
Coolidge was ridiculed for saying . . . 'The chief business of the United States
is business,' but that is a fact."

Although foreign trade comprised only 6 percent of the gross national
product in 1945, State Department planners hoped to use U.S. economic
power to persuade Great Britain, France, and the Soviet Union to open their
trading blocs to U.S. businesses. When these nations applied for U.S. loans in
1945 to replace the wartime assistance, negotiators delayed action to win trading concessions. Nearly bankrupted by the war, Britain reluctantly accepted
U.S. conditions; so did France. But the Soviet Union, although devastated by
the war, refused to agree.

While Soviet leaders continued to advocate the Marxist-Leninist doctrine
of worldwide communist revolution, Josef Stalin rejected trade deals with
Western capitalists and decided to rebuild his war-ravaged country with German reparations. Stalin also demanded "friendly governments" in eastern Europe to prevent another invasion of his country and rejected free elections in
some areas occupied by Soviet troops. In Poland, the Red Army repressed political freedom to promote a pro-Soviet regime. During the war, Roosevelt
had minimized the problem of Soviet expansion in eastern Europe, largely
because he could do nothing about it and needed to preserve the Grand Alliance against Hitler. Although he remained suspicious of Stalin and refused
to share information about the atomic bomb, the president tried to treat the
Soviet Union as a "normal" state that was only protecting its national interests.

But Roosevelt failed to attract public support for this approach. Fearful of
a resurgence of isolationism, he hesitated to move ahead of public opinion. Nor
did he challenge the popular view that the United Nations, like the League of

Nations, would be based on President Woodrow Wilson's principle of equal representation for all nations. Yet Roosevelt believed that the UN could succeed where the League had failed only if the Big Powers dominated international diplomacy. He assumed that the Big Four (Britain, China, the United States, and the Soviet Union) would use their veto power in the UN's Security Council to protect their national interests. At the 1945 Yalta Conference, Roosevelt and Churchill acknowledged Soviet dominance in eastern Europe, the British claimed special privileges in the Mediterranean, and the United States sought to maintain power in Latin America. Roosevelt accepted these realities because he understood the special interests of each Allied nation.

At Roosevelt's death, Truman knew little about these foreign policy assumptions. Instead, the new president viewed the Soviet presence in eastern Europe as an infringement of the principle of national self-determination and a violation of the Yalta agreements. In a foreshadowing of future conflicts, Truman clashed angrily with Soviet Foreign Minister V. M. Molotov in 1945 about the undemocratic character of the Polish government and decided to withhold U.S. economic aid until Stalin retreated.

The new administration also shifted U.S. policy toward the British, Dutch, and French empires, most significantly in French Indochina. Roosevelt was opposed to French imperialism and had proposed that Indochina be placed under international trusteeship until the French colony achieved independence. When the leader of the Indochinese national liberation movement, Ho Chi Minh, drafted a declaration of independence in 1945, however, British pressure forced Roosevelt to accept the return of French troops—although with the goal of ultimately granting Indochina independence. Truman dropped that essential qualification. Instead, he agreed to return Indochina to France. Ho's sympathy toward communism had alarmed State Department officials. Equally important, Truman wished to retain French support in Europe, where France could be an ally against the Soviet Union. In 1945 the United States helped to transport French troops back to Indochina. Thereafter, the State Department ignored Ho Chi Minh's appeals for support.

While restoring French colonialism in Southeast Asia, Truman proceeded with prewar plans to grant independence to the Philippine Islands, first seized from Spain in 1898. Yet before departing from that strategic region, Washington negotiated long-term treaties providing for military bases and the stationing of U.S. troops in the Philippines. Besides ensuring military security, the treaty protected U.S. economic investments and reinforced the rule of its entrenched allies. Similar arrangements brought the United States a string of military bases in Iceland, in North Africa, in Okinawa (an island near Japan), and in the Azores (a group of islands in the Atlantic Ocean). In Spain, Truman legitimized the fascist dictator Francisco Franco as a defender against socialist revolution and Soviet influence.

Despite basic disagreements, the Big Three—(left to right) Prime Minister Winston Churchill, President Harry Truman, and Premier Josef Stalin—pose amicably at the Potsdam Conference in 1945. Days later, Churchill's defeat at the polls forced his replacement by Clement Atlee.

THE COLD WAR BEGINS

After the defeat of Germany, the three major Allies met in Potsdam in July 1945 but failed to resolve their differences about a peace settlement in Europe. Stalin continued to demand German reparations and expressed no interest in reducing Soviet influence in eastern Europe. Truman, emboldened by the first successful atomic bomb test that month, rejected such a Soviet sphere of influence. He proposed smaller reparations from Germany in hopes of maintaining Soviet dependence on U.S. exports. Since they failed to reach agreement, the Big Three postponed these issues until a subsequent Foreign Ministers Conference in London. Frustrated by Soviet stubbornness, Truman decided to exclude the Soviet Union from participation in the eventual occupation of Japan.

The atomic bombings of Japan in August 1945 reinforced Truman's confidence but aroused Soviet suspicions. At the London conference, the Soviets offered minor concessions on elections in Bulgaria and Hungary, but Washington demanded Western-style elections. Again, the diplomats could not agree. This failure showed the futility of atomic bomb diplomacy. When Molotov asked jokingly whether Secretary of State Byrnes had an atomic bomb in his

EXHIBIT **8-3** **ORIGINS OF THE COLD WAR, 1945–1949**

Year	Event
1945	Yalta Conference VE Day: Germany surrenders Potsdam Conference Atomic bombing of Japan; Japan surrenders (VJ Day)
1946	Kennan telegram Churchill's "Iron Curtain" speech Soviet occupation of northern Iran Acheson-Lilienthal plans for atomic energy Atomic Energy Act (creates AEC—Atomic Energy Commission)
1947	Truman Doctrine Federal Employee Loyalty Program National Security Act
1948	Communist coup in Czechoslovakia Marshall Plan—European Recovery Program Berlin airlift
1949	NATO Soviet A-bomb detonated Communist victory over Chinese Nationalists

pocket, Byrnes replied, "If you don't cut out all this stalling . . . I am going to pull an atomic bomb out of my hip pocket and let you have it!" To the surprise of U.S. negotiators, the Soviet Union would not be coerced into accepting Truman's demands. Secretary of War Henry Stimson, who had once viewed the bomb as a diplomatic lever, now saw an opportunity to ease tensions by sharing atomic secrets with the Soviets. "If we fail to approach them now and merely continue to negotiate with them, having this weapon rather ostentatiously on our hip," he warned, "their suspicions and their distrust . . . will increase." Yet after a high-level policy debate, the president chose to maintain the atomic monopoly.

Despite doubts about further negotiations, Secretary of State Byrnes met with Stalin in Moscow in December 1945. The meeting produced tentative agreements about portions of eastern Europe, Korea, and a United Nations Atomic Energy Commission. Yet pressure from congressional conservatives, who opposed any concessions to Stalin, forced Truman to adopt a more rigid position, and he abruptly disavowed Byrnes's agreements. "Unless Russia is faced with an iron fist and strong language, another war is in the making," he declared. "I'm tired of babying the Soviets." Meanwhile, Stalin rejected participation in the International Monetary Fund, asserting the Soviet desire to maintain economic independence.

Truman's firmness won support within the State Department from George F. Kennan, a longtime analyst of Soviet affairs, who insisted that it was not possible to gain concessions from Stalin through negotiation. "We have here," Kennan cabled from Moscow in February 1946, "a political force committed fanatically to the belief that . . . it is desirable and necessary that the internal harmony of our society be disrupted, our traditional way of life destroyed, the international authority of our state be broken if Soviet power is to be secure." Kennan's "long telegram" confirmed the president's belief that there could be no compromise with communist nations. One month later, Truman accompanied Winston Churchill to Fulton, Missouri, where the former prime minister attacked the Soviet Union for drawing an "iron curtain" around eastern Europe. The speech, approved by Truman, brought wide editorial criticism but publicized the change in foreign policy.

The United States also challenged the Soviet Union within the United Nations. The first major crisis involved Soviet occupation of northern Iran in 1946. The problem was oil. During the war, the Soviets, the British, and the Americans had occupied Iran jointly, but the Soviets hesitated to leave until they received oil concessions similar to those won by the British. Fearing a Soviet attempt to control vital oil resources, the White House supported Iran in the Security Council, where the United States controlled a preponderance of votes. Such diplomatic pressure forced Iran and the Soviet Union to negotiate oil concessions in exchange for a Soviet withdrawal. Afterward, Iran repudiated the agreement. Using UN institutions, the United States had thwarted Soviet expansion.

The United Nations also sanctioned the U.S. decision to maintain a monopoly on atomic weapons. In 1946, to ease public fear of atomic war, the Truman administration announced the Acheson-Lilienthal plan, which proposed that atomic energy become an internationally shared technology. The United States would relinquish control of atomic weapons in stages. During the transition, the United States would maintain a monopoly, and other countries would be required to allow international inspection. The United States "should not under any circumstances throw away our gun until we are sure the rest of the world cannot arm against us," said Truman. In presenting the program to the United Nations, Truman's advisor, financier Bernard Baruch, added other conditions, including the surrender of the UN Security Council veto on atomic energy issues and the imposition of "condign punishments" against violators of the plan by a majority vote (which was controlled by U.S. allies). Although fearful of the U.S. atomic monopoly, the Soviet Union was rushing to build its own atomic bombs and rejected the Baruch plan. Instead, the Soviets suggested immediate nuclear disarmament and sharing of atomic secrets. Truman considered the Soviet alternative unacceptable.

Frustrated by Soviet negotiators, U.S. leaders believed that Stalin could not be trusted. The Soviet leader's ruthless killing of his domestic rivals (as well as millions of innocent citizens), his cynicism in signing a nonaggression pact with Nazi Germany in 1939, and his determination to extend Soviet influence as far as possible—all reinforced fears of a communist plan to undermine U.S. national security. Defining Soviet communism as "red fascism,"

U.S. leaders were determined to avoid a repetition of the "appeasement" that had allowed Germany to control Europe in the 1930s. "The language of military power is the only language which disciples of power politics understand," presidential adviser Clark Clifford assured Truman in 1946. Moreover, in identifying the Soviet Union with Nazi Germany, Truman broadened support for his policy. Under the principle of "bipartisanship," Republicans, led by Senator Arthur Vandenberg and foreign policy expert John Foster Dulles, supported Truman's diplomacy, at least in Europe.

As a Cold War consensus crystallized in Washington, one former New Dealer emerged as a major critic—Henry A. Wallace, secretary of agriculture during the 1930s, Roosevelt's third-term vice president, and now Truman's secretary of commerce. In September 1946, after gaining Truman's approval, Wallace spoke publicly at Madison Square Garden in New York City, arguing that the United States had "no more business in the political affairs of Eastern Europe than Russia had in the political affairs of Latin America, Western Europe, and the United States." Yet when other members of the administration protested the speech, Truman abruptly fired Wallace. "The Reds, phonies, and the 'parlor pinks,'" Truman wrote, "seem to be banded together and are becoming a national danger."

Fear of communist influence permeated the nation. Preparing for a Soviet attack, FBI Director J. Edgar Hoover developed a Custodial Detention Program and compiled lists of suspected subversives who would be arrested at the outbreak of war. When the White House tried to minimize the communist threat, Hoover aligned with more militant anticommunists in Congress. "Communism," Hoover told the House Committee on Un-American Activities (HUAC), "is . . . an evil and malignant way of life." Persuaded by such testimony, Congress voted to provide more funds for FBI investigations of government workers. These political pressures pushed Truman toward a more militant anticommunist position.

The dismissal of Wallace revealed the administration's growing intolerance of positions that had seemed acceptable only a year before. After conservative Republican victories in the 1946 elections, some liberals deserted Truman and formed a coalition group, Progressive Citizens of America (PCA). The PCA complained that the Democratic Party had departed from Roosevelt's New Deal and urged a return to liberal principles or the creation of a third party. Although the PCA did not discriminate against members of the Communist Party, most liberals opposed communism and especially resented conservative accusations that liberals were tools of Soviet foreign policy. In January 1947 these anticommunist liberals formed Americans for Democratic Action (ADA). Like the PCA, the ADA endorsed expansion of the New Deal, the United Nations, and civil rights, but the ADA explicitly rejected any association with communists.

EXHIBIT **8-4**   GREECE, TURKEY, AND THE MEDITERRANEAN, 1947

THE TRUMAN DOCTRINE

Early in 1947 U.S. intelligence detected a relaxation of Soviet policy, but the State Department concluded that such changes were deliberately deceptive. This mistrust was reinforced by growing concern about the slow pace of economic recovery in Europe. Washington feared that economic unrest would encourage political instability and communist expansion and undermine U.S. interests. Matters climaxed in February 1947 when Britain announced it could no longer provide aid to Greece, a client state it had supported since World War II in a civil war against communist guerrillas. Truman welcomed the opportunity to replace Britain in the area, but U.S. intervention required congressional approval at a time when conservatives sought to cut government expenses. Moreover, the public appeared uninterested in Greek affairs. Truman decided, as Vandenberg put it, to "scare hell out of the American people."

   In an impassioned speech, the president personally presented the "Truman Doctrine" to a special session of Congress in March 1947, requesting $400 million in economic and military assistance for Greece and Turkey.

Condemning a communist system based on "terror and oppression, a controlled press and radio, fixed elections and the suppression of political freedoms," Truman depicted an emergency situation that forced the United States to "support free peoples who are resisting attempted subjugation by armed minorities or by outside pressures."

The Truman Doctrine represented a major turning point in foreign policy, announcing that threatened communist expansion obliged the United States to initiate unilateral action without consulting the United Nations. The new policy was later called "containment." Truman had abandoned the idea of effecting changes within the Soviet sphere of influence and stressed instead the importance of containing Soviet expansion. The doctrine, in effect, drew a line, dividing the globe into areas of "freedom" and zones of "terror and oppression." Such language allowed no room for compromise: All communists were dangerous; all communist threats became equally critical. The Truman Doctrine expanded the definition of "national security" to encompass conflicts anywhere in the world. "Wherever aggression, direct or indirect, threatened the peace," Truman later explained, "the security of the United States was involved."

Truman's belief that communism represented a monolithic threat placed the United States on the side of authoritarian governments in Greece and Turkey. Because he viewed Greek communists as minions of Moscow, Truman supported a conservative monarchy that had little popular support. In Turkey, the United States backed a repressive regime that had cooperated with the Germans during World War II and continued to crush internal dissent. The administration justified these alliances by articulating what later became known as the "domino" theory: "If Greece and then Turkey succumb," one State Department official advised, "the whole Middle East will be lost. France may then capitulate to the communists. As France goes, all Western Europe and North Africa will go."

Truman's commitment to interventionism on a global scale alarmed conservatives and liberals alike. Republican Senator Taft protested that Truman had made fundamental policy choices without adequately consulting Congress. Meanwhile, the liberal Wallace broadcast a scathing critique: "There is no regime too reactionary" to receive U.S. aid, he said, "provided it stands in Russia's expansionist path." Despite such criticism, the announcement of the Truman Doctrine rapidly boosted the president's approval ratings. Yet U.S. aid neither suppressed the Greek rebellion nor made the monarchy less oppressive. "There is no use pretending . . . that for $400 million we have bought peace," admitted Vandenberg. "It is merely a down payment."

Meanwhile, the slowness of European economic recovery disturbed U.S. leaders concerned about the lack of markets and the potential for social unrest. Secretary of State George C. Marshall, seeking to end economic shortages in Europe, stabilize economic growth, and stimulate U.S. trade, unveiled the administration's innovative European Recovery Program in a highly publicized speech at the Harvard University commencement in June 1947. Marshall described severe economic problems in Europe and called for a massive program of economic aid that offered assistance to all European nations, including communist governments. "Our policy is directed not against any country or doctrine," he stated, "but against hunger, poverty, desperation, and chaos." However, the Marshall Plan's purportedly unselfish offer of aid to the Soviets was deceptive because the plan threatened the independence of the Soviet economy. In addition, the program attempted to return to the prewar conditions that had left eastern Europe less industrialized than the West. Instead of receiving reparations, the Soviet Union might have to contribute food to other countries. Finally, the plan would rebuild the German economy and hasten German integration with western trade.

The State Department correctly predicted that the Soviet Union would reject participation in what came to be known as the Marshall Plan and would force its satellite states in eastern Europe to do the same. But sixteen nations drafted a four-year program of economic recovery and gladly accepted $17 billion in U.S. aid. This economic power allowed Washington to persuade political leaders in Italy and France to exclude the Communist Party from participation in their coalition governments.

Despite the anticommunist aspects of the Marshall Plan, the conservative majority in Congress remained suspicious of executive power, foreign aid, and potential benefits to large exporters rather than domestically oriented small firms. Moreover, as late as November 1947, 40 percent of the public had never heard of the Marshall Plan. But as economic conditions in western Europe continued to deteriorate and Communist parties throughout Europe organized protests, street demonstrations, and strikes, the White House moved quickly to arouse domestic opinion, launching a major lobby effort in Congress.

"We'll either have to provide a program of interim aid relief until the Marshall program gets going," Truman warned congressional leaders, "or the governments of France and Italy will fall, Austria too, and for all practical purposes, Europe will be Communist." Drawing on his personal standing among Republican leaders, Marshall sold Congress on the program. The idea that Europe would be saved from communism undermined conservative scruples about government spending abroad. Truman summoned a special session of Congress, played down the economic basis of the plan, and returned to the militant anticommunist rhetoric of the Truman Doctrine. The strategy worked, and Congress passed an interim aid measure. By 1950 the program had delivered $35 billion in government grants and loans to European countries and was credited with restoring morale and revitalizing political moderates.

George Catlett Marshall *(1880–1959)*

When Indiana Senator William Jenner opposed George Marshall's nomination as secretary of defense in 1950 by dismissing the general as a "living lie . . . a front man for traitors," it was as if someone had attacked the integrity of George Washington. Described by President Truman as "the greatest living American," Marshall had designed and coordinated World War II's Normandy invasion. He served as secretary of state from 1947 to 1949 and headed the Defense Department from 1950 to 1951. He was the key architect of the European Recovery Program, known as the Marshall Plan, and in 1953 he became the first career soldier to win the Nobel Peace Prize.

The Granger Collection, New York

"We are now concerned with the peace of the world," Marshall declared as World War II ended. One day after the general resigned from the military, Truman appointed him special presidential emissary to China with orders to seek an accord between warring Nationalists and Maoist communists. American officials worried that a victory by Maoists would strengthen Soviet influence in Asia. Marshall arrived in China in 1946 and used the lever of U.S. aid to compel the Nationalist government of Chiang Kai-shek to institute democratic reforms. Meanwhile, he tried to convince the communists to agree to a coalition government and unified army under Chiang's leadership.

THE RED SCARE

Anticommunist foreign policy paralleled an anticommunist crusade at home. Washington not only viewed the Soviet Union as a hostile and expansionist foreign power but also viewed the U.S. Communist Party as Stalin's domestic agent. Indeed, since the 1930s, various American Communists had provided information to the Soviet state, including aspects of atomic bomb research. Some evidence of Soviet espionage had surfaced in two highly publicized scandals: the discovery in 1945 of stolen secret documents in the offices of *Amerasia,* a left-wing diplomatic journal, and the capture of Soviet spies in

Aware that political pressures in the United States precluded a complete cessation of U.S. aid to an anticommunist ally, Chiang ignored Marshall's pleadings and launched a major military offensive. Perceiving that negotiations had "reached an impasse," Marshall warned Washington that "the Communists have lost cities and towns but they have not lost their armies." After more than 300 meetings with the disputing parties, Marshall returned home in 1947, citing "complete, almost overwhelming" mutual suspicion as "the greatest obstacle to peace."

The failure of the China mission underscored Marshall's conviction that military effectiveness was limited by political and social conditions. Believing that armed strategy should serve policy, not drive it, he recommended the firing of Korean War commander General Douglas MacArthur in 1951. Months later, Senator Joseph McCarthy denounced Marshall as an accessory to the 1949 victory of the Chinese Maoists and a coconspirator in the communist quest for world domination.

"God bless democracy," Marshall once had exclaimed. "I approve of it highly but suffer from it extremely." The general had popularized the Marshall Plan as a fight against the enemies of "hunger, poverty, desperation, and chaos." Yet the "fall" of China challenged U.S. plans for global peace, prosperity, and democracy, and the principal architect of the postwar world became the centerpiece of recriminating debates that tore at the Cold War consensus.

Canada in 1946. Republican candidates, such as Richard Nixon and Joseph McCarthy, had exploited this issue in winning election to Congress.

After the Republican victories in 1946, Truman attempted to defuse the explosive issue of communist influence in government by creating a Temporary Commission on Employee Loyalty. Nine days after enunciating the Truman Doctrine, the president created a permanent Federal Employee Loyalty program to eliminate subversives from government. The announcement reflected continuing pressures from congressional conservatives as well as anticommunist attitudes within the administration. In 1947 the House Committee on Un-American Activities (HUAC) opened new investigations of communist infiltration of government, Hollywood, education, and labor unions. HUAC's inquiry into the movie industry resulted in contempt charges against the "Hollywood Ten," a group of writers and directors who refused on First Amendment grounds to answer questions about their political activities. After the Supreme Court refused to hear their appeals, the Hollywood Ten went to prison.

Truman attempted to preempt similar investigations of government employees by issuing an executive order that mandated loyalty investigations of all federal workers and job applicants. The president also ordered dismissal of workers for whom "reasonable grounds" for suspicion of disloyalty existed. He instructed Attorney General Tom Clark to publicize a list of "subversive" organizations, and ninety-one groups were so designated in 1947. The Justice Department contended that these groups were "fronts" for the Communist Party. Federal investigators would treat membership in such organizations as grounds for further inquiries of individuals thus suspected of disloyalty. "There are many Communists in America," the attorney general declared. "They are everywhere—in factories, offices, butcher shops, on street corners, in private businesses—and each carries with him the germs of death for society." Perhaps it was no coincidence that 1947 witnessed the first UFO scare as Americans in thirty-five states and in Canada reported seeing flying saucers or "unidentified flying objects." In any case, the belief in a pervasive conspiracy allowed the administration to ignore due process protections in stigmatizing opponents of government policy and members of so-called subversive groups.

"What," asked a HUAC pamphlet, "is the difference in fact between a Communist and a Fascist? Answer: None worth noticing." In 1947 J. Edgar Hoover published a widely circulated article, "Red Fascism in the United States Today," warning of the imminent danger of communist subversion. To obtain judicial sanction for further surveillance and detention programs, Hoover pressed the Justice Department to prosecute leaders of the Communist Party for violating the Smith Act of 1940. That law made it a crime to advocate the overthrow of government by force or to belong to a group with such a goal. In 1948 the Justice Department charged twelve leading Communists with violations of the Smith Act, winning convictions and stiff prison sentences.

Even though cases of espionage by U.S. Communists and sympathizers certainly occurred before 1945, the political danger of domestic communism appeared minimal. At its peak strength during World War II, the U.S. Communist Party could claim fewer than 100,000 members. Most of them had no interest in subversive activities or the overthrow of the U.S. government. They did, however, hold political positions outside the prevailing consensus. The Communist Party had strenuously opposed racist policies in the South; and the party itself was one of the few racially integrated political organizations in the country. Communists demanded government support of social welfare programs, such as unemployment and health insurance, and preached of a more equitable economic order that gave incentives not for profit but for social benefit.

Although politicians warned about communist subversion, espionage, and other illegal activities, the core of anticommunism lay in public perceptions of its ideology. A wave of novels, movies, essays, and newspaper stories portrayed communism as the epitome of heartless atheism, deadening bureaucracy, and ruthless totalitarianism. Many eastern European ethnic groups hated the Soviets for invading their homelands and destroying Christian churches. Many Americans believed that communism jeopardized traditional values of religion, family, individual liberty, and personal initiative. "Communism is secularism on the march," J. Edgar Hoover told a Methodist gathering. "It is a moral foe of Christianity."

Ironically, the growth of government bureaucracy, big corporations, and impersonal, homogenized communities already threatened traditional values. "Our problem is not outside ourselves," admitted Republican presidential candidate Thomas E. Dewey in 1948. "Our problem is within ourselves." Anticommunist spokesmen such as Joseph McCarthy, J. Edgar Hoover, and Richard Nixon saw themselves as defending individualism, religion, and free enterprise. Their wrath focused not so much on actual Communists as on the sophisticated, cosmopolitan leadership that they saw tolerating communists in government and accommodating the Soviet Union. "I look at that fellow," Senator Hugh Butler of Nebraska remarked about Secretary of State Dean Acheson. "I watch his smart-aleck manner and his British clothes and that New Dealism, everlasting New Dealism in everything he says and does, and I want to shout, 'Get out, Get out. You stand for everything that has been wrong with the United States.'"

Conservative Republicans such as Nixon and McCarthy exploited anticommunist feelings to attack Democrats and the New Deal tradition. Public distrust of elites who were not accountable to voters—government bureaucrats, intellectuals, scientists, media and entertainment leaders—encouraged loyalty oaths, "naming names" of alleged communist associates, blacklists, and legal persecution. Mickey Spillane's detective novel *One Lonely Night* (1951), which sold 7 million copies, advocated another method to eliminate communists: "Don't arrest them, don't treat them with the dignity of the democratic process of courts of law . . . do the same thing that they'd do to you! Treat 'em to the inglorious taste of sudden death."

Thus backed by public opinion and the courts, law enforcement officials and anticommunist activists faced few obstacles in purging "red" elements from American life. As the FBI budget increased from $35 million in 1947 to $53 million in 1950, the agency's watchdogs processed nearly 5 million loyalty forms between 1947 and 1954. Under Truman, more than seven thousand federal government employees lost their jobs; thousands more were never hired in the first place. State and municipal governments adopted similar programs barring "subversives" from public employment. Workers and managers in private industry cooperated to harass suspected employees. Teachers, union leaders, even factory workers were forced to sign loyalty oaths—refusal usually meant dismissal. New York City high school students had to sign loyalty oaths to collect their diplomas. And the U.S. Post Office intercepted and opened mail from certain communist countries. "If ignorant people read it," said one censor, "they might begin to believe it."

Such excesses might have been checked by an independent judiciary, but Truman's appointments to the Supreme Court, including Attorney General Clark, consistently voted against civil liberties. In the *Dennis* case (1951) the Court upheld the convictions of eleven Communist Party leaders, ruling that "communist speech" was not protected by constitutional guarantees because communists participated in an international movement. As a result of 141 indictments and other harassment, many Communist Party leaders went "underground," and the party lost half its membership.

THE MILITARY CRISIS

The sense of national emergency stimulated the reorganization of the military services. The National Security Act of 1947 unified command over the armed services within the new Department of Defense, formalized the Joint Chiefs of Staff, and created an independent air force. The law also established the National Security Council (NSC) and the Central Intelligence Agency (CIA) as secret bureaus responsible only to the president. The NSC would coordinate and refine foreign policy for the White House and act as the president's liaison to the security bureaucracy. The CIA would preside over the gathering of intelligence information. The agency's congressional charter also provided for "such other functions as the Director of Central Intelligence shall, from time to time, deem appropriate." This loophole allowed the agency to develop secret military and political projects overseas. Amendments to the charter in 1949 exempted the CIA from budgetary accounting requirements, thereby releasing the agency from strict congressional oversight.

The National Security Act consolidated the power of the executive branch. Foreign policy decisions increasingly became insulated from external scrutiny. In a critical choice of military strategy, Truman opted in 1948 for an "air-atomic" plan that made strategic bombing, including nuclear weapons, the primary military force. Yet the United States possessed few atomic bombs or technicians capable of assembling more. To the budget-conscious president, air-atomic technology seemed an inexpensive way to build an unassailable defense. The plan had the additional advantage of reducing the need for a large army.

The decision to rebuild U.S. military strength faced opposition from both conservatives and liberals. Wallace, who announced his presidential candidacy as leader of the new Progressive Party, chastised Truman for ignoring the United Nations and provoking the Soviet Union. More powerful opposition came from Republicans such as Taft, who denounced the swollen federal budget and argued that the war with communism was ultimately a contest of ideas, not military might. When the president requested funds for the air-atomic plan in 1948, Congress seemed uninterested. "The outlook for greatly increased aviation budgets is not bright," the trade journal *Aviation Week* lamented early in 1948.

Congress abruptly snapped to attention, however, when communists seized power in Soviet-occupied Czechoslovakia in February 1948. Although the State Department had treated Czechoslovakia as part of the Soviet bloc, news of the communist coup shocked the public, confirming fears of Soviet aggression through internal subversion. Truman resolved not to repeat the Munich sellout of Czechoslovakia of 1938, when British and French "appeasement" had permitted Hitler to occupy Czech territory.

Speaking to a joint session of Congress in March 1948, the president warned that the United States was on the verge of war. The Soviet Union had "destroyed the independence and democratic character of a whole series of nations," said Truman, and so revealed "the clear design" to conquer "the remaining free nations of Europe." "There is some risk involved in action— there always is," he admitted, "but there is far more risk in failure to act." The somber speech persuaded Congress to approve the Marshall Plan and to reestablish the military draft. Conservatives managed to defeat a proposal for universal military training, but Congress allocated $3.5 billion for military purposes, 25 percent more than the White House had requested.

Military confrontation came one step closer when the Soviet Union blockaded Berlin in June 1948. Since the end of the war, the great powers had failed to sign a final peace settlement. While Truman and Stalin argued about German reparations, the former enemy remained divided into occupied zones. Because the United States and Britain planned to merge their occupied zones into a single unit, Stalin realized that the Western powers were hastening German independence to bring Germany into the Western alliance. In response the Soviets blocked access to Berlin through East Germany.

Truman saw war on the horizon. Determined to support Berlin, the president ordered a massive airlift of food and supplies that lasted eleven months. Stalin was unwilling to go to war and had to accept U.S. plans for West Germany. Yet the crisis escalated the level of conflict. In July 1948 Truman ordered B-29 bombers to England. These were the only planes capable of dropping atomic bombs in Europe, although (unknown to the Soviets) they were not modified for such work until 1949. For the first time, atomic weapons had become an explicit instrument of foreign policy.

EXHIBIT **8-5**   **BERLIN BLOCKADE, 1948**

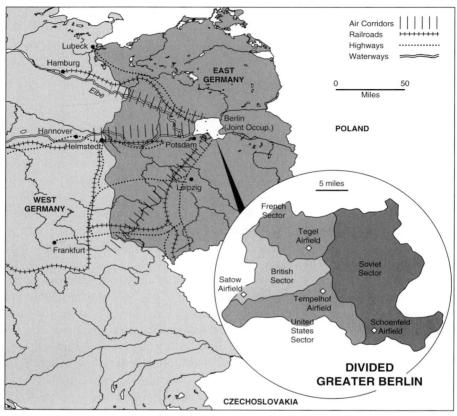

The Cold War crisis enabled Congress to reverse Truman's policies in Asia. In China, the corruption of Chiang Kai-shek's Nationalist regime and the success of Mao Zedong's communists had persuaded the president to allow the Chinese civil war to run its course. However, the Truman Doctrine suggested that any communist expansion threatened U.S. interests. Influenced by a well-funded pressure group known as the China Lobby, congressional conservatives insisted on a literal interpretation of the Truman Doctrine. Contrary to White House intentions, Congress proceeded to appropriate funds to support Chiang's regime, committing the United States to a repressive but noncommunist government and influencing subsequent foreign policy in Asia for three decades. Meanwhile, Truman's decision to abandon Chiang accelerated accommodation with Japan, a noncommunist ally. In 1947 Truman extended economic assistance to Japan and strengthened U.S. military forces there.

Washington also solidified its sphere of influence in Latin America. The Rio Pact of 1947 provided for collective self-defense of the Western Hemisphere. In 1948 the Bogota Treaty created the Organization of American States to coordinate policy, and the United States disavowed intervention in the affairs of other states. In creating this alliance, Washington avoided economic commitments, preferring to support private development. Yet in a series of bilateral agreements, the administration offered military assistance, including the training of Latin American armies. Such support stabilized military and landed elites throughout the region and increased dependence on U.S. trade.

THE ELECTION OF 1948

With the nation facing a series of foreign policy crises, political pundits questioned Truman's leadership. A March 1948 Gallup poll showed that the Democrats would lose the presidential election to any one of several Republican challengers: New York Governor Thomas E. Dewey, Vandenberg, former Minnesota Governor Harold Stassen, or General Douglas MacArthur. Meanwhile, Henry Wallace announced an independent candidacy. "There is no real fight between a Truman and a Republican," said Wallace. "Both stand for a policy which opens the door to war in our lifetime and makes war certain for our children." Yet military mobilization against Soviet communism worked to the president's advantage. By identifying Wallace as procommunist, the president kept most liberals in the Democratic Party.

Truman also moved to rebuild the New Deal coalition. Despite inherent conflicts between white southern Democrats and northern black voters, he opted to endorse civil rights, issuing an executive order to desegregate the military. The choice strengthened his appeal among both African Americans and northern liberals who might have backed Wallace. His veto of Taft-Hartley restored his support among organized workers. Truman also improved his standing among Jews by recognizing the new state of Israel in 1948.

The Wallace insurgency emboldened Republicans. They nominated Dewey for president and adopted a moderate platform that called for federal support of housing, farm payments, abolition of poll taxes, a permanent Fair Employment Practices Commission (FEPC), and increases in Social Security benefits. Confident of an election victory, Republicans deliberately excluded foreign policy issues from debate, which freed Truman from having to defend his positions. The president then undermined the Republicans by calling the Eightieth Congress into special session and daring the Republican majority to enact their party platform.

Truman also confronted divisions within the Democratic Party. At the Democratic National Convention, liberals, led by Minneapolis Mayor Hubert Humphrey, demanded a commitment to civil rights legislation. "The time has arrived for the Democratic Party to get out of the shadow of states' rights," Humphrey declared, "and walk forthrightly into the bright sunshine of human rights." Democrats responded by backing a strong civil rights plank. Angry

EXHIBIT **8-6**   **THE ELECTION OF 1948**

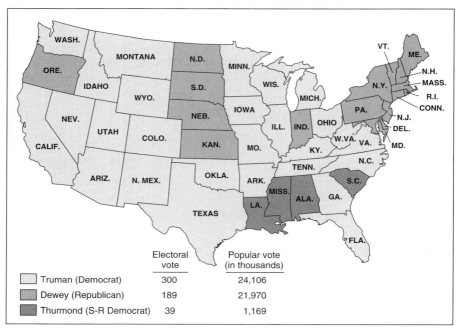

	Electoral vote	Popular vote (in thousands)
Truman (Democrat)	300	24,106
Dewey (Republican)	189	21,970
Thurmond (S-R Democrat)	39	1,169

southern delegates who opposed this plank left the convention. Three days later, these Dixiecrats met in Birmingham, Alabama, formed the States' Rights Party, and nominated South Carolina's Strom Thurmond for president. Other southern Democrats stayed in the party, but ignored the party platform. Lyndon B. Johnson, running in Texas for the Senate, attacked the FEPC ("because if a man can tell you whom you must hire, he can tell you whom you cannot employ"), and opposed proposals to end the discriminatory poll tax or enact federal antilynching laws.

Supporters of Henry Wallace proceeded to organize the Progressive Party and launched another independent campaign. Although communists held important positions in the party, the platform primarily reflected liberal principles. The Progressives challenged Truman's Cold War and Dewey's bipartisanship by arguing that "ending the tragic prospect of war is a joint responsibility of the Soviet Union and the United States." Yet the Progressives could never overcome their association with communism. "Politicians of both major parties have tried to pin the Communist tag on the followers of . . . Wallace," observed pollster George Gallup. "Apparently their efforts have succeeded." The Wallace campaign encountered harassment, mob violence, and denial of public meeting places, particularly in southern states that refused to permit racially mixed gatherings.

While Dixiecrats and Progressives attacked Truman, the special session of the Eightieth Congress convened. If Republicans enacted their platform, Truman would get credit for goading them to act; if not, they would appear hypocritical. After much discussion, Congress adjourned without passing significant legislation. The decision gave Truman campaign ammunition against "do-nothing" Republicans. Preelection polls forecast a Republican victory, but Truman launched a personal "whistle-stop" campaign that covered more than 20,000 miles. "Give 'em hell, Harry!" became a rallying cry as Truman appealed to anxious farmers about Republican threats to the price support program and became the first president to campaign for the African American vote in Harlem.

The results brought a surprise Democratic victory in November when Truman topped Dewey by more than 2 million votes. "The publishers' press is a very small part of our population," gloated Truman. The Electoral College gave Truman 304 votes, Dewey 189, Thurmond 34 (all in the South), and Wallace none. Each third-party candidate attracted slightly more than 1 million votes, but Truman did best among farmers, organized labor, and blacks—all groups that supported Roosevelt's New Deal.

THE FAIR DEAL

"Every segment of our population and every individual," Truman told the Eighty-first Congress, "has a right to expect from our Government a fair deal." With a Democratic majority again in Congress, the president called for increased Social Security benefits and minimum wages, civil rights legislation, federal aid to education, national health insurance, and repeal of the Taft-Hartley Act. However, White House proposals soon met resistance from the true majority in Congress—a conservative coalition of southern Democrats and midwestern Republicans. By controlling the congressional committee system, these groups prevented consideration of Truman's program. Although Congress passed the Housing Act of 1949, providing for slum clearance and low-income housing, insufficient appropriations limited the program. In addition, civil rights legislation died in committee. Truman, choosing to avoid a hopeless skirmish, did not push for its passage.

Truman's support of civil rights appeared ambiguous. Despite the president's 1948 order to desegregate the armed services, the military evaded enforcement. In Truman's inauguration parade of 1949, black soldiers marched with whites, but the army blocked full integration by segregating platoons. Truman's Department of Justice supported civil rights suits, but the Federal Housing Authority continued to accept residential segregation, even after the Supreme Court outlawed restrictive covenants in 1948. As for equal employment opportunity, the president hesitated to reestablish the FEPC, then failed to halt discrimination in war industries. Nonetheless, African Americans praised Truman's moral support. "No occupant of the White House since the nation was born," wrote black leader Walter White, "has taken so frontal or constant a stand against racial discrimination as has Harry S Truman."

The limitations of Truman's Fair Deal reflected changes in liberal thinking. After Wallace's defeat, liberals repudiated associations with communism and moved away from radical positions. Anticommunist liberals, including theologian Reinhold Niebuhr and historian Arthur M. Schlesinger Jr., argued that the search for a perfect society such as a communist utopia was naïve, self-deceptive, and led to totalitarian excesses. At a time when more middle-class citizens were enjoying personal prosperity, creating the baby boom, and celebrating conformity, U.S. liberalism understandably supported the status quo.

LIMITED BIPARTISANSHIP

Although political disagreement eventually undermined the foreign policy consensus, a bipartisan spirit prevailed on European issues. In June 1948 the Senate passed the Vandenberg Resolution, which permitted participation in a peacetime military alliance with the nations of western Europe. The next year, the United States signed the North Atlantic Treaty, a pact that provided for a collective defense against the Soviets by forming the North Atlantic Treaty Organization (NATO). The administration also moved to create a new West German state, and in 1949 the Federal Republic of Germany joined the Western alliance. Although the treaty obligated the United States to send military assistance to European allies, its purposes appeared less military than political. First, NATO served as a deterrent to Soviet expansion. Second, the alliance ensured U.S. domination of western Europe by obliging its members to adopt a united, U.S.-influenced approach to the region's security. Third, the pact linked German industrial and military power with the rest of western Europe to avoid old rivalries. Taft, who was opposed to permanent military commitments, led the fight against the treaty's ratification in the senate, but could not overcome the president's supporters. The House, however, hesitated to allocate funds to implement the treaty's provisions. Then, in September 1949, the president announced that the Soviet Union had exploded an atomic bomb. Within a week, the House provided the NATO funding.

Perceiving the Soviet Union as a relentless enemy that now possessed devastating weapons of destruction, Republicans and Democrats alike felt increasingly vulnerable to attack both at home and abroad. Although Soviet spies accelerated the development of a Soviet atomic bomb (probably by fewer than two years), fears of domestic subversion assumed nightmarish proportions.

EXHIBIT **8-7 THE NORTH ATLANTIC TREATY ORGANIZATION (NATO)**

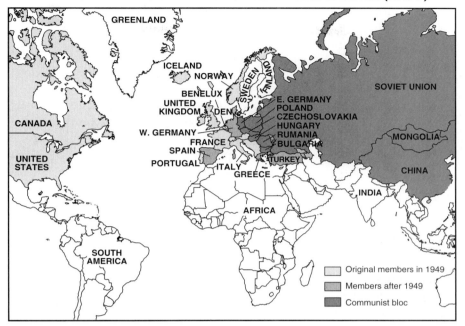

GREENLAND

ICELAND
NORWAY
BENELUX
UNITED
KINGDOM   DEN.
W. GERMANY
FRANCE
SPAIN
PORTUGAL   ITALY
GREECE

CANADA

UNITED
STATES

SWEDEN   FINLAND

E. GERMANY
POLAND
CZECHOSLOVAKIA
HUNGARY
RUMANIA
BULGARIA
TURKEY

SOVIET UNION

MONGOLIA

CHINA

INDIA

AFRICA

SOUTH
AMERICA

Original members in 1949
Members after 1949
Communist bloc

Allegations that government "traitors" such as former State Department official Alger Hiss had passed secret documents to communist agents reinforced
the climate of suspicion. Yet Washington recognized that the Soviet Union
lacked the military capacity to launch an atomic attack. Even so, Truman opted
to strengthen U.S. military power. During the fall of 1949, top administration
advisors debated whether the country should proceed to build a "superbomb."
Despite unanimous objections by scientists and civilians on the Atomic Energy Commission's General Advisory Council, commission head Lewis Strauss,
backed by physicist Edward Teller, urged the development of the new hydrogen weapon. In January 1950 Truman ended the debate by ordering development of the bomb. By the end of the next year the United States successfully
tested the new weapon; within two years the Soviet Union did the same.

Truman continued to face Republican criticism for neglecting China's
Chiang Kai-shek. Despite appropriations exceeding $1 billion for the Chinese
Nationalists, communist armies steadily destroyed Chiang's crumbling forces.
By August 1949 the State Department predicted a communist victory and
halted further assistance. "The only alternative open to the United States," asserted a State Department white paper, "was full-scale intervention in behalf
of a government which had lost the confidence of its own troops and its own
people." Yet, although it conceded the inevitability of a communist victory,

Arthur H. Vandenberg *(1884–1951)*

"The Old Guard dies but never surrenders," wrote journalist Milton S. Mayer of the last-ditch noninterventionists in 1940; "Vandenberg surrenders, but never dies." Michigan Senator Arthur H. Vandenberg blazed the trail for those conservative Americans who made the transition from prewar anti-interventionism to postwar internationalism.

Although staunch Old Guard Republicans such as Robert Taft of Ohio refused to compromise their "America-first" principles, Vandenberg believed that national security required a new internationalist commitment. He insisted that the Soviet Union constituted a threat to U.S. interests around the world and worked with the Truman administration to build a national consensus in support of the Cold War.

Born in Grand Rapids, Michigan, Vandenberg embraced the traditionalist middle-class and midwestern values of his surroundings. Yet Pearl Harbor and the requirements of World War II prompted him to embrace internationalism, leading to the senator's support for a postwar United Nations. To win Republican backing of the postwar settlement,

the administration rejected accommodation with the Chinese insurgents. Four months later Mao Zedong's communist forces swept into power, forcing Chiang to abandon the mainland and flee to the island of Taiwan (Formosa).

Given the logic of containment, the communist victory in China could only be seen as a defeat of U.S. policy, especially after Mao signed a mutual assistance pact with the Soviet Union in 1950. The China Lobby, which included leading Republican senators, attacked the administration for failing to support an anticommunist ally. Such criticism reinforced Truman's reluctance to negotiate with the Chinese communists. Instead, the United States adopted a policy of nonrecognition that lasted for more than two decades.

Truman chose Vandenberg to attend the first United Nations conference in San Francisco in 1945, where the delegate persuaded his colleagues to adopt Article 51 of the UN Charter, providing for regional alliances. Intended to protect U.S. influence in Latin America, this proviso later provided the basis for NATO and other regional pacts.

As the leading internationalist in the Republican Party, Vandenberg demanded a voice in foreign policy in exchange for bipartisan support of the Cold War. Criticizing any sign of "appeasement" of the Soviet Union, he denounced negotiations to internationalize atomic energy in 1946. His vanity, though, made him easily subject to flattery and pressure. Using the principle of bipartisanship, the administration won his support of the Truman Doctrine, Marshall Plan, and NATO. Vandenberg also intervened with Republican leaders to prevent any serious debate of foreign policy during the 1948 presidential election.

Unlike Taft, Vandenberg did not question the high cost of the Cold War or the growth of a national security state. Taft's opposition to the military state prevented him from winning the Republican nomination in 1948 and 1952. Yet Vandenberg, whose foreign policy position seemed more popular, failed to win the respect of his colleagues and never became a party leader.

The so-called loss of China, the explosion of a Soviet atomic bomb, allegations of communists in government—all disturbed the search for security that had followed World War II. Two days after Truman announced the first Soviet atomic test in September 1949, a young evangelical Baptist named Billy Graham opened a tent revival meeting in Los Angeles and addressed the most pressing question of the age. "Time is desperately short," he warned; "prepare to meet thy God." Worried citizens had to wonder how the country had moved so rapidly from the optimism of peace in 1945 to the perils of atomic warfare with the Soviet "anti-Christ."

AMERICAN HISTORY RESOURCE CENTER

To explore documents, images, audio and video clips, articles, and commentary related to the material in this chapter, visit the source collections at ushistory.wadsworth.com and and use the Search function with the following key terms:

Cold War	George Kennan
Harry Truman	J. Edgar Hoover
George Marshall	

RECOMMENDED READINGS

Gary A. Donaldson, *Truman Defeats Dewey* (1999). A study of postwar election politics, this book describes Truman's success at rebuilding the New Deal coalition in 1948.

Rosalyn Baxandall and Elizabeth Ewen, *Picture Windows: How the Suburbs Happened* (2000). The authors place postwar suburban growth in a century-long context of housing issues and public policy.

Melvyn P. Leffler, *A Preponderance of Power: National Security, the Truman Administration, and the Cold War* (1992). A thorough and balanced analysis of postwar foreign policy, this volume explains U.S. motivations in the emerging Cold War.

William Graebner, *The Age of Doubt: American Thought and Culture in the 1940s* (1991). This book explores wartime and postwar cultural expression, including media, literature, and the arts, emphasizing the underlying anxieties caused by political events.

Additional Readings

The major issues of the Truman years are explored in Alonzo L. Hamby, *Beyond the New Deal: Harry S. Truman and American Liberalism* (1973). Two good biographies are Robert H. Ferrell, *Harry S. Truman: A Life* (1994), and Alonzo L. Hamby, *Man of the People: A Life of Harry S. Truman* (1995). Also useful as an introduction to the period is an anthology, Barton J. Bernstein, ed., *Politics and Policies of the Truman Administration* (1970). A convenient collection of primary sources is Barton J. Bernstein and Allen Matusow, eds., *The Truman Administration* (1966). See also Gary W. Reichard, *Politics as Usual: The Age of Truman and Eisenhower* (1988).

The postwar relationship between government and business is illuminated in Elizabeth A. Fones-Wolf, *Selling Free Enterprise: The Business Assault on Labor and Liberalism, 1945–1960* (1994). For a fine study of the relationship between technology and industrial development, see David F. Noble, *Forces of Production: A Social History of Industrial Automation* (1986). Government support of science and technology is the major theme of three valuable studies: Walter A. McDougall, *The Heavens and the Earth: A Political History of the Space Age* (1985); Richard Rhodes, *Dark Sun: The Making of the Hydrogen Bomb* (1995); and Kenneth Flamm, *Creating the Computer: Government, Industry, and High Technology* (1988). For the impact of the atomic bomb on U.S. society, see Paul Boyer, *By the Bomb's Early Light: American Thought and Culture at the Dawn of the Atomic Age* (1985), and Spencer R. Weart, *Nuclear Fear: A History of Images* (1988). For Truman's farm policies, see Allen Matusow, *Farm Policies and Politics in the Truman Years* (1967); for labor, see R. Alton Lee, *Truman and Taft-Hartley* (1966).

The consequences of the high postwar birthrate are described in Landon Y. Jones, *America and the Baby Boom Generation* (1980). For the influence of pediatrician Benjamin Spock, see Julia Grant, *Raising Baby by the Book: The Education of American Mothers* (1998). The broader problems of economic class and wealth are well analyzed in George Lipsitz, *Rainbow at Midnight: Labor and Culture in the 1940s* (1994). A survey of women's history can be found in Elaine Tyler May's *Homeward Bound: American Families in the Cold War Era* (1988), which can be supplemented with Rochelle Gatlin, *American Women Since 1945* (1987).

The literature on the Cold War is vast. A sensible and readable introduction is Walter Lafeber, *America, Russia, and the Cold War* (1985), as is Bernard Weisberger, *Cold War, Cold Peace* (1984). John Lewis Gaddis's *Now We Know: Rethinking Cold War History* (1997) places Soviet-American conflict in a longer perspective. An excellent analysis of the creation of the new national defense policies is Michael J. Hogan, *A Cross of Iron: Harry S. Truman and the Origins of the National Security State* (1998). See also Daniel Yergin, *Shattered Peace: Origins of the Cold War and the National Security State* (1977). The importance of the atomic bomb in foreign policy and military planning is analyzed carefully in Gregg Harken, *The Winning Weapon: The Atomic Bomb in the Cold War, 1945–1950* (1980). For the sources of economic conflict, see Robert A. Pollard, *Economic Security and the Origins of the Cold War, 1945–1950* (1985). The close relationship between domestic anticommunism and foreign policy is presented in Richard M. Freeland, *The Truman Doctrine and the Origins of McCarthyism* (1972).

The impact of the Red Scare is thoroughly documented in David Caute, *The Great Fear: The Anti-Communist Purge Under Truman and Eisenhower* (1978). Also illuminating is Les Adler, *The Red Image: American Attitudes Toward Communism in the Cold War Era* (1991). A series of recent volumes, based on declassified but often ambiguous evidence, depicts Soviet espionage activities: see Harvey Klehr and Ronald Radosh, *The Amerasia Spy Case: Prelude to McCarthyism* (1996); John Earl Haynes and Harvey Klehr, *Venona: Recoding Soviet Espionage in America* (1999); and Allen Weinstein and Alexander Vassiliev, *The Haunted Wood: Soviet Espionage in America—the Stalin Era* (1999).

The political consequences of anticommunism are explored in Francis H. Thompson, *The Frustration of Politics: Truman, Congress, and the Loyalty Drive, 1945–1953* (1979); in Athan Theoharis, *Seeds of Repression: Harry S. Truman and the Origins of McCarthyism* (1971); and in Alan D. Harper, *The Politics of Loyalty* (1969). The investigations of Hollywood are detailed in Larry Ceplair and Steven Englund, *The Inquisition in Hollywood: Politics in the Film Community, 1930–1960* (1980), and in Victor Navasky, *Naming Names* (1980). For the effect of the new political climate on the movie industry, see Lary May, *The Big Tomorrow: Hollywood and the Politics of the American Way* (2000). An oral history exploring these issues can be found in Griffin Fariello, *Red Scare: Memories of the American Inquisition* (1995).

The Wallace candidacy of 1948 is described in Richard J. Walton, *Henry Wallace, Harry Truman, and the Cold War* (1976), which contains many primary sources, and in Norman D. Markowitz, *The Rise and Fall of the People's Century: Henry A. Wallace and American Liberalism* (1973). James T. Patterson's *Mr. Republican: A Biography of Robert A. Taft* (1972) examines the career of the leading conservative. For the early career of Lyndon B. Johnson, see the second volume of Robert Caro's *The Years of Lyndon Johnson: Means of Ascent* (1990).

The role of key personalities in policymaking emerges in Robert L. Messer, *The End of an Alliance: James F. Byrnes, Roosevelt, Truman, and the Origins of the Cold War* (1982). See also Michael J. Hogan, *The Marshall Plan: America, Britain, and the Reconstruction of Western Europe* (1987). The persistence of isolationism is the subject of Justus D. Doenecke, *Not to the Swift: The Old Isolationists in the Cold War* (1979). A useful anthology on the dissenters from Truman's policies is Thomas G. Paterson, ed., *Cold War Critics* (1971).

The Cold War in Asia is described in Robert M. Blum, *Drawing the Line: The Origin of the American Containment Policy in East Asia* (1982); in William Whitney Stueck Jr., *The Road to Confrontation: American Policy Toward China and Korea, 1947–1950* (1981); and in Nancy Tucker, *Patterns in the Dust: Chinese-American Relations and the Recognition Controversy, 1949–1950* (1983). A good analysis of postwar Asian policy can be found in Gordon H. Chang, *Friends and Enemies: The United States, China, and the Soviet Union, 1948–1972* (1990). For U.S. policy in Indochina, see the relevant chapters of Lloyd C. Gardner, *Approaching Vietnam: From World War II Through Dienbienphu, 1941–1954* (1988).

American policy in the Middle East is presented in Aaron David Miller, *The Search for Security: Saudi Arabian Oil and American Foreign Policy, 1939–1949* (1980); in Barry Rubin, *Paved with Good Intentions: American Experience in Iran* (1980); and in Zvi Ganin, *Truman, American Jewry, and Israel, 1945–1948* (1979). For international economic affairs, see Fred L. Block, *The Origins of International Economic Disorder* (1977). Also insightful is Ernest R. May, *"Lessons" of the Past: The Use and Misuse of History in American Foreign Policy* (1973).

REPUBLICAN LEADERSHIP AND THE ANTICOMMUNIST CRUSADE, 1950–1954

The 1950s began ominously, accentuating public anxieties about the Soviet atom bomb and the communist victory in China. In January a jury waded through hours of allegations and denial and found former State Department official Alger Hiss guilty of perjury for denying that he had passed classified documents to erstwhile Communist Whittaker Chambers in the 1930s. The sensational case confirmed conservative fears that a link existed between Hiss's New Deal liberalism and communist influence in government. The case further embarrassed Democrats because President Harry Truman had labeled the congressional investigation of Hiss "a red herring" and had issued a 1948 executive order barring Congress from access to government loyalty files without presidential approval.

The Hiss case solidified the Cold War suspicion that association with the U.S. Communist Party was equivalent to service for the Soviet state. Indeed, recent revelations from Soviet archives show that the Russians had found willing agents among some U.S. Communist Party members, although the nature of their activities remains unclear. However, most U.S. communists attempted to affect policy through more conventional political activities, such as participation in labor groups, elections, or public events. Nonetheless, Richard Nixon, who had sparked the Hiss investigation for the House Committee on Un-American Activities (HUAC), denounced "high officials" for concealing a larger subversive "conspiracy." Thereafter, anticommunist liberals would disassociate themselves from political activities that might prove embarrassing.

Truman, in any case, had no intention of relaxing the nation's defenses. In January 1950, the commander in chief rebuffed the objections of some civilian scientists and ordered the Atomic Energy Commission (AEC) to proceed with the development of a thermonuclear or hydrogen bomb, a thousand times more powerful than atomic weapons. In February the Soviet Union and the People's Republic of China signed a treaty of friendship, alliance, and mutual assistance and both communist states extended recognition to Indochina's rebels, the Vietminh. That month, British authorities arrested physicist Klaus Fuchs on suspicion of passing atomic secrets to the Soviet Union during World War II. The Fuchs case set off a string of arrests that netted other accused atomic spies, including U.S. citizens Julius and Ethel Rosenberg. Meanwhile, the National Security Council (NSC) began to put the finishing touches on a secret comprehensive plan of global defense labeled NSC-68, which warned that the public was suffering from "a false sense of security."

In this climate of mounting global tension, Wisconsin Senator Joseph R. McCarthy presented a Lincoln Day address to the Women's Republican Club in Wheeling, West Virginia, that stunned the nation. "Five years after a world war has been won, men's hearts should anticipate a long peace," he said, "and men's minds should be free from the heavy weight that comes with war." Instead, he declared, the country was engaged in a frightening Cold War between "communistic atheism and Christianity." In defining the conflict with Soviet communism as a religious crusade, McCarthy offered a secularized version of total war between good and evil in which the outcome remained uncertain.

The Wisconsin senator also presented a startling revelation about the cause of the country's unexpected and dangerous predicament. According to McCarthy, America's crisis resulted from a conspiracy against the U.S. government. "I have in my hands," said McCarthy, "a list of 205 [government employees] that were made known to the secretary of state as being members of the Communist Party and who nevertheless are still working and shaping policy in the State Department." In later versions of his speech, McCarthy changed the specific number of alleged communists—facts, to McCarthy, were slippery items—but he vigorously affirmed the charge that subversives permeated the federal bureaucracy.

McCarthy's attacks on communism stamped his name indelibly on the era. Of course, the anticommunist crusade had preceded his election to Congress in 1946, and other conservative leaders, such as California's Richard Nixon and South Dakota's Karl Mundt, had warned about communist subversion of government. President Truman had created a loyalty security program to identify and purge spies and subversives (see Chapter 8). But McCarthy's rhetorical style—his claims of possessing evidence and proof of conspiracy—added to the sense of emergency. Moreover, McCarthy disdained the legal steps of due process associated with government investigations. A contentious, tough-talking ex-Marine, the Wisconsin senator often drank to excess, insulted witnesses, swore at his critics, and assaulted a Washington journalist who challenged his conspiratorial claims. Such behavior would ultimately prove McCarthy's undoing. But between 1950 and 1954, he hurled innumerable charges of communism at upstanding citizens and created a climate of persecution that his critics compared to a witch hunt.

THE RED SCARE

McCarthy's success reflected the national mood. In June 1950 the arrest of Julius and Ethel Rosenberg, who were charged with transmitting atomic bomb secrets to the Soviet Union during World War II, underscored the domestic threat. That month the "Hollywood Ten," who had refused to testify to HUAC about their political associations, began to serve one-year prison sentences for "contempt" of Congress. By then, the movie industry had established a blacklist, refusing to employ alleged communists in films. A new movie, *The Flying Saucer,* claimed that UFOs were Soviet airplanes "designed for one purpose—to carry an atomic bomb," while the science fiction thriller *Destination Moon* had U.S. business leaders racing to beat the Russians to the uranium-rich lunar surface. "I cannot tell you when or where the attack will come," admitted President Truman as he announced the first national civil defense program. "I can only remind you that we must be ready when it does come."

The belief in a pervasive communist conspiracy prompted efforts to identify and control all communist activities. In 1950 Nevada's Democratic Senator Patrick McCarran introduced the Internal Security Act, which banned communists from employment in defense industries, established a Subversive Activities Control Board to monitor communist organizations, required communists to register with the attorney general, and barred communists from obtaining passports. Senate liberals, hoping to defeat the measure, offered an alternative bill that authorized the president to declare an "internal security emergency" and to detain suspected dissidents. But then the Senate combined and passed both proposals. Truman vetoed the bill "because any governmental stifling of the free expression of opinion is a long step toward totalitarianism." Congress overrode the veto by an overwhelming margin. Terrified by the prospect of an atomic war with the Soviet Union, the public supported such anticommunist measures.

McCarthy's accusations concerning communists in government won the support of most conservative Republicans, who, despite occasional misgivings about his tactics, endorsed attacks on the Truman administration. One exception was Maine Republican Margaret Chase Smith, the only woman in the Senate. Responding to the climate of "fear and frustration," she drafted a "Declaration of Conscience" that denounced her party's support of "fear, ignorance, bigotry and smear." In 1950 a Senate investigating committee chaired by Maryland Democrat Millard Tydings found no evidence to support McCarthy's charges and concluded that the allegations were "a fraud and a hoax." Yet the Senate responded to the report along strict party lines. Such party loyalty enabled McCarthy to remain a presence if not a decisive factor in the 1950 congressional elections. In Maryland, McCarthy smeared Tydings as a procommunist and contributed to Tydings's defeat. In California, Nixon defeated liberal Democrat Helen Gahagan Douglas, whom he dubbed the "Pink Lady," to win election to the Senate.

After the 1950 elections, McCarran's Senate Internal Security subcommittee focused on communist influence at the United Nations, and HUAC resumed investigations of Hollywood figures in 1951. Meanwhile, McCarthy's accusations that communists were employed in the State Department gained wide public attention. Truman called McCarthy a liar. Yet the administration reacted to the charges not by defending the civil liberties of the accused but by affirming its own anticommunist credentials. In April 1951 Truman issued an executive order introducing a new standard for ferreting out subversives: A federal employee could be fired not when there were "reasonable grounds" but rather when there was "reasonable doubt" about the person's loyalty. The burden of proof thus shifted from the accuser to the accused.

In 1952 Congress endeavored to protect U.S. borders by establishing new rules for immigration. The McCarran-Walter Immigration Act, passed over Truman's veto, gave the president power to exclude any foreigner deemed "detrimental" to the national interest. The law continued previous immigration policies by favoring immigrants from northern and western European countries and sharply limiting immigrants from the colonies of those countries. The act slightly increased Asian immigration quotas and permitted wider immigration from Latin America, but reduced immigration from the West Indies and Africa. Consistent with the anticommunist crusade, the McCarran-Walter Act also limited immigration from countries under communist control and facilitated expulsion of "undesirable" aliens and naturalized citizens.

THE WAR IN KOREA

By the spring of 1950 the National Security Council had completed the secret analysis of U.S. foreign policy, NSC-68. Asserting that "the Soviet Union . . . is animated by a new fanatic faith . . . and seeks to impose its absolute authority over the rest of the world," the report emphasized the possibility of immediate war and recommended that the United States be prepared to halt Soviet expansion throughout the world. Such a goal demanded a global defense system that included hydrogen bombs, expansion of conventional military forces, and a network of international alliances. To finance this policy, NSC-68 recommended quadrupling the $13 billion national defense budget. This costly plan faced considerable opposition in Congress, particularly because the Soviet Union had avoided any overt action since 1948 that justified U.S. military intervention. Meanwhile, in secret meetings, the administration debated plans to defend Taiwan from invasion by Chinese communists.

EXHIBIT **9-1**   **THE KOREAN WAR**

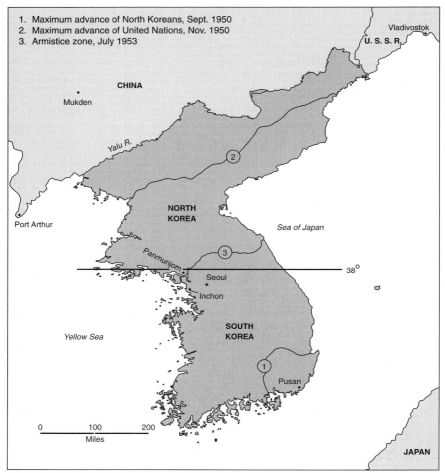

1. Maximum advance of North Koreans, Sept. 1950
2. Maximum advance of United Nations, Nov. 1950
3. Armistice zone, July 1953

The tense peace was shattered on June 25, 1950, when North Korean troops suddenly invaded South Korea. Six months earlier, Secretary of State Dean Acheson had remarked in a speech to the National Press Club that Korea and Taiwan lay beyond the U.S. "defense perimeter" in the Pacific. The statement, though challenged by Republican conservatives, had justified a reduction of aid to the Chinese Nationalist regime of Chiang Kai-shek. But as North Korean armies advanced quickly, Truman ordered military assistance to South Korea and directed the Seventh Fleet to sail between mainland China and Taiwan to prevent an invasion of the Nationalist-held island. The next day the White House called an emergency session of the UN Security Council, which branded North Korea an aggressor. (The Soviet delegation, boycotting the Security Council because of U.S. refusal to discuss the admission of communist China, missed the critical vote.)

As the South Korean army collapsed, Truman saw the North Korean invasion as equivalent to the 1941 attack on Pearl Harbor and ordered U.S. troops into action. "The attack upon Korea," he declared, "makes it plain beyond all doubt that communism has passed beyond the use of subversion to conquer independent nations." The United Nations later approved Truman's action, giving international sanction to U.S. policy. Sixteen nations eventually participated in the war, but the United States provided most of the resources and leadership.

Intervention in Korea stemmed from the conviction that the United States had to "draw the line" against communist aggression and demonstrate its willingness to fight the Soviets anywhere in the world. As with the earlier decisions of challenging the Berlin blockade and developing hydrogen bombs, the president bypassed consultation with congressional leaders, thereby setting important precedents for successors. Although Senator Robert A. Taft denounced Truman's "complete usurpation . . . of authority to use the armed forces," public opinion supported the president's action. Indeed, Truman's claim to be enforcing UN policy won favor among liberals, even though the U.S. military commander, General Douglas MacArthur, took orders directly and exclusively from Washington.

American troops landed in Korea just in time to stop a complete North Korean victory. After hard fighting near the southern port of Pusan, the Allied armies forced the enemy to retreat. At the start of the war, the administration insisted that fighting was "solely for the purpose of restoring the Republic of Korea to its status prior to the invasion." In September 1950, however, Truman authorized a military advance north of the thirty-eighth parallel, the border between North and South Korea, in an effort to liberate North Korea from communism before the U.S. congressional elections. General MacArthur promised victory by Christmas. In October Truman conferred with MacArthur at Wake Island and agreed to allow UN troops to proceed to the Yalu River, which bordered China. This advance aroused Chinese concerns about U.S. intentions, and China decided to protect North Korea. By November Chinese "volunteers" were fighting in Korea. The UN advance soon stalled, and the combined communist armies proceeded to drive the UN forces into a retreat south of the thirty-eighth parallel.

The confrontation with Chinese troops raised the possibility of another world war, which might include the use of nuclear weapons. Truman, however, exercised his power as commander in chief to restrain MacArthur and prevent an attack on China. By 1951, battle lines again stabilized around the thirty-eighth parallel, but MacArthur criticized the limits of U.S. involvement. "There is no substitute for victory," he declared. Unfamiliar with the concept of limited war, public opinion appeared ambivalent, showing both strong support for the use of atomic bombs and a desire to withdraw from the war altogether. When Truman announced a stalemated cease-fire, MacArthur,

General Douglas MacArthur greets President Truman at Wake Island in the Pacific to discuss Korean War strategy in 1950. It was the only time the two met. Truman fired the general the next year.

harboring his own presidential ambitions, publicly criticized the president's "no-win" policy.

Exasperated by MacArthur's insubordination, Truman fired the general in 1951. The decision infuriated Republican leaders, who spoke of impeaching the president and welcomed MacArthur home with parades and a unique address to a joint session of Congress. The general took the opportunity to condemn the idea of limited war. Yet the removal of MacArthur facilitated the opening of truce negotiations, which began in 1951. These talks lasted for two years, while the fighting continued under the command of General Matthew Ridgeway. (Truman's refusal to repatriate communist prisoners of war who declined to return to their homelands stalled the negotiations.) The impasse ended only after the inauguration of the next administration in 1953. In the end, the limited war cost 34,000 U.S. lives.

The Korean crisis nevertheless justified the military buildup envisioned in NSC-68. Wartime appropriations expanded the armed forces and nuclear arsenal and increased the number of overseas bases. Funding for aircraft research and development escalated from $1.8 billion to $3.1 billion. Furthermore, the CIA expanded in size and scope of operations and increased its staff from fewer than 5,000 in 1950 to 15,000 by 1955. The war led the president to hold regular meetings with the NSC, setting a precedent for Truman's successors. On the home front, Congress gave Truman authority to establish wage, price, and rent controls. In December 1950 the president declared a "national emergency" and implemented those economic powers, stabilizing the cost-of-living index for the remainder of the war. When steelworkers went on strike in 1952, Truman seized operations of the steel industry, but the Supreme Court later ruled the act unconstitutional.

The Korean War also prompted the administration to proceed with plans to rearm Germany. When France objected, Truman offered to station U.S. troops in Europe to ensure stability. Congressional conservatives, worried that waging the Cold War would create a "garrison state" at home, protested these unprecedented peacetime military commitments. In the "Great Debate" of 1951, Republicans ended the bipartisan foreign policy that had characterized Cold War politics since 1947. Attacking the limited war in Korea and expressing frustration that Chiang Kai-shek had not been permitted to enter the fray, Republicans focused on Truman's unilateral military decisions and insisted that Congress have a role in foreign policy. Republicans then sponsored a Senate resolution that blocked U.S. troops from being sent to Europe without approval from Congress. Although testimony from NATO's supreme commander, General Dwight D. Eisenhower, blunted some of the Republicans' criticism, Congress passed a compromise version of the resolution that limited troop deployments to four divisions.

The Korean War also stimulated a more aggressive U.S. policy in Asia. Although the administration had been prepared to accept a communist Chinese invasion of Taiwan in early 1950, the Korean conflict provided an excuse to send the Seventh Fleet to protect the besieged island. Truman also deepened U.S. involvement in Indochina. When Ho Chi Minh, leader of the anti-French liberation movement, accepted support from China and the Soviet Union, the United States increased aid to France. After the Korean War began, Truman permitted U.S. military personnel to assist French forces. "If Indochina went," explained a State Department official in 1951, "the fall of Burma and the fall of Thailand would be absolutely inevitable." According to the State Department, the "fall" of these countries would be followed by communist victories in Malaysia and India. Such assumptions led to increasing commitments in Southeast Asia that culminated in the Vietnam War.

Investment in the French empire contrasted with lack of support for colonized peoples. In his 1949 inauguration address, Truman introduced the Point Four program, asserting that the United States had a responsibility to spread "the benefits of our scientific advances and industrial progress" to the "underdeveloped areas" of the world. Yet Point Four foreign aid offered no alternatives to existing economic relations: "Underdeveloped areas" were seen only as suppliers of raw materials and consumers of industrial goods. Rather than a humanitarian program, Point Four funded economic studies to facilitate private business investment. Even so, the administration could not persuade Congress to appropriate more than a token $27 million in 1950.

Such priorities reflected the huge emphasis on using pro-capitalist countries as allies in the Cold War. After Japan accepted a new constitution in 1947 that disavowed war, the United States brought Japan's rebuilt economy into an Asian anticommunist network, which included South Korea, Taiwan, and Indochina, to stabilize relations in the Pacific. A new treaty of 1951 restored Japanese control of their home islands, but it also allowed U.S. occupation of Okinawa and the stationing of troops on Japanese territory. To overcome objections from Japan's former enemies in the Pacific, the United States promised to protect Australia and New Zealand from attack, an agreement formalized in the ANZUS treaty of 1951. With such alliances, Washington established an anticommunist barrier against Chinese and Soviet expansion in the Pacific.

Alliances with former enemies included support of Italy and Spain. In 1951 the Western Allies lifted military restrictions imposed on Italy at the end of World War II. At the same time, Truman entered negotiations with Franco's Spain, which culminated in a 1953 treaty that allowed U.S. military bases in Spain in exchange for economic and military assistance. (Meanwhile, on the home front, the attorney general placed Veterans of the Abraham Lincoln Brigade, whose members had fought against Franco in the Spanish Civil War, on a list of subversive organizations.) In supporting Spain, Italy, Germany, and Japan against China and the Soviet Union, Truman had ironically reversed the Grand Alliance of World War II.

By 1952 the Cold War had undermined Truman's initial foreign and domestic policies. The commitment to Soviet containment had ended earlier State Department hopes for expanded international trade; U.S. exports to eastern Europe and China remained minimal. Even worse, containment had bogged down in the "limited" Korean War, which promised neither victory nor an early end. High military expenditures, in turn, weakened the president's Fair Deal agenda of social legislation at home. Congressional conservatives worried that high budgets and big government bureaucracies would stifle the very freedoms for which the country was fighting overseas. Meanwhile, McCarthy continued a campaign to expose alleged communists in government. Revelations of corruption by administration officials compounded Truman's difficulties. Republican leaders expected to change government policy by capturing the White House in 1952.

THE ELECTION OF 1952

The Republican campaign slogan of 1952 summarized the troubles of the incumbent administration—"K1C2": Korea, Communism, Corruption. The phrase offered a convenient formula for tapping voter dissatisfaction. According to opinion polls, the limited war in Korea remained the primary public concern. As part of the Cold War, moreover, the Korean conflict intensified fear of atomic war. Congress appropriated $3 billion for bomb shelters, but officials admitted that less than 1 percent of the population would be protected from an atomic strike. In New York and San Francisco, public schools routinely issued dog tags to pupils to help identify victims of nuclear war. The Hollywood science fiction film *The Thing* (1951) ended by advising audiences to "Watch the skies!"

Republicans expected to benefit from this climate of fear. The party's front-runner, Senator Taft of Ohio, appealed to conservatives by demanding a retreat from expensive international commitments and a reduction in the size and scope of government programs. "The greatest enemy of liberty," he declared, "is the concentration of power in Washington." Taft's conservatism attracted midwestern and western Republicans, but his strident hostility to big government alarmed more liberal eastern Republicans, particularly big-business leaders. These "corporate liberals" preferred an internationalist foreign policy to stabilize world trade and recognized that New Deal programs such as Social Security bolstered purchasing power and helped to prevent social unrest at home.

Fearing that Taft's conservatism would doom the party at the polls, eastern Republicans led by Massachusetts Senator Henry Cabot Lodge Jr. and former Governor Thomas Dewey of New York turned to a candidate who claimed to have no interest in presidential politics: General Dwight David ("Ike") Eisenhower. As supreme commander of NATO forces in Europe, Eisenhower's political views appeared sufficiently ambiguous for Truman to hint at giving him the Democratic nomination. Eisenhower, however, was too conservative to run as a Democrat. Yet, unlike Taft, the general believed in the importance of the U.S. military presence in Europe. After a series of successful primary showings, including a surprise victory in New Hampshire, Eisenhower came home from Europe in June 1952 to seek the Republican presidential nomination. Benefiting from his immense popularity and some astute maneuvering at the convention by Lodge, the general captured a first-ballot nomination. As a concession to conservatives, Eisenhower chose Richard Nixon as his running mate.

While Eisenhower promised "to lead a great crusade . . . for freedom," K1C2 dictated the Republican platform. "There are no Communists in the Republican Party," it boasted, whereas Democrats "shielded Traitors . . . in high places." Denouncing Truman's containment policy as "negative, futile, and immoral," Republicans vowed to bring "genuine independence" to the "captive peoples" of eastern Europe—a promise that appealed to eastern European ethnics, who usually voted for Democrats. The platform showed the Republicans' conservative position on civil rights by insisting that state governments had primary responsibility in that area.

Billy Graham (1918–)

The most famous religious figures of the 1950s were two southerners in the Baptist tradition, Billy Graham and Martin Luther King Jr. But whereas King challenged U.S. society with a stinging moral critique on behalf of the dispossessed, Graham won access to the rich and powerful with a message palatable with social conventions.

Handsome, charismatic, and committed, Graham threw himself into evangelism early in life, honing his skills while traveling the country after World War II for a fledgling fundamentalist group, Youth for Christ. His big break came during the fourth week of a 1949 Los Angeles revival, when the powerful newspaper publisher William Randolph Hearst sent a blunt telegram to the editors of his newspapers: "Puff Graham." Attracted to the anticommunist themes of Graham's sermons, Hearst was the first of many powerful figures eager to use the preacher's sincerity and popularity to advance their own agendas. Within a year, Graham had been the subject of feature articles in the major magazines; within a decade, he was the most popular religious figure in the country.

Like evangelists before him, Graham blended familiar hymns and an altar call with a dynamic and polished pulpit style. Cutting through

The Democratic spotlight flashed briefly on Tennessee's Senator Estes Kefauver, who won a series of primary contests. But Democratic leaders feared that Kefauver's televised investigations of organized crime would hurt the party in the cities and preferred Governor Adlai Stevenson of Illinois. A cultivated liberal, Stevenson presented himself as a voice of reason. He criticized McCarthyism ("we want no shackles on the mind . . . no iron conformity," he said) and promised to "talk sense to the American people." To balance the ticket in the South, Stevenson chose Alabama Senator John Sparkman as his running mate.

Despite the Democratic candidate's efforts to distance himself from the Truman administration, Stevenson stood for a continuity of principles and policies. He defended the Korean War as "a long step toward building a security system in Asia" and echoed the White House attack on domestic commu-

the apparent complexities of the "age of anxiety," he called on listeners to heal their lives through a personal commitment to Jesus. To a nation that had survived depression and war only to find itself in the midst of the nuclear age, the simplicity and directness of Graham's message had enormous appeal. Although Graham traveled constantly, conducting six major crusades a year, he and his associates soon realized that print, films, radio, and television offered enormous opportunities to broaden their ministry even further. His direct-mail techniques were so sophisticated that representatives of both political parties visited his headquarters to study them. This pioneering work in marketing and media techniques paved the way for the televangelists of later years.

Although Graham has declared himself to be "completely neutral in politics," his fundamentalist, eschatological theology made him a particular favorite of conservative Republicans. Called by some a "Gabriel in gabardine," Graham spent much of his career preaching a gospel that upheld traditional values while calling for domestic consensus against overseas communist expansion. Even though he insisted that his crusade audiences be integrated even before the Supreme Court's *Brown* decision, Graham typically emphasized otherworldly solutions to social problems. "My message is so intensely personal," he explained, "that people miss the overwhelming social content."

nism. But unlike Truman, Stevenson took a quiet position on civil rights by emphasizing the importance of state sovereignty. Only after intense criticism from liberals did he endorse a permanent Fair Employment Practices Commission (FEPC). This belated gesture cost Stevenson support among African Americans while offending southern whites. Stevenson further angered Gulf Coast Democrats by opposing state control of offshore oil wells. The candidate's hesitancy to attack the Taft-Hartley labor law also alienated the traditional Democratic labor constituency.

Eisenhower, meanwhile, stood as a candidate above parties, a middle-of-the-road moderate with leadership experience that reflected caution, restraint, and common sense. After making peace with Taft, the general scrupulously avoided antagonizing Old Guard Republicans. Although personally insulted by McCarthy's rhetorical attack on former Secretary of State George Marshall,

Eisenhower's wartime superior officer, the nominee quietly deleted a defense of Marshall when speaking in McCarthy's home state of Wisconsin. The candidate also played up allegations of Democratic corruption. "Let's clean up the mess in Washington!" said Ike, in the first political advertising to appear on television in 1952. Coached by Hollywood actor Robert Montgomery and a leading advertising agency, Eisenhower's campaign proved the political value of the new media. Usually Eisenhower left the partisan oratory to Nixon, who denounced "Adlai the appeaser . . . who got a Ph.D. from Dean Acheson's College of Cowardly Communist Containment."

Nixon's verbal ammunition exploded when newspapers reported that the vice presidential candidate had a secret "millionaire's" fund to defray his political expenses. When Democrats used the issue to reply to Republican accusations about the "mess in Washington," Eisenhower's advisers urged him to drop Nixon from the ticket. Nixon responded by buying television time to defend his personal honesty. Emphasizing that his family had not profited from politics, Nixon said his wife still wore a "plain Republican cloth coat" and that despite criticism he would not return a gift his daughter had received, a cocker spaniel named Checkers.

The sentimental performance proved effective. As public support for Nixon increased, Eisenhower kept him on the ticket. For the first time, political pundits saw the immense influence of television. This recognition highlighted the importance of a candidate's image and suggested that a politician could effectively appeal to the voters over the heads of party leaders. As for Nixon, the speech gave him confidence in the power of television. In later years he returned to the small screen to win vindication of other aspects of his career, although seldom with the success of his 1952 effort.

Supporting the basic premises of Truman's Cold War, Eisenhower avoided the militant rhetoric of the Republican platform on matters of foreign policy. He approved of Truman's intervention in Korea but opposed General MacArthur's call for all-out war. When Stevenson argued that the only "answer" to Korea was to "keep it up as long as we have to," Eisenhower hinted at alternative policies. His military experience enabled him to speak with authority. In a late campaign speech, Eisenhower suggested that ending the war required his personal attention. "I shall go to Korea," he declared. Eisenhower's promise ignited the hopes of a war-weary nation.

Eisenhower achieved a stunning victory. He captured nearly 34 million votes (55 percent) to Stevenson's 27 million (44 percent) and swept the Electoral College 442–89. The Republican ticket carried four southern states, breaking the Democrats' "solid South" for the first time since Al Smith's defeat in 1928. Eisenhower attracted traditional Democrats in the big cities— African Americans, Catholics, and white ethnics. His coattails pulled a Republican majority into both houses of Congress for the first time since the Great Depression.

EXHIBIT **9-2**   **THE ELECTION OF 1952**

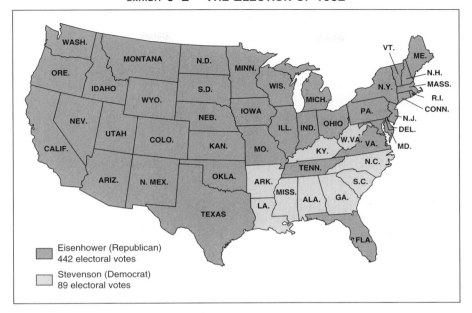

Eisenhower (Republican)
442 electoral votes

Stevenson (Democrat)
89 electoral votes

Republicans exulted in the destruction of the New Deal coalition. The reelection of conservatives like McCarthy and the defeat of several of McCarthy's critics seemed to vindicate the anticommunist crusade. However, statistics also showed that Eisenhower ran far ahead of other Republicans, including McCarthy. The election of 1952 was an Eisenhower victory, not a Republican landslide; the party controlled the House by only eight seats, the Senate by one. During the 1950s voters seemed less interested in political ideology and appeared more sensitive to short-term issues or party affiliation. Yet Eisenhower managed to attract independent voters and Democrats, including a well-funded "Democrats for Eisenhower" organization headed by Hollywood actor Ronald Reagan. The breadth of Eisenhower's support reflected not only his personal popularity but also a political consensus based on internationalism abroad and minimum social welfare at home.

THE GENERAL TAKES COMMAND

Eisenhower's success among Democrats reinforced his political philosophy of consensus. As a career military officer, the former general represented the new managerial middle class of the twentieth century. In a world dominated by large corporate bureaucracies, he emphasized the importance of voluntary cooperation between government and business. Nearly all the members of his cabinet—including Secretary of State John Foster Dulles, Secretary of Defense Charles E. Wilson, Secretary of the Treasury George M. Humphrey, and Attorney General Herbert Brownell Jr.—came from the highest ranks of corporate management and law. (The exception was Secretary of Labor Martin Durkin, a plumber, who soon resigned and was replaced by a department store personnel manager.) Eisenhower believed these leaders could apply conservative principles to the management of government without turning back the clock or canceling promises of social justice.

To streamline administration, Eisenhower relied more heavily than Truman had on the National Security Council (NSC), but the president frequently overrode the advice of the Joint Chiefs of Staff. Eisenhower distrusted special interests, partisan conflicts, and mass movements. Contrary to the wishes of Old Guard Republicans, he preserved the New Deal and even established a cabinet-level Department of Health, Education, and Welfare in 1953. However, the president initiated no social welfare legislation; he believed that expansion of government services would stultify a free, capitalist society. "We cannot risk living all our lifetime under emergency measures," he said in ending economic controls established by Truman during the Korean War.

Eisenhower envisioned a world order based on free trade and protected by restrained military power. On many occasions, he resisted pressure to increase the Pentagon budget or to rush rashly into war. "I just don't believe you can buy 100 percent security in every little corner of the world," the president said in 1954. Yet Eisenhower permitted the nuclear arsenal to expand from hundreds to thousands of weapons and ordered the deployment of nuclear weapons overseas. He also relied increasingly on covert operations by the CIA, headed by Allen Dulles, brother of the secretary of state. Always the cold warrior, Eisenhower assumed that the United States should maintain military superiority over communist nations. "Forces of good and evil are massed and armed and opposed as rarely before in history," he explained in his inaugural address. "Freedom is pitted against slavery; lightness against the dark. . . . In the final choice, a soldier's pack is not so heavy a burden as a prisoner's chains."

These metaphors of morality and struggle reflected the new administration's approach to foreign policy. Determined to take the initiative in the Cold War, Eisenhower and Secretary of State Dulles replaced the Democratic strategy of containment with a new doctrine of "massive retaliation." Dulles argued that neither public opinion nor the nation's economy could sustain a series of limited conventional wars like the Korean War. Instead, he echoed conservative policy by calling for reliance upon air and naval superiority, a position Eisenhower supported.

The nations of the "free world," the president proclaimed, would be prepared "to retaliate instantly" against the Soviet Union "by means and at places of our own choosing." Nuclear weapons aimed at the Kremlin—not at some border area—would deter further communist expansion. In military terms, massive retaliation reaffirmed the air-atomic strategy approved by Truman and updated his policy of containment with the doctrine of nuclear deterrence. Eisenhower never intended to go to war to overturn communist control of "captive nations" in eastern Europe. However, his administration hoped to use the nuclear arsenal as a symbolic weapon—and an ever-present threat—in the political crusade for anticommunist liberation.

A policy of massive retaliation had distinct domestic advantages. Conservative Republicans led by Taft had long opposed soaring military budgets. Eisenhower shared these sentiments, although he believed that cost-cutting should not compromise the nation's strength. Air power and nuclear weapons provided a cheaper solution. Eisenhower's "new look" in military policy enabled the Pentagon to reduce the size of conventional forces. This policy cut $7 billion from Truman's projected budget. Subsequent opinion polls found wide support for these reductions.

Eisenhower's enormous prestige and electoral popularity enabled him to accomplish in Korea what Truman had been reluctant to suggest. After fulfilling his campaign promise to visit Korea, the new president recognized that a continuation of the ground war would only bleed the army and the federal budget. Secretary Dulles joined conservative senators such as Styles Bridges and William Knowland in advocating complete victory. Yet Eisenhower, primarily concerned with reaching a political settlement, rejected the use of atomic weapons. The president instead used a show of force to persuade the enemy to negotiate. In his inaugural address Eisenhower announced the removal of the Seventh Fleet from the area separating Taiwan from the Chinese mainland and hinted that he might "unleash" Chiang Kai-shek against the communist enemy. The White House also used diplomatic channels to notify China that the United States might use nuclear weapons if negotiations failed. The death of Josef Stalin in March 1953 added to China's uncertainties about Soviet support.

Both China and Eisenhower understood and accepted the limits of military struggle in Korea. The main stumbling block now involved the return of prisoners of war. Hoping to discourage communist China's future reliance on its troops, the United States refused to require the repatriation of communist prisoners who did not wish to go home. After Washington made additional threats to use atomic weapons, China accepted the idea of voluntary repatriation of prisoners of war. At the last minute, South Korea's dictator, Syngman Rhee, nearly thwarted the truce by suddenly releasing 27,000 prisoners, who promptly disappeared into the countryside. The move violated the armistice agreement, but Eisenhower ignored Rhee's action, and the United States signed a truce in July 1953. "We have won an armistice on a single battlefield—not peace in the world," Eisenhower reminded the nation. "We may not now relax our guard nor cease our quest."

The end of the Korean War brought not a sense of celebration but plain relief. Nearly 34,000 U.S. soldiers had died to defend an area that in 1950

Secretary of State Dean Acheson had acknowledged lay beyond the nation's strategic defense perimeter. Sensitive to criticism from conservatives about selling out Korea to the communists, the White House reiterated the possibility of massive retaliation against any further aggression. The retention of U.S. military bases in South Korea added credibility to those threats. Eisenhower also approved a multibillion-dollar program of economic and military assistance to bolster South Korea. The Korean armistice, then, actually formalized Truman's policy of communist containment in Asia.

Frustrated by the Korean compromise, nationalist Republicans criticized Eisenhower's version of containment. In 1951 Republican Senator John Bricker of Ohio had introduced a constitutional amendment requiring congressional approval of all international agreements. Through this partisan move, Bricker had sought to limit Truman's executive independence, but the measure never came to the Senate floor. The 1952 Republican Party platform kept the issue alive by promising to "repudiate all commitments contained in secret understandings." This position reflected strong congressional opposition to presidential control of foreign policy. In 1954 Bricker reintroduced his constitutional amendment. Eisenhower strongly opposed the proposal. Yet because the president believed in a rigid separation of powers, he exercised minimal leadership in the Senate debates. Democrats led by Lyndon Johnson saved the president from his own party's militants. Although the Bricker amendment won a 60–31 majority, it fell one vote short of the necessary two-thirds required for the passage of constitutional amendments. The White House, not Congress, would continue to control foreign policy.

Eisenhower's European policies revealed basic continuities with those of Truman. Although the new administration talked about liberating eastern Europe, the principles of massive retaliation appeared too inflexible to respond effectively to minor crises. When East German workers staged anticommunist protests in June 1953, Dulles could offer only moral encouragement and $15 million in food.

Eisenhower also made gestures to reduce Cold War tensions, but they were more symbolic than real. In 1953 the president addressed the UN General Assembly, presenting a dramatic "atoms for peace" proposal that urged international control of atomic weapons. In offering to join the Soviet Union in pooling nuclear resources for peaceful purposes, the president hoped to overcome the mutual hostility that set the two powers on a deadly course. Yet Eisenhower knew, as did the Soviets, that his proposal would preserve U.S. nuclear superiority. When the Soviet Union reacted unfavorably, the president settled for the propaganda advantages and made no counteroffer. Eisenhower had no intention of reducing the nation's military preparedness.

Like Truman, Eisenhower worked instead to strengthen U.S. allies in western Europe. When the Soviet Union proposed a treaty that would make Germany a neutral country, Eisenhower saw the plan as a ruse to divide the

Western Alliance and rejected the Soviet overture. More concerned with bringing Germany into the West's political camp, the administration urged the formation of a European Defense Community. When France objected to rearming Germany, however, the president chose an alternative policy that enabled Germany to rearm under NATO. "These agreements are founded upon the profound yearning for peace which is shared by all the Atlantic peoples," Eisenhower declared. "The agreements endanger no nation." Yet the entry of West Germany into NATO assured a long-term division of central Europe. In 1955 the Soviet Union created the Warsaw Pact, a military alliance that attempted to balance the power of NATO.

SECRET FOREIGN POLICY

While exercising restraint in Korea and Europe, Eisenhower pursued an aggressive but secret foreign policy beyond the scrutiny of Congress and the public. Under the Central Intelligence Agency Act of 1949, the CIA had a multibillion-dollar, top-secret budget that was exempt from congressional accountability and control. Initially intended to obtain and assess intelligence, the CIA under Eisenhower became an interventionist force as well. In one secret mission, the agency built an underground tunnel beneath East Berlin and used wiretaps and recording devices to obtain an intelligence windfall. Besides establishing spy networks around the world, the CIA performed secret, illegal operations that promoted the State Department's formal policy. For example, the CIA regularly supported disruptive raids launched from Taiwan onto the Chinese mainland. When such activities were discovered, the United States denied all allegations and used the episodes to denounce its enemies. In 1955 Democratic Senator Mike Mansfield proposed the creation of a congressional intelligence oversight committee, but the White House effectively blocked such interference with foreign policy management by the executive branch.

The intervention of the CIA proved especially effective on the new battlefronts of the Cold War in the developing ("third") world. In 1953 the United States instigated a coup d'état in Iran, then denied complicity in the affair. Two years earlier, the premier of Iran, Dr. Mohammed Mossadegh, had attempted to end British exploitation by nationalizing Iran's oil wells. Western-owned companies retaliated by boycotting Iranian oil. Mossadegh appealed to Eisenhower for assistance, but the president rebuffed him, stating, "It would not be fair to American taxpayers." Mossadegh then turned to the Soviet Union.

Eisenhower responded by ordering the CIA to intervene in Iran's internal affairs. In August 1953 U.S. agents provided crucial military support that enabled the hereditary shah to topple the Mossadegh regime and return to power. In the ensuing negotiations, Iran agreed to replace the nationalized oil wells with an international consortium in which U.S.-owned companies held a

40 percent interest. The Western oil companies then agreed to limit Iranian oil production to maximize their profits at the expense of Iran. By overthrowing Mossadegh, the United States not only broke the British oil monopoly but also placed Iran safely in the noncommunist camp. Continued economic and military aid to the shah strengthened this realignment. Yet the CIA never acknowledged its role in the coup; even today, the relevant documents remain classified.

The CIA also implemented Eisenhower's foreign policy in Guatemala in 1954. As in Iran, a popular leader, Colonel Jacobo Arbenz, attempted to improve economic conditions by enacting land reform and nationalizing the holdings of the U.S. United Fruit Company. Arbenz offered compensation for the expropriated property, but United Fruit, backed by the State Department, rejected the sum. The administration then began planning the overthrow of Arbenz with the help of a CIA invasion army trained in Nicaragua and Honduras.

To justify this new version of dollar diplomacy, the United States described Arbenz as a front man for "international communism," someone who imperiled the entire hemisphere. In 1954 Washington sponsored a resolution at the Tenth Inter-American Conference, declaring that communist control of "any American State" endangered "the peace of America." Guatemala alone voted against resolution. Two months later, Arbenz received a shipment of arms from Czechoslovakia, which confirmed administration fears. The next month a CIA-backed rebel army and mercenary force invaded and bombed Guatemala and defeated Arbenz. The invasion won bipartisan approval at home. "There is no question here of United States interference in the domestic affairs of any American State," insisted Senator Lyndon Johnson.

Claiming to have saved Guatemala from an international conspiracy, the administration supported the regime of Colonel Carlos Armas with $90 million in economic and military aid. Armas returned the nationalized land to United Fruit, provided tax benefits for the corporation, crushed the labor union movement, and disenfranchised illiterate people, who constituted 70 percent of the population. Restoring conditions favorable to U.S. investment, the administration then supported military government in Central America.

BUILDING A CORPORATE COMMONWEALTH

Like Truman, Eisenhower believed in preserving a balanced budget; and like his predecessor he accepted the necessity of high military expenditures to wage the Cold War. But where Truman preferred more spending for social welfare programs, such as health insurance, Eisenhower had little interest in liberal policies. Yet Eisenhower did not oppose modest domestic programs. Rather, he believed that government should be used to moderate economic

Charles E. Wilson, shown with models of some of the Pentagon's best toys, went from being head of General Motors to a job that seemed much the same—head of the Defense Department.

conflict and sustain growth without threatening private enterprise or becoming too burdensome, and he attempted to steer a middle course between unregulated capitalism and an activist government.

Eisenhower saw the government's role as a mediator among society's interests and hoped that cooperation and consensus, not coercion, would direct the nation toward social harmony. Instead of prosecuting violations of antitrust laws, for example, the administration preferred negotiated settlements between government and business. The president also resolved to reduce the scope of federal government activities and supported Secretary of the Treasury George Humphrey's efforts to balance the federal budget by reducing expenses. However, Eisenhower would not agree to drop basic New Deal programs such as Social Security and the minimum wage. To balance the budget, therefore, the White House reluctantly delayed a tax cut. Despite Humphrey's efforts to promote frugality and the sharp criticism of conservative Republicans, government expenditures remained a basic prop of the economy.

Although Eisenhower joined "corporate liberals" in retaining New Deal regulations and social welfare nets, he sided with conservatives in defending the petroleum industry against federal regulation. The president believed that a prosperous oil industry reinforced national defense. For more than a decade, the federal government had contested the claim of several coastal states, particularly Texas, Louisiana, and California, to jurisdiction over offshore oil. Because the major petroleum companies expected beneficial legislation from state governments, they supported the state claims. Conservative Republicans opposed federal control of private business and also supported the states' claims. So did southern Democrats, who saw state control of oil as not only in their economic interests but also as a defense of states' rights. In 1946 and again in 1952 Congress passed legislation giving control of offshore oil to the states. Truman vetoed both measures and before leaving office reserved offshore oil for the navy. Eisenhower reversed his predecessor's position. In 1953 Republicans cooperated with southern Democrats to pass a measure giving control of offshore oil to the states.

The White House also opposed public control of electric power projects. In 1954 Eisenhower recommended a revision of the Atomic Energy Act to allow private manufacture and operation of atomic reactors. This legislation led to the first privately run nuclear power plants. The administration's decision to bypass the Tennessee Valley Authority (TVA) in providing electricity for the Atomic Energy Commission (AEC) facilities proved more controversial. By ignoring the TVA, long a symbol of New Deal liberalism, the policy attacked federal support of public power. Hints of political corruption weakened the president's position, and a compromise ended the controversy. The administration did succeed in blocking public power projects in other parts of the country, such as Hell's Canyon on the Snake River.

Despite his military background—or because of it—Eisenhower strove to strengthen civilian control over military decisions. Following precedents established by Truman, the administration relied on a presidential Science Advisory Committee to obtain expert opinion about technological issues and questions of research and development. Such counsel gave Eisenhower independent information to respond to proposals made by the armed services. Thus while military leaders urged the expansion of the nation's offensive weapons for massive retaliation, science advisors advocated greater continental defense against Soviet attack. Such discussions culminated in the 1954 agreement between the United States and Canada to construct a distant early warning (DEW) line of radar installations across North America. The president's science advisors would later play an important role in negotiating nuclear test restrictions with the Soviet Union.

THE ANTICOMMUNIST CRUSADE

Although Eisenhower, the hero of World War II, appeared as the consummate cold warrior, his personal popularity could not shield him from criticism of militant anticommunists who alleged that communists continued to influence the government. Indeed, the president's efforts to stand above controversy strengthened the most fervent congressional anticommunists, particularly Joseph McCarthy. Yet the administration had hardly ignored the problem. Soon after taking office in 1953, the president agreed to appoint Scott McLeod, a McCarthy supporter, to head the State Department's personnel program, accelerating the dismissal of alleged subversives. Eisenhower also revised Truman's loyalty program, issuing Executive Order 10450, which established new standards for dismissal of government employees. Although Truman had required evidence of disloyalty or subversion, Eisenhower authorized dismissal on the grounds that an individual's employment "may not be clearly consistent with the interests of national security." Under the new guidelines, Eisenhower removed 2,200 "security risks" in his first year in office. Few were actually charged with disloyalty.

The administration's definition of security risks revealed the underlying cultural assumptions within the Cold War consensus. Besides obvious cases of negligence, criminality, and insanity, Eisenhower's criteria for dismissal included "notoriously disgraceful conduct, habitual use of intoxicants to excess, drug addiction, or sexual perversion." Persons practicing such acts were considered risks because they were vulnerable to blackmail, and government loyalty boards frequently dismissed homosexuals from their jobs (making such people *more* vulnerable to blackmail). Ironically, to protect themselves from government reprisals, the homosexual activists who organized the Mattachine Society in Los Angeles deliberately adopted the structure of the Communist Party to avoid entrapment.

The insistence on ideological conformity also demanded the suppression of political dissent. Shortly after moving into the State Department, Dulles fired several career diplomats, including prestigious China experts such as John Carter Vincent and John Paton Davies, who had predicted Mao Zedong's victory in China in 1949. Dulles also encouraged the departure of George Kennan, viewed as the architect of containment. To replace Kennan as ambassador to the Soviet Union, the administration supported Charles E.

J. Robert Oppenheimer (1904–1967)

The security status of one of the nation's leading atomic physicists provoked a dramatic closed-door clash in 1954 between traditional freedom of scientific inquiry and Cold War demands for absolute conformity. The ensuing top-secret hearings into the matter of J. Robert Oppenheimer re-

vealed both changing standards of political propriety and a growing concern about "national security" in an age of fundamental anxiety.

Oppenheimer was a secular Jew who had studied quantum mechanics at Harvard, Cambridge, and the University of Gottenburg. He helped to make the University of California at Berkeley the global center of theoretical physics in the 1930s. Yet the Depression-era poverty of his students and anti-Semitism in Nazi Germany encouraged the affluent bachelor to support progressive social causes promoted by the Communist Party.

Appointed head of the wartime Los Alamos Laboratory charged with developing the atom bomb, Oppenheimer became a postwar advocate of international control of nuclear energy. As chief advisor to the Atomic Energy Commission, he led efforts to oppose research on the hydrogen fusion bomb, which he regarded as a "weapon of genocide." He called for the use of tactical nuclear weapons for continental defense instead of the massive strategic bombing preferred by the air force. He also insisted that it was technically premature to build nuclear-powered aircraft and opposed construction of atomic submarines.

Bohlen. However, rigid anticommunists questioned the nomination, pointing out that Bohlen had acted as a translator for President Franklin D. Roosevelt at international conferences with the Russians. Rumors of the nominee's homosexuality also surfaced. Unwilling to drop one of his first appointees, Eisenhower accepted a compromise, permitting two senators to examine Bohlen's confidential FBI file. Their favorable report led to senatorial confirmation. Nonetheless, Taft warned the president: "No more Bohlens."

J. Robert Oppenheimer, the celebrated physicist who had directed the development of the atomic bomb, also fell victim to the loyalty controversy. Fearing that Oppenheimer's moral doubts about the hydrogen bomb might

The AEC gave Oppenheimer security clearance in 1947, but six years later a former congressional staffer sent the FBI a detailed list of accusations against the physicist. A subsequent report prompted President Eisenhower to demand that a "blank wall" be erected between Oppenheimer and sensitive information. Eisenhower feared that the highly respected scientist might persuade other researchers to abandon the superbomb project. The president also wished to head off potentially embarrassing investigations by McCarthy. Consequently, the White House asked the AEC to initiate hearings on Oppenheimer's security clearance.

Although Oppenheimer apologized to the inquiry for naïve associations with "fellow travelers" and for occasional lapses of candor, colleague Edward Teller testified that the physicist lacked the "wisdom and judgment" for a security clearance. This finding was upheld by the AEC, which ruled that the father of the atomic bomb had "placed himself outside the rules that govern others" and "exhibited a willful disregard of the normal and proper obligations of society."

By focusing on Oppenheimer's character, the AEC rejected the view that scientists should be judged differently from military and government personnel. By 1954, many Americans distrusted intellectual cosmopolitans such as Oppenheimer and believed that loyalty to the struggle against communism was the most important qualification for public service. Deprived of a security clearance, Oppenheimer returned to teaching at Princeton University and never again worked for the government.

influence other scientists, Eisenhower supported the AEC's decision to lift the scientist's security clearance. In yet another controversial case, the president refused to provide clemency to the convicted atomic spies Julius and Ethel Rosenberg, exaggerating their activities by claiming that the couple "may have condemned to death tens of million of innocent people all over the world." Despite ambiguous evidence about Ethel Rosenberg's espionage activities, the unrepentant couple was electrocuted in 1953.

"In America," protested the playwright Arthur Miller in *The Crucible,* a 1953 version of the Salem witch trials, "any man who is not reactionary in his views is open to the charge of alliance with the Red hell." The next year,

Congress underscored the religious stakes by adding to the Pledge of Allegiance the words "under God." Meanwhile, church membership in all denominations in the United States increased—from 64 million in 1940 to 115 million in 1960, or from 50 percent to 63 percent of the population. The Cold War remained a struggle between the godly and the damned.

Through the first years of the Eisenhower presidency, the nation's foremost witch hunter remained Senator McCarthy, a crude, intemperate inquisitor who disregarded courtesy and due process in his quest for communist sympathizers. Even after Eisenhower's inauguration, McCarthy continued to attack communist influence in government. As chairman of a Senate subcommittee on government operations, McCarthy held public hearings in 1953 about the Voice of America, the government's overseas radio stations, and claimed that the State Department's propaganda organ served as a front for communists.

With the tacit consent of Secretary Dulles, McCarthy meddled in other State Department affairs. Two members of McCarthy's staff, Roy Cohn and G. David Schine, embarked on a chaotic investigation of the United States Information Agency (USIA) in Europe. Their scrutiny of USIA libraries unearthed many "subversive" works by authors such as novelist Theodore Dreiser and historian Arthur M. Schlesinger Jr. Fearing McCarthy's wrath, the agency removed several thousand volumes from library shelves.

"I will not get into the gutter with that guy," said Eisenhower, avoiding direct confrontation with the vitriolic senator. Wishing to prevent a split in Republican ranks, the president hoped that if he ignored McCarthy the senator would recede from the limelight. Instead, McCarthy felt emboldened to attack the administration. In September 1953 he launched an investigation of army security procedures at Fort Monmouth, New Jersey. Concerned about the routine promotion of a Communist dentist, McCarthy clashed publicly with military leaders, chastising one officer for defending "Communist conspirators." The army responded by releasing documents showing that McCarthy sought special privileges for Cohn's coworker, Private David Schine. McCarthy then ordered a full investigation of the army, including Eisenhower's Secretary of the Army Robert Stevens.

The president now entered the conflict, refusing to cooperate with the Senate investigation. "In opposing Communism," he told a March 1954 press conference, "we are defeating ourselves if we use methods that do not conform to the American sense of justice." Although Attorney General Brownell could find no legal precedents for denying subpoenaed documents, Eisenhower invoked the right of executive privilege to block McCarthy's access to his staff. Eisenhower was concerned that McCarthy's indiscriminate investigations would uncover the continuing Oppenheimer controversy and disturb scientific work on the hydrogen bomb. "We've got to handle this so that all our scientists are not made out to be Reds," Eisenhower remarked.

"That goddamn McCarthy is just likely to try such a thing." To Eisenhower's alarm, McCarthy was threatening to penetrate the secrets of the national security state.

McCarthy also showed disdain for the Democratic leadership. "Those who wear the label—Democrat," he said, "wear it with the stain of an historic betrayal." Yet precisely because of such charges, Democrats hesitated to attack McCarthy directly. In 1954 a Senate appropriations committee voted nearly unanimously to continue funding McCarthy's subcommittee. Indeed, some liberal Democrats attempted to deflect McCarthy's rhetoric by demonstrating their own anticommunist credentials. Minnesota liberal Hubert Humphrey introduced the Communist Control Act in 1954 to make membership in the Communist Party illegal. Democrat Paul Douglas of Illinois supported the measure, explaining that "we liberals must destroy the Communists if this dirty game is to stop."

As McCarthy pursued the investigation of army security procedures and the army made accusations against him, Senate leaders looked for an opportunity to weaken McCarthy's power. To show the public the extent of McCarthy's malice, Majority Leader Lyndon Johnson demanded that the public hearings be televised. Beginning in March 1954 the three major television networks broadcast the much-heralded Army-McCarthy hearings. The spectacle once again demonstrated the new medium's power to influence public opinion. For thirty-six days viewers witnessed McCarthy's erratic, stormy behavior.

As the senator attacked colleagues, threatened witnesses, and ignored legal procedures, his favorable public opinion ratings declined from 50 percent to 34 percent. The hearings climaxed when McCarthy chastised a young army lawyer for once belonging to the National Lawyers Guild, which was, in McCarthy's words, "the legal bulwark of the Communist Party." Chief Army Counsel Joseph Welch used the episode to strike back at McCarthy. "Little did I dream you could be so reckless and so cruel," Welch berated McCarthy before the cameras. "Have you no sense of decency, sir, at long last? Have you left no sense of decency?"

When McCarthy amended his denunciation of "twenty years of treason" to "twenty-*one* years," thus implicating the Eisenhower presidency in a cover-up of communism, his reach exceeded his grasp. "Were the junior Senator from Wisconsin in the pay of Communists," Republican Senator Ralph Flanders of Vermont declared, "he could not have done a better job for them." In July 1954 Flanders introduced a resolution that called for McCarthy's censure by the Senate.

In a carefully orchestrated proceeding, a panel of conservative senators—chaired by Republican Arthur Watkins of Utah—recommended censure for conduct that "tended to bring the Senate into dishonor and disrepute." McCarthy continued to rage against his adversaries, accusing the Senate of

J. Edgar Hoover *(1895–1972)*

Without question, J. Edgar Hoover was the most successful bureaucrat in U.S. history. Raised a few blocks from the Capitol, Hoover graduated from George Washington University, took a clerical job with the Department of Justice, and assumed the directorship of the agency that became

the Federal Bureau of Investigation in 1924, a post he held for the rest of his life. Energetic and capable, Hoover professionalized the bureau and cultivated a positive image through well-publicized and successful manhunts for celebrated gangsters.

During World War II, the FBI broke up Nazi spy rings in the United States and South America. As the Cold War ensued, Hoover turned the bureau's attention to alleged Soviet espionage and perceived threats of "red fascism." Critics charged that the director ignored the spread of organized crime and white-collar felonies to pursue conspiratorial notions of communist subversion at the expense of individual civil liberties. Yet Hoover insisted that an ever-broadening front of alien radicals was seeking to transform the United States into a land of class struggle, that communism embraced a materialistic religion that inflamed its adherents with destructive fanaticism.

serving the communists, but half the Republicans joined the unanimous Democrats to censure McCarthy by a vote of 67–22. Vice President Nixon, presiding in the Senate, deleted the word *censure* from the final document. It was a formality that made no difference. McCarthy had lost his power. He remained in the Senate, politically ineffective, until his death, attributed to alcoholism, in 1957.

McCarthy's fall created an illusion that communist witch hunts had ended, but the attack on communism extended beyond Congress and assumed the power of a national obsession. Libraries removed controversial books; school boards and universities fired radical teachers; industries established blacklists to prevent employment of suspected communists. Many high school students had to sign loyalty oaths to receive their diplomas. And the Hollywood black-

As public opinion hardened against government controls, domestic labor unrest, and Soviet expansionism in the years following World War II, Hoover assumed a prominent role in the coalition of political activists, government prosecutors, congressional staffers, and conservative clergy who comprised the anticommunist lobby. Members of the group depicted communism as a menace to U.S. security, democratic freedoms, individual privacy, and religious values. Hoover liked to say that Soviet agents were corrupting society through covert propaganda and confidence tricks.

Acting on these principles, Hoover pushed the FBI into full participation in the postwar Red Scare. The bureau maintained thousands of files on domestic dissidents, did the fieldwork for government employee loyalty investigations, provided intelligence on high-profile defendants such as Alger Hiss and the Rosenbergs, and leaked information to friendly politicians and the press when it served the director's interests.

The culmination of Hoover's anticommunist activities came in the 1950s when the bureau adopted a variety of counterintelligence techniques and "dirty tricks" designed to disrupt the Communist Party. The director's covert methods, racial paranoia, and tendency to associate domestic political groups with subversion would come under heavy criticism in subsequent years. But at the height of the Cold War, Hoover's reputation was virtually untarnished as a protector of the "American Way of Life."

list continued. In 1954 the winner of eight Oscars, including Best Picture, was Elia Kazan's *On the Waterfront*, a movie that celebrated "naming names" to government investigators.

Encouraged by the anticommunist consensus, FBI Director J. Edgar Hoover stepped up his attacks on the Communist Party. Because the Communist Control Act stated that the Communist Party was "not entitled to any of the rights, privileges, and immunities . . . [of] legal bodies," Hoover moved to disrupt the organization with a Counterintelligence Program (COINTELPRO) introduced in 1956. Using informants, infiltrators, wiretaps, and a variety of "dirty tricks" (forged letters, anonymous telephone calls, police harassment), the FBI doggedly attacked the dwindling communist movement. This harassment, together with revelations of Stalin's totalitarianism and Soviet aggression in eastern Europe, drastically reduced the party's membership. From a peak membership of 75,000 during World War II, the party dwindled to fewer than 3,500 members by the end of 1957.

A SHAKY CONSENSUS

The political demise of Senator McCarthy contributed to a mood of consensus. Republican leaders expected the anticommunist crusade to remain an effective campaign weapon in the 1954 congressional elections. True to his dispassionate style of leadership, Eisenhower avoided the emotionally charged issue. Nixon repeated his performance of 1952 and attacked the Democrats for tolerating communists in government. Yet neither Eisenhower's prestige nor Nixon's rhetoric could overcome the political effects of the economic recession that followed the Korean War. Although Eisenhower could attract independent voters, other Republicans were linked with traditional party labels. In the end, Democrats gained small majorities in both houses of Congress.

Instead of creating partisan conflict between the branches of government, the Democratic congressional victories actually encouraged cooperation. Senate Majority Leader Johnson and House Speaker Sam Rayburn, both of Texas, accepted a political consensus and a balance of power between the parties. Because congressional committee assignments depended on seniority, southerners, who came from a one-party region, enjoyed advantages. Patterns of congressional representation also strengthened conservative groups. Urban areas, which usually supported liberals, were underrepresented in Congress because state legislatures divided voting districts to suit local needs and felt no obligation to provide representation based on population. (Not until 1962 did the Supreme Court uphold the principle of equal representation in the case of *Baker* v. *Carr.*)

Eisenhower did not identify with the conservative wing of the Republican Party that held strong antigovernment views. In a 1953 speech to the nation's newspaper editors, he warned that the costly arms race would rob society of other valuable assets. He lamented that the cost of one heavy bomber deprived the country of "a modern brick school in more than thirty cities" and that funds for one fighter plane could buy half a million bushels of wheat. He also acknowledged that the federal government "must do its part to advance human welfare and encourage economic growth with constructive actions."

The administration thus continued to subsidize farm prices, even though Secretary of Agriculture Ezra Taft Benson persuaded Congress to lower the level of supports. The president also backed a slight expansion of Social Security to include self-employed workers and approved modest housing legislation. Using the justification of "national security," Eisenhower signed legislation in 1954 to build the St. Lawrence Seaway to connect the Great Lakes to ocean ports.

Committed to such "modern Republicanism," Eisenhower presided over a national consensus that unified moderates in both political parties through vigorous pursuit of the Cold War. Democrats and Republicans alike shared a belief in the communist menace and agreed to seek military superiority. The correlation between military expenditures and economic prosperity also assured minimal resistance to administration requests for large Pentagon budgets.

Even as the Army-McCarthy hearings focused public attention on the communist threat in the spring of 1954, however, two other issues of immense potential revealed the shaky foundations of the national consensus. The first occurred in distant Indochina when Vietminh guerrillas surrounded the French garrison at Dien Bien Phu, threatening France's colonial domination and forcing Eisenhower to face the choice of U.S. intervention in that remote part of the world. The second occurred in Washington, D.C., on May 17, 1954, when the U.S. Supreme Court ruled in the case *Brown* v. *Board of Education of Topeka* that racial segregation in public schools was unconstitutional. Each situation raised questions that existed outside the Cold War consensus, and each forced the American people to confront unexpected conflicts within the nation's identity.

AMERICAN HISTORY RESOURCE CENTER

To explore documents, images, audio and video clips, articles, and commentary related to the material in this chapter, visit the source collections at ushistory.wadsworth.com and and use the Search function with the following key terms:

Dwight D. Eisenhower	CIA, History
Korean War	J. Robert Oppenheimer
Alger Hiss	Elections: 1952

RECOMMENDED READINGS

Ellen Schrecker, *Many Are the Crimes: McCarthyism in America* (1998). This study of the anticommunist crusade examines the major political issues, weighing the conflict between national security and civil liberty.

Greg Mitchell, *Tricky Dick and the Pink Lady: Richard Nixon vs. Helen Gahagan Douglas—Sexual Politics and the Red Scare, 1950* (1998). Focusing on the 1950 California Senate race, the author describes the increasing importance of communism as the primary domestic issue.

Victor Navasky, *Naming Names* (1980). The author presents a sensitive analysis of the moral, psychological, and ideological dimensions of anticommunism in the entertainment industry.

Richard Whelen, *Drawing the Line: The Korean War, 1950–1953* (1990). This book provides a clear, balanced account of the global issues and military dimension of the conflict.

Additional Readings

The domestic anticommunist crusade is described by Richard M. Fried, *Nightmare in Red: The McCarthy Era in Perspective* (1990). For Joseph McCarthy, the best starting point is David M. Oshinsky, *A Conspiracy So Immense: The World of Joe McCarthy* (1983); but see also Thomas C. Reeves, *The Life and Times of Joe McCarthy* (1981); Mark Landis, *Joseph McCarthy: The Politics of Chaos* (1987); and Robert Griffith, *The Politics of Fear: Joseph R. McCarthy and the Senate* (1988). McCarthy's attack on one State Department official is told in Robert P. Newman, *Owen Lattimore and the "Loss" of China* (1992). The relationship between the Cold War and male identity is explored in Robert D. Dean, *Imperial Brotherhood: Gender and the Making of Cold War Foreign Policy* (2001). The related attack on homosexuals is described in David K. Johnson, *The Lavender Scare: The Cold War Persecution of Gays and Lesbians in the Federal Government* (2004).

For the impact of McCarthyism in academia, see Ellen W. Schrecker, *No Ivory Tower: McCarthyism and the Universities* (1986). An interesting collection of case studies appears in Bud Schultz and Ruth Schultz, eds., *It Did Happen Here: Recollections of Political Repression in America* (1989). Also helpful in understanding McCarthy's support are Michael Paul Rogin, *The Intellectuals and McCarthy* (1967), and David M. Oshinsky, *Senator Joseph McCarthy and the American Labor Movement* (1976). A recent effort to rehabilitate McCarthy's reputation can be found in Arthur Herman, *Joseph McCarthy: Reexamining the Life and Legacy of America's Most Hated Senator* (2000).

There are numerous books about the dramatic political trials of the era. A good background to such trials is Stanley Kutler, *The American Inquisition: Justice and Injustice in the Cold War* (1982). Also see Allan Weinstein, *Perjury: The Hiss-Chambers Case* (1978); and Ronald Radosh and Joyce Milton, *The Rosenberg File* (1987), which asserts the guilt of Julius Rosenberg (not Ethel Rosenberg). For the harassment of U.S. Spanish Civil War veterans, see Peter N. Carroll, *The Odyssey of the Abraham Lincoln Brigade: Americans in the Spanish Civil War* (1994). More sympathetic to the anticommunist crusade is Richard Gid Powers, *Not Without Honor: The History of American Anticommunism* (1995). The role of the FBI is detailed in Richard Gid Powers, *Secrecy and Power: The Life of J. Edgar Hoover* (1987), and in Athan G. Theoharis and John Stuart Cox, *The Boss: J. Edgar Hoover and the Great American Inquisition* (1988).

The background of the Korean War is best studied in James Irving Matray, *The Reluctant Crusade: American Foreign Policy in Korea, 1941–1950* (1985); in Jian Chen, *China's Road to the Korean War: The Making of the Sino-American Confrontation* (1994); and in William Whitney Stueck Jr., *The Korean War: An International History* (1995), which may be supplemented by Bruce Cumings's two-volume study, *The Origins of the Korean War* (1981–1990), and Rosemary Foot's *The Wrong War: American Policy and the Dimensions of the Korean Conflict, 1950–1953* (1985). Still valuable is Ronald Caridi, *The Korean War and American Politics* (1968). One wartime legal case dealing with the relation between government and business is the subject of Maeva Marcus, *Truman and the Steel Seizure Case* (1977).

The traditional view of Eisenhower as a laissez-faire president can be found in Peter Lyon, *Eisenhower: Portrait of a Hero* (1974). This view has been challenged persuasively in Blanche Wiesen Cook, *The Declassified Eisenhower: A Divided Legacy* (1981), and Fred Greenstein, *The Hidden Hand Presidency: Eisenhower as Leader* (1982). A detailed collection of primary sources can be found in Robert L. Branyan and Lawrence H. Larsen, *The Eisenhower Administration*, two volumes (1971).

Numerous biographies offer insight into the domestic issues of the 1950s. For a superb study of politics in the Senate, see Robert A. Caro, *The Years of Lyndon Johnson: Master of the Senate* (2002). Good studies of the leading Democrat include Jeff Broadwater, *Adlai Stevenson and American Politics: The Odyssey of a Cold War Liberal* (1994), and John Bartlow Martin's more detailed two-volume *The Life of Adlai Stevenson* (1976–1977). For the vice president's career, see Stephen E. Ambrose's biography, *Nixon: The Education of a Politician* (1987), as well as the superb analysis by Garry Wills, *Nixon Agonistes* (1970). The liberal perspective emerges in Carl Solberg's *Hubert Humphrey: A Biography* (1984). Voting behavior in the 1950s is explained in Norman H. Nie et al., *The Changing American Voter* (1976).

A good introduction to Eisenhower's foreign policy is Walter Lafeber, *America, Russia, and the Cold War* (1985). A more favorable account is Robert A. Divine, *Eisenhower and the Cold War* (1981). These works should be supplemented by the suggestive articles in Richard A. Melanson and David Mayers, eds., *Reevaluating Eisenhower: American Foreign Policy in the 1950s* (1987). Eisenhower's economic foreign policy is the subject of Burton I. Kaufman's *Trade and Aid: Eisenhower's Foreign Economic Policy, 1953–61* (1982). U.S. interest in Iran and oil is analyzed in Mary Ann Heiss,

Empire and Nationhood: The United States, Great Britain, and Iranian Oil, 1950–1954 (1997).

U.S. intervention in Central America is best described in Piero Gleijeses, *Shattered Hope: The Guatemalan Revolution and the United States, 1944–1954* (1991); see also R. H. Immerman, *The CIA in Guatemala: The Foreign Policy of Intervention* (1982), and Stephen C. Schlesinger and Stephen Kinzer, *Bitter Fruit: The Untold Story of the American Coup in Guatemala* (1982).

White House anticommunism is the theme of Jeff Broadwater's *Eisenhower and the Anti-Communist Crusade* (1992). For the Oppenheimer case, see Peter J. Goodchild, *J. Robert Oppenheimer: Shatterer of Worlds* (1981). For the impact of Cold War anticommunism on popular culture, see Margot A. Henriksen, *Dr. Strangelove's America: Society and Culture in the Atomic Age* (1997).

EISENHOWER'S TROUBLED CONSENSUS, 1954–1960

By the middle of the 1950s, the United States stood as the most powerful and prosperous nation on earth. Although its inhabitants constituted just 6 percent of the world's population in 1955, they made two-thirds of the world's manufactured goods. In addition to this industrial strength, the number of jobs in the service sector of the economy—sales, clerical, and other white-collar occupations—exceeded the number of manufacturing occupations for the first time in 1956, heralding a new postindustrial society based on technological innovation and labor productivity. But although economists such as John Kenneth Galbraith depicted "the affluent society," deep pockets of poverty remained untouched by technological progress and economic growth. Persistent disparities of wealth between the elderly and the young, between racial minorities and whites, between city dwellers and suburbanites stimulated concerns about social inequities.

Foreign policy issues appeared equally problematic. The anticommunist crusade had effectively silenced dissent against mounting government expenditures for national security or the preoccupation with political loyalty. But although President Dwight D. Eisenhower endorsed the expansion of a vast military arsenal, the Cold War with the Soviet Union remained unresolved, and crises erupted continually around the world—in Southeast Asia, Taiwan, the Middle East, Berlin, and Latin America. Fear of nuclear warfare permeated the land, prompting increased concern about civil defense and the high cost of domestic security. Eisenhower himself lamented the growth of a "military-industrial complex" that threatened to swamp traditional freedoms and the entrepreneurial spirit. The Cold War consensus thus rested on a shaky foundation, both at home and abroad.

CRISIS RELATIONS IN ASIA

In the spring of 1954—at the same time that Senator Joseph McCarthy presided over televised investigations of the U.S. Army and Eisenhower quietly canceled the security clearance of physicist J. Robert Oppenheimer—a Vietnamese guerrilla force was surrounding the French garrison at Dien Bien Phu in Vietnam. Facing military disaster that would doom the French empire in the region, France appealed to Eisenhower for U.S. military intervention. Since the outbreak of the Korean War, the United States had provided major support for French attempts to suppress the Vietminh rebels led by Ho Chi Minh. By 1954 Washington had spent $1.2 billion on military assistance and was financing nearly 80 percent of France's total war costs. These expenses included several hundred "technical" advisers. The administration justified intervention on the grounds that Vietnam provided valuable raw materials such as tin and rubber and remained a vital strategic link in the attempt to halt communist expansion. Yet, although Washington supported the French in Southeast Asia, administration leaders repeatedly expressed frustration at France's failure to develop support among noncommunist Vietnamese.

Despite U.S. aid, the French position worsened. As a new crisis loomed in 1954, Eisenhower faced critical choices. Sensitive to the limited success in Korea, he hesitated to commit U.S. military forces unilaterally. Although the Central Intelligence Agency (CIA) flew relief missions to the French garrison and conducted reconnaissance flights, the doctrine of massive retaliation—by which the United States threatened nuclear reprisals against communist enemies—had limited use in jungle warfare in Indochina. Tactical air strikes, perhaps with atomic weapons, alarmed British allies, who worried that all-out war in Indochina would trigger Chinese intervention, particularly against Hong Kong and Malaysia. The British also feared Soviet retaliation and an atomic war. Without British support, moreover, congressional Democrats led by Senator Richard Russell refused to sanction military action. Democratic Majority Leader Lyndon Johnson told Secretary of State John Foster Dulles, "No more Koreas with the United States furnishing 90 percent of the manpower."

For Eisenhower, Vietnam held the future of Asia. And in 1954 a special National Security Council (NSC) committee called for military victory "to provide tangible evidence of Western strength and determination to defeat Communism." At a press conference that year the president buttressed this position with the "falling domino" theory: "You have a row of dominos set up, you knock over the first one, and what will happen to the last one is the certainty that it will go over very quickly." The fall of Vietnam would mean that "many human beings pass under a dictatorship that is inimical to the free world." It would interfere with the acquisition of precious resources, imperil Japanese trade, and force that ally "toward the Communist areas in order to live."

EXHIBIT **10-1**   INDOCHINA AFTER THE GENEVA ACCORDS OF 1954

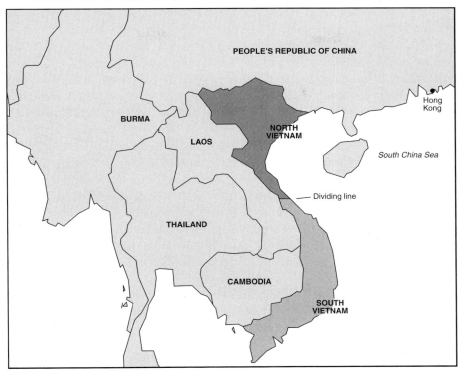

Eisenhower never wavered from the belief that the Vietminh were not an anticolonial force, but part of an international communist conspiracy. But the commander in chief had learned from the Korean experience. Without British support and explicit approval from Congress, Eisenhower refused to commit ground forces to another war in Asia. Yet when the French finally surrendered to the Vietminh in May 1954, Senator Johnson criticized the White House's failure to act. "American foreign policy had never in all its history suffered such a stunning reversal," he declared.

The French defeat made a diplomatic settlement imperative. In July 1954 France signed the Geneva Accords and ended eight years of war by accepting the independence of Vietnam, Laos, and Cambodia. The agreement divided Vietnam militarily at the seventeenth parallel, but this temporary line did not imply a political separation. The agreement called for national elections, supervised by an international commission, to be held within two years. By acknowledging a Vietminh government, if only in North Vietnam, the Geneva settlement represented a defeat of Eisenhower's anticommunist foreign policy. The United States announced it would respect the Geneva Accords; but the administration refused to sign the document, and Secretary of State John Foster Dulles referred to South Vietnam as a "country."

The United States soon began to violate the Geneva agreement by continuing a secret war against the Vietminh. Instead of accepting a communist Vietnam, Washington worked to build an anticommunist nationalist movement in South Vietnam led by Ngo Dinh Diem, a U.S.-educated Catholic. Installed as premier of the French-controlled portion of the country, Diem welcomed a U.S. military mission, which organized a South Vietnamese army and launched acts of sabotage and a propaganda campaign against the Vietminh in the north. Meanwhile, the CIA distributed $12 million to bribe Diem's rivals into neutrality.

Eisenhower also moved to replace France's influence in Vietnam. Washington bypassed French officials and transmitted aid directly to Diem, thus avoiding the appearance of supporting French colonialism. Such policies led France to withdraw from Vietnam before the 1956 election deadline. Quickly stepping into the power vacuum, U.S. advisers began to train a large South Vietnamese army "to deter Vietminh aggression." Acknowledging that Ho Chi Minh would win national elections, the administration worked to stop national unification under the terms of the Geneva Accords. Diem made these policies explicit in 1955 by announcing his rejection of national elections. Unlike France and Britain, the United States backed Diem. Eisenhower welcomed him in Washington, where the two leaders reaffirmed the struggle against "continuing Communist subversive capabilities."

During the next five years, when Vietnam seldom attracted attention in the U.S. media, Washington sent nearly $1.5 billion in economic and military aid to South Vietnam to finance most of Diem's government expenses. Such support enabled the dictator to suppress his political rivals by arresting both communist and noncommunist opponents. Diem also ended land reform begun by the Vietminh. By 1959 these repressive policies triggered another guerrilla revolt. Although the United States urged Diem to allow political and social reforms, the South Vietnamese leader refused, prompting the U.S. ambassador to suggest "it may become necessary . . . to begin consideration of alternative courses of actions and leaders." Eisenhower passed this unresolved predicament to the next U.S. presidential administration in 1961.

While adopting unilateral action in Vietnam, Eisenhower instituted collective security plans to prevent the spread of communism in Asia. In 1954 Dulles signed a Southeast Asia Treaty Organization (SEATO) pact with Britain, France, Australia, New Zealand, Thailand, Pakistan, and the Philippines. This accord provided for mutual defense against armed attack, subversion, or indirect aggression. "An attack on the treaty area would occasion a reaction so united, so strong, and so well placed," said Dulles, "that the aggressor would lose more than it could hope to gain." Yet the SEATO agreement had inherent limitations, including the refusal of neutral India to participate and the difficulty of using massive retaliation against subversion. The Senate rati-

EXHIBIT **10-2**   **TAIWAN AND THE PEOPLE'S REPUBLIC OF CHINA**

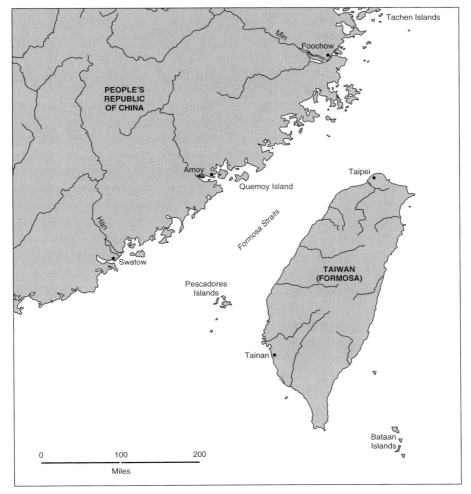

EXHIBIT **10-2**   **TAIWAN AND THE PEOPLE'S REPUBLIC OF CHINA**

fied the treaty with little dissent, but the military provisions were never invoked, and the treaty ended in 1977.

Even as Dulles was flying to Manila to negotiate the SEATO pact in 1954, the weaknesses of the treaty became apparent. Without warning or obvious provocation, Chinese artillery suddenly began to bombard Quemoy, one of the small islands (along with Matsu and the Tachen Islands) between China and Taiwan. The attacks moved Washington to prepare for war, including considering atomic bombing of China. Although Eisenhower recognized that the islands were not crucial to the defense of Taiwan, he defined the Taiwan regime as part of the "backbone" of international security. The government of China began to prepare for an atomic attack. As war fever rose, Dulles negotiated a mutual defense pact with Taiwan but made no mention of the disputed islands.

When China captured one of the Tachen Islands, Eisenhower asked Congress for authority to use armed forces to defend Taiwan and the nearby islands. Approved by nearly unanimous votes of both houses of Congress in 1955, the so-called Formosa Resolution gave the president discretionary power to declare war, a virtual blank check for future presidential foreign policy. As China continued to bomb the islands, Eisenhower indirectly reiterated the threat of atomic attack. At the same time, however, the Soviet Union was seeking a relaxation of global tensions and hoping for an arms control agreement in Europe. Soviet pressure, combined with Eisenhower's threats, persuaded China to break the deadlock. As abruptly as it began, the crisis passed.

Eisenhower's threats to use atomic bombs moved the People's Republic of China to develop its own nuclear capacities. Meanwhile, the Taiwanese government proceeded to strengthen fortifications on the disputed offshore islands. Tensions between the two Chinas kept the world on edge. Then, in 1958, the People's Republic abruptly reopened the crisis by launching a steady bombardment of Quemoy. This time, as the administration rushed military aid to Taiwan, Eisenhower avoided reference to nuclear weapons. By then both the United States and the Soviet Union were discussing an arms control agreement, and scientists meeting in Geneva had announced "a workable and effective control system for the detection of violations." The refusal of the Soviet Union to support China's attack intensified the rift between the communist allies. Yet neither the United States nor the Soviet Union could abandon their rival Chinese clients. The result was the preservation of the two-China status quo. Eisenhower and Dulles had accomplished no more than Truman's policy of containment had.

A VIGILANT THAW

The Cold War climate of mutual suspicion made negotiations with the Soviet Union difficult and unrewarding. During his first years in office, Eisenhower avoided presidential diplomacy, preferring Dulles to handle direct talks. But by 1955, Democrats in Congress urged the president to make some gesture of reconciliation to ease world tensions. As a precondition to meeting with other leaders, Eisenhower insisted that the Allies of World War II first sign a peace treaty with Austria. When the Soviets agreed in 1955, Eisenhower flew to a summit meeting in Geneva with British, French, and Soviet leaders. The international press heralded the meeting as a "thaw" in the Cold War.

The main topics on the global agenda—the status of Germany and disarmament—could not be settled. Hoping to break the stalemate of suspicion, Eisenhower introduced a new plan, known as the "open-skies" proposal, which would permit aircraft to fly freely over foreign countries to inspect military installations and thus avert the risk of a surprise attack. Yet the plan clearly offered advantages to the less-secretive United States, and the Soviet Union rejected the scheme. After the conference ended, Eisenhower proceeded with plans to use a new secret spy plane (the U-2) to achieve the goal that the open-skies plan had intended. Both superpowers continued to test hydrogen bombs and intercontinental missiles, but the Geneva meeting did ease world tensions. "Communist tactics against the free nations have shifted," observed Eisenhower in 1956, "from reliance on violence to reliance on division."

The thaw in the Cold War had obvious limits. When Poland and then Hungary tried to establish more liberal communist governments in 1956, Americans celebrated what appeared to be a collapse of the Soviet empire. However, when Soviet tanks crushed the uprising in Budapest, massive retaliation proved worthless. Although the U.S. government's Radio Free Europe broadcast moral support to the Hungarian rebels, Eisenhower could only condemn Soviet aggression and allow 20,000 Hungarian refugees to enter the country. Both sides remained vigilant and mistrustful.

The arms race continued, leading the federal government to invest heavily in military technology, such as jet aircraft, missiles, electronic transistors, and computers. Between 1950 and 1959, the federal government sponsored $12 billion in research and development (R&D), including $300 million per year for university research. Aircraft manufacturing, one of the leading growth industries, drew 80 percent of its business from military contracts. The government also backed electronics, which grew 15 percent per year, making it the fifth largest industry by 1960. Secret military programs for nuclear weapons, missiles, and cryptography also demanded complicated mathematical calculations that boosted the computer industry.

Among the most sophisticated R&D programs was the plan to launch an artificial satellite that would orbit the earth in 1958. Indeed, it was the prospect of this technological breakthrough that had inspired Eisenhower to make the open-skies proposal. But before U.S. scientists could achieve a satellite launch, the Soviet Union surprised the world in October 1957 by sending the 184-pound *Sputnik* satellite into space. The event sent psychological shock waves across the nation, suggesting both a technological defeat for U.S. science and a military threat in the Cold War.

"The time has clearly come," said one Republican critic, "to be less concerned with the depth of pile on the new broadloom rug or the height of the tail fin on the car and to be more prepared to shed blood, sweat, and tears if this country and the Free World are to survive." "The Soviets have beaten us at our own game," declared Senator Johnson, "daring scientific advances in the atomic age." Besides the philosophic shock caused by the triumph over the earth's gravitation, *Sputnik* aroused fear that the communist enemy could deliver intercontinental ballistic missiles armed with nuclear weapons before the United States could muster sufficient retaliatory power. This belief in a missile gap fed widespread fear of nuclear annihilation. Best-selling books such as Nevil Shute's *On the Beach* (1957) and Walt Miller's *A Canticle for Leibowitz* (1959) dramatized the imminence of holocaust.

Although military intelligence understood that U.S. rocketry remained competitive with the Soviet achievement, public fears stimulated greater government support for scientific research. In 1958 Congress created the National Aeronautics and Space Administration (NASA), a civilian space program, and increased appropriations for missile and satellite research. Government expenditures for R&D jumped from $6.2 billion in 1955 to $14.3 billion six years later, a 131 percent increase.

Throughout the *Sputnik* crisis, Eisenhower denied U.S. military weakness and rejected plans to build fallout shelters around the country. In any case, the country was soon prepared to match the Soviet achievement. After a few highly publicized failures, the army lofted the *Explorer* satellite into orbit in 1958. The president also created a White House Science Advisory Committee headed by the Massachusetts Institute of Technology's James Killian. By bringing scientists into the administration, Eisenhower for the first time had access to authoritative opinions about a range of technological issues. These scientists would later contradict the advice of the Atomic Energy Commission (AEC) and the Pentagon and suggest that the nuclear arms race could be controlled, paving the way for negotiations about restricting nuclear testing.

The administration also proceeded with a program to explore outer space. In 1959 NASA unveiled Project Mercury, a program for manned space flight, and introduced the first seven astronauts to the public. In the international "space race," U.S. rocketry at first lagged behind Soviet successes. Early Soviet missiles carried more than a ton of cargo (and even a dog), whereas the first U.S. satellite weighed only 30 pounds. However, in the next decade, electronic miniaturization and the development of intercontinental ballistic missiles (ICBMs) brought primacy to U.S. rocketry. The space program thus benefited from military defense research.

CRISES IN THE MIDDLE EAST

Huge expenditures for military aircraft and transportation underscored the importance of petroleum resources for waging the Cold War and reinforced the strategic role of Middle East countries. Although the United States had supported the independence of Israel in 1948, Presidents Truman and Eisenhower encouraged U.S. oil companies to provide Arab states with subsidies, which were tacitly repaid by the federal government in the form of tax deductions. Eisenhower also backed British influence in the Middle East to

EXHIBIT **10-3**   **THE MIDDLE EAST, 1956–1958**

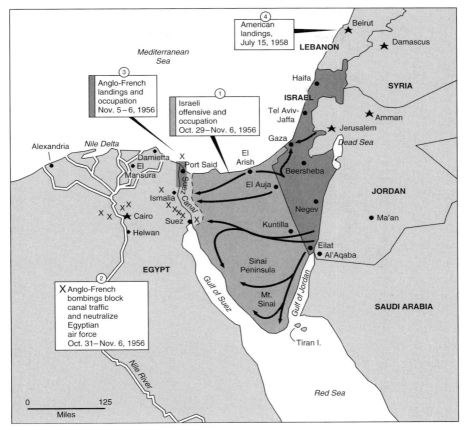

check Soviet expansion and supported a British plan for regional cooperation through the Baghdad Pact of 1955.

This anticommunist alliance alarmed Egyptian leader Gamal Abdel Nasser, a nationalist who needed economic and military assistance to strengthen his country. As Nasser negotiated with communist Czechoslovakia to purchase arms, Washington offered to finance the Aswan Dam, a giant hydroelectric project that promised to modernize Egypt. But when Nasser announced his recognition of the People's Republic of China in 1956, U.S. cooperation ceased. "Do nations which play both sides get better treatment than nations which are stalwart and work with us?" asked Dulles angrily. Eisenhower promptly withdrew the offer to build the dam. The reversal humiliated Nasser. One week later, the Egyptian leader nationalized the Suez Canal, thereby jeopardizing western Europe's access to oil and Israel's shipping rights.

Although Britain and France threatened military reprisal, Eisenhower opposed a reassertion of colonialism. The two countries then resolved to take action without U.S. participation, using Israel as an instigator. In October 1956 the Israelis launched a surprise attack on Egypt, which provided Britain and France with an excuse to intervene to protect the canal. The invasion coincided with the Soviet suppression of the Hungarian uprising. Faced with a double crisis, Eisenhower demanded the withdrawal of troops from Egypt. So did Premier Nikita Khrushchev, who warned the Western nations of a retaliatory attack and expressed interest in a Soviet presence in the Middle East. To prevent such Soviet expansion, Eisenhower increased pressure on the allies by halting oil shipments to western Europe. The embargo forced the British and French to remove their forces from the Middle East by the end of the year.

To fill the resulting power vacuum in the Middle East, Eisenhower presented a plan, known as the Eisenhower Doctrine, in 1957. The president asked Congress to approve unspecified economic and military assistance and also requested a resolution announcing that "overt armed aggression from any nation controlled by international Communism" would be met by U.S. military force. Congress agreed. Once again, the United States would police the world against communist influence, confusing Arab nationalism with communist expansion.

The Eisenhower Doctrine gave the White House extensive authority to intervene in the Middle East. In 1957 Jordan's King Hussein claimed that a nationalist rebellion in his country constituted a communist attack. Although Eisenhower understood the king's duplicity, he sent the Sixth Fleet to protect the political status quo. In 1958 a similar distortion of events led the president to order the marines into Lebanon. This dramatic gesture served notice to Arab nationalists that the United States was determined to protect access to Middle Eastern oil.

"What makes the Soviet threat unique in history," the president stated in 1958, "is its all-inclusiveness. . . . Trade, economic development, military power, arts, science, education, the whole world of ideas—all are harnessed to the same chariot of expansion." Fear of Soviet influence in economically underdeveloped countries stimulated a reappraisal of U.S. economic foreign policy. As a proponent of free enterprise, Eisenhower hoped that foreign trade and private investment would assure U.S. influence without adding to government expenditures. Foreign aid remained largely military and was justified on grounds of national security.

But increased Soviet competition persuaded the president to endorse foreign aid as a way of accelerating the economic development of other countries and linking their interests to the West. In 1957 Congress established the Development Loan Fund and two years later created the Inter-American Loan Bank for Latin America. Both projects provided relatively small sums and emphasized private investment. Eisenhower defined such assistance not as an attempt to reduce poverty but rather as a defense of national security in the fight against communism. Moreover, foreign military aid far exceeded economic assistance and caused a severe imbalance in international payments that weakened the dollar abroad. Yet Eisenhower's commitment to foreign economic development provided a precedent for later administrations.

THE POLITICS OF MODERATION

Surveying the political spectrum in 1956, Democratic contender Adlai Stevenson concluded that "moderation is the spirit of the times." Although liberals such as Hubert Humphrey and Paul Douglas spoke eloquently about social reform, Democrats worked closely with Eisenhower's "modern" Republicans to enact minimal social legislation, such as raising the minimum wage slightly and constructing limited public housing.

The grandfatherly Eisenhower remained extremely popular. Although the president's 1955 heart attack shook public confidence, he recovered rapidly and resolved to seek a second term. After slight hesitation, Ike agreed to keep Vice President Richard Nixon on the Republican ticket. Democratic chances seemed slim. Stevenson won a first-ballot nomination and then, in a dramatic moment, opened the vice presidential choice to the whole Democratic National Convention. In the exciting floor fight, Tennessee Senator Estes Kefauver managed to defeat Senator John F. Kennedy of Massachusetts.

The Democrats then adopted a moderate platform. Hoping to regain the southern white voters, the party waffled on the issue of racial segregation. The party also echoed Eisenhower's Cold War principles. Stevenson did introduce two controversial proposals by calling for an end to the military draft and suggesting a moratorium on hydrogen bomb testing. However, both issues played to Eisenhower's reputation as an experienced military leader. "The butchers of the Kremlin," said Nixon, "would make mincemeat of Stevenson over a conference table."

Eisenhower's 1956 margin of victory exceeded the totals of his first election. He captured 58 percent of the popular vote and carried all but seven states. Other Republican candidates ran far behind, and Democrats strengthened their control of both houses of Congress. This anomalous situation reflected the persistence of party voting habits. With 50 percent more registered Democrats than Republicans, congressional Democrats coasted to victory in 1956. But unlike congressional candidates, Eisenhower could attract voters from all parts of the political spectrum because specific issues appeared relatively unimportant. One exception to the rule was the African American vote. In 1956, 40 percent of black voters, including Martin Luther King Jr., supported the Republican Party against Democratic racists who controlled southern politics.

Emboldened by their success in the congressional elections, Democrats moved to clarify their political position and define their differences with the

Estes Kefauver (1903–1963)

In an era of political consensus and corporate expansion, Tennessee's Senator Estes Kefauver flourished as a maverick politician and a champion of the ordinary citizen against big business and political corruption. Running for the Senate in 1948, he broke with Tennessee's political machine and adopted a coonskin cap as a symbol of his frontier independence. The folksy style became his political trademark. Kefauver's image as a populist, enhanced by televised broadcasts of his Senate hearings on organized crime in 1950 and 1951, catapulted him to national fame and made the senator a strong Democratic presidential contender. Yet his individualism created many enemies. In the end, he was deemed too much a southerner for liberals, too much a liberal for southerners.

© Stock Montage

Born in eastern Tennessee, Kefauver studied law at Yale and worked as a corporate lawyer before being elected to Congress in 1939. He supported small business interests against corporate concentration, advocated congressional reform, and coauthored the book *A Twentieth Century Congress* (1947). Although Kefauver was sensitive to civil liberties issues, he placated his southern constitutents by opposing a federal Fair Employment Practices Commission and antilynching legislation. But, unlike most racial opportunists, he urged repeal of poll taxes because they disenfranchised the poor of both races, and he opposed the use of the filibuster to kill civil rights legislation. Indeed, after the Supreme Court overturned school segregation in 1954, he readily accepted the idea of racial integration.

Republican agenda. Eisenhower's success in the black neighborhoods of northern cities goaded congressional liberals into action. "I don't think a party should run on 'trouble,' on economic difficulty," declared Hubert Humphrey. "We must design a new liberal program." Led by Humphrey and Douglas, liberal senators presented a sixteen-point "Democratic Declaration" that advocated civil rights legislation, public housing, unemployment compensation, and other reforms. Meanwhile, Democratic leaders organized a Democratic

Kefauver's investigation of organized crime in the first televised Senate hearings created a national sensation in 1950. Exposure of national crime networks and widespread political graft underscored an abiding fear in the Cold War era that secret forces—"government-within-a-government," as he put it—were threatening national values. For Kefauver, it was crime and corruption, not communism, that were the prime menace. Significantly, he opposed provisions of the 1954 communist control bill that made Communist Party membership a felony. Kefauver's crime hearings also showed the political power of television. In his book, *Crime in America* (1951), the senator estimated that more than 20 million people watched the hearings. As a result, Kefauver suddenly became a nationally known politician.

Capitalizing on this popularity, Kefauver donned his coonskin cap in 1952 and entered a series of Democratic presidential primaries as the first major candidate to recognize the potential of grassroots support. He surprised the country by defeating President Truman in New Hampshire, but his unorthodox style did not allow him to build a national organization. Kefauver's nonpartisan investigations of organized crime also alarmed the Democratic leadership, which feared a loss of party strength in the cities. Meanwhile, his spotty record on civil rights weakened his support among liberals, and his opposition to filibusters cut into his southern base.

Twice defeated for the presidential nomination by Adlai Stevenson, Kefauver staged a dramatic floor rally in 1956 to win the vice presidential slot over Massachusetts Senator John F. Kennedy. After the presidential loss, Kefauver returned to the Senate. In 1963 he collapsed during a floor speech and died a few days later.

Advisory Council distinct from the cautious congressional leadership of Lyndon Johnson and Sam Rayburn to press for a liberal agenda.

The revitalization of Democratic liberals produced greater conflict with the Republican administration. The first controversy erupted when the president presented a $73.3 billion budget request, the highest appropriation ever requested in peacetime, for fiscal year 1958. Committed to a balanced budget, Treasury Secretary George Humphrey predicted that such expenditures would cause a depression. Eisenhower complicated the situation by inviting Congress to reduce government expenditures. The result was a bitter legislative "battle of the budget" as Congress picked apart the president's entire program, shaving the budget by $4 billion. For Eisenhower, the outcome was an embarrassing personal defeat.

Instead of boosting the economy, however, the reduction of government expenditures slowed economic growth. By mid-1957, industrial production had dropped and unemployment had increased. Eisenhower remained skeptical about the ability of government spending to stimulate the economy. But the Democratic Congress had fewer reservations. Increased appropriations, including public works projects, added more than $8 billion to the budget and halted the recession. Yet continued government spending resulted in large budget deficits.

THE CULTURE OF CONSUMPTION

The debates about government spending underscored the role of big business in shaping society and culture during the 1950s. In supporting what Eisenhower called the military-industrial complex, government agencies awarded most contracts to the country's largest corporations. Only 4 percent of R&D funds reached small businesses. Although convenient for government administrators, support of big business did not reduce costs. Without competitive bidding, federal budgets routinely absorbed business cost overruns. Nothing better showed the marriage between the federal government and big business than the Interstate Highway Act of 1956, which facilitated the integration of national roadways in the name of national defense. The law committed the federal government to spend more than $30 billion to develop a continental freeway system. Not coincidentally, national automobile registration increased from 40 million in 1950 to 62 million in 1960. There was little irony, then, when Eisenhower's secretary of defense, Charles E. Wilson, the former president of General Motors, said: "For years I thought what was good for the country was good for General Motors, and vice versa."

Spurred by the baby boom, suburban growth, and the expansion of white-collar jobs, corporate prosperity increased and stimulated tremendous confidence in the economic future. "Not only do the younger people accept the beneficent society as normal," observed author William H. Whyte Jr., "they accept improvement, considerable and constant, as normal too." Peaceful labor-management relations had brought unprecedented prosperity to the nation's workers. Between 1955 and 1960, average hourly earnings rose more than 22 percent, twice the rate of inflation. Long-term union contracts assured blue-collar employees regular cost-of-living wage hikes as well as paid vacations.

EXHIBIT **10-4   GROSS NATIONAL PRODUCT, 1954–1958**
(IN ROUNDED BILLIONS OF DOLLARS)

1954	372
1958	457

Source: *Economic Report of the President* (1988).

Although economic recessions occurred three times after the war—in 1948–1949, 1953–1954, and 1957–1958—private consumption steadily increased each year. In the immediate postwar years consumers exhausted their savings to buy durable household goods such as appliances, furniture, and automobiles—some 21 million cars, 20 million refrigerators, 5 million stoves, and 12 million TVs. Then they relied on borrowed money to purchase disposable goods and services such as insurance, entertainment, and travel. In 1950 Diner's Club introduced the personal credit card to allow businessmen to charge their meals. By the end of the decade Carte Blanche, American Express, and BankAmericard extended easy credit to predominantly male members. (Most married women could not obtain personal credit until the 1970s.) Installment credit soared from $4 billion in 1954 to $43 billion in 1960.

Some consumer spending reflected the age-specific demands of the baby boom: children's clothing, toys, "family-size" products. In 1956, for the first time, the airline industry attracted as many passengers as did railroads; in 1958 the Boeing 707 brought jet speed to commercial aviation. Planned obsolescence made consumption appear to be an end in itself. Men's clothing styles began following women's fashions by undergoing annual changes that made serviceable wardrobes outmoded. By emphasizing cosmetic innovations such as fender "fins," annual changes in automobile models encouraged frequent trade-ins.

Advertising, not coincidentally, became one of the major growth industries of the postwar period. Although best-selling books such as Vance Packard's *The Hidden Persuaders* (1957) publicized the psychological techniques of advertising, market research found that consumers remained more responsive to emotional appeals than to product substance. As advertising touted consumer disposables and luxuries such as tobacco, beverages, drugs, amusements, and extra home furnishings, annual advertising expenditures exceeded $10 billion by 1960. Postwar advertising relied increasingly on national media, such as network television and mass circulation magazines, rather than local radio stations or newspapers. The new outlets facilitated product recognition for a population that increasingly migrated around the country. Advertisers also geared their pitches to market segments identified by demographic factors such as age, income, education, and lifestyle. And in 1952, Eisenhower became the first presidential candidate to film televised commercials.

The growth of advertising paralleled the expansion of all service industries. Each year consumers spent ever-larger sums for insurance, automobile repairs, medical care, and travel. These expanding service industries also had a major impact on the nature of work. As part of a long historical trend, technological innovation increased individual worker productivity, which in turn reduced the proportion of blue-collar jobs. Meanwhile, the growth of corporations created new managerial jobs for employees who administered business activities rather than producing commodities. In 1956 the number of people employed in service industries exceeded the number of producers for the first time, which heralded the postindustrial society. Government bureaucracies also swelled on all levels. State and local government increased by 2 million employees during the 1950s, an increase of 52 percent. By 1960, nearly 8.5 million employees drew government paychecks, largely for white-collar employment.

Skilled work now took another form. In the growing corporate and government bureaucracies, managerial expertise focused on increasing the productivity of white-collar workers and touted new values such as teamwork and administrative efficiency. The requirements of the corporate workplace contributed to an emphasis on consensus in postwar society. College students appeared greatly concerned about the need to conform and to "get along." Dubbed the "silent generation," many young people preferred courses in business administration and education to those in the liberal arts.

In the social sciences, William Whyte observed a "bias against conflict" among scholars who viewed terms such as "disharmony, disequilibrium, maladjustment, disorganization" as "bad things." Sociologists and political scientists stressed social "pluralism," a belief that a diversity of interest groups competed on an equal basis and adjusted their differences through reason and compromise. Liberal theory held that democracy was unworkable if people maintained loyalties to social classes, ethnic groups, or ideologies. Indeed, sociologist Daniel Bell declared that ideology was "dead." Historians Louis Hartz, Richard Hofstadter, and Daniel Boorstin described the national past in terms of a homogenized culture that succeeded because it avoided major social conflicts.

Postwar consensus was also reflected in the resurgence of church membership in all denominations—from 64 million in 1940 to 115 million in 1960, or from 50 percent to 63 percent of the population. This interest in spiritual security partly demonstrated the underlying anxieties of a rootless society and the search for identity in new communities. Religious leaders of the 1950s offered less a promise of salvation than a sense of secular reassurance and solace. "Believe in yourself!" the Reverend Norman Vincent Peale proclaimed in the popular tract, *The Power of Positive Thinking* (1952). "Have faith in your abilities! Without a humble but reasonable confidence in your own powers you cannot succeed." Worshippers spent $1 billion building churches in 1960 alone.

The postwar consensus also influenced the values of young people. "I would like to be able to fly if everybody else did," a twelve-year-old girl told sociologist David Riesman, "but it would be kind of conspicuous." Critics contended that conformity had worked its way into the public schools through a perversion of John Dewey's philosophy of progressive education. Instead of encouraging students to question social values, as Dewey had urged, teachers typically stressed the values of social adjustment. Yet, ironically, progressive education became the target of further attacks when the Soviet *Sputnik* launch of 1957 abruptly challenged the pedagogical status quo. Shocked by this Cold War "defeat," educational reformers scurried to improve academic standards. Congress quickly passed the National Defense Education Act of 1958, the first major federal aid to education, to encourage the study of science, mathematics, and foreign languages. This government support, which later included such subjects vital to the "national defense" as U.S. history, financed the vast expansion of higher education in the next decade.

Mass Culture and the Youth Cult

Rising personal consumption brought larger postwar recreation expenditures, which jumped from $11 billion in 1950 to more than $18 billion in 1959. Professional baseball truly became the national pastime in 1958 when major league teams moved to San Francisco and Los Angeles. Television proved to be the major innovation in postwar entertainment. In 1947 ten TV broadcasting stations reached about 20,000 TV sets. The next year TV sales suddenly skyrocketed. By 1957 U.S. households owned 40 million TV sets and could select programs from as many as seven broadcasting channels at a time. Television quickly became part of family life—seen by promoters as a modern "hearth" to encourage "togetherness" and by critics as an omnipresent salesman's foot in the door.

Although a new industry, television was controlled by the same corporations that dominated radio. Advertising rather than programming content determined the broadcast schedule. In 1951 the first coaxial cable linked the East and West Coasts and enabled national audiences to see the same thing at the same time. That year TV commercial sales surpassed radio advertising revenue for the first time. Although a host of young writers and performers produced brilliant examples of live drama and spontaneous comedy, the pressure to increase network ratings mostly generated formulaic series, variety programs, and quiz shows.

Television nonetheless eclipsed the other popular media such as radio, newspapers, magazines, and motion pictures. During the immediate postwar years, Hollywood had examined such controversial subjects as racism (*Home of the Brave*, 1948); anti-Semitism (*Crossfire*, 1947; *Gentlemen's Agreement*,

1947); and mental illness (*The Snake Pit*, 1949). Yet the investigation of Hollywood for communist subversion sent a chill through the industry and discouraged social criticism. Hollywood also suffered from declining movie attendance. By 1953 ticket sales were half of their 1946 record highs. The postwar baby boom, which tended to keep young adults at home, contributed to the drop. However, enthusiasm for TV—by 1953 more than 43 percent of U.S. families owned a set—swamped the old entertainment. Hoping to recapture audiences, Hollywood introduced production innovations such as 3-D, wide screens, and more color, which were unavailable on TV; but as movie mogul Sam Goldwyn predicted in 1949, people were "unwilling to pay to see poor pictures when they can stay at home and see something which is, at least, no worse."

Hollywood's recourse was to concentrate on psychological themes, daring sex, and films geared to the youth culture. Television's family audiences limited sexual content to vague double meanings or slapstick comedy. Although the motion picture industry still prohibited nudity or explicit sexuality, movies exploited the sexuality of stars like Marilyn Monroe, who combined provocative costumes with an uncanny sense of humor. Although many of Monroe's films portrayed sexual pleasure as a reward of affluence, the actress was a complex figure. A working-class woman who had escaped the dreariness of Los Angeles factory life, Monroe resented being judged by appearances even as she mastered the art of cinematic seduction.

Hollywood achieved greater success in exploiting a growing youth culture with sensitive young actors such as James Dean, Montgomery Clift, and Marlon Brando. "What are you rebelling against?" a teenage waitress asks a motorcycle tough in the Hollywood epic, *The Wild One* (1954). "What do ya got?" replies Brando. Popular movies about youth culture, such as *Rebel Without a Cause* (1955), portrayed a young generation that rejected the materialistic values of its parents. These films also expressed a lack of confidence in the older generation's ability to guide the young. "No longer is it thought to be the child's job to understand the adult world as the adult sees it," complained David Riesman in his classic study, *The Lonely Crowd* (1950).

Searching for peer approval and a sense of belonging, many adolescents turned to clubs, cliques, and gangs and experimented with cigarettes, alcohol, and sex. The antiauthoritarian *Mad* magazine, scoffing at mainstream culture, politicians, teachers, and parents, emerged as an instant hit among high school and college students. However, the primary form of social rebellion among postwar youth involved rock-and-roll music, a derivative of black rhythm and blues that was introduced to wider audiences by Cleveland disc jockey Allan Freed. Records by African American performers such as Chuck Berry and Little Richard often contained themes that rejected adult authority and assumed knowledge of sexual matters. By 1956 Elvis Presley, a sideburned white southerner whose music was based on the country rockabilly tradition, had

In the 1955 film *Rebel Without a Cause,* teenage delinquents in leather jackets seemed more concerned with social conformity than alternative lifestyles.

achieved cult status by blatantly mixing pelvic thrusts with raunchy blues shouts. The introduction of a new dance, the twist, by Chubby Checker in 1959 turned suggestive body expression into a national fad and hinted at the social integration of blacks and whites in postwar society.

Clergy and moral authorities professed shock at the frankness of rock and roll and its roots in the working-class cultures of blacks and southerners. In Boston police banned a live show staged by Freed and claimed that the loud and heavy beat excited teenagers to violence and delinquency. Yet for all its symbolic rebellion, rock and roll served more as a collective ritual for adolescents experiencing the traumas of puberty. Even "delinquents" in black leather jackets and motorcycle boots emulated the adult world by participating in consumer culture. And, after *The Blackboard Jungle* (1955) used Bill Haley's "Rock Around the Clock" in its soundtrack, Hollywood began to tailor its products to the burgeoning youth market. Other youth-oriented commodities included clothing, records, jewelry, cosmetics, soft drinks, and automobiles. Meanwhile, the music of white country legends such as Hank Williams, Patsy Cline, and Bob Wills and the Texas Playboys continued to express the joys and hardships of sexual love for working-class audiences. By 1955 annual record sales in the United States reached $225 million.

Economic abundance thus appeared in the 1950s as the epitome of national virtue. When Vice President Nixon visited Moscow in 1959 to accompany a traveling exhibition of U.S. home furnishings, he engaged in a highly publicized "kitchen debate" with Premier Khrushchev about the superiority of the U.S. way of life. While communists clung to a belief in a class revolution that would offer equality to all workers, Nixon pointed to the products of U.S. abundance—"44 million families with their 56 million cars, 50 million televisions and 143 million radios"—which showed the triumph of a truly "classless society." The superiority of the United States, said Nixon, could be seen in the multitude of its conveniences and its beautiful housewives.

Such political rhetoric disguised two enduring problems that would soon shatter the political consensus at home. The first concerned a growing realization that the fruits of U.S. capitalism did not reach all people equally. The second involved criticism from cultural outsiders who lamented corporate conformity and the homogenization of middle-class social roles and values.

Race, Poverty, and the Urban Crisis

"The saving grace of the American social system," boasted *Life* magazine in 1949, "is . . . the phenomenon of social 'mobility'—the opportunity to move rapidly upward through the levels of society." Indeed, the postwar period saw an era of unprecedented prosperity as family earnings among all recipients of income increased by at least 2.4 percent per year until 1973. Yet even in the prosperous 1950s unemployment rates remained between 3 and 8 percent, and unemployment insurance reimbursed only 20 percent of lost income. While touting middle-class success, social commentators typically ignored what author Michael Harrington called "the other America"—the numerous subcultures of poverty.

Among the poorest people were those older than sixty-five. A 1960 Senate report found that "at least one-half of the aged—approximately 8 million people—cannot afford today decent housing, proper nutrition, adequate medical care, preventive or acute, or necessary recreation." Mandatory retirement programs drove many able-bodied workers into poverty. During the 1950s the number of people entitled to Social Security benefits increased fivefold to 9.6 million, but government assistance filled a small fraction of their needs. More than half of the households headed by people older than sixty-five had incomes less than $3,000 a year in 1960.

Another pocket of poverty consisted of migrant farmworkers. On Thanksgiving Day 1960, Edward R. Murrow's TV broadcast, "Harvest of Shame," stunned the nation by revealing the poverty of rural workers. At the end of the 1950s, 1.5 million farmworkers, five-sixths of them white, had net yearly incomes less than $3,000. Most lived in the South in dilapidated housing without electricity and plumbing. Migrant farmworkers of every nationality had

Many Native Americans, like this man in a remote village in Alaska, still obtained water from unsafe or contaminated sources in the 1950s, despite the increasing affluence of other social groups.

virtually no protection from illegal labor practices that kept them poor and dependent.

Minority workers—Puerto Ricans, Mexican Americans, Native Americans, and Asian Americans—also earned extremely low incomes in occupations unprotected by minimum wage laws. Eighty percent of New York City's Puerto Rican families earned less than the government's estimated minimum levels for "modest but adequate" living standards. In California the average yearly income of Japanese and Chinese American families in 1959 was a lowly $3,000, but even that was higher than the income of Spanish-speaking workers. Native Americans appeared poorest of all nonwhites and lived in such squalor that their death rate was three times the national average.

American Indian peoples continued to struggle with problems of poverty and assimilation. Stimulated by wartime migrations, the urban Native American population more than doubled during the 1940s and reached 56,000 by 1950, but many faced severe economic hardships and discriminatory policies. In two southwestern states, Native American citizens were denied the vote until 1948, and officials routinely prevented them from receiving veterans' benefits and from making other civil claims.

Hoping to end Native American dependence on government, Congress passed the Indian Claims Commission Act of 1946, which allowed tribes to bring legal action against the federal government for violations of previous treaties. The Bureau of Indian Affairs (BIA) and congressional conservatives saw the measure primarily as an opportunity to terminate government responsibility for native peoples. Although many assimilated American Indians welcomed the opportunity to claim compensation for past wrongs, traditionalist leaders warned that termination would leave native peoples vulnerable to economic problems and cultural isolation. Yet Congress embraced detribalization by passing a series of termination laws in 1954 to dissolve tribal structures, disburse tribal assets, and end federal assistance. For the Menominee of Wisconsin and the Klamath of Oregon as well as 100 smaller groups, the policy created severe economic and social dislocation.

Unemployment rates on reservations were staggering—more than 70 percent among the Blackfeet of Montana and the Hopi of New Mexico and more than 86 percent among the Choctaw of Mississippi. Many job-seekers moved to nearby cities, where they lived in poverty. Off the reservations, traditional tribal rituals became less important, and the number of spoken Native American languages declined. Yet Indian peoples also mobilized resistance to white culture. Thus the postwar period also saw a revitalization of Native American religion and identity, particularly among the young. Assertions of American Indian pride helped block the termination program in the 1960s.

The economic situation among African Americans was more complex. As middle-class whites assumed new lifestyles in the suburbs between 1940 and 1970, 5 million blacks left southern farms for the North and West. By 1960 half the nation's African Americans lived in central cities. Migration to industrial areas helped to increase their incomes. Although less than 17 percent of the nation's blacks were in the middle-income category in 1940, nearly 47 percent were middle-income earners by 1970. Black social mobility was symbolized by the eradication of the color barrier in organized sports. In 1947 Jackie Robinson signed a contract with the Brooklyn Dodgers, becoming the first African American to play major league baseball in more than sixty years. By 1960 professional basketball and football had become racially integrated sports followed by millions of television viewers.

Despite such dramatic gains, black migrants to the cities often faced limited job opportunities. As technological advances reduced the number of blue-collar jobs, white-collar opportunities were shifting to the suburbs. Moreover, racial policies created disparities of salaries. African American women earned less as factory workers than white women did, and they continued to be relegated to unskilled or semiskilled jobs such as housekeeping, waitressing, and practical nursing. Similarly, black men earned a fraction of the wages paid to white men.

African American urban dwellers also confronted severe problems in acquiring satisfactory housing. Although Congress passed the Housing Act of 1949, authorizing slum clearance and construction of low-rent housing, the federal program was undermined by budget cutbacks and by uncooperative real estate interests, which blocked loan programs in inner cities. City planners found loopholes in the law that permitted the destruction of old buildings without replacement by low-cost rentals. One million postwar residential units faced the wrecking ball, but fewer than 350,000 took their place. Urban renewal programs worsened the situation. Such programs replaced old residential neighborhoods with convention centers, office buildings, parking lots, and other nonresidential units. During the postwar period every large city had a skid row with from 5,000 to 10,000 homeless people.

Urban newcomers also encountered patterns of racial discrimination supported by government policy. Through "restrictive covenants," white property owners and real estate agents adopted legal agreements to avoid selling or renting dwellings to minorities. "If a neighborhood is to retain stability," advised one federal guideline, "it is necessary that properties shall continue to be occupied by the same social and racial classes." In a practice known as redlining, the Federal Housing Authority (FHA) denied insurance coverage to racially integrated housing projects and discouraged loans to residents of older, racially mixed neighborhoods.

In 1948 the Supreme Court responded to a lawsuit, sponsored by the National Association for the Advancement of Colored People (NAACP)—*Shelley* v. *Kraemer*—by ruling that restrictive covenants were illegal. However, residential segregation persisted and affected African Americans and other minorities. Levittown, for example, did not accept African Americans until 1960. Of the nearly 1 million Puerto Ricans residing in New York City in 1960, 40 percent lived in inadequate dwellings, yet rent absorbed as much as one-third of their incomes. In higher income brackets, residential segregation affected such groups as Jews, Chinese Americans, and Japanese Americans, who tended to cluster in homogeneous communities.

City dwellers also found that the suburbanization of middle-class taxpayers decreased the urban tax base and curtailed municipal services. The increased use of automobiles resulted in a deterioration of mass transit for want of passengers. In cities such as Los Angeles, St. Louis, Philadelphia, and Salt Lake City, municipal officials accepted bribes from General Motors to replace inexpensive electric trolley cars with the company's gas-consuming buses. The resulting traffic congestion could not be eased even by the construction of new freeways in most major cities.

African Americans in southern states faced far harsher conditions than their northern counterparts did. Under the 1896 *Plessy* doctrine of "separate but equal," seventeen states required segregated public school facilities in

Earl Warren (1891–1974)

Of his eight years in the White House, President Eisenhower later said that the nomination of Earl Warren as Chief Justice of the Supreme Court in 1953 was "the biggest damnfool decision I ever made." Warren produced a number of constitutional surprises for the Republican White

House. In making the choice, Eisenhower had fulfilled a political debt. As the three-term governor of California, Warren represented the liberal wing of the Republican Party. He had run for vice president (with Thomas Dewey) in 1948 and remained an important "dark horse" candidate four years later.

Warren's political background had offered few clues to his subsequent career. As a California district attorney and state attorney general, he earned a reputation as a tough law enforcement officer. During World War II he advocated the confinement of all Japanese Americans regardless of their political beliefs. His position reflected an undisguised racism that viewed "Orientals" as essentially unassimilable. Elected governor in 1942, Warren supported liberal legislation in such areas as health insurance and prison reform.

Warren's appointment to the Supreme Court led to dramatic reversals of legal precedent. In his first major decision, *Brown* v. *Board of Ed-*

1951. Southern boards of education typically spent twice as much to teach white children as black children, and whites were four times as likely as blacks to finish high school. During the postwar era, civil rights groups led by NAACP lawyer Thurgood Marshall initiated legal suits to end academic discrimination. Benefiting from postwar criticism of racism, Marshall won legal victories against segregated law schools and graduate schools by arguing that the alternative black institutions were unequal in quality to white schools. Emboldened by these legal victories, the NAACP attacked public school segregation by denying that educational systems could be racially separate and still equal.

Using psychological evidence to argue that "prejudice and segregation have definitely detrimental effects on the personality development of the Negro child," Marshall persuaded the Supreme Court to reconsider the *Plessy*

ucation (1954), the Chief Justice dismantled the doctrine of "separate but equal" and paved the way for fundamental changes in race relations. Eight years later he carried the principle of democracy further by mandating the reapportionment of all legislative districts according to the principle of one person, one vote in *Baker* v. *Carr*. As in the *Brown* ruling, the decision attacked traditional political structures—in this case, state legislatures—that had enabled rural interests to ignore numeric majorities.

The California jurist also emerged as a strong defender of individual civil liberties. In the *Yates* decision (1957), he concurred in reversing the conviction of leading communists by differentiating between the theory of subversion and its actual practice. This position led to the eventual overthrow of certain loyalty oaths and state laws against communists. Under the principle of due process of law, he defended the rights of criminals to legal counsel (*Escobedo,* 1964) and to fair treatment by police (*Miranda,* 1966). The Warren-led Court tightened the interpretation of obscenity to protect the rights of free speech and freedom of the press from censorship. In 1962 the Court supported a rigid separation of church and state by denying prayer and Bible reading in public schools. Such opinions earned Warren the hatred of right-wing groups such as the John Birch Society, which called for his impeachment and stimulated the rise of populist conservativism after the 1960s.

doctrine. In a historic ruling delivered in May 1954 in *Brown* v. *Board of Education of Topeka*, the Supreme Court declared that segregating children "because of their race generates a feeling of inferiority . . . that may affect their hearts and minds in a way unlikely ever to be undone." In public education, the Court concluded, "'separate, but equal' has no place. Separate educational facilities are inherently unequal."

THE BIRTH OF A NEW CIVIL RIGHTS MOVEMENT

The *Brown* ruling landed like a bombshell on the political scene, forcing complacent politicians to rethink the goals of U.S. education and heralding a new era of civil rights protest. African Americans and southern whites alike perceived a new political force emerging to topple the old social order based on race and discrimination. Black leaders such as Thurgood Marshall believed that by attacking race prejudice in schools, the youngest Americans would learn the lesson that discrimination was undemocratic; other segregated institutions would soon disappear. The Council of Negro Education placed the ruling in the context of the Cold War against totalitarian communism. "We hail the decision, because it dramatically distinguishes our way of life in a democracy. . . . Here in the United States great social wrongs can be and are righted without bloodshed and without revolutionary means."

As African Americans and liberals expected the end of racial segregation in all aspects of social life, however, conservatives warned about the dangers of rapid upheaval. Responding to concern about implementing the *Brown* decision, the Supreme Court issued a second decree in 1955 ordering compliance with desegregation not immediately but "with all deliberate speed" and gave the responsibility for desegregation to federal district courts, which were dominated by traditional segregationist judges. The ruling opened a broad loophole for local defiance. "You are not required to obey any court which passes out such a ruling," advised Mississippi Senator James Eastland. "In fact, you are obligated to defy it." Some southerners opposed any alteration of traditional race relations; others resented the expansion of federal power over states' rights. Either way, segregationists endorsed "massive resistance" to public school integration.

As southern leaders defended segregation, African Americans took the initiative by organizing a grassroots civil rights movement that changed the face of U.S. life. The crusade began on a public transit bus in Montgomery, Alabama, in December 1955, when Rosa Parks, a local NAACP worker, refused to obey a law requiring segregated seating. Overnight, her arrest produced a carefully orchestrated citywide bus boycott led by Baptist minister Martin Luther King Jr. "We have known humiliation, we have known abusive language, we have been plunged into the abyss of oppression," King declared from the pulpit of the Dexter Avenue Baptist Church. "And we decided to rise up only with the weapon of protest. It is one of the greatest glories of America that we have the right to protest." The year-long boycott unified the African American community, but the Supreme Court had to intervene before municipal officials accepted bus desegregation. Montgomery showed the power of organized black protest and inaugurated the mass actions of the civil rights movement.

As African Americans adopted direct action protests against racial discrimination, southern resistance increased. State legislatures passed new laws making voter registration more difficult, harassed civil rights organizations (the NAACP was outlawed in several states), and sanctioned police violations of legal rights. Whites also created local citizens councils, which implemented economic reprisals against blacks who attempted to exercise their rights to vote or register their children in integrated schools. The rejuvenated Ku Klux Klan responded with acts of violence and a rash of bombings that targeted integrated schools, black churches, and Jewish synagogues. In 1955, fourteen-year-old Emmett Till, a Chicago youth visiting relatives in Mississippi, was murdered for whistling at a white woman. The acquittal of his accused killers showed that local law enforcement had failed. But the Eisenhower administration refused to intervene.

Affirming this policy of massive resistance, 101 defiant southern congressmen issued a "Declaration of Constitutional Principles" in 1956 that denied the power of the federal government to order desegregation in the states. Eisenhower, who personally opposed the *Brown* ruling, declared, "The final battle against intolerance is to be fought—not in the chambers of any legislature—but in the hearts of men." The president firmly rebuffed suggestions that he take a stand supporting the desegregation of public schools. But in response to appeals from Harlem Congressman Adam Clayton Powell, the White House ordered the desegregation of employment in southern navy yards and worked quietly to desegregate public facilities such as movie theaters in the District of Columbia. In 1956 Attorney General Herbert Brownell proposed legislation to protect African Americans' voting rights, but the measure died in a southern-controlled committee in the Senate. In the absence of clear support from the federal government, violence and coercion reduced the number of registered black voters in some southern states.

"Give us the ballot," declared Martin Luther King, "and we will no longer have to worry the federal government about our basic rights." On the third anniversary of the *Brown* ruling in 1957, African American leaders organized a Prayer Pilgrimage to Washington that attracted 30,000 protesters against racial discrimination. That year Eisenhower again requested legislation to protect the right to vote. This time the proposal won support from Senate Majority Leader Lyndon Johnson, who sought to broaden his national political appeal. Working behind the scenes, Johnson persuaded southern leaders to drop the filibuster in exchange for a mild bill. The new law called for a weak Civil Rights Commission and authorized the attorney general to seek injunctions for violations of voting rights. The measure was the first civil rights legislation since Reconstruction. However, in 1960 only 25 percent of eligible African Americans could exercise the right to vote.

Direct action by blacks soon forced the president to support desegregation. In September 1957 Governor Orval Faubus of Arkansas mobilized the National Guard to prevent the integration of Central High School in Little Rock, an action that violated a federal court order. While armed soldiers prevented nine black students from attending the school, Eisenhower remained aloof. Yet Faubus's defiance of federal authority threatened the constitutional system of government, and national protests aroused Eisenhower to action. "Law cannot be flaunted with impunity by any individual or mob of extremists," he

Richard B. Russell Jr. *(1897–1971)*

One of the great barons of the U.S. Senate at mid-century was Richard Russell. Styled as the "boy wonder" of Georgia politics, he was elected governor in 1930 at the age of thirty-three. Two years later he won a seat in the Senate, where he remained for the rest of his life. A bachelor who had spartan habits, Russell devoted himself completely to the Senate, and over the years as his seniority and his shrewdness grew, he became one of its most powerful members. Always mindful of details, he read every line of the *Congressional Record* daily and was an acknowledged master of parliamentary maneuver. Although he rejected an opportunity to become majority leader in 1953, Russell functioned as "dean of the Senate establishment," presiding over the informal inner club that largely dominated its affairs.

AP/Wide World Photos

Russell's career illustrated both the power and the frustration of ambitious southern politicians in an era of segregation. The systematic disenfranchisement of blacks, poor whites, and city dwellers produced a political system that generally did not challenge entrenched leadership.

conceded. The president then federalized the National Guard and ordered paratroopers to enforce the court decision. Despite continuing mob violence, black students began attending the school under federal military protection. Faubus managed to close the school the next year, but a court order ended Little Rock school segregation in 1959. Elsewhere in the South, school desegregation continued to provoke violence. By 1960 less than 1 percent of African American children attended integrated schools in southern states. In the North the Supreme Court decision did not address de facto segregation.

Despite southern white resistance, black activists kept the issue of segregation alive. In 1957 black religious leaders, including Martin Luther King, formed a coalition group, the Southern Christian Leadership Conference (SCLC). Committed to nonviolent civil disobedience, the group emphasized the spiritual righteousness of the cause and endeavored to touch the conscience

Once elected, members of Congress could expect a long tenure. Consequently, Russell, like many other southerners, steadily accumulated great power in a legislative branch that stressed seniority of membership. When the system assured them chairs of major committees, they could channel federal dollars to their constituents. An advocate of military preparedness almost from his earliest days in Congress, Russell became chair of the Senate Armed Services Committee in 1951. By 1960, Georgia had some fifteen military installations employing 40,000 people and was home to the major defense contractor Lockheed Aircraft.

Although the southern political system was an important element in Russell's power, it ultimately thwarted his broader ambitions by making him unacceptable to a national Democratic constituency. He tried to move the party away from reforms that would threaten states' rights by seeking the presidential nomination in 1952, but he was resoundingly defeated. A disappointed man, Russell increasingly devoted his energy and talents to opposing civil rights legislation. If the integrationists "overwhelm us," he declared, "you will find me in the last ditch." Tragically, both for his region and his own career, too much of Russell's talent and energy went into a misguided defense of what he considered to be "the Southern way of life."

of whites. A new generation of African Americans educated after World War II rejected compromise with racial injustice and demanded the full rights of citizens. Many were encouraged by the emergence of the new nations of black Africa in the late 1950s, which inspired hopes of freedom at home.

"All of Africa will be free," exclaimed novelist James Baldwin, "before we can get a lousy cup of coffee." Such anger and frustration provoked a series of disciplined nonviolent sit-in protests by African American college students at the lunch counters of Greensboro, North Carolina, in February 1960. The idea spread like wildfire through the southern states. Instead of waiting for legislative or judicial sanction, young blacks simply violated segregation laws and went to jail. These actions won support among white liberals, who joined African Americans in a national crusade for civil rights. During the next decade, these protests would alter forever the nation's political and cultural landscape.

CRITICIZING MASS CULTURE

The emergence of the black civil rights movement demonstrated deep cracks within the national consensus. But even middle-class beneficiaries of corporate capitalism raised questions about the moral tone and social values of postwar society. Although most agreed that U.S. business could provide superior economic satisfaction, many questioned the poverty of the nation's spiritual life. "The religion that actually prevails among Americans today has lost much of its authentic . . . content," observed Will Herberg, author of the popular *Protestant Catholic Jew* (1956).

The blandness of spirituality reflected a larger problem of alienation. "When white-collar people get jobs," cautioned sociologist C. Wright Mills in *White Collar* (1951), "they sell not only their time and energy but their personalities as well." Similar warnings came from such works as David Riesman's *The Lonely Crowd* (1950), Herbert Marcuse's *Eros and Civilization* (1955), and William Whyte's *The Organization Man* (1957). These books attacked the prevalence of social conformity, the decline in individual initiative, and the obsession with security in business and private life.

While critics of U.S. conformity lamented the loss of older male values of danger, risk, and virility, more and more middle-class women rejected the ideals of domesticity that endeavored to separate women from the male world of work. Despite the postwar baby boom, women curtailed childbearing at a relatively young age (slightly above thirty), leaving many years for active careers. Indeed, during the 1950s middle-class women—particularly married women with school-age children—entered the workforce in unprecedented numbers. Their private decisions added up to a mass movement of women's employment that would become a typical pattern in the next decade. Meanwhile, individual women decried the price of idealizing domesticity. The young poet Sylvia Plath put it succinctly by describing herself as living inside a "bell jar" of conformity.

Alternative voices also emerged in art, music, and comedy. Although the public preferred the representational painting of Thomas Hart Benton, Grant Wood, and Grandma Moses, a new group, abstract expressionists, turned New York City into an international center of nonrepresentational action painting. Jackson Pollock, Willem de Kooning, and Mark Rothko painted with vigorous line and color that compelled viewers to find meaning in the work on their own. Abstract painters also celebrated traditional national subjects, but suggested that surfaces could be deceiving. Larry Rivers's blurry, tongue-in-cheek version of *Washington Crossing the Delaware* (1953), for example, or Jasper Johns's numerous depictions of the American flag hinted at unease with patriotic subjects. In music, teenagers danced to rock and roll while their parents worked and shopped to Muzak. The bebop sound of Charlie

EXHIBIT **10-5**   **U.S. NATIONAL DEFENSE AND VETERANS OUTLAYS, 1955–1960 (IN BILLIONS OF DOLLARS)**

1955	47.4
1960	53.5

Source: *Statistical Abstract of the United States* (1987).

Parker and Dizzy Gillespie brought new vitality to jazz by offering hard-driving rhythms and complex, nonlinear harmonies. Nightclubs featured a new breed of "sick" comedians—Mort Sahl, Lenny Bruce, Dick Gregory—who derided social convention.

The strongest voices of protest came from a group of poets and writers who congregated in New York and San Francisco—the Beats. Jack Kerouac, William Burroughs, Lawrence Ferlinghetti, and Gary Snyder condemned the alienating effects of bureaucratic culture and called for a new spiritualism that would merge the body and the spirit. The Beats emphasized the spoken word and celebrated the human voice as an alternative to mass media. Most eloquent was poet Allen Ginsberg. In *Howl,* read aloud in 1955 and published the next year, he indicted a sterile society that watched "the best minds of my generation destroyed by madness." Strong, rolling cadences condemned "scholars of war" with their "demonic industries" and "monstrous bombs." Ginsberg pleaded with America to "end the human war." Here, in the cultural underground, lay the roots of protest and transcendence that would puncture middle-class illusions of stability and security in the 1960s.

THE END OF AN ERA

The emergence of dissident voices, the reawakening of the civil rights movement, the appearance of a youth culture, the shock of *Sputnik,* an economic recession in 1958, and the continuing Cold War with the Soviet Union—all fed a growing frustration with Eisenhower and the Republican leadership. In 1958 Democrats achieved landslide election victories and shifted the congressional leadership in a liberal direction. Since they now controlled the House by seventy votes and the Senate by thirty, the Democrats rejected the president's fiscal austerity and promptly voted to increase the military budget. Congress also admitted Alaska and Hawaii into the union in 1959 but carefully reversed the administration's priorities by welcoming the Democratic Alaska first. For the first time since 1925, the Senate rejected a White House cabinet nominee—Lewis Strauss, Eisenhower's choice to head the Department of Commerce—because of political disagreements. Despite these disputes, however, the administration worked with Congress to enact the National Defense Education Act of 1958 and the Landrum-Griffin labor law.

Lenny Bruce *(1926–1966)*

Lenny Bruce, a stand-up nightclub performer, emerged as the most controversial comedian of the postwar era. Using a jazz soloist's style, Bruce blended plain street talk with Yiddish and black idiom to satirize and demystify social conventions. His most scathing routines focused on reli-

gious hypocrisy, the artificiality of traditional sexual relationships, and racial prejudice. Because of his brutal honesty, the established media labeled Bruce and his colleague Mort Sahl "sick" comedians. "I'm not a comedian," Bruce retorted. "And I'm not sick. The world is sick and I'm the doctor. I'm a surgeon with a scalpel for false values. I don't have an act. I just talk." Even the title of his autobiography—*How to Talk Dirty and Influence People*—made fun of the popular homilies for success.

Born Leonard Schneider in New York, he joined the navy at the age of sixteen and saw active service in the Mediterranean. After the war Bruce hustled as a con artist for phony charities before drifting into comedy work in sleazy nightclubs and dance halls. But, by the mid-1950s, his brand of comedy captured national attention. He appeared on network television, made popular records, and captivated audiences at top nightclubs across the country.

Bruce's comic routines illuminated the anxieties and unspoken assumptions of postwar society. Although middle-class ethnic groups embraced homogenized suburban values (including, as in Bruce's case, the

After the death of Secretary of State Dulles in 1959, Eisenhower engaged more openly in personal diplomacy. In 1958 he sent Nixon on a goodwill tour of Latin America, but hostile crowds vigorously protested U.S. economic and political exploitation. The administration dismissed these demonstrations as examples of communist propaganda. Democrats disagreed. "It is foolish . . . to attribute anti-Americanism just to Communist agitation," explained Adlai Stevenson after a trip to Latin America in 1960. Rather, the Eisenhower administration "has been basically concerned with making Latin America safe for American business, not for democracy," especially by supporting "hated dictators."

changing of ethnic names), the comedian's sketches reaffirmed the vitality of ethnic, religious, and racial identity. While middle-class media celebrated traditional monogamous marriage despite a soaring divorce rate, Bruce spoke about alternative, premarital, extramarital, and homosexual relationships. He attacked middle-class consumption patterns, raged against bureaucracy and organized religion, and noted the absurdity of a Christian country waging endless war.

"All my humor is based on destruction and despair," he admitted. "If the whole world were tranquil, without disease and violence, I'd be standing on the breadline right in back of J. Edgar Hoover and . . . Dr. Jonas Salk." Bruce's insistence on creative freedom led him to attack legal censorship of free speech. "What's wrong with appealing to the prurient interest?" he wanted to know. "We appeal to the killing interest." His use of explicit language brought police reprisals, and he endured a series of arrests and court trials in several cities on charges of obscenity. He was also accused of using illegal drugs. The endless litigation drained his energy, and the subject of legal harassment came to dominate his nightclub act. "The halls of justice," quipped Bruce. "That's the only place you see the justice . . . in the halls."

As police departments worked with municipal courts to silence the irreverent comedian, Bruce died of a heroin overdose. His obscenity conviction, however, was overturned posthumously. Bruce's quarrel with censorship and his ability to merge humor about sex, race, and politics foreshadowed the radical and counterculture sensibilities that would influence U.S society after his death.

Attention soon focused on Cuba. After backing dictator Fulgencio Batista since 1952, Eisenhower reacted cautiously to the revolutionary government established by Fidel Castro in 1959. Although the United States offered Castro economic aid, the administration opposed Castro's agrarian reform laws because they nationalized private U.S. holdings. Eisenhower cut aid to Cuba and demanded immediate compensation. As relations between the two nations worsened in 1960, Castro announced the sale of sugar to the Soviet Union in exchange for economic and military assistance.

Eisenhower responded with a two-pronged attack. In 1960 the president ordered the CIA "to organize the training of Cuban exiles mainly in

Guatemala against a possible future day when they might return to their homeland." Meanwhile, the president exerted economic pressure by decreasing purchases of Cuban sugar. Castro protested that the reduction in U.S. sugar imports was a prelude to an invasion, and Soviet leader Khrushchev announced that his country would protect the Cuban government. Frustrated by Castro's audacity, Eisenhower severed diplomatic relations with Cuba in January 1961 and left the problem for his successor.

Eisenhower attempted nonetheless to reduce conflict with the Soviet Union. Since his "atoms for peace" proposal of 1953, the president had emphasized inspection and control as a precondition for disarmament. In 1956 he had sneered at Stevenson's call for a halt in nuclear testing, but a diplomatic conference among scientists in Geneva in 1958 indicated that controls could be implemented. Domestic science advisors also warned Eisenhower that strontium 90, an element of radioactive fallout from atomic testing, was threatening to poison the nation's food chain. Consequently, the president announced in 1958 that the United States was ending further nuclear testing. The Soviet Union performed a final series of tests before it too halted such explosions.

Despite these accommodations, Eisenhower vigorously resisted Khrushchev's demands that Allied forces depart from Berlin. "Any sign of Western weakness at this forward position," he declared in 1958, "could be misinterpreted with grievous consequences." Both powers now spoke about World War III, but in the next year tensions abated when Khrushchev and Eisenhower agreed to engage in personal diplomacy. In 1959 the Soviet leader toured the United States and met amicably with the president at Camp David. Although substantive issues remained unresolved, the two powers were close to agreement about nuclear arms.

The loss of a U-2 airplane destroyed those hopes. In May 1960, on the eve of a summit conference to discuss arms control, Khrushchev announced that the Soviet Union had shot down a U.S. spy plane. The administration immediately denied the charge and claimed that a "weather plane" had merely strayed off course. To Eisenhower's embarrassment, Khrushchev produced the CIA pilot, Francis Gary Powers, thereby revealing the president's lie. While the whole world watched anxiously, the State Department acknowledged the U-2 mission and justified such flights with the open-skies reasoning that the Soviets had rejected in 1955.

Eisenhower still hoped to salvage the summit conference. By claiming ignorance of the U-2 program, the president attempted to avoid complicity in the spy flight. Yet Eisenhower's disavowal of knowledge of the mission implied that subordinates were controlling crucial foreign policy decisions. The situation threatened the president's credibility as a political leader. Reluctantly, Eisenhower acknowledged his involvement. "It is a distasteful but vital necessity," he declared, reminding the public of the lessons of Pearl Harbor.

Eisenhower's admission destroyed the summit meeting. At the Paris session, Khrushchev denounced the president and refused to negotiate.

The intensification of the Cold War had a profound effect on public opinion. Democratic politicians criticized the president's clumsy diplomacy. More fundamentally, the U-2 affair shocked the public by revealing the government's dishonesty. Eisenhower, who strove to rise above parties, had lied not only to Khrushchev but to his own citizens. The notion of a credibility gap between the people and their government would haunt politicians for the next two decades. Together with the new voices of dissidence and the larger frustrations of corporate capitalism, some Americans would demand fresh answers to abiding social issues.

AMERICAN HISTORY RESOURCE CENTER

To explore documents, images, audio and video clips, articles, and commentary related to the material in this chapter, visit the source collections at ushistory.wadsworth.com and and use the Search function with the following key terms:

Ho Chi Minh
Montgomery Bus Boycott
Cuban Revolution
John Kenneth Galbraith

Southeast Asia Treaty Organization
Sputnik
Martin Luther King Jr.

RECOMMENDED READINGS

Stephen E. Ambrose, *Eisenhower* (1984). The second volume of a large biography of the president, this study provides a thorough and sympathetic account of administration policies at home and abroad.

Taylor Branch, *Parting the Waters: America in the King Years, 1954–1963* (1988). This detailed narrative of the civil rights crusade places the protest movement in historical context and underscores the great human effort involved in seeking change.

Jessica Weiss, *To Have and To Hold: Marriage, the Baby Boom, and Social Change* (2000). Placing marriage and family patterns of the 1950s in a longer historical perspective, this study stresses the innovative roles of postwar women in pursuing careers.

Daniel Belgrad, *The Culture of Spontaneity: Improvisation and the Arts in Postwar America* (1998). This book explores new styles of expression in art, poetry, music, and dance as a response to the values of corporate conformity.

Additional Readings

Eisenhower's response to the Vietnam crisis is described in James R. Arnold, *The First Domino: Eisenhower, the Military, and America's Intervention in Vietnam* (1991); in Melanie Billings-Yun, *Decision Against War: Eisenhower and Dien Bien Phu, 1954* (1988); and in the relevant chapters of Lloyd Gardner, *Approaching Vietnam* (1990). For China and the offshore islands issue, see Gordon H. Chang, *Friends and Enemies* (1990). The origin of the space race is analyzed in Walter A. McDougall, *The Heavens and the Earth: A Political History of the Space Age* (1985), as well as in Robert A. Divine, *Sputnik Challenge* (1993). For the disarmament question, see Robert A. Divine, *Blowing on the Wind: The Nuclear Test Ban Debate, 1954–1960* (1978). African American views about international affairs are discussed in Brenda Gayle Plummer, *Rising Wind: Black Americans and U.S. Foreign Affairs, 1935–1960* (1996). The links between foreign policy and domestic civil rights are examined in Thomas Borstelmann, *The Cold War and the Color Line: American Race Relations in the Global Arena* (2001).

For surveys of the postwar civil rights movement, see Harvard Sitkoff, *The Struggle for Black Equality: 1954–1980* (1981), and Manning Marable, *Race, Reform, and Rebellion: The Second Reconstruction in Black America, 1945–1982* (1991). The legal struggle to end racial discrimination is brilliantly described in Richard Kluger, *Simple Justice: The History of Brown v. Board of Education and Black America's Struggle for Equality* (1976). Also valuable are the first four volumes of *The Papers of Martin Luther King, Jr.* (1992–1999), edited by Clayborne Carson. An excellent study of the relationship between sports and race can be found in Jules Tygiel, *Baseball's Great Experiment: Jackie Robinson and His Legacy* (1983).

African American voting is treated in two books by Steven F. Lawson: *Black Ballots: Voting Rights in the South, 1944–1969* (1976), and *Running for Freedom: Civil Rights and Black Politics in America Since 1941* (1991). Federal jurisdiction is analyzed in Michael R. Belknap's *Federal Law and Southern Order: Racial Violence and Constitutional Conflict in the Post Brown South* (1987). Other studies include William Chafe, *Civilities and Civil Rights: Greensboro, North Carolina, and the Black Struggle for Freedom* (1980); Robert F. Burk, *The Eisenhower Administration and Black Civil Rights* (1980); and Juan Williams, *Eyes on the Prize: America's Civil Rights Years, 1954–1965* (1987). For an excellent single-state study, see John Dittmer, *Local People: The Struggle for Civil Rights in Mississippi* (1994). For the origins of the Southern Christian Leadership Conference, see Adam Fairclough, *To Redeem the Soul of America: The Southern Christian Leadership Conference and Martin Luther King, Jr.* (1987). Changes in southern society are described in Pete Daniel, *Lost Revolutions: The South in the 1950s* (2000); see also Jack Bass and Walter DeVries, *The Transformation of Southern Politics: Social Change and Political Consequence Since 1945* (1976).

For the Warren Court, see the relevant chapters of Paul L. Murphy, *The Constitution in Crisis Times: 1918–1969* (1972), and two fine biographies: G. Edward White, *Earl Warren: A Public Life* (1982), and Bernard Schwartz, *Super Chief: Earl Warren and His Supreme Court: A Judicial Biography* (1983).

Government policy toward Native Americans is described in Donald L. Fixico, *Termination and Relocation: Federal Indian Policy, 1945–1960* (1986); in Vine Deloria Jr., *Custer Died for Your Sins: An Indian Manifesto* (1969); and in the relevant chapters of Richard Drinnon, *Keeper of Concentration Camps: Dillon S. Myer and American Racism* (1987). The emergence of homosexual communities is well treated in John D'Emilio, *Sexual Politics, Sexual Communities: The Making of a Homosexual Minority in the United States, 1940–1970* (1983), and in Marc Stein, *City of Sisterly and Brotherly Loves: Lesbian and Gay Philadelphia, 1945–1972* (2000). See also Stephanie Coontz, *The Way We Never Were: American Families and the Nostalgia Trap* (1992).

The problems of youth are described in James Gilbert, *A Cycle of Outrage: America's Reaction to the Juvenile Delinquent in the 1950s* (1986). For the history of early rock and roll, see James M. Salem, *The Late Great Johnny Ace and the Transition from R&B to Rock 'n' Roll* (1999); Charlie Gillett, *The Sound of the City: The Rise of Rock and Roll* (1983); and Nelson George, *The Death of Rhythm and Blues* (1988). An examination of TV's impact on postwar society can be found in Lawrence R. Samuel, *Brought to You By: Postwar Television and the American Dream* (2001), and Lynn Spigel, *Make Room for TV: Television and the Family Ideal in Postwar America* (1992). Erik Barnouw's *The Image Empire* (1970) describes the television industry. Also interesting is Jeff Kisseloff's *The Box: An Oral History of Television, 1920–1961* (1995). For the movies, see Peter Biskind, *Seeing Is Believing: How Hollywood Taught Us to Stop Worrying and Love the Fifties* (1983), and Thomas Doherty, *Teenagers and Teenpics: The Juvenilization of American Movies in the 1950s* (1988). James Gunn's *Alternative Worlds: The Illustrated History of Science Fiction* (1975) surveys the genre. For the bebop revolt and social attitudes of black musicians, see the relevant chapters of Ben Sidran, *Black Talk* (1981). The fine arts are the subject of two excellent books: Serge Guilbaut, *How New York Stole the Idea of Modern Art: Abstract Expressionism, Freedom, and the Cold War* (1983), and Sidra Stich, *Made in USA: An Americanization in Modern Art, the '50s and '60s* (1987).

For a survey of dissident intellectuals, see Andrew Jamison and Ron Eyerman, *Seeds of the Sixties* (1994). Postwar novels and novelists are discussed in Josephine Hendin's *Vulnerable People: A View of American Fiction Since 1945* (1978). For the Beat writers, see Lawrence Lipton, *The Holy Barbarians* (1959); John Tytell, *Naked Angels* (1976); Dennis McNally, *Desolate Angels* (1979); and Michael Davidson, *The San Francisco Renaissance: Poetics and Community at Mid-Century* (1989).

THE AGE OF LIBERAL ACTIVISM, 1960–1965

"Somehow the wind is beginning to change," wrote liberal historian Arthur M. Schlesinger Jr. in the first month of 1960. "People—not everyone by a long way, but enough to disturb the prevailing mood—seem to seek a renewal of conviction, a new sense of national purpose." Writing in *Esquire* magazine, Schlesinger proposed a liberal agenda that ranged from education reform to equal rights for minorities, from more foreign aid to improved weapons. "Thus," he predicted, "the Sixties will probably be spirited, articulate, inventive, incoherent, turbulent, with energy shooting off wildly in all directions. Above all, there will be a sense of motion, of leadership and of hope."

Few historians have been so prophetic. Indeed, the 1960s introduced a new era of liberal activism. Rejecting Dwight Eisenhower's belief in limited government, Democratic Presidents John F. Kennedy and Lyndon B. Johnson advocated an active federal government to achieve economic and social progress. As African Americans and other minorities pleaded for political equality, liberal programs brought greater government benefits to disadvantaged groups. Such policies improved the rights and roles of minorities, but also accentuated conflicts between competing interests.

Kennedy and Johnson also pursued an assertive Cold War foreign policy that intensified global conflicts. Accepting the notion of a monolithic international communist conspiracy aimed at overthrowing capitalist democracies, the Democratic administrations focused attention not only on the Soviet menace but also on the status of smaller countries in the so-called third world. Prepared to defend such nations from communist infiltration, Washington boldly intervened overseas in Cuba and Southeast Asia. But in the new climate of the 1960s, such policies also provoked criticism and opposition at home, triggering a militant antiwar movement. By the end of the decade, the Cold War consensus had been replaced by bitter strife about the proper use of U.S. power at home and abroad.

THE ELECTION OF 1960

"The American people are tired of the drift in our national course," said Massachusetts Senator John Kennedy in launching his run for the presidency in 1960. For eight years Eisenhower had extolled the warrior virtues of strength and power. Yet the grandfatherly Ike, then the oldest man to serve as president, seemed helpless against Soviet Premier Nikita Khrushchev's indignation, the eruption of liberation movements in Asia and Africa, and anti-U.S. protests in Latin America and Japan. At home, voters blamed the administration for the recession of 1957–1958. "Wind up the Eisenhower doll," ran a popular joke, "and it does nothing for eight years."

Kennedy, at forty-two, was youthful in appearance (and concealing serious chronic illnesses), and he symbolized strength, vigor, and energy. In the Senate, he attacked the administration for creating a "missile gap" between Soviet and U.S. arsenals. "This is not a call of despair," he stated. "It is a call for action."

Kennedy's ambition benefited from great personal wealth, but his Roman Catholic religion remained a major handicap. Only one Catholic, Al Smith, had run for president, and he had suffered a devastating defeat in 1928. Kennedy challenged religious prejudices directly, entering a series of primaries against his major rival, Minnesota Senator Hubert H. Humphrey. Kennedy won their first contest in Wisconsin, but voting analysis showed that he carried Catholic districts, whereas Humphrey attracted Protestants. The race moved to West Virginia, an impoverished state with a 95 percent Protestant population. Humphrey shamelessly used the theme song, "Give Me That Old-Time Religion." Kennedy responded with an expensive campaign that emphasized his commitment to New Deal liberalism. A decisive victory over Humphrey overcame the issue of religion, and Kennedy went on to win a first-ballot nomination for the presidency. To balance the Democratic ticket in the South, he chose as his running mate Senate Majority Leader Lyndon Johnson of Texas.

Kennedy's Catholicism remained a controversial issue in the campaign against Vice President Richard M. Nixon. "I am not a Catholic candidate," Kennedy insisted. "I am the Democratic Party's candidate, . . . who happens also to be a Catholic." Vowing to maintain the separation of church and state, the nominee expressed disbelief that 40 million citizens "lost their chance of being president on the day they were baptized." Although since 1945 white ethnics had been accepted in many educational, business, and social organizations, religious prejudices still influenced political behavior. In the election, Kennedy won a high proportion of Catholic supporters but lost among Protestants. One exception was Kennedy's appeal to black evangelical Protestants.

Brown Brothers

John F. Kennedy responds to opponent Richard M. Nixon at their televised debate during the 1960 presidential contest.

When civil rights activist Martin Luther King Jr. was sentenced to prison for trespassing in a segregated restaurant in Georgia, a much-publicized telephone call from Kennedy to King's family revealed the candidate's genuine compassion as well as his astute political calculation. By appealing both to African Americans and white ethnics, Kennedy restored the New Deal coalition, but subsequent voting analysis suggested that the issue of religion probably cost him more votes than it won for him.

Religion seemed important in 1960 because the differences between Kennedy and Nixon remained small. Four nationally televised debates, which attracted more than 100 million viewers, spotlighted their similarities. Both candidates were cold warriors who vowed to end communist expansion and disagreed only about whether to defend the islands between mainland China and Taiwan. Both stressed the importance of economic growth. Both used the phrase "new frontiers" to evoke a spirit of opportunity and expansion. "Mr. Nixon says, 'We never had it so good,'" Kennedy stated in a typical remark. "I say we can do better."

Despite these common assumptions, television illuminated not the candidates' words but their manner of presentation. Radio listeners, who were not distracted by visual appearances, reacted favorably to Nixon's speeches; but television cameras accentuated the vice president's shadowy face and dripping makeup. In contrast, Kennedy projected self-confidence. Polls indicated that the debates may have swayed 4 million voters, three-quarters of whom supported Kennedy.

EXHIBIT **11-1   THE ELECTION OF 1960**

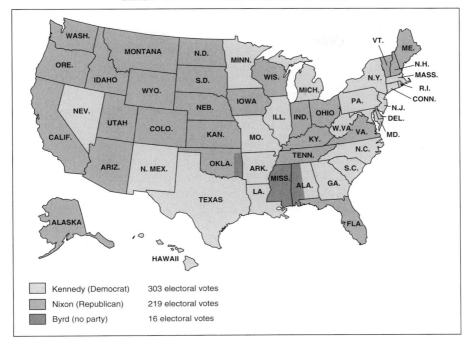

	Kennedy (Democrat)	303 electoral votes
	Nixon (Republican)	219 electoral votes
	Byrd (no party)	16 electoral votes

Such intangible factors had immense significance because the balloting was extremely close. Kennedy's popular majority was only 118,000—a margin of one-tenth of 1 percent. The Electoral College vote was 303–219, but these figures concealed paper-thin majorities and probable fraud in such key states as Illinois and Texas. Kennedy also trailed behind Democratic congressional candidates. Although the Democrats held control of both houses of Congress, most of the sixty-three new legislators subsequently voted against the White House on important issues. Because southern Democrats frequently aligned with Republicans, Kennedy lacked a working majority in Congress.

LAUNCHING THE NEW FRONTIER

Kennedy labeled his program the "New Frontier." "Let the word go forth that the torch has been passed to a new generation of Americans," he declared. With his slender majority, Kennedy's inaugural speech avoided domestic topics and focused exclusively on the international peril. Indeed, he exaggerated the Soviet threat. Although Khrushchev had recently advocated wars of national liberation, the Soviet leader was addressing criticism from his more radical Chinese ally rather than the United States. To Kennedy, however,

Khrushchev's speech had brought the nation to "its hour of maximum danger," and he stressed the "burden" of "relentless struggle." Said Kennedy: "Ask not what your country can do for you—ask what you can do for your country," but despite his dynamic language, he lacked a political base to initiate bold policy departures.

Kennedy's leadership reflected the era's distrust of emotionalism and ideology and extolled the virtues of scientific management and cold reason. "Most of the problems . . . that we now face are technical problems, are administrative problems," he said in 1962. "They are very sophisticated judgments which do not lend themselves to the great sort of 'passionate movements' which have stirred this country so often in the past." Matters of foreign policy, the president suggested, "are so sophisticated and so technical that people who are not intimately involved week after week, month after month, reach judgments which are based on emotion rather than knowledge of the real alternatives."

Secretary of Defense Robert S. McNamara typified the liberal leadership. Taking charge of the Pentagon, the former head of the Ford Motor Company initiated a program of rigorous cost-benefit accounting to determine military priorities. In place of Eisenhower's "massive retaliation," the new administration preferred flexibility, conventional arms for "brushfire" wars, and the elite Special Forces (Green Berets) for guerrilla warfare. Unlike Eisenhower, Kennedy rejected the use of nuclear weapons outside the strategic struggle with the Soviet Union. However, he did demand additional nuclear missiles even after learning that no "missile gap" existed. Within a month of the inauguration, the White House requested funds for missiles, warheads, and electronic support systems such as computer databases and orbiting communications and spy satellites. This emphasis on technological developments in turn encouraged a managerial revolution within the Pentagon. Under McNamara, the Defense Department centralized research and development and created a Defense Intelligence Agency to coordinate information.

Enthusiasm for technical management flourished in the space program. Five months after taking office, Kennedy used the continuing rivalry with the Soviets to call for a human landing on the moon by the end of the decade. "No single space project," he said, "will be more impressive to mankind." Vice President Johnson, author of the 1958 legislation that established the National Aeronautics and Space Administration (NASA), now served as chair of the National Aeronautics and Space Council and shared Kennedy's zeal. To Secretary McNamara, the space program promised to compensate the aerospace industry for cuts in military contracting demanded by cost-benefit analysis. Concerned about winning support from big business, Kennedy and Johnson endorsed private ownership of a communications satellite corporation and worked vigorously to overcome a 1962 Senate filibuster led by Tennessee's Estes Kefauver to block this federally supported private monopoly.

A carefully orchestrated public relations program reinforced popular support for space exploration. The media portrayed the first astronauts as all-American pioneers and heralded John Glenn's 1962 flight around Earth as a Cold War victory. As NASA planned Project Mercury (the circumnavigation of Earth by single astronauts, 1962); Project Gemini (multi-manned flights, rendezvous in space, and spacewalks, 1964–1965); and Project Apollo (moon landing, 1969), the space budget leaped fivefold by 1964 and accounted for 78 percent of all U.S. research and development. Although the White House emphasized the prestige of space exploration, expenditures served essential military functions involving ballistic missiles, communications, and intelligence gathering. For national security reasons, this aspect of the space program remained secret. Moreover, although the Outer Space Treaty—signed by sixty-two nations in 1967—would prohibit nuclear weapons in space and declare the moon a demilitarized zone, the defense strategy of both superpowers depended on continuing military operations in space.

THE POLITICS OF ECONOMIC GROWTH

As Kennedy took office in 1961, a Gallup poll found that 42 percent of the public hoped the president would pursue moderate policies; 24 percent hoped he would be conservative; and 23 percent desired a liberal position. This middle-of-the-road climate reinforced the cautious congressional leadership. Despite growing public concern about poverty, especially after the publication of Michael Harrington's influential book, *The Other America* (1962), Congress thwarted social reform. Although legislators responded favorably to Kennedy's request in 1961 for an Area Development Agency to stimulate industrial development in economically depressed areas such as Appalachia, Congress never provided sufficient funds to implement the program of road construction or encourage business relocation. By 1963 the entire state of West Virginia had gained only 350 jobs. Similarly, public housing legislation in 1961 permitted the razing of slums but failed to mandate adequate replacements. By 1967 some 400,000 buildings had been demolished, which resulted in more than 1.4 million displaced residents. Kennedy lacked enough political support even to introduce legislation providing hospital insurance for the elderly.

During the presidential campaign, Kennedy promised to produce a 5 percent annual rate of economic growth. This goal seemed especially relevant because the unemployment rate was 7.7 percent in January 1961. White House economic advisors, particularly the liberal Walter Heller, urged more vigorous federal spending. However, except for military appropriations, the president declined to request additional programs. Instead, Kennedy proposed a tax credit to encourage business investment in new plant equipment. By stimulating capital investment, he believed the measure would simultaneously attack

John H. Glenn Jr. (1921–)

"We have stressed the team effort in Project Mercury," said the nation's newest hero three days after becoming the first American to circumnavigate the Earth from outer space on February 20, 1962. "It goes across the board . . . sort of a crosscut of Americana, of industry and military and civil service, government workers, contractors—a crosscut of American effort in the technical field." At this moment of awesome technological achievement, however, astronaut John Glenn also symbolized the vitality of traditional earthbound virtues: love of family, religion, and patriotism.

NASA

Born and raised in small-town Ohio in the 1920s and 1930s, Glenn left home to become a Marine aviator during World War II and remained in the military as a combat flyer in Korea and later as a test pilot of jet aircraft. In 1957 he set the coast-to-coast speed record in a plane that required three midair refuelings with high-flying tankers. Such technical proficiency and iron-willed self-discipline qualified Glenn to become one of the seven original astronauts.

Glenn deliberately blended his enthusiasm for modern technology with old-fashioned Manifest Destiny. "I take my religion very seriously," the Presbyterian stated at the first Project Mercury press conference in 1959. "We are placed here with certain talents and capabilities. . . . I think we would be most remiss in our duty if we didn't make the full use

unemployment and stimulate long-term growth. To compensate for the loss of tax revenue, Kennedy requested the elimination of corporate tax loopholes such as expense accounts and tax-exempt foreign income. But these reforms adversely affected influential corporate leaders, and Congress delayed action until 1962. Meanwhile, large military expenditures boosted the sagging economy.

Concern about recession was soon supplanted by fear of inflation. In 1962 the president's Council of Economic Advisers announced wage-price "guideposts" to discourage inflationary increases. However, corporate leaders resisted efforts to regulate business costs and profits. The disagreement climaxed in a major clash between the White House and the nation's largest industry—

of our talents in volunteering for something . . . as important as this is to our country and to the world in general right now."

Framed by the Cold War with the Soviet Union, the space race pitted free-enterprise capitalism against state-supported technological planning. The U.S. astronauts were the human side of the competition. To the public's dismay, however, the nation appeared to be running second. Soviet cosmonaut Yuri Gagarin circumnavigated the globe in April 1961, a month before Project Mercury's first suborbital flight. Thus, despite serious technological malfunctions aboard Glenn's *Friendship 7* capsule, the mission restored national confidence in the space program. "This is the new ocean," declared Kennedy moments after Glenn splashed down in the Atlantic, "and I believe the United States must sail on it and be . . . second to none."

The public spontaneously embraced the sunny-faced astronaut. "I still get a hard-to-define feeling inside when the flag goes by," Glenn told a joint session of Congress, which interrupted his patriotic remarks twenty-five times with applause. Four million people—equivalent to half the population of New York City—lined the streets of lower Manhattan to form the largest ticker-tape parade crowd in history. During the next year Glenn received more than half a million letters of encouragement from around the country, was named Father of the Year, and was saluted for his patriotism by the Daughters of the American Revolution. Treated as a prophet of the space age, Glenn set his eyes on a Senate seat from Ohio, which he eventually won in 1974.

steel—in 1962. When the U.S. Steel company led other producers in increasing prices 3.5 percent, an amount the administration considered inflationary, the president responded by using the government's economic power to force the industry to retreat. McNamara instructed the Department of Defense to purchase steel only from noninflationary companies, and Attorney General Robert F. Kennedy ordered investigations of price-fixing. These pressures led one company to reject the price increase, a retreat that spread throughout the industry. Kennedy had effectively defended his economic strategy.

Although lower steel prices reduced costs for other manufacturers, business leaders bitterly resented this show of government economic power. A slumping stock market intensified their anger. In May 1962 Wall Street prices reached their lowest point since the Crash of 1929. The downturn reflected the belated impact of the 1960–1961 recession, which had reduced corporate earnings. However, the president's stand on steel prices disheartened elements of the business community, which blamed the administration for the slump. Kennedy responded by emphasizing his support of business, and the administration moved quickly to support corporate prosperity. The Treasury Department liberalized depreciation allowances for business equipment, thereby encouraging the replacement of older machinery. Congress finally enacted the proposed tax credit for new investments as well as tax reforms that gave business specific benefits. Kennedy endorsed new legislation favorable to the drug industry and lobbied Congress to permit private control of space communications.

This commitment to business culminated in the president's support of foreign trade. Since the late 1950s the economy had suffered imbalances of foreign payments, largely because of heavy spending for military bases abroad. In 1961 Kennedy created a new position in the Pentagon to encourage sales of U.S. arms to foreign nations. By 1962 the White House persuaded Congress to pass a foreign trade expansion bill.

Departing from the tradition of strict balanced budgets, Kennedy also embraced the "new economics" of John Maynard Keynes, who advocated deficit spending to stimulate the economy. Taking the advice of Keynes's disciples on the Council of Economic Advisers, Kennedy came to accept the theory that a tax cut would increase consumer spending and increase the rate of economic growth. In 1963 the president submitted a bill calling for a $13.6 billion reduction in taxes, mostly on individual incomes, as well as reforms that would shift the tax burden to upper-income brackets. The move set the stage for unprecedented economic growth.

THE CIVIL RIGHTS CRISIS

Despite campaign promises to the black community, Kennedy dragged his feet on civil rights. Recognizing the power of southern Democrats, the White House appeased regional demands for patronage by awarding federal construction projects to southern states, raising price supports on cotton, and declining to introduce civil rights legislation. Instead, the president took moderate executive actions such as creating the Commission on Equal Employment Opportunity (CEEO) in 1961. Headed by Vice President Johnson, the CEEO sought to end employment discrimination in work done under government contract. However, the commission preferred voluntary compliance and seldom punished violators.

Although Kennedy claimed during the 1960 campaign that Eisenhower could eliminate federal support of segregated housing "with the stroke of a pen," the president became remarkably silent when that power passed into his own hands. Civil rights leaders began sending pens to the White House. Hoping to win congressional approval for a Department of Urban Affairs, Kennedy refused to challenge segregated housing. Only after Congress defeated his efforts in 1962 did the president act to end segregation in federally funded housing. More than previous presidents, however, Kennedy appointed African Americans to government positions and allowed them to work in areas other than race relations.

Kennedy showed a similar lack of interest in women's rights. Although the president personally accepted the sexual revolution, he never connected changing sexual values with issues of power. The "new woman," according to Helen Gurley Brown's 1962 best-seller, *Sex and the Single Girl*, "took the pill and lived in an apartment with a double bed. She spent money on herself and men spent attention on her. She was the old feminist ideal of the independent woman with a new twist—she was sexy." Rising female employment and the sexual revolution bolstered a growing sense of female autonomy. By 1960 nearly 40 percent of women more than sixteen years old held jobs outside the home. Yet women workers earned only three-fifths of what men received and seldom held political power.

Although the radical National Woman's Party continued to press for an equal rights amendment to the Constitution that would guarantee legal equality to both sexes, Kennedy, like his predecessors, listened primarily to the liberals in the government's Woman's Bureau who advocated economic gains without threatening the existing laws that provided specific protections for women workers. In 1962 he created the President's Commission on the Status of Women, charged with making policy recommendations. "Equality of rights . . . for all persons, male or female, is . . . basic to democracy," the commission reported in 1963. That year Congress passed the Equal Pay Act, which provided equal wages for "equal work." However, the law excluded numerous jobs and lacked enforcement provisions, and the traditional segregation of occupations by gender further eroded the concept of "equal work." Still, at a time when the proportion of women in the workforce continued to increase, the federal government had begun to address widespread economic inequalities.

Kennedy's limited support of equal rights reflected the values of liberal reformism. Believing that changes in social relations could not be forced on the nation, the White House intended to follow rather than lead public opinion. The president appointed few women to significant offices. So while issues of gender equality were largely ignored, problems of race moved to the forefront of the national agenda. Kennedy had hoped to limit government action on race issues to enforcement of the voting rights provisions of the Civil Rights

Acts of 1957 and 1960. Yet his fear of white southern political power led him to appoint segregationist judges to federal courts in the South. One appointee openly referred to blacks as "niggers" and "chimpanzees."

African American activists resolved to move ahead of the White House to challenge legal segregation and force the federal government to protect equal rights. Following the nonviolent, direct action strategy of Martin Luther King and the sit-in demonstrators of 1960, the Congress of Racial Equality (CORE) embarked on interracial "freedom rides" in 1961 to desegregate interstate bus travel and commerce. As expected, violent mobs throughout the South viciously attacked the travelers, and local and state law enforcement authorities failed to provide minimal protection. The raw violence, coming on the eve of a summit meeting between Kennedy and Khrushchev, embarrassed the White House and compelled the federal government to intervene in areas of law enforcement that traditionally had been handled by the states. The president ordered federal marshals into the South and obtained court injunctions against interference with interstate travel. At the same time, however, the president's brother, Attorney General Robert Kennedy, asked the freedom riders for a "cooling-off period." "If we got any cooler," protested James Farmer, organizer of the freedom rides, "we'd be in a deep freeze." Meanwhile, the attorney general petitioned the Interstate Commerce Commission (ICC) to end segregation in interstate travel. Administration pressure led to the desired ICC ruling in 1961.

Thus, despite Kennedy's effort to remain aloof from the civil rights controversy, black activism and white intransigence demanded presidential intervention. In 1962 James Meredith, an African American air force veteran, won a federal court order to enter the all-white University of Mississippi. Governor Ross Barnett spoke for the southern leadership when he announced his refusal to comply with the ruling. Following Eisenhower's precedent of 1957, Kennedy federalized the National Guard and sent federal marshals and soldiers into the university town of Oxford. After a night of violence and bloodshed, Meredith gained entry into the university. However, Kennedy tried to avoid further antagonism of southern leaders by limiting federal interference to minimal legal protection and by refusing responsibility for local law enforcement.

While the White House sought to avoid racial confrontations, the Student Nonviolent Coordinating Committee (SNCC) proceeded with a voter registration campaign among disenfranchised blacks. This Voter Education Project, funded by northern liberal foundations but implemented primarily by courageous white and black students, soon provoked a violent reign of terror—beatings, bombings, and murders—to prevent the expansion of the African American electorate.

As in the case of the freedom rides, civil rights workers discovered that the federal government failed to provide adequate protection on the grounds that it lacked a statutory right to intervene. As liberals and activists protested White House inertia, the president introduced a civil rights bill in February 1963 that called for prosecution of voting rights violations, federal funds to encourage school desegregation, and extension of the Civil Rights Commission. "We are committed to achieving true equality of opportunity," said Kennedy, "because it is right."

African American leaders, however, wanted more fundamental changes and rejected Kennedy's modest proposal. In the spring of 1963 King's Southern Christian Leadership Conference (SCLC) carried the civil rights crusade to Birmingham, Alabama, purportedly "the most thoroughly segregated big city" in the nation. The movement's nonviolent strategy aimed at producing so much "creative tension" that segregationist leaders would feel compelled to negotiate a peaceful settlement. As noisy but peaceful marchers paraded downtown, local police chief "Bull" Connor ordered violent arrests that filled the jails. After weeks of futile demonstrations, civil rights leaders feared the crusade would fail for want of volunteers who could afford to be arrested and rearrested. African American leaders decided to find recruits among the city's youth, some as young as six years old. Birmingham police proceeded to attack the children with clubs, fire hoses, and vicious dogs. The brutality not only steeled the nerves of black protesters, but because of wide television coverage, it sent waves of outrage throughout the land.

Southern resistance flared again a few weeks later when Governor George Wallace stood in a doorway at the University of Alabama and tried to block the court-ordered admission of two black students. Federal marshals accompanying the students obliged the governor to step aside, but the ritualistic gesture of defiance encouraged President Kennedy to reaffirm his commitment to federal authority and civil rights. "We face . . . a moral crisis as a country and as a people," he told a television audience. "It cannot be met by repressive police action. It cannot be left to increased demonstrations in the streets." Kennedy's speech signaled the administration's determination to enact civil rights laws. But that night Mississippi's NAACP leader Medgar Evers was shot to death outside his home. Kennedy immediately introduced a broad new civil rights bill to prohibit racial discrimination in public accommodations, to authorize the Justice Department to initiate suits to desegregate public schools, to improve black employment opportunities, and to protect voting rights. Although African American leaders questioned loopholes in the proposal, few doubted the clarity of Kennedy's moral position.

As Congress began to consider the civil rights bill, black leaders staged a show of strength by organizing a March on Washington. The president initially discouraged the demonstration, but civil rights activists refused to retreat. On August 28, 1963, about 250,000 marchers converged at the Lincoln Memorial in the nation's capital and heard Martin Luther King Jr. proclaim, "I have a dream . . . that the sons of former slaves and the sons of former slave owners will be able to sit together at the table of brotherhood." King's passionate language electrified the crowd. However, other voices in Washington indicated differences within the African American community. John Lewis of SNCC attacked the administration for its "immoral compromises" with conservative politicians. "If any radical social, political, and economic changes are to take place in our society," he said, "the people, the masses must bring them about. . . . We must seek more than mere civil rights; we must work for the community of love, peace, and true brotherhood."

While liberals like Senator Hubert Humphrey lined up votes for the civil rights bill, southern representatives vowed to kill the measure by parliamentary procedures. But southern extremists spoke louder by detonating a bomb in a Birmingham church, killing four black girls. No local officials apologized for the violence. Such intransigence fed a counterresponse from black nationalist Malcolm X, who had ridiculed the March on Washington. Recognizing the importance of achieving political power as a precondition for racial progress, Malcolm rejected the limited horizons of racial integration. "A revolutionary," he asserted in 1963, "is a black nationalist."

THE COLD WAR ON NEW FRONTIERS

In continuing the Cold War, Kennedy kept his eye on Moscow and Beijing; but the president also believed that the nations of Asia, Africa, and Latin America held the key to victory. To energize the nation's youth for that struggle, Kennedy created the Peace Corps in 1961, encouraging volunteers to serve "on a mission of freedom" around the world. Kennedy also launched a Food for Peace program to send surplus food to poor countries. By 1963 the plan was feeding 93 million people each day. Nor did Kennedy, unlike Eisenhower, insist that neutral nations take sides in the Cold War. In the former Belgian colony of the Congo, for example, the United States supported a United Nations peace mission to back a neutral government, although the White House allowed the CIA to provide secret payments and military aid to friendly Congolese politicians.

Kennedy also proposed "a new alliance for progress" in Latin America. Promising technical expertise and capital investment, the president envisioned major agrarian reform and public welfare within democratic institutions. In 1961 the administration pledged $20 billion to alleviate poverty and bring social reform. These funds boosted U.S. prestige, but Kennedy had no intention of altering Latin American politics. Instead, Washington continued to cooperate with conservative landed elites and their military allies.

American corporations also hesitated to invest in unstable countries. In 1962 Congress approved the Hickenlooper Amendment, which stopped foreign aid to countries that nationalized or excessively taxed corporate property.

The Executive Committee of the National Security Council deliberating during the Kennedy administration.

The next year the Foreign Assistance Act established an investment guaranty program that required recipients of U.S. aid to insure investors against losses due to nationalization. Most aid to Latin America went in the form of loans, rather than grants, and had to be repaid with interest and service charges (usually amounting to half the face value of the loan). And even these limited funds had to be spent within the United States at prevailing prices.

The Alliance for Progress aimed to blunt the appeal of Fidel Castro's revolutionary Cuba. During his last days in office, Eisenhower had broken diplomatic relations with Cuba and ordered the CIA to plan a military coup. As a presidential candidate, Kennedy endorsed the overthrow of Castro. Believing that Castro did not represent the Cuban people and could be toppled with sufficient pressure, Kennedy urged business leaders to boycott Cuba and banned the importation of Cuban sugar.

Anti-Castro activities culminated in a military invasion of Cuba at the Bay of Pigs in April 1961, by 1,400 Cuban exiles trained and organized by the CIA. But the CIA planned badly, choosing an indefensible landing position and mismanaging air attacks. Recognizing an imminent disaster, the White House refused to provide additional air support, which doomed the mission. Most seriously, the president had underestimated the strength of Castro's political base.

Although U.S. media had received unofficial leaks about the Bay of Pigs operation, the administration persuaded publications such as the *New York*

Times to suppress the story. "There will not be, under any conditions, an intervention in Cuba," the president told a press conference five days before the mission. Secretary of State Dean Rusk lied blatantly: "The American people are entitled to know whether we are intervening in Cuba or intend to do so in the future," he said on the morning of the invasion. "The answer to that question is no. What happens in Cuba is for the Cuban people to decide." In justifying the invasion, Kennedy saw Castro as a pawn in the Cold War. "We are opposed around the world by a monolithic and ruthless conspiracy," he told the nation's leading news editors, "that relies primarily on covert means for expanding its sphere of influence." The president urged the news media to limit reporting of world events. "Every democracy," he claimed, "recognizes the necessary restraints of national security."

In the aftermath of the Bay of Pigs fiasco, Kennedy permitted the CIA to conduct illegal military activities against Castro, provided they were "plausibly deniable." The CIA proceeded to disrupt Cuban trade with the Soviet Union, in one case contaminating a shipload of sugar with bad-tasting chemicals. Secret CIA operations included support of anti-Castro exiles and underworld gangsters who attempted to assassinate the Cuban leader. Kennedy also exerted economic pressure by prohibiting trade with the island. Such destabilization efforts drew Castro closer to the Soviet Union.

Having failed in Cuba, however, Kennedy resolved to prove his strength on the issue of Germany. Although the Soviet Union wanted to formalize the existence of two German states—one linked to the communist bloc, the other to the West—and thereby force the Western Allies to leave Berlin, Washington demanded the unification of Germany through free elections (in which the larger population of West Germany would predominate). Soon after taking office, Kennedy asked Congress for increased military appropriations to build a preponderance of power that would force the Kremlin to accept U.S. terms. In this spirit he agreed to meet Khrushchev in Vienna in June 1961.

Kennedy underestimated Soviet resolve. In a blistering encounter, Khrushchev reminded the president that World War II had ended sixteen years earlier and demanded that the Western powers sign a final peace treaty that recognized the two German states and terminated the military occupation of Berlin. Kennedy refused to abandon Berlin. Instead of easing international tensions, the summit conference intensified the Cold War.

The president now asked Congress for another $3 billion military appropriation, which doubled the total military spending package in his first six months in office. Kennedy also called up military reserves and extended the draft. Finally, in a gesture that spread horror throughout the land, the president requested increased appropriations for civil defense and bomb shelters. Khrushchev then ordered the erection of a military barrier between East and West Berlin in August 1961, which ended the flood of refugees from East Germany and showed his determination to preserve two German states. Despite an extreme atmosphere of crisis, Kennedy resolved to test Soviet strategy by ordering 1,500 battle-ready troops to drive from West Germany into West Berlin, where they would be met by Vice President Johnson. Khrushchev decided not to worsen the situation. After U.S. troops entered West Berlin, Khrushchev scrapped his deadline for settling the Berlin question, and the crisis passed.

The Cold War intensified that same month when the Soviet leader announced the resumption of nuclear bomb testing. Within a week, Kennedy declared that the United States would also resume underground testing. Two days later *Life* magazine published an article, endorsed by Kennedy, asserting (erroneously) that a national program of fallout shelters would ensure a 97 percent survival rate in the event of nuclear war. The news precipitated the first major protests against nuclear testing by peace organizations such as the National Committee for a Sane Nuclear Policy (SANE) and the Student Peace Union. As Soviet tests escalated to the 50-megaton level, the White House heightened tensions by revealing to Khrushchev that U.S. intelligence knew the extent of Soviet military weakness. The president proposed disarmament talks that would preserve the U.S. advantage. When the Soviets objected to international inspection, Kennedy ordered a resumption of atmospheric tests.

THE CUBAN MISSILE CRISIS

In admitting the nonexistence of a "missile gap," Kennedy increased Soviet concerns about the imbalance of power. The White House accentuated the problem by announcing a shift in nuclear strategy in 1962. Hereafter, U.S. missiles would be aimed not at Soviet cities but at nuclear missile sites. Such targets meant that a U.S. first strike could destroy Soviet power to retaliate. This disadvantage may have influenced Khrushchev's decision to place less expensive short-range missiles in Cuba. In the aftermath of *Sputnik*, the United States had pursued a similar policy by establishing missile bases in Turkey and Italy. Khrushchev also wanted to discourage U.S. military action in Cuba.

During the summer of 1962, Soviet troops in Cuba began building sites to base missiles with a striking range of 2,000 miles, sufficient to reach East Coast cities or the Panama Canal. The Soviets had also placed nearly 100 nuclear warheads on the island—most attached to tactical rockets with a 15- to 20-mile range. The United States did not learn about the presence of the warheads until the 1990s, but when U-2 spy planes confirmed intelligence reports of the missiles, Kennedy summoned a top-level executive committee in October 1962 to consider U.S. responses. The choices ranged from immediate military attack (a "Pearl Harbor in reverse," objected Robert Kennedy) to a diplomatic retreat by closing U.S. missile bases in Turkey if the Soviets removed theirs from Cuba. A consensus eventually emerged that considered armed intervention only as a last resort. Kennedy also overruled his more militant advisers—the

EXHIBIT **11-2**   **CUBAN MISSILE CRISIS**

Joint Chiefs of Staff, National Security Adviser McGeorge Bundy, Secretary Rusk—and agreed to trade the removal of U.S. missiles in Turkey and Italy for Soviet missiles in Cuba. He did not reveal this concession to many in his administration nor to the public, lest he face criticism for "appeasement" of communism.

In a dramatic televised speech, Kennedy described Soviet intervention as "deliberately provocative" and demanded the removal of all missiles. "We will not prematurely or unnecessarily risk the cost of worldwide nuclear war in which the fruits of victory would be ashes in our mouth," he promised, "but neither will we shrink from that risk at any time it must be faced." As the world approached a nuclear holocaust, Kennedy announced the establishment of a "quarantine"—a naval blockade—to keep offensive weapons from Cuba.

Khrushchev had not anticipated Kennedy's outraged reaction. In a private letter to the president, the Soviet leader protested the demand for unconditional surrender. Yet Khrushchev did not want to start a war that "would not be in our power to stop." In a second, emotional letter, the Soviet leader emphasized that Soviet ships in the mid-Atlantic carried nonmilitary goods and that the missiles had already arrived in Cuba. He offered to remove the weapons provided that the United States end the blockade and agree to respect Cuban independence. "Only a madman," Khrushchev wrote, "can believe that armaments are the principal means in the life of a society."

The next day the president received still another message from Khrushchev that stiffened the terms for removal of the missiles. The Soviet leader now demanded the withdrawal of missiles from Turkey in exchange for withdrawal of those in Cuba. Months earlier, Kennedy had questioned the value of those outmoded weapons; but during the crisis, the White House publicly refused to discuss the question, fearing to suggest a wavering of national policy.

Kennedy decided to ignore Khrushchev's last letter and answer only the more conciliatory message that preceded it. The formal reply therefore made no mention of U.S. missiles in Europe; only privately did Kennedy agree to remove them from Turkey and Italy. Khrushchev then accepted the arrangement, and the crisis passed. Two months later, Kennedy admitted that the Cuban missiles would not have changed the military balance of power. "But it would have politically changed the balance of power," he explained. "It would have appeared to, and appearances contribute to reality." Although Khrushchev's retreat enhanced the president's reputation, the diplomatic victory obscured Washington's failure to change the government of Cuba. While Castro remained in power, the frustrated administration continued a secret program to assassinate the Cuban leader and overthrow the communist regime.

TOWARD DÉTENTE

The brush with nuclear war convinced both Kennedy and Khrushchev to seek an end to nuclear testing. At the same time, the international balance of power shifted dramatically when Soviet and Chinese leaders split over the issue of the future of world communism. The breakup of the Sino-Soviet alliance, although still incomplete, persuaded Moscow to seek accommodation with the West. One remaining stumbling block was Khrushchev's refusal to allow on-site inspections to verify compliance with a test ban treaty.

As the two superpowers resumed negotiations, Kennedy placed his faith in U.S. technology—satellite photographs and distant seismography. In a dramatic speech at American University in June 1963, the president introduced a major reevaluation of the Cold War. Explaining that the United States did not seek "a Pax Americana enforced . . . by American weapons of war," he assured the nation that "we can help make the world safe for diversity." Kennedy announced he was sending a mission to Moscow to negotiate a test ban treaty, and in an act of "good faith" he ordered a halt on nuclear testing.

As questions of inspection and underground testing were set aside, negotiators quickly reached agreement. Yet the treaty required the approval of the Senate, the Pentagon, and public opinion. In seeking this support, the administration emphasized that the test ban constituted a victory because the United States held a clear lead in nuclear technology. Kennedy also assured the Pentagon that underground tests would continue, promises that were fulfilled after the Senate ratified the treaty in September 1963.

Although Kennedy expressed interest in improving relations with the Soviet Union and approved the sale of surplus U.S. wheat to Russia, he worried about a weakening of the Western Alliance. During the summer of 1963 the president journeyed to Europe and reaffirmed the impossibility of compromising with communism. "Today, in the world of freedom," he told a cheering throng in West Berlin, "the proudest boast is 'Ich bin ein Berliner.'" ("I am a Berliner.") Kennedy never wavered from his Cold War stance. In his last, undelivered speech, the president defined his sense of his historic mission: "We in this country, in this generation, are, by destiny rather than choice, the watchmen on the walls of world freedom."

COMMITMENTS IN VIETNAM

In seeking greater flexibility in the Cold War, Kennedy argued in 1961 that "the great battlefield for the defense and expansion of freedom today is the whole southern half of the globe—Asia, Latin America, Africa, and the Middle East—the lands of the rising peoples." Here the president saw communism "nibbling away" at the forces of freedom. Having been humiliated at the Bay of Pigs and having agreed in Vienna to a neutral Laos, Kennedy resolved to act decisively in Vietnam. Kennedy thus followed Eisenhower's policies, continued to reject the 1954 Geneva Accords, and refused to consider a neutral Vietnam state.

By 1961 the U.S.-backed regime of Ngo Dinh Diem was rapidly losing support to the newly established communist National Liberation Front (known as the Vietcong) as well as to noncommunist dissidents such as Buddhist priests. Kennedy responded to this pressure by increasing the number of military advisors and dispatching Green Berets and intelligence agents to engage in covert warfare in 1961. Although presidential advisors recommended additional military assistance, Kennedy hesitated to commit conventional forces and risk a repetition of the Korean War. The White House also urged Diem to offer political reforms to broaden support among Buddhists and the peasantry, but without success.

With increased U.S. military aid, the level of violence increased. In 1962 the Vietcong indicated a willingness to negotiate the neutralization of South

Vietnam, but the White House remained optimistic about military victory and rebuffed the approach. Meanwhile, U.S. advisors persuaded Diem to experiment with counterinsurgency based on "strategic hamlets." Assuming that guerrilla armies required a popular base of support, advisors proposed the encampment of the peasant population behind barbed wire. Depriving the Vietcong of their support base would cause them to disappear. However, the hamlets could not be defended, and the peasants resented being forcibly uprooted.

"Every quantitative measurement we have," declared McNamara with his faith in numbers, "shows we're winning this war." The State Department confirmed this optimism, announcing that 30,000 Vietcong were killed in 1962. Yet that figure was twice the estimated number of the entire Vietcong organization at the beginning of the year. Exaggerated administration claims stemmed not only from poor calculations but also from a deliberate effort to deceive Congress and the nation about the nature of the U.S. commitment. When the *New York Times*'s Saigon reporter David Halberstam reported failures of U.S. policy, Kennedy personally asked the newspaper to reassign him elsewhere.

By 1963 the Vietcong were stepping up terrorist attacks against the Diem regime. Yet Diem refused to institute political reforms. Tensions exploded in 1963 when South Vietnamese troops fired on a crowd of demonstrators and Buddhist priests set themselves on fire to protest political abuses. These events embarrassed the administration, but Kennedy took refuge in the domino theory. "For us to withdraw from that effort," he said, "would mean a collapse not only of South Vietnam, but Southeast Asia. So we are going to stay there." But the administration began to plan a military coup to remove Diem from power. On November 2, 1963, South Vietnamese army officers, encouraged by the U.S. embassy, killed their president.

The murder shocked Kennedy but did not alter his Vietnam policy. By November 1963 the administration had stationed 16,000 troops in South Vietnam. The previous month, Kennedy had announced the withdrawal of one thousand men by the end of the year and said that the U.S. commitment would end in 1965. His words probably reflected the same misplaced optimism that characterized U.S. policy toward Vietnam throughout the decade. Recently declassified audiotapes suggest that Kennedy still believed a military victory was possible. Perhaps, with Diem dead, the president would have considered a political solution to the war, just as he proposed a political response to the Cuban missile crisis. The remaining evidence provides no perfect answer.

ASSASSINATION AND THE YOUTH MOVEMENT

Kennedy did not live to fulfill his programs. On a political junket to Texas designed to strengthen the Democrats in the 1964 elections, the president was shot and killed by sniper fire in Dallas on November 22, 1963. The alleged assailant, Lee Harvey Oswald, denied his guilt but was killed in police custody by mobster Jack Ruby before he could testify. The mystery surrounding Kennedy's death contributed to the political turmoil of the decade. Although a special presidential commission headed by Chief Justice Earl Warren reported in 1964 that Oswald was a "loner" and had acted alone, the public widely believed the murder was part of a conspiracy. A 1966 Gallup poll found that a majority doubted the validity of the Warren report, although a majority also opposed reopening the case.

The assassination shocked the nation—not only because of the sudden death of the president but also because of the disruption of the normal continuity of public life. To most citizens the events surrounding the assassination emerged as a shared emotional experience. Surveys found that 92 percent of the public learned of the assassination within 2 hours, and that more than half of the entire population watched the same television coverage of the story. (For three days, the networks canceled all advertising!) Millions watched Jack Ruby shoot Oswald. The mass public mourning greatly magnified the slain president's stature. Local governments named and renamed public buildings in his honor; Kennedy's grave at Arlington National Cemetery became a national shrine; Kennedy memorabilia (picture books, coins, paintings, and jewelry) proliferated. Ironically, Kennedy created in death what had eluded him in life—a broad affirmation of consensus that transcended the differences of traditional politics.

The emotional intensity of the Kennedy assassination coincided with the coming of age of the first baby boomers (the cohort born just after World War II). Twice as numerous as their parents, teenagers formed a distinctive, self-conscious culture whose sheer numbers exerted tremendous economic and political power. Having grown up in the prosperous 1950s, the rising generation accepted affluence and consumption as expressions of its uniqueness. As children, baby boomers created an enormous market for diaper services, toys, and toddlers' shoes; as teenagers, the same generation consumed vast quantities of records, costume jewelry, and apparel. Purchasing power set the stage for the youth rebellion of the 1960s.

Nothing better expressed the teenagers' quest for personal independence than rock and roll. Just months after the Kennedy assassination, the British Beatles launched their first U.S. tour and instantly became icons of antiestablishment feelings. During the 1960s teenagers and college students crowded dance floors that reverberated to the rhythms of the "Motown sound," a hard-driving "soul" music named for the black Detroit record company that produced it. Black performers such as Ray Charles, James Brown, Otis Redding, Aretha Franklin, the Supremes, and the Temptations offered the new generation an alternative to sexually repressed music. Meanwhile, the arrival of British fashions such as long hair, miniskirts, and working-class blue jeans encouraged liberation of the body and a new confidence in defying social decorum.

The idea of choosing one's "lifestyle" reflected a changing morality associated with the "sexual revolution." Even before the introduction of the birth control pill in 1960, couples were engaging more frequently in nonmarital intercourse. The trend accelerated and received more attention during the 1960s. Surveys showed that the age of first sexual experience continued to decline and that the frequency of sexual intercourse within all social classes increased. Easier attitudes toward sexuality also led to a rise in unwanted pregnancies and an average of half a million illegal abortions each year.

The sexual revolution also undermined traditional definitions of obscenity and pornography. In a series of landmark cases in the late 1950s, the Supreme Court outlawed censorship of such literary classics as *Fanny Hill*, D. H. Lawrence's *Lady Chatterley's Lover,* and Henry Miller's *Tropic of Cancer.* By the mid-1960s Hollywood had replaced its 1930s production code with a rating system that permitted nudity and obscene language as well as "mature" themes. Traditional morality and censorship persisted on television, but commercial advertising increasingly introduced sexual themes and suggestive comments. Images of women, for example, shifted from dutiful housewives to sexually seductive singles.

The sheer number of baby boomers precipitated a large assault on adult institutions. As a result of economic prosperity and the service industry's demands for extended education, college enrollment doubled to 10 million in the 1960s. Increasingly independent college youth no longer accepted control of their private lives by student deans, who customarily had used curfews, sexual segregation, and threats of expulsion to dictate social behavior. During the 1960s most campuses abolished the doctrine of *in loco parentis* ("in place of parents"), which treated students as children rather than young adults. Students won the right to live in coeducational dormitories, to have opposite-sex visitors, and to stay out at night. This freedom of personal expression extended to campus political rights, including the publication of uncensored newspapers and magazines, the recruitment of political support, and public demonstrations.

Drugs became one of the most controversial routes to youth independence. Although earlier generations had consumed alcohol to defy adult morality, teenagers and college students increasingly used marijuana as a rite of initiation into youth culture. Harvard University psychologists Timothy Leary and Richard Alpert experimented with the government-provided hallucinogen LSD ("acid") and discovered states of "expanded" consciousness that approached religious ecstasy. When the university fired them for unprofessional conduct in 1963, Leary assumed the role of LSD "guru," advising a generation of students to "turn on, tune in, and drop out."

The cultural rebellion of middle-class youth paralleled an emerging political movement among a smaller segment of college students known as the "New Left." Student-led civil rights activity in the South had ignited radical dissent across the country. After the sit-ins of 1960, veteran activist Ella Baker

Bob Dylan *(1941–)*

Bob Dylan's intense musical style and provocative songs made him a major catalyst and symbol of the cultural crisis of the 1960s. Dylan first captured national attention by merging blues and country music with the left-wing political content of the urban folk music scene. Then in

AP/Wide World Photos

1965 he abruptly adopted the raucous sounds and electrified motifs of rock and roll, which he combined with surreal images and poetic phrasing to attack prevailing middle-class values and institutions.

Born Robert Zimmerman and raised in a small town on Minnesota's Iron Range in the 1950s, the young musician identified with the alienation expressed by actor James Dean and, like the Beat writers, concocted fantasies of escape. In 1960 he changed his name to Dylan and took off for New York in search of his hero, folksinger Woody Guthrie, troubadour for radical causes since the 1930s.

Dylan began singing in folk clubs in Greenwich Village, responding to the events and themes of the sixties. His 1962 song, "Blowin' in the Wind," denounced the complacence of middle-class society and quickly became an anthem of liberal dissent. He wrote many songs in support of the civil rights movement ("Oxford Town," "Who Killed Davey Moore?") and performed at the March on Washington in 1963. The Cuban missile crisis inspired "A Hard Rain's Gonna Fall." "Every line of it is actually

helped young African Americans organize the Student Nonviolent Coordinating Committee (SNCC), which combined a Christian social ethic with a commitment to participatory democracy. The courageous attacks on segregation by SNCC leaders such as John Lewis, Diana Nash, and Robert Moses inspired many liberal white students to engage in political struggle. Equally important was the young generation's despair at the continuing Cold War. Campus radicals organized Students for a Democratic Society (SDS) in 1962, issuing a manifesto called the Port Huron Statement, drafted by University of Michigan activist Tom Hayden. "We may be the last generation in the experiment with living," SDS announced. Attacking a complacent acceptance of poverty,

the start of a whole song," he said, "but when I wrote it, I thought I wouldn't have enough time alive to write all those songs so I put all I could into this one."

Dylan's political faith eroded further after the Kennedy assassination. When given the Tom Paine Award in December 1963 by the Emergency Civil Liberties Committee at a swank New York hotel, he saw only the "mink and jewels." "It took me a long time to get young," he told the liberal audience, ". . . and I'm proud of it." For Dylan, the immense success of the Beatles' U.S. tour in 1964 suggested a way to reach the mass audience he had always sought. He began to perform with rock musicians and electrified his guitar to add a pulsating beat to his lyrical style. The result was 1965's "Like a Rolling Stone," Dylan's first major hit. With this success, he liberated political music from the enclaves of folk and brought lyrical protest into the cultural mainstream.

During the 1960s Dylan's gravelly voice resonated with the discontent of the youth movement. His lyrics became more metaphoric and symbolic; their juxtaposition of familiar Americana and surreal imagery suggested the absurdity and harsh hypocrisy of contemporary life. At the peak of his success in 1966, Dylan nearly died in a motorcycle crash, and he retreated from public view. When he returned two years later, he began to experiment with country music and gospel. Yet he would always be associated with the modern folk and rock music that he helped pioneer.

racism, and militarism, the student New Left called for participatory democracy to overcome the alienation caused by bureaucratic decision making.

The first massive student protest erupted at the University of California at Berkeley in 1964 when administrators banned political recruiting on campus. Borrowing tactics from the civil rights struggle, the ensuing Free Speech Movement (FSM) organized a sit-in at which 800 students submitted to arrest. "There's a time when the operation of the machine becomes so odious," declared FSM leader Mario Savio, "that you can't take part . . . and you've got to put your bodies upon the gears . . . and you've got to make it stop." Otherwise, FSM warned, education merely prepared students to take their places in an oppressive corporate order. "You can't trust anybody over thirty," FSM activist Jack Weinberg taunted. A generation once courted by President Kennedy had now set its own agenda.

BUILDING THE GREAT SOCIETY

Five days after Kennedy was killed, President Lyndon Johnson stood before a joint session of Congress and pleaded earnestly, "Let us continue." Determined to preserve the liberal agenda, the new president now called for a "Great Society" to end poverty and racial injustice. Taking advantage of the public grief, he pushed legislation that Kennedy had initiated but failed to pass through Congress. By early 1964 Johnson had signed major laws involving economic development, social welfare, and civil rights. Ironically, this success diminished Johnson's appeal. Whereas Kennedy had appeared quick, witty, and inspired, Johnson emerged as a consummate politician, immensely experienced and skilled in political affairs but never quite reliable or sincere. The tall Texan was notorious for bullying subordinates and ignoring political criticism. Failing to charm the public, Johnson eventually personified the duplicity of government and widened the "credibility gap" between the presidency and the people.

In his first legislative triumph, Johnson persuaded Congress to pass Kennedy's tax reform program. The Revenue Act of 1964 affirmed the principle of deficit spending and stimulated a 7 percent boost in the gross national product (GNP) during its first year. To all appearances, government management had created unique economic expansion. The new tax laws encouraged productivity while reducing unemployment and inflation and brought prosperity for U.S. corporations. Profits jumped 57 percent between 1960 and 1964 as innovative technology, including pneumatic conveyors, copying machines, piggyback freight, and containerized shipping, increased efficiency and profits. Military and space contracts, particularly in the "Sunbelt" states of the South and Southwest, stimulated prosperity and corporate consolidation. By the end of the decade, 71 percent of manufacturing profits went to the nation's 400 largest firms.

In the reformist climate of the 1960s, however, the scope of corporate enterprise became an issue of public policy. In 1962 biologist Rachel Carson's best-selling book, *Silent Spring*, depicted the poisonous effects of environmental pollution and urged regulation of hazardous chemicals. Other critics charged that the interaction between private business and government threatened public interests, and that personnel shifted too easily between corporate management and federal regulatory boards that set industry standards. Few government officials attempted to remedy the situation or protect consumer interests. But a private lawyer named Ralph Nader emerged as a consumer

1960	515
1962	575
1964	650

Source: *Economic Report of the President* (1988).

advocate. After his book *Unsafe at Any Speed* (1965) exposed the hazards of General Motors' Corvair, Senate hearings revealed that the world's largest corporation had investigated Nader's personal life in an effort to discredit his findings. Nader used a resulting jury award to start research centers to monitor the quality of consumer products as well as to investigate tax inequities, mine safety, radiation hazards, and pollution.

Prosperity both reflected and encouraged U.S. enterprise abroad. During the 1960s investment in western Europe doubled, and the total value of U.S.-owned overseas plants and equipment surpassed $100 billion. While U.S. firms exported $35 billion in goods each year, foreign subsidiaries of multinational businesses sold another $45 billion in goods. By the end of the decade the United States controlled nearly three-quarters of the world's oil and produced most of its machinery, electronics, and chemicals.

Amid prosperity, however, income distribution remained lopsided. The wealthiest fifth of U.S. families received more than 45 percent of the nation's personal income, whereas the poorest fifth earned 3.7 percent. Tax loopholes accentuated the problem. Tax-exempt bonds, a refuge for wealthy investors, amounted to nearly $86 billion in 1963. More than 150 persons with incomes exceeding $200,000 paid no taxes. Corporations benefited from similar loopholes. The percent of federal revenues derived from corporate income taxes decreased from 20 percent in 1955 to 12 percent in 1970. Yet nearly one-quarter of all U.S. citizens still lived in poverty.

Concerned about such inequities, Johnson vowed to wage an "unconditional war on poverty." Raised in the tradition of southern populism and having been a congressional New Dealer, Johnson believed that medical care, education, job training, and racial equality could complete the New Deal. Indeed, the ensuing legislative accomplishment dazzled the country, and the media compared Johnson's mastery of Congress to the achievement of the first hundred days of Roosevelt's New Deal of 1933.

The Economic Opportunity Act of 1964 created the Office of Economic Opportunity (OEO), launched training programs for the young, and offered loans and grants for self-help projects initiated by local communities. The bill's Community Action Program bypassed traditional leadership and called for a "participatory democracy" of the poor in shaping government-funded projects. The law mandated a Job Corps for youth and Volunteers in Service to America (VISTA), which assigned volunteers to assist needy communities. The OEO also introduced the Head Start program to provide preschool aid to children of the poor.

By the end of 1964 Congress had enacted most of Johnson's social welfare program, including $1 billion in housing legislation, federal grants for mass transportation, loans for college students, and aid for college construction. The president also expanded a food stamp program for the working poor. The Great Society thus promised to alleviate economic misery and social injustice for previously ignored citizens. The Kennedy administration had initiated some of these programs; but Johnson had greatly enlarged the agenda, and his legislative skill translated liberal intentions into public policy.

EXPANDING CIVIL RIGHTS

Johnson's political genius also ensured passage of new civil rights laws. Although Kennedy had lined up support for his proposal in 1963, southern senators expected to weaken its provisions. Kennedy's death abruptly changed the political climate. "No memorial or eulogy," Johnson told a stunned joint session of Congress five days after Kennedy's death, "could more eloquently honor Kennedy's memory than the earliest possible passage of the Civil Rights Bill for which he fought so long." Linking the new measure to the martyred president, Johnson refused to compromise on its major provisions. With the support of northern Republicans, two-thirds of the Senate voted to end a southern filibuster—the first time the Senate halted such obstruction of a civil rights measure.

The Civil Rights Act of 1964 gave the federal government the power to sue to desegregate public accommodations and schools. The law also prohibited denial of equal job opportunities in all but the smallest businesses and unions and created the Equal Employment Opportunity Commission (EEOC) to sue for compliance. To be illegal, however, racial imbalances in employment had to be the result of deliberate intent, and the law prohibited the use of quotas or preferential treatment to accomplish racial balance. African Americans and liberals nonetheless celebrated this landmark step toward equal opportunity. But conservatives such as Arizona Senator Barry Goldwater attacked the law's extension of federal power. Die-hard southern segregationists such as Alabama's George Wallace detected a communist conspiracy at work.

Passage of the Civil Rights Act also opened an unexpected area for social change. During the debate in Congress, the National Woman's Party protested that prohibition of discrimination because of "race, color, religion, or national origin" had omitted the word *sex*. Virginia Democrat Howard Smith, an opponent of the entire bill, then introduced an amendment adding the missing category. Although some suggested he was merely making a mockery of the measure, Smith probably sought to extend to white women the same rights now offered to blacks. Whatever his motives, nearly all the women in Congress endorsed the change, which carried both houses.

Subsequent failure of the EEOC to push for compliance with the anti-sex-discrimination law frustrated women reformers. Encouraged by the popularity of her book, *The Feminine Mystique* (1963), Betty Friedan joined other activists in forming the National Organization for Women (NOW) in 1966 to exert pressure on the government. Pledged to "take the actions needed to bring women into the mainstream of American society," NOW pushed for legal abortions, maternity leave, tax-deductible child care, and an equal rights amendment to end sex discrimination. Simultaneously, a younger generation of women working within the civil rights movement developed a commitment to equality for all groups and demanded equal treatment for themselves. The two strands of feminist reform later converged in the women's liberation movement.

THE ELECTION OF 1964

"I think we just delivered the South to the Republican Party," Johnson told an aide as he signed the Civil Rights Act of 1964. Angered at government interference in the private sector, Republican conservatives rallied behind Senator Goldwater, author of the best-selling book, *The Conscience of a Conservative* (1960). "Extremism in the defense of liberty is no vice," declared Goldwater in his acceptance speech to the stormy Republican National Convention. "Moderation in the pursuit of justice is no virtue." The Republican nominee lamented crime in the streets, political corruption, aimlessness among youth, anxiety among the elderly, and the loss of spiritual meaning. His was the first candidacy to embrace the "social issue," the discomfort experienced by many voters over personally frightening aspects of social change in the 1960s. "I will give you back your freedom," said Goldwater. Meanwhile, his militant foreign policy speeches made Johnson look like a dove.

Alabama Governor George Wallace echoed Goldwater's agenda and captured national attention by winning one-third of the Democratic primary vote in Wisconsin, Indiana, and Maryland. Political commentators described Wallace's victories as a backlash against civil rights agitation and integration, but the conservative Democrat aimed his criticism at liberal paternalism and big government. "The American people," he said, "are fed up with the continuing trend toward a socialist state which subjects the individual to the dictates of an all-powerful central government." Wallace's surprising success revealed deep dissatisfactions among lower-middle-class whites about liberal support of African Americans instead of solutions to their own economic and social

Betty Friedan *(1924–)*

At a time when psychologists insisted that a normal woman would achieve maximum fulfillment as wife, mother, housewife, and homemaker, author Betty Friedan challenged the cult of domesticity in her best-selling 1963 book, *The Feminine Mystique.* According to Friedan,

middle-class women responded to traditional expectations of domestic bliss with a bewildered "Is that all?" Her book sold 3 million copies, reached an estimated readership five times as large, and provoked a fundamental reexamination of women's place in U.S. society. Scarcely a single family was unaffected by its message.

From Peoria, Illinois, and the daughter of immigrant Jewish parents, Friedan had studied psychology and social science at Smith College and the University of California at Berkeley. "I didn't want to be like my mother," she later recalled. She worked as a journalist during World War II but lost her job to a returning war veteran. Despite a union contract forbidding such actions, she was fired from another job because of pregnancy. In 1949, she explained, no term existed to describe "sex discrimination."

During the 1950s Friedan lived in the suburbs of New York, where she raised three children and continued to pursue a journalism career as a freelance magazine writer. For a piece about her Smith College classmates fifteen years after graduation, she conducted a survey of their attitudes and feelings. Her research revealed a profound unhappiness among college-educated, middle-class women; but the article contra-

problems. Recognizing that Wallace threatened his support in the South, Goldwater persuaded the Alabaman to withdraw.

Johnson, himself a southerner, worried more about black activism and tried to silence further civil rights reform. African Americans defied his wishes. In 1964 the Student Nonviolent Coordinating Committee (SNCC) invited hundreds of white volunteers to participate in a voter registration campaign in Mississippi during the summer vacation. The integrated Mississippi Summer Project encountered violent repression from vigilantes and local offi-

dicted the assumptions of the day, and the editors of women's magazines refused to publish her findings.

Friedan decided to write a book. "Something is very wrong with the way American women are trying to live their lives today," she began. "It is no longer possible to . . . dismiss the desperation of so many American women." Friedan proceeded to demolish the "happy housewife" image of postwar society, arguing that middle-class women required a source of personal fulfillment, a career, to achieve satisfaction.

Having identified a major social problem, Friedan joined other feminists in seeking a solution. Her philosophy was quintessentially liberal. She demanded that women be given opportunities equal to those of men to achieve economic and political citizenship. In 1966 she helped found the National Organization for Women (NOW) "to bring women into full participation in the mainstream of American society now" and served as its first president until 1970. Besides demanding employment opportunities and legal rights, NOW advocated child-care centers and "the right of women to control their reproductive rights." Working within the liberal consensus, Friedan also helped establish the National Women's Political Caucus in 1971 to pressure the major political parties to accept greater female participation.

Friedan's liberal agenda clashed not only with sexist values but also with a more radical feminism that emerged in the late 1960s. Viewing politics in traditional terms, she rejected the idea that "the personal is political" and dismissed the activism of lesbians within the women's movement as internally divisive. Nevertheless, Friedan continued to enjoy considerable stature as a foremother of contemporary feminism.

cials, which resulted in mass arrests, bombings, arson, beatings, and the murder of civil rights workers. Although only 1,200 blacks dared to register to vote during the summer's bloody events, a contingent of SNCC workers and new black voters went to the Democratic National Convention in Atlantic City to demand political representation.

Calling themselves the Mississippi Freedom Democratic Party, they argued that the all-white Mississippi delegation should be unseated because African Americans could not participate in their selection. Johnson feared

Lyndon Johnson used the politics of consensus to win a 61 percent plurality in the 1964 election. Having signed civil rights legislation that year, he captured more than 90 percent of the black vote.

such reforms would cost white support and offered the delegates two at-large seats. In the end, no compromise was acceptable. The regular Mississippi Democrats, most of whom backed Goldwater, left the convention, and the unseated blacks remained embittered by liberal hypocrisy. As a gesture of reconciliation, Johnson chose the liberal Hubert Humphrey as his running mate; but many African Americans lost confidence in and respect for their white Democratic allies.

Johnson and Humphrey sought a politics of consensus in 1964 by defending civil rights legislation and promising moderation in Vietnam. "We seek no wider war," said the president, denouncing those who would "supply American boys to do the job that Asian boys should do." In the election, the Johnson-Humphrey liberal agenda received a record 61 percent plurality and amassed 43 million votes. The Democrats won more than 90 percent of the black vote but lost five states in the Deep South. The landslide gave the president greater than two-to-one majorities in both houses of Congress. Even without the white South, the president could now attempt to fulfill the promises of the liberal agenda.

THE TRIUMPH OF LIBERALISM

Johnson treated his election as a mandate and proceeded to expand his Great Society agenda, persuading Congress to enact a variety of programs for social reform. In 1965 he signed an education bill that based federal aid on the number of low-income families in each school district. The law enabled the federal government to influence local political decisions. For example, the Commissioner of Education ruled that school districts had to show a "good faith substantial start" toward desegregation or lose federal funds. In 1966 the Office of Education issued tighter guidelines and declared an end to "paper compliance with desegregation orders." Conservatives objected that federal aid was threatening local control over schools.

Johnson also pushed for health care for the elderly, leading to the pioneering Medicare program in 1965. The core of the legislative package provided for hospital and nursing-home care for elderly citizens through payroll taxes administered by Social Security. The law also provided Medicaid grants to states that enacted health programs for poor people of all ages. By 1970 the cost of state health care nearly equaled that of Medicare. To accommodate conservative concerns about free enterprise, however, the law did not allow the government to control service fees.

The Great Society program peaked in 1965. Johnson signed a $1 billion Appalachia Assistance program, most of which went for road building in the economically depressed region. A portion of the $7.8 billion housing bill included rent supplements for low-income families. Johnson made the Department of Housing and Urban Development a cabinet-level office and followed that with approval of the Demonstration Cities and Metropolitan Development Act, which appropriated nearly $1 billion to attack urban blight. Congress also abolished the national-origins quota system for immigration, underscoring the rejection of race in federal policy. The Immigration Act of 1965 limited admission to 300,000 people a year but favored relatives of U.S. citizens and those with special skills rather than particular nationalities and encouraged a considerable increase in immigration from Asia and Latin America.

GUNS AND BUTTER

Despite the popularity of Johnson's initiatives, conservatives criticized the growth of government power and bureaucracy and resented the tax burdens to finance social reform. Southern leaders also objected to civil rights measures that demanded desegregation of public accommodations. Yet Johnson defended his program passionately, not only because it brought him political support but also because it satisfied a personal desire to be remembered as a caring president. He would later compare his commitment to domestic reform to a love affair with a beautiful woman.

Johnson understood nevertheless that his ambitious program depended on preserving a political consensus that would support deficit spending for social legislation. He was constantly afraid that political opponents would undermine his support, and he feared that any weakness in Cold War foreign policy would open him to criticism. In this context, he faced critical decisions about the continuing war in Vietnam. "I knew from the start that I was bound to be crucified either way I moved," he told biographer Doris Kearns after he completed his term in office. "If I left the woman I really loved—the Great Society—in order to get involved with that bitch of a war on the other side of the world, then I would lose everything at home. All my programs. All my hopes to feed the hungry and shelter the homeless. All my dreams to provide education and health care to the browns and the blacks and the lame and the poor." Yet Johnson believed, initially at least, that the country would support both "guns and butter"—the war in Asia and the War on Poverty.

Like Kennedy, Johnson recognized the importance of undeveloped countries in the Cold War and opposed political or economic changes that might destabilize U.S. interests. In 1965 he ordered U.S. troops into the Dominican Republic when he suspected that communists controlled a constitutional movement to seize power from the army. Johnson also followed Kennedy's precedents in authorizing the CIA to promote friendly governments abroad.

In any case, U.S. military power appeared awesome and continued to grow. By the late 1960s, the armed forces operated more than 3,000 military bases in 30 countries and had 1 million military personnel overseas. The nation's arsenal included 1,000 nuclear-armed intercontinental missiles and 70 nuclear-armed and -powered submarines. The nuclear storehouse amounted to the equivalent of 15 tons of dynamite for every person in the world. Total navy tonnage exceeded that of all other nations combined. The cost of the military establishment exceeded $216 million a day. Between 1945 and 1970, U.S. taxpayers spent $1 trillion for military purposes. Yet the late 1960s brought the United States the worst military and political disaster in its history.

Just hours after the assassination of President Kennedy, Johnson conferred with the U.S. ambassador to South Vietnam, Henry Cabot Lodge, to assess the status of the war. When Lodge reported that the Vietcong had escalated military activity, Johnson replied that he was "not going to be the President who saw Southeast Asia go the way China went." Instead, he canceled Kennedy's order to withdraw troops from South Vietnam. Although South Vietnam had failed to compete effectively against the Vietcong politically or militarily, Johnson believed that U.S. military force would ensure victory in the Vietnamese civil war. By early 1964, the White House approved plans to expand the war across the border separating South and North Vietnam.

EXHIBIT **11-4**   **VIETNAM**

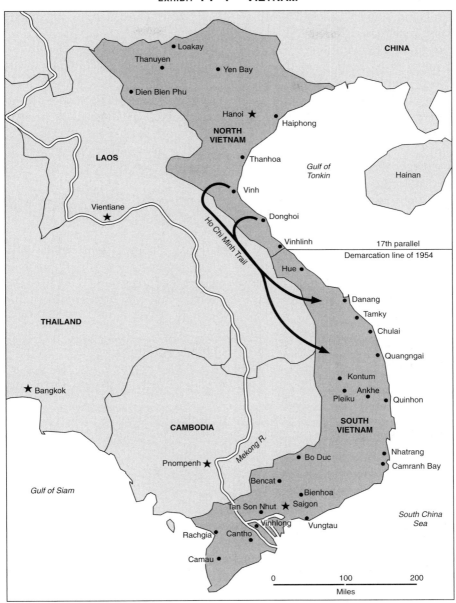

To be sure, Johnson was determined to keep Vietnam from becoming an issue in the presidential election. His 1964 State of the Union address made no mention of foreign policy—the first such silence since the end of World War II. Yet behind the scenes, top administration officials monitored the war closely and made decisions that brought the nation closer to military intervention.

During the spring of 1964, U.S. destroyers patrolled the Gulf of Tonkin, and PT boats occasionally attacked North Vietnamese coastal installations. As military clashes increased, the State Department secretly drafted a congressional resolution for a declaration of war in May 1964. Two months later, South Vietnamese ships, accompanied by U.S. intelligence vessels, began bombarding North Vietnamese territory in the Gulf of Tonkin. When North Vietnamese patrol boats fired on one of the destroyers, U.S. fighter planes strafed the attackers. Secretary McNamara openly lied to Congress in denying U.S. involvement in these attacks. On August 4 the navy reported a second attack on U.S. ships, although subsequent analysis blamed "freak weather effects, and an overeager sonar man" for that claim. Newly opened records show that the second attack never occurred.

Johnson nevertheless used the allegation to order air reprisals on North Vietnamese bases. Insisting that the United States sought "no wider war," the president presented Congress with a reworded version of the secretly prepared May declaration of war, which stated that "Congress approves and supports the determination of the President as commander-in-chief to take all necessary measures to repel any attack against the forces of the United States and to prevent further aggression." The Tonkin Gulf Resolution passed in the House unanimously and in the Senate with only two dissenters, Wayne Morse of Oregon and Ernest Gruening of Alaska. A Harris poll showed 85 percent approval of air strikes against North Vietnam. Although Congress stopped short of a full declaration of war, which might have drawn China and the Soviet Union into the conflict, Johnson had won a free hand to conduct the war as he chose.

During the election campaign, Johnson stood as the candidate least likely to embroil the nation in a Vietnam war. But after his victory, he moved swiftly to approve measures to escalate U.S. military involvement. In December 1964 the president approved plans to begin a sustained bombing campaign of North Vietnam and accepted the deployment of U.S. ground forces to support the air war and engage the enemy in combat. These plans were made unilaterally, often in defiance of the opinion of such U.S. allies as France, Britain, even South Vietnam. Indeed, when South Vietnamese leaders suggested the possibility of opening negotiations with the National Liberation Front, U.S. officials refused to consider the possibility of a peaceful neutralization of the region. Moreover, Johnson feared that publicizing his military decision would increase international pressure to negotiate and would undermine congressional support for the Great Society. The decision to escalate the war thus remained secret.

The White House merely waited for an opportunity to begin the bombing campaign of North Vietnam. The excuse came after the Vietcong attacked a U.S. base at Pleiku in February 1965. Vowing not to be scared out of Vietnam, Johnson ordered air strikes, known as Operation Rolling Thunder, against

North Vietnam. Claiming the bombings were merely retaliatory, the White House concealed the deepening commitment of air power from the public. The air war also required more ground troops to protect U.S. bases, and Johnson ordered 100,000 additional soldiers to Vietnam. In this way he hoped to maintain enough force to prevent the communists from winning, but not enough to precipitate Chinese intervention.

The war against North Vietnam thus began as a policy change soon after Johnson came to office. Although a few administration officials, such as presidential advisor George Ball, opposed escalation of the war, Rusk, McNamara, Bundy, and the Joint Chiefs of Staff advocated a military solution to the political struggles in Indochina. Kennedy had resisted their pleas; Johnson, less confident about foreign policy and fearing the wrath of conservatives should he be responsible for "losing" Vietnam, determined to uphold an independent South Vietnam with ties to the Western alliance. In 1965 a Gallup poll found that 61 percent of the public approved increased troop deployments, indicating that Johnson was not running ahead of public opinion. But as the cost of the war became apparent, support for Johnson's war steadily weakened. And, tragically for Johnson, so did support for "the woman [he] really loved—the Great Society."

AMERICAN HISTORY RESOURCE CENTER

To explore documents, images, audio and video clips, articles, and commentary related to the material in this chapter, visit the source collections at ushistory.wadsworth.com and and use the Search function with the following key terms:

John F. Kennedy	Great Society
Cuban Missile Crisis	Lyndon Johnson
New Left	Student Nonviolent Coordinating Committee

RECOMMENDED READINGS

Taylor Branch, *Pillar of Fire: America in the King Years, 1963–1965* (1998). A thorough analysis of the civil rights movement, this volume emphasizes the role of individual participants.

Rebecca E. Klatch, *A Generation Divided: The New Left, the New Right, and the 1960s* (1999). A sociological study of political activism, this work examines the choices of activists on both sides of the spectrum.

Fredrik Logevall, *Choosing War: The Lost Chance for Peace and the Escalation of War in Vietnam* (1999). This study of U.S. policymaking between 1963 and 1965 describes the decisions that led to war in Vietnam.

Michael R. Beschloss, ed., *Taking Charge: The Johnson White House Tapes, 1963–1964* (1997). Based on transcriptions of White House telephone conversations, this volume vividly depicts the transition of power from Kennedy to Johnson.

Additional Readings

Although numerous authors have addressed the sixties, most confuse protest movements with the larger historical context. Good overviews include David Steigerwald, *The Sixties and the End of Modern America* (1995); David Farber, *The Age of Great Dreams: America in the 1960s* (1994); and Maurice Isserman and Michael Kazin, *America Divided: The Civil War of the 1960s* (2000). More speculative is Edward P. Morgan's *The Sixties Experience: Hard Lessons about Modern America* (1991). One political history critical of the liberal consensus is Allen J. Matusow, *The Unraveling of America: A History of Liberalism in the 1960s* (1984).

A balanced discussion of the Kennedy administration appears in James N. Giglio's *The Presidency of John F. Kennedy* (1991), which may be supplemented with the second volume of Herbert S. Parmet's biography, *JFK: The Presidency of John F. Kennedy* (1983). More critical is Bruce Miroff's *Pragmatic Illusions: The Presidential Politics of John F. Kennedy* (1976). A briefer book is David Burner's *John F. Kennedy and a New Generation* (1988). For an insightful study of the impact of personality, see Garry Wills, *The Kennedy Imprisonment* (1982). A fine study of U.S. leadership can be found in David Halberstam, *The Best and the Brightest* (1972). Historians' views of Kennedy are studied in Thomas Brown, *JFK: History of an Image* (1988).

Kennedy's problems with Congress are explored in Tom Wicker, *JFK and LBJ: The Influence of Personality upon Politics* (1968). The space program is well treated in Walter A. McDougall, *The Heavens and the Earth: A Political History of the Space Age* (1985); in Clayton R. Koppes, *JPL and the American Space Program: A History of the Jet Propulsion Lab* (1982); and in Tom Wolfe's journalistic *The Right Stuff* (1979). Problems of economic policy are described in Jim F. Heath's *John F. Kennedy and the Business Community* (1969). For the Peace Corps, see Gerard T. Rice, *The Bold Experiment: John F. Kennedy's Peace Corps* (1985). Women's politics are covered in Cynthia Harrison, *On Account of Sex: The Politics of Women's Issues, 1945–1968* (1988). The career of a leading feminist is described in Daniel Horowitz, *Betty Friedan and the Making of the Feminine Mystique: The American Left, the Cold War, and Modern Feminism* (1998). For the experience of younger women, see Sara Evans, *Personal Politics: The Root of Women's Liberation in the Civil Rights Movement and the New Left* (1979).

A good survey of the civil rights movement can be found in Robert Weisbrot, *Freedom Bound: A History of America's Civil Rights Movement* (1990). Kennedy's relationship to civil rights is analyzed critically in Victor S. Navasky, *Kennedy Justice* (1971), and more favorably in Carl M. Brauer, *John F. Kennedy and the Second Reconstruction* (1977). For Martin Luther King Jr., see Stephen B. Oates, *Let the Trumpet Sound: The Life of Martin Luther King, Jr.* (1982), and David J. Garrow, *Bearing the Cross: Martin Luther King, Jr., and the Southern Christian Leadership Conference* (1986). King's organization is studied in Adam Fairclough, *To Redeem the Soul of America: The Southern Christian Leadership Conference and Martin Luther King, Jr.* (1987). The legal framework is explained in Michael R. Belknap, *Federal Law and Southern Order: Racial Violence and Constitutional Conflict in the Post-Brown South* (1987). See also Hugh Davis Graham, *The Civil Rights Era: Origins and Development of National Policy* (1990). Another facet of government policy emerges in David J. Garrow, *The FBI and Martin Luther King, Jr.* (1981). The role of student activists is presented in Clayborne Carson, *In Struggle: SNCC and the Black Awakening of the 1960s* (1981). A fine oral history is Howell Raines's *My Soul Is Rested: The Story of the Civil Rights Movement in the Deep South* (1983).

For a thorough discussion of Kennedy's handling of the Cold War, see Michael R. Beschloss, *The Crisis Years: Kennedy and Khrushchev, 1960–1963* (1991). For the Bay of Pigs, see Trumbull Higgins, *The Perfect Failure: Kennedy, Eisenhower, and the CIA at the Bay of Pigs* (1988). The Cuban missile crisis is discussed in Robert Weisbrot, *Maximum Danger: Kennedy, the Missiles, and the Crisis of American Confidence* (2001), and Sheldon M. Stern, *Averting "The Final Failure": John F. Kennedy and the Secret Cuban Missile Crisis Meetings* (2002). A detailed study of the German conflict can be found in Curtis Cate, *The Ides of August: The Berlin Wall Crisis, 1961* (1978). Another aspect of Kennedy policy emerges in Richard D. Mahoney, *JFK: Ordeal in Africa* (1983).

The Kennedy assassination has created a vast literature. A good starting point is Gerald L. Posner's *Case Closed: Lee Harvey Oswald and the Assassination of JFK* (1993).

For Lyndon Johnson, a good starting point is Irving Bernstein, *Guns or Butter: The Presidency of Lyndon B. Johnson* (1996), and Robert Dallek, *Flawed Giant: Lyndon Johnson and His Times, 1961–1973* (1998). Also insightful is Doris Kearns, *Lyndon Johnson and the American Dream* (1976). The internal workings of the administration are covered in Emmette S. Redford and Richard T. McCulley, *White House Operations: The Johnson Presidency* (1986). See also Carl Solberg's biography of the vice president, *Hubert Humphrey* (1984).

The Republican opposition is described in Mary C. Brennan's *Turning Right in the Sixties: The Conservative Capture of the GOP* (1995), and Robert Alan Goldberg, *Barry Goldwater* (1995). See also Stephan Lesher, *George*

Wallace: American Populist (1994), and Jody Carlson, *George C. Wallace and the Politics of Powerlessness: The Wallace Campaigns for the Presidency* (1981).

The decision to intervene in Vietnam is described in David Kaiser, *American Tragedy: Kennedy, Johnson, and the Vietnam War* (2000). Other overviews of the Vietnam War include Marilyn B. Young, *The Vietnam Wars, 1945–1990* (1991), and George L. Herring, *America's Longest War: The United States and Vietnam, 1950–1975* (1986). Another excellent introduction is Neil Sheehan, *A Bright and Shining Lie: John Paul Vann and America in Vietnam* (1988). Also useful are Stanley Karnow, *Vietnam: A History* (1983), and William S. Turley, *The Second Indochina War: A Short Political and Military History* (1986).

The best study of the Tonkin Gulf incident is Edwin E. Moise, *Tonkin Gulf and the Escalation of the Vietnam War* (1996). The limits of leadership are covered in Lloyd C. Gardner, *Pay Any Price: Lyndon Johnson and the Wars for Vietnam* (1995), and in Larry Berman, *Lyndon Johnson's War: The Road to Stalemate in Vietnam* (1989). A fine study of one leading official is Paul Hendrickson's *The Living and the Dead: Robert McNamara and Five Lives of a Lost War* (1996).

POLARIZED AMERICA: RACIAL TURMOIL AND VIETNAM, 1965–1968

President Lyndon Johnson dreamed of enlisting Americans behind a Great Society program of racial harmony and social reform. Yet Johnson could not contain the widening agenda of the civil rights movement, whose focus moved from nonviolent campaigns in the South to nationwide demands for African American political power and community control. Nor was the president able to forge a consensus for the fight for an anticommunist government in South Vietnam. As Johnson unleashed a bombing campaign against North Vietnam and sent the first U.S. combat troops to the South, he vowed that "come hell or high water, we're gonna stay there." Yet escalation of the U.S. role in Vietnam unleashed a torrent of dissent, led by a small but vocal antiwar movement, some of it infused with countercultural values.

Despite general prosperity, divisions over race relations, the Vietnam War, and social morality polarized public life. By articulating a conservative critique of "pseudo-intellectual government," Governor George Wallace mobilized a third-party race for the presidency. Wallace asserted that the "average man in the street" supported "a change on the domestic scene in this country." Meanwhile, Richard Nixon sought the White House by focusing on middle-class concerns about "social issues" such as crime, violence, and student protest. By 1968, the nation confronted the worst crisis since the Civil War.

THE VOTING RIGHTS CRUSADE

Many African Americans benefited from the widespread prosperity and made significant economic strides during Lyndon Johnson's tenure. As the ratio between black and white family income narrowed, black median family income increased by more than one-third between 1964 and 1969. Over the decade, the proportion of African American families living in poverty decreased from nearly 50 percent to less than 30 percent. Seeking to extend the benefits of inclusion to those left out of New Deal reforms, Johnson appointed African Americans to high-profile offices. Robert Weaver was named to head the Department of Housing and Urban Development, which the president upgraded to cabinet status, and became the first black in U.S. history to serve in such a high position. The president also selected Thurgood Marshall, former counsel for the National Association for the Advancement of Colored People (NAACP), to be the first black justice to serve on the Supreme Court. Meanwhile, Massachusetts voters elected Edward Brooke to the Senate in 1966; he was the first African American to sit in that body since Reconstruction.

Civil rights activists built on widespread liberal sympathy to win long-denied voting rights for African Americans. The Twenty-Fourth Amendment to the Constitution, ratified in 1964, outlawed the poll tax, a historic barrier to black political participation in the South. But many southern states still used "literacy tests" to disqualify potential voters on the basis of race. When the Student Nonviolent Coordinating Committee (SNCC) initiated a voter registration drive in Selma, Alabama, local officials refused to cooperate, leading organizers to ask for help from Martin Luther King Jr. After King's nonviolent street demonstrations resulted in police harassment, 600 civil rights activists mounted a march to the state capital in Montgomery. On "Bloody Sunday"—March 7, 1965—state troopers used clubs and tear gas in a vicious attack on the peaceful protest. Broadcast on national television, the atrocity forced the White House to intervene. Johnson then summoned a joint session of Congress to request federal protection for black voter registrants. Borrowing the language of the civil rights movement, the first southern president since Woodrow Wilson declared, "All of us . . . must overcome the crippling legacy of bigotry and injustice—and we *shall* overcome."

As hundreds of clergy and civil rights supporters answered King's call to come to Selma, a federal judge nationalized the Alabama National Guard, permitting the Montgomery march to take place with official protection. Even so, Viola Liuzzo, a white volunteer from Detroit, was killed by racist vigilantes; she was the third casualty of the Alabama campaign. Violence against the protests helped to rally public opinion in support of the Voting Rights Act of 1965, a landmark piece of legislation that produced a revolution in southern politics. The new law abolished literacy tests and empowered the attorney general to assign federal examiners to register voters in states practicing racial discrimination. In one year, federal officials registered more than 400,000 African American voters. By 1968, 1 million southern blacks had qualified to vote. Although the voting rights measure remained a central pillar of the civil rights revolution, it led to a new form of racial separation in the South's political structure as blacks enlisted on the Democratic rolls and whites increasingly voted Republican.

RACIAL TURMOIL AND IDENTITY POLITICS

The Voting Rights Act marked the culmination of the effort to achieve racial integration in the South. After passage of the act, national attention shifted to the majority of African Americans, who resided outside the region. Northern blacks lived primarily in decaying ghettos in the older industrial cities, where the exodus of manufacturing plants to the suburbs and Sunbelt states decimated urban tax bases and increased joblessness. In 1968 the Department of Labor reported that the black unemployment rate was three times as high as the white rate. Despite rising expenditures, welfare programs such as Aid to Families with Dependent Children (AFDC) failed to meet the needs of impoverished families. Federally funded urban renewal projects added to the problem by destroying low-income housing without replacing it. As the black population of the central cities increased by 6 million between 1960 and 1977, 4 million whites moved out. Washington's heralded War on Poverty could not erase the fact that ghetto life remained depressingly bleak.

Moderate black leaders could not contain the mixture of impatience, rage, and militant consciousness that accompanied heightened aspirations and unchanging realities for most African Americans. Between 1964 and 1967, more than 100 urban riots and rebellions occurred as angry blacks attacked retail property in their communities in response to economic abuses and police harassment. Chanting "burn, baby, burn," young blacks in the Los Angeles community of Watts damaged nearly $750 million of property while dozens were killed and thousands injured in one explosive outbreak in the summer of 1965. The next year, black violence erupted in Chicago when angry whites attacked Martin Luther King's "open city" housing campaign. In 1967 central Detroit went up in smoke as African Americans and some whites went on a week-long rampage that brought out the National Guard and federal troops. A six-day riot in Newark, New Jersey, left twenty-seven dead, resulting in a special report to the governor that blamed law enforcement officials for "excessive and unjustified force." SNCC leader H. "Rap" Brown expressed the bitter mood of 1967, urging demonstrators in Cambridge, Maryland, to "burn this town down if this town don't turn around and grant the demand of Negroes."

Johnson reacted to the violence by appointing a National Advisory Commission on Civil Disorders, chaired by Illinois Governor Otto Kerner. In a widely read report, the Kerner Commission concluded in 1968 that the nation was "moving toward two societies, one black, one white, separate and unequal." Blaming the riots on white racism and white institutional power, the commission urged a massive commitment to housing, education, jobs, and welfare as well as better law enforcement techniques. However, by then the White House was preoccupied with foreign policy and remained silent on the findings.

Stokely Carmichael (1941–1998)

No single figure embodied the radicalization of 1960s protest among African Americans as much as Stokely Carmichael did. Born in Trinidad, Carmichael went to public high school in the Bronx, New York, and graduated from predominantly black Howard University with a degree in

philosophy. Initiating his activism in the Deep South in 1961, he served several months in prison when he was arrested as a Freedom Rider, the first of thirty-five incarcerations he would experience.

After participating in the Mississippi Freedom Summer Project of 1964, Carmichael assumed the directorship of SNCC's voter registration campaign in Lowndes County, Alabama. There he proposed to arm field organizers and adopted the image of a snarling black panther as the insignia for a separate black political party. After succeeding John Lewis as SNCC chair in 1966, Carmichael warned of a "long hot summer" among discontented African American youth in the nation's ghettos.

A few days after Carmichael's election to the SNCC post, he virtually assumed leadership of James Meredith's March Against Fear in Mississippi by chanting the slogan "Black Power, Black Power" to sharecrop-

The explosion of black anger after 1965 effectively killed the biracial, nonviolent civil rights coalition. Limited gains from liberal reform, the persistence of black poverty, and a vocal white backlash encouraged African Americans to see all whites as part of a rigid "establishment." When James Meredith, the first black to enroll at the University of Mississippi, launched a solitary March Against Fear through Mississippi in 1966—only to be shot by a sniper, civil rights leaders rushed forward to continue the demonstration. Then SNCC's Stokely Carmichael brushed aside talk of nonviolence and proclaimed "Black Power!" The words electrified the media and terrified whites. Martin Luther King urged Carmichael to adopt a more moderate slogan, but black pride and cultural identity could no longer be contained by nonviolent rhetoric. Refashioning itself as the Student National Coordinating Commit-

pers along the highway. "We are determined to win political power . . . by any means necessary," he stated. Carmichael coauthored a book entitled *Black Power: The Politics of Liberation in America* (1967) that urged the black community to abandon its "dependent colonial status" and "win its freedom while preserving its cultural integrity."

"Before a group can enter the open society, it must first close ranks," wrote the authors of *Black Power*. Carmichael implemented this philosophy by purging whites from SNCC. "If we are to proceed toward true liberation," he explained, "we must set ourselves off from white people." In seeking to shift the movement's focus from integration to black liberation, he dropped the word *nonviolent* from SNCC's name. One year later, Carmichael expressed sympathy for communism on a trip to Cuba and warned that black anti-imperialists in the United States were "preparing groups of urban guerrillas for our defense in the cities . . . a fight to the death."

Carmichael resigned from SNCC in 1967 and became prime minister of the Black Panther Party the following year. Yet his association with the Panthers was short-lived. Converted to Pan-Africanism, he soon proclaimed that socialism was "not an ideology suited for black people. . . . It's not a question of right or left. It's a question of black." He left the United States in 1969 and settled permanently in the African nation of Guinea until his death in 1998.

tee, SNCC removed the word *nonviolent* from its name. As the organization purged nonblacks from leadership positions, Carmichael dismissed integration as "a subterfuge for the maintenance of white supremacy."

The magnetism of Black Power revealed widespread frustration within African American communities. "To be a Negro in this country," explained novelist James Baldwin, "is to be in a rage all the time." Eldridge Cleaver, an emerging leader of the Black Panther Party, expressed similar fury in his bestselling *Soul on Ice* (1968). For many young blacks, failure to gain equal rights, economic advancement, and cultural respect produced a powerful identity crisis, forcing a conversion from "Negro" values of assimilation and integration to "black" affirmations of ethnicity. Many blacks followed the lead of Malcolm X and changed their "slave" names to African or Muslim names. In Los Angeles,

Maulana Ron Karenga formed the US Organization to promote "back to black" cultural traditions and popularized Kwanzaa as an African American alternative holiday to Christmas.

Through his posthumously published autobiography, Malcolm X emerged as an important cultural force. Born Malcolm Little, he had converted to the black Nation of Islam (Black Muslims) religion while in prison and changed his name to symbolize independence from white domination. A persuasive, charismatic speaker, he initially opposed interracial cooperation and warned that any association with "evil whites" would thwart social justice. However, after breaking with the Black Muslims in 1964, Malcolm argued that capitalism functioned as an oppressive force and that people of all colors must cooperate to achieve a socialist alternative. Assassinated in Harlem in 1965, allegedly by associates of the Nation of Islam, Malcolm remained a prophet for black and white radicals seeking interracial cooperation.

The cultural aspects of Black Power—Afro hairstyles, soul food, ethnic identity—paralleled efforts to organize a black political movement. In 1967, Bobby Seale and Huey Newton founded the Black Panther Party in Oakland, California, to address the overwhelming problems of ghetto life. The Panthers considered urban riots as self-destructive and instead formed a community defense league to monitor local police. To dramatize the right to bear arms against the "occupation" of their communities by white authorities, Panthers marched into the California legislature with loaded rifles. By 1968, the Black Panther Party had devised a ten-point program embracing Marxist concepts of self-determination and opposition to "welfare colonialism." The Panthers also distributed a national weekly newspaper, established local health clinics, and provided free breakfasts and schools for black children. In 1968 Panther leaders won white radical support for the Peace and Freedom Party, which ran one of their members, Eldridge Cleaver, for president; but the movement exerted minimal influence on the election.

While the Black Panthers, SNCC, and Martin Luther King jockeyed for African American leadership, the cry of Black Power emboldened other ethnic groups. By the late 1960s, Mexican Americans in the Southwest and California proclaimed their "Chicano" pride. Chicano consciousness, however, could not hide the bleak facts of Mexican American economic existence, particularly for agricultural field workers. To improve such conditions, California's Cesar Chavez and the United Farm Workers union used Christian nonviolence and product boycotts to win collective bargaining rights for the small but militant union.

Native Americans also moved from liberal reformism to militant assertions of cultural identity. When the state of Washington attempted to abridge native treaty rights to salmon fishing in the interests of conservation in 1964, local tribes invited the National Indian Youth Council to stage "fish-in" demonstrations. Four years later, the U.S. Supreme Court upheld the Indian position. Meanwhile, the Taos Pueblo in New Mexico rejected a federal offer of compensation for seizing sacred waters and initiated protests that led to a reversal of government policies. In 1966 Indian leaders adopted the phrase "self-determination" to oppose federal termination programs. Two years later, President Johnson embraced that language to demand "equality and dignity" for native peoples, and Congress passed the Indian Civil Rights Act, requiring tribal consent to state jurisdiction over civil or criminal matters. That year, young activists formed the American Indian Movement (AIM), raised the cry "Red Power," and vowed to continue the struggle for cultural and political autonomy.

JOHNSON'S WAR

When Johnson authorized the Rolling Thunder air strikes against North Vietnam in 1965, he merely implemented an earlier decision to preserve the South Vietnamese government at all costs. Yet poor target accuracy and enemy anti-aircraft fire produced a high loss of planes and led to indiscriminate bombing of civilian targets, increasing the need for ground troops. By the summer of 1965, U.S. forces had begun large-scale combat operations in the South, engaging in "search-and-destroy" missions against the Vietcong (the National Liberation Front) while B-52s flew from Guam to bomb suspected enemy targets. By the end of the year, 180,000 U.S. ground troops were "in country," and the air force was attacking industrial areas in the North. "It used to be a war of the South Vietnamese assisted by the Americans," noted newspaper columnist Walter Lippmann. "It is now becoming an American war very inefficiently assisted by the South Vietnamese."

Johnson consistently had ruled out negotiations with the communists. During Christmas of 1965, however, the president ordered a bombing moratorium and sent diplomats across the globe to explore possibilities for peace. Yet the White House refused to recognize the National Liberation Front as a political force independent of North Vietnam. Contending that Hanoi had invaded South Vietnam in an instance of territorial aggression, Johnson denied that the United States had become involved in a civil war.

As troop commitments approached 400,000 in 1966, some members of Congress began to express reservations about the war. J. William Fulbright, chair of the Senate Foreign Relations Committee, held open hearings criticizing White House policy. And even though intelligence reports noted that air power was militarily ineffective, Johnson ordered the bombing of Hanoi. "We must continue to raise the price of aggression," he explained. The goal of the bombing had changed from breaking the enemy's will to cutting supply lines. The president promised to end the attacks if North Vietnam pledged to send no more troops south, but Hanoi responded that peace depended on withdrawal of U.S. forces. Because Johnson insisted that South Vietnam's independence must be preserved, he rejected Hanoi's demands.

Despite tremendous firepower, the president's limited war could not defeat the enemy. Military advisors repeatedly made the error of assuming that a reduction of Vietcong operations indicated diminished military capability rather than changes in strategy. In late 1966 Defense Secretary McNamara commissioned a study, later known as the Pentagon Papers, to evaluate the entire war policy; but the bombing continued, and reliable journalists in Vietnam denounced administration claims about the minimal number of civilian casualties.

By 1968 Johnson had ordered 500,000 soldiers to South Vietnam. As ground forces began to confront North Vietnamese regulars as well as Vietcong guerrillas, casualty figures soared. Meanwhile, the Vietcong controlled the timing and terms of 80 percent of all military confrontations. To destroy enemy bases, U.S. planes dropped napalm, jungle defoliants, and lethal herbicides throughout the country in a war in which it was difficult to distinguish between combatants and civilians. American fragmentation bombs left victims riddled with millions of tiny particles that could not be detected by x-rays. The Central Intelligence Agency (CIA) also launched Operation Phoenix, an assassination program against alleged Vietcong civilian leaders that claimed at least 20,000 victims.

THE ANTIWAR MOVEMENT

Less than a month after Johnson ordered the full-scale bombing of North Vietnam in 1965, 20,000 protesters participated in a Washington, D.C., demonstration sponsored by Students for a Democratic Society (SDS). College students, vulnerable to the draft and increasingly concerned about issues of social justice and personal freedom, denounced the war. "Teach-in" protests spread to major universities. At the University of California, Berkeley, 12,000 students and faculty participated in Vietnam Day in 1965. Draft calls reached 40,000 a month the following year, and rallies, marches, and draft-card burnings multiplied. Young men refused induction orders, thousands deserted the armed forces, and even more fled to Canada and Europe to avoid conscription. Protesters occupied military induction centers and harassed on-campus job recruiters for the military and the CIA.

The antiwar movement saw the use of technological violence against an economically impoverished people as equivalent to genocide. Defense contractors such as Dow Chemical, which manufactured napalm used to kill civilians in Vietnam, and Honeywell, which made antipersonnel fragmentation bombs, faced militant protests by activists. Carl Oglesby of SDS considered the conflict a laboratory for developing imperial techniques to halt social revolution in the third world. Yet most demonstrators identified with the spirit of Joseph Heller's cult novel, *Catch-22* (1960), an absurdist view of World War II that suggested that escape was the only sane response to war. Bolstered by celebrity activists such as folksingers Joan Baez and Phil Ochs, antiwar assemblies became instant communities in which outrage merged with political action.

African American organizers such as Stokely Carmichael played a key role in the antiwar crusade. Identifying with the colonized peoples of the third world and aware that blacks suffered disproportionate casualties in Vietnam, Carmichael made SNCC the first civil rights group to oppose the war in 1966. Coining the slogan "Hell No, We Won't Go!" the organization urged blacks to resist the draft. The next year, African American heavyweight champion Muhammad Ali refused military induction based on his status as a Muslim minister and remained defiant when boxing authorities stripped him of his crown. "No Viet Cong ever called me nigger," Ali explained.

Martin Luther King also responded to rising antiwar sentiment in the black community and issued a "declaration of independence" from the Vietnam War in 1967. The United States was the world's leading purveyor of violence, King asserted from the pulpit. As antiwar protest evolved into massive resistance, however, the movement struggled to maintain peaceful methods. A "stop-the-draft" week at the Oakland, California, Induction Center resulted in street battles between police and 20,000 activists. Late in 1967, 300,000 antiwar protesters rallied in New York City. The same day, the National Mobilization Against the War (MOBE) gathered more than 100,000 marchers to surround the Pentagon. When several hundred stormed the citadel, many protesters were arrested by military police, an event recorded in Norman Mailer's prize-winning *Armies of the Night* (1968).

Clergy from all three major denominations figured strongly in the antiwar crusade. In 1967, Catholic activists, including Father Philip Berrigan, poured blood on draft files in Baltimore. As efforts to destroy selective service records spread across the country, conscientious objectors in the military refused assignment to Vietnam. By 1968, the antiwar SDS boasted nearly 300 chapters and a national membership of 100,000. For many of the nation's increasingly politicized students and peace activists, the Vietnam War had become a symbol of all that was wrong with America.

THE COUNTERCULTURE

"There's battle lines being drawn / Nobody's right if everybody's wrong," suggested a popular rock song of the period. Alienation from the Vietnam War was enhanced by the spread of countercultural values and youth-oriented lifestyles—components of a changing morality associated with the questioning of social authority and the spread of the "sexual revolution." Flaunting the breakdown of old barriers, rock songs such as the Rolling Stones' "Let's Spend the Night Together" directly described sexual longing. "Life was free and so was sex," novelist Sara Davidson later wrote in *Loose Change,* a novel set in Berkeley in the sixties.

Public fascination with new sexual standards and casual intimacy surfaced in books such as *The Harrad Experiment* (1967), a best-selling novel about a utopian sexual community of college students; in Ian Fleming's popular James Bond series; and in the pulp fiction of Jacqueline Susann, the most successful novelist of the period. Hollywood contributed to the shift in mores by replacing its 1930s production code with a rating system that permitted nudity and obscene language as well as "mature" themes. Television shows such as *The Smothers Brothers* and *Laugh-In* also broke precedent by joking about non-marital sex, divorce, and "uptight" behavior. In country music, once the bastion of traditional morality, the widespread use of birth control pills and enhanced sexual frankness were reflected in the songs of superstars Tammy Wynette and Loretta Lynn.

As a psychedelic counterculture blossomed from Beat roots in San Francisco's Haight-Ashbury district, the mass media discovered the "hippie." "I never hold back, man. I'm always on the outer limits of possibility," declared Haight rock vocalist Janis Joplin. Young cultural dissidents wore their hair defiantly long and dressed in a free-form fashion that included bells, feathers, bandanas, beads, and earrings. Many survived in crash pads or in shared housing by panhandling, making crafts, selling "underground" newspapers, and dealing drugs. Some, like the communal Diggers, started free kitchens and health clinics. The most important facet of hippie culture involved its attempt to reject the mainstream's competitive individualism, materialism, and middle-class pretensions. Instead, the alternative culture prided itself on honest affection, physical pleasure, sharing, experimentation, and absolute inner freedom.

Few college students actually traveled to San Francisco during 1967's "Summer of Love" or identified themselves as hippies. Yet many sensed the counterculture's possibilities for social change and refashioned their private lives to emulate it. Many middle-class rebels believed their cultural lifestyles should reflect their political sensibilities and left the cities to form thousands of rural communes. Others published underground comics and newspapers, produced "guerrilla" theater and alternative film documentaries, created color-crazed "pop art" posters, or sought expression in traditional disciplines such as musical composition, dance, poetry, or prose. Many more adopted antiestablishment attitudes, spoke in "hip" language, wore blue jeans, and experimented with sexual freedom, marijuana, and rock music.

"Psychedelic" or "acid" rock bands such as the Jefferson Airplane, the Grateful Dead, and Joplin's Big Brother and the Holding Company integrated electric guitars with elaborate light shows, developing the piercing "San Francisco" sound. As introspective lyrics and "spaced-out" musical styles spread to the Beatles and Rolling Stones as well as to Bob Dylan, the Byrds, Jimi Hendrix, and The Doors, performers sought to fuse high art with popular culture. The underground culture was highly irreverent, a mood captured in essayist Tom Wolfe's *The Electric Kool-Aid Acid Test* (1968), a description of the exploits of writer Ken Kesey, whose Merry Pranksters traveled around the country in a psychedelically painted bus while promoting liberation through drugs, sex, and rock music. Satirical novels by Kesey, Kurt Vonnegut, and Thomas Pynchon won huge followings with absurdist portraits of "straight" life and social conventions. Youth culture received even wider exposure in provocative Hollywood films such as *Bonnie and Clyde* (1967), *The Graduate* (1967), and *Easy Rider* (1969).

Counterculture authors offered validation for alternative values that cherished the spiritual life and transcended competitive ego. Herbert Marcuse's *Eros and Civilization* (1955, 1962) condemned the use of sexual repression to bolster elite rule; Carlos Castaneda's *The Teachings of Don Juan: A Yaqui Way of Knowledge* (1968) rejected the narrowness of materialist rationality; R. D. Laing's *The Politics of Experience* (1966) depicted society's neglect of the inner self as insane. A popularized version of the new perspective found its way into Charles A. Reich's *The Greening of America* (1970), which predicted that the revolutionary counterculture was moving the nation toward an epoch of shared love and community.

Although radical activists insisted on the counterculture's hostility to consumer capitalism, the two forces were undeniably intertwined. Advertisers sought to tap expanded consumer tastes in a period of unprecedented prosperity by tying brand identity to youthful images and countercultural fantasies of liberation and revolution. By associating automobiles, carbonated beverages, cosmetics, and other products with the "rebellion" of the "Now Generation," "hip" marketers encouraged the public to adopt changing styles and fashions as a way of satisfying psychological needs for authenticity and individuality. Pop artist Andy Warhol illustrated the compatibility of the two worlds by creating silk-screened representations of everyday commodities such as soup and soda cans. The purpose of art was to alter consciousness and explore new sensibilities, not to elevate formal culture above popular expressions, lectured essayist Susan Sontag in her influential *Against Interpretation* (1964).

Radical feminists, however, remained adamantly hostile to the temptations of consumer capitalism. Drawing inspiration from the civil rights slogan, "The Personal Is Political," movement activists such as Casey Hayden and Mary King began to organize women against the male domination of SNCC, SDS, and other groups. Despite the radical community's espousal of egalitarian values, they asserted, New Left men mirrored establishment culture by relegating women to office duties and other minor tasks. Feminists also complained

EXHIBIT **12-1**   **ARRESTS OF PERSONS UNDER AGE 18, 1966–1969**
(IN ROUNDED FIGURES)

1966	1,149,000
1969	1,500,000

Source: *Historical Statistics of the United States, Colonial Times to 1970* (1975).

that the male-oriented sexual revolution furthered female debasement by treating women as mere playthings and objects of conquest.

While their male colleagues greeted their efforts with ridicule and outright hostility, New Left women initiated "rap" sessions to share their grievances and address gender identity issues. In 1968, 200 radical feminists went public by organizing the first women's liberation demonstration. Calling themselves the Women's International Terrorist Conspiracy from Hell (WITCH), activists protested against "sexism" and capitalism's "objectification" of women's bodies by picketing the Miss America Pageant and throwing "instruments of torture" such as brassieres and high-heeled shoes into a "freedom trash can." Feminists focused on women's control of their own bodies by embracing an agenda that included the right to legal abortions, dissemination of birth control literature, and passage of tougher laws against rape and spousal abuse.

THE WAR AT HOME

As dissent against the Vietnam War increased, the White House fought to curtail public criticism. Since the early 1960s, FBI Director J. Edgar Hoover had directed counterintelligence (COINTEL) efforts against both the Ku Klux Klan and the civil rights movement. The FBI program was soon expanded to include the wiretapping and bugging of Martin Luther King, whom the director feared as a potential "black messiah." Black Panther militancy toward local police aroused Hoover's anger in 1967, and he ordered counterintelligence activities to "expose, disrupt, misdirect, discredit, or otherwise neutralize the activities of black nationalists." After King joined SNCC leaders in opposing the Vietnam War, the FBI broadened its covert capabilities to disrupting the New Left. The COINTEL program also targeted women's liberation groups.

Other government agencies initiated similar operations against the antiwar movement. Since many campuses encouraged antigovernment activity, Johnson ordered Army Intelligence to join the FBI in putting thousands of students and faculty under surveillance. By 1968 the army had compiled 100,000 dossiers on antiwar dissidents. The president also authorized the CIA's Operation Chaos to conduct domestic surveillance—in violation of the agency's charter—against activists, demonstrators, and even "suspicious" members of Congress. When the CIA notified Johnson that domestic dissent appeared to be independent of foreign funding, he rejected the finding. The

EXHIBIT **12-2**   **U.S. NATIONAL DEFENSE AND VETERANS OUTLAYS, 1966–1968 (IN BILLIONS OF DOLLARS)**

1966	64.0
1968	88.8

Source: *Statistical Abstract of the United States* (1987).

EXHIBIT **12-3**   **CONSUMER PRICE INDEX, 1966–1968 (IN ROUNDED PERCENTS) (1967 = 100)**

1966	97
1967	100
1968	104

Source: *Historical Statistics of the United States, Colonial Times to 1970* (1975).

courts were also used to impede the antiwar movement, as when the Justice Department indicted pediatrician Dr. Benjamin Spock and Yale chaplain William Sloane Coffin for promoting draft evasion.

Johnson thought he could fight poverty and communism simultaneously, that he could finance the Vietnam War without cutting Great Society funding. Yet as military costs rose to $2 billion a month in 1966, the president admitted the impossibility of spending large sums for both "guns and butter." Civil rights demonstrations, urban rioting, and campus protests added to a weakened liberal position. In Chicago, Martin Luther King's open-housing marches into white ethnic neighborhoods provoked violent retaliation. When the White House submitted a federal equal housing bill, two attempts to end a Senate filibuster failed, and the administration settled for a modest rat-control appropriation. In a year of record federal expenditures, Congress abolished the school milk program and cut appropriations for education. The War on Poverty also faced reductions when big-city mayors complained that the community action program had been taken over by minority professionals and other patronage entrepreneurs.

Congressional uneasiness with domestic programs also reflected the soaring inflation caused by war spending. Johnson persuaded Capitol Hill to suspend Kennedy's investment tax credit and accelerated depreciation allowances in 1966, but these minor tax increases provided insufficient funds to finance the war. The president suffered a severe legislative setback when Congress refused to accept a war tax surcharge and preferred spending cuts or tax reform. Although the White House won a small tax surcharge in 1968, the delay in increasing taxation encouraged a crippling inflation that would retard economic growth for the next twenty-five years and bring into question the use of government spending as national policy. Rising prices and war outlays produced a phenomenal rise in the federal deficit, which more than doubled between 1966 and 1967 and nearly tripled during 1968 to more than $25 billion.

Democrats warned that education, jobs, housing reforms, and an end to discrimination were necessary to end domestic strife. Yet voters responded to escalating welfare costs, rising inflation, higher crime rates, black militancy, and antiwar demonstrations by participating in a conservative backlash in the 1966 congressional elections. By stressing increasing crime and the need for law and order, Republican candidates made large gains in both houses of Congress. In California, former movie actor Ronald Reagan, an ex-Democrat, captured the governorship by blaming a cultural elite of liberal politicians, intellectuals, and bureaucrats for the expanding welfare state.

The conservative backlash enabled Alabama's George Wallace to attract a national following. "A bearded professor . . . thinks he knows how to settle the Vietnam War," Wallace told one audience, but he "hasn't got enough sense to park his bicycle straight." Wallace articulated deeply held resentments against liberal government programs, ghetto rioting, and student rebellions and appealed to working people concerned about the rising crime rate and fearful of the loss of traditional values. In 1968 he launched a presidential campaign through the American Independent Party, calling for repeal of civil rights laws and for a military victory in Vietnam. "When I become your president," he declared, "I'm going to ask my attorney general to seek an indictment against any college professor who calls for a communist victory. . . . That's treason."

Despite Wallace's popularity among workers, blue-collar support of the war barely outpaced that of the rest of the nation in a period marked by increasing skepticism over Johnson's credibility. Yet a majority of voters saw peace demonstrations as "acts of disloyalty against the boys fighting in Vietnam." To "hawk" and "dove" alike, the war had become a volatile political issue. Organized labor, led by AFL-CIO President George Meany, remained loyal to the Democratic Party and backed the Vietnam crusade. In 1967 a New York City march "supporting our men in Vietnam" attracted 70,000 people. Nevertheless, Johnson's Democratic consensus seemed to be unraveling.

THE CHAOS OF 1968

Disaffected from the Vietnam War he had helped to orchestrate, Defense Secretary Robert McNamara resigned in late 1967 to head the World Bank. On the eve of Tet (the Vietnamese New Year) early the next year, disaster struck. As Johnson deployed immense firepower to repel the siege of a desolated marine outpost at Khe Sanh, the Vietcong launched a coordinated attack on every major population center in South Vietnam. In Saigon, commandos penetrated the U.S. embassy grounds. In Hue, communist forces executed police officials and political enemies while the South Vietnamese army retaliated against Buddhists, students, and teachers who appeared to be "VC col-

EXHIBIT **12-4**   **THE TET OFFENSIVE**

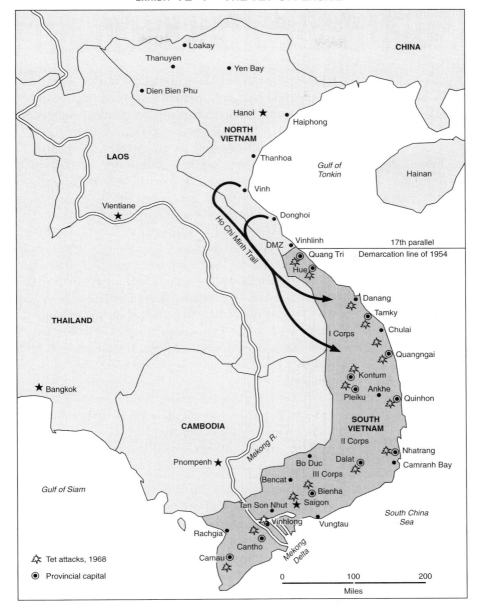

laborators." By the time the cities were once again under Saigon's control, the United States had lost 4,000 soldiers and suffered nearly 20,000 injuries.

The Tet Offensive had cost the lives of 32,000 communist insurgents and greatly depleted Vietcong strength, forcing Hanoi to rely on regular troops to pursue its military objectives. Yet the campaign showed the futility of the U.S.

William Childs Westmoreland (1914–)

General William Childs Westmoreland, the commander of U.S. military forces in Vietnam from 1964 to 1968, embodied the strengths and weaknesses of the U.S. presence in Southeast Asia. A picture-book soldier, he was ramrod straight, 6 feet tall, jut-jawed, brave, meticulous, and self-disciplined. In Vietnam he was determined to prove that superior technology and organization skills could defeat a guerrilla army—but, like civilian leaders, he underestimated the passion and power of the enemy, and he failed to appreciate the political dimensions of the war.

Born in Spartanburg, South Carolina, Westmoreland devoted his entire life to the military. He attended West Point, saw service in World War II, and commanded a parachute troop in Korea. He then went to the Pentagon's manpower office and enrolled in an advanced management program at the Harvard School of Business. Indistinguishable from the other corporate executives in the seminars, the young general became a proficient administrator and later used his association with former classmates who had become defense contractors to increase worker performance and productivity in military procurement and manpower allocation. In 1960 President Dwight Eisenhower appointed him superintendent of West Point.

strategy. In one telling instance, a general ordered the army to destroy a "friendly" village to "save" it from the communists, highlighting the difficulty of assessing civilian loyalty in a civil war. As documentation of military atrocities surfaced in coming months, the public would learn the moral consequences of waging war in Vietnam. Yet the immediate lesson of Tet was that the enemy merely had to survive to prevent the United States from "winning." The offensive also exposed the inability of South Vietnamese troops to defend positions without U.S. assistance or air strikes.

By drastically undermining support for Johnson's war policy at home, Tet provoked one of the most tumultuous years in U.S. political history. Although General William Westmoreland insisted that the tide in Vietnam had turned, he then requested another 200,000 troops and mobilization of the reserves— proposals that would have added $12 billion to war costs already reaching

Chosen to lead U.S. troops in Vietnam in 1964, Westmoreland drew upon his vast administrative skill. Even to the general's critics, his logistic achievements seemed astounding. Under his command, the military constructed deep-water ports, jet airfields, tactical airstrips, hundreds of helicopter pads, storage facilities, and miles of telephone cable and radio grids, as well as bridges, roads, canals, and seaways. Westmoreland's demand for troops also appeared voracious and increased from 16,000 in 1964 to 520,000 in 1968.

Such power inflicted immense damage but could not defeat the elusive enemy. Nor could the seemingly unending war justify the tremendous drain on U.S. resources. When political leaders recognized that victory could not be achieved, President Johnson appointed Westmoreland Chief of Staff of the Army in 1968 and ordered him back to Washington. "We have curtailed the tide of Communist aggression," Westmoreland stated in his final report on the war; ". . . the enemy has not won a single major victory."

The general never accepted responsibility for the defeat in Vietnam. "However desirable the American system of civilian control of the military," he argued in his memoirs, "it was a mistake to permit appointive civilian officials lacking military experience and knowledge . . . to wield undue influence in the decision-making process."

$30 billion a year. As opposition to the conflict intensified, newly appointed Defense Secretary Clark Clifford found extensive dove sentiment within the Pentagon. In March 1968 antiwar Senator Eugene McCarthy of Minnesota astounded the nation by taking 42 percent of the vote in the New Hampshire Democratic presidential primary, a serious political defeat for the White House. Days later, New York Senator Robert Kennedy announced his candidacy. Within a week, Johnson relieved Westmoreland of the Vietnam command and summoned a meeting of senior advisors to reassess the war effort.

The White House conference included twelve of the most prestigious members of the nation's foreign policy, business, and legal establishment. Nearly all had supported the escalation of bombing in 1967. But now they concluded that the present policy could not achieve its objectives without full citizen support and major budgetary sacrifices, and they warned that the war

President Johnson listened somberly to the advice of the administration's "wise men" at a meeting in the Oval Office on March 26, 1968. Five days later, Johnson withdrew from the presidential contest.

threatened the position of the U.S. dollar abroad. The bombing of North Vietnam had damaged the administration in Washington more than the regime in Hanoi, scolded former Secretary of State Dean Acheson. Johnson agonized about his response. Then, on the evening of March 31, 1968, he gave a dramatic televised speech announcing the suspension of the bombing of North Vietnam and a willingness to negotiate with the communist enemy. In a surprising postscript, he also announced his withdrawal from the presidential race.

Four days later, on the day North Vietnam agreed to peace talks, a self-proclaimed racist named James Earl Ray assassinated Martin Luther King in Memphis, Tennessee. King had come to the city to support a strike of predominantly African American sanitation workers. The murder provoked a spasm of racial violence and riots in more than 100 cities and sent smoke from black neighborhoods circling above the Capitol Dome in Washington, D.C. King had hoped to draw attention to the need for jobs and housing with a Poor People's March on Washington that spring, but without his presence the demonstration lost focus. Goaded by his assassination, Congress at last passed the long-delayed open-housing bill, which banned discrimination in the sale and rental of about four-fifths of the nation's housing and provided more than $5 billion in mortgage and rent subsidies.

Johnson's withdrawal from presidential politics emboldened sentiment for a negotiated end to the war and sparked heated campaigns by peace candidates Senators McCarthy and Kennedy. The White House choice, Vice President Hubert Humphrey, remained on the sidelines; but in June, Kennedy won the California primary—only to be killed minutes after his victory by Sirhan Sirhan, a Palestinian opposed to the senator's support for Israel. Bitterly divided over the Vietnam War and related social issues, the Democratic Party drifted for want of leadership.

The assassinations of King and Kennedy underscored the national political and cultural crisis. At New York's Columbia University, cooperation between African American activists and SDS briefly surfaced in the spring of 1968 when the two groups separately occupied university buildings to protest campus ties to the war as well as planned expansion into a Harlem community park. Yet blacks called off their action just before New York City police viciously smashed the SDS occupation. The confrontation, which brought nearly 700 arrests, set the tone for clashes at every major university—more than three thousand campus protests occurred during 1968. Public opinion polls found that most respondents blamed the demonstrators, not the police, for the violence.

As the Democratic Party prepared to nominate Vice President Humphrey, several thousand peace activists and young radicals descended on Chicago to hold a "festival of life" and demonstrate at the national convention. Their protest was coordinated by a coalition of antiestablishment groups, including the Youth International Party (Yippies), a group of cultural dissidents organized by antiwar leaders Jerry Rubin and Abbie Hoffman. Mayor Richard Daley refused to allow demonstrators to protest in the streets or camp in city parks and ordered mass arrests and the use of indiscriminate force, permitting what a presidential commission later called a "police riot." While street crowds chanted, "The whole world is watching!" police attacked protesters, passersby, and the media with clubs and mace. Inside the convention, party leaders defeated a dovish platform and proceeded to nominate Hubert Humphrey.

THE "NEW" NIXON

With his party split, Humphrey's chances seemed slim against Republican nominee Richard Nixon. After losing a bitter race for the California governorship in 1962, Nixon had joined a prestigious New York law firm and refurbished his image as an elder statesman with extensive world travel that provided him with the opportunity to consult foreign leaders. Vowing to "bring the American people together," the candidate declared that 1968 was the "time for a complete housecleaning" in Washington. Regarding Vietnam, Nixon promised to "end the war and win the peace in the Pacific," although he provided no specifics other than to hint at a Great Power settlement. "We're going to build this country up so that no one will dare use the U.S. flag for a doormat again," he stated.

Robert Francis Kennedy *(1925–1968)*

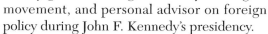

Robert Kennedy's assassination signaled the end of hope in a turbulent era desperately in need of conciliation. Kennedy had served as the New Frontier's principal power broker. He was his brother's presidential campaign manager in 1960, attorney general during the stormy civil rights movement, and personal advisor on foreign policy during John F. Kennedy's presidency.

As a tough Irish American, Kennedy helped to shape counterinsurgency in Vietnam, personally supervised the CIA's covert campaigns in Cuba, and had a reputation as a cool-handed operator with a ruthless streak. Dallas changed all that. The heir apparent to the presidency, Bobby Kennedy began a new career in 1964 as the junior senator from New York. Deeply affected by his loss, he used his prestige to push for greater commitments to those without privilege or power. He visited Cesar Chavez's striking farmworkers in California, heard testimony on malnutrition in Mississippi, and held hearings on the squalor of reservation life in New Mexico. Kennedy warned in 1967 that "we cannot measure national spirit by the Dow-Jones Average, nor national achievement by the gross national product."

The senator was not among the first to question the Vietnam War. However, early in 1966 he issued a cautious call for a coalition government in Saigon. A year later he took the floor to condemn the Johnson administration's bombing: "We are all participants. . . . We must also feel as men the anguish of what it is we are doing." In 1967 Kennedy delivered a spontaneous tirade on national television against U.S. slaughter of the Vietnamese people. Commentators began to speculate on his

Nixon's most emphatic message addressed voter fears concerning domestic instability and safety on the streets. "The first civil right of every American," he declared, was to be free of violence. In the face of student protests and ghetto riots, the nominee called for recognition of "the Silent Americans"—working people "forgotten" by high-minded liberals and unruly radicals. Nixon's vice presidential running mate, Governor Spiro Agnew of Mary-

availability as a presidential candidate, but Kennedy was too much of a professional to risk splitting the Democratic Party in a personal vendetta against an incumbent president. Johnson's political fall in 1968 moved the senator to action.

The eighty-five-day presidential campaign of Robert Kennedy stirred an emotional groundswell seldom seen in election politics. Kennedy's proposals for a draft lottery, corporate development of the ghettos, and Vietnam negotiations were modest; but he symbolized the lost idealism of the New Frontier, the flickering hope that all classes and races could share in the American Dream. He campaigned on the streets with his jacket off, tie loose, and sleeves rolled up. Excited crowds swarmed the primary trail just to touch his hand.

When Martin Luther King was assassinated, Kennedy went directly to a ghetto street gathering in Indianapolis and shared his own feelings of loss by quoting the Greek poet Aeschylus. A nearby graffito explained his remarkable following among African Americans: "Kennedy white but alright / The one before, he opened the door." Yet the secret to the Kennedy campaign was the compassion he expressed toward all the nation's working people and dispossessed. Despite his stance against the war, the strict Catholic and father of ten scored large primary pluralities in white districts that had previously supported George Wallace.

Kennedy was the only leader of his era who might have united white working people, antiwar students, and racial minorities in a coalition for change. His assassination by a Palestinian Arab incensed at the candidate's support for Israel was a harsh blow to the nation. At the Democratic Convention in Chicago, delegates wept and sang the "Battle Hymn of the Republic" in his memory.

land, a Greek American, had achieved national prominence by attacking violent black power and antiwar demonstrators and by espousing the traditional social values and law-and-order requirements of white ethnics and George Wallace supporters.

The conservative Nixon campaign enhanced its prospects by advancing the political use of television advertising. Professional marketers merged the candidate's calm voice with a series of still black-and-white images, associating the nominee with serene competence, respect for tradition, and faith in the American people. Campaign operatives also staged ten regional live broadcasts enabling Nixon to answer questions from specially selected panels of "ordinary" citizens. Nixon used these opportunities to court the traditional Democratic constituency of white southerners, northern Catholics, lower-middle-class Jews, and blue-collar workers—the so-called middle Americans who resented liberal preoccupation with racial minorities and who despised the influence of counterculture values. "Our objective in the next four years should not be to get more people on welfare rolls—we want to get more people on payrolls," Nixon declared. His TV commercials carried this warning: "VOTE AS IF YOUR WHOLE WORLD DEPENDED ON IT."

As the seriousness of the Republican challenge intensified, President Johnson moved toward a settlement of the Vietnam War. In September, Johnson had rejected private North Vietnamese overtures. But in the following month the president announced a complete halt of the bombing and began active campaigning for Humphrey. However, Republican operatives, fearing Nixon's defeat, used intermediaries to urge the South Vietnamese government to refuse participation in the peace talks and wait for a better deal once the Democrats lost. The Saigon regime then opposed the seating of the National Liberation Front at the Paris negotiations. Although FBI wiretaps of the South Vietnamese Embassy and other sources confirmed the arrangement, the Johnson administration had no evidence of Nixon's personal involvement and feared a constitutional crisis should the deal be exposed.

Despite Humphrey's dramatic narrowing of Nixon's lead in the last week of the campaign, he never overcame the burden of White House incumbency or the Democratic Party's association with lawlessness and the disorder of the Chicago convention. In the North, Humphrey managed to preserve the historic New Deal coalition of labor, blacks, Jews, and Catholics. Yet the Democrats took only 35 percent of the overall white vote and failed to retain the loyalty of sufficient numbers of middle-class citizens. By positioning himself as a moderate capable of healing the nation's bitter social divisions, Nixon won the 1968 election by less than 1 percentage point in one of the closest races in U.S. history. Wallace's American Independent Party, which had hoped to force the contest into the House of Representatives, amassed nearly 14 percent of the vote and claimed 45 electoral votes in the Deep South. Together, Nixon and Wallace carried 57 percent of the national electorate, although Democrats maintained control of both houses of Congress by substantial margins.

The turbulence of 1968 shook public faith in the political system. As the credibility gap and violent dissent brought widespread alienation from the White House and conventional politics, the U.S. death toll in Vietnam passed 30,000. At year's end more than 500,000 soldiers remained in that distant out-

EXHIBIT **12-5**   **THE ELECTION OF 1968**

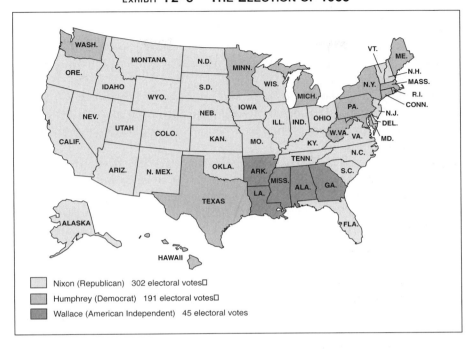

Nixon (Republican)   302 electoral votes☐

Humphrey (Democrat)   191 electoral votes☐

Wallace (American Independent)   45 electoral votes

post of national aspirations. Fatigued by bitter divisions of war, race, and culture, a weary nation looked to Richard Nixon to restore tranquility at home, achieve a dignified peace abroad, and stabilize the domestic economy.

AMERICAN HISTORY
RESOURCE CENTER

To explore documents, images, audio and video clips, articles, and commentary related to the material in this chapter, visit the source collections at ushistory.wadsworth.com and and use the Search function with the following key terms:

Tet Offensive   Cesar Chavez
Malcolm X   George Wallace
Richard Nixon   Black Panther Party
Thurgood Marshall

RECOMMENDED READINGS

Robert D. Schulzinger, *A Time for War: The United States and Vietnam, 1941–1975* (1997). This overview of the Vietnam War places Johnson's escalation in full context.

Douglas C. Rossinow, *The Politics of Authenticity: Liberalism, Christianity, and the New Left in America* (1998). The author breaks new ground by tying antiwar activism and participatory democracy to Protestant moralism in Texas and the South.

Dan T. Carter, *The Politics of Rage: George Wallace, the Origins of the New Conservatism, and the Transformation of American Politics* (1995). A key source for understanding the rise of populist conservatism in the 1960s.

Thomas Frank, *The Conquest of Cool: Business Culture, Counterculture, and the Rise of Hip Consumerism* (1997). This innovative work establishes connections between countercultural values and the 1960s innovations of Madison Avenue.

Additional Readings

For overviews of the 1965–1968 period, descriptions of the Johnson administration, and accounts of civil rights and ethnic identity movements, see the sources listed in Chapter 11. Additional overviews of the 1960s include David Burner, *Making Peace with the Sixties* (1996); Douglas T. Miller, *On Our Own: Americans in the 1960s* (1996); and Irwin Unger and Debi Unger, *America in the 1960s* (1988). Accounts of reform and its limitations include Irwin Unger, *The Best of Intentions: The Triumph of the Great Society Under Kennedy, Johnson, and Nixon* (1996), and Jill Quadagno, *The Color of Welfare: How Racism Undermined the War on Poverty* (1994).

For further discussion of African American radicalism, see Philip S. Foner, ed., *The Black Panther Party: A Brief History with Documents* (1996). The definitive history of feminism can be found in Ruth Rosen's *The World Split Open: How the Modern Women's Movement Changed America* (2000). The origins of radical feminism are traced in Sara Evans, *Personal Politics: The Root of Women's Liberation in the Civil Rights Movement and the New Left* (1979).

Surveys of the Vietnam War are listed in the readings for Chapter 11. For criticism of the notion that a liberal media helped to lose the war, see Clarence R. Wyatt, *Paper Soldiers: The American Press and the Vietnam War* (1993).

For the antiwar movement, student activism, and the counterculture, see the listings in Chapter 13. Additional sources include Terry Anderson, *The Movement and the Sixties: Protest in America from Greensboro to Wounded Knee* (1995). See also the perceptive Peter Levy, *The New Left and Labor in the 1960s* (1994). Media treatment of dissidents is described in Melvin Small, *Covering Dissent: The Media and the Anti-Vietnam War Movement* (1994), and Todd Gitlin, *The Whole World Is Watching: Mass Media and the Making and Unmaking of the New Left* (1980).

Changes in sexual conventions are outlined in David Allyn, *Make Love, Not War: The Sexual Revolution, An Unfettered History* (2000). Drugs and the counterculture are discussed in Jay Stevens, *Storming Heaven: LSD and the American Dream* (1987), and Martin A. Lee and Bruce Shlain, *Acid Dreams: The CIA, LSD, and the Sixties Rebellion* (1985). For the intellectual roots of the counterculture, see Theodore Roszak, *The Making of the Counter Culture* (1969). A good study of cultural dissent can be found in Jonah Raskin, *For the Hell of It: The Life and Times of Abbie Hoffman* (1997). For popular culture, see David Pichaske, *A Generation in Motion: Popular Music and Culture in the Sixties* (1989), and Jon Weiner, *Come Together: John Lennon in His Time* (1991). Youth-oriented Hollywood films are analyzed in portions of Michael Ryan and Douglas Kellner, *Camera Politica: The Politics and Ideology of Contemporary Hollywood Film* (1990).

For FBI activities, see David J. Garrow, *The FBI and Martin Luther King, Jr.* (1981); Richard Gid Powers, *Secrecy and Power: The Life of J. Edgar Hoover* (1987); and Athan G. Theoharis and John Stuart Cox, *The Boss: J. Edgar Hoover and the Great American Inquisition* (1988). Conservative political activism is described in Stephan Lesher, *George Wallace: American Populist* (1994); in Kent Schuparra, *Triumph of the Right: The Rise of the California Conservative Movement, 1945–1966* (1998); and in segments of Jerome L. Himmelstein, *To the Right: The Transformation of American Conservatism* (1990).

For the politics of 1968, see William H. Chafe, *Never Stop Running: Allard Lowenstein and the Struggle to Save American Liberalism* (1993); David Halberstam, *The Unfinished Odyssey of Robert Kennedy* (1968); and David Farber, *Chicago '68* (1988). The Nixon campaign is described in the relevant segment of Roger Morris, *Richard Milhous Nixon: The Rise of an American Politician* (1990); in Stephen E. Ambrose, *Nixon: The Triumph of a Politician, 1962–1972* (1989); and in William C. Berman, *America's Right Turn: From Nixon to Bush* (1994).

THE EMBATTLED PRESIDENCY, 1968–1976

Richard Nixon's election revealed widespread impatience with liberal social values and positioned the Republican Party as an advocate of George Wallace's populist conservatism. Nevertheless, the Nixon administration embodied enormous contradictions. While defending individual responsibility and demanding reduced federal power, the president expanded the welfare state and broadened the scope of regulatory reform, making strong commitments to environmental policy. Overseas, the White House worked with National Security Assistant Henry Kissinger to sustain respect for U.S. power and military strength. Yet the Nixon administration ended the nation's painful commitment to Vietnam and pulled off the most dramatic diplomatic triumph of the entire Cold War era by forging a détente with historic communist rivals.

Nixon also brought his personal demons to the White House. Having forged his reputation in Congress and the vice presidency as a bitter anticommunist, he resented the social superiority of affluent reformers like the Kennedys. Nixon hoped to use the presidency to get back at a "soft" liberal establishment he believed to have been "poisoned by the elite universities and the media." Despite its accomplishments, Nixon's presidency unraveled because his animosity toward adversaries led to the political abuses associated with the Watergate scandal. As Gerald Ford served out his predecessor's second term, disillusionment over Vietnam and Watergate threatened to erode national confidence and public trust in government.

THE INDOCHINA BIND AND THE NEW FEDERALISM AT HOME

Aware that massive commitments of military force in Vietnam had destroyed Lyndon Johnson's presidency, Nixon sought to prevail in Southeast Asia by combining Cold War diplomacy with the selective use of force. He believed

424

that the Soviet Union might be willing to pressure North Vietnam into a nego-tiated settlement in exchange for superpower negotiations about arms control and Berlin. Yet within one month of taking office, the administration faced a North Vietnamese military offensive. Responding assertively but hoping to limit public criticism from neutralist Cambodia, the president dispatched B-52 bombers in a secret campaign against communist sanctuaries located within Vietnam's southwest neighbor. Meanwhile, the White House sent Henry Kissinger to engage the North Vietnamese in secret talks in Paris.

Although negotiations floundered over Hanoi's insistence that North Viet-namese troops remain in the South and that the Saigon government be re-placed with a coalition, the new president announced what appeared to be a policy change in the spring of 1969. In what was called the Nixon Doctrine, Nixon promised that "Vietnamization" of the war would permit gradual with-drawal of U.S. ground troops while expanding the air campaign against the North. Meanwhile, Saigon would receive sufficient military assistance to com-plete the struggle against the communists. Yet Hanoi continued to ignore U.S. threats, leading Kissinger to fume that "a little fourth-rate power like North Vietnam" had to "have a breaking point." As polls during the fall of 1969 re-vealed that 57 percent of Americans favored a specific deadline for total dis-engagement in Vietnam, domestic public opinion became a serious obstacle to the White House's Indochina strategy.

The administration's major challenge at home was the maintenance of economic prosperity. Since the end of World War II, the Bretton Woods sys-tem of international exchange rates and the open market arrangements of the General Agreement on Tariffs and Trade (GATT) had provided enormous ad-vantages for U.S. business. During the 1960s, U.S. multinational corporations took part in an unprecedented wave of mergers. Reduced tariffs and lower in-vestment barriers enhanced their global position. Between 1960 and 1974, the foreign assets of U.S. banks leaped from $3 billion to $155 billion. Inte-gration into the world economy was of great interest to financial figures such as David Rockefeller, who in 1973 created the Trilateral Commission, a "think tank" of business leaders, social planners, and politicians from western Eu-rope, Japan, and the United States devoted to such issues as long-term devel-opment and global stability.

As U.S. military spending, foreign aid, and overseas investment diverted capital from the economy at home, however, the "golden age" of postwar pros-perity appeared to be increasingly fragile. These trends accelerated in 1971 when the Organization of Petroleum Exporting Countries (OPEC) raised oil prices, tripling the U.S. balance of trade deficit. The "dollar drain" reduced U.S. gold reserves and lowered currency values. As inflation set in, corporate debt and government budget deficits intensified the competition for credit, leading to a rise in interest rates. As a result of both trends—inflation and higher interest rates—consumers suffered a substantial reduction in spending

EXHIBIT **13-1**   **U.S. NATIONAL DEFENSE AND VETERANS OUTLAYS, 1968–1976 (IN BILLIONS OF DOLLARS)**

1968	88.8
1970	90.4
1972	89.9
1974	92.7
1976	108.0

Source: *Statistical Abstract of the United States* (1987).

power and a threat to savings. The deterioration of "real" wages also encouraged labor unrest, leading to a wildcat strike by the Teamsters Union, an extended walkout by automakers, and a brief disruption of mail delivery by postal workers during the first strike by federal employees in U.S. history.

Nixon acted to reduce inflation by cutting government spending and by encouraging higher interest rates, but these measures merely brought "stagflation"—a combination of rising prices and high unemployment. Desperate to reverse negative economic trends, the president suspended gold payments for dollars in 1971, thereby taking the nation off the gold standard and ending participation in the Bretton Woods system. Nixon established the first peacetime economic controls since 1947 and ordered a ninety-day freeze on wages, prices, and rents; he also placed a surtax on imports. Such unprecedented administrative measures ironically came from a Republican chief executive who claimed to support smaller government. Even though Nixon created a Cost of Living Council to monitor rising costs, continuing stagflation compelled him to end the import surtax after devaluing the dollar.

Because of the continuing structural weaknesses of the economy, Nixon ignored his own warnings and stepped up the federal government's social welfare activity. Under the leadership of White House advisors John Ehrlichman and Harvard sociologist Daniel Patrick Moynihan, the administration created a new set of executive agencies—including the Office of Management and Budget (OMB), the Domestic Council, and the Urban Affairs Council—which worked with the Democratic Congress to expand Great Society reform. By indexing Social Security payments to the cost of living, the government enabled millions of older Americans to raise their incomes above the poverty level. Nixon nearly tripled the caseload of Aid to Families with Dependent Children (AFDC), the nation's largest welfare program. Congress also quadrupled food stamp coverage when midwestern agricultural interests lobbied to extend the program to the able-bodied and to the nonelderly poor. In 1969 the White House introduced a $6 billion Family Assistance Plan that offered a guaranteed annual income to needy families and proposed to triple the number of welfare recipients. Nixon also called for a comprehensive health-care plan based on employer mandates. And even without the additional welfare benefits, federal income maintenance costs surpassed defense outlays for the first time in history.

EXHIBIT **13-2** **CONSUMER PRICE INDEX, 1968–1976 (1967 = 100)**

1968	104.2
1970	116.3
1972	125.3
1974	147.4
1976	170.5

Source: *Economic Report of the President* (1988).

EXHIBIT **13-3** **U.S. GOVERNMENT SPENDING AS A PERCENTAGE OF GROSS NATIONAL PRODUCT, 1969–1976**

1969	30.5
1976	33.9

Source: *Historical Statistics of the United States, Colonial Times to 1970* (1975); *Economic Report of the President* (1977).

Nixon also responded to public concern about environmental deterioration and safety issues and substantially broadened federal regulatory power. In 1970 the president approved creation of the Occupational Safety and Health Administration (OSHA), an agency empowered to set mandatory standards to protect employees from workplace hazards. Nixon made environmental protection a matter of national priority. After signing the Endangered Species Act in 1969, the president endorsed the National Environmental Policy Act, which required the government to issue ecological impact statements about pending legislation or programs. The Clean Air Act of 1970 set emission standards for new cars and reorganized antipollution agencies into the Environmental Protection Agency (EPA). The new bureau outlawed the use of the pesticide DDT and implemented a congressional ban on the production and stockpiling of biological and chemical weapons. Environmental rules contributed to a sixfold increase in the length of the *Federal Register*'s guide to regulations during the Nixon presidency.

Although the Republican administration expanded government power, Nixon courted public opinion by packaging his reforms as a limitation on Washington's influence. For example, the president described his Family Assistance Plan as "workfare" because it contained employment requirements for some recipients. When Democrats complained of inadequate support levels for the proposal, however, they joined antiwelfare conservatives in defeating the measure in Congress. Angered by the lack of cooperation from liberals, Nixon made major cuts in Head Start, the Job Corps, and the War on Poverty. He also introduced a "revenue sharing" plan to reduce government spending, which had reached nearly one-third the gross national product, and sought to give the states primary responsibility for welfare programs. Despite Nixon's much-heralded "new federalism," however, federal budget deficits continued to mount.

AFFIRMATIVE ACTION AND THE BURGER COURT

The Nixon White House assumed a wildly contradictory approach to race relations, an area of government activism often criticized by social conservatives. In the South, radio crusaders such as Reverends Carl McIntyre and Billy James Hargis had contributed to a conservative social climate in the 1960s by combining evangelical enthusiasm with harsh assaults on liberal social programs as communist inspired. As population in the Sunbelt exploded in the next two decades (the Southwest would claim five of the nation's ten largest cities by 1980), evangelical churches expanded their traditional influence. Between 1965 and 1974, the Southern Baptist Convention gained almost 2 million followers, and its total membership reached 12.5 million. Meanwhile, mainstream liberal Protestant denominations lost members to charismatic sects whose leaders professed divinely inspired powers of healing and prophecy.

Resentment of Washington's civil rights agenda also resonated among George Wallace's supporters in northern and midwestern industrial cities. Blue-collar and middle-class white ethnic descendants of immigrants often invoked traditional virtues such as patriotism, religion, the work ethic, and family loyalty. Hostile to the counterculture and the national media, millions of Italian, Greek, and Slavic Americans centered their families and social lives around communal practices from the past, a phenomenon reflected in such Hollywood films as *The Godfather, Parts I and II* (1971, 1974), *Rocky* (1976), and *Saturday Night Fever* (1977).

Many working-class whites blamed "permissive" schools, "liberal" media, misguided judges, and amoral officials for rising welfare costs, higher taxes, increased drug use, and criminal activity (crime rates doubled between 1960 and 1980). In cities such as Philadelphia, voters elected tough law-and-order mayors like Police Commissioner Frank Rizzo. Neighborhood anticrime groups such as the Guardian Angels and New York's Jewish Defense League (JDL) established foot patrols to protect city residents, leading to increased racial tensions in some cases. The most controversial expression of white ethnic power centered on the campaign against court-ordered busing. Busing, which was designed to achieve racial integration in northern public schools, raised fears that inner-city youth would bring crime, drug use, and poverty into stable, white neighborhoods. Grassroots antibusing activists such as Boston's Louise Day Hicks led demonstrations and boycotts in the 1970s to protest the imposition of school integration by liberal government officials.

As federal courts integrated public schools in the South and reduced the region's proportion of African Americans in segregated educational facilities to 8 percent, Nixon professed to endorse racial equality and due process. Yet in northern suburbs, the White House tailored civil rights enforcement to

meet the preferences of white Wallace supporters and Republican conservatives. When the Supreme Court unanimously sanctioned busing to promote
school integration in 1973, Nixon rejected use of "arbitrary" guidelines and
proposed a congressional moratorium on the forced transfer of pupils. Federal judges responded by slowing racial integration in the North, and the
Supreme Court confined busing to districts that intentionally segregated. By
1974 half of African American students in northern and western states remained in schools whose racial composition was at least 95 percent black.

Insisting that "black capitalism" offered the surest road to equal opportunity, Nixon followed White House advisor Moynihan's call for a civil rights
policy of "benign neglect." The president denounced racial quotas as "a dangerous detour away from the traditional value of measuring a person on the
basis of ability." Yet the Nixon administration quietly extended the implementation of affirmative action (the principle of compensatory racial justice) to include employment and union membership practices. Affirmative action drove
a wedge between Democratic constituencies in organized labor and in the
civil rights movement. Lyndon Johnson's Department of Labor had responded to historic patterns of racial prejudice by requiring government construction contractors to end job discrimination. In 1969 Nixon's Secretary of
Labor George P. Shultz introduced the "Philadelphia Plan," a program that
applied a proportional system of minority hiring in federally funded construction and required contractors to file affirmative action policies with the Labor
Department.

In 1971 the Supreme Court upheld preferential hiring in *Griggs* v. *Duke
Power Co.* (1971) by ruling that job applicants could not be subjected to apti-
tude tests or arbitrary job qualifications if such policies sustained discriminatory patterns. The decision paved the way for antibias suits against fire and
police departments and against building contractors. Congress advanced affirmative action by expanding the enforcement powers of the Equal Employment Opportunity Commission (EEOC). By 1974 the Washington bureaucracy provided more than $240 million a year in "set-asides" for minority
contractors. By then, racial and ethnic minorities constituted one-fifth of the
federal government's civilian labor force, and affirmative action affected one-
third of the nation's workforce.

The Labor Department had not originally targeted women workers, but
in 1970 Nixon approved an agency directive that ordered equal treatment of
both sexes in recruitment, job opportunities, pay, and the granting of seniority rights. Congress supplemented such coverage in 1972 by prohibiting sex
discrimination in all federally funded educational programs and thereby leg-
islated equal support for men and women in collegiate athletics. Democratic
pressure also led the administration to continue civil rights reform when
Congress renewed the Voting Rights Act in 1970. The law retained federal

registrars in southern states and suspended literacy tests for another five years. It also triggered the deployment of registrars anywhere in the country where more than half of the minority population of voting age had failed to register.

Nixon's support for minority voting rights played a key role in the president's "southern strategy." Anticipating that newly enfranchised African Americans would vote Democratic, the president hoped to attract white southerners to the Republican Party and end Democratic domination of the region. The White House courted white votes in the South by balancing its qualified support for civil rights with a series of controversial nominations to the Supreme Court. As a presidential candidate, Nixon had denounced the court for "permissiveness" for abolishing compulsory prayer in public schools and for requiring procedural protections for criminal suspects. When Chief Justice Earl Warren retired in 1969, the president chose Minnesota moderate Warren E. Burger to replace him. When a second vacancy occurred that year, the White House nominated South Carolina Judge Clement F. Haynsworth. After the Democratic Senate questioned the conservative Haynsworth about a judicial conflict of interest, however, he became the first Supreme Court nominee to be rejected in forty years.

The president responded to the Haynsworth defeat by nominating another southerner, G. Harold Carswell, but the Florida judge failed to win Senate confirmation after revelations concerning white supremacist statements made earlier in his career. Infuriated, the president denounced "regional discrimination" and claimed that the power of appointment had been abrogated by liberals hostile to a strict interpretation of the Constitution. Yet the White House eased tensions by selecting Harry A. Blackmun, a well-qualified moderate, whom the Senate easily confirmed. When two more vacancies occurred in 1971, the appointments of Lewis F. Powell Jr. and William Rehnquist provided Nixon with the conservative ideological consistency he desired.

Despite White House efforts to mold a conservative majority, however, the Burger Court had a mixed record. The high tribunal outlawed domestic national security wiretaps without judicial permission in 1972 and ruled the death penalty unconstitutional because of its cruelty and inconsistent application. In *Roe* v. *Wade* (1973), its most controversial decision, the Court struck down state abortion laws covering the initial three months of pregnancy as a violation of a woman's right to privacy and an intrusion into the physician-client relationship, although the justices said that states could prohibit abortions during the final term and regulate midterm pregnancies affecting a woman's health. The Court balanced these "liberal" decisions by limiting the immunity of witnesses from prosecution, permitting nonunanimous jury verdicts in state criminal cases, and compelling journalists to testify before grand juries. Moreover, in 1975 the Court reversed earlier rulings by providing a "local option" for obscenity and pornography censorship. The following year the Court approved death penalty statutes if they were carefully constructed and applied without discrimination.

RADICAL CULTURE AND IDENTITY POLITICS

President Nixon's continuation of the war in Vietnam and his conservative policies at home inspired the spread of a broad radical movement infused with counterculture values and identity politics. One expression of the dissident culture occurred during the summer of 1969 at Woodstock, an upstate New York rock music festival whose 400,000 participants gathered to celebrate love, community, and peace. As leading bands performed, many in the crowd shared marijuana, shed their clothes, and celebrated the rise of an idealistic "new generation" and spiritually advanced "Age of Aquarius." Woodstock marked the coming of age of a youth-oriented popular culture devoted to personal liberation, affinity with nature, and rejection of traditional authorities. Yet as rock music developed into a $1 billion industry, the youth market embraced capitalist commodities such as blue jeans, waterbeds, granola, "hip" cosmetics, specialized hair accessories, and Hollywood movie hits like the documentary *Woodstock* (1970).

Countercultural interest in spirituality stimulated new concern about ecological issues. The focus on planet Earth initially surfaced as a result of the U.S. space program. In 1969 the landing of astronauts Neil A. Armstrong and Colonel Edwin E. Aldrin Jr. on the Moon in the *Apollo 11* spacecraft was televised worldwide. "That's one small step for a man," said Armstrong, "one giant leap for mankind." Space photographs confirmed that Earth was a small and frail island of life in an immense universe. Environmentalists like Barry Commoner explained that humans lived within Earth's atmosphere and needed to limit air pollution from manufacturing and auto exhausts. In *The Closing Circle* (1971), Commoner declared that the industrial system interfered with nature's attempts to regulate Earth's air, water, and soil. An international study, *The Limits to Growth* (1972), concluded that economic growth threatened to exhaust the planet's resources by the end of the twentieth century.

By April 1970, when environmentalists organized university teach-ins to celebrate the first Earth Day, a national ecological movement had begun. Activists directed attention toward toxic residues from fossil fuels and petrochemical fertilizers, nonbiodegradable waste from plastics and detergents, industrial pollutants that turned rivers into fire hazards, and damage to the atmosphere's ozone layer from aerosol sprays and other chemicals. The environmental movement took its cues from such writers as E. F. Schumacher, author of *Small Is Beautiful* (1973), who criticized the materialism of Western capitalism and insisted that human survival depended on a harmonious relationship with nature that required a livable technology of solar, geothermal, and wind power. Urban cooperative stores and rural communes sought to simplify consumer habits through use of organic foods and natural fibers.

Radical culture also embraced the feminist revolution, which used liberatory "rap groups" and "consciousness-raising" sessions to build collective self-esteem among growing numbers of middle-class women. Inspired by the politics of identity, Gloria Steinem launched *Ms.* magazine in 1971. Calls for the restructuring of patriarchy and capitalism appeared in such provocative books as Kate Millett's *Sexual Politics* (1969), Shulamith Firestone's *The Dialectic of Sex: The Case for Feminist Revolution* (1970), and Robin Morgan's *Sisterhood Is Powerful* (1970). These works not only inspired the spread of women's studies classes and programs but also contributed to bonds of solidarity among radical women whose empowerment derived from their criticism of the social and moral conventions of the status quo.

Opponents of economic discrimination against women constituted another segment of the feminist movement. Demanding that the market treat women equally as individuals, these activists worked with such groups as the National Organization for Women (NOW), the academic Women's Equity Action League (WEAL), and the Professional Women's Caucus (PWC). While reformers promoted "equal pay for equal work," groups like the National Women's Political Caucus helped to break down gender barriers to holding office. As congresswomen such as Shirley Chisholm and Bella Abzug assumed prominence in the early 1970s, radical and reformist feminists joined forces to endorse the Equal Rights Amendment (ERA), which Congress approved and sent to the states for ratification in 1972. The following year, women's rights activists celebrated *Roe* v. *Wade,* the Supreme Court's landmark decision on abortion, as a victory for women's freedom to control their bodies. After 1973, abortion clinics and hospitals performed more than 1.5 million legal abortion procedures each year. Meanwhile, a growing feminist health movement explored alternative methods of birthing, healing, and treatment of women's diseases such as breast cancer.

The women's liberation movement inspired protests among homosexuals of both genders. The movement originated in 1969, when New York City police raided the Stonewall Inn, a gay men's bar in Greenwich Village, and angry patrons fought back against harassment for the first time. Gay men and lesbians soon announced a national gay power and civil rights movement that portrayed homosexuality as a chosen lifestyle instead of as a disease or criminal pastime. Their efforts at self-validation inspired the American Psychiatric Society to drop its classification of homosexuality as a mental disorder in 1975. The anniversary of the Stonewall riot continues to serve as an occasion for yearly marches to celebrate gay pride.

Native Americans, seeking to overcome a legacy of economic devastation, government abuse, and social demoralization, also turned to identity politics. In 1969 members of the American Indian Movement (AIM) began an eighteen-month occupation of San Francisco Bay's Alcatraz Island, the site of a former federal prison, to demand that the government permit them to establish a cultural center on its grounds. The protest was part of an effort by Indian leaders to revive historical traditions of worship, dance, poetry, and healing in community centers and university Native American studies programs. Activists also pursued economic and political goals. Passage of the Alaska Native Land Claims Act in 1971 returned nearly $1 billion and 40 million acres to that state's original inhabitants. Yet the overall plight of indigenous peoples remained abysmal. As the Native American population neared 1 million, average income remained less than that of African Americans.

In 1972 AIM protested government corruption and neglect of Native Americans by mounting a "Trail of Broken Treaties" march to Washington that resulted in a takeover of the Bureau of Indian Affairs. The following spring AIM focused attention on the Pine Ridge reservation in South Dakota, where Sioux dissidents were protesting federal collusion in tribal corruption. Hundreds of AIM activists occupied the village of Wounded Knee, took hostages, and confronted federal marshals in a series of armed clashes. The siege lasted seventy-one days, but U.S. officials refused to reopen disputed treaty talks.

Mexican Americans comprised another group that turned to radical politics to assert ethnic identity. During the 1970s population growth and endemic poverty in Mexico encouraged between 3.5 and 6 million residents to immigrate illegally to the United States. These "undocumented aliens" willingly accepted low-paying jobs, mainly in the Southwest, and eventually constituted 10 percent of California's labor pool. Although Chicanos continued to work as migrant field hands, a larger number found employment in the service sector or worked for nonunion subcontractors in the garment trades. Unionization of Mexican American women became a national issue in the early 1970s when the Amalgamated Clothing Workers organized a consumer boycott to support a strike against the manufacturer of Farah pants. After the workers gained a union contract, the company gradually moved its operations to Mexico. As a contingent labor force, Mexican Americans received only 70 percent of median white income. By 1980 one-fifth of the Chicano community lived in poverty, and median educational levels for Chicanos remained below tenth grade.

Building on the success of Cesar Chavez's farmworkers union, Mexican American activists such as Corky Gonzales and Jose Angel Gutierrez organized civil rights protests in Denver and south Texas in the late 1960s and early 1970s. In Los Angeles and Denver, young Chicanos asserted independence from Anglo authorities by wielding weapons as Brown Berets. The rural

Phyllis Schlafly (1924–)

"Politics is too important to be left to politicians," declared conservative Republican Phyllis Schlafly in 1969. "More women should strive for the elected positions now held by men, and more women should support those who do." Women's leadership, she added, "can raise the moral

© Bettmann/CORBIS

tone of politics. They keep their ideals while playing the game." Although spoken in the language of feminism, Schlafly's appeal did not reflect a feminist agenda. In fact, it was just the opposite. During the 1970s she would emerge as the nation's most vocal opponent of the proposed Equal Rights Amendment (ERA).

Long involved in Republican politics, Schlafly preferred to identify herself as an Alton, Illinois, "housewife" and mother of six. Born into a pious Roman Catholic family in Depression-era St. Louis, she had watched her mother enter the workforce when her father lost his job. After achieving academic success at Radcliffe and obtaining a government job in Washington, she married a wealthy corporate lawyer—"who rescued me from the life of a working girl," she later said—and moved to southern Illinois. While busy as a homemaker, Schlafly still found time to participate in community organizations and Republican politics. As a supporter of the conservative Robert Taft, she ran unsuccessfully as a "powder-puff" candidate for Congress in 1952.

Endorsing the anticommunist crusade of the 1950s, Schlafly cultivated expertise on national defense issues as a leader of the Daughters of the American Revolution. In 1963 Schlafly was the only woman to testify in the Senate in opposition to the ratification of the nuclear test ban treaty. She achieved celebrity status in Republican circles the next year when her campaign biography of Barry Goldwater, *A Choice, Not an Echo,* sold

New Mexican activist Reies Lopez Tijerina also armed followers to protest the loss of historic land claims. Mexican American students at southwestern universities adopted confrontational tactics to establish Chicano studies programs and assert ethnic pride. The cultural awakening produced scholarly journals such as *Aztlan,* the popular magazines *El Grito* and *La Raza,* and moving ex-

3 million copies. Goldwater's loss failed to dampen her spirits. Pursuing her enthusiastic opposition to détente, Schlafly proceeded to coauthor a series of small books exposing Soviet perfidy and the failure of liberals to stand up to the communist menace. When her ardent conservatism cost her the leadership of the National Federation of Republican Women, she organized an independent network of her supporters and began publishing a newsletter called "The Phyllis Schlafly Report."

Because she worked outside the Republican establishment, Schlafly earned no rewards from Nixon's victory in 1968. When the president opened diplomatic relations with China and signed the SALT disarmament treaty, she broke with the administration. But congressional passage of the ERA in 1972 rejuvenated her career. "Their motive is totally radical," she said of the new feminists. "They hate men, marriage, and children. They are out to destroy morality and the family. They look upon husbands as exploiters, children as an evil to be avoided (by abortion if necessary), and the family as an institution which keeps women in 'second-class citizenship.'" She announced a new lobbying group called Stop-ERA and led her conservative army into battle.

Arguing that feminists were selfish and socially irresponsible, Schlafly wrote articles, gave lectures, organized public demonstrations, and sought private meetings with key legislators in the states. Her 1977 book, *The Power of the Positive Woman,* warned that the ERA would "mandate the gender-free, rigid, absolute equality of treatment of men and women" and would create "a constitutional mandate that the husband no longer has the primary duty to support his wife and child." She also protested that the ERA would permit women to serve equally with men in the armed forces. Schlafly's moment of greatest triumph occurred when the ERA failed to gain ratification by the necessary three-fourths of the states in 1982.

plorations of Chicano roots by novelists and poets such as Raymond Barrio, Rudolfo Anaya, Lorna Dee Cervantes, and Angela de Hoyos.

As Mexican Americans gained an economic foothold, middle-class and professional organizations substituted political lobbying for protest. By the 1970s the Congress of Mexican American Unity served as an umbrella for 200 civic groups, and Mexican Americans played a major role in the National Council of La Raza, a consortium of twenty-six Hispanic organizations. In the Los Angeles area and in San Antonio, Mexican Americans elected public officials, used political clout to fight discrimination, and campaigned for bilingual education. In 1974 the Supreme Court ruled in *Lau* v. *Nichols* that public schools were required to teach children in a language they understood.

Radical African Americans engaged in the most bitterly contested assertions of identity politics. Activists organized an extended student strike at San Francisco State and an armed march on a building at Cornell University to demand the creation of black studies programs and more hiring of minority faculty. Meanwhile, the Black Panthers continued to face the wrath of the FBI and local police, resulting in the death of some forty activists by December 1969. In one episode, Chicago police and state officers raided the apartment of Panther leaders Fred Hampton and Mark Clark and shot them to death while they slept. Even so, the Black Panthers continued organizing, even in the nation's prisons. In California, several bloody confrontations led to the shooting death in 1970 of Panther prisoner George Jackson. The following year, New York Governor Nelson Rockefeller ordered state troopers to storm Attica prison, where white, Puerto Rican, and black inmates had taken over the facility to protest degrading conditions. The confrontation resulted in the killing of thirty-three prisoners and ten guards held as hostages. By mid decade, control of the Panthers had shifted to African American women, including Elaine Brown and Erika Huggins.

ANTIWAR PROTEST, KENT STATE, AND POLITICAL STALEMATE

Amid declining public support for the Vietnam War in the fall of 1969, peace activists organized a series of huge antiwar rallies. On October 15, Vietnam Moratorium Day, more than 200,000 protesters, many of them demonstrating for the first time, marched in Boston, New York, and Washington, D.C. One month later, 250,000 marched to the Washington Monument. When 10,000 demonstrators were teargassed after breaking away from the rally to storm the Justice Department, Attorney General John Mitchell remarked that "it looked like the Russian Revolution."

President Nixon responded to antiwar activism by assuring the nation in a televised speech that protest was not necessary, since the administration was "Vietnamizing the search for peace." "Precipitate withdrawal" from Vietnam would be a "popular and easy course," he acknowledged, but defeat and humiliation would bring the "collapse of confidence in American leadership." Promising an all-volunteer army and an end to the draft, Nixon marginalized

Vice President Spiro T. Agnew executed the Nixon administration's rhetorical campaign against anti–Vietnam War dissenters and other critics.

protesters as a "vocal minority" in contrast to the compliant "silent majority." Vice President Spiro Agnew dismissed demonstrators and news commentators as an "effete corps of impudent snobs who characterized themselves as intellectuals." Complaining that the media legitimized the antiwar message, Agnew took particular aim at the "tiny enclosed fraternity of privileged men" in TV journalism that offered "instant analysis" of presidential speeches.

The White House's difficulty in managing wartime information surfaced when newspapers published the first photographs of the recently uncovered My Lai massacre. After the Tet Offensive of 1968, U.S. troops under the command of Lieutenant William Calley massacred 347 unarmed South Vietnamese peasants—mostly women, children, and the elderly. The case epitomized the bitter divisions caused by the Vietnam War. Whereas critics described the act as racially motivated genocide, defenders argued that villages like My Lai were often staging grounds for Vietcong attacks on U.S. troops. Others contended that the beleaguered company had cracked under the strains of a war in which commanders were expected to produce high enemy body counts. Although Nixon expressed sympathy for Calley, a military court convicted the lieutenant of murder in 1971. After the president reduced Calley's sentence, the lieutenant was paroled and received an honorable discharge in 1974.

Nixon hoped to build support for a peace agreement that would leave the South Vietnamese government in place. By the spring of 1970 the president had withdrawn 110,000 U.S. troops from Southeast Asia as part of Vietnamization. To impress the North Vietnamese with U.S. resolve, however, the White House decided to expand the war to Cambodia. On April 30, 1970, Nixon went on television to tell a stunned nation that 25,000 U.S. and South Vietnamese troops had entered Cambodia in an "incursion" designed to "shorten the war." He described the operation's purpose as "cleaning out major North Vietnamese and Vietcong occupied territories" and destroying the "main headquarters for the entire Communist military operation in South Vietnam." The president also hoped to bolster the anticommunist military regime that recently had taken control of the Cambodian capital. Proclaiming that the United States could not act "like a pitiful, helpless giant," Nixon protested that he would rather be a one-term president than allow the nation to become a "second-rate power."

The Cambodian invasion revitalized the antiwar movement. As student protests spread, Nixon dismissed activists as "bums," and Ohio Governor James Rhodes ordered the National Guard to police several dissident campuses. At Kent State, antiwar protesters trashed the town business district and burned the university's Reserve Officers' Training Corps (ROTC) building. The next day, May 4, 1970, a small number of campus demonstrators failed to respond to an order to disperse during a noon rally and threw rocks and bottles at guardsmen deploying tear gas. Several of the tense troopers wheeled around and fired into the crowd. The attack wounded nine and killed four, including two students leaving class. The Kent State deaths electrified a nation already shocked by news of the Cambodian invasion. University presidents had warned Nixon that peace could not be restored on campuses without ending the war, but Vice President Agnew attributed the violence to "elitist" permissiveness toward "psychotic and criminal elements . . . traitors and thieves and perverts . . . in our midst." Public opinion polls showed that majorities sympathized not with the students, but with the National Guard.

In the most extensive student unrest in U.S. history, post–Kent State strikes closed 350 universities and colleges and mobilized millions of demonstrators, many first-time protesters. At Mississippi's Jackson State, two more students were killed when state police responded to antiwar activism at the

EXHIBIT **13-4**   **THE THRUST INTO CAMBODIA, 1970**

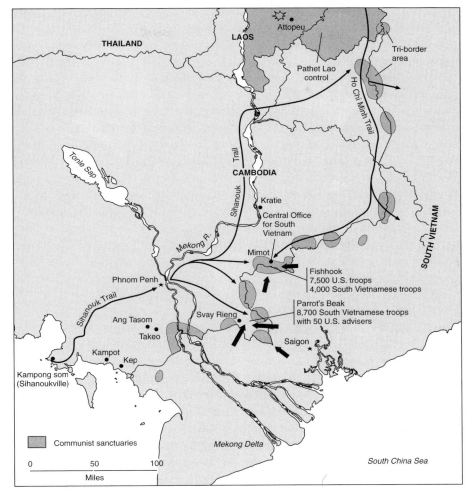

predominantly African American college by firing on a dormitory. Later that summer, the National Chicano Moratorium organized a peaceful march of 20,000 protesters in Los Angeles to emphasize that Mexican Americans accounted for nearly one-fifth of the Vietnam War casualties from the Southwest. At an ensuing street festival, county deputies made mass arrests that resulted in the death of Chicano journalist Ruben Salazar.

Despite Nixon's showdown with the antiwar movement, the president withdrew U.S. troops from Cambodia two months later. Aware of the military's failure to uncover communist installations and sensitive to growing peace sentiment, Congress set a summer deadline on the Cambodian deployment, the first such limit imposed on the commander in chief during the Indochinese conflict. While the administration mounted "protective-reaction" air strikes to increase the pressure on North Vietnam in the fall of 1970, the Pentagon continued to withdraw ground forces. With the decline in draft quotas and U.S. casualties, the press curtailed coverage of the war. Yet Nixon purposely taunted antiwar demonstrators as he campaigned for Republican congressional candidates.

While the White House sought a position of strength from which to negotiate with North Vietnam, the president announced early in 1971 that U.S. and South Vietnamese troops had invaded Laos, where the CIA had organized covert bombing campaigns against communist insurgents since the 1960s. The new escalation inspired spring marches of hundreds of thousands of protesters, including two thousand members of Vietnam Veterans Against the War (VVAW), who threw their military decorations on the Capitol steps. In one demonstration, 30,000 activists blocked Washington commuter traffic. Monitored by a unit jointly commanded by the CIA and local police, 12,000 dissidents were swept off the streets in the largest mass arrest in U.S. history. Such police activity involved widespread suspension of legal procedures, however, and federal courts later awarded the victims modest damages.

POPULIST CONSERVATISM AND THE WAR AGAINST DISSENT

Domestic conflict over the Vietnam War revealed profound class divisions. Many Americans viewed the blatant sexuality and drug use of the radical counterculture as self-indulgent and destructive. Indeed, an "underground" trade in drugs took its toll in substance-related deaths, including three rock superstars—Jimi Hendrix, Janis Joplin, and Jim Morrison. Drug use led Charles Manson's self-styled "family" of hippie revolutionaries to murder seven wealthy Hollywood Hills residents in 1969, a case that received extensive media attention and drew comments from President Nixon.

Movement extremists also generated criticism for revolutionary rhetoric and violence. Some members of Students for a Democratic Society (SDS) formed the "Weathermen" and went underground to escape police. Other young radicals aligned themselves with "third world" Marxists and attacked the United States as racist and imperialist. Intent on "bringing the war home," secret affinity groups bombed at least fourteen government and military installations between 1969 and 1974. Three members of the Weathermen lost their lives in a 1970 explosion in a Greenwich Village townhouse used to assemble bombs. That year a bomb planted at a mathematics research facility at the University of Wisconsin killed a graduate student. Activists and police engaged in repeated confrontations—from Santa Barbara, California, where street people reacted to police harassment by burning down a branch of the

Bank of America, to the University of California at Berkeley, where thousands of residents protested police destruction of a "people's park" built on university property.

Until the inauguration of the Selective Service lottery system in 1969, predominantly middle-class activists were exempted from the draft as college students—only 20 percent of the 3 million who served in Vietnam came from middle- or upper-class families. In contrast, limited educational and job opportunities pushed poor and working-class men into military service, although the most effective draft evaders often were inner-city blacks who simply ignored Selective Service requirements. Polls of white northern workers revealed that nearly half supported the immediate withdrawal of troops by 1970. Yet fully half of those favoring disengagement were hostile to antiwar actions. Although the peace movement depicted ordinary soldiers as pawns of higher-ups, many citizens viewed attacks on the armed services and on the war as extensions of class privilege legitimizing escape from military duty.

Working-class criticism of antiwar protest and counterculture lifestyles often found expression in white country music, as in Merle Haggard's "Okie from Muskogee" (1969) or in "The Fightin' Side of Me" (1970), a song confronting those who were "runnin' down our country." Similar convictions about the immorality of protest surfaced in 1970 when New York City construction workers assaulted college students participating in a nonviolent antiwar demonstration on Wall Street. After receiving praise for their patriotism from President Nixon, the labor unions mobilized thousands of supporters in a "Victory in Vietnam" parade down New York City's Broadway.

Convinced that domestic disunity would undermine Kissinger's secret diplomacy, Nixon turned to coercive measures to create a wartime consensus. When the liberal *New York Times* reported the secret bombing of Cambodia, the White House ordered "national security" wiretaps on the telephone lines of four journalists and thirteen administration aides. To ascertain the source of future "leaks," Nixon officials hired private investigators to make additional wiretaps. Federal prosecutors also accused Father Philip Berrigan and other Catholic radicals of participating in an alleged plot to kidnap Henry Kissinger, although the defendants were acquitted. In another case, the administration indicted eight organizers of the demonstrations outside Chicago's 1968 Democratic Convention for conspiracy to violate antiriot laws. Led by Yippies Abbie Hoffman and Jerry Rubin, the defendants used the trial to showcase the revolutionary culture of the protest movement and mocked the court and government prosecutors. The judge reacted to continuing protests by defendant Bobby Seale by having the Black Panther leader gagged and chained. After five months of contentious testimony and repeated contempt citations, the jury rejected nearly all of the government's arguments.

Nixon officials used the increased militancy among dissidents to press for a more formal program of domestic intelligence. In 1970 presidential aide

Tom Huston proposed an interagency intelligence unit composed of the FBI, CIA, National Security Agency, and Pentagon intelligence groups that would conduct illegal burglaries, wiretappings, mail openings, solicitation of campus informants, and interceptions of international communications. After the Huston plan had been approved by the president and had been implemented for five days, however, J. Edgar Hoover squelched the plan because it threatened FBI control of domestic security. But government agencies continued to rely on secret and illegal methods to monitor and disrupt domestic dissenters. The Internal Revenue Service used tax audits to harass individuals and organizations with "extremist views and philosophies."

The Nixon administration faced another public relations challenge in 1971 when the *New York Times* began to publish the secret Pentagon Papers. The documents, a history of the Vietnam War commissioned by former Defense Secretary Robert McNamara, illustrated the continuity of government duplicity during the Kennedy and Johnson administrations. Fearing that future leaks might threaten Soviet and Chinese confidence in U.S. ability to conduct secret negotiations, the administration sought a court order to stop publication of the papers; but the Supreme Court ruled that the government had no grounds for preemptive censorship. Dissatisfied with the Court's finding, the White House ordered a Special Investigations Unit (the "plumbers") to investigate Daniel Ellsberg, a former Defense Department planner who had confessed to releasing the Pentagon Papers. After the Justice Department indicted Ellsberg for espionage and conspiracy, the plumbers burglarized the office of Ellsberg's psychiatrist to gain confidential information on the defendant.

DÉTENTE, CHILE, AND THE ELECTION OF 1972

Seeking to press the North Vietnamese to accept a workable settlement of the Indochinese war, Nixon turned for help to the People's Republic of China and the Soviet Union. Washington had refused to recognize China since the communist revolution of 1949. Cold warriors like Nixon had continually warned that recognition would lead to the abandonment of the Nationalist government on Taiwan (Formosa) and would legitimize communist subversion of established regimes. However, when the Chinese made diplomatic overtures in 1969, Nixon reasoned that he could win concessions from both Beijing and Moscow and could stabilize global tensions if he took advantage of the deepening rift between the two communist rivals.

Nixon and National Security Assistant Kissinger initiated the new balance of power by easing restrictions on U.S. travel to mainland China. In 1971 the United States announced the end of a twenty-one-year embargo on Chinese trade. Washington also accepted the People's Republic of China's admission to the United Nations, even though China claimed the seat of the Republic of

China located on Nationalist Taiwan. In 1972 Nixon formalized détente when he visited China and signed a joint communiqué with Chinese Premier Zhou Enlai (Chou En-lai) in which the two nations pledged "peaceful mutuality." The most important part of the negotiations involved a U.S. promise to withdraw military forces from Taiwan.

Nixon followed the agreement with China by traveling to Moscow for disarmament negotiations. The resulting Strategic Arms Limitation Treaty (SALT) of 1972 limited the construction of antiballistic missile sites and nuclear delivery systems. Although the accord did not rule out the development of new weapons, it represented the Cold War's first advance toward regulating existing arsenals and was the biggest step toward nuclear disarmament since the atmospheric test ban treaty of 1963. The Nixon-Brezhnev talks also produced consensus on the status quo in divided Berlin and a trade pact providing for the sale of nearly one-fourth of the U.S. grain crop to the Soviets. When Secretary Leonid I. Brezhnev visited Washington in 1973, the two leaders signed additional agreements covering nuclear arms, cultural exchange, and the peaceful use of atomic energy.

Recognizing the limits of U.S. strength, Nixon and Kissinger acknowledged the Soviet Union as a superpower with virtual nuclear parity. Despite this acceptance, détente reaffirmed the president's conviction that communist negotiating partners only respected military strength and that Washington should never appear weak. The White House saw U.S. hegemony in the Western Hemisphere as a symbol of national credibility and power. Thus, the administration reacted harshly to the election of Marxist Salvador Allende as president of Chile in 1970. Although Nixon shared Kennedy's and Johnson's distrust of the CIA's intelligence capability, he and Kissinger ordered the agency to destabilize the Allende regime. The CIA provided secret funds to opposing politicians, friendly media, and anticommunist unions, and the U.S. government and private lending agencies refused to provide credit to Chile, thereby creating severe economic shortages and political chaos. Allende was assassinated in a bloody 1973 coup by Chilean military leaders, who executed thousands of dissidents and abolished democracy.

As the administration prepared for the 1972 presidential election, the Democratic Party became the main political vehicle for antiwar criticism, demands for social justice by racial minorities, and women's rights. Under the "McGovern rules," instituted after 1968, Democratic convention delegates and nominees were chosen in open primaries, not by party bosses. The new procedures also required proportional representation of women and racial minorities—the percentage of female delegates jumped from 10 percent to 40 percent between 1968 and 1972. Because upper-middle-class citizens more frequently participated in primaries than did working-class voters, the new system favored consideration of the cultural issues endorsed by the more affluent. As a result, delegates openly debated abortion rights, the legalization

Daniel Ellsberg *(1931–)*

Converted from righteous advocate of the Cold War crusade to antiwar activist, Daniel Ellsberg played a central role in bringing down the Nixon presidency. Born in Chicago during the Depression, Ellsberg attended an exclusive preparatory school on a full scholarship before getting an

economics degree from Harvard. Yet he abandoned the academic life in 1954 by volunteering for the Marines and by becoming an infantry sharpshooter. Two years later, Ellsberg resumed his studies at Harvard and Cambridge. His Ph.D. thesis in economics focused on strategic military planning.

A tall, lean man with a sharp-featured, narrow face, Ellsberg embraced the Cold War as an advisor to Senator John Kennedy on foreign policy. In 1959 he signed on with the Rand Corporation, a California consultant to the Defense Department, as a strategic analyst whose specialty was nuclear warfare. By 1964, Ellsberg had become convinced that the future of democracy hinged on the war in Vietnam. He served as a special international security aide in the Pentagon. Then he volunteered to become State Department liaison with the counterinsurgency effort in the Vietnamese countryside. By 1967, he was special assistant to the deputy ambassador.

With a Boy Scout's enthusiasm for containing communist aggression, Ellsberg often donned military gear to accompany counterinsurgency teams on "clearing operations" in Vietnam. Yet by 1966 he began to note the failure of pacification campaigns, the rising number of civilian casualties, widespread corruption in the South Vietnamese govern-

of marijuana, and gay liberation. More than 100 convention participants publicly acknowledged their homosexuality in 1972.

The Democratic Convention nominated South Dakota's George McGovern, a liberal senator who had criticized the Vietnam War. McGovern called for a "politics of conscience" embracing tax reform and a shift from defense spending to social needs. Citing Nixon's ties to big business, he castigated the Republican administration as "the most corrupt in history." Yet the Democratic candidate's plan for a guaranteed national income lacked credi-

ment and military, and repeated reports of the torture of Vietcong prisoners. Ellsberg informed Defense Secretary McNamara that, although the war was stalemated, its level of violence continued to increase and that official reporting was not telling decision makers what they needed to know. On leaving Saigon in 1967 he proposed a high-level study of U.S. policy in Vietnam. By the time McNamara ordered such an assessment, Ellsberg had returned to Rand and became one of thirty-six researchers to work on the project.

The Pentagon study convinced Ellsberg that the war stemmed from a sordid history of aggression perpetuated by several presidents. Seeing no justification for U.S. policy and feeling guilty about his complicity in pacification, Ellsberg made copies of the secret study report, soon to be known as the Pentagon Papers, and resigned from Rand in 1970. Once he became convinced that the Nixon administration was about to repeat the mistakes and deception of its predecessors, he released portions of the Pentagon Papers to the *New York Times.*

Although a court injunction temporarily halted publication of the Pentagon Papers, the Supreme Court overruled any prior restraint on publishing them. Nevertheless, the Nixon administration indicted Ellsberg for conspiracy, theft, and violation of espionage laws. To discredit the disaffected strategist, the White House assigned his case to a newly formed Special Investigations Unit. In September 1971 the "plumbers" broke into the Los Angeles office of Ellsberg's psychiatrist. This government misconduct resulted in dismissal of all charges against the man who had leaked the Pentagon Papers and the prosecution of leading White House aides for subverting the Fourth Amendment.

bility, and he was forced to replace his vice presidential running mate when press reports announced that the nominee had repeatedly been hospitalized for depression. The McGovern campaign hoped to take advantage of the Twenty-Sixth Amendment, which in 1971 gave the vote to eighteen-year-olds. Yet young voters tended to support Wallace. By crusading against busing and the "suffocating bureaucracy in Washington," Wallace won Democratic primary victories in Florida, Michigan, and Maryland before being paralyzed by an assassin's bullet in May 1972.

EXHIBIT **13-5   U.S. NATIONAL DEFENSE AS A PERCENTAGE OF TOTAL FEDERAL OUTLAYS, 1968–1976**

1968	46.0
1970	41.8
1972	34.3
1974	29.5
1976	24.1

Source: *Statistical Abstract of the United States* (1987).

Nixon's campaign followed the strategies of Kevin Phillips's *The Emerging Republican Majority* (1969), which sought to refashion the New Deal electoral coalition by recruiting Wallace voters, white southerners, urban supporters in the Southwest, working-class Catholics, suburbanites, and rural Americans. These voters were philosophically opposed to the costly welfare programs established in the 1960s and clung to traditional moral and social values. Acknowledging such disaffection, Nixon instructed aides about the "gut" issues of the campaign—crime, busing, drugs, welfare, and inflation. The president called for a congressional moratorium on busing, denounced "arbitrary" government orders, and attacked racial quotas. "The way to end discrimination against some," he declared, was "not to begin discrimination against others." The White House also pointed to Kissinger's prediction that peace was "at hand" in the Vietnam negotiations.

Nixon won 61 percent of the popular vote and the entire Electoral College except for Massachusetts and the District of Columbia and nearly equaled Lyndon Johnson's landslide of 1964. While McGovern received only 29 percent of the vote in the South, the president became the first twentieth-century Republican to win a majority of white Catholic and working-class voters. The Republicans also took nearly 80 percent of the Wallace vote and thereby signaled an end to the New Deal electoral coalition of the 1930s.

ENDING THE VIETNAM WAR

Empowered by a mandate at the polls, Nixon and Kissinger continued to press for an acceptable resolution of the Vietnam War. In the spring of 1971, Washington dropped its demand that a peace agreement provide for the North's withdrawal of troops from the South. Yet the administration faced a new crisis a year later when North Vietnamese regulars invaded the central highlands, forcing further retreat by Saigon's army. Emboldened by South Vietnam's successes with pacification, however, the president refused to be intimidated by the communist advances. Denouncing Hanoi's leaders as "international outlaws," the commander in chief ordered the mining of the North's ports. He also authorized massive B-52 air strikes against enemy industrial sites, flood-control dikes, and railroad lines leading to the People's Republic of China. Within months, Hanoi dropped demands that a peace accord provide for the replacement of the Saigon government. In turn, the United States agreed to stop bombing the North. Kissinger and North Vietnamese negotiators secretly agreed to a military cease-fire in October 1972. Yet the White House allowed the South Vietnamese to veto the truce, and Kissinger abruptly announced the suspension of negotiations and the resumption of the air war.

After the 1972 presidential election, Kissinger won minor changes in the prospective agreement with the North Vietnamese. When communist negotiators consulted with their superiors in Hanoi, however, the president charged them with breaking off the talks. In the "Christmas Bombing" of 1972—the most intensive air attack in military history—B-52s targeted populated areas in North Vietnam. As the campaign resulted in the loss of 15 U.S. bombers and the 121 members of the crews, congressional critics charged that Nixon and Kissinger were conducting war "by temper tantrum." Yet the attack supported the administration's repeated contention that brute force would push Hanoi toward peace on U.S. terms. By the end of the year Nixon had caused nearly 4 million tons of bombs to be dropped on Indochina—twice the amount ordered by Johnson and 1.5 times the total tonnage deployed by all armies in World War II.

Having demonstrated U.S. military power, Nixon announced in January 1973 that Kissinger had brokered an agreement that would "end the war and bring peace with honor." The Paris Peace Accord provided for the withdrawal from the South of remaining U.S. troops in exchange for North Vietnam's repatriation of 587 U.S. prisoners of war. Under the terms of the treaty, Washington recognized the Vietnamese National Liberation Front (Vietcong) and resolved the nineteen-year controversy over the two Vietnams by declaring that the seventeenth parallel was a provisional boundary instead of a political or territorial line. American military involvement in Vietnam ended in March 1973 with the withdrawal of the last combat troops and a televised homecoming of U.S. prisoners of war. Although Kissinger and his Vietnamese counterpart shared the 1973 Nobel Peace Prize, the terms of the accord hardly varied from those of the preelection agreement and were virtually identical to the ones Nixon had opposed in 1968.

WATERGATE

Even though Nixon had ended the divisive U.S. presence in Vietnam, his second term would be remembered by Watergate, a series of political scandals arising from the president's desire to forge a Vietnam consensus and win a re-election landslide. As early as 1969, White House officials had ordered "national security" investigators to conduct surveillance of Senator Edward M.

Kennedy, a potential Democratic candidate for the presidency. Kennedy had delayed reporting a late-night accident in which he had driven his car off a coastal bridge, drowning Mary Jo Kopechne, a former campaign aide. Nixon officials organized the Committee to Re-Elect the President (CREEP) in 1971. The panel created 400 dummy corporations to channel secret contributions and collected $55 million from corporate donors seeking preferential treatment. The committee also used "dirty tricks" such as signing the names of Democratic candidates to misleading literature to discredit presidential contenders.

Seeking information on Democratic National Chairman Lawrence O'Brien, CREEP Director John Mitchell approved covert entry into Democratic headquarters at Washington's Watergate complex in June 1972. When an electronic listening device malfunctioned, five CREEP operatives returned for a second entry and were arrested. Although Nixon press secretary Ron Ziegler dismissed the crime as a "third-rate burglary," an address book notation linked the team to White House "plumbers" G. Gordon Liddy and E. Howard Hunt. Immediately, CREEP and White House aides began a cover-up, destroying campaign records, lying to the FBI and to the grand jury, removing incriminating evidence from a White House safe, and pressuring law enforcement agencies for "cooperation." Although the disclosure would not be made for two years, Nixon initiated the Watergate cover-up by personally ordering aides to request that the CIA stop the FBI from tracing the source of Watergate funds.

By the time the trial of the Watergate burglars opened in early 1973, two of the men had received promises of executive clemency in return for continued silence. In March, White House counselor John Dean brought new demands to Nixon at an Oval Office meeting in which he warned of a "cancer on the presidency" and estimated that eventual hush-money payments could reach $1 million. However, the next day Nixon ordered Mitchell to continue the cover-up. Despite these precautions, news reports soon linked top White House aides to the Watergate affair. Attempting to place responsibility on Dean, Nixon fired the White House counsel and asked for the resignation of his key assistants, John Ehrlichman and H. R. Haldeman. The president also acceded to the appointment of a special Watergate prosecutor.

As a Senate Select Committee chaired by Democrat Sam Ervin began dramatic televised hearings on the scandal in 1973, Dean testified about the president's knowledge of the cover-up. He also produced evidence of the plumbers unit, the illegal Huston plan, and an administration "enemies list" submitted to the Internal Revenue Service (IRS) for possible audits. Even more astounding, White House aide Alexander Butterfield revealed that Nixon had installed secret tape-recording devices in the Oval Office. Although the president's attorneys claimed that executive privilege and the separation of powers gave him the right to preserve the confidentiality of conversations with advisors, a federal court ordered him to turn over nine tapes to the courts.

When Special Prosecutor Archibald Cox refused White House demands to stop subpoenas and cited the president's "noncompliance" with court orders, Nixon stunned the nation by ordering Attorney General Elliot Richardson to fire Cox and to abolish the special prosecutor's office. Richardson refused and resigned in protest. When Deputy Attorney General William Ruckelshaus objected to the presidential order, Nixon fired him and secured the compliance of Solicitor General Robert F. Bork. The "Saturday Night Massacre" produced wide protests, and Nixon agreed to relinquish the tapes and appoint a new special prosecutor. Yet three of the subpoenaed tapes were missing, and evidence revealed that extensive blank spots on the others had been caused by manual erasures.

By the fall of 1973 both President Nixon and Vice President Agnew faced income tax problems. Agnew had been under investigation for participation in a kickback scheme with Maryland contractors. In October the vice president pleaded "no contest" to tax evasion and resigned. Adhering to the succession provisions of the Twenty-Fifth Amendment, ratified in 1967, Nixon nominated House Republican leader Gerald R. Ford for the vice presidency, and Congress quickly confirmed his choice. When the IRS announced that it was reexamining Nixon's tax deductions for the donation of his vice presidential papers, he assured a televised meeting of newspaper editors that "I'm not a crook." The agency subsequently reported that the president owed $450,000 in back taxes and penalties.

NIXON'S FALL

Weakened by Watergate, Nixon found the implementation of his foreign policy constrained. As the military draft expired in 1973, the army adopted voluntary recruitment for the first time since 1948. Moreover, the president was forced to submit to a congressionally imposed deadline of August 1973 for funding combat activities in Indochina. The compromise finally ended the bombing of Cambodia—one of Nixon's most fiercely protected projects. Congress also overrode a presidential veto to pass the War Powers Act of 1973. The landmark legislation required the chief executive to inform Congress within forty-eight hours of the deployment of overseas military forces and established a sixty-day limit on the commitment of troops without congressional consent. Although no president has ever acknowledged the constitutionality of the statute, the War Powers Act provided the most important limitation on executive military initiative since the dawn of the Cold War.

Nixon's ability to assert U.S. power also was challenged by a new Middle East war. Just as Watergate revelations climaxed in the fall of 1973, Egyptian and Syrian troops invaded territories claimed by Israel. When the Soviet Union airlifted supplies to Egypt, the United States responded by providing

John Sirica (1904–1992)

Beneath the dark judicial robes of John Sirica sat the oldest son of a poor Italian immigrant barber. Although in 1973 he was chief judge of the federal district court in Washington, D.C., John Sirica never forgot his humble beginnings. "I came up rough-and-tough," he liked to say. "If it

had not been for the Republican Party, I might never have done much better than my father." And now standing before him were four members of the Spanish-speaking Cuban exile community of Miami who were on trial for their participation in the Watergate break-in. They triggered an instinctive sympathy. If it had not been for the Republican Party, the judge suspected, they might not be in his courtroom either.

Sirica had barely worked his way through law school. Poorly educated and unsuccessful as a lawyer, he managed to get a job as an assistant government attorney in 1929. Returning to an unprofitable private practice, he served as chief counsel for a congressional committee investigating corruption in the Federal Communications Commission in 1944; but to his annoyance, Democratic politicians squashed the case. After World War II, Sirica strengthened his position in Republican circles by campaigning actively for Eisenhower. He was also a close friend of Senator Joseph McCarthy. In recognition of the attorney's loyalty, Eisenhower appointed him to the federal court in 1957. The judge soon gained a reputation for brusqueness and impatience with abstruse legal argument. The severity of his sentences earned him the nickname "Maximum John," but many of his decisions were overturned on appeal.

By 1973, Sirica's seniority made him chief judge of the Washington, D.C., district court. As a loyal Republican, he felt a special obligation to

military equipment for the Israelis. In response, Arab oil producers ended the sale of petroleum products to nations friendly to Israel. After the United Nations brokered a cease-fire, the Soviets threatened to move troops to the Middle East to supervise the truce. Nixon immediately placed U.S. forces on worldwide alert, forcing Moscow to agree to the creation of a UN peacekeeping force. Kissinger then resumed diplomatic relations that had been broken

ensure a fair trial for the seven men accused of organizing the break-in at Democratic Party headquarters at the Watergate complex in June 1972. When—to establish a conspiracy of silence—they all pleaded guilty, Sirica replied: "I don't think we should sit up here like nincompoops."

Exercising his authority as a federal judge, Sirica interrupted the courtroom examinations to ask specific questions about payments and uncovered additional incriminating evidence. After a jury convicted the burglars, Sirica delayed sentencing to pressure the defendants to talk. To his delight, one of the men broke his silence under pressure, and Sirica eventually presided over the trials of many high-level coconspirators. Meanwhile, congressional investigators issued a subpoena for tape-recorded evidence to President Nixon, but the White House rejected the request on grounds of executive privilege. The constitutional dispute came to Sirica's docket. "One question kept nagging at me," he recalled. "If Nixon himself were not involved why would he stand on such an abstract principle . . . when by voluntarily turning over the tapes he could prove himself innocent and put the Watergate case behind him?" Sirica ordered the release of the subpoenaed material.

Nixon's compliance merely intensified the judge's outrage because, while listening to the presidential tapes, he discovered that the man he had supported in 1972 was vulgar, devious, and dishonest. On the day before his seventieth birthday, in his last act as chief judge, Sirica ordered the release of grand jury files to the House of Representatives, which was debating Nixon's impeachment. This material contained explosive and incriminating evidence that forced the president to resign. "I was often described as an 'obscure federal judge' and that was true," Sirica observed, "but I was not a damn fool."

off with Egypt since 1967 and used "shuttle diplomacy" to arrange for UN buffer units to monitor the fragile cease-fire.

Despite Kissinger's triumphs, the Arab oil embargo dramatized U.S. dependence on foreign energy sources and intensified chronic inflation. Fearing recession, Nixon had relaxed wage and price guidelines in 1973. When the sale of 8.5 million tons of grain to the Soviet Union led to an increase in retail food prices, however, the president imposed a second freeze and again raised the dollar price of gold. After failing to lower inflation and reduce the trade deficit, Nixon conceded defeat in 1974 and allowed price controls to expire. However, the oil boycott quadrupled the price of petroleum and dramatically inflated the cost of gasoline, diesel fuel, heating oil, plastics, fertilizers, and synthetic fibers. Dwindling supplies produced endless lines at the gas pumps and generated public criticism of energy hoarding by industry. Meanwhile, inflation reached a twenty-five-year high of 12 percent.

Higher energy costs compelled federal officials to promote the use of domestic fuel sources. With only 6 percent of the world's population, the United States consumed 30 percent of global energy production. Nearly 40 percent of this amount came from overseas. Congress reacted to the oil embargo in late 1973 by authorizing construction of a controversial pipeline across Alaska. Rejecting plans to ration oil or tax oil-company profits, Nixon created a Federal Energy Administration to develop nuclear reactors and coal-burning facilities. "We can't live in a Garden of Eden and still have a technological society," Atomic Energy Commissioner Dixie Lee Ray scolded in 1974. After launching what he termed "Project Independence," the president ordered government thermostats to be lowered to 68 degrees Fahrenheit, cut official air travel, requested the relaxation of environmental regulations affecting energy consumption, and reduced the speed limit on interstate freeways to 55 miles per hour.

Richard Nixon's presidency did not survive the energy crisis. In March 1974 a grand jury indicted former White House aides Haldeman, Ehrlichman, Mitchell, and four others for perjury and hush-money payments and named the president himself as an unindicted coconspirator. Four months later, Ehrlichman and former aide Charles Colson were convicted of ordering the burglary of Ellsberg's medical records. This verdict was supported by a federal court ruling that a president has no constitutional right to authorize a break-in, even if he were targeting foreign intelligence operatives or threats to national security. The House of Representatives voted 406–4 to investigate whether sufficient grounds existed for Nixon's impeachment, and the Burger Court unanimously ruled that the president had to surrender all subpoenaed tapes. "When the claim of privilege is based only on a generalized interest in confidentiality," ruled the Court, "it cannot prevail over the fundamental demands of due process." The House Judiciary Committee then passed three bills of impeachment against Nixon and charged him with obstruction of justice, abuse of power, and unconstitutional defiance of its subpoenas.

The "smoking gun" of Watergate emerged when subpoenaed tapes revealed that the president had played a key role in the early cover-up. As a result, on August 9, 1974, Richard Nixon became the first chief executive in U.S. history to resign from office. "Our long national nightmare is over," newly inaugurated President Ford told the nation. "Our Constitution works. Our great re-

EXHIBIT **13-6**   THE MIDDLE EAST

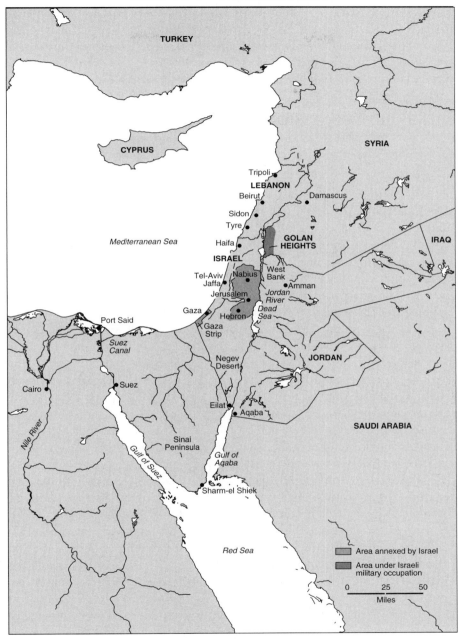

public is a government of laws and not of men." As the first White House
occupant not elected as either president or vice president, Ford faced a nation
whose faith in leaders had been shaken by Vietnam and Watergate. Public

opinion was stunned, therefore, by the announcement that the new president was pardoning Nixon "for all offenses against the United States." In personal testimony before Congress, Ford insisted there had been "no deal," that he had granted the pardon to remove the disruptive Watergate issue from the national spotlight. The president also offered clemency to Vietnam-era draft law violators and deserters, but only 6 percent of the 350,000 eligible applied.

THE FORD SUCCESSION

Ford chose former New York Governor Nelson D. Rockefeller as his vice president, although the Empire State billionaire faced hostile questions about his political finances. Sensitivity to political ethics also resulted in passage of the Campaign Finance Law of 1974. Although the Supreme Court later invalidated the act's spending limits, the law established checkoffs on federal income tax returns to finance elections and created strict disclosure requirements for campaign contributions. Two years later, Congress restricted the proliferation of political action committees. Meanwhile, lawmakers updated the Freedom of Information Act of 1966 by setting deadlines for government response to citizen requests for documents.

In foreign policy, Ford relied on Nixon's Secretary of State Henry Kissinger to pursue the policy of détente. Late in 1974 the president went to Vladivostok to discuss arms limitations with the Soviet Union and agreed to an accord setting negotiating guidelines. At Helsinki in 1975, Ford and Soviet leader Brezhnev joined European leaders in signing a declaration that acknowledged the primacy of human rights and recognized the territorial boundaries that emerged after World War II. As Cold War tensions eased, Kissinger sought stability in the strategically important Middle East by pushing Israel and Egypt to accept an interim peace pact.

However, the Ford administration faced a Congress that sought to regain the initiative in formulating foreign policy. Criticizing the Helsinki Accords for implicitly recognizing communist annexations and satellite regimes in eastern Europe, congressional leaders denied the Soviets most-favored-nation trade status until Moscow relaxed emigration restrictions on Jews and other dissenters. Congress also sought to control the CIA in 1974 by passing the Hughes-Ryan Amendment, which required the president to report covert actions to Congress "in a timely fashion." The administration soon faced a test case in west Africa's Angola, where it opposed a nationalist movement supported by the Soviets and Cubans. Ford authorized funding for a covert operation in the civil war, but Democrats voted to cut off this aid in 1976. Congressional distrust of the CIA intensified when a select committee led by Senator Frank Church exposed agency involvement in foreign assassination plots and other covert actions.

Congress also defeated administration pleas for increased South Vietnamese military aid. Without such support, the Saigon government could not stop communist advances. On April 30, 1975, one day after military helicopters evacuated one thousand citizens from the U.S. embassy, North Vietnamese troops marched into Saigon and renamed it Ho Chi Minh City. A symbol of the limits of U.S. power, the war in Southeast Asia brought the deaths of 1.5 million Vietnamese and left 10 million homeless. More than 58,000 members of the U.S. armed forces died in Vietnam, more than 300,000 were wounded, and the conflict's financial cost surpassed $150 billion. Although the United States rescued 120,000 Vietnamese refugees as hostilities ended, the humiliating defeat was an incalculable blow to U.S. national cohesion and pride.

Two weeks before the fall of Saigon, Khmer Rouge rebels had taken control of the Cambodian capital while the U.S.-supported government fled. In May 1975 a patrol boat under orders from the revolutionary regime seized the U.S. merchant ship *Mayaguez*. Just as the vessel was being released, Ford ordered aerial bombing and a coastal island assault. Fifteen marines were killed in the ensuing combat, and twenty-three others died in a helicopter crash. Yet the Ford administration used the confrontation to suggest that the United States had resumed world leadership after the Vietnam War.

At home, inflation and unemployment continued to plague an economy suffering from international competition, sagging growth and profits, and rising social welfare costs. As the era of post–World War II prosperity drew to a close in 1974, Congress appropriated funds for housing, public schools, transportation, and educational benefits for Vietnam veterans. In response, Ford campaigned for Republican congressional candidates by introducing a Whip Inflation Now (WIN) program of reduced government spending. Yet Watergate, the Nixon pardon, and the ailing economy helped to assure the Democrats a two-thirds majority in the House and added strength in the Senate. After the election, Ford agreed to the Comprehensive Employment and Training Act (CETA), a program that provided temporary jobs in state and local governments for skilled workers. The empowered Democrats then raised Social Security stipends and extended unemployment benefits in states hit by the recession. While agreeing to some tax relief, Congress also ended oil depletion write-offs for large energy corporations and curbed investment-related tax shelters.

Seeking to bring the nation together amid the Vietnam War and continuing racial turmoil, Richard Nixon had adopted a two-track policy. Overseas, the president turned to the creative diplomacy of Henry Kissinger to establish détente with the communist Soviet Union and the People's Republic of China. Yet the easing of Cold War tensions failed to bring the anticipated "peace with honor" in Southeast Asia. On the domestic front, Nixon embraced environmental regulation, price control, increased social welfare spending, affirmative action, and racial integration of some public schools. Nevertheless, the president's obsession with a Vietnam consensus and his political competitiveness intensified polarization at home. Facing mounting antiwar protests and criticism from liberals, Nixon turned to repressive tactics, resulting in the Watergate scandal that destroyed his presidency. As Gerald Ford presided over the final chapter of the Vietnam saga and struggled to deal with a sagging economy, Americans looked for leaders to restore morale and address the nation's problems.

AMERICAN HISTORY RESOURCE CENTER

To explore documents, images, audio and video clips, articles, and commentary related to the material in this chapter, visit the source collections at ushistory.wadsworth.com and and use the Search function with the following key terms:

Henry Kissinger	Equal Rights Amendment
Organization of Petroleum	Kent State
Exporting Countries	Pentagon Papers
Busing	Watergate
Roe v. *Wade*	Gerald Ford

RECOMMENDED READINGS

Jeffrey Kimball, *Nixon's Vietnam War* (1998). This provocative study attributes the president's military escalations to the "mad bomber theory"—the belief that Hanoi's fear of an unpredictable adversary would produce a favorable settlement.

Lewis Sorley, *The Better War: The Unexamined Victories and the Final Tragedy of America's Last Years in Vietnam* (1999). The author presents a fresh approach to the subject by highlighting the surprising success of pacification under Nixon.

Stanley I. Kutler, ed., *Abuse of Power: The New Nixon Tapes* (1997). The transcripts of uncensored Nixon Watergate conversations are presented in this well-edited collection, providing chilling insights into the president's personal foibles and obsessions.

Jill Quadagno, *The Color of Welfare: How Racism Undermined the War on Poverty* (1994). This analysis includes a critical view of the Nixon administration's politicalized approach to the needs of racial minorities and the poor.

Additional Readings

The definitive work on the Nixon administration is Melvin Small's *The Presidency of Richard Nixon* (1999). For a critical perspective, see the relevant portions of Stephen E. Ambrose, *Nixon: The Triumph of a Politician, 1962–1972* (1989), and of *Nixon: Ruin and Recovery, 1973–1990* (1991). A more sympathetic view appears in Joan Hoff, *Nixon Reconsidered* (1994). See also the relevant segments of Roger Morris, *Richard Milhous Nixon: The Rise of an American Politician* (1990), and of John Robert Greene, *The Limits of Power: The Nixon and Ford Administrations* (1992). For Nixon's domestic policies, see Allen J. Matusow, *Nixon's Economy: Booms, Busts, Dollars, and Votes* (1998).

Nixon's social policies are treated in the relevant segments of Irwin Unger, *The Best of Intentions: The Triumph of the Great Society Under Kennedy, Johnson, and Nixon* (1996). For racial matters, see Hugh Davis Graham, *The Civil Rights Era: Origins and Development of National Policy* (1990), and the first segments of Dan T. Carter, *From George Wallace to Newt Gingrich: Race in the Conservative Counterrevolution, 1963–1994* (1996). Nixon's political activities are described in the early sections of William C. Berman, *America's Right Turn: From Nixon to Bush* (1994). See also Dan T. Carter, *The Politics of Rage: George Wallace, the Origins of the New Conservatism, and the Transformation of American Politics* (1995).

For global diplomacy in the Nixon years, see Robert S. Litwak, *Détente and the Nixon Doctrine: American Foreign Policy and the Pursuit of Stability* (1984), and Robert D. Schulzinger, *Henry Kissinger: Doctor of Diplomacy* (1989). The later stages of the Indochina War can be followed in many of the sources listed in Chapters 11 and 12. Other important works include Harry G. Summers Jr., *On Strategy: The Vietnam War in Context* (1981), and Michael P. Sullivan, *The Vietnam War: A Study in the Making of American Policy* (1985). For war-related controversies, see Stuart I. Rochester and Frederick Kiley, *Honor Bound: The History of American Prisoners of War in Southeast Asia, 1961–1973* (1998), and Jerry Lembcke, *The Spitting Image: Myth, Memory, and the Legacy of Vietnam* (1998).

Antiwar activism during Nixon's presidency is treated in the relevant portions of Tom Wells, *The War Within: America's Battle Over Vietnam* (1994), and in Kenneth J. Heineman, *Campus Wars: The Peace Movement at American State Universities in the Vietnam War Era* (1993). For working-class responses to student protest and the New Left, see Christian G. Appy, *Working-Class War: American Combat Soldiers and Vietnam* (1993), and the last segment of Peter B. Levy, *The New Left and Labor in the 1960s* (1994). The relationship between antiwar politics and the counterculture is discussed in Peter N. Carroll, *It Seemed Like Nothing Happened: America in the 1970s* (2000). For cultural history, see Michael X. Delli Carpini, *Stability and Change in Ameri-*

can Politics: The Coming of Age of the Generation of the 1960s (1986), and the relevant portions of John D'Emilio and Estelle Freedman, *Intimate Matters: A History of Sexuality in America* (1988).

Space technology and its implications are explored in the relevant segments of Walter A. McDougall, *The Heavens and the Earth: A Political History of the Space Age* (1985). The best overview of the environmental movement is Samuel Hays and Barbara D. Hays's *Beauty, Health, and Permanence: Environmental Politics in the United States, 1955–1985* (1987). For ecological controversies in the resource-rich western states, see Richard White, *It's Your Misfortune and None of My Own: A History of the American West* (1991).

Feminist agitation in the 1970s is the subject of the appropriate segments of Ruth Rosen, *The World Split Open: How the Modern Women's Movement Changed America* (2000), and of Alice Nichols, *Daring to Be Bad: Radical Feminism in America, 1967–1975* (1989). The ERA is described in Donald G. Mathews and Jane Sherron De Hart, *Sex, Gender, and the Politics of ERA* (1990), and in the provocative work by Mary Frances Berry, *Why ERA Failed: Politics, Women's Rights and the Amending Process of the Constitution* (1986). For the abortion rights controversy, see David Garrow, *Liberty and Sexuality: The Right to Privacy and the Making of* Roe v. Wade (1994), and Kristin Luker, *Abortion and the Politics of Womanhood* (1984). Struggles for homosexual rights are described in Barry D. Adam, *The Rise of a Gay and Lesbian Movement* (1987), and in the relevant sections of D'Emilio and Freedman, *Intimate Matters*.

Mexican American history of the 1970s can be found in Rodolfo Acuña, *Occupied America: A History of Chicanos* (2004), and in Juan Gomez Quinones, *Chicano Politics: Reality and Promise, 1940–1990* (1990). For Native Americans, see Philip Reno, *Mother Earth, Father Sky, and Economic Development* (1981), and the later segments of Francis Paul Prucha, *The Great Father: The United States Government and the American Indians, Volume II* (1984).

Assertions of black power in the early 1970s are treated in segments of William L. Van Deburg, *New Day in Babylon: The Black Power Movement and American Culture, 1965–1975* (1992), and in Harvard Sitkoff, *The Struggle for Black Equality, 1954–1980* (1981). For the Black Panthers, see Philip S. Foner, ed., *The Black Panthers Speak* (1995). For African American political activity, see Katherine Tate, *From Protest to Politics: The New Black Voters in American Elections* (1993).

White ethnicity and populist conservatism are the focus of Richard D. Alba, *Italian Americans: The Twilight of Ethnicity* (1985), and of Richard Krickus, *Pursuing the American Dream: White Ethnics and the New Populism* (1976). Two excellent case studies are Ronald P. Formisano, *Boston Against Busing: Race, Class, and Ethnicity in the 1960s and 1970s* (1991), and Jonathan Rieder, *Canarsie: The Jews and Italians of Brooklyn Against Liberalism* (1985). For conservatism, see Mark Gerson, *The Neoconservative Vision: From the Cold War to the Culture Wars* (1995), and Jerome L. Himmelstein, *To the Right: The Transformation of American Conservatism* (1990).

Reassessments of the radical political and cultural movements of the Nixon era appear in the relevant portions of Todd Gitlin, *The Twilight of Common Dreams: Why America Is Wracked by Culture Wars* (1995); in E. J. Dionne Jr., *Why Americans Hate Politics* (1991); and in Maurice Isserman and Michael Kazin, *America Divided: The Civil War of the 1960s* (2000). Far more critical is Peter Collier and David J. Horowitz, *Destructive Generation: Second Thoughts About the '60s* (1989). The political consequences of radical activism and liberal social policy are graphically portrayed in Thomas Byrne Edsall with Mary D. Edsall, *Chain Reaction: The Impact of Race, Rights, and Taxes on American Politics* (1991).

Watergate is summarized in Stanley I. Kutler, *The Wars of Watergate* (1990). For a view of the scandal sympathetic to Nixon, see Len Colodny and Robert Gettlin, *Silent Coup* (1992). See also Michael Schudson, *Watergate in American Memory: How We Remember, Forget, and Reconstruct the Past* (1992). For FBI abuses, see Richard Gid Powers, *Secrecy and Power: The Life of J. Edgar Hoover* (1987), and Athan G. Theoharis and John Stuart Cox, *The Boss: J. Edgar Hoover and the Great American Inquisition* (1988). For Ford's presidency, see John Robert Greene, *The Limits of Power and the Presidency of Gerald R. Ford* (1995). See also James L. Sundquist, *The Decline and Resurgence of Congress* (1981).

Struggling Giant: The Carter and Reagan Years, 1976–1988

"We want to have faith again. We want to be proud again," declared newly elected President Jimmy Carter. Promising to overcome the legacies of Vietnam and Watergate, Carter pledged to restore public trust in government. But energy shortages, severe economic dislocation, and global instability combined to sink esteem for the White House. As a wave of populist conservatism swept the nation in the late 1970s, Republican Ronald Reagan offered to rekindle the national sense of mission.

Reagan mobilized a new coalition of social conservatives, free-market advocates, and foreign policy hawks in response to economic stagnation at home and declining influence abroad. His ambitious program of government deregulation, welfare cuts, tax relief, and increased military spending led to the most dramatic change of government since the New Deal. Although "Reaganomics" was credited with the business boom that dominated the 1980s, trade imbalances and federal budget deficits threatened to eradicate prosperity. Meanwhile, the country was divided over identity politics, cultural allegiances, and conflicting social values.

Jimmy Carter: The Energy Crisis and Economic Stagnation

Gerald Ford hoped to translate public goodwill into victory at the polls in 1976. The president was the object of sympathy when two female assailants botched separate assassination attempts, leaving him unharmed. Ford and running mate Senator Robert Dole of Kansas campaigned against excessive federal spending. Yet they faced a formidable Democratic opponent in former Georgia Governor James ("Jimmy") Earl Carter Jr., a virtual unknown. As chair of the Democratic Campaign Committee, Carter had helped the party dominate the congres-

Promising to restore public trust in government after the Vietnam War and Watergate, newcomer Jimmy Carter refashioned the Democratic Party's electoral coalition in 1976.

sional elections of 1974. Yet, except for his service in the navy, the Georgia politician had never worked for the federal government.

Carter played up his outsider status by attacking a "confused and overlapping and wasteful federal bureaucracy" and by calling for tax reform, a national health program, and a comprehensive energy policy. Supported by African American leaders such as Atlanta's Andrew Young, the candidate also sought to capture the votes of white southerners who had deserted the Democrats in the previous two presidential elections. Indeed, the Georgian's credentials as a "born-again" Christian helped to defeat George Wallace in the southern primaries. Yet Carter also took pride in his experience as a nuclear engineer and member of the business-oriented Trilateral Commission. Defeating a wide

EXHIBIT **14-1**   **U.S. GROSS NATIONAL PRODUCT, 1976–1980**
(IN CURRENT BILLIONS OF DOLLARS)

1976	1782.8
1978	2243.7
1980	2732.0

Source: *Economic Report of the President* (1988).

range of candidates in the early primaries, Carter easily won the Democratic nomination. To bring geographic and ideological unity to the ticket, the nominee chose Senator Walter F. Mondale, a Minnesota liberal, as his running mate.

Although Carter called for "a time of healing" after Vietnam and Watergate, he also expressed populist anger toward elites. "It's time for the people to run the government," the candidate stated softly, "and not the other way around." When Carter accused Ford of trying to "hide" in the White House Rose Garden, the president agreed to hold three televised debates, the first such exercise since 1960. The TV exposure quickly transformed the challenger into a viable candidate.

By receiving a majority of the white male vote, Ford swept the West and carried three key midwestern states. Yet Democrats rebuilt the New Deal coalition by winning overwhelmingly among northeastern union workers, African Americans, and middle-class liberals. Because of strong support from black and white evangelicals, Carter captured all southern states except Virginia—90 percent of the candidate's national plurality came from the South. Winning by a margin of 2 percent of the popular vote, Carter edged past Ford in a 297–240 victory in the Electoral College, the closest finish since 1916. Despite the tightness of the race and the candidates' sole reliance on public campaign financing for the first time in U.S. history, voter participation remained less than 55 percent.

As Carter assumed the presidency, he faced a stagnating economy whose performance was worsened by inflation, federal budget deficits, and increased national debt. Delays in the modernization of manufacturing facilities had produced a sharp decline in worker productivity by the 1970s. Foreign competition particularly hurt the automobile industry, whose managers were slow to recognize consumer demand for smaller, energy-efficient cars in an era of rising gas prices. By the following decade, Japan would produce more autos and trucks than the United States for the first time in history and rank as the world's largest steel manufacturer. Plant and mill closings devastated midwestern "rust belt" cities such as Detroit, Gary, and Youngstown and contributed to declining property values and the failure of regional businesses. Western mining operations were also victimized by the recession.

Pressed by organized labor to respond to the recession, Congress passed an emergency public works program in 1977. The next year Carter signed the

EXHIBIT **14-2**   **U.S. CONSUMER CREDIT OUTSTANDING, 1977–1980 (IN ROUNDED BILLIONS OF DOLLARS)**

1977	279
1980	369

Source: *Economic Report of the President* (1988).

EXHIBIT **14-3**   **U.S. FEDERAL SOCIAL WELFARE EXPENDITURES, 1976–1980 (IN BILLIONS OF DOLLARS)**

1976	197.0
1978	239.7
1980	302.6

Source: *Statistical Abstract of the United States* (1987).

Humphrey-Hawkins Act, which set a ceiling on acceptable inflation rates and sought to reduce unemployment by making the federal government the employer of last resort. The president also approved a generous price-support system for farmers suffering from commodity surpluses. Yet Republicans embraced proposals advanced by Senator William Roth and Representative Jack Kemp that called for a 30 percent reduction in federal income taxes and government spending cuts. Carter encouraged the Federal Reserve Board to fight inflation by raising interest rates while the president established voluntary guidelines for wage and price increases. Responding to a tax rebellion initiated by California voters, the president also promised future tax relief.

Despite the administration's attempts to control spending, spiraling energy costs continued to spur inflation. In a major television address, Carter depicted the emergency as the "moral equivalent of war." Pleading for the conservation of electricity and fuel, he called for limits on oil imports and for subsidies to develop alternative energy. The White House also proposed a tax on excessive energy consumption and a contingency plan for gas rationing. In 1979 the crisis deepened when the Organization of Petroleum Exporting Countries (OPEC) hiked oil prices another 50 percent. After convening a domestic summit, Carter returned to television to depict the nation's inability to deal with its problems as a national "crisis of confidence." The president outlined a massive, ten-year energy program but faced congressional opposition from those who wanted to cut consumption by deregulating prices. The stalemate was resolved when Carter accepted gradual deregulation of domestic energy prices and limited rationing powers. Congress also agreed to impose a windfall profits tax on oil companies and to fund a Department of Energy and synthetic fuels program. Per capita energy use declined 20 percent between 1978 and 1981.

Reverend Andrew Young *(1932-)*

Andrew Young often recalled an old slavery proverb: "The Lord can make a way out of no way." The son of an African American dentist who raised his family in a racially integrated neighborhood of New Orleans, Young graduated from Howard University and received a degree from

© Stock Boston

Hartford Theological Seminary. He presided over small Congregational churches in Georgia and Alabama in the late 1950s and led early voter registration drives. Appointed assistant director of the National Council of Churches in 1959, he channeled funds into the burgeoning civil rights movement.

Young joined the Southern Christian Leadership Conference (SCLC) in Atlanta in the early 1960s, where he pursued voter registration, served as a trusted aide to Martin

Luther King Jr., and rose through the organizational hierarchy. In 1972 he became the first African American from Georgia to be elected to the House of Representatives in more than a century. Four years later, Young supported Jimmy Carter for president because the former Georgia governor had compiled an excellent civil rights record and had a positive working relationship with black leaders.

Seeking to fashion a foreign policy that fused U.S. ideals and interests, Carter chose Young as his United Nations spokesperson. The new

---

The energy crisis placed new emphasis on the use of nuclear reactors as a source of electrical power. Vowing to reverse this trend, environmental activists turned to civil disobedience at sites such as Seabrook, New Hampshire, to call attention to the health, safety, and financial dangers associated with atomic plants. In 1979 a near "meltdown" of the reactor core at a nuclear facility at Three Mile Island, Pennsylvania, focused public attention on the credibility of energy company managers and government regulators. "The history of the nuclear power industry," consumer advocate Ralph Nader told more than 100,000 demonstrators gathered in Washington, "is replete with cover-ups, deceptions, outright lies, error, negligence, arrogance, greed."

While the economy stagnated, Carter sought to establish a consumer protection agency and a hospital cost-control plan. Although the administration

ambassador enhanced Washington's global image by denouncing white minority rule in South Africa and Rhodesia. Yet the administration soon discovered the difficulty of applying evangelical principles to foreign policy.

As Carter brokered peace talks between Israel and Egypt at Camp David, Jewish leaders criticized the president for inadequate support of Israeli interests. Relations with the Jewish community deteriorated in 1979 when the president's brother hosted a Libyan business delegation and blamed criticism of the meeting on the "Jewish media." Carter was slow to distance himself from such remarks and courted further trouble by comparing the zeal of the guerrilla Palestine Liberation Organization (PLO) to that of the nonviolent U.S. civil rights movement. Two weeks later, in his role as temporary UN Security Council president, Young discussed the timing of a PLO resolution with the organization's UN representative, a Columbia University professor.

Young believed he had taken a "risk for peace" by encouraging the PLO to recognize the state of Israel. Yet he was forced to resign because he misled State Department officials about engaging in a meeting contrary to U.S. policy. Portrayed as a conservative by civil rights activists and as a moderate by Congress, he began to attract criticism as a radical. Despite the setback, Young would be elected mayor of Atlanta in the 1980s and would continue to emphasize the spiritual component to the quest for equal rights.

met defeat for these proposals in Congress, it succeeded in getting legislation to create a Department of Education, to establish a chemical contamination cleanup fund, to control strip mining, and to restrict the development of federal lands in Alaska. Carter also signed measures that deregulated the airline, railroad, trucking, communications, and banking industries and that authorized a multibillion dollar loan to save automaker Chrysler from bankruptcy. Pressed by Republican advocates of tax relief, Carter finally agreed to substantial cuts, although he postponed implementing them until 1981.

Unable to protect Democratic constituencies from rising oil prices and economic structural problems, the administration watched helplessly as "stagflation" worsened. Annual inflation reached 13.5 percent for 1980—the highest level since 1947—and the prime lending rate exceeded 22 percent. As loan rates surpassed the limits of potential home and car purchasers, economic stagnation pushed unemployment to more than 7 percent. When bloated budget deficits forced government borrowing, foreign investors sold off depreciated dollars, and the crisis worsened.

Carter's unfamiliarity with Washington compounded his political difficulties. Billing himself as an outsider, the Georgian chose advisors who lacked experience in congressional dealings and who could not win confidence on Capitol Hill. Carter attributed his legislative failures to narrow economic interests and single-issue lobbyists. Yet he often failed to follow his visionary televised appeals with detailed political negotiations among congressional leaders. As the president's approval ratings fell from a high of 75 percent upon taking office to less than 25 percent, the public viewed the nation's leader as hesitant, evasive, and removed from their problems.

Superpower Limits and the Iran Hostage Crisis

Having promised to cut defense spending and to take a fresh approach to foreign policy, Carter canceled production of the B-1 bomber, which air force leaders wanted as a replacement for the aging B-52. The president proclaimed that the United States was at last free "of the inordinate fear of communism . . . the fear that led to the moral poverty of Vietnam." Carter also deferred development of the neutron bomb and proposed to withdraw ground troops from South Korea. Building on the foundations laid by Nixon and Ford, the president stabilized relations with the Soviet Union by signing a second Strategic Arms Limitation Treaty (SALT II) in 1979. The new accord set limits on the number of long-range missiles, bombers, and nuclear warheads that could be held by the superpowers. Such cooperation reflected an easing of Cold War tensions in Europe, where West Germany had opened diplomatic and trade relations with the Soviet bloc. Washington also exchanged ambassadors with China and agreed to sever diplomatic ties with Taiwan.

The search for political stability in the oil-rich Middle East and the chance to exert global leadership led the White House to promote peace between Egypt and Israel. After a dramatic visit to Jerusalem by Egypt's Anwar Sadat in 1977, Carter brought the Egyptian leader and Israeli Prime Minister Menachem Begin to Maryland's Camp David for a summit. When further negotiations stalled two years later, the president flew to the Middle East to continue low-key diplomacy. Egypt and Israel finally signed a historic peace treaty in Washington in 1979. Yet Palestinian Arabs living in Israeli-occupied territories were not part of the accord and remained the most important stumbling block to regional peace.

EXHIBIT **14-4**   **U.S. NATIONAL DEFENSE AND VETERANS OUTLAYS, 1976–1980 (IN BILLIONS OF DOLLARS)**

1976	108.0
1978	123.5
1980	155.2

Source: *Statistical Abstract of the United States* (1987).

Carter had greater success in linking foreign policy to the aspirations of third-world people. Stressing the importance of human rights in his global strategy, he became the first president to visit black Africa. Andrew Young, the administration's African American ambassador to the United Nations, denounced apartheid in South Africa and defended the president's refusal to recognize the white minority government of Rhodesia (now Zimbabwe) until blacks were given political rights.

Carter also continued Nixon's and Ford's negotiations to return the Panama Canal to Panama by 2000. Despite strong opposition by Republican conservatives and a lengthy Senate debate, the president signed the Panama Canal treaty in 1978, although the United States reserved the right to intervene to preserve the Canal Zone's neutrality. By awarding Panama $1 billion and by negotiating the canal's sovereignty, the Carter administration removed the most obvious symbol of U.S. military aggression in the hemisphere. Congress also approved a small amount of emergency aid for Nicaragua when a 1979 revolution by Sandinista nationalists overthrew a brutal military dictatorship once supported by Washington.

Despite such achievements, Carter was devastated when the Soviet Union sought to contain Islamic nationalism on its southern flanks by invading neighboring Afghanistan in 1979. Placing the action in a Cold War context, the president raised alarms about "the most severe threat to world peace since the second World War." Carter promptly suspended grain sales to the Soviets and ordered a boycott of the 1980 Olympic Games in Moscow. The president also asked the Senate to shelve ratification of SALT II. Defense-minded senators from both parties had denounced the treaty for restricting development of cruise missiles while permitting the Soviets to improve "Backfire" bombers and other weapons. Yet the main objection to the accord centered on difficulties in verifying compliance, a persistent point of contention between the two superpowers. Another area of disagreement involved charges that the Soviets habitually violated the human rights of domestic dissidents.

Fearing that the Afghan operation signaled a Soviet move into Africa and the oil-rich Persian Gulf, the White House issued the Carter Doctrine of 1980. "An attempt by any outside force to gain control of the Gulf region," it proclaimed, would be regarded as an assault on U.S. "vital interests" and would be

468

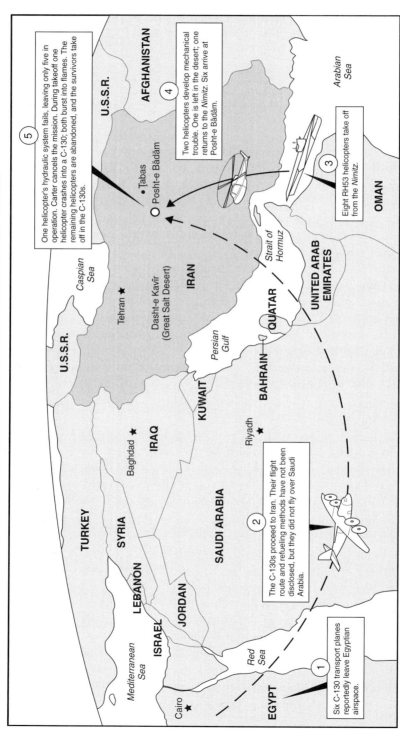

EXHIBIT **14-5**   LOCATION OF U.S. HOSTAGE RESCUE EFFORT IN IRAN

5 One helicopter's hydraulic system fails, leaving only five in operation. Carter cancels the mission. During takeoff one helicopter crashes into a C-130; both burst into flames. The remaining helicopters are abandoned, and the survivors take off in the C-130s.

4 Two helicopters develop mechanical trouble. One is left in the desert; one returns to the *Nimitz*. Six arrive at Posht-e Bādām.

3 Eight RH53 helicopters take off from the *Nimitz*.

2 The C-130s proceed to Iran. Their flight route and refueling methods have not been disclosed, but they did not fly over Saudi Arabia.

1 Six C-130 transport planes reportedly leave Egyptian airspace.

U.S.S.R.

AFGHANISTAN

Arabian Sea

OMAN

UNITED ARAB EMIRATES

Strait of Hormuz

QUATAR

BAHRAIN

KUWAIT

Persian Gulf

IRAN

• Tabas
○ Posht-e Bādām

Dasht-e Kavīr (Great Salt Desert)

Tehran ★

Caspian Sea

U.S.S.R.

IRAQ

Baghdad ★

SAUDI ARABIA

Riyadh ★

TURKEY

SYRIA

LEBANON

JORDAN

ISRAEL

Mediterranean Sea

Cairo ★

EGYPT

Red Sea

repelled "by any means necessary." To demonstrate national resolve, Carter prevailed upon Congress to resume registration for the draft. He also proposed a 25 percent growth in defense spending in the next five years. The administration already had responded to claims that the U.S. military had deteriorated after the Vietnam War by increasing annual outlays by nearly 50 percent. Carter provided additional support for the military by endorsing Pentagon plans for the deployment of Trident submarines armed with nuclear missiles.

Ironically, the Soviet Union did not present Carter with his most daunting foreign policy challenge. Instead, the administration floundered as a result of a crisis arising from the 1979 overthrow of Iran's pro-Western Shah Mohammed Reza Pahlavi. Led by Moslem cleric Ayatollah Ruhollah Khomeini, Shiite fundamentalists demanded a religious state that would end ties with the United States and that would purge Western secularism and materialism. Many Iranians remained embittered by the CIA coup that had restored the shah in 1953. Like Nixon and Kissinger, Carter recognized Iran's importance as an oil-rich nation that bordered the Soviet Union, purchased U.S. arms, and functioned as a reliable client state. The president first supported the shah but then watched helplessly as the dictator's regime crumbled. Forced into exile, the deposed leader sought medical treatment in the United States. When Kissinger and the Rockefeller family convinced Carter to grant the shah's request for U.S. entry on humanitarian grounds, outraged Iranian militants seized the U.S. embassy in Tehran, took embassy personnel hostage, and demanded repatriation of the shah and his fortune.

After the United States refused to negotiate with the militants in Tehran, the Iranian government assumed control of the hostages. Carter then froze Iran's assets in the United States, severed diplomatic relations, and ordered trade sanctions. By portraying the president as singularly committed to the release of U.S. citizens, the White House dramatized their plight. Months later, under pressure to break the deadlock, Carter ordered a military rescue; but two helicopters malfunctioned in a desert sandstorm, eight commandos were killed, and the mission failed. Protesting the decision to resolve the crisis through military means, Cyrus R. Vance became the first secretary of state to resign because of a disagreement about policy since William Jennings Bryan did so in 1915.

After engaging in complex negotiations with intermediaries regarding Iranian assets held in U.S. banks, Tehran agreed to release the fifty-two remaining hostages—but only after Jimmy Carter left office. Hours after the inauguration of a new president on January 20, 1981, the captives ended 444 days of incarceration. The Iranian standoff remained a bitter symbol of the diminished global power of the United States in the post–Vietnam War era and helped to produce a major power shift in Washington.

Reverend Jerry Falwell *(1933–)*

As leader of the Moral Majority, a political and social lobby for Protestant fundamentalists, Jerry Falwell was America's most influential conservative voice of the 1980s. His Sunday evening cable TV program reached into 34 million homes. His enterprises and holdings included

television's National Christian Network, Liberty Baptist College, and an 18,000-member Baptist Church in Lynchburg, Virginia. Falwell traveled 200,000 air miles each year by private jet to raise the annual $100 million needed to sustain these interests. Once described as the "sleeping giant" of U.S. politics, the Virginia preacher was credited with controlling the votes of an estimated 21 million evangelicals.

Falwell came from a successful but disreputable Lynchburg family that included bootlegging and a dance hall among its enterprises. A bright student and an accomplished athlete with a flair for rowdiness, he studied mechanical engineering at a local college. One night Falwell attended a Baptist service, fell in love with (and subsequently married) the church pianist, and instantly became a born-again Christian. Two months later he decided to enter the ministry and transferred to a Baptist Bible college in Missouri. Upon graduation in 1956, Falwell returned to Lynchburg to found an independent fundamentalist church in an abandoned bottling facility.

Falwell immediately arranged to broadcast services by radio. Six months later, his *Old Time Gospel Hour*, which merely recorded the service as it occurred, made it to television. A 6-footer with a large waistline and a deep, booming voice, the minister wore dark suits and always carried a Bible. His upbeat theology conveyed images of success and messages of hope and redemption. At the same time, Falwell never strayed

THE CHRISTIAN RIGHT AND SOCIAL CONSERVATISM

The evolving political climate in Washington reflected a major upsurge in conservative social views. As the number of one-parent families in the United States increased by 79 percent in the 1970s and the birth rate declined to

from the fundamentalist belief in the accuracy of the Bible or from resistance to anything that conflicted with spiritual command.

In 1977 the Lynchburg preacher reversed long-standing fundamentalist isolation from social action and politics by affirming a religious leader's right to disseminate views on abortion, pornography, and homosexuality. During that year, Falwell helped singer Anita Bryant lead a political campaign to repeal a Florida county ordinance granting equal rights to homosexuals, whom the minister accused of "perversion and immorality." In 1978 and 1979 he fashioned "Clean Up America" campaigns to counteract "a tide of permissiveness and moral decay." These efforts climaxed in the founding of the Moral Majority in 1979.

Falwell described the independent Moral Majority as a united front for God and country. He professed to speak for the vast majority of citizens who subscribed to traditional values in opposition to the "godless minority" that ruled the country. In *Listen America!* (1980), Falwell explained that this "coalition of God-fearing moral Americans" would "reverse the politicalization of immorality." The enemy was "secular humanism" in government—the attempt to solve problems apart from God. "I believe in the separation of church and state but not in the separation of God and government," Falwell remarked.

After signing up more than 2 million members, the Moral Majority registered twice that number as new voters for the 1980 elections and urged another 10 million to vote. Falwell had created a massive political action movement. Yet he rejected party affiliations and simply chose to identify himself as "a noisy Baptist" who had a "divine mandate" to fight for laws to save America. Politicizing the struggle between "good and evil," Falwell's mobilization of evangelical social conservatives dramatically realigned national politics and helped set the stage for the election of Ronald Reagan.

record lows, evangelical Christians began to denounce increased tolerance of birth control, abortion, premarital sex, divorce, and pornography. In 1979 Reverend Jerry Falwell founded the Moral Majority and used his televised pulpit to mobilize evangelical Protestants who sought a Christian republic. By revitalizing political involvement and social activism among fundamentalists of the Southwest and the West, Falwell fused anticommunism with a condemnation of "modernist" teachings such as evolution. The movement complained that a liberal "Eastern Establishment" had destroyed reverence for religion and proper education by imposing "value-free" standards on churches and schools.

Condemning secular humanism as a misguided philosophy that placed man above God, fundamentalists preached against "sin" and "moral decadence" and attacked abortion, the Equal Rights Amendment (ERA), gay rights, and "satanic" rock music. They also struggled to replace evolutionist teachings with creationist doctrines that conformed to biblical teaching. Using computer lists, direct mail, telephone marketing, and audiocassettes, the Christian Right organized 50 million born-again Protestants. The new religious conservatism fostered a variety of popular television evangelists such as Pat Robertson, who went on to create cable TV's Christian Broadcasting Network (CBN).

The most intense debate over family values centered on abortion. Insisting that the fetus was a sacred form of human life, the Roman Catholic Church and groups such as National Right to Life denounced legalized abortion as murder of the unborn. Conservatives like Phyllis Schlafly argued that abortion placed the individual needs of the potential mother above those of family and society. Abortion opponents viewed sex as a procreative ritual and childbearing as a God-given privilege, so they also objected to family planning. A broad movement of conservative Catholics, Protestants, and Jews began to picket abortion clinics and mount massive demonstrations in the late 1970s. Although the Supreme Court refused to reverse *Roe* v. *Wade* or grant states the power to outlaw abortion outright, pro-lifers succeeded in limiting taxpayer support of the procedure. In 1976 Congress passed an amendment introduced by Illinois's Henry J. Hyde barring the use of Medicaid funds for abortions for women on welfare.

The ERA became another focal point of the conservative cultural crusade. Stop-ERA organizer Schlafly lobbied furiously against the measure by claiming it would "neuterize" society and would relieve men of the obligation to support their families. Fearing that the ERA would force women into the male-dominated labor market and require placement of children in day care, opponents linked the amendment to an attack on the family. As the debate shifted from issues of equality to a conflict over traditional values, anti-ERA activists raised the specter of a military draft that would place women in combat. Feminists appeared to cut themselves off from less-privileged cohorts by suggesting that women should discard the traditional protections offered by men. The ERA fell three states short of ratification in 1982 and six votes shy of reconsideration the following year. Nine states in the traditional South were among those that rejected the measure.

The ERA controversy illustrated the conflict between individual rights and traditional obligations. Similar polarization marked the confrontation over affirmative action. As the courts and regulatory agencies seemed to penalize nonminorities for the past policies of employers, the costs of civil rights reform became more broadly distributed, and whites complained of reverse discrimination. The controversy was particularly bitter in higher education, where institutions set aside admissions slots for minority students even if their grades and test scores were lower than those of rejected white applicants. In the *Bakke* case of 1978 the Supreme Court ruled that affirmative action numeric quotas in medical school admissions violated civil rights law, although race could be considered in order to secure a more diverse student body.

THE 1980 ELECTION AND REAGANOMICS

Having responded to inflation with reduced federal spending and tight monetary policies, President Carter faced an uprising of traditional Democratic constituencies in the labor and civil rights movements. When Senator Edward Kennedy challenged Carter for the 1980 presidential nomination, the White House used the powers of incumbency to prevail in the party primaries. Yet Carter faced a more effective opponent when Ronald Reagan defeated George Bush in the race for the Republican nomination. A minor star in 1940s movies, Reagan had forged anticommunist credentials as president of the Screen Actors Guild during the Hollywood Red Scare. As his movie career declined in the early 1950s, the actor became the national spokesperson for defense contractor General Electric. Moving into politics, Reagan espoused fiscal and social conservatism and Cold War interventionism. After winning the governorship of California in 1966, he attracted attention as a militant opponent of student activism, as a critic of government bureaucracy, and as a supporter of the Vietnam War.

By 1980 Reagan had become the leading voice of the nation's conservatives by questioning détente with the Soviets, by demanding a strong defense, and by attacking government social spending as inflationary. The Republican candidate promised to "take the government off the backs of the people" by cutting government "waste, extravagance, abuse, and outright fraud." He also identified with the social values advanced by the Christian Right and Reverend Falwell. By promoting family cohesion, religious worship, and traditional education, the nominee expressed the desire of Protestant evangelicals and conservative Catholics to redeem the nation from moral permissiveness and collectivist values.

Asking voters if they were "better off" than they had been four years earlier, Reagan assured a frustrated electorate that it did "not have to go on sharing scarcity." Instead, the candidate proclaimed "an era of national renewal" and promised to restore U.S. global power. Democratic allusions to Reagan as a right-wing threat to peace backfired when the challenger appeared relaxed and amiable in a nationally televised debate. Although Reagan won support

EXHIBIT **14-6**   THE ELECTION OF 1980

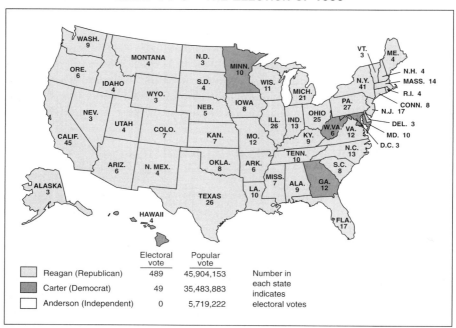

	Electoral vote	Popular vote	
Reagan (Republican)	489	45,904,153	Number in each state indicates electoral votes
Carter (Democrat)	49	35,483,883	
Anderson (Independent)	0	5,719,222	

from corporate leaders seeking to reduce social costs and to regain a competitive edge in the world economy, his rejection of Carter's notion of "limits" attracted a broad coalition of upscale professionals, young entrepreneurs, and blue-collar workers anxious about economic opportunity. As the White House waited in vain for settlement of the Iranian hostage crisis, Reagan and vice presidential candidate George Bush captured 51 percent of the popular vote, compared with 41 percent for Carter and Mondale. Running as an independent, Representative John B. Anderson, a moderate Illinois Republican, received nearly 7 percent of presidential ballots.

The one-sided nature of the 1980 contest surfaced in the Electoral College vote, where the Republicans prevailed by an overwhelming 489–49. His support of a constitutional amendment to ban abortion allowed Reagan to attract more than three-fifths of born-again white Protestants, who helped him capture seven southern states that Carter had carried in the previous contest. Meanwhile, Republicans won control of the Senate for the first time since 1952.

George Bush had accused Reagan of espousing "voodoo economics" during the Republican primaries. Yet the former governor insisted that he could reduce government spending while increasing outlays for defense, could lower taxes while balancing the federal budget, and could simultaneously restore economic prosperity. Such reasoning originated with "supply-side" economists such as Arthur Laffer of the University of Southern California and consultants associated with conservative think tanks such as the Heritage Foundation and the American Enterprise Institute. These advisors insisted that government regulations and high taxes held back production and inflated prices. Supply-side policy called for generous tax cuts and government deregulation. Reagan argued that investors would anticipate improvements from his economic program and would spur market recovery. As supply-side economics gained ground in Congress, the president called for the largest tax cut in U.S. history.

While many Democrats lashed out against "Reaganomics," Office of Management and Budget Director David Stockman appeared before Congress to demonstrate that tax relief would not interfere with a balanced budget, even if accompanied by added military spending. Although Stockman acknowledged that tax cuts served the interests of the administration's wealthy supporters, he insisted that the budget plan could sustain economic growth without inflation. Accordingly, Democrats cooperated in passing the Economic Recovery Act of 1981, which enacted a three-year individual income tax reduction of 25 percent. The law offered incentives for individual retirement accounts (IRAs), reduced capital gains taxes and maximum tax rates, increased amounts exempted from estate and gift taxes, and indexed returns to inflation. Congress also lowered corporate tax rates, accelerated depreciation allowances, and reduced the windfall profits tax on oil. Although House Democrats subsequently tightened loopholes and restored some cuts, Reagan's tax relief pumped billions of dollars into the economy.

REAGAN DEREGULATION

Reagan sought to implement a conservative agenda by altering the direction of the Supreme Court. In 1981 he appointed Arizona judge and free-market advocate Sandra Day O'Connor as the first female justice to sit on the Court, despite her moderate support for abortion rights. When Chief Justice Warren Burger retired in 1986, the White House chose Antonin Scalia, a conservative academic, to fill the vacancy and elevated William Rehnquist, the panel's most conservative member, to the presiding chair. Reagan anticipated further judicial influence when he selected constitutional scholar Robert H. Bork to fill a third vacancy in 1987. However, Democrats and Republican moderates rejected Bork's strict interpretation of constitutional rights protections as "extremist." Forced to abandon the nominee after a campaign by feminists and civil rights activists, the president settled on the less abrasive Anthony M. Kennedy, a California judge.

The Reagan administration also pursued conservative policies by abandoning suits in favor of affirmative action and school desegregation, by opposing busing, by reducing legal services budgets for the poor, and by stacking civil rights agencies with obstructive appointees. Most important, the president sought to lessen Washington's commitment to the welfare system. Viewing discretionary social spending as counterproductive and inflationary, the White House hoped to restore post–World War II prosperity by returning to a budget in which safety net functions were confined to Social Security. Accordingly, Reagan and Congress cut $35 billion from domestic programs in 1981 through a drastic reduction of welfare. Confining the provision of benefits to the "truly needy," the government removed 400,000 families from Aid to Families with Dependent Children (AFDC) and took nearly 1 million people off the food stamp rolls. Discretionary social expenditure as a share of gross national product declined by more than a third during Reagan's tenure.

Committed to free-market reform, Reagan's administration accelerated Carter's steps toward deregulation. A 1982 court order divested American Telephone and Telegraph (AT&T) of local telephone service business and permitted its subsidiaries to enter computer processing and information fields. The Banking Act of 1982 enabled lenders to increase new services such as interest-bearing checking and money market accounts. Meanwhile, continued federal airline deregulation introduced lower fares and more flexible schedules. However, the policy soon led to conflicts with organized labor. When Reagan reduced the authority of the Occupational Safety and Health Administration (OSHA) in 1981, union leaders complained that the government had abandoned workers to suffer from excessive noise levels and lethal chemical exposures. After airline controls were lifted, air traffic controllers protested that the Federal Aviation Administration (FAA) had not allocated sufficient resources to deal with increased domestic flights. When 12,000 controllers went on strike, the president dissolved their union and ordered the FAA to replace them with military personnel. This antiunion strategy signaled the government's support for reduced labor costs amid global competition.

The administration also provoked the ire of environmentalists when it cut Carter's energy windfall profits tax and eliminated federal funding for alternative fuels. Further conflict emerged when Secretary of the Interior James G. Watt leased offshore drilling rights to oil and gas interests and proposed the harvesting of timber from national parks. After activists won Watt's resignation in 1983, the head of the Environmental Protection Agency (EPA) was forced to resign; another official was convicted of perjury in a scandal involving EPA collusion with industrial polluters. Congress responded with legislation imposing stricter handling of hazardous wastes, agreed to a new Superfund to clean toxic dumps, and overrode a presidential veto to appropriate billions of dollars to combat water pollution. Experts estimated that the cleanup costs for three U.S. government nuclear waste disposal sites alone would surpass $100 billion.

Responding to the White House's lack of interest in environmental regulation, ecologists warned that pollution crossed national boundaries. For example, depletion of Amazon rain forests by developers and fast-food cattle interests was dangerously lowering global atmospheric oxygen levels. Sulfuric emissions from the burning of cheap coal by U.S. factories and power plants resulted in acid rain that was defoliating trees and contaminating lakes in Canada and the northern Midwest. As the federal government moderated regulations to accommodate industrial interests, figures revealed that Earth's atmosphere had lost 2.3 percent of its ozone layer—an essential shield against ultraviolet rays that cause skin cancer and excessive heating by the sun.

Despite Reagan's conservative agenda, however, the White House often compromised with congressional Democrats. As unemployment approached 11 percent in 1982, the president approved a gas tax that funded a four-year outlay for highway and other transportation projects. After Reagan created a bipartisan commission on the impending bankruptcy of the Social Security system, he signed the commission's recommendations for increased payroll taxes into law. Yet Congress refused to implement the White House's "new federalism," a proposal to shift welfare programs to the poorly funded states. Congress also ignored the president's plan to provide tuition tax credits for private school education because the plan was perceived as a threat to public schooling and racial integration. Nor did Congress approve requests to abolish the Departments of Education and Energy. Constitutional amendments concerning balanced budgets, abortion, and public school prayer also met defeat.

REELECTION AND THE REAGAN DOCTRINE

Reagan's tax cuts coincided with a sharp drop in global oil prices and a return of prosperity. "We Brought America Back," the White House announced in 1984. Seeking to strengthen voter faith in the Republican Party as the promoter of opportunity, campaign videos proclaimed that it was "Morning in America." Democrats disagreed on how to regain the electorate's confidence. African American minister and civil rights advocate Jesse Jackson represented a "rainbow coalition" of racial minorities, feminists, peace activists, and the poor. Senator Gary Hart of Colorado cultivated urban professionals involved in the high-tech service economy. Yet former Vice President Mondale emerged as the 1984 Democratic presidential nominee by deferring to party power bases in labor, education, and the big cities. At the urging of feminists, Mondale chose Representative Geraldine A. Ferraro of New York as his running mate—the first woman nominated for national executive office by a major party.

Democrats tried to preserve the alliance of unions, beneficiaries of big government, and urban developers that had financed their party's presidential races since World War II. Yet global competition reduced tolerance of government regulation and social spending among business interests that had

EXHIBIT **14-7   VOTER PARTICIPATION, 1980–1984**
(AS A PERCENTAGE OF ALL ELIGIBLE VOTERS)

1980	52.8
1984	53.3

Source: *Statistical Abstract of the United States* (1996).

once been friendly to the Democratic Party. Meanwhile, the diminished role of manufacturing eroded union membership and bargaining power. Both parties now competed for financial backing by relying on election specialists, media advisors, and legal consultants. Democrats increasingly leaned on their upper-middle-class base by combining calls for fiscal integrity with a focus on education, the environment, and civil rights.

Although Mondale won the AFL-CIO's first-ever presidential endorsement in 1984, he lost the confidence of many voters by acknowledging that he would raise taxes to ease the budget deficit without shifting the burden to the affluent. The Democrats emerged from the election with 90 percent of African American ballots, nearly two-thirds of the Hispanic vote, and a hefty majority among the working poor. Yet Reagan's communications skills fused with sophisticated polling and advertising techniques to produce a stunning Republican victory.

The president won 59 percent of the popular vote and captured majorities in every state but Mondale's Minnesota and the District of Columbia. Republicans did particularly well among evangelical Christians, southern whites, white males, and the affluent. More surprising was Reagan's comfortable majority among eighteen- to twenty-nine year-olds, a group who preferred Republican promises of economic growth to the status-quo politics of the losers. The election dramatized the conversion of "Reagan Democrats"—Republican voters from working-class families once loyal to the New Deal—who were more comfortable with the president's pro-market policies than with the Democrats' social liberalism.

Reagan contrasted the "evil empire" of the Soviet Union with the moral superiority of the United States—the "blessed land" of a "chosen people." President Carter had translated this moral imperative into a demand that allies such as Chile and El Salvador adhere to high standards in guaranteeing human rights. In contrast, Reagan's UN Ambassador Jeane J. Kirkpatrick rejected this policy as naïve and insisted that right-wing "authoritarian" dictatorships were capable of democratic change, whereas left-wing "totalitarian" regimes were not. Blaming "world terrorism" and most global conflict on Soviet adventurism in developing nations, national security planners fashioned an unofficial "Reagan Doctrine" to rebuild the Central Intelligence Agency's (CIA) capabilities. The president persuaded Congress to lift the Carter-era restrictions in Angola and personally designated the anticommunist UNITA to be the recipient of military aid. The United States also supplied anticommunist rebels in Afghanistan, Cambodia, Ethiopia, and Nicaragua.

Although the administration insisted that communism contributed to the worst human rights abuses, the White House faced intense congressional pressure when the white minority government of South Africa violently suppressed black demonstrations. As U.S. civil rights leaders led daily antiapartheid protests at Washington's South African embassy, conservative Republicans embraced the campaign to demonstrate opposition to racism. Reagan responded with a policy of "constructive engagement" that called for peaceful persuasion of an anticommunist ally. Not satisfied, Congress then handed the president his most dramatic foreign policy reversal by overriding his veto of South African trade sanctions in 1986. After the defeat, Reagan recognized the government of reformer Corazon Aquino when Philippine dictator Ferdinand E. Marcos was ousted by a democratic movement. American officials also escorted dictator Jean-Claude Duvalier out of Haiti. As relations cooled with military governments in Chile and Paraguay, Reagan announced that the United States encouraged democratic movements among right-wing allies.

THE MIDDLE EAST QUAGMIRE

The United States faced its most daunting challenges in the Middle East, where it sought to protect regional oil fields and shipping lanes and to support Israel and "moderate" Arab leaders. When Reagan sent a contingent of marines to act as peacekeepers during a civil war in Lebanon in 1982, the troops clashed with Syrian forces and with Moslem militias allied with Iran. Islamic revolutionaries deployed massive truck bombs to destroy the U.S. embassy and marine headquarters, killing 241 U.S. servicemen. For the first time in history, Congress invoked the War Powers Act. Although Reagan did not recognize the statute's constitutionality, he agreed to withdraw all troops within eighteen months. Like its predecessors, the Reagan administration underestimated the region's pervasive currents of nationalism and fundamentalism and failed to address the ongoing dispute between Israel and the Palestinians.

Perceived as a supporter of Israeli expansion and as an imperial power in the Middle East, the United States continued to be the target of violent attacks, kidnappings, and hijackings. After declaring a trade embargo against radical Libya, which the White House accused of supporting terror campaigns, the president unleashed an air and naval attack in 1986. Once Washington linked the Libyans to the bombing of a West German discotheque frequented by U.S. soldiers, the administration orchestrated a second military attack against Libya that destroyed the family quarters of Libyan leader Muammar al-Qaddafi.

The administration also sought to contain revolutionary Iran. Reagan embargoed military shipments to Tehran and pledged never to negotiate with

EXHIBIT **14-8**   **LEBANON, 1983**

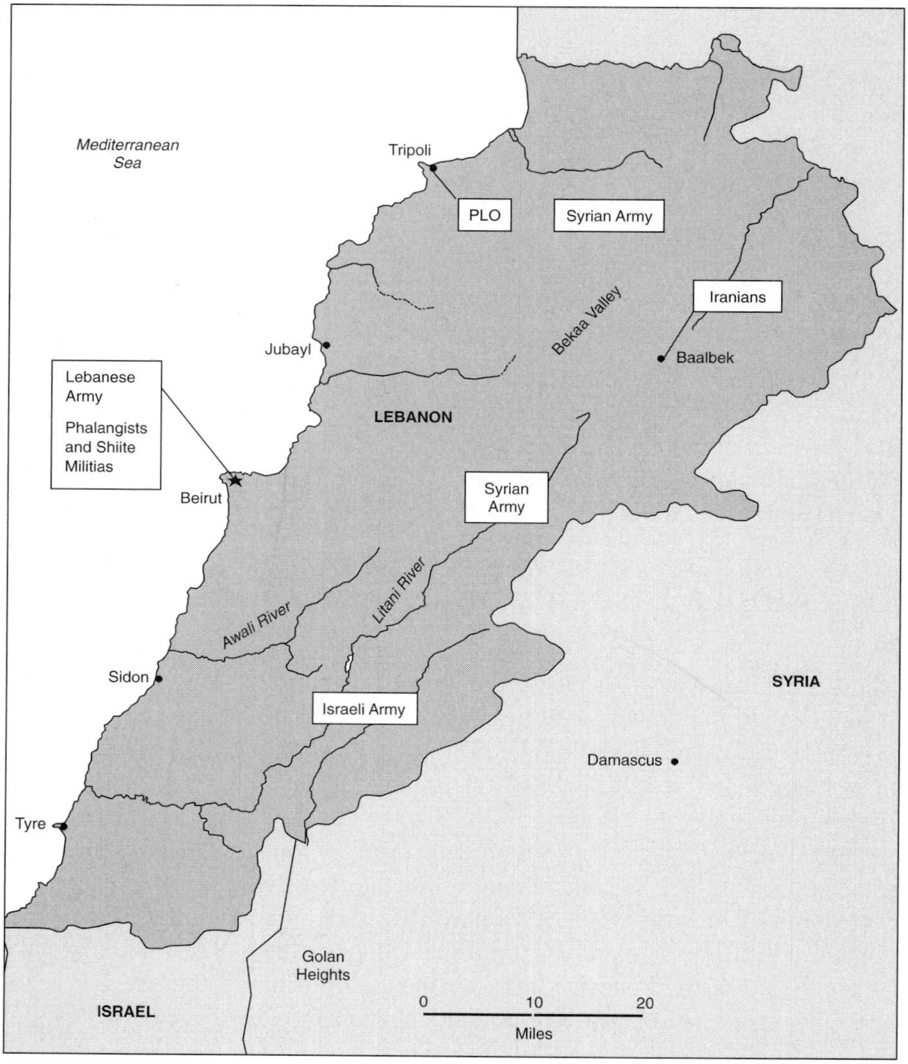

terrorists. Nevertheless, in 1985 the president permitted National Security Council officials to arrange a secret exchange of U.S. weapons to Iran for the release of U.S. hostages in Lebanon. When a Beirut newspaper leaked details of the arms-for-hostage accord in 1986, the administration abruptly ended the relationship. Reagan subsequently sent naval forces to the Persian Gulf to protect the passage of Middle East oil tankers. Yet the covert arrangement with Tehran would haunt the president for the remainder of his term.

EXHIBIT **14-9** PERSIAN GULF SHIPPING LANES

EXHIBIT **14-9** PERSIAN GULF SHIPPING LANES

SOVIET UNION

Black Sea

Caspian Sea

Ankara

TURKEY

SYRIA

IRAQ

Tehran

Beirut

Damascus

LEBANON

Baghdad

ISRAEL

IRAN

AFGHANISTAN

Jerusalem

Amman

JORDAN

KUWAIT

Cairo

Kuwait

PAKISTAN

Persian Gulf

Strait of Hormuz

Bahrain

EGYPT

Qatar

Doha

Gulf of Oman

Riyadh

Muscat

Red Sea

SAUDI ARABIA

UNITED ARAB EMIRATES

YEMEN ARAB REPUBLIC (NORTH YEMEN)

OMAN

Khartoum

San'a

PEOPLE'S DEMOCRATIC REPUBLIC OF YEMEN (SOUTH YEMEN)

SUDAN

Aden

Gulf of Aden

Arabian Sea

DJIBOUTI

SOMALIA

ETHIOPIA

0   500

Nautical Miles

UGANDA   KENYA

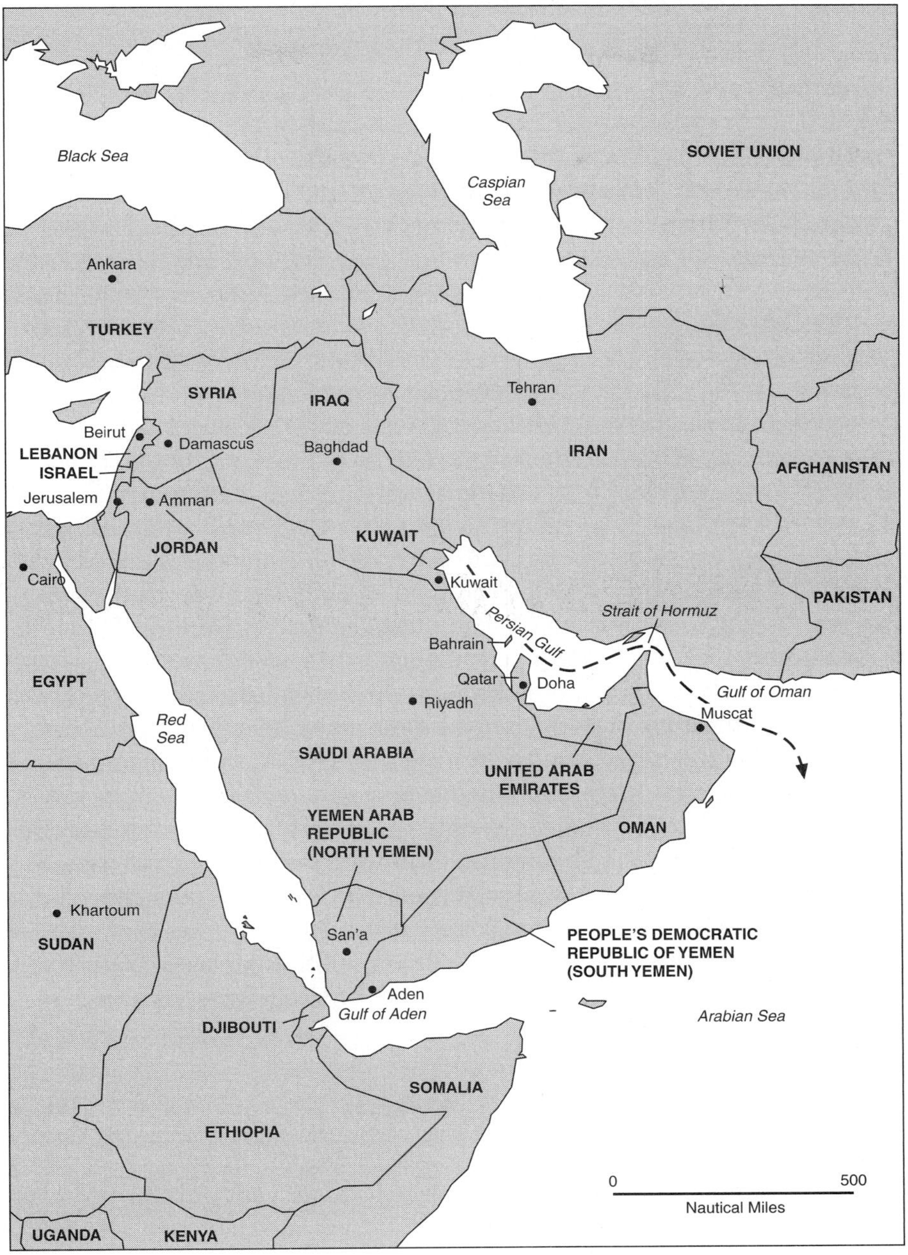

Jeane J. Kirkpatrick *(1926–)*

Like her boss Ronald Reagan, Jeane Kirkpatrick became a prominent Republican after years of loyalty to the Democratic Party. While a staunch Democrat, Kirkpatrick went to Barnard College and Columbia University but delayed her career to meet family responsibilities. She returned to

academic life in the early 1960s, joined the faculty of Georgetown University, and completed her Ph.D. in political science at Columbia in 1968. Quickly establishing herself as a prolific and respected scholar, Kirkpatrick did important work on U.S. politics and foreign policy.

Kirkpatrick grew steadily estranged from liberal politics after 1968. She particularly objected to the influx of Democratic dissidents she described as "antiwar, antigrowth, antibusiness, antilabor." As a result of the Vietnam War, moreover, she found that Democrats expressed a reluctance to wield military power to defend U.S. interests against Soviet and other threats. Kirkpatrick preferred an older version of liberalism best articulated in the 1970s by Senators Henry Jackson of Washington and Hubert Humphrey of Minnesota. Characterizing herself as a "welfare conservative," she defended the "noble tradition of caring in domestic affairs, of . . . providing minimum standards of well-being" while simultaneously contrasting the success of American society to "the failure and tyranny of communist societies."

The issue of foreign policy finally prompted her break with the Democratic Party during the Carter administration, whose approach to

THE CRUSADE IN CENTRAL AMERICA

Pushing for supremacy in the Cold War, Reagan officials pursued a vigilant anticommunist policy in the Caribbean and Central America. Cuba's Fidel Castro had permitted 125,000 exiles to flee to Florida in 1980, but the United States charged that many were criminals, mental patients, or social undesirables. As relations between Havana and Washington worsened, Castro consolidated ties with the Marxist government of the tiny Caribbean island of Grenada. When dissident communists murdered Grenada's prime minister

world affairs she saw as guilt-ridden and irresolute. Kirkpatrick voiced these concerns in a biting article for the conservative journal *Commentary*. Titled "Dictatorships and Double Standards," her polemic attacked the failure of Carter's foreign policy as "clear to everyone except its architects." Kirkpatrick particularly scorned the administration for opposing pro–U.S., right-wing authoritarians while tolerating leftist or revolutionary regimes unfriendly to the United States. She argued that for all their faults, right-wing authoritarians more easily accepted democratic reforms than did left-wing totalitarians. "Liberal idealism," she concluded, "need not be identical with masochism, and need not be incompatible with the defense of freedom and the national interest."

Impressed by the article, Reagan appointed Kirkpatrick ambassador to the United Nations shortly after his election in 1980. During her five years at the UN, she acquired a reputation as a combative advocate of U.S. policy, but her role as UN ambassador increasingly frustrated her. Kirkpatrick called the body a "dismal show" where conflicts never were resolved. When Reagan did not appoint her to a high-level policymaking position, she resigned in 1985 and returned to Georgetown. Almost simultaneously, she joined the Republican Party.

One of the few prominent women to serve in the Reagan administration, Kirkpatrick often received press consideration as a possible candidate for elective office or for a future political appointment. Adored by conservatives and vilified by liberals, Jeane Kirkpatrick remained an outspoken beacon of plain talk and provocative viewpoints.

and other leaders in 1983, Reagan used the pretext of civil strife to mount an invasion against Cuba's ally. Labeling the operation a "rescue mission" to protect one thousand U.S. medical students, the president dispatched a small force of marines, rangers, and paratroopers to take control of the island. Polls revealed public endorsement of the nation's first military "victory" in the post–Vietnam War era.

In Central America's impoverished El Salvador, the Reagan administration pursued a more controversial policy by arming a right-wing military government whose security forces and "death squads" killed 30,000 civilians in a

EXHIBIT **14-10**   **CENTRAL AMERICA AND THE CARIBBEAN**

bloody civil war in the early 1980s. When a centrist leader won internationally supervised elections in 1984, Congress approved additional funding to defeat left-wing guerrillas. Yet efforts to incorporate the rebels into the political structure were threatened in 1988 when right-wingers regained control of El Salvador's legislature. In neighboring Nicaragua, Reagan authorized the CIA to support a rebel army of "contras" to overthrow the Sandinista government, which the White House saw as a front for communist expansion. Administration policy in Central America was strongly opposed by many religious leaders, particularly in the Catholic community. After learning of CIA assassination manuals and the secret mining of Nicaraguan ports, Congress passed the Boland Amendments of 1982 and 1984, which prohibited the use of military or intelligence funds for covert action against Nicaragua's government.

Frustrated by congressional interference with so-called freedom fighters, Reagan officials violated Boland Amendment restrictions by secretly raising more than $36 million from private donors and conservative allies such as Saudi Arabia and Taiwan. Meanwhile, CIA Director William Casey, National Security Advisor Rear Admiral John M. Poindexter, and National Security Council aide Lieutenant Colonel Oliver North coordinated an illegal scheme to help the contras by diverting unlawful profits from the illegal Iranian arms sales. The top-secret campaign depended on illegal CIA operations and pressure on the governments of Honduras and Costa Rica to permit Nicaraguan contra rebels to operate from their territory.

Disclosure of the Iran-Contra fund diversion in 1986 created the greatest crisis of Reagan's tenure. Having weathered an assassin's bullet in his first months in office, the president had forged a reputation as a "Teflon" leader who survived both misfortune and criticism with ease. However, after denying the arms sale to Iran had ever occurred and after insisting that missiles were not traded for hostages, Reagan faced questions about his involvement in the violations of the Boland Amendments. A commission led by former Senator John Tower concluded in 1987 that the commander in chief had mismanaged his staff but had no knowledge of the contra funding. Reagan fired North, accepted Poindexter's resignation, and agreed to the appointment of a special prosecutor. After televised hearings in which North gave a passionate defense of his actions, a joint panel of the House and Senate cited the administration for violating congressional restrictions on covert activity and for "pervasive dishonesty and inordinate secrecy." When the Nicaraguan government agreed to peace talks with its domestic rivals in 1988, Congress ended military aid to the contras.

Despite embarrassment, the Reagan administration managed to survive the scandal. After Special Prosecutor Lawrence Walsh won convictions of North and Poindexter for obstructing Congress, an appeals court reversed the verdicts because the Iran-Contra committee had granted the defendants limited immunity. After the perjury indictment of Defense Secretary Caspar W. Weinberger, public consideration of the matter was closed when Weinberger and five other officials received presidential pardons from Reagan's successor in 1992. Although the president had been compelled to testify as a witness in court proceedings, he never accepted legal or moral responsibility for the actions committed in his name, nor acknowledged how Iran-Contra had diminished his political effectiveness.

COLD WAR CATHARSIS

Having won the White House with promises to revitalize national defense, Reagan initiated the largest peacetime military buildup in U.S. history. Congress approved an $18 billion increase in defense spending in a 1981 budget that embraced construction of neutron bombs, production of the B-1 bomber canceled by Carter, and creation of a rapid deployment force. Insisting that the United States could win the Cold War by forcing the Soviets to spend beyond their means, Reagan prevailed on Congress to raise annual military expenditures by nearly 50 percent between 1981 and 1986. The most controversial feature of the president's plan was the Strategic Defense Initiative (SDI), introduced in a 1983 television address. Dubbed "Star Wars," the massive research and development project sought to explore the use of space satellites and laser weapons to fend off nuclear missiles. Although Congress appropriated a fraction of the proposed funding, many scientists joined the Soviets in expressing concerns about the potential militarization of space.

EXHIBIT **14-11**   **NATIONAL DEFENSE SPENDING, 1980–1988 (IN BILLIONS OF DOLLARS)**

1980	134.0
1982	185.3
1984	227.4
1986	273.4
1988	290.4

Source: *Statistical Abstract of the United States* (1996).

Because Reagan viewed arms control as an inadequate response to an aggressive Soviet military machine, he acknowledged the possibility of a "limited" nuclear war in which damage might be confined to Europe. By 1982, however, grassroots activists on both sides of the Atlantic had mounted a "nuclear freeze" movement, demanding that the superpowers declare a verifiable moratorium on testing, deployment, and production of atomic weapons. Public concern about the dangers of nuclear war mounted under Reagan. Three chilling cult movie classics—*Mad Max* (1980), *Road Warrior* (1981), and *Blade Runner* (1982)—portrayed the bleak human and physical landscapes resulting from nuclear apocalypse. In 1983 astronomer Carl Sagan gave credence to such fears by warning that radioactive dust clouds from atomic war might block the sun's rays and produce a "nuclear winter" that would condemn the human species to imminent death. That year's television special, "The Day After," graphically illustrated the potential effects of a nuclear explosion on a typical midwestern town.

Strategic thinkers such as Daniel Ellsberg and Robert McNamara led campaigns for nuclear disarmament, and 600,000 protesters rallied in New York City's Central Park in the largest demonstration to that point in U.S. history. When the nuclear freeze resolution came before the House, the White House argued that passage would weaken the U.S. bargaining position in the SALT negotiations, and the proposal met a narrow 204–202 defeat. Nevertheless, the president declared that nuclear war should be deterred at all costs and committed the nation to SALT II. Congress moderated the arms race in 1985 by eliminating funding for half the MX missiles the administration requested.

Despite militant anticommunism, Reagan embraced some accommodation with the Soviet Union. In 1981 he responded to the agricultural lobby by ending the Carter embargo on grain sales to Moscow. Two years later Reagan negotiated a five-year wheat sales pact. As the Soviets initiated democratic political reforms, European allies and Congress pushed the White House toward negotiations with Soviet Communist Party leader Mikhail Gorbachev. At the Geneva conference of 1985, the first summit in six years, Gorbachev expressed a desire for *glasnost* ("openness") at home and abroad. Seeking to modernize his economy through Western investment and lower defense costs, the Soviet leader persuaded Reagan to work toward a 50 percent cut in nuclear weapons.

Soviet Secretary Gorbachev and President Reagan at the Geneva summit of 1985, the first of four such meetings between the two superpower leaders.

When Reagan and Gorbachev met again in Iceland in 1986, they nearly reached consensus on major arms reduction, but the Soviets insisted that the United States first confine development of Star Wars to laboratory research. Nevertheless, the summit resulted in an Intermediate-range Nuclear Forces (INF) treaty the following year that allowed Reagan to keep Star Wars but provided for the dismantling of thousands of medium- and short-range missiles in Europe. The pact included the most extensive system of weapons surveillance ever negotiated by the two superpowers. Following Moscow's announcement in 1988 that it intended to withdraw troops from Afghanistan, the U.S. Senate took a major step toward ending the Cold War by ratifying the INF treaty.

THE NEW ECONOMY

As Cold War tensions eased, the U.S. economy thrived with innovations in information services and expanded international trade. By 1980 more than two-fifths of the workforce was employed in the "knowledge" sector, accounting for more than one-third of the gross national product. As electronics firms

EXHIBIT **14-12**   **U.S. GROSS NATIONAL PRODUCT, 1981–1987**
(IN BILLIONS OF DOLLARS)

1981	3,052.6
1983	3,405.7
1985	4,010.3
1987	4,486.2

Source: *Economics Report of the President* (1988).

introduced desktop computers with silicon chips to digitally process, store, and display information, innovations such as electronic mail and the Internet communications "web" accelerated the pace of data transmission. Other applications of electronic technology included mobile telephones, facsimile (fax) machines, telephone answering devices, videocassette recorders, and compact disc players.

Telecommunications increasingly shaped the way Americans did business and filled leisure time. The National Aeronautics and Space Administration (NASA) had established a global communications system in the 1960s by deploying satellite relay stations in space. When the development of fiber-optic cables and photonic amplifiers stimulated the growth of cable television in the 1980s, space satellites began transmitting TV signals worldwide. By the early 1990s, cable and satellite networks offered twenty-four-hour news, sports, music, movie, and shopping channels to more than 60 percent of U.S. households.

High-tech products also reached consumers through new retail facilities and manufacturers' outlets in suburban shopping malls. In 1989 the largest shopping complex in the nation—Mall of America—opened in Bloomington, Minnesota. Urban strip malls, discount stores, mail-order sales, TV shopping channels, amusement "theme" parks, and credit card services helped to push consumer debt to more than $744 billion by 1991. Fast-food outlets provided another key to economic growth. Begun in 1954 by Ray Kroc, McDonald's grew into a hamburger franchising operation with nearly 10,000 worldwide outlets. The diversified fast-food industry proliferated around the world with formula-produced soft drinks, pizza, fried chicken, and ice cream products.

The high-tech, global service economy created new clusters of corporate power and influence. As U.S. trade with Asia surpassed that with Europe in the 1980s, San Francisco became a major center of international business and global investment planning. The growth in the service sector, which accounted for nearly three-quarters of all employment by the 1990s, attracted professional and white-collar workers to the capital cities of the Midwest and to computer software centers like California's Silicon Valley. Meanwhile, tourism and the retirement industry served as development magnets in the Sunbelt states of Arizona, California, Florida, and Texas, where half the nation's population growth occurred in the 1980s.

EXHIBIT **14-13**   **U.S. CONSUMER CREDIT OUTSTANDING, 1980–1987**
(IN ROUNDED BILLIONS OF DOLLARS AS OF DECEMBER OF EACH YEAR)

1980	369
1981	390
1983	468
1985	657
1987	756

Source: *Economics Report of the President* (1988).

Spurred by investment from Japan and the Middle East, U.S. financial managers prospered in the 1980s. Yet profits were sustained partially through questionable techniques such as the sale of high-risk "junk" bonds, an innovation of Wall Street broker Michael R. Milken that permitted small companies to borrow huge sums to absorb larger firms. Stocks benefited from leveraged buyouts, with which executives staged hostile corporate takeovers by purchasing the equity of other shareholders. Mergers and acquisitions consolidated the airlines, communications, and banking industries. Yet the resulting volatility contributed to the greatest one-day loss in stock market history in 1987 when the Dow Jones average lost nearly one-fourth of its value. The market regained its footing only when the Federal Reserve poured capital into the banking system. Federal authorities then sought to discourage further abuse by prosecuting junk-bond dealer Milken for securities fraud and charging several Wall Street brokers with insider trading and stock fraud.

The banking boom also generated economic instability. Beginning in 1980, federal deregulation phased out interest rate ceilings on savings accounts and increased federal deposit insurance to $100,000. Commercial banks could then extend high-interest loans to developing nations and engage in risky real estate development at home. Congress also permitted savings and loans (S&Ls) to invest in the money market and to pump funds into commercial real estate. Subsequent mismanagement and fraud led to the bankruptcy of hundreds of financial institutions by the decade's end.

Congress responded to the S&L crisis in 1989 with a bailout to cover depositor losses and a massive fund for buying and selling off failed institutions. Taxpayers paid for this expensive intervention, eroding confidence in the government's ability to monitor financial greed. Five U.S. senators were reprimanded by colleagues for exerting improper influence on behalf of one banker.

YOUNG URBAN PROFESSIONALS AND THE NEW AGE

The global economy and information age provided expanded opportunities for the skilled college graduates of the baby boom era. Clustered around high-tech service centers, young urban professionals ("yuppies") specialized in law,

Madonna Louise Veronica Ciccone (1958–)

"I was born and raised in Detroit," an unknown Madonna Ciccone scribbled in an audition statement for a New York movie producer, "where I began my career in petulance and preciousness. By the time I was in fifth grade, I knew I either wanted to be a nun or a movie star. During high school I became slightly schizophrenic as I couldn't choose between class virgin or the other kind."

© Bettmann/CORBIS

Known simply as Madonna, Ciccone emerged as a major cultural icon of the 1980s, the most financially successful female entertainer in history. One of eight children in a middle-class Catholic family, she was devastated at the age of six by the death of her mother. In 1978 she dropped out of the University of Michigan and flew to New York with $37 in her pocket. After enrolling for classes with the third-string troupe of the prestigious American Dance Center, she rented a fourth-floor "walk-up" in Manhattan's East Village, worked at Dunkin' Donuts, posed in the nude for art classes, and sifted through garbage for food.

After a one-year stint in France as a backup vocalist and dancer for a Parisian disco act, Madonna returned to the United States and began singing with "alternative" music bands and lip-synching on the Lower Manhattan disco and hip-hop club circuit. Adopting a trampy, punk look that featured rags, safety pins, and the use of underwear as outer garments, the aspiring performer set her mind on a pop music career. Building on personal contacts with club musicians and disk jockeys, Madonna garnered a Warner Bros. recording commitment in 1983. Her first album, the disco-oriented *Madonna,* attracted little attention until the vocalist took it upon herself to promote club exposure and airplay. The

marketing, computer trades, the media, health services, and government. Their intensity and informality revitalized U.S. business with team play, networking skills, and a strong entrepreneurial spirit. Urban professionals such as Apple Computer cofounder Stephen Jobs saw the workplace as an arena for translating personal growth goals into practical life strategies. Attorneys in "public interest" law organized class-action lawsuits against corporate polluters, cigarette companies, and employers charged with discriminatory labor policies.

collection eventually sold 9 million copies, and three of its cuts rose to the Top Ten.

Madonna benefited from the immense popularity of MTV, whose twenty-four-hour cable television programming placed her videos on "heavy" rotation. An appearance as a charming street-waif in the film *Desperately Seeking Susan* (1984) contributed to the performer's mystique. Abandoning bracelets and crucifixes for a white silk wedding dress and for a belt buckle reading "Boy Toy," Madonna cut a new song titled "Like a Virgin" (1984). The album of the same name sold 11 million copies and featured "Material Girl," a simultaneous tribute to and parody of Marilyn Monroe. Another collection, *True Blue* (1988), reached sales of 17 million and included the controversial "Papa Don't Preach," a portrait of a pregnant single woman who chooses to keep her baby.

Aware of Madonna's loyal following among young women, including many African American and Hispanic fans, the Pepsi Corporation agreed to sponsor a 1989 concert tour and to pay the performer $5 million for three commercials. When the video for "Like a Prayer," the title song of Madonna's new album, included footage of the singer kissing a black saint and dancing provocatively before burning crosses, the company pulled the commercial and severed its relationship with the star. "Express Yourself," the album's second hit, told listeners never to settle for "second best"—for anything less than truth and self-respect.

During the 1990s Madonna leveraged her fame and financial success into careers as a movie performer, book publisher, record company owner, and producer. The star's mixture of toughness and vulnerability continued to speak to many women. Sampling a diversity of postures and styles, she brilliantly embodied the era's postmodern synthesis of high and mass culture.

By emphasizing countercultural values such as self-fulfillment and openness to change, the new professionals helped to reshape consumption patterns. "Postmodern" condominiums, theaters, and specialty shops contributed to the gentrification of urban neighborhoods. Although the high rents that accompanied renovation of historical districts often displaced less-affluent tenants and shopkeepers, the new middle class played an active role in neighborhood associations and campaigns to make cities safer and more livable.

Improvement also took on a personal character. Instructional workout videos and manuals produced by actress Jane Fonda led millions in daily exercise routines. Jogging, bicycling, body building, indoor sports, and hot tubs provided convenient outlets for professionals with limited recreational time and disposable income. Such activities would be supplanted in the 1990s by more "extreme" pursuits that included rollerblading, snowboarding, hang gliding, windsurfing, and bungee jumping.

Eating habits also changed. Urban professionals opted for tasty, lower-calorie, nutritional meals that did not require extensive preparation. Carry-home specialties (often reheated in microwave ovens) replaced home-cooked meals. The new diet featured natural and organic foods, frozen yogurt desserts, fresh-ground coffees, domestic wines, "light" beers, and mineral waters. A proliferation of gourmet restaurants included specialists in "California cuisine"—an aesthetically presented cookery that replaced salty and fatty foods with fresh fish, poultry, and vegetables. Espresso bars and microbreweries served as additional gathering places for young urbanites.

Trends in popular music reflected the diversity of cultures made possible by enhanced communications. Although country and western, gospel, soul, and rock music continued to attract loyal fans, the disco rhythms of big-city gay and black dance clubs found their way to the airwaves and recording studios in the mid-1970s. In turn, disco and mainstream rock soon were supplanted by the more confrontational sounds of heavy metal and punk. After the launching in 1981 of MTV (Music Television), a twenty-four-hour cable outlet originally devoted to rock videos, young consumers could sample musical styles ranging from techno-pop, reggae, rap, and hip-hop to grunge, alternative rock, and new folk.

Facing competition from specialized cable programming, network television struggled to attract new audiences. Widely viewed 1980s TV series—*Hill Street Blues, Miami Vice, St. Elsewhere,* and *L.A. Law*—explored the work life of urban professionals. In the film industry, new computer technologies produced sophisticated animations such as *Who Framed Roger Rabbit?* (1988), Disney's *The Little Mermaid* (1989), and Steven Spielberg's dinosaur saga, *Jurassic Park* (1993).

Countercultural lifestyles also influenced the spiritual practices of many urban professionals. As second marriages, stepparenting, and two-income families became more common, some religious denominations offered greater roles for women and increased involvement in such social issues as homelessness. Alternative religions also prospered—by 1987, 20 percent of Americans between eighteen and twenty-four years of age (31 percent on the West Coast) claimed a religious belief outside the mainstream faiths. Young cultural dissidents of the 1960s and 1970s had experimented with Asian spiritual traditions such as Zen Buddhism, Tibetan Buddhism, yoga, the *I Ching*, and martial arts. These interests led some to join such sects as the Church of Scientology, the Hari Krishnas, and the Unification Church of Korea's Reverend Sun Myung Moon. Others experimented with "New Age" fusions of science and spirituality that embraced holistic practices associated with natural medicine, acupuncture, biofeedback, and meditation.

MULTICULTURAL POPULATIONS

The global economy, together with overseas political repression, stimulated the mobility of labor, leading 20 million people to immigrate legally to the United States between 1950 and 1990. More than 8.3 million newcomers arrived in the 1980s, the most numerous of whom were Hispanics, two-thirds of whom came from Mexico. Although Chicanos faced a struggle for survival, they established significant power bases in southwestern cities like Los Angeles and San Antonio, producing national leaders such as future cabinet official Henry G. Cisneros. Film director Louis Valdez captured the authentic textures of Mexican American life in films such as *Boulevard Nights* (1979), *Zoot Suit* (1981), and *La Bamba* (1987).

Impoverished migrants from Central America and the Caribbean contributed to the stream of newcomers. Cuban Americans ranked as one of the most successful of the recent immigrants. An annual average of 20,000 Cubans had migrated to the United States through the 1960s, most skilled professionals or white-collar workers. In the following decades, working-class Cubans joined the exodus, particularly when Fidel Castro allowed thousands to leave the island in 1980. As the Cuban American population reached 1 million, its leaders made Miami the financial and cultural center of Latin America. Yet the poverty of the city's underclass and its geographic location attracted the international narcotics trade in the 1980s. The multibillion-dollar industry brought rising cocaine addiction, rampant police corruption, soaring crime and homicide rates, and schemes for laundering proceeds from drug sales.

Los Angeles replaced New York as the leading port of entry in the 1970s, because Asian immigrants accounted for more than 40 percent of newcomers to the United States. A half-million Filipinos immigrated to America during the 1980s. Taking advantage of the liberal provisions of the Immigration Act of 1965, more than 6 million newcomers from China, Taiwan, Hong Kong, and Korea arrived between 1970 and 1995. Many of these immigrants established small businesses, particularly retail food stores and restaurants. Asian Americans also worked in low-wage service and garment trades, sometimes as "sweatshop" seamstresses who received minimal pay and no benefits from unregulated clothing subcontractors. Yet the children of Asian immigrants frequently sought college training. The richness of Chinese ethnic culture and family life was conveyed in Amy Tan's popular novel, *The Joy Luck Club*

1980	531,000
1985	570,000
1990	1,500,000

Source: *Statistical Abstract of the United States* (1996).

(1989). Nearly 840,000 refugees from the Indochina War, some aided by government relocation funds, also came to the United States.

Public reaction to immigration depended upon perceived labor needs. When officeholders in the Southwest and West complained that poor migrants created excessive social welfare burdens, several states passed laws to make English their official language. Under the Immigration Act of 1986, employers could be fined for knowingly hiring illegal aliens or undocumented laborers, although the law provided amnesty to some illegal immigrants. Ironically, professionally trained foreigners were actively pursued by U.S. corporations, research facilities, and medical institutions. Seeking to exploit the "brain drain" from eastern Europe and Asia, Congress passed the Immigration Act of 1990, which increased the legal immigration quota and made allowances for skilled newcomers, particularly engineers, scientists, and professionals. To encourage aliens to become citizens, naturalization procedures were moved from the courts to the Justice Department. By the mid-1990s legal immigration to the United States had risen to an annual 900,000.

Native Americans also sought opportunities for economic development and control of natural resources. Beginning in 1977 more than a dozen U.S. tribes filed federal lawsuits based on historic land claims. Three years later the Supreme Court upheld an award that compensated the South Dakota Sioux for U.S. seizure of the Black Hills a century earlier. After three tribes in northern Maine won another settlement, the U.S. Civil Rights Commission asked the federal government to negotiate several eastern Indian land disputes. Native American tribes also obtained the right to federal funding on the same basis as states and received recognition of claims to fishing and other resources. These assertions of economic sovereignty were sustained by the Supreme Court and by the Indian Gaming Reservation Act of 1988, which enabled tribes to build reservation gambling casinos.

Economic vitality accompanied renewed interest in Native traditions of spirituality, dance, drumming, and storytelling. Powwows, cleansing sweats, and vision quests counteracted historical legacies of racism by enhancing Native American self-esteem and ethnic pride. Indian leaders also compelled archeologists and anthropologists to turn over ancestral remains for respectful treatment and reburial. The cultural renaissance found expression in the literary works of Leslie Marmon Silko, Gerald Vizenor, and Louise Erdrich.

Five hundred years after Columbus first explored the New World, the U.S. Native American population surpassed 2 million. Yet poverty, unemployment, alcoholism, and suicide continued to plague young people whose reservations and urban communities were untouched by capital investment or tourist development.

Like Native Americans, African Americans won added recognition of their cultural contributions during the 1980s but also saw economic opportunities decline among poorer members of the community. As black studies programs and the perspectives of people of color began to find their way into university curricula, Alex Haley's *Roots* (1976), a personal story of black genealogy, popularized African American history for a mass audience. More than 130 million viewers, or at least half the nation, watched at least one segment of the televised version of the book. African American artists considered their work an assertion of cultural independence. Race-conscious poetry emerged from literary figures such as Nikki Giovanni and Maya Angelou. Critically acclaimed black novelists included Nobel Prize winner Toni Morrison, whose *Beloved* (1987) explored psychological themes within a historical context. Alice Walker's *The Color Purple* (1982) portrayed a direct connection to the African legacy. Other significant African American novelists included Ishmael Reed, Al Young, Terry McMillan, and John Edgar Wideman.

Black creative energies had an enormous impact on the performing arts. Pulitzer Prize–winning playwright August Wilson used African techniques of storytelling and ensemble performance in *Ma Rainey's Black Bottom* (1984) and *Fences* (1987). Filmmaker Spike Lee brought black themes to mainstream audiences with provocative features such as *Do the Right Thing* (1989) and *Malcolm X* (1992). New directors like John Singleton incorporated inner-city gang life into movies such as *Boyz in the Hood* (1991). Rap music and hip-hop, products of black street subculture, spawned a new generation of African American recording artists and pop cultural icons. As black spending power reached nearly $500 billion a year, mainstream African American entertainment and sports figures such as Bill Cosby, Eddie Murphy, Michael Jackson, Whitney Houston, Michael Jordan, and Oprah Winfrey became mainstays of international television, movies, and the celebrity press.

African American consumer power was buttressed by an increasingly prosperous black middle class. Government statistics revealed that 70 percent of the African American population lived above the poverty level (compared with 90 percent for whites). The annual income of black men leaped by half in the 1980s, while wage rates for African American women rose to equal those of white women. More than a million blacks were attending college by the 1980s, and African Americans constituted an increasing percentage of the nation's social service professionals. Economic well-being translated into political power. Between 1964 and 1980 the number of elected black officials jumped from 103 to more than 4,000. In the 1980s major cities such as Chicago, Philadelphia, Los Angeles, and New York chose African American mayors, and Virginia's L. Douglas Wilder became the first black governor. By 1993, thirty-eight African Americans sat in the House of Representatives.

Despite achievements, African Americans were particularly disadvantaged by conservative tax and investment policies that drained capital from inner cities, factories, and public schools, and by the stagnant minimum wage rates of the 1980s. More than 30 percent of African Americans continued to live in poverty. By 1985, jobless rates among adult black men averaged 60 percent. Although economic opportunities for affluent African Americans broadened in the 1980s, black poverty increased. By 1990, an African American citizen was nearly three times as likely to be without a job as was a white citizen. The inability of black men to support families contributed to large numbers of African American women having babies without getting married. By the mid-1980s, 60 percent of black infants were born out of wedlock, and more than half of all African American children less than six years of age lived in poverty. Although blacks constituted less than 13 percent of the U.S. population, African American families constituted more than half of AFDC recipients.

As the inner city became the warehouse for society's unwanted, poverty and hopelessness produced an urban underclass—a population of unemployed and untrained people who relied on hustling and crime to survive. By the early 1990s violent street gangs contracted with powerful drug syndicates to sell "crack," an inexpensive but highly addictive cocaine derivative. As gang members sought territorial sovereignty, communities across the nation were terrorized and helpless to protect themselves. Government crime statistics for the 1980s showed that 30 percent of violent assaults and 60 percent of robberies were committed by blacks.

CULTURE WAR

Women activists focused identity politics on economic barriers in the 1980s, attacking the last legal bastions of sex segregation. Following the settlement of several class-action bias suits, the Supreme Court outlawed sex discrimination in private clubs and organizations. By 1980, women constituted the majority of university students and received ten times as many professional degrees as they had a decade earlier. Education improved women's occupational prospects. By the 1990s, 58 percent of women over sixteen years of age participated in the labor force, and women held nearly half of all jobs. Although women rarely reached top executive positions, they constituted nearly half of all managerial and professional employees and began to build lucrative careers as entrepreneurs. As wages for skilled female labor caught up to prevailing rates for men, however, the larger number of women in clerical, office, retail sales, and other low-status jobs continued to earn only three-quarters the rates of their male counterparts. Detecting a "feminization" of poverty, social critics noted that households headed by women were five times more likely to be destitute than those with male breadwinners.

Homosexuals also stepped up efforts to win inclusion in public life. Forming groups such as the National Gay Task Force, activists fought for local civil rights ordinances, mounted court cases against discrimination, and organized for acceptance of gays into the military and other institutions. Despite growing solidarity, however, the gay male population was decimated by the acquired immunodeficiency syndrome (AIDS) epidemic, first detected in 1981. Gays ultimately organized campaigns to close bathhouses (the scene of unprotected promiscuous sex), to limit sexual partners, and to promote the use of condoms; but activists accused the federal government of delaying AIDS research and condemned the media for failing to issue explicit warnings against dangerous sexual practices. By 1997, more than 400,000 AIDS patients had died in the United States.

Feminist, gay, and multicultural assertions of identity politics generated heated responses from social conservatives, particularly evangelical Christians who supported the televised ministries of preachers such as Jim Bakker, Jimmy Swaggart, Robert Schuler, and Oral Roberts. Even though Swaggart was defrocked for sexual misconduct and Bakker received a long prison sentence for financial irregularities, televangelists and Christian popular media remained influential forces. Pat Robertson used his national television audience to campaign for the Republican presidential nomination in 1988, although he finished poorly. Nevertheless, through Robertson's Christian Coalition, an issue-oriented political lobby, evangelical conservatives assumed a major role in the Republican Party.

As birthrates slowly rose during the 1980s, cultural traditionalists reasserted the importance of "family values" and moral authority. Insisting that social commitments were more important than individual rights, critics such as the scholar Allan Bloom attacked the dominance of secular values among professionals and academicians. Reagan's Secretary of Education, William J. Bennett, a Catholic intellectual, called for more emphasis on intellectual standards and ethical training. Defenders of family discipline also assailed the mass media for subjecting children to sex, violence, and antisocial messages. Concerned about the loss of parental control, Mary "Tipper" Gore, the wife of Tennessee Senator Al Gore, led a successful campaign in the late 1980s to convince popular music recording companies to place warning labels on products containing sexually explicit lyrics. Another parents' group, Mothers Against Drunk Driving (MADD), sponsored national advertising, pressed for tougher sentences for drinking offenders, and helped to pass legislation denying federal highway funds to states that did not raise the drinking age to twenty-one. Sensitivity to victims' rights led the Supreme Court to restrict repeated death penalty appeals in 1991 and to allow juries to consider testimony about murder victims from victims' families before sentencing.

Drug use stimulated another battle to sustain traditional values. As cocaine addiction spread to the middle class and victimized top entertainment and sports figures, some corporations began mandatory testing of job applicants and employees. After the Supreme Court upheld the right of public school officials to search students without warrants, the federal government ordered drug tests for many civilian employees. Under the Omnibus Drug Act of 1986, Congress authorized a "war on drugs" that included enforcement, education, and treatment. The United States even sent troops to Bolivia to wipe out cocaine-processing laboratories. Yet when Colombian drug cartels began to smuggle less-refined cocaine across U.S. borders, domestic dealers began producing "crack" and inner-city gang warfare intensified.

Family values advocates stepped up the campaign against abortion during the 1980s with massive demonstrations at clinics. In 1989 the Supreme Court concluded that unborn children had protectable rights and prohibited the use of tax-supported facilities for abortions not essential to save the mother's life. Two years later the tribunal upheld a congressional ban on federal funding for abortion counseling. In 1992 the Court permitted states to erect abortion restrictions that did not interfere with the privileges granted in *Roe* v. *Wade*. Social conservatives also protested that homosexuality was undeserving of government support. In *Bowers* v. *Hardwick* (1986), the Supreme Court upheld a Georgia law that made sodomy a criminal offense and thereby refused to extend constitutional rights of privacy to consensual relations between homosexuals. The issue of government endorsement of homosexuality surfaced the next year when the National Endowment for the Arts (NEA) funded a Cincinnati arts show featuring homoerotic photography by Robert Mapplethorp. Although Congress reauthorized NEA financing in 1990, it limited grants to work "sensitive to the general standard of decency."

Traditionalists also denounced sperm donation for artificial insemination and in vitro fertilization (in which an egg is fertilized before placement in the womb). When a New Jersey woman agreed to act as a paid "surrogate" mother but sued to keep the baby in 1987, a state court ruled that she had contractual obligations to surrender custody to the natural father and his infertile wife. The resulting furor inspired several state laws that prohibited compensation of surrogate mothers. Advances in artificial life support contributed to medical controversy. After the parents of a comatose patient, Karen Ann Quinlan, sued to disconnect an artificial respirator in 1975, eighteen states followed with laws declaring that legal death was defined by the cessation of brain activity, not of heartbeat. In 1990 the Supreme Court acknowledged an individual's right to refuse medical treatment but upheld legislation requiring "clear and convincing evidence" of a patient's wishes. The next year, Congress ordered health-care groups to inform clients about the right to complete "living wills" to anticipate such requests. Calling for "right-to-die" protection for terminally ill people in pain, Michigan's Dr. Jack Kevorkian began a campaign to legalize physician-assisted suicide.

THE REAGAN LEGACY

In the wake of Vietnam and Watergate, Americans yearned for a resurgence of national pride. Media events such as the 1976 Bicentennial, the 1982 dedication of the Vietnam Memorial, the 1984 Olympics, and the gala 1986 Statue of Liberty celebration sought to unite a fragmented society around patriotic values. Yet wounds like those produced by the Vietnam War continued to fester. In Hollywood movies such as *Rambo* (1982), the Vietnam War veteran emerged as a symbol of the latent anger generated by the conflict. Frank portraits of the war also appeared in such films as *Platoon* (1986), *Full Metal Jacket* (1987), and *Hamburger Hill* (1987), as well as in popular novels by veteran Timothy O'Brien.

The space program offered another chance to forge national identity. After a series of manned spaceflights resulted in linkage with a Soviet satellite in 1975, NASA used its *Skylab* space station to launch vehicles to explore the solar system and photograph the distant Milky Way. The agency also inaugurated a series of manned space flights. In 1986, however, an explosion killed seven *Challenger* space shuttle astronauts, including the project's first civilian, a New England schoolteacher. Despite the tragedy, shuttles continued to perform space missions such as synthesizing chemicals in a vacuum. Meanwhile, space technology fascinated moviegoers and video-game players. Films such as *Star Wars* (1977) and its sequels, the *Star Trek* film series (of which the first was released in 1978), and *E.T.: The Extra-Terrestrial* (1982) thrilled audiences with computer-generated morality tales involving exotic creatures, cyborgs, and rapid galactic travel.

Despite the renewal of national optimism, the Reagan administration never overcame bloated foreign trade and federal budget deficits. Because Treasury shortfalls prompted government borrowing on international exchanges, foreign consumers had fewer dollars with which to buy U.S. exports. Overseas manufacturing by U.S. multinationals also cost thousands of jobs at home. Congress sought to relieve domestic producers by curbing some imports in 1985, but Reagan vetoed the measure as protectionist. Yet as the trade deficit with Japan mounted in 1987 and Tokyo "dumped" below-cost computer chips on the U.S. market, the president overcame free-market sentiments to approve tariffs on Japanese electronic exports. He also signed a measure permitting retaliation against unfair trade practices and providing aid to

EXHIBIT **14-15**   **U.S. FEDERAL SPENDING AND BUDGET DEFICITS, 1980–1988 (IN BILLIONS OF DOLLARS)**

Year	Outlays	Deficit
1980	590.9	73.8
1982	745.7	127.9
1984	851.8	185.3
1986	990.3	221.2
1988	1,064.1	155.2

Source: *Statistical Abstract of the United States* (1996).

industries and workers facing overseas competition. When Congress passed another bill requiring manufacturers to provide sixty days' notice of plant closings and major layoffs, Reagan let it become law without his signature.

The administration's reluctance to raise taxes, combined with increased military and domestic spending, thwarted efforts to control federal budget deficits. Facing a large budget shortfall in 1985, Congress passed the Gramm-Rudman-Hollings Act. The legislation established deficit-reduction targets and required the president to make across-the-board cuts if the targets were not met. Yet the House failed to agree on spending limits, and in 1986 the Supreme Court ruled the automatic cuts unconstitutional. Concerned with containing the deficit, Congress eliminated many business deductions and raised capital gains taxes, adding some $120 billion in revenues over the next five years. Nevertheless, the federal budget deficit multiplied 2.6 times between 1985 and 1987. With the national debt soaring into the trillions by the end of Reagan's term, the United States became the world's largest borrower.

Ronald Reagan insisted that a U.S. military buildup and lower taxes would counteract the foreign policy reverses and economic stagnation of the Carter years. Yet Reagan's policies resulted in bloated trade and budget deficits as well as mixed results overseas. Seeking to extend their party's White House reign, Republican strategists searched for ways to sustain electoral goodwill amid an unevenly distributed and tenuous economic boom, continuing cultural conflicts at home, and a persistently unstable world environment.

AMERICAN HISTORY
RESOURCE CENTER

To explore documents, images, audio and video clips, articles, and commentary related to the material in this chapter, visit the source collections at ushistory.wadsworth.com and and use the Search function with the following key terms:

Jimmy Carter	Ronald Reagan
Three Mile Island	Jesse Jackson
Jerry Falwell	Iran-Contra

RECOMMENDED READINGS

David Skidmore, *Reversing Course: Carter's Foreign Policy, Domestic Politics, and the Failure of Reform* (1996). This thoughtful work explains the tragic consequences of Jimmy Carter's high-minded approaches to domestic reform and international relations.

John W. Sloan, *The Reagan Effect: Economics and Presidential Leadership* (1999). A primer in Reaganomics that explores the impact of tax cuts and reduced government.

Beth A. Fischer, *The Reagan Reversal: Foreign Policy and the End of the Cold War* (1997). The author evaluates the extent to which Reagan's military buildup led to victory in the global struggle against communism.

David M. Reimers, *Unwelcome Strangers: American Identity and the Turn Against Immigration* (1998). A valuable source for tracing anti-immigrant sentiment in the late twentieth century.

Additional Readings

Carter's rise to the Oval Office is portrayed in Patrick Anderson, *Electing Jimmy Carter: The Campaign of 1976* (1994). The Carter White House is the focus of Erwin C. Hargrove's *Jimmy Carter as President: Leadership and the Politics of the Public Good* (1988), and of Charles O. Jones's *The Trusteeship Presidency: Jimmy Carter and the United States Congress* (1988). See also Kenneth Earl Morris, *Jimmy Carter, American Moralist* (1996). Assessments of Carter's presidency appear in Burton I. Kaufman, *The Presidency of James Earl Carter* (1993), and in John Dumbrell, *The Carter Presidency: A Re-Evaluation* (1993).

For Carter's domestic policy, see Anthony S. Campagna, *Economic Policy in the Carter Administration* (1995); Laurence E. Lynn, *The Presidency as Policymaker: Jimmy Carter and Welfare Reform* (1981); and Laurence H. Shoup, *The Carter Presidency and Beyond: Power and Politics in the 1980s* (1980). A useful collection can be found in Gary M. Fink and Hugh Davis Graham, eds., *The Carter Presidency: Policy Choices in the Post–New Deal Era* (1998). Pressure group politics are discussed in William F. Grover, *The President as Prisoner: A Structural Critique of the Carter and Reagan Years* (1989).

For foreign policy, see Robert A. Strong, *Working in the World: Jimmy Carter and the Making of American Foreign Policy* (2000); Gaddis Smith, *Morality, Reason, and Power: American Diplomacy in the Carter Years* (1986); and Timothy P. Maga, *The World of Jimmy Carter: U.S. Foreign Policy,*

1977–1981 (1994). Oil diplomacy figures in portions of Daniel Yergin, *The Prize: The Epic Quest for Oil, Money, and Power* (1992), and in Michael A. Palmer, *Guardians of the Gulf: A History of America's Expanding Role in the Persian Gulf, 1933–1992* (1992).

The revitalization of evangelical Christianity is placed in historical context in George M. Marsden, *Religion and American Culture* (1990), and in Robert Wuthnow, *The Restructuring of American Religion: Society and Faith Since World War II* (1988). The social and cultural influence of religious conservatives is addressed in Steve Bruce, *The Rise and Fall of the Christian Right: Conservative Protestant Politics in America, 1978–1988* (1988); in Michael Lienesch, *Redeeming America: Piety and Politics in the New Christian Right* (1993); and in Sara Diamond, *Spiritual Warfare: The Politics of the Christian Right* (1989). For Jerry Falwell, see Dinesh D'Souza, *Falwell Before the Millennium: A Critical Biography* (1986). See also Duane M. Oldfield, *The Right and the Righteous: The Christian Right Confronts the Republican Party* (1996). Catholic conservatives are the focus of Patrick Allitt, *Catholic Intellectuals and Conservative Politics in America: 1950–1985* (1993). The abortion rights controversy is discussed in David Garrow, *Liberty and Sexuality: The Right to Privacy and the Making of* Roe v. Wade (1994), and Kristin Luker, *Abortion and the Politics of Womanhood* (1984).

The evolution of post-1945 conservative political and social thought is summarized in Mark Gerson, *The Neoconservative Vision: From the Cold War to the Culture Wars* (1995); in Melvin J. Thorne, *American Conservative Thought Since World War II: The Core Ideas* (1990); and in Jerome L. Himmelstein, *To the Right: The Transformation of American Conservatism* (1990). For the influence of secular conservatives, see J. David Hoeveler Jr., *Watch on the Right: Conservative Intellectuals in the Reagan Era* (1991); James Allen Smith, *The Idea Brokers: Think Tanks and the Rise of the New Policy Elite* (1991); and Sidney Blumenthal, *The Rise of the Counter-Establishment: From Conservative Ideology to Political Power* (1986).

The definitive introduction to the Reagan administration is William E. Pemberton, *Exit with Honor: The Life and Presidency of Ronald Reagan* (1997). See also Michael Schaller, *Reckoning with Reagan: America and Its President in the 1980s* (1992). For a controversial biography that uses a fictional narrator, see Edmund Morris, *Dutch: A Memoir of Ronald Reagan* (1999). Critical assessments of the president include Robert Dallek, *Ronald Reagan: The Politics of Symbolism* (1984), and Paul D. Erickson, *Reagan Speaks: The Making of an American Myth* (1985). For a psychological analysis, see Garry Wills, *Reagan's America: Innocents at Home* (1987).

Reagan's mastery of political discourse is explored in William K. Muir, *The Bully Pulpit: The Presidential Leadership of Ronald Reagan* (1992), and in the final chapter of David Green, *Shaping Political Consciousness: The Language of Politics in America from McKinley to Reagan* (1987). See also

Jeffrey Bell, *Populism and Elitism: Politics in the Age of Equality* (1992), and portions of William C. Berman, *America's Right Turn: From Nixon to Bush* (1994). Reagan's administrative style and conservative approach to economic growth is the subject of John W. Sloan's *The Reagan Effect: Economics and Presidential Leadership* (1999). See also Amos Kiewe and David W. Houck, *A Shining City on a Hill: Ronald Reagan's Economic Rhetoric, 1951–1989* (1991). A portrait of the president's most innovative appointment appears in Nancy Maveety, *Justice Sandra Day O'Connor: Strategist on the Supreme Court* (1996).

Reagan's cuts in domestic spending are analyzed in the final segments of Michael B. Katz, *The Undeserving Poor: From the War on Poverty to the War on Welfare* (1989). See also George Lipsitz, *The Possessive Investment in Whiteness: How White People Profit from Identity Politics* (1998). The administration's approach to race is surveyed in Robert Detlefsen, *Civil Rights Under Reagan* (1990). See also the relevant portions of Dan T. Carter, *From George Wallace to Newt Gingrich: Race in the Conservative Counterrevolution, 1963–1994* (1996).

Relationships between politics, economics, and the plight of working families are explored in Thomas Byrne Edsall, *The New Politics of Equality: How Political Power Shapes Economic Policy* (1984), and Greg J. Duncan, *Years of Poverty, Years of Plenty: The Changing Economic Fortunes of American Workers and Families* (1984). For Reagan's labor policy, see the relevant segments of James A. Gross, *Broken Promise: The Subversion of U.S. Labor Relations Policy, 1947–1994* (1995).

Environmental policy under Reagan is assessed in the last portions of Richard H. K. Vietor, *Energy Policy in America Since 1945: A Study in Business–Government Relations* (1984). For balanced evaluations of the domestic impact of the Reagan presidency, see Sidney Blumenthal and Thomas Byrne Edsall, eds., *The Reagan Legacy* (1988).

For Reagan's involvement in foreign policy, see the relevant portions of John Prados, *Keeper of the Keys: A History of the National Security Council from Truman to Bush* (1991), and of Francis P. Wormuth and Edwin P. Firmage, *To Chain the Dog of War: The Powers of Congress in History and Law* (1986). A useful analysis appears in Coral Bell, *The Reagan Paradox: American Foreign Policy in the 1980s* (1989).

Reagan's Persian Gulf policies are discussed in sections of Michael A. Palmer, *Guardians of the Gulf: A History of America's Expanding Role in the Persian Gulf, 1933–1992* (1992). For Iran-Contra, see Robert Busby, *Reagan and the Iran-Contra Affair: The Politics of Presidential Recovery* (1999), and Roxanne Y. Sutherland, *Defusing a Rhetorical Situation Through Apologia: Ronald Reagan and the Iran-Contra Affair* (1992). Central American policy is assessed in the appropriate portions of Robert Kagan, *A Twilight Struggle: American Power and Nicaragua, 1977–1990* (1995); of Raymond Bonner,

Weakness and Deceit: United States Policy and El Salvador (1984); and of William M. LeoGrande, *Our Own Backyard: The United States in Central America, 1977–1992* (1998). See also Mark P. Lagon, *The Reagan Doctrine: Sources of American Conduct in the Cold War's Last Chapter* (1994).

Cold War policy in the Reagan years is explored in Beth A. Fischer, *The Reagan Reversal: Foreign Policy and the End of the Cold War* (1997), and in Strobe Talbott, *Deadly Gambits: The Reagan Administration and the Stalemate in Nuclear Arms Control* (1984). See also Keith L. Shimko, *Images and Arms Control: Perceptions of the Soviet Union in the Reagan Administration* (1991). Star Wars is the focus of Rebecca S. Bjork, *The Strategic Defense Initiative: Symbolic Containment of the Nuclear Threat* (1992). For Cold War overviews, see the later sections of John Lewis Gaddis, *The Long Peace: Inquiries into the History of the Cold War* (1987), and of Thomas J. McCormick, *America's Half-Century: United States Foreign Policy in the Cold War* (1989).

A brief introduction to the world market can be found in Henry C. Dethloff, *The United States and the Global Economy Since 1945* (1997). See also Robert Schaeffer, *Understanding Globalization: The Social Consequences of Political and Economic Change* (1997). For the computer revolution, see Katie Hafner and Matthew Lyon, *Where Wizards Stay Up Late: The Origins of the Internet* (1996), and portions of George Basalla, *The Evolution of Technology* (1988).

The rise of upwardly mobile professionals is treated in Michael X. Carpini, *Stability and Change in American Politics: The Coming of Age of the Generation of the 1960s* (1986). See also Landon Y. Jones, *Great Expectations: America and the Baby Boom Generation* (1980). Ties between yuppie lifestyles and the earlier protest culture are addressed in Lauren Kessler, *After All These Years: Sixties Ideals in a Different World* (1991), and in Annie Gottlieb, *Do You Believe in Magic? The Second Coming of the Sixties Generation* (1987). See also Jack Whalen and Richard Flacks, *Beyond the Barricades: The Sixties Generation Grows Up* (1989). For perspectives on 1980s consumerism, see Debora Silverman, *Selling Culture: Bloomingdale's Diana Vreeland and the New Aristocracy of Taste in Reagan's America* (1986), and Warren J. Belasco, *Appetite for Change: How the Counterculture Took on the Food Industry, 1966–1988* (1990). The social ethics of professionals are the subject of Robert N. Bellah et al., *Habits of the Heart: Individualism and Commitment in American Life* (1985). A more critical account can be found in portions of Christopher Lasch's *The True and Only Heaven: Progress and Its Critics* (1991). For the New Age, see John P. Briggs and F. David Peat, *Looking Glass Universe: The Emerging Science of Wholeness* (1984), and Wade Clark Roof, *A Generation of Seekers* (1993).

The roots of 1970s feminism are vividly portrayed in Alice Echols, *Daring to Be Bad: Radical Feminism in America, 1967–1975* (1989). See also Rochelle

Gatlin, *American Women Since 1945* (1987). The ERA is the focus of Donald G. Mathews and Jane Sherron De Hart, *Sex, Gender, and the Politics of ERA* (1990), and of the provocative Mary Frances Berry, *Why ERA Failed: Politics, Women's Rights and the Amending Process of the Constitution* (1986). Struggles for homosexual rights are described in Barry D. Adam, *The Rise of a Gay and Lesbian Movement* (1987).

The postmodern roots of multiculturalism can be traced in Andreas Huyssen, *After the Great Divide: Modernism, Mass Culture, Postmodernism* (1986). For the politicization of cultural studies see Benjamin Barber, *An Aristocracy of Everyone: The Politics of Education and the Future of America* (1992). Harsh critiques of multiculturalism and "political correctness" include Allan Bloom's *The Closing of the American Mind* (1987) and Roger Kimball's *Tenured Radicals: How Politics Has Corrupted Our Higher Education* (1990). For a reassertion of ideas about pluralist democracy, see Arthur M. Schlesinger Jr., *The Disuniting of America: Reflections on a Multicultural Society* (1993). Identity politics is criticized by radical activist Todd Gitlin in *The Twilight of Common Dreams: Why America Is Wracked by Culture Wars* (1995). Historian David A. Hollinger seeks to resolve the conflict in *Postethnic America: Beyond Multiculturalism* (1995).

Treatments of the new wave of immigration include Gil Loescher and John A. Scanlan, *Calculated Kindness: Refugees and America's Half Open Door, 1945 to the Present* (1986), and David Reimers, *Still the Golden Door: The Third World Comes to America* (1985). See also the later segments of John Bodnar, *The Transplanted: A History of Immigrants in Urban America* (1985), and of Roger Daniels, *Coming to America: A History of Immigration and Ethnicity in American Life* (1991).

Asian ethnicity is the focus of Roger Daniels, *Asian America: Chinese and Japanese in the United States Since 1850* (1988); Ronald Takaki, *Strangers from a Different Shore: A History of Asian Americans* (1989); and Stephen S. Fugita and David J. O'Brien, *Japanese American Ethnicity: The Persistence of Community* (1991). For Hispanics, see Alejandro Portes and Robert L. Bach, *Latin Journey: Cuban and Mexican Immigrants in the United States* (1985). Mexican Americans are the subject of Rodolfo Acuña, *Occupied America: A History of Chicanos* (2004), and of Juan Gomez Quinones, *Chicano Politics: Reality and Promise, 1940–1990* (1990).

For native peoples, see the later segments of Francis Paul Prucha, *The Great Father: The United States Government and the American Indians, Vol. II* (1984). An overview of recent African American history is presented in Manning Marable, *Black American Politics: From the Washington Marches to Jesse Jackson* (1988). See also the useful Katherine Tate, *From Protest to Politics: The New Black Voters in American Elections* (1993). One of the most important African American leaders is portrayed in Adolph L. Reed Jr., *The Jesse Jackson Phenomenon* (1986), and in the relevant segments of Allen D.

Hertzke, *Echoes of Discontent: Jesse Jackson, Pat Robertson, and the Resurgence of Populism* (1993).

A growing literature on the postindustrial workplace includes Jon C. Teaford, *Cities of the Heartland: The Rise and Fall of the Industrial Midwest* (1993), and Kathryn Marie Dudley, *The End of the Line: Lost Jobs, New Lives in Post-Industrial America* (1994). See also Eileen Boris, *Home to Work: Motherhood and the Politics of Industrial Homework* (1994). For nonelite social perspectives, see David Halle, *America's Working Man: Work, Home, and Politics Among Blue-Collar Property Owners* (1984); Craig Reeinarman, *American States of Mind: Political Beliefs and Behavior Among Private and Public Workers* (1987); and Clarence Y. H. Lo, *Small Property Versus Big Government: Social Origins of the Property Tax Revolt* (1990).

The cultural confrontations of the post-Vietnam era are the focus of James Davison Hunter, *Culture Wars: The Struggle to Define America* (1991); of John Kenneth White, *The New Politics of Old Values* (1988); and of Ira Shor, *Culture Wars: School and Society in the Conservative Restoration, 1969–1984* (1986). See also Jeffrey Goldfarb, *The Cynical Society: The Culture of Politics and the Politics of Culture in American Life* (1991). Racial conflict is analyzed in Lawrence H. Fuchs, *The American Kaleidoscope: Race, Ethnicity, and the Civic Culture* (1990), and in Edward G. Carmines and James A. Stimson, *Issue Evolution: Race and the Transformation of American Politics* (1989).

Critical approaches to Reagan-era conservatism include Thomas Ferguson and Joel Rogers, *Right Turn: The Decline of the Democrats and the Future of American Politics* (1986); Herbert I. Schiller, *Culture, Inc.: The Corporate Takeover of Public Expression* (1989); and Michael Parenti, *Democracy for the Few* (1995). See also Donald L. Bartlett and James B. Steele, *America: What Went Wrong?* (1992).

THE TURN TO CENTRISM: BUSH, CLINTON, AND BUSH, 1988–2003

CHAPTER

15

Ronald Reagan won the highest public opinion rating any previous chief executive had received upon leaving office. Shortly thereafter, the bipolar Cold War ended with the dissolution of the Soviet Union. Despite the apparent victory, Reagan's successors faced a complex and dangerous global environment—a "new world order" in which nationalist and religious extremists continued to resort to destabilizing violence and terror. At home, Presidents George Herbert Walker Bush and Bill Clinton sought prosperity and social cohesion in a period of reduced ideological fervor but declining trust in government. Although Clinton favored a more "hands-on" political style than Bush, both leaders worked for moderate programs embracing environmental protection, volunteer services, welfare reform, and budget deficit reduction. As the global market and information revolution contributed to an economic boom in the late 1990s, the two major parties sharpened their partisan attacks while simultaneously appealing to the centrist sentiments of the huge middle class.

The Clinton economic boom reached its final stages just as George W. Bush won the presidency in the hotly disputed 2000 election. Partisan strife dominated the first months of the new administration. Then, on September 11, 2001, the United States suffered the most devastating terrorist attack in its history, leading Bush to proclaim a war against global terror. As the administration pursued military action in Afghanistan and then Iraq, critics accused the president of pursuing a unilateralist strategic policy while abridging dissent at home and ignoring the nation's economic difficulties.

GEORGE BUSH AND THE END OF THE COLD WAR

Democrats prepared for the 1988 presidential election by exploiting the weaknesses of Reaganomics. During the 1980s workers and middle-class citizens had experienced no notable increase in income. In contrast, Reagan's tax cuts helped to boost the earnings of the richest 1 percent of families by 87 percent—the greatest upward redistribution of income in U.S. history. Tax breaks and reduced federal regulation had encouraged financial speculation and corporate mergers and led cost-conscious companies to downsize and phase out skilled manufacturing positions. Democrat Jesse Jackson responded to these trends by refashioning a second presidential campaign around populist issues. Appealing to white workers and farmers as well as racial minorities, Jackson campaigned for higher taxes on corporations and the regulation of plant closings and relocations overseas.

Although Jackson received nearly a third of the Democratic primary vote, Massachusetts Governor Michael Dukakis, a political centrist, emerged as the party nominee when front-runner Gary Hart was forced out of the race by accusations of marital infidelity. A Greek American with extensive public administration experience, Dukakis heralded the use of tax incentives, an educated labor force, and a balanced budget in fashioning an economic "miracle" in his home state. Combining proposals for national health insurance and investment in education with fiscal moderation, the governor chose Senator Lloyd Bentsen, a Texas conservative with expertise in finance, as his vice presidential partner.

Aware of the uneven distribution of Reagan-era prosperity, Republican campaign strategist Lee Atwater prepared the party for the 1988 election by concentrating on social issues. Seeking a coalition of nonaffluent white southerners and middle-class voters in northern suburbs, Atwater positioned the Republicans as supporters of family values, defenders of patriotism, and opponents of crime. After defeating Senate Minority Leader Robert ("Bob") Dole in early primaries, Vice President George Bush won the party nomination. A Yale graduate, a World War II pilot, and the son of a former Republican senator from Connecticut, Bush had a successful early career in the Texas oil business. After two terms in the House, he served the Nixon White House as UN ambassador, chair of the Republican National Committee, and liaison to China. Bush spent the final year of the Ford presidency as the director of the Central Intelligence Agency (CIA). A social moderate and an internationalist, he chose Dan Quayle, a conservative Indiana senator, as his running mate.

Bush attacked Dukakis as an "ice man," a Harvard elitist whose membership in the rights-oriented American Civil Liberties Union (ACLU) betrayed liberal social values. Republicans focused on the Democratic governor's opposition to the death penalty and his vetoes of legislation requiring public school students to recite the Pledge of Allegiance and of a bill banning prison furloughs for first-degree murderers. Television ads dramatized the case of Willie Horton, a black convict serving a life sentence for murder, who had raped a white woman while on furlough from a Massachusetts prison. The Republican candidates also celebrated Reagan's restoration of national dignity and the taming of the Soviet Union. Promising to sustain Reagan's legacy of domestic pros-

EXHIBIT **15-1**   **THE ELECTION OF 1988**

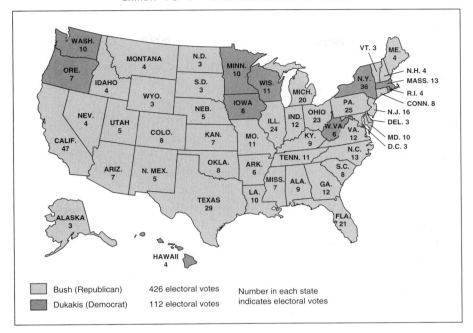

Bush (Republican)	426 electoral votes	Number in each state
Dukakis (Democrat)	112 electoral votes	indicates electoral votes

perity and deregulation, Bush issued an emphatic promise: "Read my lips—no new taxes!" To soften his image, the vice president spoke of a "kinder" and "gentler" nation whose volunteer charities formed "a thousand points of light."

Failing to respond to the Republican assault on his moral integrity and having no broad-based appeal, Dukakis suffered a humiliating defeat. In November the Bush-Quayle ticket captured 54 percent of the popular vote and swept the Republican Party to its fifth victory in the last six presidential elections. By taking nearly two-thirds of the white male vote as well as most of that of southerners and suburbanites, Republicans tightened their grip on the key "Reagan Democrats." Once again, political apathy and cynicism lowered participation rates to barely more than half of eligible voters.

As Bush took office in 1989, East Germany dismantled the Berlin Wall, and democratic movements began to replace eastern Europe's communist governments. Once the Soviet Union withdrew its troops from Afghanistan and held its first free elections at home, the president met with Soviet leader Mikhail Gorbachev in 1990, and the two leaders accepted a framework for mutual nuclear disarmament and agreed to stop producing chemical weapons. The Cold War effectively ended in that year when the Conference on Security and Cooperation in Europe (comprising thirty European nations plus the United States and Canada) sponsored a treaty drastically limiting U.S. and Soviet military presence on the continent. After signing the Strategic Arms Reduction

Jesse L. Jackson (1941–)

"God hasn't finished with me yet," Baptist minister Jesse L. Jackson told the 1984 Democratic National Convention after finishing third in the party's presidential sweepstakes. Four years later, Jackson swept across the country in a fiery presidential campaign that brought him nearly a

third of all Democratic primary votes. By the 1990s, Jackson's biracial reform agenda had earned him a reputation as the conscience of the Democratic Party and as a spokesperson for the nation's people of color.

Jackson was the illegitimate son of a teenage domestic from the cotton mill town of Greenville, South Carolina. He won an athletic scholarship to the University of Illinois but transferred to predominantly black North Carolina Agricultural and Technical College in Greensboro after Illinois placed him on academic probation. Arriving in Greensboro months after students initiated the 1960 lunch-counter sit-ins, he became the star quarterback, student body president, and leader of the demonstrations. Chosen for a Rockefeller Foundation grant, Jackson attended the Chicago Theological Seminary but left short of graduation to work with Martin Luther King Jr.

King made the young activist head of the Southern Christian Leadership Conference's Operation Breadbasket—a campaign that used boycotts and mass picketing to win jobs and contracts for black workers and businesses. Citing Jackson's lack of organizational loyalty and discipline, however, the SCLC suspended the young minister. Jackson seized the opportunity to create his own group, Operation PUSH (People United to Save Humanity).

With PUSH, Jackson sought to build a national campaign to restore African American pride. "I may be poor, but I am somebody," Jackson chanted with the black youngsters he addressed in the public schools, where he conducted self-help motivational programs that cautioned against drug abuse, teenage pregnancy, truancy, and high drop-out rates. Between 1971 and 1983, PUSH attracted $17 million in government grants and private donations, although critics pointed to the organization's chaotic financial administration and poor management. "I'm a tree-shaker, not a jelly-maker," Jackson later explained.

Jackson was an influential supporter of Jimmy Carter in 1976 and 1980 and organized voter registration drives in 1983. After the election of Chicago African American reform mayor Harold Washington, he announced his candidacy for the presidency, criticizing Democratic leaders for being "too silent" and "too passive" about Ronald Reagan's policies. Jackson promised to represent "the poor and dispossessed of this nation" and to forge a "rainbow coalition" for those who were "rejected and . . . despised." Yet his campaign faltered when a black reporter revealed that the candidate had privately referred to Jews as "hymies." Jackson apologized but never managed to repair the break with the Jewish community. Relations worsened when he was slow to disavow the support of Louis Farrakan, a Nation of Islam leader given to anti-Semitic pronouncements.

Addressing a broad constituency of peace activists, organized labor, environmentalists, farmers, and racial minorities, Jackson launched the National Rainbow Coalition and announced his second presidential candidacy in 1987. He condemned "economic violence" against those "locked out of the system." He proposed to tax corporate mergers, to enact protections against plant closings and farm foreclosures, and to invest public employee pension funds in social programs. "If I can win, you can win. We the people can win!" Jackson told voters in the 1988 Democratic presidential primaries. Astounding political professionals, the candidate finished a strong second.

Jackson continued to raise racial issues as a media commentator in the 1990s. He played a key role in popularizing the term *African American* and in convincing Congress to make Reverend King's birthday a national holiday. He campaigned against South African apartheid, supported a U.S. role in restoring democracy in Haiti, and pushed for statehood for the District of Columbia. Recognized as a prime authority on racial discrimination, he participated in negotiations to end bias in corporations, the media, and professional athletics. Ever the caretaker of souls, Jackson denounced drugs and gang violence with customary fervor. Yet he also spoke out against police brutality against people of color, "hate" crimes, and investor neglect of the inner city.

Treaty (START) in 1991, both nuclear superpowers eliminated most short-range nuclear weapons. When Gorbachev resigned as president the same year, the Soviet Union dissolved, breaking up into its constituent republics, the most powerful of which was Russia.

Although Bush waited for signs of reform before providing aid to the former Soviet republics, he welcomed Boris Yeltsin, the Russian president, as a negotiating partner. Meeting in Moscow in early 1993, the two leaders signed START II, which reduced world tensions by providing for the gradual elimination of all land-based nuclear missiles. Yet instead of bringing peace, the end of the Cold War destabilized world politics. When the communist federation in Yugoslavia dissolved in 1992, Croatian and Serbian military forces mounted armed attacks on the Muslim-dominated breakaway state of Bosnia-Herzegovina. Although the Croats soon recognized Bosnian independence, the Serbian army and nationalist militias initiated a genocidal campaign of "ethnic cleansing" to rid Bosnia of Muslims. Instead of taking unilateral action, the Bush administration joined European allies in imposing sanctions on Serbia. When the Bosnian Serbs cut off supply lines to the capital city of Sarajevo, Congress authorized the U.S. military to participate in a multilateral force charged with delivering food and medical supplies.

THE GULF WAR AND THE NEW WORLD ORDER

Although Bush hesitated to deploy military force in southeastern Europe, the administration showed greater interest in the Persian Gulf, where oil reserves provided resources for western Europe and Japan—Washington's partners in the global economy. In the summer of 1990, Iraq's President Saddam Hussein invaded his oil-rich neighbor Kuwait, annexed it, and placed troops on the Saudi Arabian border. The UN Security Council unanimously condemned Iraq as an aggressor and demanded unconditional withdrawal. The council then ordered an economic embargo against Iraq and authorized UN members to use all necessary means to liberate Kuwait. Taking the leadership in forging a military coalition with the Russians and twenty-six other countries, including Saudi Arabia, Egypt, and Syria, Bush organized Operation Desert Storm. Under the leadership of General Colin Powell—whom the president had appointed as the first African American Chair of the Joint Chiefs of Staff—and General H. Norman Schwarzkopf, 540,000 U.S. and 160,000 Allied troops participated in the largest military mobilization since World War II.

After a heated debate and a close 52–47 vote in the Senate early in 1991, Congress authorized the Bush administration to use force to back the UN mandate. The Gulf War began with a massive six-week air and missile campaign. Once Iraq's air force, communications, and weapons facilities had been destroyed, Bush set a deadline for Hussein's withdrawal from Kuwait. The United

EXHIBIT **15-2**   **THE PERSIAN GULF WAR**

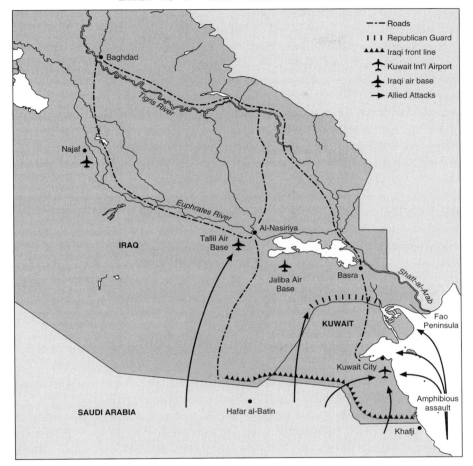

States then orchestrated a broad attack on Iraqi ground forces. Hussein's troops quickly retreated or were left isolated while his infantry fled Kuwait. Fearing the rise of nationalistic sentiment in Iraq, however, Bush sought to avoid the extensive casualties and controversy of a prolonged war. Accordingly, the White House deferred to Arab allies by terminating the one-sided rout within hours, thereby leaving Hussein in power. Nevertheless, Bush declared that the "Vietnam Syndrome" no longer paralyzed U.S. foreign policy.

The most decisive U.S. military victory since World War II, the Gulf War was heralded as the fruit of a post–Cold War "new world order." Envisioning a historic opportunity to stabilize the volatile Middle East, Bush arranged peace talks among Israel, neighboring Arab states, and Palestinians. Under U.S. and Russian auspices, the Madrid Conference of 1991 broke new ground by focusing on a "comprehensive" settlement based on exchanging "territory for peace." The following year, the administration signaled its commitment to international humanitarianism by sending troops to Somalia after famine and factional warfare prompted the UN Security Council to request military protection for food relief efforts.

In the absence of Cold War hostilities, Bush sought to promote democracy in Central America. Panamanian leader General Manuel Noriega Morena had been indicted by the Reagan administration for drug trafficking and money laundering. When Noriega halted free elections and incited violence against U.S. citizens in 1989, Bush mobilized 24,000 troops to invade Panama. After inflicting hundreds of casualties and detaining thousands, the army forced Noriega to surrender and took him to the United States to stand trial. Once U.S. military authorities installed the country's duly elected leader as president, the Bush administration granted Panama's new government nearly a half-billion dollars in aid. Congress awarded a smaller sum to Nicaragua, where a conservative defeated the leftist Sandinista government in internationally supervised elections in 1990. Tensions also eased in El Salvador when Washington brokered a peace treaty in 1992, ending a twelve-year civil war.

THE STRUGGLING ECONOMY

At home, the Bush White House pursued an activist record on environmental reform to bolster its moderate credentials. The president agreed to the Montreal Protocol of 1989, by which eighty nations banned dangerous chemicals and pledged to halve the production of ozone-depleting substances. He approved the Clean Air Act of 1990, which called for the reduced emission of industrial pollutants that cause acid rain, placed new pollution controls on autos, and phased out the use of chemicals threatening the ozone layer. Bush also signed a treaty limiting carbon dioxide emissions, cited by scientists as a cause of the greenhouse effect and global warming. After an Exxon tanker ran aground in Alaskan waters in 1989, spilling millions of gallons of crude petroleum and causing the worst environmental disaster in U.S. history, the president supported the creation of a federal cleanup fund for oil pollution. He also signed the Energy Policy Act of 1992, which encouraged natural gas development and alternative fuel use.

Other Bush reforms included federal support for volunteer service programs, child care, and transportation projects. Yet the president faced increasing controversy over his domestic agenda. When an overextended real estate market decimated the savings and loan industry, the White House was forced to ask Congress for a massive infusion of funds to reimburse investors and rehabilitate delinquent banks. Subsequent anxiety over federal budget deficits led to the greatest controversy of George Bush's tenure. In return for reduced federal spending and a promise to cut the deficit within five years, House De-

EXHIBIT **15-3** U.S. FEDERAL BUDGET DEFICITS, 1988–1992
(IN ROUNDED BILLIONS OF DOLLARS)

1988	155
1990	221
1992	290

Source: *Statistical Abstract of the United States* (1996).

EXHIBIT **15-4** PERCENTAGE DISTRIBUTION OF U.S. HOUSEHOLD
AGGREGATE INCOME, 1993

Top 1 percent of household income receivers	20.3
Top 5 percent of household income receivers	47.0

Source: *Statistical Abstract of the United States* (1996).

mocrats compelled the administration to accept a tax hike in 1990. Although the agreement stipulated that one-fourth of government savings were to come from entitlement cuts, the remainder was to be implemented through defense reductions and increased tax rates on top incomes. Complaining that federal taxation already amounted to nearly one-fifth of the gross domestic product, Republicans condemned the president for betraying his campaign promise of "no new taxes."

Bush's problems deepened as an economic recession took hold in 1991. Concerned about maintaining his credibility with conservatives, the president recommitted his administration to Reaganite policies. The White House endorsed a constitutional amendment to protect the flag, although Congress merely passed a law prohibiting flag desecration that the Supreme Court overturned on First Amendment grounds. Bush encountered further controversy when he sought to replace retiring African American Justice Thurgood Marshall with federal appeals court judge Clarence Thomas. A black conservative, Thomas had administered cuts as Reagan's chair of the Equal Employment Opportunity Commission (EEOC). The nomination became more contentious when African American law professor Anita Hill, a former EEOC employee, charged Thomas with sexual harassment, a highly sensitive issue among professional women. Anxious to address concerns over the abuse of women in the workplace, the Senate held special televised hearings on Hill's allegations. Nevertheless, Thomas won confirmation in a close 52–48 vote.

As Bush prepared to face voters in 1992, unemployment hovered at 7.5 percent. Since the 1970s, automation, plant consolidations, bankruptcies, transfer of factories overseas, and reduced union membership had contributed to a loss of skilled manufacturing jobs, stagnating wage scales, and decimated pension protection. As a result, the least affluent two-fifths of families had experienced an absolute decline in earnings, while income for the rich soared. Critics pointed to the fact that chief executive officers at large corporations

EXHIBIT **15-5**   **U.S. FEDERAL SOCIAL WELFARE SPENDING, 1980–1990**
(IN ROUNDED BILLIONS AND AS A
PERCENTAGE OF GROSS NATIONAL PRODUCT)

Year	Amount	Percentage
1980	303	11.4
1985	451	11.3
1990	617	11.1

Source: *Statistical Abstract of the United States* (1996).

made nearly 150 times the pay of the average factory employee. As the recession deepened, Bush's disinterest in domestic affairs and his opposition to government activism reinforced accusations that he was a disengaged leader out of touch with pressing needs. Enacting a ninety-day moratorium on all new government regulations in 1992, the president opposed legislation for gun control, voter registration at state motor vehicle bureaus, and additional aid to the cities. Bush also vetoed bills to permit workers to leave jobs for family emergencies, to expand civil rights protections in the workplace, and to cap campaign spending in congressional races.

BILL CLINTON AND THE 1992 ELECTION

During the height of the Gulf War, Bush's approval ratings had surpassed 90 percent. Yet the president's success in defeating Saddam Hussein removed foreign policy as a leading source of consideration and opened the door for Democratic criticism of the White House's economic policy. As the 1992 presidential campaign approached, an assortment of Democrats called for tax reform, targeted spending cuts, balanced budgets, and attention to education and the environment. The nominee turned out to be the virtually unknown governor of Arkansas—William ("Bill") Jefferson Clinton.

Raised by a widowed mother, Clinton had aspired to political life since boyhood. During the height of the Vietnam controversy in the mid-1960s, he attended Georgetown University and worked for antiwar Senator J. William Fulbright of Arkansas. Clinton was also opposed to the U.S. presence in Vietnam; he accepted a prestigious Rhodes scholarship to attend Oxford University and managed to avoid the draft. A graduate of Yale Law School, he won election as the nation's youngest governor in 1978. After cofounding the centrist Democratic Leadership Council, Clinton pushed the party to adopt moderate positions on the budget and on social issues such as abortion, crime, and welfare. With Tennessee Senator Albert ("Al") Gore Jr. as his running mate, the nominee opposed "tax and spend" liberalism and promised to "reinvent government" and to reform welfare. However, the "New Democrat" also criti-

EXHIBIT **15-6**   **THE ELECTION OF 1992**

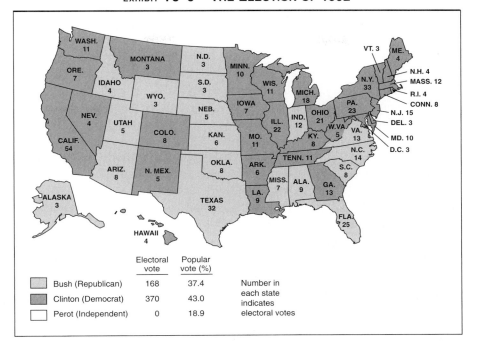

	Electoral vote	Popular vote (%)	
Bush (Republican)	168	37.4	Number in each state indicates electoral votes
Clinton (Democrat)	370	43.0	
Perot (Independent)	0	18.9	

EXHIBIT **15-7**   **U.S. VOTER PARTICIPATION, 1988–1992**
(AS A PERCENTAGE OF ELIGIBLE VOTERS)

1988	50.3
1992	55.1

Source: *Statistical Abstract of the United States* (1996).

cized the "trickle-down economics" of the Republicans. Rallying to the cry, "It's the economy, stupid," Clinton aides promoted their candidate as an agent of change who would rescue the middle class by "Putting People First."

Bush survived a spirited primary challenge from former Nixon speechwriter Patrick ("Pat") Buchanan, who fused conservative social values and economic nationalism. Yet Buchanan's strident references to "culture wars" alienated party moderates and independents, particularly the half of the electorate now living in suburbs. Bush was also hurt by the third-party candidacy of H. Ross Perot, a self-made billionaire who promised to break the Washington gridlock by taking government away from the "politicians." Launching his campaign on a cable TV talk show, Perot called for federal spending cuts and a balanced budget, tighter trade regulations, and a national industrial policy.

Although Perot performed well in three televised debates, Clinton outdid his rivals as a master of modern media. Through televised "town meetings"

Patrick ("Pat") Buchanan (1938–)

"I'm entitled to be a heretic," Pat Buchanan once declared. Combining radical conservatism and populist social values, the scrappy media commentator and Republican campaigner embodied some of the most jarring contradictions of 1990s political life.

The third of nine children, Buchanan grew up in the suburbs of Washington, D.C. A product of Catholic schooling from the primary grades to Georgetown University, Buchanan absorbed the Cold War notion that communism was the ideological enemy of Christianity. After graduating from the Columbia University School of Journalism on a scholarship, the ambitious writer found work as a reporter and editorialist for the conservative Republican *St. Louis Globe-Democrat*. An avid reader of William F. Buckley's *National Review*, Buchanan supported Barry Goldwater in 1964. Viewing Richard Nixon as the conservative hope for the next presidential race, he joined the former vice president's staff, brought Maryland Governor Spiro Agnew to his boss's attention, and served as press secretary and speech writer in the 1968 campaign.

Once Nixon won, Buchanan became a special assistant who briefed the president on media coverage. The first in the administration to grasp the significance of George Wallace's populism, Buchanan drew up press releases that contrasted the traditional values of Nixon's "new majority" of "middle Americans" with the "liberal elitism" of the media and intelligentsia. After returning to journalism to produce a widely syndicated newspaper column, Buchanan cofounded *Crossfire,* a television commentary series on the Cable News Network (CNN). During Ronald Reagan's second term, Buchanan resurfaced in public life as director of communications and supplied the media with White House rhetoric on the Nicaragua "freedom fighters."

(including an effective pitch for the youth vote on MTV), the Arkansas governor established personal rapport with voters. By positioning himself as a centrist, Clinton overcame questions concerning his personal life and captured a plurality of independent votes, equaling Bush's total among whites and making strong inroads among Republican suburbanites. Taking seven of the ten

Dissenting from Bush's globalism, Buchanan campaigned furiously against U.S. involvement in the Gulf War. "There are only two groups that are beating the drums for war in the Middle East," he declared on television, "the Israeli Defense Ministry and its amen corner in the United States." If the United States went to war, he warned, fighting would be done by "kids with names like McAllister, Murphy, Gonzales, and Leroy Brown." Buchanan expanded upon such populism when he challenged Bush for the Republican presidential nomination in 1992. Portraying the incumbent as rich, indifferent, and out of touch, Buchanan tapped voter frustration about economic stagnation by taking 40 percent of the New Hampshire primary vote. At the Republican Convention, he expanded his perspective to warn of an emerging "cultural war . . . for the soul of America."

Mobilizing against Republican front-runner Bob Dole in 1996, Buchanan forged a coalition of Reagan Democrats, protectionists, social conservatives, and supporters of the far right. A bitter opponent of the North American Free Trade Agreement (NAFTA), he agreed with labor leaders and progressive activists such as Ralph Nader in condemning corporate plant closings and overseas relocations. Buchanan shocked Republican officials by denouncing "blood-sucking multinational banks" and "the money lenders of the Fortune 500." Yet he also blamed unemployment on illegal immigration, a problem he sought to rectify with a security fence across the entire border with Mexico.

After a narrow victory over Dole in New Hampshire, Buchanan sought to rally the Christian right by stressing opposition to abortion, but consensus-oriented politicians minimized the candidate's exposure at the 1996 convention. A dissident among Republican supporters of the global economy, Pat Buchanan had become a politician with no institutional base. Four years later, he won the presidential nomination of a badly split Reform Party but managed to win less than 0.5 percent of the popular vote.

largest states and several southern states, Clinton scored 43 percent in contrast to 37 percent for Bush and 19 percent for Perot—certainly not a mandate. In winning only their second presidential contest since 1964, however, the Democrats benefited from a voter turnout of 55 percent of eligible voters, the highest rate in twenty years.

CLINTON'S POST–COLD WAR DIPLOMACY

Clinton's inaugural address focused on economic revitalization and citizen assumption of personal responsibility. However, amid the instabilities of the post–Cold War period, global politics assumed a more important role than the leader of the world's sole superpower anticipated. The president responded to this challenge by engaging in personal diplomacy and leading the United States into multilateral commitments overseas. Yet without the focus of the anticommunist crusade, U.S. foreign policy appeared to lack cohesion and direction.

Weeks after taking office, Clinton met with Russian President Yeltsin. As the two nations extended a mutual moratorium on nuclear testing, the White House promised emergency aid to the struggling Russians. When Yeltsin sent the army to the province of Chechnya in 1994 to subdue a separatist revolt, poorly equipped troops suffered major losses and inflicted huge civilian casualties. Yet after continued support from Clinton, the Russian leader prevailed in his country's first democratic elections and temporarily withdrew the military from Chechnya.

Anxious to preserve stability in the Middle East, the Clinton administration continued Bush's enforcement of economic sanctions against Iraq until international inspectors certified the dismantling of Baghdad's chemical, biological, and nuclear weapons. After receiving information that Saddam Hussein had sponsored a plan to assassinate former President Bush, Clinton unleashed cruise missile attacks on Baghdad intelligence headquarters in 1993. The White House orchestrated a second series of strikes after Hussein attacked Kurdish enclaves in northern Iraq. When Baghdad mobilized a large military force at Kuwait's border in 1994, the president redeployed troops to the region before the Iraqis withdrew. Hardened by these provocations, the United States insisted on enforcing sanctions despite their huge toll on Iraq's civilians and children. By 1996, Iraq agreed to permit the United Nations to administer its foreign oil sales and to channel oil revenues to food and medical relief, although reports of suffering persisted. Meanwhile, U.S. aircraft and missile power enforced the "no fly" zone with periodic raids on Iraqi installations.

The complexities of post–Cold War policy emerged in Somalia, where the U.S. military turned the food relief effort begun by Bush over to the United Nations in 1993. Finding themselves in the middle of factional strife, commanders initiated a campaign to capture General Mohammed Farah Aidid, a powerful warlord who refused to engage in peace talks. When fighting erupted, Aidid's followers killed eighteen U.S. soldiers and paraded their bodies before jubilant crowds. Under intense congressional pressure, Clinton ordered more troops to Somalia, but only to assure an orderly withdrawal. Condemned for allowing the Somalia operation to drift from humanitarian aid to involvement in a civil war under multilateral auspices, the White House promised to seek purely political solutions to the conflict.

Although peacemaking failed in Somalia, the Clinton administration continued to seek an important role as an international power broker. After a military coup overthrew Haiti's freely elected Jean-Bertrand Aristide in 1991, President Bush had supported a UN oil and arms embargo against the regime but returned thousands of refugees who had entered the United States after fleeing the Caribbean island. Clinton upheld the refugee policy but supervised an agreement to restore democracy. When Haitian ships blocked a U.S. attempt to implement the accord, the president backed reimposition of the UN embargo and threatened an invasion. In a final attempt to win a peaceful transition of leadership, Clinton sent personal emissaries to negotiate a settlement. Once the Haitian military accepted Washington's offers of relocation and financial assistance in 1994, the president dispatched troops to the island to maintain order while Aristide completed his term of office. Although opposed by many in Congress, the deployment restored democracy.

Anxious to please the large population of Cuban Americans in southern Florida, Clinton mixed conciliatory and hard-line stances toward the communist government of Cuba's Fidel Castro. Once Cuba's subsidies from the Soviet Union disappeared, the Bush administration had sought to expedite the overthrow of Cuban communism by tightening trade sanctions. Clinton followed a different course by relaxing travel restrictions and by permitting humanitarian relief and cultural exchanges with the island. Yet in 1996 the president signed the Helms-Burton bill, permitting citizens to sue some foreign companies that did business with the Cuban government, although Clinton postponed enactment of the controversial law.

Although the Cold War was over, communist North Korea aroused U.S. anxiety when it appeared to be assembling materials to develop nuclear weapons. Clinton dispatched Jimmy Carter to forge an agreement by which Japan and South Korea financed construction of atomic reactors incapable of producing weapons-grade materials. In another effort at alleviating tensions with a communist power, the administration prevailed on Vietnam to assist efforts to locate the remains of more than two thousand U.S. servicemen missing in action from the Vietnam War. While extending formal diplomatic recognition to the former adversary in 1995, Clinton celebrated "the opportunity to bind up our wounds." In yet another effort at personal diplomacy, the White House appointed former Senator George Mitchell to coordinate peace talks on British-held Northern Ireland. After the nationalist Irish Republican Army (IRA) agreed to a cease-fire and supervision of its arsenal in 2000, Britain turned power over to a self-ruling assembly of all factions.

The struggle to realize a peaceful and stable new world order received its greatest challenge in Bosnia. As Serbian militias continued ethnic cleansing and shelled the capital city of Sarajevo, Clinton called for North Atlantic

EXHIBIT 15-8   BOSNIA, 1995

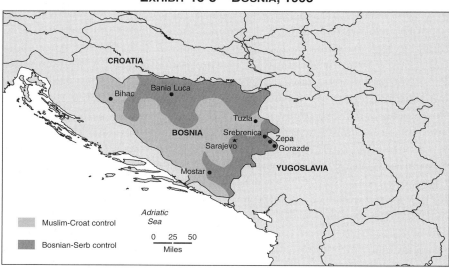

Treaty Organization (NATO) air strikes against Serbian positions. In 1995 the president convened a peace conference near Dayton, Ohio, which established a cease-fire between the warring parties and organized internationally supervised elections. The agreement also called for the deployment of U.S. troops to the region as part of a NATO peacekeeping force, a multilateral provision that Congress acceded to but did not endorse.

Clinton exerted his strongest efforts at personal diplomacy in the Middle East. After the Israelis conducted secret talks in Norway with Yasir Arafat's Palestine Liberation Organization, the president invited Arafat and Israeli Prime Minister Yitzhak Rabin to Washington in 1993 to sign a Declaration of Principles. Marked by a historic handshake between the former adversaries, the pact provided for mutual recognition and a renunciation of armed conflict. It also established an interim period of Palestinian self-rule in territories occupied by Israel, to be followed by negotiations for a permanent settlement. One year later, Israel and Jordan signed another treaty. Although the Israelis and Palestinians remained far apart in views, the Clinton administration sought to preserve the peace process—though without success.

CLINTON AND THE DOMESTIC AGENDA

As Americans reassessed the importance of government in the post–Cold War era, the Clinton administration struggled to redefine Washington's role at home. Relying for support on Democratic interest groups, the new president initially stumbled. Clinton was forced to withdraw the nominations of several women to the Justice Department when his staff conducted inadequate background checks. White House sponsorship of diversity also suffered when the president prepared an executive order ending discrimination against homosexuals in the armed forces. Having made campaign promises to gay activists, and viewing bias as an obstacle to the optimal use of human resources, Clinton did not anticipate the firestorm of opposition that erupted from the military and Congress. Under intense criticism for undermining the morale of the armed forces, he amended the order to permit homosexuals to serve only if they did not publicly acknowledge their sexual orientation or engage in homosexual acts ("don't ask, don't tell"). Satisfying neither gays nor conservatives, the policy remained a source of controversy and branded Clinton with a reputation for "waffling" on his principles.

Accepting the advice of Democratic congressional leaders, the president proposed to enact an energy tax to fund a massive jobs program. Yet as the economy showed signs of recovery, the measure came under strong attack from critics of government spending. Reversing direction, Clinton moved toward fiscal conservatism by accepting the idea that prosperity would not be restored until reduced federal budget deficits lowered interest rates and ensured investors against inflation. The White House then produced a five-year budget that cut defense outlays, payments to Medicare providers, and discretionary spending while increasing taxes on gasoline, wealthy income receivers, and affluent Social Security recipients. In the House, where not one Republican supported the budget, the measure passed by a single vote; in the Senate, Vice President Gore was forced to break a tie in favor of passage.

Democrats heralded the fiscal discipline of the 1993 budget as the cornerstone of the decade's prosperity. Acknowledging public discomfort with big government, Clinton assigned Gore to chair a committee to trim government bureaucracy. Meanwhile, the administration contrasted itself from its Republican predecessor by addressing reforms that appealed to the middle class. The president signed three measures opposed or vetoed by George Bush—motor voter registration legislation, the family leave act, and the Brady bill for establishing a five-day waiting period for handgun purchases. Clinton also won approval for a National Service Plan, which provided college students with earnings from community service to help pay for tuition. Another statute extended the terms of tuition loans without using private lenders. The president moved closer to the political center by appointing moderates Ruth Bader Ginsburg and Stephen G. Breyer to the Supreme Court.

Viewing U.S. participation in the global economy as essential to national prosperity, the Clinton administration emphasized the need to ratify the North American Free Trade Agreement (NAFTA), which Bush had signed in 1992. The treaty eliminated taxes or rules impeding the flow of commerce between the United States, Mexico, and Canada. Seeking to overcome the objections of union activists and environmentalists, Clinton had completed supplemental agreements establishing labor and pollution standards. Nevertheless, the AFL-CIO joined nationalists such as Ross Perot in arguing that lower trade barriers would encourage multinational corporations to desert the United States for cheaper labor in Mexico. Ironically, Republican free-trade supporters such as House Minority Leader Newt Gingrich provided the administration with the necessary votes to overcome the resistance of Democratic protectionists and human rights reformers. After the enactment of NAFTA, ten nations at the Pacific Summit joined the United States in calling for extended trade liberalization.

Despite the accomplishments of its first term, the Clinton administration suffered a devastating defeat when Congress refused to act on a national health insurance plan advanced by a panel led by the president's wife, Hillary Rodham Clinton. As advances in medical technology prolonged life but increased costs, health-care spending accounted for nearly 12 percent of the gross national product. Seeking to contain costs through comprehensive coverage and to establish medical care as a civil right, the administration proposal divided responsibility between government and private business. The White House task force proposed to enroll consumers in health-care alliances that would contract for medical coverage with private insurers. Government regulation of premiums, costs, and quality would assure "managed competition" in a system in which employers absorbed most costs. Once the complex regulations of the proposal were made known, however, public anxieties about government bureaucracy merged with opposition by medical industry interests to kill the measure.

Immobilized by the failure of its central reform, the administration returned to more modest proposals in 1994. Congress passed Clinton's Goals 2000 legislation, a program to establish the first national educational standards. The president also received funding to encourage defense contractors to diversify production for civilian markets. Yet polls showed that crime remained the most important and troubling issue for Americans. Overall crime rates had remained static or declined since the early 1980s. Yet violent offenses by juveniles had increased 50 percent since 1988—young offenders accounted for one-fifth of violent crime arrests in 1994. Disturbed by the random violence emanating from an urban youth culture of weapons, drugs, and gangs, voters demanded that the federal government provide greater support for local law enforcement.

The Clinton administration responded with the Omnibus Crime Act. A patchwork of differing philosophies, the law appealed to conservatives by providing grants to the states to hire more police and build prisons. It also expanded the federal death penalty and mandated life imprisonment for three-time violent federal offenders ("three strikes, you're out"). Yet the legislation addressed liberal concerns by funding crime prevention programs, banning many assault weapons, appropriating money to fight violence against women, and setting up special courts to rehabilitate nonviolent drug abusers. Despite such concessions, civil rights activists were furious that the law's penalties for possession of crack cocaine, a mainstay of inner-city street life, were far more stringent than the punishment for more expensive powder cocaine, consumed by affluent whites.

Disregarding the centrist nature of the Clinton program, Republican politicians insisted that the Democrat-led Congress was politically vulnerable. Following exposure of a series of financial scandals involving House leaders in 1992, the states had ratified a constitutional amendment that outlawed pay raises for sitting members of Congress. By 1994, less than one-fifth of Americans believed that government would "always" do what was right. Charging the Democratic leadership with a forty-year record of cronyism and greed, House Minority Leader Gingrich prepared to take control of the House by drafting a campaign manifesto called the "Contract with America." Signed by 350 Republican House incumbents and candidates, the document promised action on mandatory term limits, a balanced budget amendment, welfare reform, tougher law enforcement, government deregulation, pro-family legislation, and a strong national defense.

REINVENTING REFORM

The Contract with America helped Republicans regain majorities in both houses of Congress. Although Democrats retained a majority of the women's vote in 1994, they carried less than 40 percent of white males. Ideologically opposed to big government, first-year Republicans influenced the most independent Congress since 1947. The House opened the new session by eliminating many of its own committees and reducing the size of its staff. Under Gingrich's leadership, Congress curbed unfunded federal government mandates and enacted a presidential line-item veto on spending measures. A constitutional amendment requiring a balanced budget passed the House but twice fell short of the required two-thirds Senate majority. Another amendment to limit congressional terms to twelve years failed to receive sufficient support.

Stunned by his party's loss of Congress, Clinton declared that the era of big government was over. Yet Republicans overplayed their hand. Promising a 1995 budget that would eliminate the federal deficit in seven years, Gingrich and Senate Majority Leader Dole combined substantial tax cuts with reductions in the growth of Medicare and Medicaid and decreased aid to education and the environment. Following a Democratic television campaign, Clinton vetoed the Republican budget and the government shut down twice. To the dismay of voters, Washington beltway politicians appeared to be engaged in a destructive game of gridlock—the result of capture of the White House by one political party and control of Congress by its opponents. Yet public opinion placed more of the blame on Gingrich and Dole than on the president.

With public support, Clinton eventually embraced moderate reductions in domestic spending that spared popular social programs. As the 1996 election approached, chagrined Republicans accepted a minimum wage increase they formerly had opposed. In turn, Democrats agreed to a telecommunications bill that promised lower consumer costs and required manufacturers to equip large-screen televisions with V-chips that allowed parents to block offensive programming. (Studies showed that young people watched five hours of television daily and that cartoons and other children's programming contained more violence than prime-time shows.) Continuing to seek centrist credentials, Clinton signed the Kennedy-Kassenbaum bill, which enabled workers to carry health insurance from job to job and increased medical insurance tax deductions.

The high point of bipartisan cooperation emerged with the Welfare Reform Act of 1996, the most far-reaching change to federal public assistance since its inception in the 1930s. Half of African American and Hispanic families headed by women lived in poverty. Critics had long pointed to the need to break the cycle of "dependence" among "welfare mothers" who were recipients of Aid to Families with Dependent Children (AFDC). Declaring that government assistance provided a second chance, not a way of life, Clinton promoted welfare reform as a means of bringing the poor into the economic mainstream. The new law returned aid programs to the states through federal block grants, compelled nearly a half-million adult recipients to find work in two years, and placed a five-year limit on help to the needy. When liberals accused the president of abandoning women and the poor, he promised to seek tax incentives for businesses that hired former welfare recipients and to provide extra funds for job training.

As the presidential election approached, Clinton readdressed the needs of middle-class families. Responding to continuing concerns about excessive sex and violence on television, he asked the networks to adopt a ratings system to protect young viewers. Attacking cigarette smoking as "the most significant public health hazard facing our people," the president authorized the Food and Drug Administration (FDA) to limit the marketing of tobacco to minors. Appropriating the middle ground of social controversy, Clinton signed the Sanctity of Marriage Act, a Republican measure prohibiting federal recognition of same-sex unions.

THE ELECTION OF 1996 AND THE CENTRIST AGENDA

Hoping to benefit by Clinton's midterm slip in the polls, Republican presidential candidates included former education secretary Lamar Alexander, publishing magnate Steve Forbes, and free-trade opponent Pat Buchanan.

EXHIBIT **15-9   THE ELECTION OF 1996**

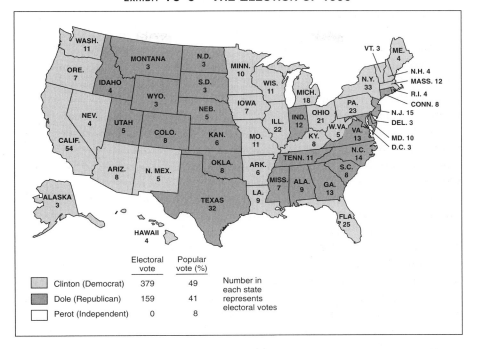

	Electoral vote	Popular vote (%)	
Clinton (Democrat)	379	49	Number in each state represents electoral votes
Dole (Republican)	159	41	
Perot (Independent)	0	8	

Nevertheless, Dole emerged as the Republican nominee by winning key southern primaries. Dole and running mate Jack Kemp called for economic growth through a tax cut, reduced government regulation, and delegation of welfare and anticrime programs to the states. Yet Dole's campaign focused primarily on Whitewater, a scandal involving financial abuses during Clinton's governorship in Arkansas, and on allegations of improper fund-raising by the Democrats. Once again, Perot's Reform Party entered the fray by focusing on campaign finance reform.

Running for reelection, Clinton and Gore targeted the votes of baby-boomer parents and suburban women ("soccer moms") by promoting education, job training, and computer literacy as a "bridge to the twenty-first century" information age. Democratic "attack ads" also lambasted Republicans for trying to cut Medicare. Benefiting by a booming economy, Clinton breezed to victory by accumulating 49 percent of the popular vote compared to 41 percent for Dole and 8 percent for Perot. Although Dole and Kemp carried most of the mountain West and the Southeast, Democrats took seven of the eight largest states, equaled the Republican total among men, outpaced their opponents among independents, and consolidated their hold among suburbanites and women. Yet voters once again ensured divided government by allowing Republicans to maintain control of Congress.

Clinton used his second term to pursue the centrist agenda favored by the middle class. On the environmental front, the White House protected millions of acres of federal wilderness and created national parks and monuments in western states such as California and Utah. In the Pacific Northwest the administration sought to preserve old-growth forests and salmon runs by limiting the timber harvest in national forests. Yet the Senate blocked U.S. implementation of a treaty on the prevention of global warning.

Finely tuned to consumer needs, Clinton approved a bailout that saved the Amtrak railroad system from bankruptcy, signed a massive transportation appropriation, and agreed to legislation allowing competition among banks, security firms, and insurance companies. The administration addressed the needs of working families by creating a medical insurance program for poor children, raising minimum wages, and expanding the earned income tax credit. To respond to charges of excessive spending and to keep interest rates at historic lows, the president endorsed a Republican plan to balance the budget. By consenting to reduce capital gains and corporate taxes, Clinton authorized the largest tax cut since Ronald Reagan. He also pleased Republicans by agreeing to a congressional moratorium on state taxation of Internet commerce. Spending cuts and continued prosperity produced results: In 1998 the United States experienced the first federal budget surplus in decades, and the Treasury predicted even larger surpluses in the new century.

Convinced that U.S. prosperity rested on ties to the global economy, Clinton promoted participation in the World Trade Organization (WTO), which had replaced the General Agreement on Tariffs and Trade (GATT) in 1995. Although Congress failed to grant the White House fast-track negotiating authority for trade pacts, it extended permanent trading partner status to the People's Republic of China despite Beijing's poor human rights and labor record. The president also fostered economic ties with communist regimes in Cuba, North Korea, and Vietnam.

Seeking a stable Europe, Clinton asked that peacekeepers remain in Bosnia and received congressional support for the admission of Poland, Hungary, and the Czech Republic into NATO. Yet the absence of a single enemy increased the partisan nature of foreign policy. After 224 people were killed in the bombing of U.S. embassies in Kenya and Tanzania in 1998, the White House ordered raids on suspected terrorist installations in Sudan and Afghanistan—only to be criticized for the poor reliability of its intelligence. The next year the president led a brief but violent NATO air campaign against Serbia when a civil war resulted in the brutal suppression of that country's Albanian Muslims. Skeptical that U.S. interests were at stake, the Republican House failed to support a resolution authorizing the Kosovo bombing. When the administration pleaded for ratification of the comprehensive nuclear test ban treaty it had carefully negotiated, the Senate fell three votes shy of agreement.

A Divided Society

Blessed with declining unemployment and negligible inflation, the Clinton era witnessed the most sustained economic boom in U.S. history. Detroit played a large role in the recovery by producing minivans, light trucks, and sports utility vehicles that tapped the huge family market at home and abroad. Yet the most dramatic growth occurred in the information and telecommunications industries, where computer technology and software applications stimulated an economic revolution. By 2000, about half of all households contained at least one personal computer, and over two-fifths of adults used the World Wide Web (the Internet), first organized in 1991. Although more than three-quarters of electronic commerce involved business-to-business transactions, an increasing number of consumers went online to make retail purchases, engage in financial transactions, arrange for travel and entertainment, download music and graphics, access information, pursue schoolwork, or socialize in chat rooms related to special interests or preferences. Millions of others communicated by electronic mail, creating a virtual subculture of global computer users.

Commercial Web sites and Internet services produced a crop of "dot.com" millionaires whose start-up companies helped to fuel the strongest stock market in history. By 2000, well over half of U.S. families held Wall Street investments. Nevertheless, as financial conglomerates organized mergers in banking, utilities, retailing, publishing, entertainment, and telecommunications, critics such as Noam Chomsky raised fears concerning corporate control of information and news. The segmented nature of the workforce also belied promises of economic democracy. In a job market dependent upon high-tech skills and training, only 25 percent of working-age people possessed college degrees. Unskilled and semiskilled employees, usually African Americans, Hispanics, or women, often filled menial and service positions bereft of health-care plans, pensions, or other benefits.

At the close of the century, national poverty rates remained at 13 percent—the same percentage prevailing at the height of Lyndon Johnson's Great Society. Anticorporate activists such as Ralph Nader contended that the highly touted global market contributed to the polarization of social classes by exporting high-wage jobs and rewarding reduced employee costs. When the World Trade Organization met in Seattle in 1999, labor union and human rights proponents received national attention when they protested that international capital exploited workers and natural resources as mere commodities.

Given society's disparities of income and privilege, race relations remained a central problem of U.S. life. Civil rights leaders insisted that racial discrimination continued to victimize Hispanics and people of color and accused police of racial profiling, a technique by which nonwhites were singled

William ("Bill") Henry Gates III (1955-)

"I wrote my first software program when I was thirteen," recalled Bill Gates, the richest person in the world. "It was for playing tic-tac-toe." Gates became enamored with computers when a system was installed at the Seattle private school he attended. He and childhood friend Paul

Allen took entry-level software programming jobs to pay for computer play time. While at Harvard in 1977, Gates read about a personal computer (PC) kit that featured a powerful microprocessor (a transistor chip that performed basic calculations). Gates and Allen realized that computers needed software programs to instruct them to perform complex tasks such as word processing and data retrieval. After dropping out of college, Gates joined Allen in forming Microsoft—the company that would personalize the computer revolution and become the information age's most successful enterprise.

Microsoft's task was facilitated by corporate giant International Business Machines (IBM), which licensed Microsoft's software for its personal computers instead of purchasing it outright. This arrangement allowed Gates and Allen to offer software to other manufacturers, who marketed their PCs as "IBM-compatible." Yet as Microsoft sought to capture the consumer market in the 1980s, it had difficulty replacing words with pictures to signal programming commands. The company did not develop a user-friendly format until 1990, when Windows 3.0 adopted the graphic commands of Apple Computer's Macintosh, and it did not achieve the full potential of Apple's "point and click" system until five years later.

Microsoft established a distinctive, informal work climate for its 17,000 employees, who were hired on the basis of intellectual curiosity and teamwork skills instead of previous expertise. A similar disdain for

out for unreasonable searches, arrest, or violence. In 1992 the most devastating race riot in U.S. history occurred in Los Angeles after an all-white jury acquitted several policemen of assault following the videotaped beating of black motorist Rodney King. Three years later, former athlete and African Ameri-

traditional methods framed Gates's view of the future. Addressing a Las Vegas computer trade show as keynote speaker in 1994, Gates tied his company's prospects to the World Wide Web—the Internet that would do away with "middlemen" and "distributors" and create an "ultimate market" of "friction-free capitalism." This "world's central department store," he insisted, would include "digital wallets," videoconferencing, and global library browsing and would be a place to do business or just "hang out."

Gates announced in 1995 that every Microsoft division would refocus on products to access and browse the Internet. The following year he negotiated a partnership with NBC to create a cable television news channel and Web site. In 1997 Microsoft revealed plans to develop "Web TV"—a product that would allow consumers to receive online services through home television monitors and thus would erase the need for expensive computer hardware. Having set software standards for 90 percent of the world's personal computers in a $100 billion industry, Gates prepared to expand Microsoft's presence in computerized banking, retailing, and telecommunications. His autobiography, *The Road Ahead* (1995), an instant best-seller, presented the blueprint for innovation on the "information highway."

"We're about making great software, that's our deal," explained Gates in 1996. Yet industry critics contended that Microsoft's market dominance resulted from monopolistic practices similar to those of nineteenth-century industrial robber barons. After the company included software for its own Internet services in Windows 95, federal prosecutors mounted an antitrust suit that resulted in a judge's finding of "monopoly power." Gates argued that the competitive basis of technological innovation did not give anyone "a lock." As Microsoft prepared for an extended series of court appeals, the multibillionaire who still used the word *cool* insisted that postindustrial capitalism offered limitless opportunities for creativity and profits.

can media star O. J. Simpson was acquitted of a double murder when a predominantly black jury questioned L.A. police procedures and discounted the testimony of a white officer who had used racial slurs. Disturbed by racist images of African American men and seeking to renew black family cohesion,

EXHIBIT **15-10   THE EIGHT LARGEST SOURCES OF LEGAL IMMIGRATION TO THE UNITED STATES IN FISCAL YEAR 1994 (IN ROUNDED FIGURES)**

Mexico	111,000
Former Soviet Union	63,000
China/Taiwan	54,000
Philippines	54,000
Dominican Republic	51,000
Vietnam	41,000
India	35,000
Poland	28,000

Source: *Statistical Abstract of the United States* (1996).

Nation of Islam minister Louis Farrakhan convened a "Million Man March" in Washington, D.C. Meanwhile, a federal report revealed that one-third of black men in their twenties were either in prison, on probation, or on parole.

As nonwhites and Hispanics came to comprise more than one-fourth of the U.S. population, racial perceptions assumed a prominent role in the nation's policy disputes. In 1993 the Supreme Court ruled that congressional districts could not be drawn solely on the basis of race. In California, where whites were a statistical minority by decade's end, the University of California abandoned affirmative action, and voters passed a ballot initiative ending bilingual instruction in public schools. Responding to conservative concerns about cultural unity and mastery of fundamentals, politicians of both political parties pushed for national testing of public schoolteachers and students.

While critics characterized affirmative action as special preference, the nation witnessed an outpouring of white supremacy and militant nationalism. In Texas, a resurgent Ku Klux Klan accused Vietnamese immigrants of taking over the Gulf shrimping industry and vowed to stop illegal immigration from Mexico. Rival Klansmen lynched a young African American man in Alabama, although a suit by civil rights activists forced the group to sell off its assets and cease operations. David Duke, a former Klansman, won election as a Louisiana state legislator and drew headlines in close races for public office. Meanwhile, activists such as Tom Metzger of White Aryan Resistance (WAR) organized gangs of young racist "skinheads" in major cities, particularly on the West Coast.

Arming themselves for race war and civil strife, "patriot" groups such as the Order, the Aryan Nation, and Christian Identity confronted government authorities over weapons violations and tax issues. At Ruby Ridge, the Idaho home of white supremacist leader Randy Weaver, a controversial shoot-out in 1992 killed Weaver's wife and son and a federal marshal. Another confrontation led to the murder-suicide of seventy-five adults and children near Waco, Texas, in 1993, when government agents ended a fifty-one-day siege by attacking the compound of the armed Branch Davidian sect. White supremacist and antigovernment views also dominated the independent militia movement, active in the western states. Federal prosecutors tied extreme radicalism to two men convicted of the murder of 165 people in the 1995 bombing of the federal building in Oklahoma City—the worst act of domestic terrorism in U.S. history. Responding to a rash of black church burnings and individual acts of racial violence, civil rights activists pressed for federal legislation against hate crimes.

Reacting to such violent rhetoric and sensational crime, critics challenged the popular culture industries to curtail presentations of violence and sexuality. Cultural commentators also worried about the nihilistic messages of punk and grunge bands such as Pearl Jam and Nirvana. A series of grisly public school shootings between 1998 and 1999 prompted a national debate over the relative dangers of guns versus the impact of violent movies, video games, hip-hop lyrics, and cult Web sites. By 2000, politicians in both parties were demanding that media and communications giants practice self-restraint or face government interference.

In a climate of affluence and cultural ferment, social conservatives desperately sought to bolster traditional values. As the twentieth century ended, nuclear families—married parents living with children—constituted only one-fourth of all households and were only slightly more numerous than those consisting of single people. Fifteen million families were headed by one parent, usually a woman. Conservatives focused on abortion as a symbol of rampant self-indulgence and persuaded the Republican Congress to ban "partial-birth" procedures. Clinton vetoed the bill because it failed to provide adequate provisions concerning the mother's health. More radical right-to-life groups such as Operation Rescue organized blockades of abortion centers. Following a series of clinic bombings and fatal shootings, however, Congress prohibited the use of force or intimidation against women entering abortion facilities, and the Supreme Court upheld the right of local authorities to regulate antiabortion protesters in 1997.

2001 AND BEYOND

Political and social divisions helped to shape the controversial impeachment of President Clinton. Following the 1996 election, both houses of Congress investigated a series of Democratic campaign abuses, including the acceptance of illegal foreign contributions, improper solicitations by Vice President Gore, and the use of White House facilities for political fund-raising. The administration responded to critics by insisting that it supported the campaign finance legislation proposed by Republican Senator John McCain and Democrat Russell D. Feingold. In 1998, however, the Republican Senate failed to stop a filibuster against the reformers' proposal to ban unregulated "soft money" donations to political parties. By that time, Clinton faced the greatest crisis of his political career.

Federico F. Peña *(1947–)*

The rapid rise of Energy Secretary Federico Peña illustrated the ethnic dimension of the "New Democrat" political movement. A member of a prominent South Texas Hispanic family, Peña grew up in Brownsville. The son of a cotton broker who stressed discipline, he served as an altar

boy before attending the University of Texas at Austin. Peña joined protests against the Vietnam War before earning his law degree in 1972. He then moved to Denver, where he became a staff lawyer for the Mexican American Legal Defense and Educational Fund. Peña concentrated on police brutality and voting rights cases before signing on as legal advisor to the Chicano Education Project, which involved him in efforts to promote bilingual education.

At thirty-one, Peña began his political career with election to the Colorado legislature, where he was chosen as Democratic minority speaker. He built on these successes in 1983 by running for mayor of Denver against a fourteen-year incumbent and won the election. Yet in the mid-1980s an economic slump in the oil, mining, and high-tech industries produced high vacancy rates in downtown Denver offices.

In 1997 the Supreme Court ruled that an Arkansas woman could pursue a sexual harassment civil suit against former governor Clinton. Shortly after the president made history by testifying in the case, press reports alleged that he had conducted a sexual affair with a former White House intern and had denied the relationship under oath. As rumors flew, Clinton used a television interview to emphatically deny involvement in an extramarital sexual relationship. Attorney General Janet Reno then permitted Special Whitewater Prosecutor Kenneth W. Starr to investigate whether the White House had encouraged the former intern to lie. Although the sexual harassment case was dismissed (Clinton ultimately settled it for $800,000), the president was compelled to appear before a federal grand jury in 1998.

Although he had misled aides, family, and the public, Clinton insisted he had been "legally correct" in his original testimony before the civil court. Seeking to take advantage of the president's evasiveness, Republicans prevailed

When Peña stood for reelection in 1987, he faced a 22-point deficit in the polls. Resorting to negative advertising, he portrayed his Republican opponent as a tool of big business and scored another close victory, which he used to gain public support for a convention center, a new airport, and a major league baseball team.

Success at the local level permitted Peña to enter the national arena. Seeking to implement a campaign promise that executive appointments would reflect diversity, President Clinton opened his first cabinet to an unprecedented number of women, African Americans, and Hispanics and named Peña as Secretary of Transportation. The cabinet officer enforced strict fuel economy standards and encouraged the establishment of new airlines to compete with the major carriers. He also developed plans for environmentally protective high-speed trains and directed the investment of pension funds in the modernization of transportation systems.

Peña perfectly combined the virtues of urban professionalism with long-standing traditions of ethnic identity and urban politics. When a vacancy occurred in the Department of Energy in 1997, Clinton responded to the large Democratic vote among Hispanics by naming Peña to the high-profile post, a position he held for a year prior to returning to the private sector.

upon the House of Representatives to release the salacious details of Starr's report and to approve two articles of impeachment for perjury before the grand jury and obstruction of justice. Although Clinton's personal approval ratings plummeted, most voters opposed removing him from office for non-political offenses. As televised impeachment proceedings shifted to the Senate in 1999, a majority of senators failed to vote for conviction on either article, falling far short of the two-thirds margin required to replace a president.

At the end of a presidential term marked by unprecedented budget surpluses and the longest run of prosperity in U.S. history, the nation still struggled over its political identity. Arizona Senator McCain sought to make campaign finance reform the focal point of an insurgent run for the White House in 2000. Yet the Republican nomination went to Texas Governor George W. Bush, son of the former president. Offering himself as a "compassionate conservative" who emphasized the importance of inclusion, Bush promised to reinvigorate the nation's public education with a combined program of federal funding, performance standards, and vouchers for private schools. While calling for less government and greater accountability from citizens, Bush proposed to place caps on civil suit settlements, enact across-the-board tax reduction and reform of the Internal Revenue Service, and privatize aspects of Social Security. To illustrate his commitment to military readiness and deployment of a missile protection system, Bush chose Dick Cheney, his father's defense secretary, as his running mate. The Republicans addressed conservative social issues by opposing affirmative action quotas and demanding prohibition of partial-birth abortions.

Seeking to separate himself from Clinton's personal scandals without distancing himself from the administration's accomplishments, Democratic candidate Al Gore asked Connecticut Senator and Clinton critic Joseph I. Lieberman to be his vice presidential standard bearer, making Lieberman the first Jew to run for national office on a major party ticket. Gore supported McCain's campaign finance reforms, gun control, prescription drugs for all Medicare recipients, a children's health-care bill, and managed health-care reform. Calling for more federal aid for public schools, he offered carefully targeted tax cuts to compensate middle-class families for medical insurance, child care, and higher-education expenses.

In a period in which the economy continued to boom but the public remained divided about the moral issues raised by Clinton's tenure, the election produced one of the closest and most bitterly contested presidential races in U.S. history. Green Party candidate Ralph Nader took 2.7 percent of the vote, while minor party candidates captured another 1 percent. Nearly all the remaining ballots were split between the Republican and Democratic candidates. Gore won the popular tally by over 539,000 votes (0.3 percent of the total) and took the West Coast and most of the industrial states of the Northeast and Upper Middle West. In the evenly divided Electoral College, the selection of president came down to the vote in Florida, where George W. Bush initially emerged with a miniscule plurality of several hundred votes.

When Democrats protested that antiquated voting machines had failed to register thousands of partially punched or indented ballots in their strongholds in south Florida, the state supreme court ordered officials to ignore an election certification deadline and accept the results of manual recounts from three counties. Yet Gore's attorneys contested the certification when only one of the three counties completed its tally before the court's new deadline. The Democrats suffered another blow when a state trial judge rejected the vice president's contest on legal and evidentiary grounds. Yet the Florida Supreme Court reversed the ruling, 4–3, in a surprising decision that ordered a statewide recount of all ballots showing no vote for president. Five weeks after the election, however, the saga came to a dramatic climax when the U.S. Supreme Court halted the recount by a 5–4 vote. In a controversial ruling, the

Court concluded that the absence of statewide recount standards amounted to a violation of the "equal protection" clause of the Fourteenth Amendment. It also cited difficulties in completing the recount by deadlines established by state law.

As a result of the Court's intervention, Florida's twenty-five electoral votes were recorded for George W. Bush, who emerged with a narrow 271–266 victory in the Electoral College. The evenly divided election also produced a 50–50 tie in the Senate when the Democrats picked up four seats. In the House, the Republican plurality was reduced to a mere ten votes. Having lost the popular vote in a bitter election marked by legal maneuvering on both sides, Bush promised to restore the luster of the presidency by pursuing a bipartisan agenda with muted acrimony. Yet as Democrats and Republicans competed for the ideological center, personal rancor and partisanship took on unprecedented dimensions in U.S. politics.

The early months of the Bush presidency focused on domestic issues. Promising to "leave no child behind," the administration agreed to an educational reform bill that mandated competency testing of public school students but did not include a White House proposal for vouchers to offset private school tuition. Despite the compromise, critics assailed the plan for providing inadequate financial assistance to public education. The heart of Bush's domestic policy was a controversial $1.2 trillion tax cut to be applied over ten years. Because the wealthy paid more taxes, most of the benefits tilted to the affluent. Democratic opponents accused the administration of rewarding the rich even further when Congress subsequently reduced the dividends tax and all but eliminated inheritance levies. Because political pressures forced budget planners to guarantee Social Security payments to the elderly, Bush's fiscal policy served Republican goals by slashing federal discretionary and state social welfare spending.

The conservative Bush program intensified strains within the Republican congressional caucus, leading Vermont Senator James Jeffords to abandon the party and align with the Democrats, who now assumed control of the Senate. When critics charged that private energy traders had colluded in spiking electricity prices in the key state of California, the administration came under additional attack for its close relationship with leading energy conglomerates. Revelations subsequently demonstrated massive accounting fraud by Enron, an energy trading company, as well as by WorldCom, the telecommunications giant.

The events of September 11, 2001, completely overshadowed the partisan rancor and domestic focus of Bush's first year. In the deadliest domestic violence since the Civil War, nineteen Islamic fundamentalists utilized box cutters to hijack four U.S. airliners. Two planes flew into the towers of New York's World Trade Center, causing the buildings to collapse. Nearly three thousand people, including police and firefighters who rushed to the scene, perished in the catastrophe. A third airplane hit the Pentagon outside Washington, D.C., while the fourth crashed in western Pennsylvania when passengers with cell phones learned of the other hijackings and successfully thwarted the mission.

Fifteen of the nineteen "martyrdom" operatives turned out to be Saudi Arabian nationals. All were affiliated with Al Qaeda, a terrorist network based in Afghanistan under the charismatic leadership of Osama bin Laden, a reclusive Saudi billionaire. A veteran of fundamentalist Islamic resistance to the Soviet occupation of Afghanistan, bin Laden opposed the stationing of U.S. troops in Saudi Arabia, resented U.S. support for Israel, and objected to U.S.-led sanctions against Iraq.

Reaction to the September 11th atrocities produced an unprecedented outpouring of emotion, ranging from renewed community spirit and support for the victims' families to militant patriotism and calls for revenge. As NATO declared the incident an attack on all its member states, Bush bonded with hard-hat rescue workers by pledging that those responsible would be held accountable for the disaster. Appearing before a joint session of Congress, a somber president dedicated his administration to protecting the American people through a war against terrorism and its sponsors. As Bush singled out the fundamentalist Taliban regime in Afghanistan, known to harbor Al Qaeda, he vowed that "either we will bring them to justice or we will bring justice to them." White House approval ratings skyrocketed to over 90 percent.

Distressed that government agencies had failed to collect useful intelligence warning of the September 11th attacks, Congress quickly approved creation of the Homeland Security Office. The bureau supervised enhanced airport security, assumed control of immigration, coordinated interagency intelligence gathering, and inaugurated a graded system of terrorism alerts for public consumption. Congress also passed the landmark Patriot Act of 2001. Although presidential rhetoric distinguished evildoers from law-abiding Muslim Americans, the federal government used the law to detain over one thousand foreign nationals on visa violations and minor charges, to question thousands of others, and to monitor foreign-born individuals suspected of ties to terrorist organizations or charities that sustained them. Despite outrage by civil libertarians at the government's precedent-setting disregard for the rights of Muslims, Arabs, and others, little public outcry accompanied the increased emphasis on security.

Having elicited popular support for rallying Americans in a time of danger, Bush initiated the war against the Taliban, labeled Operation Enduring Freedom. After a brief U.S. bombing campaign and ground attacks by anti-Taliban forces in northern Afghanistan, the Islamic government collapsed at the end of 2001. As the United States and NATO allies installed Hamid Karzai—a moderate Taliban opponent—as Afghan leader, United Nations peacekeepers deployed to the capital city of Kabul. Yet powerful warlords maintained control of the countryside, where they profited from harvests of the traditional opium poppy crop.

As the United States prevailed in Afghanistan, over 500 suspected terrorists from the battlefront were incarcerated without charges at the U.S. naval base at Guantanamo, Cuba, where they were denied prisoner-of-war status. Yet information from the detainees did not lead to the main goal of the Afghan War—the apprehension of bin Laden—although several key Al Qaeda operatives were captured or killed and the group's numerical strength was cut by more than half. By 2002, when Bush announced the existence of an "axis of evil" consisting of North Korea, Iran, and Iraq, White House attention had shifted to "rogue" nations capable of wielding weapons of mass destruction—chemical, biological, or nuclear devices. Months later, the president declared that deterrence was not a sufficient strategy for opposing global terrorism and suggested that when U.S. national security was at stake, preemptive military action might be appropriate, even against states merely supporting terrorism by others.

By the summer of 2002, the administration was demanding that Iraqi dictator Saddam Hussein account for or destroy weapons of mass destruction (WMD), as required by the United Nations after the Gulf War of 1991. Congress gave the president ultimate authority to use force to disarm Iraq, although many members hoped that military action would be coordinated with the UN. Taking advantage of Bush's high approval ratings, Republicans increased their House majority and retook control of the Senate in the 2002 elections, further strengthening the president's hand. As the United States and Britain sent 300,000 troops to the Persian Gulf, the UN Security Council unanimously passed a resolution requiring Iraq to destroy its WMD or face "serious consequences." Iraq then admitted UN weapons inspectors, who found no weapons stockpiles but reported limited compliance with disarmament requirements.

Tying the Iraqi dictatorship to unaccounted WMD, regional instability, and potential collaboration with terrorists, the White House stepped up the call for a "regime change." Yet as massive antiwar demonstrations rocked Europe, Asia, and parts of the United States, the administration failed to win a second Security Council resolution authorizing force. Undeterred, Bush and British Prime Minister Tony Blair claimed that the UN already had extended sufficient authority for mounting a "coalition of the willing" to disarm Iraq. After a three-week bombing campaign and ground invasion met little resistance in the spring of 2003, the Iraqi government collapsed. Although most Iraqis were elated that the murderous dictatorship had been overthrown, they resented the failure of the occupying forces to provide security against crime and criticized the slow pace in restoring civilian services such as electricity and sanitation.

Having premised the Iraq War on the imminent dangers of WMD, the administration was forced to explain why no weapons stockpiles were discovered well after the cessation of hostilities. Bush's credibility was further damaged when the White House admitted that it had erred in accusing Baghdad of seeking to obtain weapons-grade uranium. Although U.S. forces captured Saddam Hussein and most top-ranking Baathist leaders were either killed or captured, coalition officials were reluctant to grant Iraqis self-rule too quickly in a chaotic environment. As the United States found few nations willing to share the enormous costs of reconstruction and peacekeeping, continued resistance from Saddam loyalists, Islamic radicals, and Iraqi nationalists pushed U.S. military casualties over 700 by mid-2004. Accordingly, the Bush administration came under increasing criticism at home for misstating the grounds for war, for inadequate diplomacy, and for poor postwar planning.

The Iraq War raised serious questions about the orientation of U.S. foreign policy. Did the threat of global terrorism, as the president suggested, make deterrence an outmoded strategy? If so, what were the circumstances that legitimated preemptive military activity? How important was international goodwill in pursuing U.S. objectives? Could the United States afford a unilateralist approach to international affairs in economic as well as political terms? What role did substantive grievances about the deployment of U.S. power play in the spread of terrorism among disaffected groups? Would the threat of terrorism unify the American people, as the Cold War had done, or would increasing tensions intensify partisan bickering and sharpen the "blame game" if things went badly? Finally, would political leaders be able to maintain the sufficient balance between security and freedom required of a democratic society?

As a collapse of the high-tech market induced a sharp economic recession early in 2001, many of the issues framing public discourse since the 1890s received additional attention. What were the proper duties and limits of government, and how was prosperity to be maintained? How effective was government regulation in monitoring the behavior of private interests such as corporations? Could public policy play a role in enabling more citizens to share in the American Dream? What actions might contribute to erasing technological barriers to economic opportunity? Were social welfare programs, particularly Social Security and Medicare, financially viable without a more disciplined use of resources? Could national leaders facilitate social peace among the country's diverse ethnic and cultural groups? Could life in the twenty-first century be reconciled to traditional moral values and continuity with the past?

As Americans looked to the future for assurances of greater affluence and security, they appeared to share the same hopes and fears that had inaugurated the twentieth century. Accustomed to the persistent dangers of an unstable world and wary of political promises, they could only hope that national leaders would confront the awesome complexities and challenges of modern life with vision, courage, and integrity.

AMERICAN HISTORY RESOURCE CENTER

To explore documents, images, audio and video clips, articles, and commentary related to the material in this chapter, visit the source collections at ushistory.wadsworth.com and and use the Search function with the following key terms:

Berlin Wall, Fall   Ross Perot
Gulf War, History   Boris Yeltsin
Clarence Thomas, Hearings   Newt Gingrich
Bill Clinton, Presidency   Saddam Hussein
Bill Clinton, Impeachment   War on Terrorism

RECOMMENDED READINGS

Alex Roberto Hybel, *Power over Rationality: The Bush Administration and the Gulf Crisis* (1993). A detailed monograph and survey covering the high point of the first Bush presidency.

Stanley Allen Renshon, *High Hopes: The Clinton Presidency and the Politics of Ambition* (1996). This psychological biography provides an intriguing analysis of Clinton's personal strengths and weaknesses and offers a fitting preview to the impeachment crisis.

Theda Skocpol, *Boomerang: Clinton's Health Security Effort and the Turn Against Government in U.S. Politics* (1996). More than a eulogy on failed health-care reform, this thoughtful analysis by a scholar and policy consultant addresses eroding faith in government in the post-Reagan era.

Michael Lind, *The Next American Nation: The New Nationalism and the Fourth American Revolution* (1995). An assessment of how migration patterns have altered the ethnic and cultural mix of U.S. society.

Additional Readings

For overviews of the George H. W. Bush administration, see John Robert Greene, *The Presidency of George Bush* (2000); Michael Duffy, *Marching in Place: The Status-Quo Presidency of George Bush* (1992); and Charles Kolb, *White House Daze: The Unmaking of Domestic Policy in the Bush Years* (1994). Ecological issues are the focus of the relevant segments of Robert A. Shanley, *Presidential Influence and Environmental Policy* (1992). Bush's economic and social policies are contextualized in the appropriate chapters of William C.

Berman, *America's Right Turn: From Nixon to Bush* (1994), and of Alonzo L. Hamby, *Liberalism and Its Challengers: From F.D.R. to Bush* (rev. ed., 1992). See also Kitty Calavita et al., *Big Money Crimes: Fraud and Politics in the Savings and Loan Crisis* (1997).

The end of the Cold War stimulated an outpouring of scholarship. For the involvement of peace groups, see John Lofland, *Polite Protesters: The American Peace Movement of the 1980s* (1993), and David Cortright, *Peace Works: The Citizen's Role in Ending the Cold War* (1993). Overviews of the Cold War include H. W. Brands, *The Devil We Knew: Americans and the Cold War* (1993); Warren I. Cohen, *America in the Age of Soviet Power, 1945–1991* (1993); Michael J. Hogan, ed., *The End of the Cold War: Its Meaning and Implications* (1992); and Richard Ned Lebow and Janice Gross Stein, *We All Lost the Cold War* (1994).

Background to the Gulf War is provided in the relevant segments of Michael A. Palmer, *Guardians of the Gulf: A History of America's Expanding Role in the Persian Gulf, 1933–1992* (1992). See also Richard J. Barnet, *The Rockets' Red Glare: War, Politics, and the American Presidency* (1991). On foreign-policy decision making, see the relevant portions of Harold Koh, *The National Security Constitution: Sharing Power After the Iran-Contra Affair* (1992), and of Louis Fisher, *Presidential War Powers* (1995).

Political journalists continue to monopolize the work on the Clinton administration. See Elizabeth Drew, *On the Edge: The Clinton Presidency* (1994). For policymaking and politics, see Bob Woodward, *Inside the Clinton White House* (1994), and *The Choice* (1996). Another view can be found in James B. Stewart, *Blood Sport: The President and His Adversaries* (1996). For the president and first lady, see Roger Morris, *Partners in Power: The Clintons and Their America* (1996).

For the 1996 election, see John Hohenberg, *Reelecting Bill Clinton: Why America Chose a "New" Democrat* (1997). Clinton policies are discussed in Charles O. Jones, *Clinton and Congress, 1993–1996* (1999), and in Jacob S. Hacker, *The Road to Nowhere: The Genesis of President's Clinton's Plan for Health Security* (1997).

Political alienation is the topic of William Greider, *Who Will Tell the People: The Betrayal of American Democracy* (1992), and Stanley Greenberg, *Middle-Class Dreams: The Politics and Power of the New American Majority* (1996). See also Michael F. Spath, *Dangerous Delusions: America on the Brink* (1995).

For racial politics, see the last segments of Dan T. Carter, *From George Wallace to Newt Gingrich: Race in the Conservative Counterrevolution, 1963–1994* (1996), and George Lipsitz, *The Possessive Investment in Whiteness: How White People Profit from Identity Politics* (1998). See also Orlando Patterson, *The Ordeal of Integration: Progress and Resentment in America's "Racial" Crisis* (1997). Immigrant issues are explored in David M. Reimers,

Unwelcome Strangers: American Identity and the Turn Against Immigration (1998). A useful case study can be found in Lisa Lowe, *Immigrant Acts: On Asian American Cultural Politics* (1996). For the "patriot" movement, see Michael Barkun, *Religion and the Racist Right: The Origins of the Christian Identity Movement* (1994).

INDEX

Women *(continued)*
  and Progressive reform, 39–44, 57–59,
    62–63, 68, 84, 98–99, 139, 188–189
  and purity reform, 41–42, 54, 98–99,
    139–140, 142–144
  and race, before 1945, 23, 25, 130, 156,
    191, 194, 196
  and race, since 1945, 344, 386–387, 496,
    526
  as radical feminists, before 1945, 35, 42, 63,
    98, 99, 157, 189
  as radical feminists, since 1945, 387, 389,
    409–410, 432, 472, 497
  as social activists, since 1945, 369, 387, 389,
    496, 524
  as social feminists, 23, 39–44, 59, 120–121,
    139, 174–175, 188–191
  and social relations, 1880–1929, 35–36,
    114, 120, 129, 133, 138, 139, 143
  and suffrage, 44, 57–58, 85, 98–99, 117
  during World War I, 92, 97, 98–99
  during World War II, 226, 227, 229–230,
    238
Women Accepted for Volunteer Emergency
    Service (WAVES), 226
Women's Army Auxiliary Corps (Women's
    Army Corps — WAC), 226
Women's Christian Temperance Union
    (WCTU), 40
Women's Committee of the Council of Na-
    tional Defense, 98
Women's Equity Action League (WEAL), 432
Women's International Terrorist Conspiracy
    from Hell (WITCH), 410
Women's Joint Congressional Committee, 121
Women's liberation, 387, 389, 409–410, 432,
    472, 497
Wood, Grant, 196, 352
Wood, Leonard, 54
Woodstock Festival (1969), 431
Woolworth chain, 115
Workers' compensation, 59, 65, 68, 80, 83, 160
"Workfare," 427
Works Progress Administration (WPA),
    169–171, 185, 188, 196, 199, 233
World Bank, 223, 245, 412
WorldCom, 537
World Court. *See* Permanent Court of Inter-
    national Justice
World's Christian Fundamentals Association
    (WCFA), 141
World Trade Center, 537
World Trade Organization (WTO), 528, 529
World War I, 68
  domestic impact, 113, 116, 121, 128, 138,
    231, 238
  domestic opposition, 90–92, 95, 98,
    101–103, 124, 206, 228
  home front, 94–100, 118, 232, 235
  legacy, 201–202
  military action, 92–95, 107
  origins, 87–92

  postwar settlement, 103–106, 126, 152
  veterans, 161–162
World War II
  and African Americans, 226–230, 232,
    235–236
  and atomic weapons, 245, 262, 265–266,
    291, 292
  combat veterans, 220–221, 236, 366, 370,
    414, 508
  in Europe and Africa, 204–210, 217–221,
    239, 266, 270, 299
  and European ethnics, 207, 232
  and Grand Alliance, 204–210, 214–223,
    239–240, 263–266
  and Hollywood, 207, 231, 232–233
  home front, 208, 214, 223–239, 292, 316,
    346
  legacy, 207–208, 214, 220–221, 224, 225,
    238–240, 374, 407
  and organized labor, 230
  origins, 200–210, 214, 221
  in Pacific, 214–218, 220–221, 240, 245,
    265, 366, 414, 508
  postwar impact at home, 245–248,
    253–260, 262, 267, 380, 407
  postwar impact overseas, 245–246, 253,
    270, 298, 374, 454
  and postwar veteran benefits, 230, 233,
    247, 255–256, 388
  and postwar veteran experience, 221, 236,
    250, 343
World Wide Web. *See* Internet
Wounded Knee occupation (1973), 433
Wright, Orville and Wilbur, 12–13
Wright, Richard, 194, 198
Wynette, Tammy, 408

Yalta Conference (1945), 220–222, 239, 240,
    264, 266
Yates decision (1957), 347
"Yellow dog" contracts, 120, 161
"Yellow journalism," 17, 53
Yeltsin, Boris, 512, 520
Yiddish culture, 5, 21–22
Young, Al, 495
Young, Andrew, 461, 464–465, 467
Young, Owen D., 152, 164–165
Young Men's Christian Association (YMCA), 42
Young Plan (1929), 152, 165
Young Women's Christian Association
    (YWCA), 42
Youth culture
  between 1920 and 1941, 114, 116,
    135–140, 154, 197
  between 1945 and 1960, 262–262,
    340–341, 352, 380
  between 1960 and 1980, 380–384,
    407–409, 417, 431, 433, 438–441, 445
  since 1980, 490–492, 496, 497, 525, 526
  in Progressive era, 35, 36, 42
  during World War II, 227, 237–238
Youth for Christ, 300